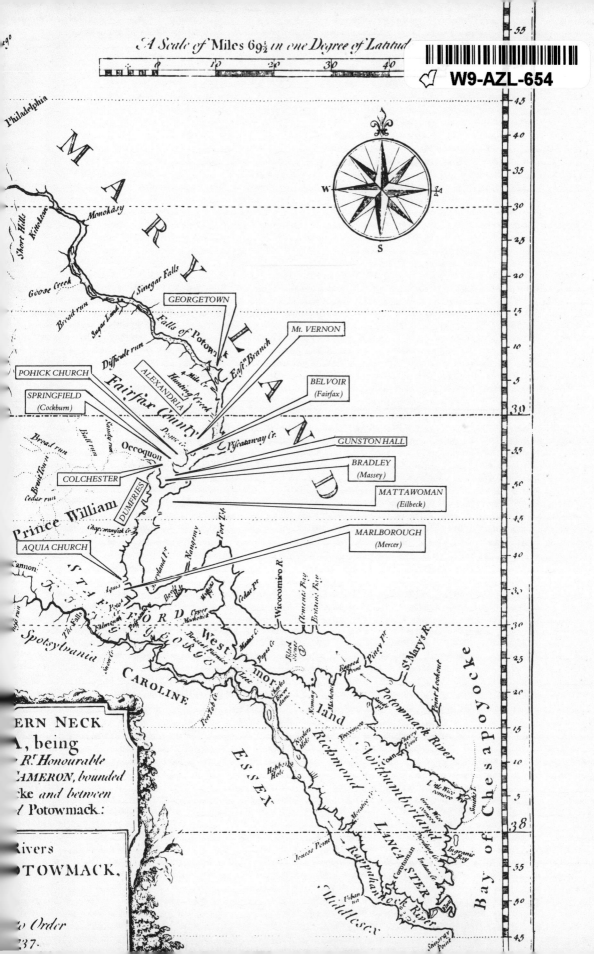

A Scale of Miles 69½ in one Degree of Latitud

0    10    20    30    40

45
40
35
30
25
20
15
10
5
30
55
50
45
40
35
30
25
20
15
10
5
38
35
50
45

W ← → A

N
S

Philadelphia

MARYLAND

Short Hills

Kittoktan

Monokäsy

Goose Creek

Broad run

Sinegar Falls

Sugar Land

Falls of Potowmk

Difficult run

4 Mile Cr.

Hunting Creek

East Branch

GEORGETOWN

Mt. VERNON

BELVOIR
(Fairfax)

POHICK CHURCH

ALEXANDRIA

Fairfax County

SPRINGFIELD
(Cockburn)

Bull run

Sandy run

Occoquon

Piscataway Cr.

Broad run

GUNSTON HALL

BRADLEY
(Massey)

Brent Town

Cedar run

COLCHESTER

DUMFRIES

MATTAWOMAN
(Eilbeck)

Prince William

Chapawamsick Cr.

MARLBOROUGH
(Mercer)

AQUIA CHURCH

Cannon

STAF

Aquia

Boyds Hole

Nanjemy

Port Tob:

Wicocomico R.

Clements Bay

Britons Bay

Potowmack River

St. Marys R.

Point Lookout

FORD

The Falls

Falmouth

Upper Machodock

West

mor

land

Regard Point

Piney Pt.

Spotsylvania

CAROLINE

GEORG

Great Wicomoco

Massey Cr.

Popes Cr.

Third Islands

Coan

Yeocomico

Cherry Point

Cornmill

ESSEX

Highbibbs Hole

Romany R.

Charles Brents down

Naylors Hole

Richmond

Northumberland

L. dle Wico comico

Great Wico comico

Little Wico

Cortomam

Bay of Chesapoyocke

Ingrams Bay

LANCASTER

Rappahannock River

Jeones Point

Indian Cr.

Urbanna

Piankitank R.

Middlesex

Stingray Point

ERN NECK
A, being
R.t Honourable
AMERON, bounded
ke and between
d Potowmack:

Rivers

OTOWMACK,

o Order
237.

# GEORGE MASON

*Gentleman Revolutionary*

*George Mason by Dominic W. Boudet, French refugee and former pupil of Jacques Louis David, after an original of 1750 by John Hesselius; one of three copies commissioned by John Mason in 1811 (courtesy, S. Cooper Dawson, Alexandria, Virginia; photo, Morton Broffman)*

# GEORGE MASON
## *Gentleman Revolutionary*

*by Helen Hill Miller*

*The University of North Carolina Press* / *Chapel Hill*

*End paper: "A Survey of the Northern Neck of Virginia," 1736–1737*
*(courtesy, The Colonial Williamsburg Collection)*

Library of Congress Cataloging in Publication Data

*Miller, Helen Day Hill, 1899—*
  *George Mason, gentleman revolutionary.*

  *Includes bibliographical references and index.*
  *1. Mason, George, 1725–1792. I. Title.*
*E302.6.M45M53      973.3'092'4 [B]      75–1377*
*ISBN 0–8078–1250–1*

# Contents

Foreword   *vii*

I.  Landscape with Figures   *3*

II.  A Start in Life   *25*

III.  Gunston Hall   *44*

IV.  County and Colony   *63*

V.  The Sharpening of the Issue   *88*

VI.  The Shadow Government   *101*

VII.  The Declaration of Independence
and the Virginia Bill of Rights   *133*

VIII.  To Govern a New State   *156*

IX.  Half the Territory of the United States   *177*

X.  Virginia at War   *197*

XI.  The Works of Peace   *214*

XII.  Building the Federal Structure   *229*

XIII.  Mason's Change of Attitude   *257*

XIV.  For and Against   *269*

XV.  Ratification with a Bill of Rights   *285*

XVI.  The French Counterpart   *301*

XVII.  Legacies   *319*

Appendixes   *337*

Notes   *345*

References   *361*

Index   *371*

*St. George Tucker, engraved by Charles
Balthazar Julien Sevret de St. Memin*
(courtesy, National Portrait Gallery,
Smithsonian Institution, Washington, D.C.)

# Foreword

*Judge St. George Tucker of Virginia, when William Wirt asked him for help* on his life of Patrick Henry in 1813, replied with some general reflections on the writing of biographies of the Virginians of the second half of the eighteenth century:

How would you be able to give any Entertainment to your readers, in the life of P. H. without the Aid of some of his Speeches. . . ? The same may be said of Lee—P[endleton] & W[ythe]—and the same may be said of every other Man of *real Merit* in Virginia. They have all glided down the current of Life so smoothly (except as public Men) that no body ever thought of noticing how they lived, or what they did; for to live and act *like Gentlemen* was a thing once so common in Virginia that nobody though of noticing it. . . . I very much doubt if a single speech of Richard H. Lee's can be produced at this day. Nevertheless he was the most mellifluous Orator that I ever listened to. Who knows anything of Peyton Randolph once the most popular man in Virginia. . . ? Who remembers Thompson Mason, esteemed the first Lawyer at the Bar? Or his Brother George Mason, of whom I have heard Mr. Madison (the present president) say, that he possessed the greatest Talents for debate, of any Man he had ever seen, or heard speak."*

To the judge, and others who had shared the jostling, the zest, the cross-purposes, and the concerted action of the times, these men without their voices were like the dear departed amid the feisty talk at a Virginia political funeral.

Yet the judge's paraphrase of François Villon's *Ballad of Lost Lords* loses its poignancy with time. To generations that never heard their voices, lives of these men can be absorbing instances of politics at work at a crucial period in American life. Political distinction was the common quality of their generation of Virginians—St. George Tucker is right that what was remarkable and exceptional about them was to be found in their character as public men.

Theirs was a letter-writing society, and if the timbre of their speech has vanished along with the scratch of their quills, what they thought privately about public affairs remains today in considerable abundance, a lively explanatory chorus to the formal words of their public speeches and the official documents that record their major acts.

It is on this contemporary material that I have relied in recounting Mason's story, using it to place him in the midst of the group pressures and individual proclivities, the milieu in which the risks, the failures, and the successes of political life take place. My long years as a journalist in Washington have made such a reliance congenial:

direct quotes leave little doubt as to what an individual actually said and thought—and the same is true of what his friends and his enemies said and thought about him. Allowing the future to become the present in due course, I have avoided hindsight, not only presenting events as they occurred but choosing for illustrations sketches, cartoons, and portraits closely contemporary to the text. (One regret: of all the voices that are silent, none was as compelling an instrument as Patrick Henry's, issuing from a body far less impressive than that of most of the men to whom he spoke. The miniature painted from life in 1795 gives no impression of his power; for that, a viewer should turn to the magnetic portrait adapted from it by Thomas Sully in 1815.) Convinced that those who have been to the places about which they write understand what they report better, I have covered the ground of Mason's interests in some detail.

Down the years, George Mason's contribution to the constitution-making period, state and national, has been relatively little recognized. He died in 1792 at just the time when his chief colleagues became actors on the newly available national stage. He was seven years older than Washington, who survived him by just that interval. He was older than Jefferson by eighteen years, than Madison by twenty-six, than Marshall by thirty, than Monroe by thirty-three. Because of his disappearance from the political scene at the moment of their emergence before the united country, their names survived while his tended to be lost to sight. But during the years from 1765 to 1789, he was in the forefront of Virginia's participation in great events, one of the chief political thinkers, draftsmen, and negotiators who gave the new state, and later the new nation, its form.

At the time of the Stamp Act in 1765, he helped prepare the text of an association to boycott trade until grievances over taxation were removed. He served in the prerevolutionary Convention of 1775 and on the Committee of Safety that exercised executive powers as the break with the mother country neared. When Virginia assumed statehood in 1776, he wrote the first Bill of Rights to be adopted on the American continent and took a large part in framing the first written constitution of the modern world.

In Virginia's postrevolutionary House of Delegates, he engaged in the day-to-day struggle to prosecute the war and to convert the newly adopted paper provisions for a new and freer society into functioning institutions under revised laws.

Aware throughout his life of the value of Virginia's land beyond the Appalachians, as the long-term treasurer of the Ohio Company, he doggedly pursued its claims; friend and counselor as well as legislator, he backed the expedition by which George Rogers Clark captured the Northwest Territory in 1778.

An active member of the Virginia delegation to the Philadelphia Convention of 1787 that drafted the Constitution of the United States, he contributed to the debate on all of its major clauses. At the end of the session, repelled by the deal between New England and the Deep South that exchanged a clause favorable to northern commerce for a clause protecting southern slavery, alarmed by the extent of powers allotted to the central government, and rebuffed by the Convention's refusal to put a bill of rights into the national document, he withheld his signature. In the state convention at which Virginia acceded to the plan in 1788, he opposed ratification without prior amendment while urging prompt revision featuring a bill of rights.

His opposition had positive results. In the conventions of other crucial states, the lack of a bill of rights had become a common denominator of the recommendations submitted for immediate consideration by the new national government. Accordingly, at the first session of the United States Congress, Madison brought forward a group of amendments which, soon ratified by the states, guarantee, in the nation's fundamental document, the basic liberties of the American people as individuals.

Contemporary with the American bill of rights on the national level, and drawing extensively on its Virginia sources, was the *Déclaration européene des droits de l'homme et du citoyen* that Lafayette brought forward in the early months of the French Revolution, the immediate precursor of the *Déclaration des droits de l'homme et du citoyen* adopted by the National Constituent Assembly in August 1789.

Mason's base of public activity—and the scene of his private life—was his Northern Neck plantation, Gunston Hall, where he contentedly lived the life of a Virginia gentleman and managed an establishment of several hundred persons, both slave and free. The Chesapeake world—the family had estates on both shores of the Potomac—was his life-long habitat. With the exception of his single journey to Philadelphia for the federal constitution-making Convention, his goings and comings were encompassed by a triangle with points at Alexandria, Williamsburg, and Richmond. His interests were wide-ranging—from Virginia's western lands to his son John's merchandizing venture in Bordeaux, and his political ideas, in keeping with the humanist philosophy of the Enlightenment, encompassed all mankind in their concern. Yet he was withal a very local man.

There were contributory reasons for his remaining rooted in Virginia. The death of his wife, Ann Eilbeck Mason, who died in 1773 leaving nine children aged three to twenty, and the persistent ill health—gout and "convulsive cholic"—that afflicted him from his young manhood until his death combined to prevent his acceptance of public office outside the state, though during the revolutionary years he was repeatedly offered membership in Virginia's delegation to the Continental Congress. His service at the Philadelphia Convention of 1787 came after his second marriage to Sarah Brent in 1780. He retired after the Virginia ratifying convention of 1788 and died at sixty-seven in 1792, patriarchally surrounded by children and grandchildren.

Primary sources for the type of biography I set out to write are currently available in unprecedented profusion. Regrettable gaps continue and probably always will exist in what is known of Mason's life, but scholarly, annotated publication of his collected papers and those of many of his contemporaries has for a number of years been in process and, in several important cases, is complete through most or all of Mason's life. The *Papers of George Mason, 1725–1792,* edited by Robert A. Rutland, was issued in 1971. The *Papers of Thomas Jefferson,* edited by Julian P. Boyd; the *James Madison Papers,* edited at the start by William T. Hutchinson and William M. E. Rachal and currently by Robert A. Rutland and William M. E. Rachal; and the *Adams Papers,* edited by Lyman M. Butterfield, have many volumes still to come, but those already published extend into the 1790s. For the latter years of these men, and for Washington throughout, reliance has to be on their earlier collected *Writings.* The *Washington Papers,* now in preparation under Donald Jackson, will bring together not only his outgoing mail, which John C. Fitzpatrick assembled at the time of the Washington bicentennary in 1932 as *The Writings of George Washington,* but his incoming mail, until now only scantily gathered.

Other recently published and annotated papers, diaries, or writings of men with whom Mason was in some degree associated include those of Benjamin Franklin, Robert Morris, and Alexander Hamilton on the national scene, and such Virginians as Edmund Pendleton, Landon Carter, and Edmund Randolph, as well as the "tours" of observers of the Old Dominion and the new Commonwealth down the course of the eighteenth century. Lee Papers at the University of Virginia and elsewhere have recently been assembled on microfilm, though not in printed form.

A sense of Mason's surroundings, social and political, can likewise be gained from such recent scholarly biographies of his contemporaries as Douglas Southall Freeman's and James Flexner's volumes on Washington, Dumas Malone's on Jefferson, Irving Brand's on Madison, Robert D. Meade's and Richard B. Beeman's on Patrick Henry, and from data assembled by statistically minded political scientists interested in voting records and historians probing such developments as the Chesapeake tobacco trade.

Two books about Mason should have special mention. Mason's first full-length biographer was Kate Mason Rowland, whose two-volume *Life of George Mason, 1725–1792* was published just a hundred years after her distinguished ancestor died. Her tireless research and her access to family papers, many of which have since disappeared, preserved much material that would otherwise be unknown and unrecoverable today. New genealogical material appeared in 1975 in *The Five George Masons: Patriots and Planters of Virginia and Maryland* by Pamela C. Copeland, honorary first regent of Gunston Hall, and Richard K. MacMaster.

Further resources are the unpublished manuscripts gathered and preserved by nineteenth-century collectors, corporate and individual;

by such men, to name only two, as Lyman C. Draper at Wisconsin and Dr. Thomas Addis Emmet in New York and by historical societies and clubs—again to name only two—such as those of Massachusetts and Virginia.

Beyond my debts to manuscripts and printed works are my many obligations to persons, though my faults in using their aid are my own. This book began in the mind of Jameson Parker, director of Gunston Hall Plantation from 1965 until his tragic death in 1972; it was he who proposed that I undertake it. Some months later, the National Endowment for the Humanities made a grant, hereby gratefully acknowledged, that covered travel, secretarial assistance, acquisition of material from collections, and assembly of illustrations.

Gratitude of long standing is owed to the memories of Louis Hertle and R. Walton Moore of Fairfax, who first introduced me to George Mason and Gunston Hall. Mrs. Frederick Frelinghuysen, currently first regent of the Board of Regents of Gunston Hall Plantation, National Society of the Colonial Dames of America, and Captain Walter W. Price, Jr., the plantation's present director, and their staff, have been most kind in the course of my present venture. S. Cooper Dawson, Jr., of Alexandria, great-great-great-grandson of George and Ann Mason, has permitted photography of their portraits.

My abundant thanks are likewise extended to the historians who have shared insights and to the many archivists and librarians, from front offices to stacks and photo-labs, who have guided and aided me in Boston, New York, Washington, Alexandria, Callao, Mount Vernon, Gunston Hall, Richmond, Williamsburg, Louisville, and Madison; in Glasgow, Carlisle, Whitehaven, and London; in Paris, Nantes, and Bordeaux. Descriptions of cartoons used in the text have been abstracted from Dorothy M. George, *English Political Caricature to 1792* (Oxford: Clarendon Press, 1959), vols. 2 and 3. The first draft of the manuscript was typed by Mrs. Nevin Wescott; later and final versions by Mrs. Margaret S. Raper and Mrs. Lourenda G. Raper.

The spirit and skill of the staff of The University of North Carolina Press have long been familiar to me. It was a particular joy that Lambert Davis, my publisher from his early days as editor of the *Virginia Quarterly Review* through his time as director of the Press, should in retirement have been willing to apply his critical eye to what I wrote, paraphrasing Franklin's story—see pages 146–47—of the hatter and his sign.

# GEORGE MASON

*Gentleman Revolutionary*

*Statue of Charles II, formerly on west
front of Lichfield Cathedral*
(courtesy, The Dean and Chapter,
Lichfield Cathedral)

# Chapter I
# Landscape with Figures

*The landscape, social and geographic, of the Northern Neck of Virginia, into* which George Mason of Gunston Hall, fourth of his name and line in America, was born in 1725, had been taking shape for close to a century, and for some seventy-five years of that time his forebears had been readily visible figures on its various contours.

In his *Present State of Virginia,* published in London in 1724, the Reverend Hugh Jones, lately professor of mathematics at the College of William and Mary and chaplain to Virginia's House of Burgesses, described the migration of which they were part: "one particular occasion that sent several families of good birth and fortune to settle there, was the civil wars in England; for Sir William Barkley the governor being strong for the King, held out the last of all the King's dominions against the usurper; and likewise proclaimed King Charles II before the Restoration. . . . This safe receptacle enticed over several Cavalier families."[1] Among them were two of the revolutionary George Mason's great-grandfathers: the first of the name in Virginia and Gerard Fowke, whose granddaughter married this George Mason's son.

Few of the emigrants who crossed the ocean after the loss of the battle of Worcester in 1651 extinguished hopes of an early Restoration came from an area so intimately concerned with the fortunes of the ousted Stuarts as the Fowkes of South Staffordshire. The Fowke family's holdings included the manor house of Brewood, some fourteen miles west of the cathedral town of Lichfield, and the farm named Gunston* just below it; in addition to their farming interests, its seventeenth-century members were active in the Midlands' rising metal industry.

Lichfield and its immediate environs had been a fought-over island of Royalist sentiment;† for an active partisan on the losing side, there was considerable incentive to emigrate after the Cromwellians won the Civil War. The escape of the fugitive Charles II which took place in the Fowkes' immediate neighborhood became a Cavalier legend. From Gunston to the manor house of Boscobel is less than six miles; it was to this refuge, owned by Col. Charles Gifford and tenanted by the five warmly Royalist Penderel brothers, that Charles, dressed as a rustic and mounted on a mill-horse, was brought for concealment when his plan to escape across the Severn after Worcester failed. The Cromwellian pursuit was so hot—and so thorough—that even though Boscobel contained two priest holes, the royal safety was committed to a nearby (and still flourishing) oak, where the king sat all day before starting south, again in disguise, on his successful flight through the West Country to sanctuary in France.

On arrival in Virginia, two Fowke brothers, Thomas and Gerard, and George Mason I established themselves on the Potomac at the upper limits of settlement. The records of Westmoreland County show a George Mason who was a juryman in late November 1652, and in 1656 a Captain George Mason, whose patent for nine hundred acres represented headrights of fifty acres for himself and seventeen other persons he had brought into the colony. On 4 December 1656 he sold one hundred acres of this land to one John Lear; two years later, Gerard Fowke represented Lear in a further transfer of which the record repeated the wording of Mason's original patent, dated 17 March 1655.*

Thomas Fowke, stated to be a merchant, patented 3,350 acres in Westmoreland on 10 June 1654, 2,000 of them transferred by a previous owner, and 1,350 as headrights for himself, his brother, and twenty-five other persons whom he had transported to the colony, and Gerard figured in further transactions involving five hundred acres in 1657. But immediately after the restoration of the king, Cavalier Thomas returned to England. In preparation for his departure, the two brothers entered into a "mateship and Copartnership" covering their real and personal property in Virginia, and Thomas drew a will, dated 14 May 1660,† in which he gave his brother all his Virginia holdings above the third part of his estate to which his wife Susanna was entitled. The will was probated on 24 June 1663; Gerard then became the family representative in the colony.

The early years of settlement along the Potomac, as English encroachments deprived the numerous small Indian tribes in the locality of their land, were bloodied by militia raids and retaliatory massacres. In the mid-1660s, the first George Mason, Fowke, and other county leaders were fined and deprived of office by the Virginia Assembly for proven wrongs to Wahanganoche, king of the Potomac Indians; in 1675, Mason's indiscriminate firing on an encampment of Susquehannocks while heading a militia expedition to avenge a murder committed by Doegs was one of the causes of the massacres that preceded Bacon's Rebellion.

But as the frontier moved westward, life in the Northern Neck came in many respects to resemble that in the English countryside from which the Masons, the Fowkes, and other English gentry came. Socially and politically, the county and its local institutions formed its framework; as immigrants pressed westward, counties multiplied. Until the time of the first Mason's arrival, Northumberland County, laid out in 1645, comprised the entire area between the Rappahannock and the Potomac, from their entries into Chesapeake Bay to indefinite limits beyond their fall lines some hundred miles northwest. In 1653, North-

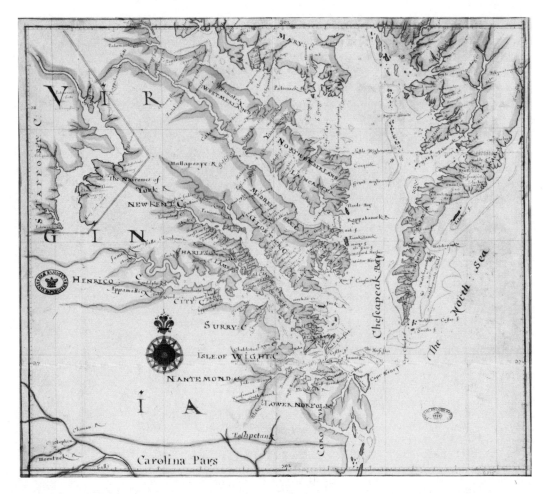

*Map of Virginia,
c. 1681*

umberland's western area became Westmoreland and Lancaster took
up its frontage on the Rappahannock. Eleven years later, western Westmoreland became Stafford; in 1730, Prince William was formed from
the upper lands of Stafford and Prince George, and itself generated three
new jurisdictions over the next three decades: Fairfax in 1742, Loudoun
in 1757, and Fauquier in 1759.

Virginia's geography was exceptionally suited to a rural society.
Chesapeake Bay, spreading its long coastline northward from Hampton
Roads behind the sea-barrier of the Eastern Shore and extending its four
great westward-penetrating tributaries—the James, the York, the Rappahannock, and the Potomac—miles inland, afforded every riparian
owner access to world trade from his own wharf. The planters had no
need for cities; Virginia developed no central commercial and financial
center like Boston, New York, Philadelphia, or Charleston. Except during sessions of the House of Burgesses and the General Court, Virginia's

colonial capitals—Jamestown in the seventeenth century and Williams-burg in the eighteenth—were sleepy villages. As late as the beginning of the Revolution, even Norfolk numbered only about six thousand. Economic differences were therefore not differences between city and country; they were differences of scale within the same rural society.

In the Northern Neck, many immigrants of small means either exercised their headrights of fifty acres to obtain modest holdings, mostly inland or above the fall lines of the rivers, that they worked as family farms or rented comparable tracts on long-term lease from larger landowners. Along the Potomac and the Rappahannock, and the lesser rivers and creeks that emptied into them, most of the riparian lands were consolidated into major plantations. The larger owners supplied both the county leadership and ranking personalities of the colony.

On this basis, the English class society reproduced itself. The autobiography of the Reverend Devereux Jarratt, a contemporary of George Mason IV, describes the gap between gentry and humble folk:

My father was brought up to the trade of a carpenter, at which he wrought till the very day before he died. . . . None of my ancestors, on either side, were either rich or great, but had the character of honesty and industry by which they lived in credit among their neighbors, free from real want, and above the frowns of the world. This was also the habit, in which my parents were. . . . Our food was altogether the produce of the farm, or plantation, except a little sugar, which was rarely used; and our raiment was altogether my mother's manufac-ture, except our hats and *shoes*, the *latter* of which we never put on, but in the winter season. We made no use of *tea* or *coffee* for breakfast, or at any other time; nor did I know a single family that made any use of them. Meat, bread and milk was the ordinary food of all my acquaintance. I suppose the *richer sort* might make use of *those* and other luxuries, but to such people I had no access. We were accustomed to look upon, what were called *gentle folks*, as beings of a superior order. For my part, I was quite shy of *them*, and kept off at a humble distance. A *periwig*, in those days, was a distinguishing badge of *gentle folk*—and when I saw a man riding the road, near our house, with a wig on, it would so alarm my fears, and give me such a disagreeable feeling, that, I dare say, I would run off, as for my life. Such ideas of the difference between *gentle* and *simple*, were, I believe, universal among all of my rank and age.[2]

To staff the local institutions, the riparian families regularly furnished the county lieutenant, named by the royal governor of Virginia on behalf of the Crown, just as the Crown named his counterpart in the shires of England. With the title of colonel, he commanded the county militia; he was the ranking gentleman justice of the county court. In both countries, the honor frequently descended from father to son, with sons usually serving apprenticeships in such posts as county sheriff, clerk of court, subordinate military officer. After filling several lesser offices, the first George Mason became county lieutenant of Stafford in the early 1670s; in the latter 1680s the second George Mason succeeded him; in 1719, the third George Mason was commissioned to the post.

The other justices of the peace, also appointed by the governor, came from similar backgrounds, along with a sprinkling of attorneys and merchants. Collectively, they comprised the county court. In Virginia, as in England, application of the law at the local level relied more heavily on common sense and practical familiarity with the neighborhood than on legal expertise. At the court's monthly meetings, moreover, the gentleman justices' agenda was not limited to the docket, which usually brought before them a miscellany of suits to collect debts, charges of immorality or theft, and occasional breaches of the peace. (Persons charged with serious crimes such as murder were remanded to the General Court at the capital.) The justices served not only as a court of law but as a local legislature, assessing the county taxes, setting the prices that inns and ordinaries could charge for bed, board, liquor, and oats, and laying out and maintaining roads.

The sheriff was the court's executive officer, enforcing ordinances and collecting taxes. While specific taxes were from time to time laid on personal possessions, from chaises to slaves, the poll tax was the chief reliance for all three of the levies to which a citizen was normally liable: the "public" levy, laid by the Assembly to fund the colony's overall government; the county levy, laid by its court; and the parish levy, laid by its vestry. Assessments were payable by free white males sixteen years of age and over and by owners of slaves on each male or female sixteen and over.

Experience as a gentleman justice was a natural preparation for candidacy for the post of county delegate in the legislature established in 1619, the House of Burgesses at Jamestown and subsequently at Williamsburg. The freeholders of each county elected two members as their representatives. Selection for this office, like membership in Parliament in England, reflected local approbation. Selection for seats on the Governor's Council, on the other hand, or designation for colony-wide offices such as governor, lieutenant governor,* or attorney general, was a sign of royal preferment. The president of the Council became acting governor in the absence of a royal appointee, and the Governor's Council sat with him as the colony's General Court, hearing both civil appeals and criminal charges.

The first and the third George Mason went to the capital by the elective route, chosen by their neighbors to represent Stafford. By contrast, the man whose daughter Ann married George Mason III in 1721 arrived with a commission from the Crown as attorney general. He was Stevens Thomson, member of the Middle Temple and eldest son of Sir William Thomson of Hollin Hall near Ripon in Yorkshire. He served the colony for a decade; Governor Alexander Spotswood notified the Lords of Trade of his death in 1714.

As in the mother country, the Church of England enjoyed a temporal status as Virginia's established church. Counties were divided into parishes; since travel was far easier by water than over the uncertain trails that served as roads, parishes were usually laid out along river banks, in blocks perhaps only ten miles deep but from thirty up to eighty miles long. Church attendance on Sunday was required by statute, but the distances at which parishioners lived gave rise to new customs with regard to other religious ceremonies, tolerantly recorded by the Reverend Hugh Jones:

> The parishes being of great extent (some sixty miles long and upwards) many dead corpses cannot be conveyed to the church to be buried: So that it is customary to bury in gardens or orchards, where whole families lye interred together, in a spot generally handsomly enclosed, planted with evergreens, and the graves kept decently: Hence likewise arises the occasion of preaching funeral sermons in houses, where at funerals are assembled a great congregation of neighbours and friends; and if you insist upon having the sermon and ceremony at church, they'll say they will be without it, unless performed after their usual custom. In houses also there is occasion, from humour, custom sometimes, from necessity most frequently, to baptize children and church women, otherwise some would go without it. In houses also they most commonly marry."[3]

When a new parish was established, the first vestry was elected by its freeholders and householders; thereafter, unless the Assembly ordered the holding of a new election, the membership was self-perpetuating. In addition to arrangements for purchases of land and erection and repair of churches, glebes, and chapels-of-ease at outlying points, vestrymen assessed parish tithes and acted as overseers of the poor, apprenticing orphans, purchasing medicine for the sick, and supplying shelter and relief for those unable to work.

Successive lists for Truro, the fourth George Mason's parish, show how election to vestries and appointment as churchwardens were steps on the ladder to county prominence, affording recognition to lesser landholders, attorneys, merchants, ship-masters, builders, and other craftsmen. On a still more local level, the vestries appointed four freeholders in each parish precinct as processioners; their duty, every four years, was to "perambulate" the bounds of the properties within their precinct, renewing markers and keeping lines fresh in local memory.

Vestrymen also had a voice in the selection of ministers. The Virginia churches were under the care of the Bishop of London, and while he had a commissary in the colony from 1689, when the Reverend James Blair became first president of the College of William and Mary, the absence of a bishop in residence affected the assignment of rectors to Virginia parishes. Qualified men were scarce; those who applied in London for colonial charges often proved of doubtful ability. As many as fourteen or fifteen of some fifty parishes were without regular ministers in the 1720s. Vestries were entitled to make one-year, renewable appointments on their own initiative; they often sought their own candidates and sent them to London for ordination. The governor, as temporal head of the established church in the colony, could give a clergyman permanent tenure by formally inducting him into a charge, but a 1724 survey covering twenty-eight incumbents showed that while only twelve had served their parishes for less than ten years, and sixteen had officiated from ten to over thirty years, only five had been inducted.*

Occasionally, the conduct of a rector induced disapproving action by the political authorities at the capital; one such flamboyant instance, with which George Mason II was closely associated, occurred at the end of the seventeenth century when the ebullient John Waugh was incumbent of Overwharton Parish in Stafford County. The cleric's first transgressions were ecclesiastical: he was suspended for six months and fined after he obliged eloping couples from across the river in Maryland with wedding ceremonies undelayed by publication of banns. But in 1690 his political actions caused his parish to seethe with serious "tumults." Stafford County contained its full share of the tensions between Whig and Tory, Anglican and Catholic, that intensified at the time of the Glorious Revolution in England. Catholic settlement in Maryland began in 1632 when Charles I carved the new colony from the Virginia area east of the Potomac and made it a county palatine with hereditary feudal rights and privileges vested in the Lords Baltimore—George Calvert, the royal favorite for whom the title was created, was a Catholic convert.

In subsequent years, various Catholics moved across the river. Following some high-level political altercations, the Brent family, with whom succeeding generations of Masons were variously associated, came to Virginia in 1650, shortly before George Mason I and the Fowkes arrived.† In 1688, the Stafford County Court issued to Giles Brent a certificate of "twenty-one years' experience of his fidelity in not seducing any persons to the Roman Catholic religion,"[4] but his nephew George, about the same time, alarmed the Anglican population by obtaining an extension of the Declaration of Indulgence afforded by King James II to his coreligionists in England. It permitted Catholics to practice their faith in Stafford on a thirty-thousand-acre area known as the Brenttown Tract.

The accession of a Catholic Stuart to the English throne had cooled the enthusiasm of a number of Virginians whose forebears had been attached to the Cavalier cause. George Mason II was among those who became ardent Whigs and rejoiced when James was ousted and the Crown settled on Anglican William and Mary in 1789. Yet at the same time the county's ranking citizens comprised men who though not Catholics remained staunch Tories, among them William Fitzhugh of Bedford, who in 1686 had succeeded the late George Mason I as county lieutenant and ranking justice of the county court.

By 1690, when the deposed James II, encouraged by his coreligionist Louis XIV of France, was plotting to regain his throne, Stafford Anglicans were uncomfortably aware of Catholic Maryland in plain view across the river. In this nervous atmosphere, citing an Indian woman as his source, Parson Waugh spread a spine-chilling rumor, in whose circulation George Mason II joined: with Indian allies, Maryland supporters of James were about to invade Stafford and use it as a staging area for occupation of Virginia by armed force. Panic led to riotous demands for military protection. Three members of the Governor's Council arrived to quell the alarm. George Brent was counseled to take refuge at Colonel Fitzhugh's. Mason was deprived of his militia command. Parson Waugh was jailed. Only after an excited interval did county ferment die away.

The rector was unperturbed. Soon after he regained his liberty, he appeared on court day and told the crowd that he had come "to correct the mistakes made by the Justices at their last sitting." William Fitzhugh was presiding; Waugh called him a papist. Fitzhugh declared he would not sit again until Waugh had been disciplined and reported him to the Governor's Council.

The Council shared the justice's outrage; in the autumn, Fitzhugh was able to inform his brother-in-law in England that Parson Waugh "has made a publick & humble acknowledgemt. In the Generall Court . . . & is appointed to do the same in our County Court, as soon as I come home, with a hearty penitence for his former faults, & a promised obedience for the future, which he sincerely prays for the accomplishment of, & for the sake of his Coat so do I too."

Yet in the same letter, Fitzhugh added plaintively: "to be disregarded nay & slighted too, & to see those mischievous active Instruments as you well know Waugh & Mason, &c, the only men in favour, & the only men taken notice thereof, grates harder than the non payment for powder shot & other disbursements."[5]

The Whigs did indeed retain their popularity, in the course of which the rector's next political activity caused the setting of a constitutional precedent. Waugh had long taken a manipulative hand in local elections and in the first choice of burgesses after the "tumult," William Fitzhugh was defeated by Martin Scarlet, a Whig. Then, in 1699, Waugh himself became a successful candidate for burgess. He was not, however, allowed to assume the position. The Assembly declared the election void, taking the view that Commissary Blair's presence in the Governor's Council corresponded to that of the English bishops in the House of Lords but that ministers were no more entitled to sit in Virginia's Lower House than in the House of Commons in England.

By the time that one last stubborn solemnizing of a runaway marriage in 1700, with its foreseeable suspension and fine, caused Waugh to end his thirty-three year ministry and retire to the ample 6,350-acre plantation he had patented in 1691, the alliance between him and Mason had become a family matter—his daughter, Elizabeth, was George Mason II's second wife. Both sides remained in politics: in 1710 Stafford's two burgesses were George Mason III and John Waugh II.

The local institutions so far mentioned, the county court and the parish vestry, duplicated with only minor modifications familiar features of the life of the English shires. The legal basis of landholding was likewise shared by the two societies. While the ease with which land could be acquired in Virginia diminished the distinction between the eldest son and the other children in a family that was normal under the English law of primogeniture and entail, the home plantation usually descended to the first-born, even though substantial provision was frequently made for his younger brothers.

In the Northern Neck, landholding resembled its counterpart in England even more closely than elsewhere in Virginia, for this area, like the entire colony of Maryland, was a proprietary, held in feudal tenure by a titled Englishman. Just as Charles I had rewarded Lord Baltimore, Charles II, in 1649, had rewarded a group of his own loyal supporters with a Virginia grant, and by the early years of the eighteenth century, Thomas, sixth Lord Fairfax, had inherited this tract as sole proprietor. Feudal law therefore applied: on both sides of the river the proprietors collected the annual quitrents that elsewhere were payable to the Crown. Four shillings per hundred acres were due the Maryland governor as the proprietor's deputy. Lord Fairfax, first through resident agents and after 1747 as the only British peer to live permanently in Virginia, collected both quitrents and percentages on extracted minerals. Numerous landowners were obligated to both proprietors, holding lands on both shores of the great central highway of the Potomac and living sometimes on one side, sometimes on the other. Just as the Brents had moved their residence to Stafford, the third George Mason moved his, about 1730, to Stumpy Point on Chickamuxon Creek in Charles County, Maryland.

Yet in the management of land, sharp differences separated the American from the English agricultural society. The lord of an English manor lived from his rents. His holdings were leased on long terms to an independent yeomanry that expected—and was expected—to assume responsibility for their cultivation. The country house was a residence, and while the squire customarily performed various local functions, the making of agricultural decisions for his tenants was not among them.

By contrast, the plantation houses of Virginia were centers of working farms. William Fitzhugh, who died owning some 54,000 potentially arable acres, observed that "without a constant care & diligent Eye, a well made plantation will run to Ruin."[6] It was the managerial judgment of the owner that saw the seedlings into the ground and the harvest off to market, and while in some Tidewater areas such responsibility was delegated to hired overseers and clerks, most Northern Neck planters, the Masons among them, exercised it themselves.

These men became specialists in the growing, curing, and marketing of tobacco. From the time of the Stuarts to the time of the Hanoverians, one staple crop, produced for shipment to the mother country, dominated Virginia's economy; by the end of the 1730s, Virginia's annual tobacco exports exceeded 28 million pounds. Planters raised enough corn, hogs, and other commodities to supply their self-contained communities, but times were good or bad depending on the growing season and the price tobacco brought in markets three thousand miles away. Its production was so general that in a country where specie was scarce, tobacco could be used as legal tender, accepted for taxes, for payment of ministers' salaries, for the settlement of debts.

No ordinary crop, from its first acclaim as a novelty by Americus Vespucius, the fragrant weed had been a subject of song and story: fine gentlemen and tavern frequenters joined Samuel Rowland's late-sixteenth-century challenge:

> Who dares dispraise tobacco,
> While the smokes is in my nose![7]

Even the king, though he forbade its growth in England, could not persuade his subjects to abandon its pleasures: James I's *Counter-blaste* of 1604 denounced "A custome loathsome to the eye, hatefull to the nose, harmefull to the braine, dangerous to the lungs, and in the blacke stinking fume thereof, neerest resembling the horrible Stigian smoake of the pit that is bottomlesse,"[8] but this monarch had not been a month in his grave when a proclamation of Charles I protected the quality of imports by restricting them to leaf grown in Virginia.

Eighteenth-century praise of the weed is typified by Isaac Hawkins Browne's *Of Smoking: Four Poems in Praise of Tobacco, An Imitation of the Style of Four Modern Poets*, published in 1736. In Pope's favorite verse-form he extols:

> Blest Leaf, whose aromatic Gales dispense
> To Templars Modesty; To Parsons Sense.
> (So raptur'd priests of fam'd Dodona's Shrine,
> Drink Inspiration from the Steam Divine)
> Poison that cures, a Vapour that affords
> Content more solid than the Smile of Lords;
> Rest to the Weary, to the Hungry, Food:
> The last kind Refuge of the Wise and Good. . . .
> Come to thy Poet, come, with healing Wings,
> And let me taste thee, Unexcis'd by Kings.[9]

Through the first half of the eighteenth century, most of the planters on the large estates of alluvial Tidewater were single-mindedly devoted to this one product, with clearing of fields, and cultivation, harvesting, and curing of the crop done by slaves.

The first Negroes in the colony had been brought in by a Dutch ship in 1619; after the middle of the century, slavery began to be a familiar institution. The English settlers were of two minds concerning this practice, but many of those who had the necessary resources bought slaves; they were indispensable to large-scale production. By 1730, they numbered some thirty thousand, about one-in-four of Virginia's population.

At the same time, enough men of influence were opposed to the traffic for the Assembly to pass repeated laws against it. Their view was succinctly expressed in the fourth George Mason's first public paper, written at the end of 1765: "The Policy of encouraging the Importation of free People & discouraging that of Slaves has never been duly considered in this Colony, or we shou'd not at this Day see one Half of our best Lands in most Parts of the Country remain unsetled, & the other cultivated with Slaves; not to mention the ill Effect such a Practice has upon the Morals & Manners of our People: one of the first Signs of the Decay, & perhaps the primary Cause of the Destruction of the most flourishing Government that ever existed was the Introduction of great Numbers of Slaves—an Evil very pathetically described by the Roman Historians."[10]

But down the decades, Virginia's prohibitory measures were uniformly disallowed by Whitehall, under pressure of English merchant interests. The only legislative discouragement permitted to stand in colonial Virginia was an import duty whose chief effect was to swell the treasury.

In extenuation of the institution, early authors such as Robert Beverley, in his *History and Present State of Virginia* published in 1705, presented a favorable contrast between the condition of Virginia slaves and that of the more humble of the English laboring classes: "Because I have heard how strangely cruel, and severe, the Service of this Country is represented in some parts of *England*; I can't forbear affirming, that the work of their Servants, and Slaves, is no other than what every common Freeman do's. Neither is any Servant requir'd to do more in a Day, than his Overseer. And I can assure you with a great deal of Truth, that generally their Slaves are not worked near so hard, nor so many Hours in a Day, as the Husbandmen, and Day-Labourers in *England*."[11]

But planters such as William Byrd II of Westover, though he dealt in slaves, viewed the social effect of the institution in a larger frame. In 1736, when General James Edward Oglethorpe was attempting to prohibit slavery in newly founded Georgia, Byrd wrote to Oglethorpe's partner, Lord Egremont: "I am sensible of many bad consequences of multiplying these Ethiopians amongst us. They blow up the pride, & ruin the Industry of our White People, who Seeing a Rank of poor Creatures below them, detest work for fear it shou'd make them look like Slaves."

Further, increasing numbers introduce an element of fear: "In case there should arise a Man of desperate courage amongst us, exasperated by a desperate fortune, he might with more advantage than Catiline kindle a Servile War." For both reasons, Byrd urged that Parliament "put an end, to this unchristian Traffick, of makeing Merchandise of our Fellow Creatures."[12]

In addition to managing the cultivation of his crops, the plantation owner had to see to the long list of other commodities—rough textiles and shoes, nails and hoes, bricks and shingles, all needed for

*George Mason, Gentleman Revolutionary*

*"A View of Port Glasgow from the
South East" by Robert Paul, Glasgow
Academy, 1768
(courtesy, The Mitchell Library, Glasgow)*

self-sufficiency. These were produced on the place by indentured white servants, specially trained slaves, or itinerant white craftsmen making regular rounds.

But self-sufficiency was not enough. On the proceeds of the year's tobacco sales depended the purchases of new land, additional slaves, and the imported luxuries, from wines and brandies,* fashions and fine fabrics, to harpsichords, books, and chaises, which were goals of prospering planters.

For both exports and imports, marketing methods changed rapidly after the Act of Union of 1707 included Scotland in the United Kingdom and enabled Scottish merchants legitimately to enter colonial trade. (In actuality, Glasgow traders had already been skirting the edge of legality by traveling as supercargo on ships loaded with Manchester goods and leased from English yards, especially those at Whitehaven just south of the border on the west coast, where trade in coal to Ireland had early stimulated a sturdy shipbuilding enterprise. Technically, the Scots thus met the requirement that commodities must travel in English bottoms under English masters.)

In little more than a generation after 1707, the tobacco trade changed Glasgow beyond recognition. Previously, the burgh had been a downhill straggle of houses along High Street from the abandoned episcopal palace to the Tolbooth beside the shallow, barely navigable Clyde. By the mid-eighteenth century, it was the second or third port of the realm, ranking only behind London and competing with Whitehaven, Liverpool, and Bristol along the western coast.

In earlier days, when Glasgow's trade outlets were confined to continental ports, the fact that its shipping must circumnavigate the British Isles was a disadvantage, and the city had little beside fish to offer. During that time, however, the rags-to-riches success story of one Walter Gibson set a pattern. In the 1680s, he caught, packed, and cured three hundred lasts of herring, rented a large Dutch ship, and sold them at £6 sterling per last at a French port. The profit was so great that he bought the Dutch ship and two others, traded to France, Spain, Scandinavia, and Virginia, developed Broomielaw harbor on the Clyde at the foot of the town, and died in a house designed by Sir William Bruce after having been provost of Glasgow.

Two generations later, a score of energetic young men, most of them from the countryside, seized the opportunities of transatlantic trade and became the tobacco lords of Glasgow. The tobacco aristocracy founded by Alexander Speirs, the two Cunninghame brothers, John Glassford, the Ritchies, a galaxy of Buchanans, and lesser traders had more in common with the way of life of the first families of Virginia than the plant that made both wealthy: they too intermarried in a close-knit cousinry, put a good part of their profits into fine houses, exercised a near-monopoly on government, and set themselves apart from lesser men. (When they retired, it was as gentry on imposing landed estates whose name was added to their own: Speirs of Elderslie, Ritchie of Craigton, Buchanan of Drumpellier.)

They continued to lease ships, mostly from Whitehaven;* they developed warehouse facilities at Port Glasgow and Greenock, some twenty miles below Glasgow at the end of the Clyde estuary where ocean-going ships could dock, and a fleet of smaller craft called gabbarts to bring samples upriver to their places of business and exchange. Shipping time from the Chesapeake Capes to home port ran some fourteen to twenty days less to Glasgow than to London, giving the Scottish merchants a differential of around halfpence per pound in freight charges, and the passage to the Atlantic through the North Channel enabled their ships to slip in and out in relative safety during the protracted periods in the eighteenth century when France and England were at war. As a result, continental buyers, led by the Farmers General purchasing for the domestic monopoly in France, became Glasgow's regular clients.

In Virginia, a new marketing system was installed as tobacco output increased in the early years of the century. When additional volume caused prices to fall, planters began to compensate for low price by shipments of trash grades. The House of Burgesses made various efforts to halt the practice, forbidding the tending of seconds—the harvesting of inferior late-season second growth—and attempting to limit plantings. Both failed. The first effective measure, taken in 1730, instituted government inspection. Thenceforth, all tobacco had to be brought to warehouses built at convenient shore points where negotiable certificates were issued against hogsheads of acceptable quality.

*"A View of Greenock," by Robert Paul, Glasgow Academy, 1768*
(courtesy, The Mitchell Library, Glasgow)

The new warehouses became the focal points of trade. Resident agents of firms in Glasgow and elsewhere built nearby stores for the display and sale of imported merchandise, and by contracting for tobacco in advance, they minimized the turn-around time of their companies' ship captains who in a few stops could deposit their incoming cargo at the stores and take on a full load of tobacco at the warehouses. The saving of time made it easily possible to complete two round-trips during the sailing season, and the competition among agents firmed up the prices paid to planters. Places of business and residence of craftsmen—ships carpenters, smiths, masons, bricklayers, joiners, harness makers, wheelwrights, weavers, and tailors—together with inns and ordinaries soon collected around this overseas commerce. The first successful towns took shape, with nearby planters and resident merchants serving as their trustees.

Although the Virginia legislature attempted periodically to encourage the growth of towns, not all survived. In 1691, the Stafford court ordered a survey of a fifty-acre site on Giles Brent's land at the tip of the pointed peninsula where Potomac Creek enters the river and contracted for the building of a new county courthouse there. Of the score of lots then sold, George Mason II bought four and received authorization to put up an ordinary to provide "a good and Sufficient maintenance and reception both for man and horse." He and William Fitzhugh, Jr., were named feoffees of the town in 1707. But the location proved inconvenient, the current Port Act was abrogated in 1710, and a few years later the courthouse burned. By 1720, the town that took the name of Marlborough after the Duke's victory at Blenheim was dead.

But at better-chosen locations, the new centers flourished. By mid-century, the Assembly had established Dumfries, Colchester, and Alexandria on the Virginia side of the Potomac, and Port Tobacco and Georgetown had been set up in Maryland. Scottish traders established themselves in each.

The third George Mason forwarded these developments so actively that his aid received recognition in Glasgow. The Glasgow Merchants House, presided over by the Dean of Gild Court, required every merchant doing business in the town to purchase a burgess ticket giving him the freedom of the city; on occasion, distinguished strangers were recognized by bestowing on them, gratis, honorary burgess tickets. Such tickets were hand-decorated by an artist who contracted to portray in color the city's coat of arms and a floral border surrounding the text.

The Act Book of the Dean of Gild Court for March 1720 lists first among four men to receive an honorary ticket, "Coll. Meston in Virginia." The ticket read: "the Honble. George Mason, Esqr., Collonel of the County of Stafford in Potomack River, Virginia, is Admitted and Received Burgess and Gild Brother of this city: and the Whole Liberties, privileges, and immunities, belonging to a Burgess and Gild Brother thereof are granted to him in most ample Form: Who gives his oath of Fidelity as Use is."[13]

Act Book,
Dean of Gild Court,
Glasgow, entry of
March 1720 showing
admission of "Coll.
Meston of Virginia"
as honorary burgess
(courtesy,
City Archives Office,
Corporation of
Glasgow)

Since tickets were individually designed and the whereabouts of Mason's, though it was seen by his biographer, Kate Mason Rowland, in the 1880s, is now unknown, its exact appearance is uncertain, but all tickets displayed symbols recalling events in the life of the Celtic saint, Kentigern (also known as Mungo), who set up a monastery on the site of the future burgh, evangelized there, and died in 603 A.D.

The covering letter that accompanied the ticket thanked Mason for "the many Extraordinary Favours you have done to our merchts. or their agents in Virginia" and expressed the hope that "in time coming you will if possible multiply your goodness towards them when you can consider them not only as strangers but as Fellow Citizens with your-self. We wish you all happiness and prosperity and do most earnestly recommend you to the protection of the Almighty."[14]

The establishment of warehouses and towns along Virginia's rivers systematized the actual marketing of tobacco, but no correspond-ing order was ever brought to the financial transactions that accom-panied it. A planter who sold his crop outright to an agent while it was

*Glasgow coat of arms*
*as shown on the ticket*
*of honorary burgess*
*Michael Newton, 1766*
(courtesy,
*The Mitchell Library,*
*Glasgow)*

still in the warehouse knew at once where he stood in earnings for the crop year. A certain number preferred this security; others preferred to consign their crops for sale at the discretion of an overseas merchant. William Fitzhugh took a grim view of the prospects of overseas consignment: "it is more uncertain for a Planter to get money by consigned Tobo. than to get a prize in a lottery, there being twenty Chances for one Chance."[15] Yet gambling was among the more popular vices of the eighteenth century, and a planter willing to accept the risk might, if the price held and his hogsheads reached port unsoaked and unsunk, realize a considerably higher profit. The proceeds of such a sale, credited to him on the merchant's books, not only covered the orders for British goods that normally accompanied his invoices but enabled him to draw drafts on his merchant negotiable for other transactions.

Exercise of such drawing rights caused enduring trouble. Accusations of bad faith and sharp dealing often culminated in court action. Because of the long lapse of time between dispatch of a crop and firm news as to what it had brought on the British exchanges, a planter's ledger-keeping often became inflated by undue optimism. The drafts he drew on his merchant then became forced loans, usually accompanied by blithe assurances that while this year's crop had been bad, next year's would undoubtedly be better. Eighteenth-century tolerance for upper-class indebtedness further encouraged loose practices. William Fitzhugh had been an exception when he accompanied a shopping list with the injunction: "rather leave some out, than bring me a penny in Debt . . . if my money falls short let it be wanting in the Dishes."[16]

When John Page, Jr., of Rosewell, the thirty-six room mansion in Gloucester whose magnificence bankrupted successive generations of the family, announced to John Norton & Sons, ranking London merchants, that he was postponing payments in May 1769, he simply mentioned "the great Scarcity of Money here, the Shortness of my Crops for four Years past, & the necessary Expences of an encreasing Family joined to the Commencement of Housekeeping in a large House;" he was still in debt in the 1790s. The following year, his kinsman Mann Page, who in 1767 had married George Mason's niece, Mary Mason Selden, in announcing a draft on the same creditor, assured him, "You shall be no sufferer" and added, "If it had pleased God the Gust we had the eighth of Sepr. had not have happened, I should have been able to have shipp'd you 130 or 140 Hhds. Tobo. this Year, but am in hopes shall send you between 70 & 80."[17]

On the other hand, a Glasgow commentator in the 1770s assigned some of the fault to the factors, "ambition for who should be possessed of the largest share of the trade took possession of them; they lent to the planters large sums of money, in order to secure them for customers, they gave them unlimited credits; and thus, by their endeavours to get the better of one another, rendered the commerce with the people of America, rather a speculative, than a solid branch of business."[18]

By continuous planting of tobacco, the Virginia planter also robbed himself of the fertility of his land. Before the seedlings were transplanted, the soil, opened by spring plowing, was formed into hills three feet apart and kept clean-cultivated thereafter. The voracious plants sucked nutrients; the often violent rains gullied the bare earth around them. Three successive years in tobacco finished a field for tobacco production. After a few further seasons in corn, also clean-cultivated, its eroded subsoil, henceforth known as an "old field," was abandoned to a straggle of scrub pine while the process was repeated in another newly opened clearing.

Because of this cycle of cultivation and destruction, groups of slaves normally worked separate clearings, called "quarters," spaced out over the plantation under the direction of a white overseer. The

*"Best Virginia," tobacco label of 1755*
*(courtesy, Arents Collections, The New York Public Library, Astor, Lenox and Tilden Foundations)*

overseer class was the least stable in the colony. Most of its members were either on their way up, with ambition to become smallholders on their own—James Monroe's grandfather, Andrew, was an example—or on their way down, after failure in some other venture. These men were the points of actual contact between the blacks in the fields and their white owners; they set the tasks and administered the discipline. In the remoteness of the separate quarters, they could be undetected practitioners of cruelty, even as they were the obvious first victims of slave uprisings.

Pressure for fresh acreage intensified an avarice for land common to all settlers. The west could be had for the taking; immigrants and established planters alike took, and took, and took. The Mason acquisitions were typical: George Mason II retained much of his father's acreage when he sold "The late mansion house of Col. George Mason deceased" at Accokeek; at the same time he bought some two thousand acres in Stafford between Potomac Creek and the Occoquan River. Continuing his purchases to the north, his last place of residence in Virginia was in Dogue's Neck, the square-ended peninsula abutting the Potomac above the Occoquan River. George Mason III lived here when his son George IV was born; before moving to Maryland, he acquired a further tract up the Potomac opposite Rock Creek. Judicious purchases in what became Loudoun County by this George Mason's widow, on behalf of her two younger children, equalized their fortunes with that of her firstborn son, George Mason of Gunston Hall. To him, Virginia's lands beyond the western mountains, all the way to the Mississippi, were a lifetime preoccupation.

By 1716, when Governor Alexander Spotswood led the company of frolicsome gentlemen whom he dubbed his "Knights of the Golden Horseshoe"—George Mason III among them—on a brief excursion westward, most of the unexplored lands of the colony were those beyond the Blue Ridge, visible in the vistas they relished from its crest. By mid-century, the frontier counties were Frederick, with its courthouse at Winchester, and Hampshire, with its county seat at Romney. In the east, Indian massacres were by that time only a memory; settlers moving west optimistically hoped by treaty and by trade to gain ground without too much bloodshed. They pushed on, thrust by a mixture of purposes: to extend the British empire in competition with the Spanish and the French; to further trade, channeling the commerce of the vast interior either to the Virginia seaboard, by connecting the Ohio with the Potomac and the James, or directly overseas, down the Ohio and the Mississippi; and to aggrandize their own wealth as individuals.

Little economic competition existed among the self-sufficient plantations of the Tidewater; their cash crop was disposed of in ports from London to Glasgow three thousand miles away. The families enjoyed each other in a context of a private life of hunting, fishing, cockfighting, horseracing, gambling; of dances, weddings, and funerals commensurate with the size of the surrounding cousinry; of churchgoing and the social season during meetings of the Assembly and General Court at Williamsburg—pleasures that their English counterparts well understood.

But the western lands opened a dimension of rivalry unknown to English county proprietors. The competitive scramble for new acres in the back country engaged the eastern gentry in a pursuit of wealth almost comparable to a gold rush. When individual land titles conflicted, they haled each other into court; united in group ventures, they carried the pursuit of wilderness sites into politics.

Beginning in the 1740s, rival companies set up claims to huge tracts along the Ohio, the Kanawha, the Kentucky, and the Tennessee rivers. Subscribers to the Ohio Company, formed in 1747, lived chiefly in the Northern Neck; Thomas Lee and Lawrence Washington were its first two presidents, and through most of its existence George Mason IV was its treasurer. The membership of the Greenbriar and the Loyal Land Company, by contrast, lived mainly in central and southside Virginia. Other equally vigorous and voracious associations were organized in Pennsylvania, Maryland, and North Carolina, frequently with participation by well-placed Virginians. Maneuvers and chicanery furthered company fortunes at the Board of Trade and Plantations in London as well as in America. The resulting feuds shaped enduring alliances in Virginia politics, influencing decisions on wholly unrelated issues. The demand for unrestricted navigation of the Mississippi was a specific factor in the close vote by which Virginia ratified the federal constitution.

The final, major difference that separated the lives of eighteenth-century Virginia plantation owners from those of their English rural counterparts was in a sense a delayed similarity. During the seventeenth century, English county families had struggled with the constitutional issue between citizen and king raised by the efforts of the first two Stuarts to secure funds by forced loans and imposts when denied military appropriations by Parliament. The Petition of Right of 1629 condemned what amounted to taxation without the consent of a representative body. And when the Glorious Revolution of 1688 ended absolute monarchy in England, the Bill of Rights promulgated by Parliament as part of the settlement of the Crown on the new sovereigns reaffirmed the illegality of such infringement of "ancient rights and liberties."

The new framework of constitutional monarchy adopted in 1689 removed the exercise of the power to tax as a domestic issue within the British Isles; but the corresponding structure of empire was not clarified. In the eighteenth century, in an imperial context, the issue reappeared. This time, the Englishmen who held their rights and liberties to have been violated lived overseas, and the author of the first American Declaration of Rights was a Virginian, George Mason of Gunston Hall.

# Chapter II
# *A Start in Life*

*In 1726, a year after George Mason IV was born, William Byrd of Westover* wrote to a British friend, "I have a large Family of my own, and my Doors are open to Every Body, yet I have no Bills to pay, and half-a-Crown will rest undisturbed in my Pocket for many Moons together. Like one of the Patriarchs, I have my Flocks and my Herds, my Bond-men and Bond-women, and every Soart of Trade amongst my own Servants, so that I live in a kind of Independence on every one but Providence."[1]

His picture was idyllic and his circumstances unsurpassed in the colony, but the contentment that breathes from his page was shared by Virginia gentry generally in his time. Nevertheless, men born during this and the next two decades became the leaders of a revolution. The formation of their characters and their intellectual preparation for new political thought occurred in circumstances of ease and enjoyment rarely associated with political upheaval. When members of the House of Burgesses reassembled at the Raleigh Tavern in Williamsburg after the royal governor prorogued them in 1774, the motto carved in the mantel of the room where they met was not inappropriate: "Hilaritas sapientiae et bonae vitae proles."

Mason's preparation was in important ways typical of his generation; it was exceptional because of an accident that occurred when he was ten. As the ferry between the mouth of Quantico Creek in Virginia and the Masons' landing stage on Chickamuxon Creek in Maryland put out on an eastbound trip in early 1735, a squall skittered over the broad Potomac and capsized the boat. Mason's father was aboard, a homeward-bound passenger. He drowned.

The widowed Ann Thomson Mason, with her three children—George, ten; Mary, four; and Thomson, two—moved from Stumpy Point back to the Virginia side of the river. Unlike most women in her situation, she did not remarry; in the Virginia of that day, a young and wealthy widow was assured of prompt offers, but she chose otherwise. For the next twenty-seven years, she lived on the dower plantation, Chopawamsic, south of the Occoquan River, devoting her very considerable abilities to managing her estate and bringing up her children.

Her accounts show her making profitable leases of family holdings in the vicinity, carefully seeking precise legal advice about terms. Under the English law of primogeniture, George was the sole heir to his father's lands. His mother equalized her children's holdings by the purchase of some ten thousand acres of western land on behalf of Mary and Thomson; these swelled Mary's dowry and supplied Thomson with the estate in Loudoun County on which he eventually built Raspberry Plain.

Her meticulous ledgers debited each child one thousand pounds of tobacco a year for support, plus special charges for unusual finery such as Thomson's ruffled linen shirts or Mary's hoop petticoat. From ten years of age to maturity, George Mason grew up in a household where competent care in economic affairs and strict avoidance of debt were daily before him.

As their coguardian, *in loco parentis*, the Mason children had their paternal uncle, John Mercer of Marlborough, a man of as strong an individuality as their mother, who provided George Mason with the means for his higher education. Born in Dublin, namesake and eldest of a Church Street merchant who died when this son was fourteen, Mercer attended Trinity College. From age sixteen, however, according to what he wrote in later years, he made his own way: "Except my education I never got a shilling of my gathers or any other relation's estate, every penny I ever got has been by my own industry & with as much fatigue as most people have undergone."[2]

Emigrating to Virginia, he began a rapid parlay of whatever capital he brought with him, trading up and down the Potomac from a sloop. At twenty-one, he made a promising landfall by marrying Catherine Mason, daughter of George Mason II and Elizabeth Waugh. The wedding ceremony signaled the groom's entry into planter society; the next year, the couple took up residence at Marlborough, renting the only remaining habitable house there from the late Parson Waugh's son David.

Little by little, lot by lot, Mercer acquired all of Marlborough. During the 1730s, he built his family a larger house and leased from the Brents, on long terms, enough land to control most of Potomac Neck. His meticulously kept land books,* his ledgers, and his diary † record every step of his advancement: the cost of timber, plank, nails for the new dwelling, and brick and oystershell for the chimney; the price of his newly acquired slaves; his orders for furniture and clothing; his purchases of lands to the west in Prince William County.

During these years also, he progressed professionally from merchant to attorney. He started to read his way into the law about the time of his marriage, and in only a few years his legal practice became his chief source of income, with earnings that rose from £291.10.12½ in 1730 to £643.18.2 a year later. His list of clients was imposing, his itineraries from courthouse to courthouse exhausting—in one year, his daily-noted mileages totaled 4,202.

Yet the motto on the scrolly ribbon beneath the heraldic design of his bookplate, "per varios casus," proved prophetic: few of his gen-

*John Mercer's bookplate
(courtesy, Bucks County
Historical Society Library,
Doylestown, Pennsylvania)*

eration experienced higher ups or lower downs than this able but irascible man. In Prince William County, the gentlemen justices found his insistence on prompt payment of fines severe, his resistance to stays of execution overemphatic, and his general manner abrasive. They brought charges against him at Williamsburg, and on 13 June 1734, the General Court suspended him from practice for six months. He used his enforced idleness to compile an abridgment of the laws of Virginia, and it was while he was thus engaged that George Mason became his ward.

Because the county courts were composed of men who for the most part were not lawyers, gentlemen justices had great need of such guides. *An Abridgment of the Laws in Force and Use in His Majesty's Plantations* had been printed in London in 1704, and in 1722 Robert Beverley had published *An Abridgment of the Publick Laws of Virginia, In Force and Use June 10, 1720: To which is added, for the Ease of the Justices and Military Officers, &c, Precedents of all Matters to be issued by them, peculiar to those Laws; and varying from the Precedents in England.* But there was room for a new abridgment after William Parks, who had set up Virginia's first permanent printing press at Williamsburg in 1730, published a definitive official transcript of all the colony's laws. The disbarred attorney subscribed to Parks's publication and went to work. On 23 April 1735, he petitioned the General Court for "leave to print an Abridgment compil'd by him of all the Laws of this Colony & to have the benefit of the

Sale thereof"[3] and also for renewal of his attorney's license. The court granted both requests, excepting only his right to practice in Prince William.

Yet for over two decades this venture was a financial failure. In August 1751, he advertised his willingness to bring the work up to date if sufficient demand were indicated, but the takers fell short of his required numbers; on 20 February 1752, he accompanied a further offer by a demand for cash on the barrel-head, "to secure myself against the base Usage I met with from the Subscribers to my former *Abridgment,* who left above 1200 of them on my Hands." Only in 1759, when a new edition was published in Glasgow, was his scholarship rewarded; the General Court then bought copies for the use of all gentlemen justices.

Mercer never learned to hold his tongue. At the end of 1738, he was again permitted to appear before the justices to whom he had given his original offense. The Council ordered that "the s'd Mercer be restored to his Practice in the s'd county, he behaving himself with that decency towards the Justices & uprightness in his practice as becomes him but if any misdemeanor shall hereafter be proved against him that then he be Suspended from practising as an Attorney in that or any other Court in this Dominion."[4] Yet a year later, though he was not disbarred in other jurisdictions, the Prince William privilege was rescinded.

In 1741, he was admitted to practice before the General Court, and in 1748, he was commissioned a gentleman justice for Stafford. Yet by 1753, he had so irritated his fellow members on the county bench that he risked dismissal—the Council's reply to their complaint, though finding in his favor, admitted their provocation:

His Conduct had been in some Respects blameable, particularly by his Intemperance opprobrious Language on the Bench, and indecent Treatment of the other Justices; and it was their Advice that his Honour [the governor] would by a Letter, to be read in open Court by the Clerk of Stafford, when the said Mercer shall be present, reprimand him for it; and also signify to him at the same Time . . . that it is expected he will alter such Parts of his Behaviour as have drawn upon him that Censure. . . . In Consideration of his having been a principal Instrument in a due Administration of Justice, and expediting the Business of the County, it has been thought proper to continue him Judge of the Court.[5]

Through the 1740s, Mercer rehabilitated a number of Marlborough buildings and put up a warehouse to replace one that burned. These were wooden structures. In 1746, however, he fired and stockpiled a large supply of bricks and, in March 1747, bought some illustrated architectural books to serve as manuals for the construction of a large and fine new house, the 108-foot-long Marlborough.

Completion of this house was the culmination of a decade in which he lived to the limit the life of a prosperous Virginia gentleman. Early in the 1740s he began to buy fine clothes, first patronizing a tailor in Stafford and later two tailors in Williamsburg, where Charles Jones made him a "full-trimm'd velvet" in 1749 and where he paid £5 for a "flower'd Velvet Waistcoat" the following year. His "gold watch, Chain

*John Mercer by an unknown artist*
*(courtesy,*
*Division of Pre-Industrial Cultural History,*
*Smithsonian Institution, Washington, D.C.)*

& Swivel," bought at William Woodford's, cost £64.6.3. William Dering, dancing master and artist at the capital, painted his portrait while Mercer lodged with him, in the still-existing Brush-Everard House on the village green, during the General Court sessions of 1748, and in 1750, a likeness of Mercer's new wife, Ann Roy of Port Royal. In late 1746, Mercer began to pay the Reverend John Phipps £100 a year to teach his children at home; in 1750, he sent George, his eldest, whose approach to young manhood he had recognized two years before by buying him a wig, to study at William and Mary.

On his rounds from courthouse to courthouse, he traveled smartly. In 1744, he bought a four-wheeled chaise locally; in 1748, he ordered a new one from the well-known London firm of Sydenham, but it proved so unsatisfactory that he refused to pay for it and replaced it with a chariot furnished by James Mills of Tappahannock for £80. His horses were worthy of his equipage: gratifying mid-century Virginian taste for English bloodstock, he assembled a score of brood mares, and a few years later the *Virginia Gazette* advertised his stallion, Ranter, at stud at forty shillings the leap.

There was indeed a cloud on his horizon—the same cloud visible in most rising planters' skies. He was in debt. By 1745, his records show him in much the same position vis-à-vis his clients as most English and Scottish merchants were vis-à-vis theirs. He supplied legal services where they supplied goods, but both went too often unpaid. He cast up a list that totaled 303 "Insolvents, bad & doubtful debts." Yet he continued to spend on the basis of what he earned rather than what he collected.

One of his major expenditures was for books. By mid-century, Mercer had assembled one of the outstanding libraries in the colony, and even in the 1730s and 1740s, it offered comprehensive grounding in most fields. Marlborough was only sixteen miles from Chopawamsic; during his minority George Mason spent at least part of his time in his uncle's home and found a university in Mercer's books.

Earlier, the boy attended one of the little schools, usually kept by clergymen, where youngsters who were not tutored at home learned their 3 R's and some Latin. In his will, Mason directed that if "Richard Hewitt, my old school fellow and Acquaintance from my childhood, Shou'd unfortunately be reduced to necessitous Circumstances, I desire and direct my Executors to Supply him with necessarys for his support."[6] His mother's account books show payments to a Mr. Williams for tutoring him during 1736-39; a Mr. Wylie received 845 pounds of tobacco for a year's schooling and books in 1738. John Mercer did not think much of tutors; years later, after troubles with those he employed for his own brood, he testily commented that most such men were "without either religion or morals, & I attribute it to George Mason's [George Mason V, then in his teens] tutor that I have long doubted with a good deal of concern, that he had very little improved in either."[7]

Mason did not go to college at William and Mary, nor did his guardians send him to London, as he, after coming of age, sent his younger brother Thomson to read law at the Inns of Court as their maternal grandfather and great-grandfather had done. But the foundations in constitutional law and in history for George Mason's later work in modeling new political institutions, the classics of legal and political theory, the case books, and the compilations of statutes were available at Marlborough, and so was his uncle's practical legal experience. A catalog of Mercer's holdings, made shortly before 1746, the year George Mason came of age, lists 404 titles, almost exactly half of them on law. That spring, he added a further 86, all except 17 on law. No equally extensive legal inventory of that date is known.*

A scattering of manuals of immediate day-to-day use, on farming and gardening, on medicine, textbooks for the children, dictionaries, guides to the drawing of simple legal instruments such as deeds, conveyances, or wills, together with a few books of sermons and devotions, were apt to be owned even by Virginians whose means limited their libraries to what their executors were likely to list as "one parcell of old bookes." Mercer's titles included all of these; his belles lettres comprised plays from Shakespeare to Wycherley; poems from Milton's *Paradise Lost* to Thomson's *Seasons*; essays and letters by Swift, Addison, Pope. Copies of the *Spectator, Tatler,* and *London Magazine* supplied current news and comment; *The Gentleman's Magazine* was particularly popular because it carried occasional items from Virginia. Works on philosophy, mathematics, and science balanced the belles lettres.

Any gentleman was expected to be familiar with the classics and to take pleasure in reading Latin authors in the original; some read Greek. In Mercer's inventory, the Greek grammar and Greek testament have George Mason's initials beside them; he owned the *Iliad*, the *Odyssey*, the *Maxims and Reflections of Plato*; his Latin works included a dozen poets, historians, and playwrights—local Virginia pride popularized Ovid's *Metamorphoses*, for the poet-treasurer of the London Company, George Sandys, when in the colony in the 1620s, had composed a translation that earned praise from Dryden.

From such books, a young reader could prepare to take his place among men with the encyclopedic interests of the period; the two further categories in which Mercer's library was strongest offered the exact materials most pertinent to the formation of one of Mason's particular bent. Mercer's law books ranged from international treatises such as Puffendorf's *Law of Nature and Nations* to some three dozen, often multivolume collections of English reports exhibiting the growth by accretion, case by case, specific instance by specific instance, distinctive of the common law.

An ample selection presented the wisdom and the views of the outstanding constitutionalists of England of the preceding century, beginning with the *Institutes* and the *Reports* of Sir Edward Coke. In 1628, when the House of Commons considered the implications of the

Five Knights' Case, a class action by men imprisoned for refusal to pay the forced loans that Charles I attempted to exact, Coke set a bench mark in his exposition of due process of law as it had developed from the time of Magna Charta. The knights sought to bring the legality of their imprisonment before the Court of King's Bench on a writ of habeas corpus. In support of the prisoners, the Commons declared the writ to be a right of every subject and further resolved that "it is the antient and undubitable right of every Freeman, that he hath a full and absolute property in his Goods and Estate; that no Tax, Tallage, Loan, Benevolence, or other like Charge ought to be commanded, or levied by the King, or any of his Ministers, without common consent by Act of Parliament."[8] These and other guarantees specified in the Petition of Right of 1629 were forerunners of the Bill of Rights adopted in 1689, when Parliament cited grievances and affirmed principles that, in their content and even in their phrasing, reappeared in the Virginia Declaration of Rights and other American affirmations of 1776.

All of Coke's major works were on Mercer's shelves, including his *Abridgment of Littleton*,* which remained the ruling authority on land tenure well into the eighteenth century. Beside them stood a succession of treatises by authors of various political affiliations during the Cromwellian and Restoration periods, bridging the years between the Petition of Right and the Glorious Revolution.

Complementing the flat legal pages, the operation of political institutions in the round was displayed in the exceptional number of English histories that Mercer had acquired. The collection stretched across the map as well as far into the English past—classical Rome, medieval Florence, Turkey, Persia, China, along with France, Hungary, Poland, and Spain. The four-volume *Universal History*, which cost Mercer £19.11.0, supplemented a thirteen-volume *History of Europe*, and a twenty-six volume *Historical Register*.

Exposure to these large concepts and broad records comprised Mason's basic education. At the same time, a young man soon to be of age and heir to a sizable estate, with the normal expectation of filling such local offices as vestryman, churchwarden, gentleman justice, and possibly burgess, like his father and grandfathers before him, could also engage in more specific preparation. Mercer's collection included *The Freeholders Companion, Keble's Assistant to Justices, The Clerk's Instruction, The Compleat Sheriff*, and *Wentworth's Office of Executors*. The shelves displayed a series of previous summaries of the laws of Virginia and the mother country, in addition to William Parks's official compilation of the Virginia statutes and Mercer's own *Abridgment*. Specific works covered *The Practice Part of the Law*: entries, equity, replevin, ejectments, bankruptcy, uses and trusts, landlords' and master and servants' law, slander, devise and revocations, the statute of limitations, tithes and laws of the clergy, wills, orphans' legacies—in short, the range of cases on the usual agenda of a county court or in which a substantial citizen and landowner might appear himself as plaintiff, defendant, executor, guardian, or trustee. For the eleven years of his wardship, these books were available to Mason; Mercer's preparation for court appearances on behalf of his many clients paralleled the texts with specific neighborhood instances.

The age of the Enlightenment expected its members to enjoy encyclopedic interests; in Virginia it also expected these interests to be combined with practical experience, whether in the conduct of public affairs, in the manifold activities of governing the sizable population of a plantation, or of meeting the needs of their household economies. Through reading and observation at Marlborough, Mason equipped himself for both.

In 1748, two years after John Mercer's guardianship ended with Mason's attainment of his majority, the now independent young man offered himself as a candidate for the House of Burgesses from Fairfax, the county north of the Occoquan River which had been separated from Prince William in 1742. It was too soon. He lost.

A man could both vote and be a candidate wherever he owned property; Mason could have tried his luck either in Stafford, where he was then living, or in Fairfax, and his decision to offer in Fairfax indicated his intention shortly to settle in the Dogue's Neck house where he had been born. He confirmed this intention the following spring by his successful candidacy in a special election for a new vestry for Truro parish.

The original Truro had been the easternmost of two parishes laid off when Prince William County was formed. Its early minister was the Reverend Charles Green, a landowner and physician of the area, whom Thomas, Lord Fairfax, recommended for ordination to the Bishop of London and who was duly installed in 1737. Its boundaries were revised when Fairfax County was organized in 1742, and again in 1749 when the parish of Cameron was carved out of Truro's western lands.

In the 1749 vestry vote, George Mason stood second to Hugh West in the list of twelve men chosen; also elected was his uncle by marriage, Jeremiah Bronaugh, second husband of Simpha Rosa Enfield Mason. Bronaugh was designated a churchwarden but died within a few months. Mason succeeded him in this office.

Up and down the river, the Assembly was giving corporate status to the newly prosperous port towns. In 1749, Dumfries was established on sixty acres belonging to the Scottish merchant John Graham. The seven town trustees, of whom Mason was one, were instructed to arrange for a public market and a quay, to sell lots, and to see that within two years purchasers "erect, build and furnish on every lot so conveyed one house of brick, stone, or wood, well-framed, of the dimensions of twenty feet square and nine feet pitch, at the least."

The same year, the Assembly authorized a new town thirty miles further up the Potomac, near the Hunting Creek tobacco warehouse that had been built in 1731; Alexandria then supplanted the hamlet of Belhaven. Ten miles beyond that, in 1751, Georgetown was established on the Maryland side of the river near the mouth of Rock Creek. Mason had interests in both.

In 1717, his father had purchased the seventy-five acre island, successively known as My Lord's Island, Barbadoes, and, during the Masons' tenure, Analostan, that lay just offshore from his Virginia plantation opposite the mouth of Rock Creek where the family had for some years maintained a Potomac ferry. Mason moved the Virginia terminus of the ferry half a mile upstream, building a causeway from the Virginia shore to the island. By placing the ferry slip on the island immediately opposite Georgetown, he supplied a link, lucrative as it was short, for travel between the two colonies.* (The Masons already operated the ferry from Quantico Creek across the Potomac to Maryland and the one plying north and south with traffic across the Occoquan River; when Ann Thomson Mason leased Occoquan Plantation to John Mercer in 1737, she was careful to do so "excepting the Ferry, with the profits thereon.")

When the first lots in Alexandria, which took its name from the family on whose land it lay, were put on sale on 13 and 14 July 1749, Mason paid seven pistoles for No. 53. Later, he bought Nos. 54, 55, and 59, at a total cost of £38.3.6. The first three lots gave him frontage on King Street, the main thoroughfare, along the entire block between Fairfax and Royal, and on the corner above Royal; the fourth was on a corner of Prince and Fairfax streets.

The original trustees of the town included several Fairfaxes: the lord proprietor, who had arrived in 1747, was still the guest of his cousin, William, at Belvoir preparatory to moving to his retreat at Greenway Court near Winchester; William, who was both agent for the proprietor's Northern Neck properties and His Majesty's collector of customs for the South Potomac; and William's son, George William, Mason's contemporary. Two other trustees, Lawrence Washington and John Carlyle of the Alexandria firm of Carlyle and Dalton, were Fairfax in-laws, the former having married William's daughter Ann and the latter his daughter Sarah. Richard Osborne, burgess, was a landowner of the area. William Ramsey, John Pagan, and Gerard Alexander were Scottish merchants: Pagan of Glasgow had recently moved to the new town from Chaptico, Maryland. Completing the roster were Hugh West, in charge of the government tobacco warehouse on Hunting Creek, and Philip Alexander of Chotank, Gerard's brother. Five years later, the town trustees' minutes for 18 June 1754 announced: "George Mason Gent: is appointed a Trustee in the Room of Philip Alexander Deceased;" Mason then built an office on his property at King and Royal.

Colchester, the town closest to Gunston Hall, was incorporated in 1753 in the southeast corner of Fairfax County, on the Occoquan River at the edge of the Dogue's Neck peninsula. This was a smaller town, laid out on twenty-five acres of land of Maj. Peter Wagener, who had married a daughter of Speaker Robinson and through his influence occupied, successively, the county clerkships of Prince William and Fairfax counties. Three years later, Mason's long-time associate, Alexander Henderson, a merhant representing John Glassford of Glasgow, arrived and started the first of what eventually became a chain of stores, with others at Occoquan, Dumfries, and Alexandria, while further south, he set up one of his clerks at Falmouth on the Rappahannock. Andrew Burnaby, in his *Travels Through the Middle Settlements in North-America in the Years 1759 and 1760*, reported seeing an iron furnace, a forge, two sawmills, and a belting mill at Occoquan—and noted that the iron ore required was brought over from Maryland because Lord Fairfax had claim to a third of the iron ore found within his proprietary.

Ever since Governor Spotswood was appointed deputy postmaster of the colonies in 1729 and established the office of New Post on his land below Fredericksburg, one of the two north-south mail routes had run through the sites of these towns.* When travel by stagecoach was established, the road became the King's Highway. For a time, all of these towns prospered. Their inns and ordinaries served men who had business to transact, from gentlemen planters and merchants to drovers, wagoners, and loggers who brought in livestock, rolled tobacco casks to the warehouse, or barged lumber downstream, and through passengers in transit.

At Colchester, Mr. Gordon's "Arms of Fairfax" was extravagantly praised late in the century by John Davis, an English tutor in the home of the Ellicott family, mill-owners on the Occoquan: "On the side of this bridge stands a tavern, where every luxury that money can purchase is to be obtained at a first summons; where the richest viands cover the table, and where ice cools the Madeira that has been thrice across the ocean. . . . The apartments are numerous and at the same time spacious; carpets of delicate texture cover the floors; and glasses are suspended from the walls in which a *Goliath* might survey himself."[9]

The variety and the volume of imported consumer goods locally available and especially convenient to customers who did not have their own accounts with British merchants is instanced by one of the semiannual orders that Alexander Henderson sent to John Glassford for his Colchester store in 1763;† the annotated invoice was dispatched in the *Catherine*, with duplicates, for safety's sake, in the *Thistle*, the *Henderson*, and the *Dunmore*.

For men, he wanted castor hats; yard goods (including some fine broadcloth); flat metal buttons for coats, glass and pearl for vests; stockings (brown and white); four gross of "garters in pairs" and one gross of scarlet ditto; shoes and pumps—"The Inhabitants of this

Country have large feet & must have large Shoes, those sent in this year are much too small"; saddles—one to be particularly fine—bridles, gunpowder, shot and lead, pipes, snuff and snuffboxes.

For the ladies, he specified sun caps and leghorn hats, scarlet cloaks, gloves, pocketbooks, stays, stockings and shoes, necklaces, a wide variety of yard goods, with needles, thimbles, and thread to make them up—the thread to be mostly brown, but also red, blue, and black—"the furnisher of the Colored thread is desired to comply with the above list exactly, & not at his pleasure mix green, Yelloe & other Colors with the above." The range of ribbons was wide: black, blue, purple, yellow, white, pink, four dozen low-priced figured ribbons and twelve dozen most fashionable silk ditto—recently "the ribbons sent are ill chosen, particularly the figured ones which are too broad, & most despicable patterns, it is therefore hoped that this will be prevented."

For family devotions and children's schooling, a dozen Bibles were ordered (without Psalms), together with hornbooks, spelling books, primers, and six common histories, also ink powder and ruled ledger books for the keeping of records.

Needed tools and housewares included blankets, sheeting, table-cloths, and cutlery; pewter and earthenware vessels, from plates, basins, and porringers to chamber pots; mortars and pestles; funnels and milk pails; corks, soap, and candles; and one hundred pounds of Bohea tea.

When all the lists were totaled, the order came to £1,096.16.0; a postscript added three carefully described high-quality guns, "at the Request of two of my very good Customers."

During the years when Dumfries was the county seat of Prince William, the town could rely on monthly crowds on court day. The Long ordinary offered simple fare; Captain George Williams's elegant brick tavern, two-story, stone-trimmed, and still standing, served the gentry who, as George Washington's diary shows, often combined entertainment with more serious business: a troupe was playing *The Recruiting Officer* in 1771 when he and Mason went down to arbitrate a case between Hector Ross of Colchester and James Semple of Occoquan Mills in which the cousins James Mercer and Thomson Mason were the opposing attorneys.

There were also the Sunday crowds at church. Another tutor, Philip Fithian of Robert Carter's Nomini Hall, describes the activities of a typical Sunday:

The three grand divisions of time at the Church on Sundays, Viz. before Service giving & receiving letters of business, reading Advertisements, consulting about the price of Tobacco, Grain &c, & settling either the lineage, Age, or qualities of favourite Horses. 2. In the Church at Service, prayrs read over in haste, a Sermon seldom under & never over twenty minutes, but always made up of sound morality, or deep studied Metaphysicks. 3. After Service is over three quarters of an hour spent in strolling round the Church among the Crowd, in which time you will be invited by several different Gentlemen home with them to dinner. The Balls, the Fish-Feasts, the Dancing-Schools, the Christ-nings, the Cock fights, the Horse-Races, the Chariots, the Ladies Masked, for it is a custom among the Westmorland Ladies whenever they go from home, to muffle up their heads, & Necks, leaving only a narrow passage for the Eyes, in Cotton or silk handkerchiefs; I was in distress for them when I first came into the Colony, for every Woman that I saw abroad, I looked upon as ill either with the *Mumps* or Tooth-Ach![10]

The letter book of Fithian's employer, listing merchants and mills in his vicinity in 1775, named eleven resident factors at Dumfries; among them was Daniel Payne, also county sheriff, who had some 350 clients. The town was likewise the scene of early efforts to set up an iron works.

In addition to Mason's assumption of economic and political responsibilities in his immediate vicinity, at the end of the 1740s, he became a partner in the Ohio Company, the vast economic and political enterprise initiated by Thomas Lee of Stratford in 1747.

Lee, president of the Council and the colony's acting governor during 1749-50, had in 1744 been a Virginia commissioner at Lancaster, Pennsylvania, during the making of the treaty with the Iroquois Indians which opened the way to new English settlement further west. Taking advice from Thomas Cresap, an experienced trader of western Maryland, the Company petitioned the Crown, in 1748, for a grant of 500,000 acres west of the mountains and south of the Forks of the Ohio,* 200,000 acres to be conveyed at once, and the remaining 300,000 on the company's fulfilment of a pledge to build a fort near the Forks and establish one hundred families around it within the space of seven years. The prominent London merchant, John Hanbury, to whom the partners offered a share, expedited the company's petition: through the good offices of the duke of Bedford, the Board of Trade approved it and instructed Virginia's Governor William Gooch to make the grant in July 1749.

The twenty original partners—the majority, like Lee himself, residents of the Northern Neck—included Lawrence and Augustine Washington; William and George William Fairfax; Landon Carter's son, Robert Wormeley; John Tayloe of Mount Airy, already a heavy speculator in western lands; as well as several well-known Marylanders, among them Thomas Cresap. Arthur Dobbs, governor of North Carolina after 1754, became a participant on his way to take up his post.

George Mason was admitted to membership on 21 June 1749; three months later, after the grant was in hand, he was made treasurer. As organization proceeded and members began to be assessed to cover costs, several of the original participants withdrew, among them the previous treasurer, Nathaniel Chapman.

Mason's earliest known letter, dated 27 May 1750, concerns Ohio Company business. Written to Lawrence Washington, it urges acceptance of the security offered by Hugh Parker, a Frederick County, Maryland, merchant experienced on the Pennsylvania frontier, and authorization for him to take a load of goods for the company's Indian trade up to Wills Creek* on the Potomac. He and Thomas Cresap had been commissioned to obtain land for a warehouse there and to clear a trail forward to the junction of the Redstone and Monongahela rivers below the Forks: "We have already given our Rivals the Pensilvns. too many advantages over us, by suffering them to engage the Interest of the Indians, & raise in them numberless Prejudices agst. the Ohio Compy while we, instead of fulfilling our Engagements & complying wth. our Promises in supplying them wth. Goods, have lain quite still, as if we were altogether unconcerned in the Matter; for these Reasons I shou'd look upon anything that put a Stop to the Trade for this Season, as utterly destructive of our whole Scheme."[11]

That September, the company commissioned Christopher Gist, who had recently explored the Ohio from the Forks to the mouth of the Scioto River, to seek out, on the south bank, "a large Quantity of good level Land, such as you think will suit the Company" for its first tract of 200,000 acres, preparing a map and keeping a journal as he went.[†] Gist proposed to settle some hundred and fifty families on the company's property; Mason and three others signed a covenant guaranteeing them fee-simple titles to land, free of quitrents for five years, upon payment within three years of £4 sterling per hundred acres. Mason made Gist an advance of £30 on his agreed fee of £150 for his voyage of reconnaissance; the explorer departed in late October and rendered a report the following May.

But almost immediate setbacks occurred. On 14 November, the company lost its well-placed president when Thomas Lee suddenly died; tuberculosis claimed his successor, Lawrence Washington, less than two years later. The company's development not only lost momentum when Lee went, it lost prestige and leverage at the capital. Both William Fairfax, Lee's successor as head of the Governor's Council, and Thomas Nelson, the colony's secretary, had been among the members who withdrew in 1749. Williamsburg's new magnet of speculative interest was Speaker Robinson, chief mover in the interlocking Loyal and Greenbriar land companies: Thomas Nelson joined him in the latter in 1751. Robinson had obtained a 100,000-acre grant on the Greenbriar River in 1745 and amplified it by a patent for 800,000 acres along Virginia's southern boundary. The constituency of these companies was drawn from central and western Virginia, including John Lewis and John Harvie of Augusta County, Dr. Thomas Walker and Peter Jefferson of Albemarle, and the English surveyor, Col. Joshua Fry; the speaker's protégé Edmund Pendleton, was the only prominent member from the Northern Neck.

To balance this accumulation of prestige, the Ohio Company reorganized in 1751: John Mercer, its new secretary and counsel, prepared revised articles of association. Virginia's newly named governor, Robert Dinwiddie, actively interested in western lands when he was

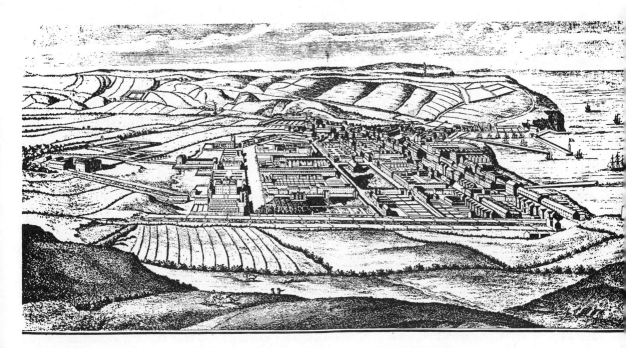

*"East Prospect of the Town and Harbour of Whitehaven," engraving by Richard Parr, based on Matthias Read's* Bird's Eye View of Whitehaven, *1738 (courtesy, Public Library and Museum, Whitehaven, Cumberland, England)*

His Majesty's surveyor general for the southern colonies, was brought in. A second new member was the nineteen-year-old George Washington, now surveyor of Culpeper County; in 1749, he had assisted in a survey of Lord Fairfax's western properties and by this time had viewed frontier lands from Frederick to Augusta.

External difficulties further complicated the company's affairs. The Virginia Charter of 1609 and the Pennsylvania Charter of 1681 overlapped on the lands around the Forks. (Even the western end of the line between Maryland and Pennsylvania was still in dispute between the Penns and the Baltimores.) During his acting governorship, Thomas Lee had initiated a correspondence on the matter with the governor of Pennsylvania, but no settlement resulted. On the spot, Pennsylvania's interests were watched over by a lusty, wily, and well-informed trader and speculator, George Croghan, who had partners, relatives, and stores up and down the Ohio River and enjoyed good relations with the Indians. The presence of the Ohio Company at the Forks was therefore certain to be protested. And uncertainty about boundaries between adjacent colonies was shortly overshadowed by a greater contest between empires, as rights to the Ohio were claimed by both the British and the French.

In the spring of 1750, George Mason, Dogue's Neck planter, Truro vestryman, Dumfries trustee, and Ohio Company partner, completed his attainment of man's estate with marriage to sixteen-year-

old Ann Eilbeck of Charles County, Maryland, only child of the owners of the plantation adjacent to that where Mason's parents lived during his father's last five years.

William Eilbeck had entered the Potomac trade in the early 1720s as a young agent of Joseph Aderton and Peter How, merchants of Whitehaven; like many other agents, he took up permanent residence in America. The canny trading instinct of his principals animated the instructions issued to him and his associate, Edward Smith, in 1725:

Alarm the planters if possible and tell them Tobacco is fallen in England—and that there will be few Ships in this Year. And let none deliver any letters, unless you see them and that they may not be prejudicial to you, which sometimes does great harm. In case of Death of either of you (which God forbid) we do empower Davy Bateman to act as one of our Agents in all Things. . . . Those goods if you think at any Time you have too much of, then endeavor by all means to get them off and abate of their price, and those, if the planters run upon, raise the price on, to keep sortable as long as you can.[12]

In 1729 or 1730, Eilbeck married Sarah, daughter of John and Joanna Edgar of Prince George's County, Maryland. Since Joanna's will, probated in 1731, excuses her son-in-law from a payment for "storage," his early business dealings on both sides of the river may have used the Edgar plantation as its base. Shortly, he began to accumulate land of his own, first an escheated estate on Mattawoman Creek in Charles County, next an adjacent property of 182 acres with a brick plantation house (known then as Mattawoman and today as Araby) that still overlooks the flood plain from a high bluff above Mattawoman Creek; and then, by inheritance from a brother-in-law, four tracts along the Potomac (called Montrose, today). Charles County land records show him continuing to add to his holdings almost to the time of his death in 1765. Mason's bride grew up at Mattawoman, the presumptive heiress of all around her; at her marriage, the *Maryland Gazette* described her as "a young Lady of distinguishing Merit and Beauty, and a handsome fortune."

The family Bible that George Mason bought toward the end of the 1750s* gives details of the marriage in his hand: "George Mason of Stafford County Virginia, aged about twenty five Years, and Ann Eilbeck (the Daughter of William Eilbeck of Charles county Maryland, Merchant) aged about sixteen Years, were married on Wednesday the 4th. Day of April in the Year 1750 by the revd. Mr. John Moncure Rector of Overwharton Parish, Stafford County Virginia."

Portraits of the young couple were painted at this time by the Maryland artist John Hesselius, under whom Charles Willson Peale received part of his training.[†] Ann's portrait bears out the description that Mason recorded in the same family Bible twenty-three years later: "She was something taller than the middle-size & elegantly shaped. Her Eyes were black, tender & lively; her Features regular & delicate; her Complexion remarkably fair & fresh—Lilies and Roses (almost without a Metaphor) were blended there—and a certain inexpressible Air of Chearfulness, Health, Innocence & Sensibility diffused over her Countenance form'd a Face the very Reverse of what is generally called masculine."

Mason's portrait shows him as a handsome, if somewhat plump and stocky, young man in a dark wig matched by heavy eyebrows; he wears a white neckcloth and ruffled shirt beneath a velvet waistcoat trimmed with gold braid and buttons; the fingers of his left hand are out of sight, inserted where waistcoat buttons have been left open, five buttons down. The waistcoat is dark blue, the topcoat over it, brown.

At the time of the wedding, Mason described himself as of Stafford County, but soon after, he moved to Dogue's Neck. His arrival occurred at about the time that George Washington inherited Mount Vernon; Washington, like Mason, had lost his father when young and, like Mason at Marlborough, had spent much of his youth in the home of his half-brother, Lawrence. Mason's first extant letter dated from Dogue's Neck is a note of sympathy written to his neighbor 29 July 1752, on learning of Lawrence Washington's death: "I came Home f[rom . . .] Yesterday, when I re[ceived your letter informing] me with the time of yr Brother['s fu]neral, & desiring my Attendance. I am very sorry it did not come to [my] Hands sooner; had I known it in [time] I wou'd by no Means have refused the last Peice of Respect to the Memory of a Gentleman, for whom, when alive, I had a sincere Regard—I

*Ann Eilbeck Mason, by Dominic W. Boudet,*
*French refugee and former pupil of Jacques Louis*
*David, after an original of 1750 by John Hesselius;*
*one of three copies commissioned by John Mason in*
*1811*
*(courtesy, S. Cooper Dawson, Jr.,*
*Alexandria, Virginia; photo, Morton Broffman)*

most heartily condole you on the Loss of so worthy a Brother & Friend & am Sir Yr. most hble Sert."[13]

As he started out in life, Mason had all advantages but one: he endured persistently wretched health. Most families suffered annual bouts with such afflictions as dysentery, which they called "the bloody flux": Mason lost an infant son in August 1757, and Washington almost died of it at the end of that same year. Malaria was common. Periodic epidemics of smallpox or yellow fever, brought in on infected ships, incapacitated whole towns. But in addition, many plantation owners, and Mason far more than most, agonized with the eighteenth century's acutely painful, if also genteel disorder, gout. While in some cases, suffering was related to over-devotion to table and wine cellar, Mason shared the abstinence to which William Fitzhugh pridefully ascribed his freedom from the disease: "As to your wonder that I have never been troubled therewith, I'll tell you Sr. I never much frequented Bacchus Orgyes, & always avoided Adoration to Ceres shrine, & never was one of Venus Votarys. . . . To speak plainly to you, I never courted unlawfull pleasures with women, avoided hard drinking as much as lay in my power, & always avoided feasting & consequently the surfeits occasioned thereby, tell your Doctor this, & he will conclude I am not near being his Patient yet."[14]

More applicable in Mason's case was the first-named of the two causes to which the disease was ascribed when the *Encyclopaedia Britannica* first appeared in 1771:

This disease seldom invades any patient till he is upwards of thirty, and men are more subject to it than women; as also persons of acute parts, who follow their studies too closely, especially in the night, with an intense application of mind. Likewise those who live high, and indulge their appetites, drinking plenty of rich generous wines; or who use acids too freely, or white eager wines; or who have been addicted too early to venereal pleasures; or whose bodies are large, gross, and full. Those also are liable to it, whose sweaty feet are too suddenly chilled; or who suffer their feet to sweat in wet shoes and stockings. Hence hunting and riding in the cold are pernicious. It may likewise be received by contagion, and is hereditary, descending from father to son."[15]

Whatever occasioned his discomfort, Mason—and, even more severely, his eldest son after him—was chronically afflicted. His letters to Washington show how, time after time, decade after decade, the malady immobilized him. Even his attendance at the convention at which he drafted his major contributions to the documents of the Revolution was jeopardized; on 18 May 1776, he wrote Richard Henry Lee from Williamsburg: "After a smart fit of the Gout, which detain'd me at Home the first of the Session, I have at last reached this Place."[16]

But in the early 1750s, accepting this persistent limitation and anticipating enjoyment of his many endowments for man's estate, he turned to an enthralling private venture—the construction, on a bluff overlooking the Potomac in the Dogue's Neck peninsula, of a fine new house.

# Chapter III
# Gunston Hall

*In 1751, Thomson Mason, his expenses paid by his older brother, set off to* London to study law; four years later, George Mason commissioned him to bring back a master carpenter and joiner to complete the house whose foundations were already laid. William Buckland's indenture paper, signed in London on 4 August 1755, accepts a four-year commitment at an annual salary of £20.

The man who became one of the earliest professional architects of Virginia and Maryland had grown up in Oxford, son of a yeoman from Burford. His uncle, James, to whom his older brother John was indentured in 1744, was a journeyman of the Worshipful Company of Joiners in London. His own seven-year apprenticeship, aided by a charity grant from Oxford's University School, began in 1748.

For a lad with Buckland's interests, the Oxford buildings were a school in themselves. Seventeenth-century woodcarving abounded in the various colleges: the garlanded panels of Trinity College Chapel were ascribed to Grinling Gibbons himself. Among major structures to go up in the years shortly before young William left home was the Radcliffe Camera, the great domed reading room of the University Library, built by James Gibbs; Gibbs's *Book of Architecture*, published in 1728, was among those Buckland later owned.

He had seen the hand of Christopher Wren in Oxford's Sheldonian Theater; in London, this master's style was everywhere plain— fifty-one churches and the new St. Paul's Cathedral had been erected under his direction after the great fire of 1666.

The young man was in training when the classical revival approached the peak of its English vogue. Almost a hundred years had passed since Inigo Jones had absorbed classical design in Italy, while collecting antiquities for the earls of Arundel and Pembroke, and obtained some of Palladio's own drawings. On his return, his plan for the Queen's House at Greenwich exhibited broken pediments for the first time in England; a few years later, he set the balanced whiteness of the new Banqueting House amid Whitehall's Tudor half-timber and red brick.

In the second quarter of the eighteenth century, new builders' manuals showing plates of classical derivation appeared almost annually. In 1727, the architect William Kent published *The Designs of*

*Inigo Jones* under the patronage of the third earl of Buckingham, then lavishing Latin inspiration on Chiswick House. The Society of Dilettanti, formed in 1734, was soon stimulating examination of Mediterranean sites east of Italy. Richard Pococke's *Description of the East* was published in 1745, and Richard Dalton's *Athenian Architecture* in 1751, the year that James Stuart and Nicholas Revett began scale drawings for their *Antiquities of Athens*. Stuart, like Buckland a poor apprentice in London, had walked most of the way to Rome in 1741; twenty years later, known as "Athenian Stuart," he was London's most fashionable architect initiating the new Greek style. It was this heritage, and this current excitement, that Buckland brought to Virginia.

Had the young man remained in London on the expiration of his apprenticeship, his advance to membership in the Worshipful Company of Joiners would have required a cash payment and the presentation of a master work. Instead, he carved his apprentice pillar in the New World; it was the interior decoration of Gunston Hall.

Under the terms of Buckland's indenture, the Masons undertook to pay his passage and thereafter to provide "all necessary Meat, Drink, Washing, Lodging, fit and convenient for him as Covenant Servants in such Cases." Satisfaction with the performance of this master builder appears in the endorsement, dated November 8, that Mason wrote on the back of Buckland's indenture when it expired in 1759: "The within named William Buckland came into Virginia with my Brother Thomson Mason, who engaged him in London, & had a very good Character of him there; during the time he lived with me he had the entire Direction of the Carpenter's & Joiner's Work of a large House; & having behaved very faithf[ully in] my Service, I can with great Justice recommend him, to any Gentlemen that may have Occasion [to] employ him, as an honest sober diligent Man, & I think a complete Master of the Carpenter's & Joiner's both in Theory & Practice."[1]

Charles Willson Peale's portrait of Buckland, begun in 1774, shows him sitting beside a table on which are the plans of the house that he completed that year for Matthias Hammond in Annapolis: viewing Buckland's subsequent work in Maryland as well as in Virginia, Mason had the pleasure of having brought to the architecture of the middle colonies the source of much of its final colonial distinction.

The back of Buckland's indenture also shows that shortly before leaving England he received an advance on his salary from Thomson Mason in two sums totaling £5; he may have bought and brought with him some of the fourteen architectural books known to have been in his possession later. Three of these titles were in any case readily available to him on arrival in Virginia, for they were the same books that John Mercer had purchased when he began construction of the elaborate brick mansion that he built at Marlborough at the end of the 1740s. Two of them were the thoroughly practical treatises, *The Gentle-*

*William Buckland by Charles Willson Peale,
begun 1774, completed 1787; plans shown on table
are of the Hammond-Harwood House, Annapolis*
(courtesy, The Mabel Brady Garvan Collection,
Yale University Art Gallery)

men's and Builders Repository on Architecture Displayed, Designs Regulated and Drawn by E. Hoppus, and engraved by B. Cole. Containing useful and requisite problems in geometry . . . etc., published in 1738, and Batty Langley's City and Country Builder's and Workman's Treasury of Design, first issued in 1740. Both contained many plates that could be directly copied. The third book was The Paladio Londonensis: or, The London Art of Building, by William Salmon, a carpenter and builder of Colchester in Essex. Andrea Palladio was the sixteenth-century Italian architect whose influence swept Europe from Sweden to the south of France and westward to England and America during the eighteenth-century classical revival. His analysis of architectural proportion in his guidebooks to classical structures in Rome and his illustrations for a new edition of the De architectura of the first-century Roman architect Vitruvius exactly suited the taste of the new humanism and set its style.

Mason's enthusiasm for a brick house instanced a fashion currently advancing up the Potomac. In the lower reaches of the Tidewater, the use of brick instead of wood as a material for residences had started early. The story-and-a-half Adam Thoroughgood house near Norfolk dates from the 1630s; near Jamestown, the Jacobean mansion, Greenspring, was erected as a summer residence for Virginia's governor in Sir William Berkeley's time. Brick churches, courthouses, and clerk's offices had been built in many areas in the seventeenth century, and after the capital was moved to Williamsburg in 1699, the new public buildings—the governor's palace, Brafferton Hall, and the President's House at the college—and several residences accelerated the trend.

The first Mann Page commenced Rosewell, in Gloucester County, shortly after his fire of 1721. In 1727, likewise because of a fire and sooner than he had planned, Thomas Lee inserted Stratford in the sequence of frame homes along the lower Potomac represented by Marmion today; he was burned out of Mount Pleasant by arsonist convicts from England whom he had sentenced for theft as presiding justice of Westmoreland County Court.* Construction of Landon Carter's Sabine Hall—classically named in honor of Horace's villa—was initiated about 1730.

But further up the Potomac, wood continued to be used for churches and courthouses as well as homes; a departure from the style of the early Mount Vernon did not come there until 1741, when William Fairfax built Belvoir on the river between the Washington plantation on Little Hunting Creek and the Mason holdings in Dogue's Neck. Then came Mercer's Marlborough, and then, Mason's Gunston Hall.

Mason's walls were laid in Flemish bond, with gauged-brick flat arches or lintels topping pairs of eighteen-paned windows on each side of the north and south entrance porches. Sandstone quoins, barged upriver from the Aquia Creek quarry, emphasized the four corners; a

*Gunston Hall, landward entrance with dogwood (courtesy, Board of Regents of Gunston Hall Plantation)*

modillioned cornice united walls and roof. Five twelve-paned dormer windows pierced the roof on each side, lighting the upstairs rooms together with three windows in the brick walls at each gable-end between pairs of interior chimneys. Near the roof peaks, light came into the attic through circular windows with a wheel design.

The house was oriented northwest by southeast. Aside from its harmonious proportions, the exterior was chiefly notable for its porches. That fronting the landward entrance was rectangular, with classical round columns topped by a Doric entablature; the arch giving access from steps to platform rose into the pediment in a Palladian design. The five-sided river entrance was more complex: classical pilasters upheld an entablature of triglyphs, metopes, and guttae and framed the high, roundheaded arch where stone steps mounted from the garden walk, but above the balustrades on either side, the arches were formed by ogival curves rising to a sharp point below the entablature. One of the plates in Batty Langley's *Gothic Architecture* shows a similar combination of classical and medieval elements.

*South view of Gunston Hall showing porch (by author)*

On the ground floor of the story-and-a-half structure, a spacious hall ran through the house from the landward entrance, where visitors on horseback or in carriages arrived from King's Highway some four miles to the west, to the garden side, where waterborne guests were received after docking at Mason's quay at the entry of Pohick Creek into the Potomac. Two interconnected rooms flanked the hall on the west side; the two on the east were separated by a narrower hall ending in a door to a brick-paved courtyard around which were grouped the domestic outbuildings.

Elliptical arches supported by pilasters and joined by a pineapple pendant spanned the division between the wide central hall and the stairwell; their keystones penetrated the deep cornice. The newel-post, banisters, double ramps of the rail at the landing, baseboards, chair rail, and cornice of the hall forecast the wealth of carving in the principal rooms that opened from the hall on the west side. Since Buckland could have found little local assistance sufficiently skilled for this phase of the work, it is unsurprising that the house was not finished until 1758—few pieces of interior woodwork are uncarved.

*Entrance hall, Gunston Hall*

*(courtesy, Board of Regents of Gunston Hall Plantation. photo, Charles Baptie)*

In the drawing room at the southwest corner, tall, seven-fluted pilasters with elaborate entablature framed the windows; interior blinds, carved in panels, were hinged to fold flush against the sides of the embrasure. Similar pilasters flanked the wide doors and the recessed cabinets on either side of the fireplace, both topped by elaborate broken pediments. The imported mantel was of carved marble; the caryatids supporting its shelf are reminiscent of Figure 11 in Salmon's *Palladio Londonensis*. Chair rail, door, and window frames were offset a fraction of an inch to permit the plain deal boards that formed the walls to be covered with brocade. The broad floorboards were of pine. Few Virginia homes of the period approached this room in variety and finesse of detail.

From the drawing room, a door led directly into the dining room; its carving was both more subdued and more innovative in style. Buckland could have seen—he is known later to have owned—Thomas Chippendale's book showing Chinese-influenced designs, or he could have looked at actual examples of their use in the showrooms and shop that Chippendale established in St. Martin's Lane in 1753. A very

*Palladian room, Gunston Hall*

*(courtesy, Board of Regents of Gunston Hall Plantation)*

promptly placed order might even. have made him familiar with the *Designs for Chinese Buildings* of William Chambers, the Scottish merchant's son born in Sweden who shipped as supercargo to Canton with the Swedish East India Company at sixteen and upon his return greatly stimulated the English taste for Chinese architecture under the patronage of George III, though Chambers came back to England only after continental study in the spring of 1755* and did not publish until two years later. Whatever its source, Buckland's Chinese room caught a trend in the making; the overmantel and the frames of the flanking closets, doors, and windows were all carved in a western version of the Chinese manner.

The memoirs of his childhood, written in his old age by Mason's fourth son, John, also describe the rooms across the hall from the more ceremonial part of the house; they convey the setting with which the children were most familiar, and afford twin sketches of his father as they saw him in it.

From the youngsters' standpoint, the rooms on which Buckland had lavished his skill most conspicuously were rather remote, associ-

*Chinese Chippendale
room, Gunston Hall
(courtesy, Board of Regents of
Gunston Hall Plantation;
photo, Charles Baptie)*

ated with grown-ups and company. The rooms where the day-to-day life of the house—their life—went on were the plainer ones opposite the formal apartments. Both had windows with window seats, a fireplace and mantel, and cupboards on either side of the chimney breast; the room beside the landward entrance was their parents' bedroom; the room whose windows looked into the garden doubled as a family dining room and as Mason's study.

In their mother's room, the conspicuous piece of furniture in the children's eyes was the very large chest of drawers that held all of their clothes, with a drawer for each article, from stockings and shoes to gowns and caps, shirts and jackets—and penalties were incurred for unauthorized rummaging. These drawers were all kept open, but at the top, two locked drawers were for Ann Mason's private use and held her valuables.

More wardrobe space was available in the two deep closets on either side of the fireplace; that to the right held the part of Ann Mason's wardrobe in current use, known to the children and servants as Momma's Closet or Mistress's Closet. That on the left was a far

*Reconstructed school-house, interior, Gunston Hall*
*(by author)*

greater attraction to the youngsters: known as THE Closet, its shelves displayed small goodies destined for delight at table. The two closets symbolized rewards and punishments, for in Momma's Closet a small green riding whip hung by the ring in its silver head. Ann Mason, who like her husband enjoyed being in the saddle, took this with her when she rode. But the children also knew it in a less happy context under the name of "the Green Doctor."

Among articles of grown-up wear, John's boyish fancy fixed on his father's wig:

It was cloth wig—with curls at the sides—that is the longest hair was turned up behind & concealed in what was called a club and tied with a black ribbon— he had several of these—and one was always kept ready dressed & powdered in a Box for exchange when occasion—they were dressed & prepared by his man James a mulatto man who attended on his person and travelled with him—But he always shaved himself—and used to shave his whole head which was covered by the wig twice a week—In summer for comfort in warm weather at home, he wore a white linen cap often changed in place of the wig—and in cooler weather—when he rode out on his plantation—or went a hunting—for untill he was advanced in life he was a great Sportsman—he wore under his hat a green velvet Cap—His habit was to bathe his head in cold water winter

& summer, on an open porch every morning immediately after rising—a practice I have heard him say he had followed all his life—and which he kept up to the time of his death—altho for many years before he had permitted his hair to grow out and a very thick Suit.[2]

Outdoors, John's inventory begins with the schoolhouse where a succession of three Scottish masters presided, tutoring the boys, while a Mrs. Newman had charge of the girls. Mason's two youngest sons, John and Thomas, were the only children schooled away from home: in the mid-1780s they were sent for a year or two to an academy in Stafford run by the minister of the Aquia and Potomac churches; John then spent a season with another Scotsman of mathematical bent in Calvert County, Maryland, and Thomas attended Fredericksburg Academy in 1788. The usual curriculum for boys was spelled out in the will of their Uncle Thomson; when he died in 1785 he left careful instructions for both the education and the character formation of John's and Thomas's cousins and contemporaries, Westwood and William Temple Mason:

I desire that my two youngest sons may be put to learning English, at one of their Guardians' houses, till Eight years of Age, and that then they be kept at Writing, Arithmetic, and reading elegant English Authors, and modern languages till they are twelve years of Age, and then to be kept at learning one Latin Language, Book Keeping, Mathematics, and other Useful branches of Literature, till the age of Eighteen, and then be put out to such Business or profession as their Genius's are best. . . . I positively direct that neither of my younger sons . . . shall reside on the South side of James River, or below Williamsburgh, before they respectively attain the Age of twenty one years, lest they should imbibe more exalted Notions of their own importance than I could wish any Child of mine to possess.[3]

West of the schoolhouse, John says a row of large English walnut trees masked the stables. To the east, the high-paled courtyard contained the kitchen and well; beyond it were the necessary house, the corncrib and granary, the poultry house, and quarters for the household slaves. Then came the hay yard and cattle pens, masked by rows of large cherry and mulberry trees. An extensive pasture for stock of all kinds ran down to the water and through it the road to the dock where waterborne persons or cargoes were landed or taken off, and boats—piraguas and canoes—kept for river transportation, fishing, and hunting. Farther east was an extensive orchard of fine fruit trees, and beyond this a high-fenced pasture for the plantation's stud stallion. "The occupant in my early days," says John, "was named Vulcan, of the best stock in the country and a direct descendant of the celebrated 'Old James.' "

Vulcan's presence reflected Mason's share in the prevailing Virginia interest in fine horseflesh. In England, careful attention to breeding and the introduction of Arabian stallions had shown results; in turn, Virginia turfmen imported English sons of outstanding sires and developed bloodlines still respected on the American track. Old Janus (John's misnomer is explained by the fact that a Mr. James owned the horse in his last days) was one of eight or ten most fancied studs, imported as a four-year-old in 1752. According to an early nineteenth-century racing source, he was

of low stature, about 14 hands and ¾ of an inch high . . . had great bone and muscle, round, very compact, large quarters, and very swift; all of which desirable qualities he imparted so perfectly to his progeny, that many of them remain in the stock at this remote period; and great speed and muscular form, are still found in many horses whose pedigrees reach him, if accurately traced through different branches; or when, as it is sometimes called, there is "a double Janus Cross." Nearly all his immediate descendants were "swift quarter nags;" they never could run far. He was the sire of an immense number of short distance racers, brood mares and stallions."[4]

While gentlemen's mounts were primarily used for riding out to inspect the quarters of their plantations, to transact business in nearby towns, and to pull the family coach for visits to neighbors or journeys further afield, they were prized for their performance at the race course and on the hunt. Washington's diary abounds in accounts of fox hunts; that of 12 December 1785 was over Mason's land:

About half after ten Oclock (being first plagued with the Dogs running Hogs) we found a fox near Colo. Masons Plantation on little Hunting Creek (West fork), having followed on his Drag more than half a Mile; and run him with Eight Dogs (the other 4 getting, as was supposed, after a second Fox) close and well for an hour. When the Dogs came to a fault, and to cold Hunting until 20 minutes after 12, When being joined by the missing Dogs they put him up afresh and in about 50 minutes killed up in an open field of Colo. Mason's. every rider and every Dog being present at the Death.[5]*

Only a few miles from Gunston was a racecourse managed by the ebullient Boggess family, whose frequent forced appearances before the Fairfax County Court did not preclude the pater familias, Robert Boggess, from service as a vestryman of Pohick Church. Mason was among the gentlemen who enjoyed the sport there; his note to Washington,† then on military duty in the west, recommending his young cousin, French Mason, for a commission and meticulously dated, "Race Ground at Boggess's Saturday 6th May 1758—5'o'Clock P: M:" conveyed the cheerful commotion around him:

The Bearer French Mason, a Relation of mine, has an Inclination to serve his Country. . . . He has lived a good while with me, & if I am not greatly deceived; he has personal Bravery that will carry him thro' any Danger with Reputation, & this Opinion I am the more confirm'd in, as he never was a flashy fellow. . . . He this Moment came up from Wms.burg, & found me here, & as I thought there was no time to be lost, I advised him to set off instantly for Winchester, as soon as I cou'd procure this Scrap of paper, & get a place in the Croud to sit down to write. . . . I have really wrote this in such a Hurry, that I am afraid it's hardly intelligible.[6]

As on any working farm, a seemingly endless number of on-going projects attracted the children's rapt attention. John listed them:

My father had among his slaves carpenters, coopers, sawyers, blacksmiths, tanners, curriers, shoemakers, spinners, weavers and knitters, and even a dis-tiller. His woods furnished timber and plank for the carpenters and coopers, and charcoal for the blacksmith; his cattle killed for his own consumption and for sale supplied skins for the tanners, curriers and shoemakers, and his sheep gave wool and his fields produced cotton and flax for the weavers and spinners, and his orchards fruit for the distiller. His carpenters and sawyers built and kept in repair all the dwelling-houses, barns, stables, ploughs, harrows, gates &c., on the plantations and the outhouses at the home house. His coopers made the hogsheads the tobacco was prized in and the tight casks to hold the cider and other liquors. . . . The distiller made every fall a good deal of apple, peach and persimmon brandy. The art of distilling from grain was not then among us, and but few public distilleries.[7]

In addition, the children could watch the itinerant shoemaker who arrived periodically to supply the family from its own leather; they could follow the annual agricultural cycle from winter fence-mending to spring gardening and births of colts and calves to fall cider-making and hog-killing in frosty November.

Underlying these activities was the field farming basic to the estate, with its staple crops of corn, wheat, and tobacco. Mason owned something over five thousand acres in Dogue's Neck, about two-thirds in virgin forest and the rest worked in four separate quarters of four hundred to five hundred acres, each under an overseer. The tract was bounded by water on three sides: Pohick Creek on the east, the Potomac on the south, the Occoquan on the west, with its Holt's Creek tributary narrowing the northern isthmus to a width of only about a mile. A stout fence crossed this neck, high enough not only to keep Mason's stock where they belonged but also to hold in the native deer.

Mason was a conservationist. In 1734, the General Assembly had forbidden the killing of deer between 1 January and 31 August, setting a fine on illicit hunters of 15/0 per head slaughtered. On 17 February 1771, Mason delivered to the Fairfax County justice, Alexander Henderson, a charge naming sixteen men and boys (including Robert Boggess, Sr., of Truro vestry) who he alleged had killed a total of fifty-two deer since the first of January. His covering letter was indignant:

There has been such shameful Havock made of the Deer during this Snow, when the poor Creatures cou'd not get out of any Body's Way, that I hope the Magistrates & Gentlemen of the County will think it their Duty to make an Example of the Offenders; and as I understand many of them intend to avoid half the Penalty by informing against each other I now make [an] information to you against such Offenders as have come to my Knowledge; a List of which with the Number of Deer kill'd by each Person, you have on the other side; so that if any of them shou'd inform agst. their Comrades, their Scheme will be disappointed by my prior Information.

If the Magistrates will exert themselves properly, I think the Fines to this Parish will be upwards of £200—for if the Informations are made by Gentlemen 'tis probable they will give their Part of the Fines to the Parish after indemnifying themselves for their Expences.[8]

The name the Masons chose for their plantation echoed that of the Gunston Hall built by the second Gerard Fowke in Charles County, Maryland, and the Gunston in Staffordshire from which the immigrant Gerard Fowke, Mason's great-grandfather, came.

*Box allée, Gunston Hall*
*(by author)*

*Garden, Gunston Hall*
*(courtesy, Board of*
*Regents of Gunston*
*Hall Plantation)*

After the debris of construction was cleared away, beginning about two hundred feet from the north door, Mason planted four avenues of trees, radiating out at carefully calculated angles, to produce a trompe l'oeil effect worthy of Palladio. According to John, his father took particular delight in displaying this conceit to visitors:

What was remarkable and most imposing in this avenue was that the four rows of trees being so alligned as to counteract that deception in our vision which, in looking down long parallel lines makes them seem to approach as they recede; advantage was taken of the circumstance and another very pleasant delusion was effected. A common center was established exactly in the middle of the outer doorway of the mansion, on that front, from which were made to diverge at a certain angle the four lines on which these trees were planted, the plantation not commencing but at a considerable distance therefrom (about two hundred feet as before mentioned) and so carefully and accurately had they been planted, and trained and dressed in accordance each with the others, as they progressed in their growth, that from the point described as taken for the common centre, and when they had got to a great size, only the first four trees were visible. More than once I have known my father, under whose special care this singular and beautiful display of trees had been arranged and preserved, and who set great value on them, amuse his friends by inviting some gentleman or lady (who visiting Gunston for the first time, may have happened to arrive after night, or may have come by the way of the river and entered by the other front, and so not have seen the avenue) to the north front to see the grounds, and then by placing them exactly in the middle of the doorway and asking "how many trees do you see before you?" 'four' would necessarily be the answer because the fact was that those at the end of the four rows next the house completely, and especially when in full leaf, concealed from that view, body and top, all the others, though more than fifty in each row. Then came the request 'Be good enough to place yourself now close to either side of the doorway, and then tell us how many you see?' The answer would now be with delight and surprise, but as necessarily, "A great number, and to a vast extent, but how many it is impossible to say!" And in truth to the eye placed at only about two feet to the right or left of the first position, there were presented, as if by magic, four long, and apparently close walls of wood made up of the bodies of the trees, and above, as many of rich foliage constituted by their boughs stretching, as seemed to an immeasurable distance.

To the south of the house, after leveling the hilltop to the point where the land fell away to the river, Mason put in an extensive orchard and garden; over the years this was where he set out the horticultural specialties exchanged with friends and neighbors and listed from time to time in Washington's diaries and Jefferson's garden book. The English box bushes with which he bordered the central walk have grown to nearly twice the height of a man. On the low land beneath the bluff a high-fenced deer park flanked the road to the landing stage.

By the spring of 1759 the family had moved in; Mason entered in the family Bible the birth of a son, named for his brother Thomson, "on Sunday the 4th. of March, 1759 abt. 11 O'Clock in the Fore-noon, at Gunston Hall & privately baptized by the revd. Mr. Charles Green." The children previously born included the couple's namesakes, George and Ann, and Mr. Eilbeck's namesake William, called after a lost baby born in April and dead of the flux in August 1757. Between 1759 and 1770 they welcomed Sarah, Mary, John, Elizabeth, and Thomas, all of whom, except John (he arrived when his parents were staying with his grandmother at Mattawoman) were born at Gunston Hall.

Once established, they took their share in the round of entertaining relatives, neighbors, friends, and strangers which diverted plantation life. John Mason observed:

At that time all the best Families of the State were seated on the Tidewater of the Rivers—great Hospitality reigned every where—and beside the Social & friendly Intercourse of the immediate neighborhood—the Habit was Families who were connected or on Friendly terms to visit each other and spend several Days or weeks at the respective mansions of each other from the distances of 50 or 100 miles—& moreover for Travellers of distinction often to call & pass a night or several Days at the Houses of the Virginia Gentlemen near the public road and during the revolutionary War particularly the officers of the different Corps of Army passing—from North to South, knowing how welcome they would always be very often took up their quarters, at these Houses for a night at least & sometimes for some Days.

Nearest of the Dogue's Neck neighbors were the Martin Cockburns at Springfield. Mason's affection for Cockburn shines through his many letters to him; John Mason recollects:

Our nearest neighbor was Mr. Cockburn, living within one mile. He was an English gentleman from Jamaica, who had settled here to enjoy life, and had married a Miss Bronaugh. . . . They made a part of our family, and the children of our family—they had no children—made a part of theirs by the most intimate and constant intercourse. . . . Among the first things I can remember were discussions and conversations upon the high-handed, tyrannical conduct of the King towards his colonial subjects in this country; for in those days the government was designated by the name of the king in all conversations. And so universal was the idea that it was treason and death to speak ill of the king that I even now remember a scene in the garden at Springfield when my father's family were spending the day there on a certain Sunday when I must have been very small. Several of the children having collected in the garden, after hearing in the house among our elders many complaints towards our country, we were talking the matter over in our own way and I *cursed the king*, but immediately begged and obtained the promise of the others not to tell on me.[9]

Across Pohick Bay was Cedar Grove, home of the McCartys; when young Daniel grew up, he married Mason's daugher Sarah. The Blackburn cousins were at the still existing Ripon Lodge near Dumfries. Three of the children of the Reverend John Moncure, rector of Aquia, had his cousin Mason as their godfather.

Among Mason's long-time friends, the current generation of the Brent family lived downriver at Woodstock. Upriver, Washington had turned in his commission, married Mrs. Martha Dandridge Custis, and was devoting himself to his estate; in 1757, George William Fairfax, whose wife was the talented Sally Cary, inherited Belvoir.

Still more valuable than John Mason's vivid descriptions of the house, the plantation, and the people of the neighborhood of Gunston Hall are his twin accounts of his father as he stood on the threshold of public service. One shows him as the genial eighteenth-century Virginia gentleman and planter, enjoying the life into which he had been born; the other, as the revolutionary thinker, single-mindedly bent on creating political forms for a new age.

As the planter, he operated without the steward or clerk employed by many of his contemporaries. Like his mother before him, he kept his own books—and maintained his ledgers free from debt. With the help of a trusty slave or two, and of his sons as they grew older, he superintended the affairs of field and farm, of processing and marketing, though during the Revolution, when imports were cut off, he engaged a white man and woman to superintend the increased weaving that was required to clothe the family and slaves from the plantation's own resources.

As gentleman host and father, entertaining, John says, "a great deal of company," he was expansive and cheerful, "fond of being ample in his conversations" with visitors and unbending and jocular with the young people who frequented the house. Gunston's wide hall accommodated children's dancing classes, with the fiddler on the landing of the broad stairway; Washington's accounts show entrance fees paid for

Patsy Custis and Milly Posey to attend the group that Mr. Christian taught at Gunston, Mount Vernon, and other plantations in 1770.

John considered his father abstemious in his drinking, but Mason had his toddy before dinner, and in the course of the day two or three glasses of claret or some other French wine when such could be obtained—during the war the British blockade made trade with the Continent difficult.

Dinner was served at two, after the bowl of toddy had circulated. The drink was made of West Indian rum, loaf sugar, and water, with a little nutmeg grated on top. All drank in turn, after an initial ceremony that John says was "a matter of civility in Society," and "belonged to the courtesy of the times,—you saw it in all good company." One of the sons presented the bowl to his father, who said, "I pledge you, Sir!" The son then put the bowl to his lips, tilted it just enough to taste the contents and handed it back to his father. "The practice," John observes, "as I have often heard it stated . . . originated during the civil wars in

England, when hard to tell Friend from Foe in mixed companies—the pledge—of drinking first—was required by him, to whom the Bowl was offered—against the possibility of a poison—in the Draught."[10]

But as the crisis deepened, Mason the constitutionalist often withdrew, body and mind, from the life of the house and family. The gardenside room across the passage from the master bedroom became his private and inviolable study. Ordinarily, it was used for family meals as well, with the formal dining room reserved for occasions when company was present. But when he was working on a public paper— "sometimes for weeks together untill late at night during the Revolutionary War when he was much absorbed in public affairs"—he isolated himself there in single-minded concentration.*

From this room, a door that opened behind the stairs into the main hall permitted him to escape directly through the outer door into his beloved garden—"thus it was in a measure detached from the rest of the House, having a direct, and [to] a degree private way." In good weather, he "would several times a day pass out of his Study and walk considerable time wrapped in meditation, and return again to his desk, without seeing or speaking to any of the family—and in these walks we all well knew, that he was not to be disturbed, more than when sitting amidst his papers—during these periods of study."

He saw the family only at meals—after the food was on the table he would be called, with nobody sitting down until he came in. He then either said himself or had one of his sons say the family grace, "God bless us, and what we are going to recieve," ate his meal, and often left the table ahead of the others. At such times, John says, "he was not morose but often taciturn . . . and I have frequently known his mind— tho' always kind & affectionate to his children so diverted from the objects around him that he would not for days together miss one the Family, that may have been absent and would sometimes at table enquire for one of my Sisters who had perhaps gone a week on a visit to some Friends of which he had known but forgotten."[11] (He was less vague about the boys, since he often busied them with copying papers or running errands about the plantation.)

For thirty years from the time he moved into Gunston Hall, Mason's study was rarely empty of public papers. During the interstices between his participation in colonial, state, or national politics at Williamsburg, Richmond, or Philadelphia, he was more often than not deeply involved in the affairs of Northern Virginia. From the late 1750s, he was a public as well as a private individual.

# Chapter IV
# County and Colony

*The concentration which, according to his son John, periodically abstracted Mason from family affairs moved its focus over a variety of preoccupations in the years 1750-74. During this quarter century, he and George Washington worked closely together at both local and colony-wide levels. Locally, he served as treasurer of the Ohio Company from 1749, town trustee of Alexandria from 1754, gentleman justice of Fairfax County from 1769, and from 1749 vestryman of a parish that initiated three new churches during the years 1763-74. At Williamsburg, he was a member of the House of Burgesses during its sessions of 1758-61 and though no longer in the legislature when the Revolutionary crisis began to develop, he became a major contributor to policy during the Stamp Act furore in 1765 and in the formation of nonimportation associations as a reply to the British tax measures that followed it.*

Among local activities, his most continuous attention was to the Ohio Company. The company had experienced difficulties almost from the moment of its 1749 grant, and now an imperial confrontation between Britain and France was shaping up along the Ohio. Soon after news of the company's intent to build a fort at the Forks reached Canada, the French governor-general at Montreal dispatched Pierre Joseph Céloron de Blainville to stake out the river as part of New France. The lead plates that he placed at strategic locations affirmed the French claim to the land on both shores in no uncertain terms. One such plate, discovered on the bank of the Kanawha River in 1843 and now in the Richmond museum of the Virginia Historical Society, reads in translation:

In the year of 1749, of the reign of Louis the 15th, King of France, we Céloron, commander of a detachment sent by Monsieur the Marquis de la Gallissonière, Governor General of New France, to reestablish tranquility in some Indian villages in these provinces, have buried this plate at the mouth of the River Chinodahichiltha on the 18th of August near the River Ohio, otherwise Beautiful River, as a monument of the renewal of the possession we have taken of the said River Ohio, and of all those which empty into it, and of all the lands on both sides as far as the sources of the said rivers, as enjoyed or ought to have been enjoyed by the kings of France preceding, and as they have there maintained themselves by arms and by treaties, especially those of Ryswick, Utrecht, and Aix la Chapelle.

Responding to the challenge, Governor Dinwiddie sent George Washington and Christopher Gist to deliver a letter to the commandant at Fort Le Boeuf below Lake Erie warning the French off the Ohio Company's lands. William Trent, a Maryland member of the company, was commissioned to select a site and start construction of a fort at the Forks; to arm it, the company ordered twenty swivel guns and other munitions from London. In 1754, Governor Dinwiddie offered free land to men who would join a regiment to protect the king's western territory.

But the French captured the fort before it was finished, renamed it Fort Duquesne for their governor-general, and at the battle of Great Meadows roundly defeated the Virginia troops of whom Washington inherited command on the death of Col. Joshua Fry. This was the initial action in the war known in America as the French and Indian War, but called the Seven Years' War by European principals more aware of its global dimensions. In March 1755, General Edward Braddock, with two British regiments, arrived in Alexandria, set up his headquarters in the house John Carlyle had built three years before, and summoned the governors of four other colonies, Massachusetts, New York, Pennsylvania, and Maryland, as well as selected Virginians, to join him in consultation. All were eager for action; William Shirley of Massachusetts, prestigious because of the capture of Louisburg from the French by Massachusetts troops a decade earlier, presented a prepared plan for offensive operations and the suggestion that the colonies be taxed to pay their share of the cost of the war. With Washington as his aide and Christopher Gist as his guide, Braddock then set forth on his road to military disaster.

In the Gunston Hall neighborhood, the war became a very personal reality. Mason's uncle-in-law, James Mercer, served as an officer with Braddock's troops; he was killed in the fighting at Albany in 1757. William Fairfax's son, Henry, died of wounds received with Wolfe in the assault on Quebec. At the same time, Mason's cousin, William Bronaugh, eldest son of his aunt Simpha Rosa, advanced from ensign to captain in Virginia's troops, and his cousin, William Fitzhugh III, son of his aunt Mary, was likewise an officer. All three of John Mercer's older boys fought with Washington: George received a wound at Fort Necessity; John Fendall, at twenty-four, was scalped by Indians in the spring of 1758; James, a captain at eighteen, commanded Fort Loudoun at Winchester. George survived his wound to become Washington's aide-de-camp.

While his younger kinsmen were in the field, Mason, along with various Alexandria merchants, busied himself supplying the Virginia forces. A letter of 9 July 1755, from Governor Dinwiddie to John (now Major) Carlyle, commissary for the 1754 Ohio expedition, urging the dispatch of flour, pork, and beef to Fort Cumberland, mentions receiving an account from Mason. The designation of Mason as "Colonel," which began at this time, may derive from an unlocated commission issued in connection with these activities. On 8 October 1755, Wash-

*Map of French
and English
possessions on the
North American
continent, c. 1755, by
R. and J. Ottens,
Amsterdam*
(courtesy, State
Historical Society of
Wisconsin)

ington instructed Capt. Thomas Wagener "if Powder and Lead cannot be had in Alexandria, you are to apply to Mr. George Mason,"[1] but eleven months later, writing to the governor on another matter, Washington states that he has "not yet heard from Colonel Mason,"[2] and a letter from Mason to Washington of 13 September 1756 is endorsed: "From Colo. Geo: Mason."

While the recapture of Fort Duquesne—thereafter known as Fort Pitt—by the British General John Forbes in 1758 ended French claims to the river, on the conclusion of hostilities British imperial policy took a turn unfavorable to the Ohio Company. Pennsylvania guaranteed the Delaware Indians not to make new settlements in their territory; the new British commander at Fort Pitt, Col. Henry Bouquet, wrote the new Virginia governor, Francis Fauquier, that Virginia also should observe this agreement and, in 1761, forbade all movement west beyond the Appalachian divide.

That September, on behalf of the Ohio Company and its grants, Mason and four others sent a petition to the king, retained a solicitor, and urged former Governor Dinwiddie, who had kept his company membership on retiring to London in 1758, to exert himself.

Two years later, with no action taken, the company requested permission of Lord Jeffrey Amherst, governor-general of British North America, to establish a town on its Wills Creek property adjoining Fort Cumberland. He refused it. The company then decided to send its own agent to London; the assignment went to George Mercer, who sailed in September 1763. In October, before he arrived, the king, as part of the treaty of peace with France, issued a further proclamation definitely precluding western settlement. For the time being, it appeared that nothing more could be done.

Matters worsened during the 1763-73 decade. Britain's policy on western settlement exacerbated colonial resentment at the same time that policy on taxation excited antagonism along the seaboard. While the Proclamation of 1763 forbade all westward movement, the nearly empty hunting grounds that it reserved for the use of the Indians proved a vacuum into which migration by individual families and speculation by associated companies inevitably moved.

George Mercer, after a trip to Virginia at the time of the Stamp Act crisis, described further on in this chapter, continued in London as the Ohio Company's representative, but there degenerated into a gentleman trifler on the fringes of preferment, perennially hopeful of lucrative employment, perennially facing debtor's prison.* His attention to the Ohio Company's affairs in the mid-1760s consisted of the petition he presented in 1765 for a compensatory grant of land in an area where the Proclamation of 1763 did not prohibit settlement, or at least for reimbursement of the company's expenditures incurred in building roads and trading posts. But the Board of Trade merely queried Governor Fauquier in 1768 on the extent of the company's expenditures and on the "effect which the encouragement of such settlement may have on the temper of the Indians."

By that time, rumors of new ventures were circulating. Robert Carter, a major Ohio Company shareholder and a member of the Governor's Council, warned Mason in February from Williamsburg that two or three new entities were expected to be created in the west. In the last weeks of his life, Governor Botetourt had requested Mason to draft a company proposal of bounds for a grant; responding, Mason suggested an acreage generally consistent with the grant of 1749 but avoiding conflict with Pennsylvania claims.

In London, Mercer published *The Case of The Ohio Company*, petitioning the Board of Trade "not to make any grant, within the limits prescribed by the royal instruction to the Company," but there was little enthusiasm for the company's claims in Williamsburg and none in Whitehall. As a negotiator at court, Mercer was now pitted against political skill and influence far superior to his. A group of Philadelphia land

Bookplate for library of the
Virginia Council chamber,
early eighteenth century;
Greek motto is from the
Iliad: "from his lips flows
speech sweeter than honey"
(courtesy, Virginia State
Library)

speculators, chief among them the wealthy Whartons and Benjamin
Franklin, together with English courtiers of influence, including Thomas
Walpole, cousin of Horace of Strawberry Hill, had formed the Grand
Ohio Company and were intent on purchasing 2.5 million acres from
the Crown on which to establish a fourteenth colony. (Their suggested
name for it, intended as a compliment to presumed ancestors of the
queen, was Vandalia.) The territory, comprising most of the present
state of West Virginia, overlapped the original Ohio Company grant.

Mercer was suborned by this group; on 7 May 1770, he agreed to
a merger, accepting two share of their Grand Ohio stock as recompense
for the Virginia Ohio Company's partners (and one share for his own
good offices) and justifying himself on the ground that the Ohio Company had given him freedom of action, had sent him no instructions, and
had left unpaid his bill for services rendered. No reply, he complained,
had come to a letter written in 1767 (but he had been home in 1768) and
to four more written after his return to England.*

While Mason "received a Letter from my kinsman Colo. Mercer
dated the 24th of July speaking very doubtfully of the Ohio Company's

affairs," the company's agent did not at once fully report his recent transaction; when the whole story became known, the partners repudiated Mercer's agreement, and in July 1772, Richard Henry Lee petitioned the Virginia Council once more for renewal of the 1749 grant, supporting his request with a detailed and heavily annotated document, *Extracts from the Virginia Charters with some Remarks upon them made in the year 1772*, in which Mason reviewed the colony's title to the western lands from the earliest times. No response was forthcoming. The company's affairs continued to languish, and at the same time Virginia's claims south of the Ohio were squeezed by a succession of North Carolinian ventures in which members of Virginia companies with holdings along the Tennessee were suspected of complicity. Mason expressed his irritation to Washington: "I suppose you have heard of the late Purchase made by some North Carolina Gentlemen from the Cherokee Indians, of all the Country between the Great Conhaway & the Tennessee Rivers. I think, considering this Colony has just expended abt. £100,000, upon the Defence of that Country, that this is a pretty bold Stroke of the Gentlemen. It is suspected some of our Virga. Gentlemen are privately concern'd in it."[3] But for the time being, other matters were proving more pressing than the future of the western lands.

In 1758, Mason had entered colony-wide political affairs. A decade after his first candidacy for the House of Burgesses, he offered again, this time with success.

Not all elections went smoothly. On receipt of a writ from the governor calling for election of a new House of Burgesses, each county sheriff set a date on which citizens gathered, usually at the courthouse steps, to hear qualified voters shout out their preferences. The canvassing that preceded and accompanied these votes often led to sharp exchanges, sometimes of words, sometimes of blows. On 11 December 1755, the three candidates for Fairfax's two seats were: an incumbent, John West; George William Fairfax, who had previously represented Frederick County on the western frontier; and William Ellzey, a Colchester trustee and Mason's attorney. Washington was a vigorous supporter of Fairfax; William Payne, a Truro vestryman with influence in the southern and inland parts of the county, was equally strong for West. When the results were tallied, West topped the poll; only two votes separated Fairfax and Ellzey.

During the canvass, words passed between Washington and Payne. Exasperated, Payne, the smaller man of the two, suddenly felled Washington with his walking stick. The embarrassment of Washington's prone position was amplified by his recent commission as commander-in-chief of Virginia's forces. The crowd that observed the encounter awaited a challenge to a duel. But reflection on what he had said convinced Washington that his remarks had indeed been offensive; he requested a meeting with Payne and declared himself in the wrong.

At the 1758 election, when Fairfax decided not to offer again, Mason replaced him. His brother, Thomson, was similarly successful in Stafford.

Among the new faces in the House that assembled that autumn, and in which Mason served for three years, were several of Mason's current and future friends and political allies, Washington included.

Washington offered in Frederick County, where he was stationed with his militia command. Three years earlier, he had been defeated there in his first contest for the House. This time, he and Lord Fairfax's nephew, Col. Thomas Bryan Martin, challenged the incumbents, and in a vigorously contested upset, both won. Col. James Wood, founder of Winchester, had acted as Washington's agent while the colonel was on duty further west; he was chaired shoulder-high around the town to huzzahs for his candidate. George William Fairfax and John Carlyle of Alexandria and Gabriel Jones of Hampshire had canvassed their tenants in Frederick; officers stationed in the area had joined the solicitation. A factor in the campaign was the antagonism of the local tavern keepers, the result of Washington's severe punishment of drunkenness among his men. Yet treating voters to drinks was a standard—if illegal— election-day practice. Given the circumstances, Washington's backers decided to spare no expense. In the thirsty heat of midsummer, the qualified voters, friends, and onlookers present consumed more than 150 gallons of rum punch, rum, brandy, wine, and beer, not to mention two gallons of cider, and brought Washington's campaign expenses to £39.6.0. But the results were highly satisfactory—Washington, 309; Martin, 239; West, 199; Swearingen, 45. Washington represented Frederick until 1765, when he became a member from Fairfax; George Mercer was the county's other burgess from 1761 until he went to England in 1763.

The new Assembly received an exceptional influx of Lees. Henry Lee of Leesylvania near Dumfries in Prince William had stood for election in 1756 but had been denied his seat on a challenge; now he was back, uncontested. "Squire Richard" of Lee Hall near Hague in Westmoreland had assumed the seat of Philip Ludwell Lee, eldest son and heir of Councillor Thomas, on Philip's elevation to the Council the previous spring; in 1758 Philip became Council president and thereafter was closer to the royal governors and their outlook than other members of the family.

Councillor Thomas Lee had had six sons: at this election, the three next in age to Philip all came to Williamsburg as new House members: Thomas Ludwell from Stafford, Richard Henry from Westmoreland, Francis Lightfoot from Loudoun. With their two junior brothers, William and Arthur, who through most of the subsequent years were strategically located abroad, this politically minded fraternity formed what was close to a self-contained faction in Virginia politics. In a partnership that began at this session and lasted through Mason's lifetime, he and Richard Henry Lee worked together.

The Williamsburg to which the new members repaired in October was described only months later by English traveler Andrew Burnaby:

*Richard Henry Lee by Charles Willson
Peale, c. 1784*
(courtesy, Independence National Historical
Park, Philadelphia)

*Reconstructed Governor's Palace, Williamsburg (by author)*

"Williamsburg . . . consists of about two hundred houses, does not contain more than one thousand souls, whites and negroes; and is far from being a place of any consequence. It is regularly laid out in parallel streets, intersected by others at right angles; has a handsome square in the center, through which runs the principal street, one of the most spacious in North-America, three quarters of a mile in length, and above a hundred feet wide. At the ends of this street are two public buildings, the college and the capitol: and although the houses are of wood, covered with shingles, and but indifferently built, the whole makes a handsome appearance. There are few public edifices that deserve to be taken notice of; those, which I have mentioned, are the principal; and they are far from being magnificent. The governor's palace, indeed, is tolerably good, one of the best upon the continent; but the church, the prison, and the other buildings, are all of them extremely indifferent. The streets are not paved, and are consequently very dusty, the soil hereabout consisting chiefly of sand: however, the situation of Williamsburg has one advantage, which few or no places in these lower parts have; that of being free from mosquitoes. Upon the whole, it is an agreeable residence; there are ten or twelve gentlemen's families constantly residing in it, besides merchants and tradesmen: and at the times of the assemblies, and general courts, it is crowded with the gentry of the country: on those occasions there are balls and other amusements; but as soon as the business is finished, they return to their plantations; and the town is in a manner deserted."[4]

Neither Mason nor Washington was new to the capital: Mason, James Scott, and John Mercer had called the first meeting of the re-organized Ohio Company into session at Mr. Wetherburn's tavern on the Duke of Gloucester Street on 7 May 1752; in January of that year, on returning from Barbadoes with his brother Lawrence, Washington had paid his respects to Governor Dinwiddie, and in October 1753, at the Governor's Palace, he had received the letter he had volunteered to deliver to the French commanding officer at Fort Le Boeuf.

By the spring of 1758, there was a new governor, Francis Fauquier having succeeded Robert Dinwiddie in the post, but the king's attorney general, Peyton Randolph, had served both in that capacity and as a burgess from 1748; John Robinson, speaker of the House and treasurer of the colony since 1738, was a man of whose power as a land speculator as well as a politician Mason and other newcomers from the Northern Neck were well aware.

At the opening of the Assembly, before crowded galleries, Washington received the thanks of the House for his military services: the occasion so overwhelmed him that he was incapable of a coherent reply. In a nineteenth-century account, Robinson is said to have terminated his confusion with a deft dismissal: "Sit down, Mr. Washington. Your modesty equals your valor, and that surpasses the power of any language that I possess."[5]

Early in the session, an issue emerged that in various forms occupied men's minds for nearly fifteen years. The year 1755 began a sequence of near failures of the tobacco crop. That December, the Assembly passed the Two Penny Act, attempting to mitigate the effects of the scarcity by permitting taxes and other dues usually calculated in tobacco to be paid, if the debtor so desired, in currency, at a rate of two pence per pound of tobacco owed.

Clergy salaries had for decades been set by statute at sixteen thousand pounds of tobacco per year. Believing that the going rate for tobacco would be materially higher than two pence, the recipients, resenting the Assembly's action, made representations through their commissary. But as the year wore on with the average price of tobacco hovering around the two-penny level, indignation died away.

The 1758 season was again bad. Landon Carter's diary describes the spring drought that turned the fields to dust: though he ordered his slaves to set his tobacco seedlings out at night, to take advantage of evening dampness and give the plants a few relatively cool hours before wilting under the morning sun, the crop shriveled. The price rose from tuppence to six-to-eight pence per pound; in October, the Assembly of which Mason was a member voted a second Two Penny Act. Representative clergy waited on the governor, urging his veto, but Fauquier, in office only since June, was not of a mind to offend the planter majority in the Assembly. The Reverend John Camm then took ship for England, where he was given an audience with the king. On 10 August 1760, the second Two Penny Act was disallowed. Various ministers brought suit against their vestries for payment of back salary, among them the Reverend James Maury of Fredericksville Parish, Hanover County.

In the Maury case, the Hanover County Court, recognizing the disallowance of the Two Penny Act, sustained the rector and empaneled a jury to assess damages. As a last resort, the defendant vestry, after its attorney withdrew from what he regarded as a hopeless cause, retained the fledgling lawyer, Patrick Henry. Exercising unexpected eloquence, Henry mesmerized the jury into setting the Reverend Mr. Maury's damages at one penny.

Many clergymen were bitter. Yet a rector's degree of bitterness at the Two Penny Acts was likely to reflect the extent of his dependence on his salary as his sole source of income. In Mason's area, the rectors were affluent. In Truro, the Reverend Charles Green was a considerable landholder; the Reverend John Moncure of Overwharton lived at Clermont, his estate on the Potomac; the Reverend James Scott, whose wife was a Mason cousin, inherited from the Reverend Andrew Scott, his brother, the plantation called Dipple, in Stafford. Scott was an active participant in the Ohio Company; both he and the Reverend John Moncure served as gentleman justices and Dumfries trustees. Lee Massey, who succeeded the Reverend Mr. Green at Truro, was a lawyer with an estate on the Occoquan before his neighbors persuaded him to take orders. In this part of the Northern Neck, no suits were brought by the clergy.

The economic crisis that brought on the Parson's Cause carried implications for the towns along the Potomac and for the growers whose tobacco alternately filled or failed to fill their warehouses. Over past decades, though farsighted planters had recognized the risks of one-crop agriculture, few had diversified. But now, increased settlement on the red clay of the Piedmont, inland from the alluvial sand of the rivers and less suitable for tobacco, was producing salable supplies of wheat. Alexandria and Georgetown drew on a large hinterland, opened up by new roads, as well as on the adjacent plantations; Dumfries was less well placed and declined when silting from upstream deforestation progressively choked its port. Enterprisers began to set up grist mills—the firm of John Carlyle and Robert Adam erected one at Alexandria; the Merchants Grist Mill was at Occoquan. Provident planters such as Mason and Washington, who put up a grist mill of his own, turned to grain.

*Washington's grist mill,*
*Fairfax County*
*(by author)*

By 1768, Washington could write the brothers Hanbury, in London, "Having discontinued the growth of tobo. myself, except at a plantation or two upon York River, I make no more of that Article than barely serves to furnish me with goods."[6]

Robert Carter's list of merchants in Alexandria in 1775 shows the extent of the shift to cereals: of twenty firms named, twelve dealt exclusively as wheat buyers; two as retailers of Philadelphia goods and buyers of both wheat and tobacco; three as retailers of British goods and buyers of tobacco. Of the remaining three, one imported rum and sugar, one was a distiller, and one was an importer and wholesaler of British goods.

Yet the change to grain production, while usefully diversifying the colony's agriculture, diminished the universality of the crop that also served as its medium of exchange. Debtors with obligations that could not be met in tobacco intensified the search for scarce specie—to meet even a minor bill in currency, a man might have to assemble a motley collection of foreign coins, each with its own exchange rate, along with some English shillings. The shortage of coin induced irate reaction when Governor Dinwiddie attempted to levy a payment of one pistole as a fee for the issuance of a land patent.

Mason retired from the legislature after the 1761 session; his next entry into colony-wide affairs, in 1765, was through papers prepared at Gunston Hall. Meanwhile, and on into the mid-1770s, he and Washington were associated in small matters and large in the neighborhood; for each, the affectionate companionship of this period was a source of subsequent nostalgia.

They exchanged condolences sometimes coupled with cautions when illness and death afflicted their households. In 1751, Mason's sister Mary had married Col. Samuel Selden of Salvington, across Potomac Creek from Marlborough; on 4 January 1758, Mason wrote Washington of her critical condition and at the same time warned his friend not to venture out too soon after his own recent serious illness: "I hope you will comply with the Opinion & Advice of all your Friends, & not risque a Journey to Winchester till a more favourable Season of the Year, or a better State of Health, will permit you to do it with Safety . . . there is nothing more certain than that a Gentleman in your Station owes the Care of his Health & Life not only to himself & his Friends, but to his Country. If you contin[ue] anytime at Mount Vernon, I will do myself the pleasure of spending a Day or two with you very soon."[7]

Four years later, on 13 November, death came to Chopawamsic, claiming Mason's mother. His father-in-law, William Eilbeck, died in 1765. Mrs. Eilbeck lived until 1780, surviving by five years a breast cancer operation regarding which Mason wrote Washington: "I return'd from Maryland but last Night, not being able to leave Mrs. Eilbeck sooner, & don't know how quickly I may be called there again, as I think she is far from being out of Danger, & the Doctor has some Apprehensions of a Mortification. I will if I can, be at Alexandria on

Monday; but it is uncertain."[8] In the intervening years, Mason devoted much time both to the administration of his father-in-law's estate and to the care of his widow.

In cases of insolvency and mismanagement on nearby plantations, Mason and Washington cooperated as advisors, arbitrators, and at times creditors. Among the most incurable debtors of the area was John Posey, their ever-hopeful, ever-improvident friend and neighbor at Ferry Farm west of Mount Vernon. In 1767, when his debts at Mount Vernon reached the limit of Washington's patience, he turned to Mason, though warned by Washington that "he tells you, in express terms and with candor that he is waiting for an opportunity of making a purchase. . . . It is as likely, therefore, that he may call for it [his money] in Six months as in a longer time, because the distress of the country and number of Estates which are daily advertising afford great prospect of purchasing to advantage."[9] Even a lucrative second marriage proved insufficient to his needs. In 1769, Posey's land and effects were sold up at auction; Washington, attending "with Colo. Mason . . . and Colo. Mason's Son George,"[10] acquired Ferry Farm and its cross-Potomac ferry.

The death of John Mercer in October 1768 not only left Mason to carry on the Ohio Company's affairs almost single-handedly but involved the two neighbors in the difficulties of the Mercer estate. Mercer had retired from the law in 1765, his health gone and his financial straits desperate. Yet instead of cutting his outlays, he had plunged into a new enterprise: he built a brewery, bought additional slaves to grow barley for it, and hired a brewmaster from abroad. The result proved barely potable. *Per varios casus.*

His son James invited Mason's and Washington's help in the doubly impossible task of settling his father's estate and meeting his brother George's debts in Britain and Virginia. A letter from Mason to Washington shows little progress to have been made by the end of 1773: "The embarrass'd Situation of my Friend Mr. Jas. Mercer's Affairs gives me much more Concern than Surprize. I always feared that his Aversion to selling the Lands & Slaves, in expectation of paying the Debts with the Crops & Profits of the Estate, whilst a heavy Interest was still accumulating, wou'd be attended with bad Consequences, independant of his Brother's Difficultys in England; having never, in a single Instance, seen these sort of Delays answer the Hopes of the Debtor."[11]

As an Alexandria trustee, Mason voted for various improvements as the town grew. He was present at a meeting on 18 June 1755, when John Carlyle was ordered to build a new warehouse at Point Lumley, and on 30 September, when, in view of the fire hazard, all wooden chimneys on houses and smiths' shops were ordered replaced by brick, otherwise to be pulled down by the sheriff. On 18 July 1759, John Carlyle and John Dalton agreed to build a "good and convenient" landing at the foot of Cameron Street, "they and their heirs to have the use of half of it as recompense for its cost."

Permission was given Thomas Fleming to start a shipbuilding venture: "This indulgence is granted this Fleming in Consideration of his usefulness as a Ship Carpenter and his Inclination to serve this Town to the utmost of his Power." The proceeds of a lottery built an Assembly Hall that included space for a grammar school. The poor condition of this building, "very much injured by the negligence of the Schoolmasters," concerned the trustees in 1767; while specifying repairs, they ordered the upper room refitted for their own monthly meetings.[12]

Regular markets and semiannual fairs in May and October were held on plots reserved for them in the center of town. From 1753, the Reverend Charles Green preached every third Sunday. Inns and ordinaries multiplied. The Royal George, brick with carved paneling and a ballroom upstairs, was the relay station for the mail and had stabling for a hundred. Gentlemen dined at the elegant City Tavern (later a part of Gadsby's*), and at David Arrell's Indian Queen on King Street across from Mason's property. The Rainbow Inn, frequented by drovers and peddlers, was at the horse market near Sharpshin Alley, the lane that took its name from the pocket-piercing pieces formed by cutting a silver coin into four bits.

A number of trustees who lived at a distance, and other men with frequent business in the town, kept offices where they could carry on transactions and spend the night. When Washington became a trustee in 1766, he built a house on Cameron Street, as Mason had done on King Street eleven years before. Near the wharves, a number of merchants put up two- or three-story brick buildings with double entrances, one leading to ground-floor showrooms and the other to spacious family quarters above stairs.

A spectacular celebration of a local election occurred in November 1761, when Alexandria's trustees organized a municipal government and, adopting a British practice, named William Ramsay lord mayor. The *Maryland Gazette* of 1 December described his installation:

There was held for the first time at Alexandria on St. Andrew's Day the election of Lord Mayor, Aldermen and Council of this city. . . . Mr. William Ramsay, first projector and founder of this promising city, was invested with a gold chain and medal. . . .

The election being ended, the Lord Mayor and Common Council, preceded by officers of State, Sword and Mace bearers, and accompanied by many gentlemen of the town and county made a grand procession to different quarters of the city, with drums, trumpets, a band of music and colors flying.

The company wore blue sashes and crosses in compliment of the day and upon the whole, made a fine appearance. . . . The shipping in the harbor displayed their flags and streamers, continuing firing guns the whole afternoon. . . . In the evening a ball was given by the Scots gentlemen, at which a numerous and brilliant company of ladies danced. The night concluded with bonfires, illuminations and other demonstrations.

The county court, after Loudoun was formed from Fairfax in 1757, no longer met at Gallow's Hill on the road from Alexandria to Leesburg near today's Tyson's Corner; a courthouse was erected in

*City Tavern
and City Hotel,
later Gadsby's,
Alexandria
(by author)*

Alexandria beside the market square, with jail, pillory, and whipping
post nearby. The green in front of it served as a parade and drill ground
for the militia and accommodated the crowds that gathered for auctions
of tax tobacco and for elections to the House of Burgesses and town
offices.

Over the ensuing years, in this courthouse and more importantly
at citizen assemblies and militia musters on the green, Washington and
Mason acted in concert. Washington was appointed a gentleman justice
in 1760 and on 16 May 1769, "George Mason Gent. having first taken
the oaths according to Law repeated and subscribed to the Teste was
sworn a Justice of this Court at common Law and in Chancery."[13] (The
Test Act, of which a manuscript copy remains in the Fairfax Courthouse,
barred Catholics from public office: "I do declare that there is no Tran-
substantiation of the Sacrament of the Lord's Supper or in the Elements
of Bread and Wine at or after the Consecration Thereof by any person
Whatsoever.")

*Mantel, City Tavern,*
*Alexandria*
*(courtesy, City of Alexandria)*

The day of Mason's induction afforded more excitement than usual. The merchant firm of Glassford and Henderson brought an action against Francis Dade; the court ruled that "on hearing the Evidences and arguments of the parties it is considered that the Plaintiffs recover against the Defendant four pounds seven shillings & an halfpenny with Costs."[14] On hearing the verdict, the defendant, who had fortified himself against it at a local tavern, castigated one of the justices so offensively that the court entered a second order: "Francis Dade having this day grossly abused Sampson Darrell Gent. in open court relating to the execution of his office as late Sheriff and being drunck and obstructing the business of the Court is fined five pounds and it is ordered that he be committed until he pays the same with Costs."[15]

The former sheriff, unwilling to let the matter end there, then obtained a third order: "On a Complaint of Sampson Darrell against Francis Dade, it appears by the Oath of Franklin Perry and Richard Leake that the said Francis Dade last night at a public ordinary abused the Justices of this Court calling them partial sons of bitches, that he would

*The William Ramsay
House, Alexandria
(by author)*

have their Ears cropt and he would turn them out of Comission which
is ordered to be certified to the next General Court."[16] Dade was escorted to jail, there to wait transfer to Williamsburg.

Actions for debt were also the most frequent item on the docket
on less exercised occasions.* The judges' agenda was likewise apt to
include citations of tobacco growers for the tending of seconds, of the
well-to-do for not declaring their coaches for tax purposes, and of persons of all stations for not attending church. More serious offenses
brought to them for judgment were births of baseborn children, usually
to servant women,† minor crimes by whites,‡ and all crimes by slaves.§

Mason and Washington were colleagues on the Truro vestry as
well as on the Fairfax bench. In 1765, when the assembly formed a new
parish, Fairfax, from the upper part of Truro, an inequitable division of
population caused dissatisfaction; even when redrawn, the line gave the
new Fairfax 1,013 and the new Truro 962 tithables. Gunston Hall was in
Truro in both cases, but Mount Vernon was in the transferred area;
Washington's membership therefore shifted from Fairfax to Truro between the election of vestry in March and that in July. Ever methodical,
Washington recorded the votes received by the twelve successful
men at each election: in that of March, Mason stood second in Truro
while he was fifth in Fairfax; in that of July, after his transfer, Mason
led the Truro list with 282 votes and he was third with 259.[17]

Following the division, the Truro vestry arranged with that of

*Aquia Church,
completed in 1757
(by author)*

Fairfax to finish building the Falls Church, started in 1763 west of Alexandria and now in its territory, and launched a building program of its own.

Mason had had vicarious experience of church building when his uncle, John Mercer, was on the vestry that in 1745 began to plan a new church for Overwharton Parish just north of Aquia Creek. Put up in 1751, it burned two years later, but rapid replacement erected the innovative cruciform brick structure, two stories tall, with two tiers of windows, stone-quoined corners and stone-framed doors, that is still in use today. The tower at its western end was one of the earliest on a Virginia church, and the earliest in the upper counties—that of Bruton Parish in Williamsburg was not added until 1769, and many others, like that of Christ Church, Alexandria, date from the early nineteenth century. Inside, a further unique feature was the triple-decked lectern-pulpit, with separate desks for the reading of the first and second lessons, and a pulpit proper that elevated the Reverend John Moncure high over his congregation for the homily of the day. A contemporary tablet commemorating completion of the edifice in 1757 lists the rector, the vestry, the undertaker of the contract, Mourning Richards, and the mason, William Copein.

With the Truro Parish levy raised from the previous range of twenty to thirty-seven pounds of tobacco per tithable to sixty pounds, on 4 February 1766 a site was agreed on for a brick church in the interior of the county to be built by Edward Payne for £ 579 Virginia currency

*Aquia Church,*
*interior*
*(by author)*

and to be completed by October 1768. Its specifications show that the terms of classical architecture were by this time in common use. The building was to be 53½ by 30 feet, with a gallery; "the Cornish to be in Proportion to the hight of the Walls (which are to be twenty two feet and an half) with Dentile Blocks . . . the Iles to be laid with Brick Tyle, the Pews to be wainscotted . . . double work on each side of the framing and raised pannel on one side." The altarpiece, 16 by 12 feet, to be "done with wainscot after the Ionic order. . . . The Pulpit, Canopy and reading Desks to be of black walnut. . . . The Gallery to be supported by Collums turned & fluted."

At the meeting that adopted these plans, a new man was recommended to His Grace the Bishop of London for ordination to replace the late Reverend Charles Green: Lee Massey, "having lived several Years amongst us and his moral Character and unexceptionable Life and Conversation being well known to most of us." Simultaneously, the vestry wrote Governor Fauquier to prevent assignment of any other rector to Truro while Massey was abroad: he "has an Intention of entering into holy Orders, provided he can have a Certainty of this Parish." Massey was installed in 1767.

Edward Payne fulfilled his contract: on 9 September 1768, when the vestry met to view the new church, Mason was ordered to make him his final payment plus an extra sum for horse blocks and benches in the churchyard.

Immediately, plans were begun for another brick structure, this one to replace the frame church on Pohick Creek, now fallen into disrepair. On 3 March 1769, Daniel French contracted to build the new Pohick about two miles north of the old at the crossroads from Hollis's to the Pohick warehouse, above Robert Boggess's racetrack. The price, based on plans drawn by James Wren and William Wait, was set at £877 Virginia currency, the work to be kept under review by a building committee consisting of George William Fairfax, George Washington, George Mason, Daniel McCarty, and Edward Payne.

The new edifice, larger and more lavishly decorated than the Falls Church, was to be 66 by 45½, with walls 28 feet high, "three bricks thick to the Water Table, and two and a half afterwards," with "the Corners of the House, the Pedistals, and Doors with the Pediment heads to be of good white freestone." Windows—"the Lights to be of the best Crown Glass"—and doorframes were to have double architraves; the cornice to be modillion outside and cove inside. On the 20 foot high and 15 foot wide altarpiece, "done with wainscot after the Ionic Order," the Apostles Creed, Lord's Prayer, and Ten Commandments were "to be neatly Painted" in black letters. Completion was stipulated for 1 September 1772. This time, horse blocks and benches under the trees were included in the contract, as well as obligation "to clear and remove all the Rubbish and litter from off the Church Lott."

In 1771, two new vestrymen, Peter Wagener and Martin Cockburn (the latter replacing John Posey, who left the area after his disposal sale), were added to the building committee, which changed the size of the altarpiece and concluded that the stone on the exterior of the church was so soft that it would have to be painted. In June 1772, the vestry arranged for the sale of pews, and for William Bernard Sears to carve ornaments on the tabernacle, canopy, and altarpiece, "guilding the Letters thereon with Gold Leaf, Presented to this Parish by the Honble. George Wm. Fairfax and George Washington Esqrs." On 4 June 1773, a stone font, copied from the upper left-hand drawing on Plate 150 of Langley's *Design*, was ordered from William Copein; a final instruction to Sears was to "gild the Ornaments within the Tabernacle Frames the Palm Branch and Drapery on the Front of the Pulpit, (also the Eggs on the Cornice of the small Frames if the Gold will hold out.)"

This church was not fully completed and accepted by the vestry until 15 February 1774; work was delayed when Daniel French died in

*Pohick Church, completed in 1774,*
*interior as restored*
*(by author)*

1771, and it was George Mason, as his executor, who assumed responsibility thereafter. The auction of pews raised a substantial fund toward its cost. Pews Nos. 1 and 2, flanking the communion table along the south wall, were reserved respectively for magistrates and strangers, and for vestrymen and merchants; those opposite on the north side, for their wives. Mason bought Nos. 3 and 4 on the south aisle, paying £14.11.8 for each. At the front of the center block of pews, facing the altar, were George William Fairfax's and George Washington's; behind Fairfax, Alexander Henderson bought two, while the Washingtons, first Lund and then George, owned a second. John Manley, whose sister was Daniel French's widow and whose wife was Massey's niece, took the third. On the north wall, Martin Cockburn's and Daniel McCarty's pews were across from the Washingtons'; that next to the pulpit was reserved for the rector's family. At the vestry meeting of 24 February 1774, deeds for these pews were delivered to their owners, and a last touch of finery added: "a cushion for the pulpit* and altar cloths of Crimson Velvett with Gold Fring, and that Colo George Washington be requested to import the same," as also two folio Prayer Books "covered with blue Turkey Leather with Name of the Parish thereon in Gold Letters, the Demensions of the said Cushion and Cloths being left to Wm. Bernard Sears who is desired to furnish Colo. Washington with proper Patterns at the Expense of the Parish."[18]

Shortly before the time that Pohick was accepted by the Truro vestry, the Fairfax vestry completed its new church in Alexandria; the Church of England in Fairfax County thus acquired four brick structures in a little over a decade, three of which survive today.

Nor was the Church of England the only form of Christian worship to take on new stature in these years. Alongside the Established ritual, by mid-century a more fervent expression of faith was gaining adherents, exhorted by such revivalists as the English George Whitefield. Trained at Oxford under the brothers Wesley, this extraordinary man made seven transatlantic visitations between 1737 and 1770, evangelizing from Savannah, Georgia, his first port of arrival, to Newburyport, Massachussetts, where he lies buried. Ousted from English pulpits because of the excitement he engendered, Whitefield early took to preaching in secular surroundings, often out-of-doors—Benjamin Franklin's *Autobiography* attests his remarkable voice to have been capable of reaching twenty-five thousand listeners. Humble folk who felt ill-at-ease in the presence of vestments and ritual were attracted, aroused, and comforted. Whitefield was not bent on schism: the diary of his first trip to Virginia laments: "If I talk of the *Spirit*, I am a *Quaker*; if I say Grace at Breakfast, and behave *seriously*, I am a *Presbyterian*. Alas! what must I do to be accounted a Member of the *Church of England!*"[19] But the Established Church would have none of him—the Bishop of London's commissary in Charleston ordered him tried for heresy, and His Grace's representative in Virginia wrote: "I cannot forebear expressing my own concern to see Schism spreading itself through a Colony

*Presbyterian Meeting House, Alexandria, begun in 1774, interior as restored (by author)*

which has been *Famous for Uniformity of Religion,*"—and as years went by the men and women who were moved by his preaching and that of other leaders in and out of holy orders began to form denominations with new names.

Presbyterian and Baptist groups multiplied as missionaries from Philadelphia and New England assembled substantial followings in Virginia. Samuel Davies, before becoming president of The College of New Jersey (later, Princeton), was instrumental in the formation of the first Virginia presbytery, set up in Hanover to the outrage of the Anglican uncle for whom Patrick Henry was named. Simultaneously, Baptist communities proliferated in the central Virginia counties from Orange to Spotsylvania; in 1768, there were ten Baptist churches in Virginia, but by 1776 there were ninety. Because of their thumping enthusiasm, Baptists, who often evangelized in taverns, were frequently jailed as disturbers of the peace. Arrests in Spotsylvania in 1768 were soon duplicated in other counties.

Mason had ample opportunity to observe the rise of these sects in his own courthouse town of Alexandria. In 1774, the Baptist Jeremiah Moore, arrested for unlicensed preaching, was sent to Alexandria jail accompanied by a mittimus to the gentlemen justices that read: "I send you herewith the body of Jeremiah Moore, who is a preacher of the gospel of Jesus Christ, and a stroller." Likewise in 1774, the Alexandria Presbyterians began the building of a brick church quite as imposing as the structure only a few blocks away that had just been finished by the Fairfax Parish vestry; thereafter, its builder, the good Presbyterian John Carlyle, who had taken over the completion of Christ Church when the vestry's original contractor failed to perform, had a church of his own persuasion.

The varied concerns in which Mason and Washington collaborated did not diminish the day-to-day domestic demands of the agriculture of their plantations. Corn to be planted:

> One for the field-mouse,
> One for the crow,
> One for the cut-worm,
> And one to grow.

Tobacco seedlings to be ready for transplanting; the old crop to be cured, its stripped leaves carefully laid in "hands," pressed into waiting casks, rolled to the warehouse, loaded on the ship. Wheat and rye to be sown after the fall plowing—and all of it dependent on the fickle chance of the weather.

Spring could be entrancing—shad in the river, a new colt in the paddock, dogwood in the forest—as when Col. Landon Carter noted: "A very fine day this indeed. I rode out and tired myself it was so very pleasant."[20] But it could also be disastrous, as in 1775 when no plantation escaped the ravages of the freak freeze that followed a May snowstorm throughout Virginia. After days of entries that recorded plantings of vegetables, on 4 May, Jefferson wrote in his *Garden Book*: "The blue ridge of mountains covered with snow," and on the fifth: "a frost which destroyed almost every thing. it killed the wheat, rye, corn, many tobacco plants, and even large saplings."[21] In Caroline County, John Clark, Sr. wrote his son Jonathan: "we are all well as to helth I thank God, but have a shockin prospect be fore us our woods are as naked as ever I saw them . . . but what is worst ther all is the wheet are kild."[22] Col. Carter lamented: "A person with a less lively confidence would dread that All things must perish, and indeed things are almost got into such a condition."[23] Washington, consigning a shipment of flour on 10 May, warned his merchant: "If these fears of ours should be realized there can be no dependance upon North America for Flour the next year, and must, I should think affect the present prices."[24] Mason wrote William Lee that "People in general have not prepared this year for Crops of Tobo. as usual; and even those who have will be able to make very little, from the uncommon Scarcity of Plants, greater than in the noted Year 1758, or perhaps than ever was known within Memory of Man, and the Season now too far advanced to raise more."[25]

Yet the frost did nothing to kill agricultural optimism. Mason and Washington were among the thirty-eight Virginia subscribers to a new company "for the Purpose of raising and making Wine, Oyl, agruminous Plants and Silk," organized by Philip Mazzei,* a Tuscan horticulturist who came to Virginia in late 1773, bringing with him ten skilled vignerons and European seeds and plants from almonds to onions. On his way to settle in the western part of the colony, he stopped at Monticello, where Jefferson, entranced, persuaded him to buy the adjacent two-thousand-acre estate, Colle. Shares in the new company cost £50; on 9 March 1775, Mason asked Washington to take the second installment of his subscription down to Williamsburg when he went, adding: "I send you the Cherry-Graffs you desire, but am afraid they are rather too forward; the bundle wth. the white Stick in it is May-Dukes; the other the large black May Cherrys."[26]†

Agricultural interest continued to urge improved access to the western parts of the colony. In 1772, Thomson Mason put through the House of Burgesses a bill for a corporation to build and maintain a canal rendering the Potomac navigable from Tidewater as far up as Fort Cumberland, though the time limit it carried was not met. In 1775, after conversations with Mason and Washington, Thomas Johnson, a speculator from across the river, obtained from the Maryland Assembly an appropriation of £3,000 for road building. On 3 November 1774, the promoter John Ballendine, author of *Proposals for Opening the Navigation of the River Potowmack,* announced in Purdie & Dixon's *Gazette* another canal-building project, naming twenty-one Virginians, including Mason, and twenty-two Marylanders as trustees. The next March, Mason sent a further river bill to Washington for comment and forwarding to Johnson, and James Mercer introduced such a measure in June, but political crisis postponed these ventures.

# Chapter V
# The Sharpening of the Issue

*A shift in the focus of Mason's attention from local affairs to policy-making for* the colony as a whole followed the British ministry's announcement of new revenue measures.

In April 1763, George Grenville, chancellor of the exchequer, introduced in the House of Commons a plan for securing more revenue in America. Though eight years before, at the Carlyle House Conference, Governor Shirley of Massachusetts had observed to General Braddock that the colonies should be made to accept responsibility for their own defense, even the expenses of civil administration in the American dominions were far from being currently met by the duties collected under the navigation acts. So the Revenue Act of 1764, the so-called Sugar Act, stating in its preamble that "it is expedient that new provisions and regulations should be established for improving the revenue of this Kingdom," tightened the customs service and authorized the use of writs of assistance (general warrants) by customs officers when searching premises for smuggled goods. The impact of this act was greater in the New England colonies than elsewhere, but the burden of its successor, the Stamp Act of 1765, was evenly distributed and quickly called forth continental resistance. Effective 1 November, it required stamps, purchased with specie, to be affixed to all newspapers and pamphlets, bills, notes, bonds, leases, other commercial and legal documents, cards, and dice.

Virginia's Stamp Act crisis erupted at the close of the spring meeting of the Assembly; that autumn, Mason's first public paper was prepared as a response.

Until 20 May, public affairs in Williamsburg had been so somnolent that many burgesses were requesting leave—or merely taking it— to go home. On that day, a proposal was advanced to empower the colony to seek a substantial loan in England, part of the proceeds to retire the paper currency issued during the late war, and part to provide an agency for the extension of credits to individuals on security of their lands. Its unclear origin may have been related to an investigation currently in process. Earlier in the session, Richard Henry Lee had shocked the Assembly by publicly implying that the treasurer's accounts might not be in order. His seniors had been aghast that even the breath of an allegation should be directed at John Robinson, holder of the treasurer's office since 1738. Robinson, acting in his other official capacity as speaker of the House, quickly appointed a commission of inquiry, consisting largely of his friends; on the twenty-ninth, its chairman, Archibald Cary, reported that all was well and that the treasury contained a comfortable cash balance; after Robinson's death, this was found to be inaccurate, but Lee was not forgiven.*

In the debate on the loan proposal, a new member from Louisa made himself heard. Special elections of burgesses had recently been held to fill vacancies in four counties: the writ that the Committee on Privileges and Elections received from Louisa showed that county's new member to be Patrick Henry of Hanover. On 24 May, in a maiden speech only days after his admission, Henry delivered a violent attack on the bill. It passed in spite of him but did not become law: in a rare and unexplained veto, the Council turned it down.

By the 29th, all except 39 of the 116 burgesses had left town. During the previous night, however, the news of the Stamp Act, or the actual text, had in Governor Fauquier's words "crept into the House."† When the day's session opened, George Johnstone of Fairfax moved that the House go into a Committee of the Whole to consider new business; as soon as his motion passed, he deferred to the gentleman from Louisa. Repudiating the act, Henry, with the oratorical flair that had won his case in the Parson's Cause, presented a series of resolves.

Two contemporary records report the ensuing proceedings. Governor Fauquier informed Whitehall that "in a Committee of the whole House five resolutions were proposed and agreed to, all by very small majorities. On Thursday the 30th they were reported and agreed to by the House, the numbers being as before in the Committee; the greatest majority being 22 to 17; for the 5th Resolution, 20 to 19 only." He added, "In the course of the debates I have heard that very indecent language was used by a Mr. Henry, a young lawyer who had not been a month a member."[1]

An eyewitness account of this language has been left by a French traveler—name unknown—who reached Williamsburg on the day of Henry's speech, went immediately to the House, and

was entertained with very strong Debates Concerning Dutys that the parlement wants to lay on the american Colonys, which they Call or Stile stamp Dutys. Shortly after I Came in one of the members stood up and said he had read that in former times tarquin and Julus had their Brutus, Charles had his Cromwell, and he Did not Doubt but some good american would stand up, in favour of his Country, but (says he) in a more moderate manner, and was going to Continue, when the speaker of the house rose and Said, he, the last that stood up had spoke traison, and was sorry to see that not one of the members of the house was loyal Enough to stop him, before he had gone so far, upon which the Same member stood up again (his name is henery) and said that if he had afronted the speaker, or the house, he was ready to ask pardon, and he would shew his loyalty to his majesty King G. the third, at the Expence of the last Drop of his blood, but what he had said must be atributed to the Interest of his Countrys Dying liberty which he had at heart. . . . Members stood up and backed him, on which that afaire was droped.[2]

Standing with this stranger in the lobby was a young William and Mary student named Thomas Jefferson; years later, he recalled hearing Peyton Randolph, who had chaired the committee, growl as he left the building, "By God, I would have given 500 guineas for a single vote!"[3] The tie created by another negative in the vote of 20 to 19 would have been reliably broken against the measure.

In all, seven resolutions were at some stage entertained by the House, though the details of their consideration are uncertain. They declared: (1) that the earliest settlers brought with them all privileges, franchises, and immunities enjoyed by the people of Britain; (2) that the two royal charters granted Virginians by King James I declared them entitled to all privileges, liberties, and immunities as if they were abiding and born within the realm of England; (3) that taxation of the people by themselves or their representatives "is the distinguishing characteristick of British Freedom, without which the ancient constitution cannot exist"; (4) that the right of being governed in respect to internal polity and taxation by laws derived from their own consent had constantly been recognized; (5) that every attempt to vest the tax power elsewhere than in the General Assembly "has a manifest tendency to destroy British as well as American freedom"; (6) that "His Majesty's liege people, the inhabitants of this Colony," are not bound to obey any tax measure other than those passed by the General Assembly; and (7) that any person who in speaking or writing asserts the opposite "shall be deemed an enemy to His Majesty's Colony."

Of these, Henry later claimed responsibility for the first five, all of which, and possibly the sixth and seventh, were accepted by the Committee of the Whole in what Jefferson recalled as "bloody" debate, with Tidewater and the upcountry pitted against each other in the voting. Since the argument closed late in the day, it was decided that the House should not consider the committee's report until morning. Tidewater hopes of using the delay to pick up enough support to defeat the measures was disappointed: the lines held while the House formally adopted five of the resolutions.

Overnight, however, the Committee on Privileges and Elections had been busy reexamining the writ certifying Henry's election; it found a flaw: Henry resided in Hanover and did not own property in Louisa. The House voted to send the writ back to the Louisa sheriff. Henry got on his horse and headed home.

Next day, observing his absence, Peyton Randolph and others saw an opportunity to expunge the offending resolutions from the record. But in the votes then taken, the first four of them were sustained and are entered in the *Journal*; only the fifth was stricken. The action was in any case irrelevant: full lists had been dispatched to other colonies, and such newspapers as the *Boston Gazette*, *Newport Mercury*, and *Mary-*

*land Gazette* shortly carried more or less complete texts. Virginia's case against the act was thus available when delegates of nine colonies convened in New York in October for the Stamp Act Congress, though no Virginians were present—by dissolving the Burgesses on 1 June, Governor Fauquier had prevented election of delegates. Citizens of the Old Dominion could only read at a distance the Declaration of Rights and Grievances there adopted.

In Fairfax County, the election for the autumn Assembly was held on 16 July. George Johnston's poor health having decided him to withdraw, Washington offered in Fairfax rather than in Frederick and led the poll with 201 votes; for the next decade, he represented his home county.

With the Stamp Act due to take effect on 1 November, Mason addressed himself to means of avoiding use of stamped paper. After conversations with Washington, who would be going to Williamsburg, and George William Fairfax, who though out of politics had a special interest in procedures related to land tenure as agent for Lord Fairfax's Northern Neck property, Mason drafted a suggested substitute for one of the most frequent court actions, recovery of goods pledged as security for rent. On 23 December, Mason wrote them a joint letter: "Inclosed is the Scheme I promised you for altering the Method of replevying Goods under Distress for Rent. . . . I beg you will alter such Parts of it as either of you think exceptionable."[4]

Rumors of Stamp Act repeal obviated the necessity of the Assembly considering Mason's proposal; repeal became a fact the following spring. But meanwhile, arrival of the stamps for Maryland and Virginia created scenes in Williamsburg which involved Mason through ties of family as well as political interest.

When his cousin, George Mercer, left for London in 1763, he had carried a recommendation from the Assembly urging that in recognition of his services in the French and Indian War he be considered for a government post; after the royal proclamation closing the western frontier forced him to become inactive as the Ohio Company's agent, he pursued the matter, and when H.M.S. *Leeds* dropped anchor in York River on Tuesday, 29 October 1765, Mercer stepped off as Virginia's stamp distributor.

The news clattered off at a gallop. The next night, in front of Westmoreland County Courthouse, the stamp distributor was burned in effigy. Meanwhile, Mercer took horse for Williamsburg. On arrival Wednesday afternoon, he was surrounded near the Capitol by a "concourse of people" whom Governor Fauquier reported he "should call a mob, if I did not know that it was chiefly if not altogether composed of gentlemen of property."[5] Its members shouted demands for Mercer's immediate resignation.

After a pause, Mercer replied that he would make a statement on the same spot at 10 A.M. on Friday and moved, still surrounded, towards Mrs. Campbell's nearby Virginia Coffee House, on whose porch the

governor, the speaker, and various Council members were staging a deliberately casual presence.

As Mercer mounted the steps and paid his respects to the governor, the rumbling crowd, regarding his manner as obsequious, appeared about to close in. Thus beset, Mercer advanced the time for his statement from 10 A.M. on Friday, the day the act became effective, to 5 P.M. Thursday afternoon. In a brittle, leaf-crunching silence, Fauquier then conducted Mercer to protection in the Governor's Palace.

Mercer resigned. His statement, reproduced in the Pennsylvania *Gazette* of 21 November, concluded with the "assurance in the meantime that I will not directly or indirectly by my deputies or myself proceed further with the Act until I receive further orders from England and not then without the assent of the General Assembly of this Colony and that no man can more ardently or sincerely wish the prosperity of than myself."

On hearing these words, the crowd huzzahed. Yesterday's villain became today's hero: all present adjourned to the Coffee House to celebrate. The *Virginia Gazette* described the episode fully. While the mood held, Mercer effected a quick departure: within ten days he was again at sea, London bound, having left the stamps with the captain of H.M.S. *Rainbow* and notified Governor Sharpe of Maryland that "I dared not let anyone know where they were, though I confess I was not a little apprehensive of an attempt to force the disclosure from me." On 10 Novem-

ber, Col. Richard Corbin informed former Governor Dinwiddie: "Mr.
Mercer, distributor of stamps, has been forced to escape his office. This
resignation has shut up the courts of justice and thrown everything into
confusion. Every evil that can be apprehended is to be dreaded from the
present temper and disposition of the people in opposition to this Act
of Parliament. If it is not repealed God only knows what the consequences will be."[6]

But if Mercer slipped away, the issue of parliamentary taxation
did not. On 1 November, the General Court convened for its regular
and usually busy semiannual session. No litigant came forward. No
stamped paper was used. The only attorney present was the attorney
general. The boycott was complete, the evidence of public solidarity
unmistakable. The court adjourned.

"The first and most obvious consequences of all this," Fauquier
noted in a report to Whitehall "must be the shutting up all the ports and
and stopping all proceedings in the Courts," though on 8 November,
feeling somewhat better, he added: "I am not altogether without hopes
that the distress the country will feel on a total stagnation of business,
will open their eyes and pave the way for the Act's executing itself. For
I am very credibly informed that some of the most busy men in opposing
the reception of Stamps are already alarmed at the consequences of the
imprudent steps they have taken."[7]

While Parliament repealed the Stamp Act in March 1766, the
Declaratory Act passed at the same time kept alive the basic issue: it

asserted the power of the king in Parliament to "make laws and statutes of sufficient force and validity to bind the colonies in all cases whatsoever." George Mason's second public paper was among the misgivings this evoked. On the last day of February 1766, a committee of London Merchants had sent an open letter to their New York counterparts. The *Virginia Gazette* reprinted it on 16 May. On 6 June, Mason sent to the *London Public Ledger* a long, closely reasoned reply signed "A Virginia Planter":

> Can the Honour of Parliament be maintained by persisting in a Measure evidently wrong? Is it any Reflection upon the Honour of Parliament to show itself wiser this Year than the last, to have profited by Experience, and to correct the Errors which Time & endubitable Evidence have pointed out? If the Declaratory Act, or Vote of Right, has asserted any unjust, oppressive, or unconstitutional Principles, to become "waste paper" wou'd be the most innocent use that cou'd be made of it: by the Copys we have seen here, the legislative authority of Great Britain is fully & positively asserted in all Cases whatsoever. But a just & necessary Distinction between Legislation & Taxation hath been made by the greatest & wisest Men in the Nation.[8]

Because of the Stamp Act repeal, however, colonists in general were less mindful of these queries than of the paragraph in Mason's communication that rejoiced:

> These Evils are, for the present, removed. Praised be Almighty God! Blessed be our most gracious Sovereign! Thanks to the present mild & prudent Temper of Parliament. Thanks to the wise & honest Conduct of the present Administration. Thanks to the unwearied Diligence of our Friends the British Merchants, & Manufacturers; Thanks to that happy Circumstance of their private Interest being so interwoven with ours, that they cou'd not be separated. Thanks to the spirited & disinterested Conduct of our own Merchants in the northern Colonys; who deserve to have their Names handed down, with Reverence & Gratitude to Posterity. Thanks to the Unanimity of the Colonys themselves. And many Thanks to our generous & able Benefactor, Mr. Pitt; who has always stood forth a Champion in the Cause of Liberty & his Country."[9]

The euphoria did not last. In view of the Declaratory Act, Mason's brother Thomson, in the Assembly that sat from late November 1766 to early April 1767, proposed that all colonies issue a declaration of their rights; he warned the Assembly that the absence of violence during the Stamp Act furore should be attributed to prudence rather than to any abandonment of a position. Then, fifteen months after repeal of the Stamp Act, the Revenue Act of 1767 became law; news of it reached Virginia in the late summer.

In the change of ministries of July 1766, Charles Townshend had become chancellor of the exchequer and "pledged himself to find a revenue in America." As a long-time member and recent president of the Board of Trade, "Champagne Charlie" intended to reorganize colonial government to give the mother country tighter political control of overseas dependencies and greater tax benefits from them. His last official act—he put the bill through Parliament in July 1767 and died in September—was projected to raise a revenue of £40,000 by taxing such articles as glass, paper, painters' colors, and tea.

In Boston, where the new Board of Customs Commissioners of the Revenue was set up, a circular letter of protest was adopted under the leadership of Samuel Adams. By the end of the year, John Dickinson's "Letters from a Farmer in Pennsylvania" were appearing, and so were the "Monitor's Letters" of Virginia's Arthur Lee. Lee, in London at the time of Stamp Act repeal, had expressed doubts of a ministerial change of heart; his judgment was corroborated when two regiments were sent to Boston, and proposals advanced to bring ringleaders in the Massachusetts disturbances to England for trial. The Massachusetts House refused to rescind its circular letter and declared removal to England would violate the ancient right to trial in the vicinage.

In a strategy of divisiveness, the ministry, having used force in Massachusetts, tried flattery in Virginia. Most of Virginia's eighteenth-century governors had in actuality been lieutenants only, but after the death of Francis Fauquier in March 1768, the next appointee was himself a noble lord, Norborne Berkeley, created baron de Botetourt four years before. He arrived in style, sent over on a ship of the line whose cargo included a state coach and white horses presented by the king's brother, Prince Henry-Frederick, duke of Cumberland.

Botetourt's administration got off to a brilliant start. The pomp of his entry, his fashionable attire, his delivery of a ceremonial speech at the opening of the Assembly in studied imitation of the Speech from the Throne by British monarchs at parliamentary openings were given due space, plus a laudatory ode, in the *Virginia Gazette*. Withal, Virginians found him a likeable man.

But as soon as the Assembly got down to work, the speaker brought in copies of the replies to the Massachusetts circular of the previous year. By mid-May, a committee consisting of Richard Henry Lee, Patrick Henry, Robert Carter Nicholas, Thomson Mason, and Benjamin Harrison, under the chairmanship of John Blair, Jr., had drafted memorials to king, lords, and Commons denouncing the proposal to transport citizens overseas for trial, maintaining the right to local taxation, and affirming the capacity of the colonies to act in concert. The Assembly circulated these with a request for concurrence by all other colonial legislatures. When Lord Botetourt learned of the action, he dissolved the House.

Members' reassembling privately, then gave attention to the resolution that Washington had brought to Williamsburg proposing formation of an association whose members would bind themselves not to import slaves, wines, or any British manufactures until the new customs act was repealed.

Mason was among the contributors to this document. Through the spring, merchants along the coast from Boston to Annapolis had urged nonimportation; two months before the new session of the Virginia Assembly, Dr. David Ross of Bladensburg, Maryland, forwarded to both Washington and Mason dossiers containing an agreement of Philadelphia merchants, signed in February; a further agreement of the

Philadelphia Merchants' Association, signed in March; and an ensuing exchange of correspondence with the merchants of Annapolis.

On 5 April, not knowing that Mason had received the same packet, Washington sent his own to his friend:

Herewith you will receive a letter and Sundry papers which were forwarded to me a day or two ago by Doctor Ross of Bladensbúrg. I transmit them with the greater pleasure, as my own desire of knowing your sentiments upon a matter of this importance exactly coincides with the Doctors inclinations. . . .

That no man shou'd scruple, or hesitate a moment to use a-ms in defence of so valuable a blessing, on which all the good and evil of life depends; is clearly my opinion; yet A-ms I wou'd beg leave to add, should be the last resource; the denier resort. Addresses to the Throne, and remonstrances to Parliament, we have already, it is said, proved the inefficacy of; how far then their attention to our rights & priviledges is to be awakened or alarmed by starving their Trade & manufactures, remains to be tryed.[10]

Mason replied with approval the same day, indicating he had already given thought to the matter and advocating an additional hint to London that in the absence of redress, nonexportation of Virginia tobacco might supplement nonimportation of British manufactures:

I entirely agree with you that no regular Plan of the Sort proposed can be entered into here before the Meeting of the Genl. Court at least, if not that of the Assembly; when a Number of Gentlemen, from the different Parts of the Country, will have an Opportunity of conferring together, & acting in Concert; in the mean Time it may be necessary to publish something preparatory to it in our Gazettes, to warn the People at least of the impending Danger, & induce them the more readily & chearfully to concur in the proper Measures to avert it; & something of this Sort I had begun; but am unluckily stop'd by a Disorder which affects my Head & Eyes in such a Manner, that I am totally incapable of Business . . . so soon as I am able, I shall resume it, & shall then write you more fully, or endeavour to see you: in the mean Time pray commit to Writing such Hints as may occur.

Our All is at Stake, & the little Conveniencys & Comforts of Life, when set in Competition with our Liberty, ought to be rejectèd not with Reluctance but with Pleasure.[11]

On 23 April, as Washington prepared to depart for Williamsburg, Mason wrote again, enclosing a further copy of the proposed articles of association; he had "made some few Alterations in it, as per Memdm. on the other Side."[12*]

In the document Washington presented to the House, political solidarity suddenly discovered itself: rapid action ensued. Boycott of the courts had proved effective against the Stamp Act; boycott of goods could combat the present levies. The nonimportation resolution, signed by eighty-eight burgesses, the clerk of the new association, and nineteen others, follows rather closely the document brought down by Washington, including most of Mason's amendments. Affirming loyalty to their sovereign, the signers lamented "the Evils which threaten the Ruin of ourselves and our Posterity" and declared that they:

having taken into our most serious Consideration the present State of the Trade of this Colony, and of the American Commerce in general, observe with Anxiety, that the Debt due to Great-Britain for Goods imported from thence is very great, and that the Means of paying this Debt, in the present Situation of Affairs,

*Statue of Lord Botetourt*
*by Richard Heyward,*
*commissioned by the*
*Virginia Assembly, 1771;*
*formerly on the grounds,*
*now in the library of the*
*College of William and Mary*
(courtesy, College of
William and Mary; Colonial
Williamsburg Photograph)

are likely to become more and more precarious; that the Difficulties, under which we now labour, are owing to the Restriction, Prohibitions, and ill advised Regulations in several late Acts of Parliament of Great-Britain, in particular, that the late unconstitutional Act, imposing Duties on Tea, Paper, Glass, &c. for the sole Purpose of raising a Revenue in America, is injurious to Property, and destructive to Liberty, hath a necessary Tendency to prevent the Payment of the Debt due from this Colony to Great-Britain, and is, of Consequence, ruinous to Trade.[13]

Subscribers bound themselves to promote industry and thrift, to discourage luxury and extravagance, not to import any of the goods, except paper, taxed for the purpose of raising revenue, nor a long list of other goods until the above named duties are repealed, nor to buy any of these from any person whatever after 1 September next. All orders hereafter placed in Great Britain were to carry the injunction not to be shipped before repeal; no slaves to be imported or purchased from importers after 1 November next; no wines not already ordered to be imported or purchased after 1 September next; and "to preserve sheep herds, no lambs yeaned before May 1 of any year to be slaughtered or sold for slaughter."

This and similar associations had effect: at one of Lord Botetourt's balls in 1769, over a hundred ladies appeared in homespun dresses; a few months later, Council President William Nelson communicated to his London merchant the disquieting news that his suit, shirts, shoes, hose, buckles, wig, and hat were made in Virginia. On 5 March 1770, Lord North moved for repeal of the Townshend Acts. But to maintain the principle of the Declaratory Act, a measure passed on 12 April retained the tax on tea.

Insofar as his official position permitted, Lord Botetourt sided with the colonists in this contest. In correspondence with Lord Hillsborough, secretary of state for the colonies, he had urged total repeal. He conveyed assurances to the November Assembly that "he would be content to be declared infamous, if he did not to the last hour of his life, at all times and in all places and upon all occasion, exert every power, with which he was or ever should be legally invested, to obtain and maintain for the continent of America that satisfaction which he had been authorized to promise that day."[14]

But because of retention of the tea tax, and because of news of fatalities in Boston when British troops fired in a hassle with lads from the harbor, the Assembly of June 1770 prepared a petition to the king expressing disappointment and determined to tighten their association further.

Enforcement was recognizably difficult. Prior to this session, Mason's long letter to Richard Henry Lee stressed the need for stricter observance:

. . . the Sense of Shame & the Fear of Reproach must be inculcated, & enforced in the strongest Manner . . . it is a just observation that if Shame was banished out of the World, she wou'd carry away with her what little Virtue is left in it. The Names of such Persons as purchase or import Goods contrary to the Association should be published, & themselves stigmatized as Enemys to their

Country. . . . I don't see how these Regulations can be effected by any other Means than appointing Committees in the Countys, to examine from Time to Time into the Imports, & to convey an Account of any Violation of the Association to the Moderator.[15]

Alexander Henderson, who though a merchant was a warm supporter of the association, assured Mason that banned cargoes could be stacked unopened in his warehouses.

But enforcement continued to be difficult. Three weeks later, the Williamsburg convention of the body of Virginia merchants known as The Cape Company joined the Burgesses in a new association of which Speaker Peyton Randolph was moderator, authorizing formation of county committees to monitor arriving goods and purchases and to publish the names of violators as suggested in Mason's letter to Lee. Their expanded list of enumerated articles included horses, and a special provision covered the troublesome question of sales in Virginia of goods "rejected by the association committees in any of our sister colonies." Delegates took printed versions back to their counties for further signatures. Washington wrote a preamble for Fairfax subscribers at the bottom of his copy; it is followed by nineteen manuscript names, mostly of merchants, ending with George Mason's. Washington, Mason, Peter Wagener, John West, and John Dalton became the Fairfax committee of surveillance.

Having registered this protest, the colony settled back into its local and personal affairs. Regret at the death of the genial Lord Botetourt in October was expressed in a subscription for purchase of the statue currently in the William and Mary library. The aging and ill Council president, John Blair, now for the third time acting governor, relinquished the position in favor of William Nelson of Yorktown, who served until John Murray, earl of Dunmore, was transferred to Virginia from the governorship of New York in the autumn of 1771. In Fairfax, Mason's local responsibilities were increased when, as Daniel French's executor, he took on the completion of Pohick Church.

Then in the spring of 1773, the pleasant tenor of domestic life at Gunston Hall came to a shattering end. On 9 March, Ann Eilbeck Mason died.

Her 1772 pregnancy had been difficult from the start, accompanied by weakness and fever. On 4 December, two months prematurely, she gave birth to twin boys. The Reverend Lee Massey baptized them Richard and James that day; they lived only until the next morning. Their mother lingered for three months, dying in the first days of spring at the age of thirty-nine. She left nine living children motherless: George her first-born was twenty, little Thomas, three; there were four girls and three boys between.

Her stunned husband wrote in the Gunston Bible: "On Teusday, the 9th. of March, 1773, about three O'Clock in the morning, died at Gunston-Hall, of a slow-fever, Mrs. Ann Mason, in the thirty-ninth year of her age, after a painful & tedious Illness of more than nine months, which she bore with truly Christian Patience & Resignation, in faithful hope of eternal Happiness in the World to come."

Her funeral sermon was preached on 27 April by the Reverend James Scott, who found his text in Psalms 73:23-25: "Nevertheless I am continually with thee: Thou hast holden me by my right hand. Thou shalt guide me with thy counsel, And afterwards receive me to glory. Whom have I in heaven but thee?" Washington's diary shows that his wife and her guests at Mount Vernon, Mrs. Calvert of Maryland and Mrs. William Augustine Washington, attended; he himself made a visit of condolence to Mason at Gunston Hall a few days later.

Though John Mason was just under seven at the time, his mother's sickness and death left a profound impression:

My Mother was attended during her illness by Dr. Craig [Craik] . . . who was afterward the Surgeon General of the Revolutionary Army—the intimate personal Friend of General Washington—as he was of my Father—among the prescriptions for her was weak milk punch to be taken in bed in the morning— little urchin as I was, it is yet Fresh on my mind, that I was called sometimes by this beloved mother to her bed side, to drink a little of this beverage, which I loved very much from the bottom of the cup,—The last that I remember of that excellent parent . . . is that, She took me one day in her arms, on her Bed—I believe it was a few days before her death—told me she was going to leave us all—gave me her blessing—and charged me in terms no doubt suitable to my age and understanding to be a Good Boy. . . . I well remember that, I had intelligence and sensibility enough to be aware of the sacredness of the charge and of the awful crisis in the Family—that it foreboded—and that I received it with a swollen heart and fell into a deep cry, which long continued. . . . I remember well my Mother's funeral—in some particulars—I know the whole Family went into deep mourning suddenly prepared—and that I was led clothed in Black to her Grave—and that I saw her Coffin lowered down—with cords covered with black cloth—and that there was a great assemblage of Friends and Neighbors— That the house was in a state of desolation, for a good while—that the Children and servants walked about in tears and in silences, or spoke in whispers—and that my Father paced the rooms, or from the House to the Grave, for it was close by, for many Days alone—with his hands crossed behind him.[16]

Unlike his neighbors—John Mercer remarried within eight weeks after the preaching of his first wife's funeral sermon, and Martha Custis's second marriage followed a less-than-three-year widowhood— Mason did not remarry for seven years. Until his youngest child was ten, he bore single-handed the confining cares of the Gunston family. His eldest daughter, Nancy, managed the household until her marriage, and during his restricted absences, the Cockburns served as foster parents, receiving frequent letters detailing what the children should do.

Eighteen days after his wife's death, Mason drew his will, setting up a "common stock" of assets for the support and maintenance of his children and providing for "the payment of their fortunes" on marriage or coming of age. So carefully was it drafted that he never changed it.

Henceforth, during his years as the lone parent at Gunston Hall, he had to balance the part that he could take in public affairs against the unremitting duties that claimed him at home.

# Chapter VI
# The Shadow Government

*During the last week of May 1774, Mason was in Williamsburg on personal* business. On the twenty-sixth, he passed on to Martin Cockburn the gist of some private conversations in which he had just taken part. The *Virginia Gazette* of 19 May had published news of the passage through Parliament of a group of acts, of which the most conspicuous closed the port of Boston; a group of Assembly members—Patrick Henry, Thomas Jefferson, Richard Henry and Francis Lightfoot Lee, and others—asked Mason to join them in considering an appropriate response. The group had been meeting ever since the *Gaspee* incident in Rhode Island in 1772, when in reprisal for the burning of a naval vessel by Providence merchants, Whitehall had proposed removal of suspects for trial overseas.[*]

These consultations afforded Mason his first opportunity to see Patrick Henry in action; in describing him to Cockburn, he went well beyond his usually measured words of praise:

At the request of the gentlemen concerned, I have spent an evening with them upon the subject, where I had an opportunity of conversing with Mr. Henry, and knowing his sentiments; as well as hearing him speak in the house since, on different occasions. He is by far the most powerful speaker I ever heard. Every word he says not only engages but commands the attention; and your passions are no longer your own when he addresses them. But his eloquence is the smallest part of his merit. He is in my opinion the first man upon this continent, as well in abilities as public virtues, and had he lived in Rome about the time of the first Punic war, when the Roman people had arrived at their meridian glory, and their virtue not tarnished, Mr. Henry's talents must have put him at the head of that glorious Commonwealth.[1]

After these associates engaged in some searching of archives for forms used by the Puritans of England and New England in Cromwell's day, the House of Burgesses set 1 June as "a day of Fasting, Humiliation, and Prayer, devoutly to implore the divine interposition, for averting the heavy Calamity which threatens destruction to our Civil Rights, and the Evils of civil War, etc.,"[2] with a sermon "suitable to the Occasion." In their capacity as private individuals, the burgesses had the resolution printed for circulation in their home counties. Mason told Cockburn that Washington would provide a copy, "and should a day of prayer and fasting be appointed in our county, please to tell my dear little family that I charge them to pay strict attention to it, and that I desire my three eldest sons, and my two eldest daughters, may attend church in mourning, if they have it, as I believe they have."[3] The fast day resolution was published in the *Gazette* of 26 May.

Up to this point, the session had exceeded even its usual gaiety. The Washingtons had reached Williamsburg in their coach and six on the twenty-third; his diary notes that he dined that day with Mr. Attorney General Randolph and the next with Mr. Speaker Randolph (spending the evening at Mrs. Campbell's Coffee House afterwards). On the twenty-fifth, there was a banquet at the Governor's Palace, and next morning Washington rode out with the governor to his farm to breakfast there; on the twenty-seventh, he dined with Mr. Treasurer Nicholas before the ball given by the House of Burgesses for Lady Dunmore, who had arrived with her children in April.

The last entertainment was held in spite of the fact that on the twenty-sixth, the Assembly had been abruptly dissolved. Governor Dunmore, on reading the fast-day resolution, held that it was conceived in terms that reflected upon "His Majesty and the Parliament of Great Britain." He terminated the session even as Mason was writing his letter to Cockburn.

Before attending the ball, eighty-nine members of the dissolved House gathered informally at the Raleigh Tavern, put their speaker in the chair, and, declaring that the attack on Massachusetts was an attack on all the colonies, resolved in favor of calling a continental congress of colonial representatives, amplifying and formalizing the committees of correspondence set up the previous year, and ending commercial regulations with the mother country if the unconstitutional tax measures currently in force should be continued.

On 29 May, letters arrived from Boston asking for immediate cutting of commercial ties; the twenty-five House members still in Williamsburg on the thirtieth summoned a convention of the people of Virginia to assemble there on 1 August.

County meetings to consider these events were promptly convened. In the Northern Neck, at Dumfries Courthouse on 6 June, Prince William citizens adopted a set of resolves proposing nonexportation as well as nonimportation; this was the measure Mason had suggested to Washington when the first association was formed five years before:

> *Resolved,* And it is the opinion of this meeting, that until the said Acts are repealed, all importation to, and exportation from, this Colony ought to be stopped, except with such Colonies or Islands in *North America* as shall adopt this measure.
> *Resolved,* And it is the opinion of this meeting, that the courts of justice in this Colony ought to decline trying any civil causes until said Acts are repealed.[4]

Mason was a Dumfries trustee, and a number of the phrases in this document recur in his known draft of the Fairfax Resolves adopted a little over a month later. In Westmoreland, where Richard Henry Lee was a burgess, a similar set of proposals was adopted on 22 June. Before the August convention met, all Virginia counties had expressed their views.

*Patrick Henry, miniature by*
*Lawrence Sully, 1795*
*(courtesy, Museum of Art,*
*Carnegie Institute, Pittsburgh)*

The first Fairfax meeting took place on 5 July: Washington's laconic diary entry reads: "Went up to Alexandria to a Meeting of the Inhabitts. of this County. Dined at Arrell's and lodgd at my own House."[5] A substantial subscription in money, flour, and wheat was collected for the relief of Boston, and a committee was appointed to ready a set of resolves for presentation at a subsequent gathering. But before that meeting, since Dunmore's sudden dissolution of the Assembly had left much public business dangling, writs had been issued for a new election of burgesses. The Fairfax vote was scheduled for 14 July.

The scenario of this election differed only slightly from the plot of a comedy, *The Candidates: or, The Humours of a Virginia Election,* written at just about this time by Col. Robert Munford, a burgess himself and a member of a Prince George County family that had moved west to Mecklenburg after the French and Indian War. It also bore out the observations on Virginia's social structure of the Scottish physician, J. F. D. Smyth, who had arrived in Williamsburg in 1770.

In his *Tour in the United State of America,* Smyth identified "three degrees of rank . . . exclusive of the negroes":

The first consists of gentlemen of the best families and fortunes in the colony, who are here much more respectable and numerous than in any other province in America. These in general have had a liberal education, possess enlightened understandings, and a thorough knowledge of the world, that furnishes them with an ease and freedom of manners and conversation, highly to their advantage in exterior, which no vicissitude of fortune or place can divest them of; they being actually, according to my ideas, the most agreeable and best companions, friends, and neighbours, that need be desired. . . .

Those of the second degree in rank are very numerous, being perhaps half the inhabitants . . . they are generous, friendly, and hospitable in the extreme; but mixed with such an appearance of rudeness, ferocity, and haughtiness, which is in fact only a want of polish. . . . Many of them possess fortunes superior to some of the first rank, but their families are not so ancient, nor respectable; a circumstance here held in some estimation. . . .

The third, or lower class of the people (who ever compose the bulk of mankind), are in Virginia more few in number, in proportion to the rest of the inhabitants, than perhaps in any other country in the universe. Even these are kind, hospitable, and generous; yet illiberal, noisy, and rude.[6]

In Colonel Munford's farce, an election crisis is provoked when a member of Smyth's first category, Mr. Worthy, who has represented his county prominently and well for some years, decides not to stand again. Less prominent and correspondingly less desirable citizens (from Smyth's second stratum)—Sir John Toddy, Mr. Wou'dbe, Mr. Strutabout, and Mr. Smallhopes—promptly offer for the vacancy. After much rollicking, Mr. Wou'dbe persuades Mr. Worthy to reconsider; the two, elected amid universal huzzahs, then address the voters:

Enter Wou'dbe and Worthy, in two chairs, raised aloft by the freeholders.
Freeholders all.—Huzza, for Wou'dbe and Worthy—Huzza, for Wou'dbe and Worthy—Huzza, for Wou'dbe and Worthy!—(they traverse the stage, and then set them down.)
Worthy. Gentlemen, I'm much obliged to you for the signal proof you have given me to-day of your regard. You may depend upon it, that I shall endeavour faithfully to discharge the trust you have reposed in me.
Wou'dbe. I have not only, gentlemen, to return you my hearty thanks for the favours you have conferred upon me, but I beg leave also to thank you for shewing such regard to the merit of my friend. You have in that, shewn your judgment, and a spirit of independence becoming Virginians.
Capt. P. So we have Mr. Wou'dbe, we have done as we ought, we have elected the ablest, according to the writ.[7]

In real life, when Washington's Fairfax County colleague, Col. John West, announced his retirement, Washington, foreseeing the candidacy of Charles Broadwater, a vestryman and a gentleman justice, but in his view a man not quite up to being a burgess, quickly proposed candidacy to both George Mason and the Proprietor's cousin, Bryan Fairfax.

Fairfax excused himself because, as he wrote Washington on 4 July, he was unprepared to go further at this time than to petition Parliament for repeal, yet he realized that "There are scarce any at Alexandria, of my opinion; and though the few I have elsewhere conversed with on the Subject are so, yet from them I could learn, that many thought otherwise; so that I believe I should at this time give general Dissatisfaction, and therefore it would be more proper to decline.[8]

Washington replied the same day:

I really think Major Broadwater, though a good man, might do as well in the discharge of his domestic concerns, as in the capacity of a legislator. And therefore I again express my wish, that either you or Colonel Mason would offer. . . .

As to your political sentiments, I would heartily join you in them, so far as relates to a humble and dutiful petition to the throne, provided there was the most distant hope of success. But have we not tried this already?. . . Does it not appear, as clear as the sun in its meridian brightness, that there is a regular, systematic plan formed to fix the right and practice of taxation upon us?[9]

When Mason, after weighing public service outside the area against his domestic responsibilities, also declined, the poll became predictable. Washington's diary for the fourteenth announces: "Went up to Alexandria to the Election where I was chosen, together with Majr. Broadwater, Burgess. Staid all Night to a Ball."[10] (This campaign cost him only £3.1.6 for general expenses, and 13/3 for cakes.)

The journal of young Nicholas Cresswell, just arrived in Virginia to seek his fortune and see the world, gives an outsider's view of this election:

Thursday, July 14th, 1774. An Election for Burgess in town (their Elections are annual). There were three Candidates, the Poll was over in about two hours and conducted with great order and regularity. The Members Col. George Washington and Major Bedwater. The Candidates gave the populace a Hogshead of Toddy (what we call Punch in England). In the evening the returned Member gave a Ball to the Freeholders and Gentlemen of the town. This was conducted with great harmony. Coffee and Chocolate, but no Tea. This Herb is in disgrace amongst them at present.[11]

The Sunday after the election, Washington "went to Pohick Church and returned to Dinner. Colo. Mason came in the afternoon and stayed all Night"; next day, they "Went up to Alexandria to a Meeting of the County."[12]

Mason had drafted a set of resolves for them to work over that evening; the following day, the freeholders and inhabitants instructed their newly elected burgesses to present the resolves "as the Sense of the People of this County, upon the Measures proper to be taken in the present alarming and dangerous Situation of America" at the Williamsburg Convention opening two weeks thence.

Washington, Mason, and twenty-two others were chosen as a Committee of Safety for the county, empowered to call meetings and "concert and adopt such measures as may be thought most expedient and necessary." Drawing on both of the upper layers of society described by Smyth, this group included the two current and two former burgesses; Alexandria's first mayor and six other merchants, together with a son of an original trustee of the town; an attorney, who became the committee's clerk; two physicians; the rectors of the county's two parishes; and eight men, either gentlemen justices or vestrymen or both, whose scattered residence assured all parts of the county a voice in decisions.

Solidarity was essential: the resolves adopted at this meeting not only reiterated—in the same phrases—some of the ideas of the nonimportation agreement of five years before but went a very considerable distance beyond them. Reaffirming the rights of Virginians to the "Privileges, Immunities and Advantages" enjoyed by their ancestors, "as if we had still continued within the Realm of England," and stating that "the most important and valuable Part of the British Constitution, upon which it's very Existence depends, is the fundamental Principle of the People's being governed by no Laws, to which they have not given their Consent, by Representatives freely chosen by themselves," they declared "that the legislative Power here can of Right be exercised only by [our] own Provincial Assemblys or Parliaments, subject to the Assent or Negative of the British Crown, to be declared within some proper limited Time."

A partial exception to this principle in the case of regulation by Parliament of trade and commerce to the mutual benefit of mother country and colonies, is acceptable because "Such a Power directed with Wisdom and Moderation, seems necessary for the general Good of that great Body-politic of which we are a Part; altho' in some Degree repugnant to the Principles of the Constitution."

The fact that the colonies recognize a duty to contribute to the defense of the empire in emergencies "was evident thro' the Course of the last War . . . no Argument can be fairly applyed to the British Parliament's taxing us, upon a Presumption that we shou'd refuse a just and reasonable Contribution."

In consequence

the Claim lately assumed and exercised by the British Parliament, of making such Laws as they think fit, to govern the People of these Colonies, and to extort from us our Money with out our Consent, is not only diametrically contrary to the first Principles of the Constitution, and the original Compacts by which we are dependant upon the British Crown and Government; but is totally incompatible with the Privileges of a free People, and the natural Rights of Mankind. . . .

Taxation and Representation are in their Nature inseperable; . . . the Right of withholding , or of giving and granting their own Money is the only effectual Security to a free People, against the Incroachments of Despotism and Tyranny; and that whenever they yield the One, they must quickly fall a Prey to the other."

The desire to retain colonial status, familiar in private correspondence* as well as public statements in previous years, is by this time baldly conditioned: "Resolved that it is our greatest Wish and Inclination, as well as Interest, to continue our Connection with, and Dependance upon the British Government; but tho' we are it's Subjects, we will use every Means which Heaven hath given us to prevent our becoming it's Slaves."[13]

Washington's recent letter to Bryan Fairfax is echoed in the affirmation that a "premeditated Design and System, formed and pursued by the British Ministry, to introduce an arbitrary Government into His Majesty's American Dominions" is evidenced by recent legislation, from the tax measures to the Boston Port Act. Since Boston is suffering in a common cause, every county should consign provisions "to some Gentleman of Character in Boston, to be distributed among the poorer Sort of People there."

The East India Company, even though it is serving as a tool of the government, should be compensated for its loss on the tea destroyed in Boston; other tea shipments now en route should be stored until money can be raised to reimburse the owners and then publicly burned; otherwise they are to remain in custody of the county committees until the tea tax is repealed. (In April, a test vote in Parliament had sustained the tax, 182 to 49.)

A firm union of the colonies is essential, and a Congress of their deputies, with wide powers, should be appointed to concert a uniform plan for defense of common rights and continued dependence on the Crown "under a just, lenient, permanent, and constitutional Form of Government." Thanks are extended to friends of liberty in Great Britain for their work to this end.

Specific measures for applying pressure through nonimportation of British goods repeat the terms of previous associations; in itemizing nonimportation of slaves, "we take this Opportunity of declaring our most earnest wishes to see an entire Stop for ever put to such a wicked cruel and unnatural Trade."

But the specifics do not stop with nonimportation; the nineteenth resolve adopts Mason's previously unsuccessful proposal of nonexportation: unless American grievances are redressed by 1 November 1775, all exports shall cease, and no more tobacco be grown. And if the forthcoming Congress adopts nonexportation, no court judgments for debt shall be thereafter rendered in the colonies, since the people will be unable to pay. A continental association should be opened; trade relations with any colony refusing to participate should be broken off; if Boston is forced to submit, the others should persevere.

The final substantive resolution contained an overt threat, inscribing in a public document the possibility that Washington had privately communicated to Mason five years before, when he wrote that "no man shou'd scruple, or hesitate a moment to use a–ms in defence of so valuable a blessing."[14] The Fairfax Resolves declared that the forthcoming Continental Congress should prepare and publish, in the papers of the principal towns of Great Britain, a petition and remonstrance to the king affirming "in the strongest Terms ou[r] Duty and Affection to his Majesty's Person, Family, [an]d Government, and our Desire to continue our Dependance upon Great Bri[tai]n; and most humbly conjuring and beseeching his Majesty, not to reduce his faithful Subjects of America to a State of desperation, and to reflect, that from our Sovereign there can be but one Appeal."[15]

This statement of the colonial case was the first of a series of documents, all preludes to action, that were the products of Mason's thought while he still maintained his private station during the years 1774–75.

While George Mason worked on the Fairfax Resolves, his

brother, Thomson, was setting forth similar views in nine letters to Rind's *Virginia Gazette* signed "A British American." The last of these, published 28 July 1774, goes even further than the final Fairfax resolution, affirming that if current grievances cannot be peacefully redressed, "you must draw your swords in a just cause, and rely upon that God, who assists the righteous, to support your endeavors to preserve the liberty he gave, and the love of which he hath implanted in your hearts as essential to your nature."

When Washington and Broadwater reached Williamsburg, they found attendance at the August Convention far larger—and far prompter—than usual at a session of the House of Burgesses. The proposals put forward by the other counties, except Middlesex and Dinwiddie, where continued reliance on petitions was preferred, generally approved the holding of a Continental Congress and the adoption of a nonimportation agreement; a number, with Fairfax's, favored nonexportation as well.* In addition to the county resolutions, great interest attached to the "Summary View of the Rights of British America," forwarded by Thomas Jefferson, delegate from Albemarle, when he fell ill and had to turn back on his way to Williamsburg.

Edmund Berkeley of Middlesex recorded the names and votes in the election of seven men to represent the colony at the Continental Congress that opened in Philadelphia's Carpenters' Hall on 5 September.[16] The top seven were the speaker of the House and moderator of the Convention, Peyton Randolph, 104; Richard Henry Lee, 100; George Washington, 98; Patrick Henry, 89; Richard Bland, 79; Benjamin Harrison, 66; Edmund Pendleton, 62. Others in the poll were Thomas Nelson and the absent Thomas Jefferson, each with 51; Thomson Mason, 16; James Mercer, 7; Francis Lightfoot Lee, Archibald Cary, and Robert Carter Nicholas, each with 4.

A spicy impression of this delegation—all of whom except Henry were physically impressive men—came to Samuel Pleasants from his brother-in-law, Roger Atkinson of Mansfield near Petersburg: Randolph "is not an orator—but he is an honest man—has knowledge, temper, experience, judgm't, & above all things Integrity"; Richard Henry Lee is "as true a trout as ever swam, as staunch a hound as ever ran." Washington is "a modest man, but sensible & speaks little—action cool, like a Bishop at his prayers"; Henry is "moderate & mild & in religious matters a Saint but ye very Devil in Politiks"; Bland is "staunch & tough as whitleather," and "has something of ye look of musty old Parchen'ts w'ch he handleth & studieth much"; Harrison, since he is Pleasants' near neighbor, needs no description; Pendleton "is ye last on ye List, I w'd willingly bring him in amongst ye first . . . a very pretty smoothtongued speaker."[17]

Mason had an opportunity for consultation with three members of the delegation at Mount Vernon on 30 August, when he, Patrick Henry, Edmund Pendleton, and Mason's relative, Thomas Triplett, spent the night with Washington at Mount Vernon, their talk continuing through dinner the following afternoon. As the delegates started north to Philadelphia, Mason turned his horse back to Gunston Hall.

Richard Henry Lee's election to the first Continental Congress permitted personal acquaintance to further the alliance between Massachusetts and Virginia which already existed on paper and had set the direction of early congressional sessions*—the Massachusetts delegation included both Samuel and John Adams. Dr. Josiah Warren of Boston, for whom Richard Henry Lee named the courthouse town of Virginia's Fauquier County, anchored the northern end of this axis as the Adamses' close associate; Mason's political partnership with Lee anchored its southern end. By mid-1775, the two colonies shared a common military incentive to force the pace: in Massachusetts, British General Thomas Gage held the capital; in Virginia, Governor Dunmore invested Norfolk while his fleet harried the Tidewater coast.

The alliance had its beginnings in London. Mason, in a letter to Richard Henry in the spring of 1775, welcomed the addition of Benjamin Franklin to Pennsylvania's congressional delegation: "I imagine no Man better knows the Intentions of the Ministry, the Temper of the Nation, & the Interest of the Minority."[18] He had perhaps not heard that Richard Henry had another reason to be pleased: Franklin's return from England in March meant new preferment in London for the youngest Lee brother, Arthur.

Dispatched from Virginia to Eton at the age of eleven, Arthur Lee had spent twenty of his next twenty-four years in England, first studying medicine at Edinburgh and then, after a brief interval of practice in Williamsburg, returning to prepare himself for admission to the English bar. He and his brother, William, had settled in London in 1768, William to marry his cousin, Hannah Phillipa Ludwell, and with her money to go into the tobacco trade, and Arthur, while reading law at the Middle Temple, to represent Virginia as the colony's London agent. Both circulated in the literary coterie centered on Boswell and Johnson, even though Johnson, a high Tory, took a low view of Americans; they were still more at ease in Whig and radical political circles, from that of Lord Shelburne to that of John Wilkes. William, in a distinction unique among colonials, was elected one of London's two sheriffs in 1773 and alderman from Aldgate in 1775. During Wilkes's term as Lord Mayor— and indeed during his earlier terms in jail—the brothers enjoyed to the full the international company, not always respectable but never dull, that gathered around this witty and profligate man; their acquaintance with Beaumarchais proved highly valuable later.

During the years 1770-75, Arthur Lee had tried persistently through his writings to reconcile the policies of his native colony and the land in which he lived: "May the liberties of England be immortal— but may Englishmen ever remember, that the same arbitrary spirit which prompts an invasion of the constitution in America, will not long leave that of England unattacked."[19] Signing himself Junius Americanus, he sent numerous communications to *The Gazetter;* his pamphlets included *An Appeal to the Justice and Interest of the People of Great Britain in the Present Disputes with America*. And he carried on a voluminous transatlantic correspondence with colonial leaders.

The alert eye of Samuel Adams of Massachusetts had early spotted him as an acute observer; on the death in 1770 of Dennys de Berdt, one of William's partners who had been the London agent of Massachusetts, Adams worked for Arthur's appointment in his place. The Massachusetts legislature preferred Franklin for the post but made Arthur his deputy; when Franklin went home, Lee moved up. Thereafter, he represented both of the colonies that were most actively pressing the constitutional cause.

It was on the strength of Arthur's connection that Richard Henry Lee had introduced himself by letter to Adams, who, in April 1773, made the same proposal to Richard Henry that Lee had made to John Dickinson in 1768, urging that "committees of correspondence for all the colonies should be formed" and "a private correspondence should be conducted between the lovers of liberty in every province." Before Adams's letter arrived, the March Virginia Assembly had named an eleven-man committee for this very purpose, the first such body to be colony wide. (While the bill creating it was framed and introduced by activists—the Lees, Patrick Henry, Thomas Jefferson, and his brother-in-law, Dabney Carr—the Assembly committed the actual correspondence to the safe hands of the speaker, the treasurer, and Dudley Digges, conservative burgess from York.) Most of the colonies rapidly took similar measures.

While the Continental Congress met, Mason was busy in Northern Virginia. The Virginia Convention had authorized formation in each county of a militia company, independent of the regular organization commanded by the governor. On 21 September, at a county gathering with Mason replacing Washington in the chair, the Fairfax Independent Company of Volunteers was organized, a one-hundred-man body whose members were to choose their own officers and meet for regular drill "In this Time of extreme Danger, with the Indian Enemy in our Country, and threat'ned with the Destruction of our Civil-rights, & Liberty, and all that is dear to British Subjects & Freemen." Its uniform was to be "Blue, turn'd up with Buff; with plain yellow metal Buttons, Buff Waist Coat & Breeches, & white Stockings"; its equipment, "a good Fire-lock & Bayonet, Sling Cartouch-Box, and Tomahawk." The men should "constantly keep by us a Stock of six pounds of Gunpowder, twenty pounds of Lead, and fifty Gun-flints, at the least."[20] The articles of association were in Mason's handwriting; Washington is thought to have specified the military details.*

The Continental Congress in Philadelphia, the Virginia Convention (scheduled to meet again in Richmond in March 1775), the county committees of safety, and the independent volunteer companies now provided Virginia with a shadow government paralleling the royal structure in all respects except a chief executive and, locally, the parish vestries and the soon-to-be-closed courts.

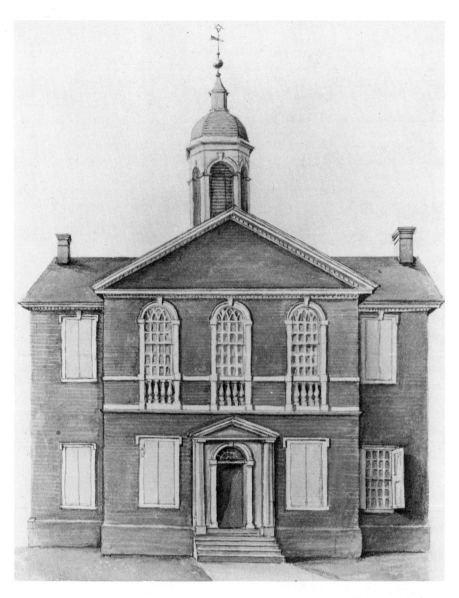

*Carpenters' Hall, Philadelphia,*
*watercolor by W. L. Breton, 1830*
*(courtesy, The Historical Society of*
*Pennsylvania)*

*John Wilkes, Esq.,*
*by William Hogarth, 1763*
(courtesy, The Trustees of the
British Museum)

Military preparations were extended in January 1775, when
Washington, back from Philadelphia, resumed the chairmanship of the
Fairfax County Committee. On the fifteenth, he discussed plans at
Mount Vernon with Mason and his son George,* Martin Cockburn,
and Daniel Dulany, member of the Maryland Governor's Council and
long-time secretary of the colony. In December, Maryland had formed
a military force whose articles of association closely paralleled the Fairfax articles. On the seventeenth, the Fairfax Committee of Safety adopted
two new resolves, of which the first proposed an assessment of three
shillings a head on all tithables, to be paid to the sheriff or other designated collector and spent on ammunition, the collector to furnish the
committee with the names of any who refused to contribute. The second
resolution concurred with the Maryland Provincial Committee "that a
well regulated Militia, composed of gentlemen freeholders, and other
freemen, is the natural strength and only stable security of a free Government, and that such Militia will relieve our mother country from any

*George Washington in British uniform*
*of the Virginia Militia*
*by Charles Willson Peale, 1772*
*(courtesy, Washington and Lee University)*

expense in our protection and defence, will obviate the pretence of a necessity for taxing us on that account, and render it unnecessary to keep Standing Armies among us—ever dangerous to liberty"; Fairfax men between sixteen and fifty were urged to choose officers, obtain firelocks, and master the book of military exercise.[21]

In February, Mason wrote and transmitted for Washington's suggestions an expanded plan for "Embodying the People:" all able-bodied freemen between the ages of eighteen and fifty were to enroll in companies of sixty-eight men each, which would then be formed into a regiment; a company of marksmen or light infantry to complement the regiment was to be composed of all who owned or understood the use of "Riphel Guns." Jefferson borrowed phrases from this document when reporting to the March Convention on behalf of its Committee to Prepare a Plan for a Militia.

At Richmond, Patrick Henry proposed that "this Colony be immediately put in a posture of defense" and supported his motion with eloquence that young hearers recalled in their old age as terminating in the cry, "I know not what course others may take; but as for me, give me liberty or give me death!" Richard Bland and Robert Carter Nicholas, urging delay, opposed the motion; Richard Henry Lee and Thomas Jefferson spoke for it. The vote went in Henry's favor. Within two days, a committee, of which he was chairman and Washington a member, brought in a plan for raising units of horse and infantry—but it had few suggestions on how they could be armed.

On 16 April, Mason went to Mount Vernon for the night, before the next day's committee meeting in Alexandria. During recent weeks, the desirability of election rather than appointment of officers in the Independent Company had been questioned. Marylanders had professed themselves shocked by this democratic procedure, and Alexandrians were proposing that the choice be confined to citizens of the town. Mason, alarmed lest the company should be tarnished "by any little dirty views of party, of mean self-interest or of low ambition"[22] supported annual elections of company officers by their men and of regimental officers by their company leaders in some "Remarks" on the fundamental principles on which the volunteer militia had been established: "No institution," he begins, "can be long preserved, but by frequent recurrence to those maxims on which it was formed." This company is no common collection of mercenary soldiers; it was assembled "upon the liberal sentiments of public good," so that "in case of absolute necessity, the people might be the better enabled to act in defence of their invaded liberty . . . gentlemen of the first fortune and character . . . have submitted to stand in the ranks as common soldiers, and to pay due obedience to the officers of their own choice."

Continuing, Mason set forth his concept of the fundamental basis of civil society:

We came equals into this world, and equals shall we go out of it. All men are by nature born equally free and independent. To protect the weaker from the

St. John's Church,
Richmond, scene of
Patrick Henry's
"liberty or death"
speech, by
J. Becker in
Leslie's Weekly,
2 September 1865
(courtesy, The
Valentine Museum,
Richmond, Virginia)

injuries and insults of the stronger were societies first formed; when men entered into compacts to give up some of their natural rights, that by union and mutual assistance they might secure the rest; but they gave up no more than the nature of the thing required. Every society, all government, and every kind of civil compact therefore, is or ought to be, calculated for the general good and safety of the community. Every power, every authority vested in particular men is, or ought to be, ultimately directed to this sole end; and whenever any power or authority whatever extends further, or is of longer duration than is in its nature necessary for these purposes, it may be called government, but it is in fact oppression. . . .

To prevent these fatal effects, and to restore mankind to its native rights . . . the most effectual means that human wisdom hath ever been able to devise, is frequently appealing to the body of the people, to those constituent members from whom authority originated, for their approbation or dissent. . . .

The application of these general principles to the subject before us is too obvious to need a minute illustration. By investing our officers with a power for life, or for an unlimited time, we are acting diametrically contrary to the principles of that liberty for which we profess to contend, and establishing a precedent which may prove fatal. By the purport of the proposed regulation every objection is obviated, every inconvenience removed; and the design of the institution strictly adhered to. It is calculated to prevent the abuse of authority, and the insolence of office on the one hand, and create a proper spirit of emulation on the other; and by an annual rotation, will in a few years breed a number of officers.[23]

Mason admitted one exception to the proposed rotation, "in favor of the gentlemen who by the unanimous voice of the company now commands it"; he called this "a very proper one, justly due to his public merit and experience; it is peculiarly suited to our circumstances, and was dictated, not by compliment, but conviction." At this time, Washington was in Philadelphia at the session of the Continental Congress; within weeks, he was commander of all continental troops.

During the night of 20-21 April, Governor Dunmore caused most of the contents of the Williamsburg magazine—some twenty barrels of powder and a supply of guns—to be moved to the *Fowey*, a 24-gun British man-of-war anchored in the James River. Irate Williamsburg citizens were prevented from rushing the Governor's Palace only by intervention of the speaker and the treasurer; a few days later, at Fredericksburg, an assembling force of six hundred cavalry was restrained from a march on Williamsburg only by a message from the speaker, then nearby at the home of Edmund Pendleton on his way to Philadelphia, and a letter from Washington to James Mercer. The decision to desist, taken in a committee of 102 chosen by the troops, was carried by a margin of a single vote. On 29 April, the new *Virginia Gazette* founded 7 February by Alexander Purdie declared: "The sword is now drawn, and God knows when it will be sheathed."

Meanwhile, the Hanover County Committee had authorized Patrick Henry and his company to advance on the capital and obtain restitution of the powder; collecting reinforcements on their way, they reached an inn sixteen miles from town on the evening of 3 May. There, an emissary of the governor received their alternative demands: either bring back the powder or pay for it. The next day, Council member Carter Braxton appeared bearing a bill of exchange for £330. Dunmore declared Henry an outlaw.

An attempt to lessen tension occurred when the governor summoned a meeting of the House of Burgesses for 1 June in order to place before it Lord North's "Olive Branch" resolutions. Speaker Randolph returned from Philadelphia for the session. The mood was grim: the response was drafted by Thomas Jefferson. From the *Fowey*, aboard which he had taken refuge after the powder incident, the governor vetoed the measure by which the House proposed to pay for "Dunmore's Indian War" of the previous autumn by levying a £5 duty on every imported slave. His refusal to leave the ship all but ended royal government in Virginia; the House attempted three further meetings, adjourning from one to the next for lack of a quorum, but its clerk wrote *finis* to the colonial record on 6 May 1776.

On 16 May, Washington sent a letter to the Fairfax County Committee from Philadelphia. It bore news of the gathering of troops to hold General Gage in Boston, but his principal purpose in writing was to urge the choice of a Convention delegate to take his place: "the necessity of a full, and able Representation at such a juncture as this, must be too obvious to need a Comment." As the election approached, weighing the conflict between duties at home and public service, Mason attempted to deflect the choice, writing William Ramsay on 11 July: "I entreat you, Sir, to reflect on the duty I owe to a poor little helpless

Thursday the 12th of October 13 Geo III. 1773.

The House met according to the Adjournment; but no more than thirty seven Members appearing, which was not a sufficient number to proceed to Business.

The House adjourned til the first Tuesday in March next.

---

Thursday the 7th of March 16 Geo. III. 1776.

The House met according to the Adjournment; but no more than thirty two Members appearing, which was not a sufficient number to proceed to Business;

The House adjourned til the first Monday in May next.

---

Monday, the 6th of May, 16 Geo. III. 1776.

Several Members met, but did neither proceed to Business, nor adjourn, as a House of Burgesses.

## FINIS.

*Last page of the* Journal of the House of Burgesses
*(courtesy, Virginia State Library)*

family of orphans to whom I now must act the part of father and mother both, and how incompatible such an office would be with the daily attention they require. This I will not enlarge on. Your own feelings will best explain it; and I rely on your friendship to excuse me to the gentlemen of the committee and my other friends."[24]

But his demurrers were ignored. When the Richmond Convention opened on 17 July, he was there; a week later, he described the body's busy schedule to Martin Cockburn: "I snatch a moment to let you know that I am well, and to desire to be kindly remembered to my dear children, and the family at 'Springfield.' I have not since I came to this place, except the fast-day and Sunday, had an hour which I could call my own. The committee (of which I am a member) appointed to prepare an ordinance for raising an armed force for the defence and protection of this colony, meet every morning at seven o'clock, sit till the Convention meets, which seldom rises before five in the afternoon, and immediately after dinner and a little refreshment sits again till nine or ten at night."[25]

Mason tried once more to sponsor a nonexportation ordinance, and on 24 July, it was "carried by a great majority." But it had to be rescinded later in the session when Maryland declined to pass a parallel measure and when the Continental Congress decided to permit exports by ship captains who would commit themselves to bring arms and ammunition on their return trips.

In August, Mason and Josiah Parker of Isle of Wight County were appointed to draft a loyalty oath to be administered by the county committees to all freemen. They proposed that subscribers should swear not to violate the nonimportation association and not take up arms or give aid or support to any power directed against the people of the colony. Persons refusing to take the oath were to be summoned before the committee, and on a second refusal to be disarmed and not permitted to go further than five miles from their homes without a special permit. But the convention deferred action on the measure: such an oath was not required until 1777.

As the time for selection of Virginia's delegation to the next Continental Congress approached, Mason was importuned by more than two-thirds of the Convention's members to allow his name to be entered in the balloting. Just up from a sickbed, he succeeded in blocking this request. The first ballot gave Peyton Randolph 89, Richard Henry Lee 88, Jefferson 85, Harrison 83, Nelson 66, Bland 61, and Wythe 58. Pressure on Mason was renewed when Bland declined because of his age. He told Cockburn:

a strong Party was form'd at the Head of which were Colo. Henry, Mr. Jefferson, & Colo. Carrington, for sending me to the Congress at all Events, laying it down as a Rule that I wou'd not refuse if ordered by my Country: in Consequence of this, just before the Ballot, I was publickly called upon in Convention, & obliged to make a public Excuse, & gave my Reasons for refusal, in doing which I felt myself more distress'd than ever I was in my Life, especially when

I saw Tears run down the President's cheeks. I took Occasion, at the same time, to recommend Colo. Francis Lee; who was accordingly chosen in the room of Colo. Bland.[26*]

The wide range of individual reaction to the heady events of 1775 had been described by Pendleton in June in a letter to Joseph Chew of Philadelphia: "The Sanguine are for rash Measures without consideration, the Flegmatic to avoid that extreme are afraid to move at all, while a third Class take the middle way and endeavor by tempering the first sort and bringing the latter into action to draw all together to a Steddy, tho' Active Point of defense."[27]

A more acid description of the difficulties of securing a sensible consensus went to Washington in Mason's letter of 14 October:

I hinted to you in my last the Partys & Factions which prevail'd at Richmond: I never was in so disagreeable a Situation, and almost despaired of a Cause which I saw so ill conducted. Mere Vexation & Disgust threw me into such an ill State of Health that before the Convention rose, I was sometimes near fainting in the House. . . .

During the first Part of the Convention Partys run so high, that we had frequently no other Way of preventing improper Measures but by Procrastination, urging the previous Question, & giving Men time to reflect: however after some Weeks, the Bablers were pretty well silenced, a few weighty Members began to take the Lead, several wholsome Regulations were made, and if the Convention had continued to sit a few Days longer, I think the public Safety wou'd have been as well provided for as our present Circumstances permit."[28]

The convention had adopted plans for uniting the independent militia of the counties into an army for the colony as a whole and furnishing it with arms; examined means of raising funds and imposing taxes; set up regulations for the election of county Committees and Convention delegates; and placed in office an eleven-man Committee of Safety.

In both his July and his August letter to Cockburn, Mason had described the Convention's deliberations on "the powers of a Committee of Safety to superintend the execution" of the measures it adopted, measures whose previously provisional character had been given new force when, as he told Washington, "The Convention, not thinking this a time to relye upon Resolves & Recommendations only, and to give obligatory Force to their Proceedings, adopted the Style & Form of Legislation, changing the Word enact into *ordain:* their Ordinances were all introduced in the Form of Bills, were regularly referred to a Committee of the whole House, and underwent three Readings before they were passed."[29]

When the ballot for committee members took place, Mason ruefully reported to Cockburn that his getting clear of the congressional appointment "has avail'd me little, as I have been since, in Spite of everything I cou'd do to the Contrary, put upon the Committee of Safety; which is even more inconvenient & disagreeable to me than going to the Congress. I endeavor'd to excuse myself, & beg'd the Convention wou'd permit me to resign; but was answer'd by an universal NO."[30]

In the ballot for the eleven-man Committee of Safety, Pendleton led with 77 votes and became chairman; Mason was next with 72. The other members—a representative group as far as the counties from which they came, but a group that was predominantly conservative in attitude—were John Page, Richard Bland, Thomas Ludwell Lee, Paul Carrington, Dudley Digges, William Cabell, Carter Braxton, James Mercer, and John Tabb.

With Dunmore gone, this committee became the colony's chief executive, vested with concentrated authority and, between conventions, subject only to its own self-restraint. By these actions, in its executive as well as its legislative function, the shadow government had assumed substance in Virginia.

Toward the end of 1775, distinct constituencies began to appear up and down the coast, with some citizens supporting the legitimate government whose substance was becoming shadow, and others, the shadow governments now substantiating themselves. For a variety of reasons, in which chance played a considerable part, Virginia enjoyed a degree of solidarity as the division took place between those who called themselves loyalists and those who took the name of patriots that made itself felt in preparing her to take the lead in May 1776.

Certain categories of men were foreseeably loyal to the Crown. Those who had long held office as acting governors or other royal officers felt obligated in honor as well as in inclination to maintain an attitude of allegiance. Governors Thomas Hutchinson in Massachusetts, Cadwalader Colden in New York, William Franklin in New Jersey, John Penn in Pennsylvania, and William Bull in South Carolina either returned to England or rusticated at a distance from their capitals. But in Virginia, no such former governor was alive at the time: John Blair had died in 1771.

Attorney General John Randolph did indeed break with his brother Peyton his predecessor in the office and currently the Convention's president, and his son, Edmund, his successor as attorney general when Virginia became a state; he left for London and died there. So did a number of Council members. Richard Corbin, receiver general for Virginia quitrents for twenty years and the intermediary between Dunmore and the Virginia Committee of Safety, was given a royal commission to be governor when Dunmore resigned but hid the commission and retired first to his estate and then to England. Philip Ludwell Lee's death in 1775 avoided a split with his five brothers. The death (probably by suicide) in 1777 of William Byrd III followed an unrequited offer of services to the king; his widow was a prominent loyalist. But other Tidewater planters like the Nelsons of Yorktown cast their lot with the Convention.

Virginia likewise had few equivalents of the men who elsewhere began as Whigs and went part way with the protesting colonists but drew back from independence. Among them New York's chief justice,

William Smith, Jr., acted as consultant to the drafters of the new state constitution in 1776, but refused to take the oath of allegiance in 1777; banished in 1778 on a second refusal to take the oath, he eventually became chief justice of Canada.

In Pennsylvania, Joseph Galloway, Assembly speaker from 1766 to 1775 and delegate to the first Continental Congress, became General Howe's civil administrator while British troops occupied Philadelphia; a loyalist spokesman in England thereafter, his Pennsylvania estates were confiscated, and his request for permission to return in the 1790s was denied.*

Mason's friend, Daniel Dulany of Maryland, was a strict constructionist; his *Considerations on the Propriety of Imposing Taxes in the British Colonies, For the Purpose of Raising a Revenue, by Act of Parliament* at the time of the Stamp Act had demolished the claim that "virtual representation" of the colonies by Parliament justified that body's revenue measures, but he held that the unconstitutionality of the act did not relieve Americans from observing it "whilst it endures."

Virginia, and the Northern Neck in particular, was again fortunate in its equivalent to a third body of natural loyalists. The proprietary heirs who controlled millions of colonial acres in Pennsylvania, New Jersey, Delaware, and Maryland were as interested in holding their own as was the Crown. But Thomas, lord Fairfax, remained in unprotesting seclusion at his home near Winchester, to die there sadly in his eighty-ninth year as the war closed; the independent state government respectfully assured his continued collection of proprietary quitrents during the entire interval. And far from being a Tory, his young relative, Mason's friend, George William Fairfax, approved the Revolution. In 1773, fully expecting to return, he resigned his Council seat and put Belvoir in Washington's charge while he and his wife went to Yorkshire to receive an inheritance. When in 1780, Washington heard that the Virginia legislature was considering confiscation of this Fairfax estate, he sent Robert Carter Nicholas a hot rebuke: "It is a well known fact that his departure for England was not only anticedent to the present rupture with Great Britain, but before there was the most distant prospect of a serious dispute with that Country, and if it is necessary to adduce proof of his attachment to the interests of America since his residence there and of the aid he has given to many of our distressed Countrymen in that Kingdm. abundant instances may be produd."[31] Washington's confidence was substantiated by a letter from Fairfax after the war: "Permit me, tho' an humble individual, and unfortunately out of the way of contributing any mite to the great, the glorious cause of Liberty, to offer my best thanks for all of your Exertions, disinterested perservance to the End of the great work . . . I glory in being called an American."[32]

In colonies where there were cities—Boston, New York, Philadelphia, Charleston—social and commercial connections with England swayed many men. When General Gage evacuated Boston in 1775, more than a thousand Massachusetts loyalists accompanied him to Halifax. British occupation of New York and Philadelphia early in the war, and of Charleston in 1780, offered congenial protection to mercantile families of those ports.

But in Virginia, the absence of a large commercial center reduced such economic magnetism. While Norfolk, the largest town, contained a substantial Tory community—mostly Scottish traders who shortly left for home—it numbered only six thousand and was burned early in the war. (But the loyalist Norfolk Goodrich family of skilled shipmasters did privateer with telling destruction against Virginia shipping around Hampton Roads, raiding plantations along the Potomac and the Chesapeake, and blocking cargoes dispatched via the North Carolina sounds at Ocracoke Inlet below Cape Hatteras.)

In partial balance with these exceptions, Virginia shared with other colonies where the Church of England was established a loyalist clergy united to the Crown both through their spiritual ties to their religious superiors in the English hierarchy and to the sovereign as head of the church, and also through the statutory tithes that paid their salaries. When the collection of tithes was suspended, a group of Virginia rectors memorialized the legislature with a reminder that they had "entered into Holy Orders expecting to receive the several Emoluments which such religious establishment offered; that from the nature of their education they are precluded from gaining a tolerable subsistence in any other way of life."[33] Yet many clergymen were planters as well, and those of Scottish origin were attracted to the growing Presbyterian strength in central and northern Virginia; such men often shared the political attitudes of their revolutionary neighbors.

The most pressing decisions based on economic considerations in Virginia were a direct result of the success, at long last, of Mason's persistent advocacy of nonexportation as well as nonimportation. With 1 September 1775 set as a cutoff date for tobacco shipments, the termination of the usefulness of the resident factors of British firms was in plain sight. Unlike the older traders of long-standing residence—the founders of Alexandria, Colchester, or Dumfries almost to a man affiliated with the American cause*— the young men in these posts felt their future to lie elsewhere.†

The Glasgow tobacco lords had been slow in accepting realities. Their prosperity was so massive as to seem impregnable. They were the importers of well over half of all tobacco coming to Britain; in their own lifetime they had opened up an entirely new section of the city, adorned with residences and public buildings in the latest neoclassical style. In front of the arcaded piazza of the new Town House and Assembly Hall in the Trongate,‡ around the equestrian statue of William III, the fenced off area known as "the Planestanes"—distinguished from surrounding cobbles by its pavement of large flat stones—was their private precinct, in which no one else was expected to set foot. When the hour of "change" sounded, they assembled in their distinctive garb—scarlet gowns over

black suits, cocked hats over curled wigs, tall gold-topped canes in hand.
An old rhyme ran:

> 'Tween twa and three, wi' daily care
> The gentry to the cross repair:
> The politician wi' grave air
> Deliberating:
> Merchants and manufact'rers there
> Negotiating.

Smaller traders stayed beyond the posts, either to deal among themselves
or to stand in patient hope of catching a lord's eye.

Some of the red-cloaked worthies made their way from Robert
Tennent's Saracen Head, the city's ranking inn, whose construction the
magistrates had encouraged in 1754 with a gift of building stone from
the former Bishop's Palace. Its principal drawing room could accommodate a hundred; its five-gallon punch bowl bore the city's coat of arms
and the motto "Success to the Town of Glasgow."

Other lords arrived directly from their town houses. William
Cunninghame's mansion survives as the central part of the Stirling
Library. In 1756, John Glassford, Alexander Henderson's principal,[*]

had sold to a fellow tobacco lord his first imposing residence, Whitehill House, on the north edge of Glasgow; around 1760, he acquired Shawfield Mansion, Glasgow's first great house, built in 1712 and in 1745 headquarters of the Young Pretender.

Provost Andrew Buchanan gave the name of Virginia Street to the road he cut through his new land west of Shawfield; in 1760, his son George built Virginia House across the head of it. An oval carriageway lined by ornamental shrubs led up to this mansion from two matching porter's lodges; grapes and peaches were pleached along the inner sides of its surrounding walls; rare plants filled Glasgow's first conservatory. Previously, when George returned from Virginia in 1756, he had built a house with a fine view of the Clyde east of Glasgow in the village of Baillieston and given it the same name that Lawrence Washington had given to his house with a fine view of the Potomac, in honor of the British Admiral Vernon. The euphoria of such magnificence made it easy to discount the possibility that Glasgow's tobacco trade might be nearing its end.

The tobacco magnates in the major markets were by no means uninformed. Two letters written from agents in Virginia in 1774 are typical of the warnings they received. On 7 June, James Parker of Norfolk started a letter to his former business associate, Charles Steuart in London, finishing it in Williamsburg ten days later, in which he reported Governor Dunmore's dismissal of the burgesses because of their declaration of a fast day and their subsequent gathering at the Raleigh Tavern to consider economic reprisals, together with almost as accurate a description of various individual attitudes: "There was some violent debate here about the association. George Mason, Pat: Henry, R. H. Lee and The Treasurer, as I am told, were for paying no Debts to Britain, no exportation or importation & no Courts here. Paul Carrington was for Paying his Debts & Exporting, on this he was joined by Carter Braxton, Mr. E. Pendleton, Thos Nielson junr & the Speaker. Tho the Whole Colony and I believe the Continent are against the Taxes without consent, Yet there are many who do not justifie the Bostonians. . . . The Present dispositions of the Merchants is to have nothing to do with either, the agreements or associations, but mind their own business."[34]

Henry Fleming,* a young Norfolk representative of several Whitehaven firms, including Eilbeck and Ross, was more alarmingly graphic:

America it's said is contending for *Liberty*! at the same time they deny the British Merchnts. resident here the liberty of pursuing their interest in a legal manner, or speaking their opinions, & almost of thinking contrary to *their* opinions. There was a pole erected upon the parade in Wmsburg when I was there with a Brush a Bag of Feathers & a Tar Barrel at its foot by order of the Burgesses to intimidate such as would dare to broach a sentiment contrary to what is called the liberties of America. . . . Our hope of redress is only in the British Parliamt. repealing the acts deem'd opressive by the Americans—otherwise our property at least must be very precarious.[35]

Only in the spring of 1775 did the lords accept the fact that a ces-

*"BOYNE*
*of Whitehaven*
*Joseph Hodgson*
*Master, 1794"*
*(courtesy, Public*
*Library and Museum,*
*Whitehaven,*
*Cumberland, England)*

sation of American supplies was upon them. Once they had done so, they acted with canny speed.* Urgent orders instructed their American agents to buy, buy, and buy; growers' eagerness to clear their stocks kept down the price. Shipping of all sorts was rushed to get the purchases under sail before the embargo date of 1 September. Ordinarily, a ship's cargo weighed less than half of its rated tonnage, but that summer, casks were even stacked in the open above decks on the Glasgow fleet: 1775 imports topped those of 1774 by over 4 million pounds for a total of 45,863,154.[†]

These consignments ended the primacy of tobacco in Britain's ranking tobacco port. By the time the next crop was ready, its destination was affected not only by the embargo that Mason had so vigorously sponsored but by the independent status that released the former colonies from the requirements of the British navigation acts. The change eliminated Glasgow's position as an entrepôt. In 1772, its merchants had exported close to 21 million pounds to France, almost 15 million to Holland, nearly 4 million to Germany. Now, American suppliers could send their cargoes directly to the buyers who had formerly frequented Glasgow's Virginia Street.[‡]

The predicament of the young factors stranded by the embargo remained to be dealt with; it was a main consideration in deciding the Virginia Convention to defer for the present the requirement of the loyalty oath drafted by Mason and Parker until most of them could find a way home. Instead, a "Resolution concerning Peaceable British Subjects Resident in Virginia" was unanimously passed, giving assurance to merchants in the form of counsel to committees of safety and ordinary citizens: "it is recommended to the Committees of the several Counties and Corporations, and others the good people of this Colony, to treat all natives of *Great Britain,* resident here, as do not show themselves enemies to the common cause of *America,* with lenity and friendship; to protect all persons whatsoever in the just enjoyment of their civil rights and liberty; to discountenance all national reflections; to preserve, to the utmost of their power, internal peace and good order; and to promote union, harmony, and mutual goodwill among all ranks of people."[36]

Yet time-consuming exceptional cases troubled various local committees of safety; with two in particular, George Mason, as chairman of the Fairfax County Committee, had to deal. Young Nicholas Cresswell's plight displayed the trivial anxieties of the innocent tourist unexpectedly caught in a rebellion; Dr. John Ferdinand Dalziel Smyth's plot exemplified the connivance of a fervent loyalist and possible British agent, who served his government so perspicaciously that he received a postwar British pension of £300 a year.

On 1 March 1774, Nicholas Cresswell had commenced a journal at Edale in the Staffordshire Peak district; "I have been studying and deliberating for a long time how to shape my course in the world, and am this day come to a determined resolution to go into America, be the consequence that it will."[37] James Kirk, currently an Alexandria merchant, was the Edale blacksmith's son; Cresswell set out for Virginia to seek his advice, and Kirk, a signer of the nonimportation resolution and a member of the Fairfax County Committee of Correspondence, took him into his home.

Cresswell found the situation alarming: tradesmen "have been tarred and feathered, others had their property burnt and destroyed by the populace. Independent Companies are raising in every County on the Continent. . . . The King is openly cursed, and his authority set at defiance. In short, everything is ripe for rebellion . . . did I not think this affair would be over in the spring, I would immediately return home. But I am very unwilling to return . . . and be laughed at by all my friends. . . . Mr. Kirk advises me to stay till Spring and take a Tour in the back Country."[38]

When Cresswell returned from exploring the Ohio, he found himself in trouble. To English friends, he had "freely declared my sentiments upon the present Rebellion"; his letters had been intercepted by the Virginia Committee of Safety and sent to the chairman of the Fairfax Committee with orders to put the author in jail. In Cresswell's absence, George Mason's brother, Thomson, now settled on his Raspberry Plain

*"The Alternative of Williams Burg," 1775; mezzotint by Philip Dawe(?) showing the choice of being tarred and feathered or signing the nonimportation association*

*(courtesy, Library of Congress)*

plantation near Leesburg, had gone surety that Cresswell, when he came back from the west, would not leave the colony without the committee's consent. The young man stayed near Leesburg until the following July, when Thomson Mason initiated a series of patient efforts to help him get home. He first requested Governor Patrick Henry to permit him to join the British fleet in Chesapeake Bay, but news came that Dunmore had been driven off and the fleet was gone. Then, at word of Lord Howe's arrival, he wrote letters to Francis Lightfoot Lee, Thomas Jefferson, and two other members of Congress in Philadelphia to obtain a pass for Cresswell to join him in New York. On approaching the city, he was recognized by a Virginian in the American army with whom he had once quarreled about politics and ordered to return to Virginia or face arrest.

When Loudoun County committeemen searched his effects for treasonable papers, the young man trembled: "My situation would have been dreadful indeed, an imprisonment of five years, or the fine of twenty thousand pounds would have been the punishment. . . . The bare idea of it makes me shudder, the thought of a prison even for debt is horrid."[39] Finally, however, to the relief of all concerned, he reached General Howe's headquarters and sailed.

The case of J. F. D. Smyth opened in Alexandria at almost the same time as Cresswell's. After practicing medicine in Williamsburg in the early 1770s, Smyth had bought a plantation in Charles County, Maryland. But as the crisis developed, he would neither take an oath to refrain from action against the colonies nor remain on his estate. Visiting Alexandria, he found "that all my precautions to remain here undiscovered were fruitless, and the first intimation I had of this was from Colonel George Mason while at dinner, who desired me to take particular notice of an unfortunate loyalist, tarred and feathered by the mob, who were that instant carrying him along as a public spectacle, emphatically observing *that it nearly concerned me.*"[40]

So on 15 October 1774, he secretly started south bent on overt service to the king. At Norfolk, after paying his respects to Lord Dunmore aboard the *William,* he "conversed for a considerable time with Lieutenant-Colonel [John] Connolly,"[41] concocting a plot that, if successful, would have threatened not only Virginia's war effort but that of the colonies as a whole.

Connolly was a son-in-law of the Pennsylvania Indian trader, George Croghan, many of whose relatives and associates were actively and effectively aiding the British in the west; he was intimately familiar with the country beyond the Alleghenies. With Dunmore and Lt. Allen Cameron, a former Indian agent of the Crown, he and Smyth set up a plan to go west via the Potomac and north to British headquarters at Detroit; there, over the winter, they would prepare a military assault on Virginia to be carried out in concert with Lord Dunmore and his fleet in early spring. First capturing Fort Pitt, they would fight their way down the Potomac while Dunmore came up the river from Chesapeake Bay. At Alexandria, their pincers would cut the continent in two:

> For the execution of this well formed, judicious, and vast undertaking, Lieutenant-Colonel Connolly was furnished with the proper and necessary powers . . . and with ample instructions for his future conduct, as well as commissions for the formation of a complete regiment at Detroit, or Pittsburg. . . . All these papers were concealed in the mail pillion-sticks on which the servant carried his portmanteau, they being made hollow, for that purpose, and covered with tin plates, and then canvass glued thereon as usual; this was so dextrously and completely executed that it could not be discovered on the strictest examination.[42]

They set out on 13 November 1774, but came to grief at an inn west of Hagerstown, Maryland: interception of a letter from Connolly to a colleague at Fort Pitt had revealed their presence in the area, and chance recognition of Connolly by a former private in his command identified them. Apprehended, they were taken to Frederick, jailed, and ordered transferred to Philadelphia. The next night Smyth escaped but was brought back after recapture twelve days later near Fort Pitt;* all three were then successfully removed to the jurisdiction of Congress in Philadelphia.

George Mason was the source of the warning that caused the Maryland Committee to act; on 29 November, he alerted its members:

*Philadelphia
from Second and
High Street
by William Birch,
c. 1800
(courtesy, The
Historical Society
of Pennsylvania)*

Having just received the following important intelligence, and not knowing whether you were apprized of the Character & dangerous designs of Majr. Connelly, I thought it proper *imediatly* to transmit it to your board, together with a copy of a letter & Intelligence, respecting him, recd. sometime ago from his excellency General Washington. . . . Connelly, we are told, had with him a Commission from Genl. Gage to raise a number of Indians, & with them to penetrate, thro' the Country, towards Alexandria in the spring, where He wou'd be met by Lord Dunmore. . . . I make no doubt but your Board will take proper measures to prevent the escape of such dangerous men.[43]

The Connolly affair startled Northern Virginians—the Fairfax County Committee transmitted their nervousness to the December Convention: "Why is this part of the Country to be left unguarded? when it appears, not only from the public Papers, but Lord Dunmore's Assignation with *Conoly* that Alexandria was to be their place of rendezvous in the Month of April next, a place well known to the Officers who were out on Genl. Braddock's Expedition, a safe Harbour for Ships of War & commanding a most material part of the Colony."[44]

The last months of 1775 were a time of uneasy waiting—the pause that in great crises is required for the majority of a community to accept the necessity of a major event. In the chemistry of Virginia society the essential elements of a decision for independence were present, but a catalyst had not appeared. For leaders whose minds were made up, it was an anxious interval.

Mason dated his decision from receipt of news of the royal proclamation of 23 August in which the king declared the colonies to be in a state of rebellion; it was a turning point for many of his associates as well. The reasoning behind their attitude then moved to a new base. Up to that date, most viewed the quarrel as a dispute concerning the rights of Englishmen, in particular their right to be governed—and taxed—by their own representatives in a colony united with others of His Majesty's dominions under the Crown.* Mason had presented this theory in the first of his Fairfax Resolves, Jefferson in his *Summary View;* so had John Adams and James Wilson in Massachusetts and Pennsylvania. As late as June and July 1775 Thomson Mason's letters in the *Virginia Gazette* had advanced a concept of empire according to which Virginia had been independent ever since 1607 in respect to its internal policy and urged that the empire be saved from the madness of Parliament. Others railed at faulty advisors who were no true friends to the king. But no challenge was offered to the Crown. During the autumn, the legislatures of New York, New Jersey, Pennsylvania, Maryland, and North Carolina all passed resolutions against independence.

Yet at the same time, a shift of ground very like that at the approach of the Glorious Revolution in England was recurring in America. In revolutionary England, John Locke had expounded the concept of the social compact between ruler and ruled, entered into by men moving from a state of nature into a state of society; in the following century, continental thinkers of the Enlightenment such as Voltaire and Rousseau explored it further as a means of upholding the rights of man under natural law.

In America, their doctrines were the more congenial because the circumstances of daily life put flesh on their abstractions. The frontiersman in his clearing fitted their description of the individual in a state of nature. And from the Mayflower Compact on, the seventeenth-century charters of the American colonies were actual and visible covenants for the formation of new societies.

In midsummer of 1774, Mason's exposition of the social compact in his "Remarks on Annual Elections for the Fairfax Independent Company" had contained the sentence: "Whenever any power or authority whatever extends further than is in its nature necessary . . . it may be called government, but is in fact oppression." By the autumn of 1775, he had accepted the implication of what he wrote. Locke, considering the options of a people "should either the executive, or the legislative, when they have got the power in their hands, design, or go about to enslave or destroy them," had declared: "The people have no other remedy in this, as in all other cases where they have no judge on earth, but to *appeal to heaven.*"[45]

At the turn of the year, the long-awaited catalyst ended the period of anxious waiting. On 10 January 1776, an anonymous, forty-seven-page pamphlet appeared in Philadelphia entitled *Common Sense.* Its author, Thomas Paine, was an Englishman whom Benjamin Franklin had counseled to emigrate as a means of extricating himself from difficulties both marital and financial, using his good offices to install Paine as editor of the *Pennsylvania Magazine*. Philadelphia's philosophical physician, Benjamin Rush, had prompted Paine to write the piece and put him in touch with a printer; he now exulted that its "effects were sudden and extensive upon the American mind."[46]* Paine had been in America less than fifteen months, but he had phrased the dynamics of the crisis so tellingly that within weeks, Washington, sensing his words to be "working a powerful change in the minds of many men," ordered the pamphlet read aloud to his troops in New York. By 31 January, he was affirming to Joseph Reed: "A few more of such flaming arguments, as were exhibited at Falmouth and Norfolk, [Dunmore's firing of the latter town took place on 1 January] added to the sound doctrine and unanswerable reasoning contained in the pamphlet *Common Sense,* will not leave numbers at a loss to decide upon the propriety of a separation."[47]

*Thomas Paine by John Wesley Jarvis*
*(courtesy, National Gallery of Art,*
*Washington, D.C., gift of*
*Marian B. Maurice)*

# Chapter VII
# *The Declaration of Independence and the*
# *Virginia Bill of Rights*

*Three months after publication, at least 120,000 copies of* Common Sense *had found avid readers.*

In Massachusetts, James Bowdoin borrowed a copy from Mercy Otis Warren, wife of the president of the provincial assembly, and declared that he and his "dear Rib" were fortified in their belief in independence by reading it. John Adams had inquired of Mercy on 8 January 1776:

Pray Madam, are you for an American monarchy or republic? Monarchy is the genteelest and most fashionable government, and I don't know why the ladies ought not to consult elegance and the fashion as well in government as in gowns, bureaus or chariots. . . .

For my own part, I am so tasteless as to prefer a republic, if we must erect an independent government in America, which you know is utterly against my inclination. . . .

It is the form of government which gives the decisive color to the manners of the people, more than any other thing. Under a well-regulated commonwealth, the people must be wise, virtuous, and cannot be otherwise. Under a monarchy they may be as vicious and foolish as they please, nay, they cannot be but vicious and foolish. As politics therefore is the science of human happiness, and human happiness is clearly best promoted by virtue, what thorough politician can hesitate who has a new government to build whether to prefer a commonwealth or a monarchy?[1]

At the other end of the seaboard, Charlestonians read the copy of *Common Sense* that Christopher Gadsden brought back from Philadelphia. The New York Committee of Safety turned a deaf ear to a printer who complained that a mob of Isaac Sears's mechanics had entered his shop and carried off to destruction the whole edition of a reply to the pamphlet, in spite of the fact that it was "entirely decent in tone."

Not everyone liked it. In Connecticut, a refutation, *Plain Truth,* appeared from the pen of James Chalmers. A Maryland landowner who signed himself "Candidus" declared that without the crown "our constitution would immediately degenerate into democracy." In Virginia, Landon Carter, though an adherent of the patriot side, came slowly to the idea of independence. He thought the pamphlet flamboyant; his first reaction, on learning it was written by Paine, was that "it is really much to be suspected of its secret intentions to fix an ill impression that the Americans are resolved not to be reconciled. And indeed that matter is incouraged under the most absured Arguments in the world."[2]

Yet when he looked back on the Virginia of these times, Edmund Randolph declared that Paine "poured forth in a style hitherto unknown, on this side of the Atlantic . . . pregnant with the most captivating figures of speech . . . the public sentiment, which a few weeks before had shuddered at the tremendous obstacles with which independance was environed, over-leaped every barrier."[3]

Paine's words were important, even essential. But words would not ward off physical attack. During the months after the August convention and the meeting of the Virginia Committee of Safety in Hanover that lasted through most of September 1775, Mason had turned his attention to the military defenses of his area. Dunmore's raids were having effect: in October, Mason wrote Washington that "Many of the principal Familys are removing from Norfolk, Hampton, York & Williamsburg, occasioned by the Behaviour of Lord Dunmore,"[4] and Lund Washington, the general's distant cousin who managed the Mount Vernon plantation during his absence, wondered if it was worthwhile to proceed with the extensive enlargement of the house which was in hand at the time of its owner's departure: from "what we are daily hearing here, it looks like lost labor to keep on with our building, for should they get burned it will be provoking; but I shall keep on until I am directed to the contrary by you."[5] On 7 November, Dunmore declared martial law, designated as traitors all men capable of bearing arms who did not "resort to His Majesty's standard," and offered freedom to slaves who would escape and join his forces.

During that autumn and winter, Mason's health was worse than usual; Lund Washington informed the general in October that "Colonel Mason has been sick ever since he came from the Convention. He looks very badly and he is quite worn out in appearance. He seems to be much disturbed that he is not able to attend the Committee of Safety. I wish he was well; we want him much and shall miss him if it pleases God to take him out of this world."[6]

By mid-January, Lund was thoroughly gloomy: "The Alexandrians expect to have their town burned by the enemy soon. They do not take any steps to prevent it. They put their trust in the Convention, and the Convention I believe, in God. . . . We are not well represented in Convention. Colonel Mason's indisposition has prevented his attendance this winter. Our other delegate you may remember, is no conjurer."[7]

In April, Mason himself told the general that while illness had "disabled me from attending the Committee of Safety this Winter, and induced me to intreat the Convention to leave me out of it . . . I hope am no less usefully employed. . . . I have in Conjunction with Mr. Dalton, the Charge of providing & equiping arm'd Vessels for the Protection of this River. The thing is new to me; but I must endeavour to improve by Experience."[8]

Mason may well have been right that the chairmanship of the Fairfax Committee was the place of his greatest usefulness; Jefferson, who declined an appointment as a negotiator with France in September 1776, later explained, "I saw, too, that the laboring oar was really at home, where much was to be done, of the most permanent interest, in new modelling our governments, and much to defend our fanes and fire-sides from the desolations of an invading enemy, pressing on our country at every point."[9]

The shortage of salt was disquieting, for without salt to cure meat, troop rations could not be accumulated, nor could civilians provide for their normal needs. In November 1775, the Fairfax Committee addressed John Hancock, president of the Congress, warning him of the need to stockpile salt over the coming winter, and urging that shipmasters who agreed to bring it in should be allowed to carry American goods abroad on the same basis as suppliers of munitions. A month later a congressional resolution validated this permission for captains from Maryland, Virginia, and North Carolina.

The Fairfax Committee likewise instructed the county's delegates to the December Convention urgently to press for additional military protection of the coasts, specifying "a few Vessells of War, to protect the Bay & Rivers, from Lord Dunmore's Pirates." More arms and ammunition are essential: "the calling a Number of Men to the lower Parts of the Colony, unaccoutred is incurring an Expence to little purpose."[10]

On 31 January, Lund Washington warned the general: "The Women & Children are leaveg Alexandria & stowg themselves into every little Hut they can get, out of the reach of the Enemys Canon as they think, every Waggon, Cart, & Pack Horse that can be got, are employ'd in moveg the goods out of town, The militia are all up (but not in arms) for Indeed they have none or at least very few. . . . I am about packg up your China Glass, &c into Barrels . . . & other things into Chests, Trunks, Bundles, &c and I then shall be able at the shortest notice, to move your things out of harms way."[11]

The Fairfax County record of slowly attained small successes, paralleled by continuous small failures, is a case history, duplicated up and down the coast, of the accumulated inadequacies that culminated in the misery of Washington's 1777-78 winter at Valley Forge.

The *Journal* and *The Account Book* of Virginia's Committee of Safety itemize that body's authorizations, orders and warrants to George Mason and John Dalton for the area of their oversight. In February, they received £1,000 "for fitting the Potowmack Navy"; in April, two payments of £3,000 each, to cover purchase of the boats; and in May, other sums for cannon, shot, etc.

In April, opening his letter with congratulations on the recovery of Boston, Mason reported progress to Washington: The *American Congress* is ready with ninety-six marines and seamen recruited to handle her; the sloops have been bought but are not yet fitted with cannon; the seven regiments voted to be raised the previous summer are "already in a Manner compleat except as to Arms, in which they are very deficient. . . . Notwithstanding the natural plenty of provisions in this Colony, I am very apprehensive of a great Scarcity of Beef & Pork among our Troops this Summer. . . . I find it extreamly difficult to lay in a Stock for about 300 men in the Marine Department of this River."

He hazards the guess that an attack by General Howe on the middle or southern colonies during the coming summer is unlikely, "a Subject, which will probably be reduced to a Certainty, one Way or other, long before this reaches your Hands." There is nostalgia in his paragraph: "when I am conversing with you, the many agreeable Hours we have spent together recur upon my Mind; I fancy myself under your hospitable Roof at Mount Vernon, and lay aside Reserve. May God grant us a return of those halcyon Days; when every Man may sit down at his Ease under the Shade of his own Vine, & his own fig-tree, & enjoy the Sweets of domestic Life! Or if this is too much, may He be pleased to inspire us with spirit & resolution, to bear our present & future Sufferings, becoming Men determined to transmit to our Posterity, unimpair'd, the Blessings we have received from our Ancestors!"[12]

As the spring burgeoned, while substantive decisions began to be expected at the forthcoming conventions up and down the coast, the possibility of a declaration of independence still provoked sharply divided reactions. On 29 March 1776, Landon Carter informed his diary, "One Robinson from Philadelphia has told somebody that Independency was thrice Proposed in the Congress, but it was each time thrown out by a Vast majority, and that to the Northward, 9/10 of the People were violently against it";[13] his cousin Francis Lightfoot Lee, when he heard of Carter's assertion, wrote to ask "Who in the name of Heaven, cou'd tell you"[14] that the question had been before Congress at all.

If the proposal had been brought to a vote during the first quarter of the year, it could well have been turned down. Yet in one county after another, the kettle of revolutionary ardor was bubbling and needed only some additional fire to boil over. The fire came from Virginia. As early as 5 April, the Committee of Safety of Cumberland County appointed a subcommittee to prepare instructions for the delegates to be chosen by the county on 22 April. John Mayo and William Fleming went to Williamsburg with a startling charge: "We therefore, your constituents, instruct you positively to declare for an independency; that you solemnly abjure any allegiance to his Brittanick Majesty and bid him good night forever, that you promote in our convention an instruction to our delegates now sitting in Continental Congress to do the same."[15] And on 23 April, neighboring Charlotte County's convention requested Paul Carrington and Isaac Read to work for "the delegates which are sent to the General Congress to be instructed immediately to cast off the British

*"The Curious Zebra"; Grenville is about to put a saddle on the animal while Lord North holds its halter; at the tail, one man represents France and the other, George Washington (courtesy, Library of Congress)*

yoke."[16] A dispatch datelined 10 May in Williamsburg forwarded these mandates for perusal in Philadelphia in the *Pennsylvania Evening Post* of 21 May.

While the counties polled, a rapid exchange of letters took place between friends in Virginia and Philadelphia. On 12 April, John Page of Rosewell estimated to Jefferson that almost every one except the treasurer* (Robert Carter Nicholas) was ready for independence and assured Richard Henry Lee that he could obtain a declaration if he attended the Convention. On 20 April, Lee urged Patrick Henry to move for separation; a month later, Jefferson urged Thomas Nelson, Jr., who had left Philadelphia to take part in events in Williamsburg, to "bring on as early as you can in convention the great question of the session"; on 8 May, from his home at Yorktown in the midst of Tory territory, Nelson wrote a convention member: "I can assure you, sir, that the spirit of the people, (except a very few in these lower parts, whose little blood has been sucked out by mosquitoes,) cry out for this declaration."

On 28 April, Robert Brent of Aquia briefed Lee on the spirited competition for convention seats in his area: "In many counties there have been warm contests. . . . Many new ones are got in . . . Colonel Mason, with great difficulty return'd for Fairfax. Our friend Harry [Col. Henry Lee of Leesylvania] much push'd in P. William. . . . Will Brent for Stafford in Room of Charles Carter."[17]

Brent was correct: over the colony as a whole, though all but one of the members of the Committee of Safety were returned, more than 40 percent of the 129 delegates were new. The session opened on 6 May. Late arrivals included George Mason and the diffident new member from Orange, young James Madison.

The conservatives were in control: Edmund Pendleton, chosen president of the December Convention following Peyton Randolph's death, was again in the chair. As chairmen of the two standing committees, Privileges and Elections, and Propositions and Grievances, he named Dudley Digges and Robert Carter Nicholas. Henry and the group that had gathered around Jefferson the previous year were left to function in their individual capacities.

Yet the events of the opening days indicated how far the center of Virginia politics had moved during the spring. Such doubts as existed about a declaration of independence concerned timing rather than substance and cut across normal political lines. Should a declaration await the certainty of foreign alliances? Should a confederation of the colonies first be assured? Both Carter Braxton and Richard Henry Lee had written Patrick Henry of the necessity of continental unity, bulwarked by overseas support; yet Gen. Charles Lee, Washington's new commander of the Southern Division, stressed the necessity of taking risk.

At the start, Henry wavered; he had written Adams that a confederation "must precede an open declaration of independency and foreign alliances." But on 11 May, when the Convention resolved itself into a Committee of the Whole on the state of the colony, he bit the bullet and moved that Virginia's congressional delegation be instructed to procure "a clear and full Declaration of Independency." During debate on 14 May, as John Page had foreseen, the idea was opposed by Robert Carter Nicholas, but next day Archibald Cary reported a compromise, drafted by Pendleton, which linked a declaration of independence, a search for foreign aid, and formation of a confederation. It likewise set, as the Convention's own immediate agenda, the framing of a declaration of rights and a plan of government for Virginia. In his seconding speech, according to Edmund Randolph, Henry stood "like a pillar of fire." When he had done, by prior agreement, Thomas Nelson, Jr., added the stamp of conservative approval. The ensuing vote, as John Augustine Washington rejoiced to Richard Henry Lee, was "by a very full house and without a dissenting voice,"—even Robert Carter Nicholas was willing to "rise or fall" with his country.

At the end of a substantial preamble listing grievances and past appeals for redress, the one hundred and twelve convention members present declared:

Wherefore, appealing to the SEARCHER OF HEARTS for the sincerity of former declarations, expressing our desire to preserve the connection with that nation, and that we are driven from that inclination by their wicked councils, and the eternal laws of self-preservation,

RESOLVED unanimously, that the delegates appointed to represent this colony in General Congress be instructed to propose to that respectable body

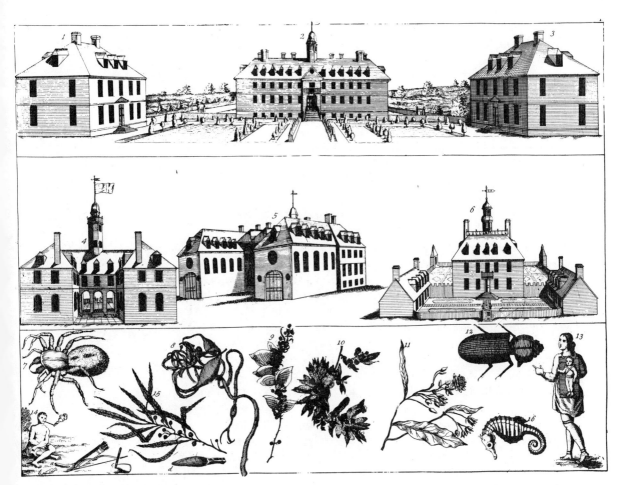

The "Bodleian"
plate of
Williamsburg,
engraved c. 1740,
possibly from a
drawing by
John Bartram; top
row: College of
William and Mary;
middle row: left to
right, southern façade
of the capitol, western
façade of the Wren
Building at the
College, and southern
façade of the
Governor's Palace
(courtesy, Library of
Congress)

to declare the United Colonies free and independent states, absolved from all allegiance to, or dependence upon, the crown or parliament of Great Britain; and that they give the assent of this colony to such declaration, and to whatever measures may be thought proper and necessary by the Congress for forming foreign alliances and a confederation of the colonies, at such time, and in the manner, as to them shall seem best: Provided, that the power of forming government for, and the regulations of the internal concerns of each colony, be left to the respective colonial legislatures.

RESOLVED, unanimously, that a committee be appointed to prepare a DECLARATION OF RIGHTS, and such a plan of government as will be most likely to maintain peace and order in this Colony, and secure substantial and equal liberty to the people.[18]

Pendleton quickly forwarded copies to the other colonies and to Virginia's delegates in Philadelphia, where the *Pennsylvania Evening Post* of 28 May carried the text; at the same time, he named Archibald Cary chairman of a large committee to prepare the proposed declaration of rights and plan of government for Virginia.

On 16 May, Williamsburg celebrated: Purdie's *Gazette* for the seventeenth, below a masthead where a makeshift design of punctuation marks replaced the royal coat of arms, announced:

In consequence of the above resolutions, universally regarded as the only door which will lead to safety and prosperity, some gentlemen made a handsome collection for the purpose of treating the soldiery, who next day were paraded in Waller's grove, before Brigadier-General Lewis, attended by the gentlemen of the committee of safety, the members of the General Convention, the inhabitants of this city, &c. The resolutions being read aloud to the army, the following toasts were given, each of them accompanied by a discharge of the artillery and small arms, and the acclamations of all present:—

1. The American Independent States.
2. The Grand Congress of the United States and their respective legislatures.
3. General Washington, and victory to the American arms.

But in reporting these rejoicings, the *Gazette* also reminded readers that Friday, the seventeenth, had been appointed by the Continental Congress as a General Fast. At a special service in Bruton Parish Church, delegates were recalled to the gravity of their task. On that day, Mason reached Williamsburg.

Both Madison, who had arrived on the sixteenth, and Mason were at once added to the Cary Committee; Mason was also named to the two standing committees, and to several ad hoc groups. In eager anticipation of the Convention's agenda, though skeptical of the capacity of some of the delegates who composed the unwieldy thirty-man committee charged with drafting the new documents, Mason hurried a letter to Richard Henry Lee into Saturday's northbound mail pouch importuning his return:

To my great Satisfaction, I find the first grand Point has been carried nem: con: The opponents being so few, that they did not think fit to divide, or contradict the general Voyce. Yr. Brother Colo. T. Lee will inclose you the Resolve. . . . We are now going upon the most important of all Subjects—Government: The Committee appointed to prepare a plan is, according to Custom, overcharged with useless Members. You know our Conventions. I need only say that it is not mended by the late Elections. We shall, in all probability have a thousand ridiculous and impracticable proposals, & of Course, a Plan form'd of hetrogenious, jarring & unintelligible Ingredients; this can be prevented only by a few Men of Integrity & Abilitys, whose Countrys Interest lies next to their Hearts, undertaking this Business, and defending it ably thro' every stage of opposition. I need not tell you how much you will be wanted here on this Occasion. . . . We can not do without you—Mr. Nellson is now on his Way to Philadelphia; & will supply your place in Congress, by keeping up the representation of this Colony. It will be some time I presume before that Assembly can be fully possess'd of the Sentiments & Instructions of the different Provinces, which I hope will afford you time to return. Pray confer with some of your ablest Friends at Congress upon the Subject of foreign Alliances; what Terms it will be expedient to offer. Nations, like Individuals, are govern'd by their Interest—Great Britain will bid against us—Whatever European Power takes us [by] the Hand must risque a War with her. We want but two things—a regular Supply of military Stores, and a naval Protection of our Trade & Coasts. . . . Our Exports shou'd not be bound as affected by Treaty. . . . In our Imports perhaps we may make Concessions as far as to give a Preference to the Manufactures as Produce of a particular Country; this wou'd indeed have the Effect of every other Monopoly: We shou'd be furnished with Goods of worse Quality, & at a higher Price than in an

"The Manner in which the American
Colonies Declared themselves
INDEPENDANT of the King of
ENGLAND, throughout the different
Provinces on July 4 1776"; engraving in
Edward Barnard's New Complete &
Authentic History of England, 1783
(courtesy, The Trustees of the British Museum)

open Market; but this wou'd only force us earlier into Manufactures. . . . I know you will excuse my loose Thoughts; which I give you in a Hurry, without Order, but without Reserve. I have not time to copy or correct having only borrowed half an Hour, before I attend the House, which is now meeting. At all Events, my dear Sir, let us see you here as soon as possible.[19]

Mason underestimated the speed with which his colleagues on the Cary Committee were prepared to act, a speed for which his membership was in part responsible. On 24 May, Pendleton wrote Jefferson: "The political cooks are busy in preparing the dish, and as Colo. Mason seems to have the Ascendancy in the great work, I have Sanguine hopes it will be framed so as to Answer it's end, Prosperity to the Community and Security to Individuals."[20]*

By the 25 May post, Thomas Ludwell Lee sent his brother a preliminary manuscript draft of the Virginia Declaration of Rights, its first ten articles in Mason's hand; at the end of the next week, he was able to forward a print of eighteen articles prepared for the Committee of the Whole. The *Pennsylvania Evening Post* made the latter available to members of Congress in its issue of 6 June, and other papers picked it up elsewhere. This draft, rather than the form finally adopted, was treated as the official version for many years.

The day after it appeared, Richard Henry Lee, as the ranking member of the Virginia delegation, moved in Congress that "these United Colonies are, and of right ought to be Free and Independent States."

By a vote of 7 to 5 (with Georgia unrepresented), action on the motion was deferred to 1 July to give delegations and sitting colonial conventions time to reflect,† but to minimize delay, a committee of five was appointed on 11 June to prepare a draft resolution to that effect—John Adams, Benjamin Franklin, Thomas Jefferson, Robert R. Livingston, and Roger Sherman.

Richard Henry Lee's name was not on the list, though under normal parliamentary procedure, as mover of the resolution, he might well have expected to be chairman of the committee. He had previously announced his intention of going home, and on 5 June, the Congress had voted him leave of absence, "his health and private affairs requiring his return to Virginia." Much later, John Adams set down several somewhat inconsistent recollections as to why Lee was not chosen and how Jefferson came to be the committee's draftsman; Jefferson's own account of proceedings is at some variance with all of Adams's versions:

Mr. Adams' memory has led him into unquestionable error. At the age of eighty-eight and forty-seven years after the transactions . . . this is not wonderful. Nor should I at the age of eighty, on the small advantage of that difference only, venture to oppose my memory to his, were it not supported by written notes, taken by myself at the moment and on the spot. . . . The committee of five met; no such thing as a sub-committee was proposed, but they unanimously pressed on myself alone to undertake the draught. I consented; I drew it; but before I reported it to the committee, I communicated it *separately* to Dr. Franklin and Mr. Adams, requesting their corrections. . . . Their alterations were two or three only, and merely verbal. I then wrote a fair copy, reported it to the committee, and from them, unaltered, to Congress."[21]

"A N.W. View of
the State House in
Philadelphia taken
1778," engraved by
J. Trenchard after
Charles Willson
Peale, 1778
(courtesy, Library of
Congress)

Jefferson's selection to draft the declaration of independence went
far to compensate him for absence from Virginia at this juncture. Most
members looked on the Continental Congress somewhat as the national
representatives who gather at sessions of the European Common Market
view that body today; while it symbolized an emerging unity, the
strength gathered around its table was the strength of the colonies from
which its members came. While Patrick Henry, in the full flood of oratory at the first Continental Congress, might declaim: "The distinctions
between Virginians, Pennsylvanians, New Yorkers, and New England-
ers, are no more. I am not a Virginian, but an American," through the
years the frequent use of the words "my country" by the delegates of
the several states showed where, with Thomas Jefferson, they thought
"the laboring oar" could be most powerfully applied. In 1775, Congress
had adjourned in July expressly to permit the Virginians to attend their
convention; on 16 May 1776, Jefferson sounded out Thomas Nelson, Jr.,
then at home, in hopes of a similar leave of absence:

Should our Convention propose to establish now a form of government perhaps it might be agreeable to recall for a short time their delegates. It is a work of
the most interesting nature and such as every individual would wish to have his
voice in. . . . But this I mention to you in confidence, as in our situation, a hint
to any other is too delicate however anxiously interesting the subject is to our
feelings. . . .
P. S. In the other colonies who have instituted government they recalled their

*Thomas Jefferson by Mather Brown, 1786*
*(courtesy, Charles Francis Adams;*
*photo, Frick Art Reference Library)*

*John Adams by Mather Brown, 1788*
*(courtesy, Library of The Boston Athenaeum;*
*photo, Cushing Photo Service)*

delegates leaving only one or two to give information to Congress on matters which might relate to their country particularly, and giving them a vote during the interval of absence.[22]

The extent to which Jefferson's thoughts were in Virginia is shown both by his use of phrases from Mason's declaration of rights in the text of the document on which he now set to work and by his preparation, even though absent, of drafts of a constitution for consideration by the delegates in Williamsburg. For seventeen days after his appointment, he closeted himself in his rented room in the home of a German bricklayer, bending over his little writing-box to phrase the document which he presented to Congress on 28 June.

On 1 July, when a vote was taken on Lee's independence resolution, a majority of the members of nine delegations voted in favor, with South Carolina and Pennsylvania against, Delaware evenly divided, and New York abstaining. Edward Rutledge of South Carolina then requested a one-day pause. The vote on the second, climaxed by the all-night, eighty-mile, storm-lashed ride of Delaware's ailing Caesar Rodney to break the tie in his delegation, showed twelve in favor; after New York's Provincial Congress, meeting at White Plains, had approved, its delegates made the endorsement unanimous on 9 July.

On 3 July, John Adams wrote his Abigail:

The Second Day of July 1776, will be the most memorable Epocha, in the History of America.—I am apt to believe that it will be celebrated, by succeeding Generations, as the great anniversay Festival, It ought to be commemorated, as the Day of Deliverance by solemn Acts of Devotion to God Almighty. It ought to be solemnized with Pomp and Parade, with Shews, Games, Sports, Guns, Bells, Bonfires and Illuminations, from one End of this Continent to the other from this Time forward forevermore.

You will think me transported with Enthusiasm but I am not.—I am well aware of the Toil and Blood and Treasure, that it will cost Us to maintain this Declaration, and support and defend these States.—Yet through all the Gloom, I can see the Rays of ravishing Light and Glory. I can see that the End is more than worth all the Means. And that Posterity will tryumph in that Days Transaction, even altho We should rue it, which I trust in God We shall not.[23]

Debate on the wording of Jefferson's draft started at once. Josiah Bartlett of New Hampshire wrote John Langdon that it was "a pretty good one. I hope it will not be spoiled by canvassing in Congress." Jefferson felt the same way. As clauses such as the one "reprobating the enslaving of the inhabitants of Africa" and the one censuring the people as well as the government of England were stricken, he squirmed silently beside Benjamin Franklin:

During the debate I was sitting by Doctor Franklin, and he observed that I was writhing a little under the acrimonious criticisms on some of its parts; and it was on that occasion, that by way of comfort, he told me the story of John Thompson, the hatter, and his new sign. . . .

"When I was a journeyman printer, one of my companions, an apprentice hatter, having served out his time was about to open shop for himself. His first concern was to have a handsome signboard with a proper inscription. He composed it in these words, 'John Thompson, *Hatter, makes and sells hats for ready money,*' with a figure of a hat subjoined. But he thought he would submit it to his friends for their amendments. The first he showed it to thought the word '*Hatter*' tautologous, because followed by the words 'makes hats' which show he was a hatter. It was struck out. The next observed that the word 'makes' might as well be omitted, because his customers would not care who made the hats. He struck it out. A third said he thought the words '*for ready money*' were useless, as it was not the custom of the place to sell on credit. Everyone who purchased expected to pay. They were parted with, and the inscription now stood, 'John Thompson sells hats.' 'Sells Hats!' says his next friend. 'Why nobody will expect you to give them away. What then is the use of that word?' It was striken out, and 'hats' followed it, the rather as there was one painted on the board. So the inscription was reduced ultimately to 'John Thompson' with the figure of a hat subjoined."[24]

On 8 July, Jefferson sent Richard Henry Lee copies of the declaration as agreed to and as originally written, with the comment, "You will judge whether it is the better or worse for the Critics."

The document, titled with first use of a new term, "A Declaration by the Representatives of the United States of America in Congress Assembled," was quickly accepted; attested on 19 July by the president of the Congress, John Hancock, and the clerk, it was ordered engrossed for signature by the delegates, beginning 2 August.

While these events were taking place in Philadelphia, Colonel Cary's committee was equally busy in Williamsburg. Between 20 and 24 May, making repeated use of wording already tried out in Fairfax County, Mason phrased the ten draft articles for a bill of rights that Thomas Ludwell Lee sent to Richard Henry Lee on 25 May, adding in his own hand a few further articles projected during preliminary talks in committee.

The document, headed "A Declaration of Rights, made by the Representatives of the good People of Virginia, assembled in full Convention; and recommended to Posterity as the Basis and Foundation of Government," contained both a general philosophy of human rights and a series of specific assurances against repetition of wrongs recently suffered. (This is given in full in Appendix 1, p. 337.)

The first article, as set forth here and used in elided form by Jefferson as the first article of the bill of rights contained in the Declaration of Independence, affirmed the desirability of a human condition that differed materially from the one existing in Virginia: "All Men are born equally free and independant," with inherent natural rights that include "the Enjoyment of Life and Liberty, with the Means of acquiring and possessing Property, and pursueing and obtaining Happiness and Safety." All men in Virginia were not free, and those that were, were by no means equal.

A group of articles then declared that government exists to secure these rights; it draws its powers from the people and is instituted for their common benefit and security. Magistrates are their trustees and servants, entitled to emoluments and privileges (none of them hereditary) only because of public service. A government that proves inadequate or acts contrary to these purposes can rightfully be reformed, altered, or abolished by decision of a majority of the community. The executive and legislative powers must be held separate from the judicial and their officials kept in touch with the body of the governed by frequent and regular elections that return them to a private station. No man's property should be taken for public use without his consent or that of his representatives, nor are citizens bound by laws other than those to which they have thus assented.

A second group of articles concerned the developing concept of due process of law, particularly a man's right "to demand the Cause and Nature of his Accusation, to be confronted with the Accusers or Witnesses, to call for Evidence in his Favour, and to a speedy Tryal by a Jury of his Vicinage . . . nor can he be compelled to give Evidence against himself."

A separate article on freedom of conscience was phrased in terms of full religious toleration by the state.

Beyond these specifics, Mason included the general statement: "That no free Government, or the Blessings of Liberty can be preserved to any People, but by a firm adherence to Justice, Moderation, Temperance, Frugality, and Virtue and by frequent Recurrence to fundamental Principles."[25]

The other articles that Thomas Ludwell Lee thought likely to be accepted included freedom of the press and fuller treatment of due process—no ex post facto laws, no general warrants, no suspension of laws or their execution. As the document emerged from committee discussion, it contained, along with minor changes and rearrangements of order, not only Mason's articles and those Lee had anticipated, but four others: on freedom of elections; on the constitution of a militia as preferable to maintenance of a standing army; against excessive bail, fines, or cruel and unusual punishments; and on maintenance of one uniform government throughout Virginia's territories. A committee print containing all these was ordered after the draft was read to the Convention on 27 May. (This is given in full in Appendix 2, p. 338.)

In correspondence in 1778, Mason dismissed the articles against general warrants and for a uniform system of government (a provision calculated to prevent erection of new jurisdictions in Virginia's western territory) as "not of a fundamental nature"; he may have had a hand in the added articles on the freedom of elections and on the suspension of laws; he specifically claimed authorship of the ban on retroactive laws. The article on a well-regulated militia is close to his wording in his "Remarks on Annual Elections for the Fairfax Independent Company." The article on excessive bail was taken almost verbatim from the English Bill of Rights of 1689.

That on freedom of the press may have been nudged into place by a communication in the center of the first page of Dixon and Hunter's *Virginia Gazette* of 18 May, which read in part:

. . . the liberty of the press is inviolably connected with the liberty of the subject. . . . The *use of speech* is a *natural right*; which must have been reserved when men gave up their natural rights for the benefit of society. *Printing* is a more extensive and improved kind of speech. Blasphemy, perjury, treason, and personal slander, are the principal offences which demand restraint; the three first are offences against the whole community; the last (personal slander) being only an offence against individuals, if the *punishment of it be carried beyond the damage sustained by the persons aggrieved,* it is not only contradictory to the principles of the constitution, but also dissonant to the laws of reason.

When the committee print of the declaration was taken up by the Convention (it was also reproduced in the Dixon and Hunter *Gazette* of 1 June) Mason squirmed even as Jefferson did a month later: in sending an early draft to a correspondent abroad in 1778, he observed: "it received few Alterations or Additions in the Virginia Convention (some of them not for the better)."

Debate started on 29 May, with the House sitting as a Committee of the Whole. Objections began with the first sentence of Article I. The conservatives, readily able to discern its revolutionary implications for a society which they found comfortable, followed Robert Carter Nicholas's lead when, with slavery in mind, he declared the phrase "born equally free" could incite "civil convulsion."

Thomas Ludwell Lee expostulated to Richard Henry:

I enclosed you by last post a copy of our declaration of rights nearly as it came thro the committee. It has since been reported to the Convention & we have ever since been stumbling at the threshold. . . . I will tell you plainly that a certain set of Aristocrates, for we have such monsters here, finding that their execrable system cannot be reared on such foundations, have to this time kept us at bay on the first line, which declares all men to be born equally free and independant. A number of absurd, or unmeaning alterations have been proposed. The words as they stand are approved by a very great majority, yet by a thousand masterly fetches & stratagems the business has been so delayed that the first clause stands yet unassented to by the Convention.[26]

Debate was then interrupted by other matters until 3 June. During the interval, Pendleton's soothing pen was applied to the challenged phrase, qualifying it by elision and insertion: rights accrue to men "when they enter into a state of society" (as slaves never do); men are "by nature" rather than "born" equally free and possessed of "certain inherent rights," omitting the word "natural." Consideration could then be resumed.

Further argument for and against other amendments, with substitutions, consolidations, and, in the case of the ban on ex post facto laws, omissions, continued in and out of the Convention until 10 June, when John Blair, Jr., delegate from the college, read out some last amendments; Committee debate then ceased. The Convention itself considered these changes on the eleventh and on the twelfth passed the document unanimously.

The final version, printed as the "Postscript" of Purdie's *Gazette* on 14 June, was not widely circulated for some years after 1776, even though it contained a major substantive change, James Madison's first contribution to political theory. (This is given in full in Appendix 3, p. 339.) To Madison, the state toleration of all sects, proposed by Mason in his article on religion, was a halfway measure. Like Mason, he had been brought up in an Anglican household; the Reverend Thomas Martin, rector of the local Brick Church, was the family tutor at Montpelier during the years 1767–69.

The Reverend Thomas, however, though ordained under the Establishment, was an enthusiastic graduate of the Presbyterian College of New Jersey; in 1769, he, his brother who would become governor of North Carolina, his young charge, and James's slave, Sawney, set forth for Nassau Hall, where the militant Presbyterian John Witherspoon of Edinburgh had just succeeded Samuel Davies as president. Graduating in 1770, Madison stayed on for another half-year of work with lodgings in Witherspoon's own home.

After his return to Montpelier, his correspondence with his former fellow-student and lifelong friend, William Bradford of Philadelphia, castigated current religious persecution in Virginia. On 24 January 1774, he cried out: "I want again to breathe your free Air. . . . That diabolical Hell-conceived principle of persecution rages among some and to their eternal Infamy the Clergy can furnish their Quota of Imps for such business. This vexes me the worst of anything whatever. There are at this [time] in the adjacent County not less than 5 or 6 well-meaning men in close Goal for publishing their religious Sentiments which in the main are very orthodox."[27]

Each man's religion, in Madison's view, was his own concern: freedom of conscience is inconsistent with toleration, either by the state or by another religious body.* He wanted complete disestablishment. Mason did not go that far: while he agreed with Locke's *Essay on Toleration* that "the care of each man's salvation belongs only to himself," he was content to affirm:

> That as Religion, or the Duty which we owe to our divine and omnipotent Creator, and the Manner of discharging it, can be governed only by Reason and Conviction, not by Force or Violence; and therefore that all Men shou'd enjoy the fullest Toleration in the Exercise of Religion, according to the Dictates of Conscience, unpunished and unrestrained by the Magistrate, unless, under Colour of Religion, any Man disturb the Peace, the Happiness, or Safety of Society, or of Individuals. And that it is the mutual Duty of all, to practice Christian Forbearance, Love and Charity towards Each other.

At the 1776 Convention, Madison experienced the diffidence of a newcomer to the political scene, but on this subject he felt strongly enough to draft an alternative reading. He secured Patrick Henry's agreement to present the wording: "That Religion or the duty we owe to our Creator, and the manner of discharging it, being under the direction of reason and conviction only, not of violence or compulsion, all men are equally entitled to the full and free exercise of it according to the dictates of Conscience, and therefore that no man or class of men ought, on account of religion to be invested with peculiar emoluments or privileges nor subjected to any penalties or disabilities unless under &c."[28] But when such staunch churchmen as Robert Carter Nicholas and Edmund Pendleton proved emphatically unprepared to support disestablishment, Henry backed away.

Madison then prepared an alternative which Pendleton himself

was willing to offer; with only two cuts, here indicated by parentheses, it was adopted.

That Religion or the duty we owe to our *CREATOR,* and the manner of discharging it, can be directed only by reason and conviction, not by force or violence; and therefore, that all men are equally entitled to (enjoy) the free exercise of religion, according to the dictates of conscience, (unpunished and unrestrained by the magistrate, Unless the preservation of equal liberty and the existence of the State are manifestly endangered;) and that it is the mutual duty of all to practice Christian forebearance, love, and charity towards each other."[29]

Madison had a readily available source for his affirmation of religious liberty in Locke, but he could have found an earlier one, with an American context, in the mid-seventeenth-century writings of the English political thinker, Sir Henry Vane the Younger. Son of an eminent courtier of Charles I, Vane quit England for New England in the 1630s in search of a freer climate. On arrival in Massachusetts Bay, his prominence thrust him suddenly into the chair of the annually elected governor. It was the year of the trial of Anne Hutchinson for heresy.* Attacked by the Puritan establishment because of his Hutchinsonian sympathies, he left Boston at the end of the summer of 1637; in Cromwellian England, he observed and experienced intolerance a second time, as a leader and speaker of the House of Commons under Cromwell. In the 1650s, he examined the nature of right government in three essays, "The Retired Man's Meditations," "A Needful Corrective," and "A Healing Question." In all, he insisted that man's spiritual freedom is absolute; he argued that government cannot have an authority possessed only by God; its power and "the exercise thereof refers to the outward man or outward concerns of man, in their bodily converse in this world." A right government "is not to intrude itself into the office and proper concerns of Christ's inward government and rule in the conscience." Even in declaring for toleration of religious beliefs, state authorities overstep their bounds: "For why shouldst thou . . . intrude into the proper office of Christ, since we are all to stand at the judgment-seat of Christ, whether governors or governed, and by His decision only are capable of being declared with certainty, to be in the right or in the wrong?"[30] This was exactly the point that Madison affirmed.

If Madison's wording of what became the final article of the Declaration of Rights was a milestone, so was Mason's last phrase in his first article, in which he specified as inherent rights "the enjoyment of life and liberty, with the means of acquiring and possessing property and pursuing and attaining happiness and safety."

Locke's trinity of life, liberty, and property was familiar to every political thinker of the period, but Mason's treatment of its third term was new, and this treatment not only led off the Virginia declaration of rights, but in elided form was incorporated in the substantive part of Jefferson's Declaration of Independence: "We hold these truths to be self-evident, that all men are created equal, that they are endowed by their creator with certain unalienable rights, that among these are life, liberty, and the pursuit of happiness."

In England and America alike, quiet possession of a man's property was agreed to be one of the good guarantees afforded citizens by the state. But opportunity for access to property, as a natural right, was new. Affirmation of America as a land of opportunity, particularly economic opportunity, expressed here in one of its earliest forms, became a major promise of the national life.

While overseas sustenance for this affirmation was not available from Locke, it could be developed from the works of a Scottish jurist widely read by Americans just before the Revolution: Henry Home, Lord Kames, Lord of Session in Edinburgh for thirty years from 1752 and described by one biographer as "a man of an ingenious and inquisitive turn of mind, and of elegant attainments, but whose disposition did not lead him to err on the side of excessive deference to authority and establishment."[31]

Irascible, often biting in his judicial opinions, he held especially strong views on some of the laws affecting property. Ten different titles by Kames were in Jefferson's library; he thought so highly of his *Principles of Equity,* first published in 1760, as to buy successive editions as they appeared. Franklin, after journeying north to visit the jurist in 1759, declared his book "will be of the greatest Advantage to the Judges in our Colonies, not only in those which have Courts of Chancery, but also in those which having no such Courts are obliged to mix Equity with Common Law. It will be of the more Service to the Colony Judges, as few of them have been bred to the Law."[32]

Kames derived property as a natural right from the sweat of the individual's own labor: "Here then is property established by the constitution of our nature, antecedent to all human conventions. We are led by nature to consider goods acquired by our industry and labour as belonging to us, and as our own. We have a sense or feeling of property, and conceive these goods to be our own, just as much as we conceive our hands, our feet, and our other members to be our own; and we have a sense or feeling equally clear of the property of others."[33]

Such an origin was consonant both with the Jeffersonian agrarian ideal of individual self-sufficiency and with the practical experience of the men who settled Virginia's west, crossing the Blue Ridge into the Valley of the Shenandoah, crossing the Alleghenies to the new county of Kentucky, who acquired their property by the bite of their own axes, the thrust of their own ploughs. When Kames said, "Now this very disposition of providing against want, which is common to man with many other creatures, involves the idea of property. The ground I cultivate, and the house I build, must be considered as mine, otherwise I labour to no purpose," he talked their language, very different from the Tidewater language of the law of primogeniture and entail.

Of entails Kames had small opinion. In his *Historical Law Tracts*, he ends his history of property with the declaration: "That entails are subversive of industry and commerce, is not the worst that justly can be said of them; they appear in a still more disagreeable light, when viewed with relation to those more immediately affected. A snare they are to the thoughtless proprietor, who, even by a single act, may be entrapped past hope of relief; to the cautious they are a perpetual source of discontent, by subverting that liberty and independency, to which all men aspire, with respect to their possessions as well as their persons."[34]

Mason, Jefferson, Madison, and Henry were all first-born; their disapproval of primogeniture and entail, under which first-born sons became the principal and sometimes the exclusive heirs of their fathers, was based on observation and reflection rather than personal experience. Richard Henry Lee, on the other hand, as the second of six boys, could attest the chagrin of being junior to a son who not only inherited Stratford and its acres but failed to pay his two youngest brothers even the relatively small sums designated for them in their father's will. Yet all were in accord that these institutions had no place in a sound legal basis for property and that legal inequality should not handicap man's natural right to the means of acquiring property in the pursuit of happiness.

Mason was indeed correct when two years later he informed a correspondent abroad that the Virginia Declaration of Rights was "afterwards closely imitated by the other United States."[35] In establishing independent frames of government, seven more of the original thirteen—Pennsylvania, Maryland, Delaware, North Carolina, Connecticut, Massachusetts, and New Hampshire—and Vermont adopted constitutions containing separate bills of rights; safeguards of certain rights, particularly those specifying due process, were comprised within the body of four others—New Jersey, Georgia, New York, and South Carolina. Rhode Island merely maintained its seventeenth-century charter.

The bill of rights passed by the Pennsylvania convention that met in July and concluded its work on 28 September 1776, the first after Virginia's, led off with an article derived directly from Mason's Article I, as phrased in the committee print published in Philadelphia, and followed it by an expanded paraphrase of Madison's wording on religious freedom. Its influence was somewhat laconically indicated by the chairman of the Delaware committee: "the Declaration of Rights—has been completed some days past but there being nothing particularly in it—I did not think it an object of much curiosity, it is made out of the Pensilvania & Maryland Draughts." Some of its phrasing, however, was taken from Mason's document and does not occur in others.

When Vermont set up its own government early in 1777, Article I of its bill of rights contained a clause outlawing slavery reminiscent of that excised from Jefferson's draft of the Declaration of Independence; Article XVI repeated Mason's emphasis on "frequent recurrence to fundamental principles."

In South Carolina, as in New Hampshire and New York, the first constitution to be adopted—in March 1776—was a fragmentary temporary framework; two years passed before a complete document was adopted. This did not contain a separate bill of rights but included an article on freedom of religion (No. XXXVIII) that proved unworkable. It was as far to the right as Madison's amendment was to the left of Mason's original proposal: proponents of establishment had been successful in phrasing a long and detailed affirmation: "That all persons and religious societies who acknowledge that there is one God, and a future state of rewards and punishments, and that God is publicly to be worshipped, shall be freely tolerated. The Christian Protestant religion shall be deemed, and is hereby constituted and declared to be, the established religion of this State. That all denominations of Christian Protestants in this State, demeaning themselves peaceably and faithfully, shall enjoy equal religious and civil privileges." Such matters as defining a denomination, however, immediately proved difficult; the constitution-makers of 1790 replaced the wording with one similar to Mason's draft.

The Massachusetts electorate, after living for two years without a governor, overwhelmingly defeated the document submitted by their convention of 1778 and warned their second convention "That a bill of rights . . . ought to be settled and established, previous to the ratification of any constitution for the State."

At this assembly, which completed its work on 2 March 1780, John Adams was the principal author, even as Mason had been in Virginia.

His Article I was very similar to Mason's, "All men are born equally free and independent, and have certain natural, essential, and unalienable rights: among which may be reckoned the right of enjoying and defending their lives and liberties; that of acquiring, possessing, and protecting their property: in fine, that of seeking and obtaining their safety and happiness," and his Article II, on religion, gathered phrases from Madison, the New Jersey bill, and Mason's original version. When New Hampshire, in October 1783, succeeded in its third attempt to frame a constitution to the liking of its citizens, Part I was a bill of rights following the Massachusetts model.

Thus from 1776 to 1790, in one or another of the several states, conventions were engaged in phrasing or rephrasing bills of rights using Mason's as a model. By the end of that time, a national bill of rights was being circulated for ratification, having been strongly recommended by various state conventions, including Virginia's, at the time of adoption of the United States Federal Constitution. And on the other side of the Atlantic, the American documents had exercised substantial influence on the preparation of the *Déclaration des droits de l'homme* of revolutionary France.

# Chapter VIII
# To Govern a New State

*In one of the pauses during final debates on the Declaration of Rights, Mason* is credited with finding time to prepare a communication "To the People of the Thirteen United Colonies; carried in the *Virginia Gazette* of 31 May and signed "Aristides"; Aristides said he had been opposed to a separation from Britain, until nine months ago—until that is, the time when the king declared the colonists to be rebels, but now he thinks no other course open. Unity is essential to its success.

Specifically, the writer justified recent action by Virginia in regard to Maryland's royal governor. The Maryland Convention had initially decided to permit Governor Eden to remain in the colony as a neutral, but correspondence between Eden and Lord George Germain, intercepted in Virginia, had indicated active collaboration between Governor Eden and Governor Dunmore and thrown doubts on the diligence exercised at Annapolis; such laxity, Aristides declared, tends "to dissolve the Union upon which alone the Salvation of American Liberty depends." The Convention, with Mason as draftsman, had sent a communication denying permission for Eden to pass through Virginia on his way home.

Once the Declaration of Rights was completed, the delegates turned to the framing of a constitution to govern a new, independent, sovereign state. The Cary committee received numerous suggestions, particularly plans drafted by or at the instance of Virginia's delegates in Philadelphia.

As early as November 1775, Richard Henry Lee had urged John Adams to sketch a plan for independent status. Adams embodied his ideas in a letter to Lee, and shortly afterwards, George Wythe invited him to expand them. With Adams's permission, the two published *Thoughts on Government: Applicable to the Present State of the American Colonies. In a letter from a Gentleman to his Friend;* Lee furnished copies to his colleagues at home.

Declaring that "the happiness of society is the end of government," Adams, after arguing against a unicameral system, proposed that in addition to a two-branch, representative legislature—"in minature an exact portrait of the people at large"—there be a council chosen by the assembly to mediate between the legislature and the executive and to exercise independent judgment with a veto power over legislation. Council and assembly together should elect a governor. The governor's powers should be limited, but should include a veto. He should command the militia and exercise the power to pardon with the advice and consent of the council. Judges should be chosen either by the governor, with the advice and consent of the council, or by joint ballot of both houses of the legislature; they should serve during good behavior. A militia law should assure defense. Public support of education would be desirable. Sumptuary laws, "curing us of vanities, levities, and fopperies" should be considered.

A "Government Scheme" along comparable lines appeared in Purdie's *Virginia Gazette* of 10 May 1776; it may have reproduced a handbill enclosed by Richard Henry Lee, who said he had had it printed before Adams prepared his paper, when he sent Adams's *Thoughts* to Patrick Henry in April.

The right-wing member of Virginia's congressional delegation, Carter Braxton,* also published a pamphlet in Philadelphia, *Address to the Convention of the Colony and Ancient Dominion of Virginia; on the Subject of Government in general and recommending a particular form to their Consideration.* Expressing the view of numbers of his Tidewater kinsfolk, it proposed a highly aristocratic structure and speculated whether, "if the [British] constitution was brought back to its original state, and its present imperfections remedied, it would not afford more happiness than any other."

Lee, who had already supplied Edmund Pendleton with a copy of Adams's plan, wrote him on 12 May to denounce Braxton's work: "The contemptible little Tract, betrays the little Knot or Junto from whence it proceeded. Confusion of ideas, aristocratic pride, contradictory reasoning, with evident ill design, put it out of danger of doing harm, and therefore I quit it."[1] Henry called it "a silly thing . . . an affront and disgrace to this country"; it was, Adams affirmed, "whispered to have been the joint production of one native of Virginia and two natives of New York."

Pendleton, however, was by no means as unsympathetic as they; on 12 May, he wrote to Braxton: "A democracy, considered as *referring determinations,* either legislative or executive, TO THE PEOPLE AT LARGE, is the worst form (of government) imaginable. Of all others, I own, I prefer the true English constitution, which consists of a proper combination of the principles of honor, virtue, and fear. I confess *there are some* objections EVEN TO THIS, which only proves that perfection is not in our power to attain."[2]

Braxton's plan was published in Dixon and Hunter's *Virginia Gazette,* but not until the issues of 8 and 15 June; its late appearance would have prevented serious consideration even if its tenor had been more widely acceptable, but its publication witnessed the existence of a respectable minority of non-Tory conservatives.

By far the most complete proposals sent from Philadelphia to Williamsburg were the successive versions of a constitution forwarded by Thomas Jefferson. Even though he participated only at a distance and his last draft did not arrive until the later stages of the committee's work, he left a distinctive mark on the final result: he supplied the preamble and supplemented the text at several points.

Meriwether Smith, Convention delegate from Essex County, is said to have prepared a draft constitution, but its text is not known. No draft in Mason's hand has been found, and he never claimed authorship of this document as he did of the Bill of Rights; but his leadership in drafting and securing the adoption of both documents was acknowledged at the time and in later accounts by various other participants. His previous preparation of public papers for Fairfax County had developed in Mason a skill in summoning the support of men eager to act while inviting the adherence of more cautious leaders. The object of the committee was not to engage in original thought; it was to set forth in clear and written form principles in which the great majority of Virginians believed and to specify means of putting them into effect on which agreement was equally general. Over subsequent years, Virginia's history recorded less riot on the left, less reticence on the right than that of any other of the newly forming states.

The most contemporary evidence of Mason's major authorship of the constitution is from William Fleming, Convention delegate from Cumberland County, who on 22 June sent Jefferson a committee print, revised to date, of the frame of government being considered by the Convention, with the notation: "the inclosed printed plan was drawn by Colo. G. Mason and by him laid before the committee."

Much of the government structure under which Virginia had lived as a colony remained usable; on the local level, it required minimum change. Most delegates were prepared to reestablish a two-house assembly and a council, preferring the bicameral system of the past to the unicameral conventions of recent years. The chief need for new ideas lay in defining the powers of the executive: recent excesses of royal governors inclined most men toward strict limitations on this branch. Discussion centered on the governor's share in appointments and the bestowal or denial of a gubernatorial right to veto legislation and to dissolve the legislature. Annual elections and rotation in office were assured.

Mason's plan, laid before the Committee of the Whole by 10 June and possibly as early as 8 June, opened with an affirmation of the importance of the separation of powers. It provided a two-branch Assembly, to meet at least annually, the lower house to consist of two representatives from each county chosen annually from freeholders upwards of twenty-four years of age, such representatives to be resident in the county for at least a year and possessed of landed estates of at least £1,000 value. For election to the upper house, the state was to be divided into twenty-four districts, in each of whose constituent counties twelve subelectors would be chosen from resident freeholders with estates of at least £500 value; these subelectors would then choose one member for the twenty-four-member upper house from resident freeholders upwards of twenty-eight years of age with landed estates of at least £2,000. For both houses, the right of suffrage was to be extended, from freeholders only, to leaseholders of lands with leases having at least seven years to run and to resident householders who were fathers of three children born in the country.

Legislation was to originate in the lower house and be approved or rejected by the Senate, or amended with the consent of the House except in the case of money bills; these were to be approved or rejected but not altered.

A salaried governor and a treasurer were to be chosen annually by joint ballot of both Houses. The governor was not to serve more than three consecutive one-year terms and to be ineligible for three years thereafter. His executive power, including command of the militia and appointment of military officers, was to be exercised with the advice of a Council of State. He was to have no veto but would be able to adjourn or prorogue the Assembly or call it into session in case of emergency and would have the power to grant reprieves and pardons.

The eight-member Council, chosen by joint ballot of both Houses, was to assist in administration, presided over by the governor but with a vice-president of its own choosing to serve in case of his death or absence; it was to be renewed by removal and replacement of two members at the end of each three years, with retiring members ineligible for three years thereafter.

Judges of the Supreme Court, judges in chancery and of admiralty, and the attorney general were to be appointed by joint ballot of the two Houses and commissioned by the governor, to be salaried, to serve during good behavior. The governor and Privy Council would appoint the justices of the county courts. In case of maladministration or corruption, government officers were to be prosecuted by the lower house in the Supreme Court. To initiate this structure, the Convention would choose twenty-four members to be an upper house, and the two Houses, by joint ballot, would select a governor and Council.

Comparison of Mason's draft with the documents available to him when he began it, especially Adams's *Thoughts* and the *Scheme* published in the *Gazette,* shows the use, on occasion verbatim, that he made of currently available ideas and also his reliance on the broad philosophical teachings of Locke, Pufendorf, and others familiar to him from his years in John Mercer's library, in addition to his own political thinking and phrasing as previously displayed in the Fairfax documents. The primacy of the representative legislature in his constitution confirmed the derivation of power from the people that was the cornerstone of new political thought from the time of Locke and even from the early phases of the Cromwellian period—the term "Commonwealth of Virginia" was not a chance selection. The emphasis on the separation of powers was an observation on the fallibility of the men in whom political power would be vested—probity was held to be relative, perfection unattainable.

Jefferson's contribution was not available when Mason began to write; his first draft dates from early June, about the time Mason's committee print was laid before the Convention, and his final version reached Williamsburg with George Wythe on 23 June.

On the twenty-fourth, a report of the Committee on the Plan of Government, on a few pages in a clerk's hand, provided a basis for nearly final amendments. It was at this point that the preamble of Jefferson's draft was placed at the head of the document and that several amendments drawing on the body of his text were inserted into it. Some of them were proposed by Wythe, who on 27 July explained to Jefferson why more were not used: "When I came here the plan of government had been committed to the whole house. To those who had the chief hand in forming it the one you put into my hands was shewn. Two or three parts of this were, with little alteration, inserted in that: but such was the impatience of sitting long enough to discuss several important points in which they differ, and so many other matters were necessarily to be dispatched before the adjournment that I was persuaded the revision of a subject the members seemed tired of would at that time have been unsuccessfully proposed.[3*]

Between Wednesday, the twenty-sixth, and Friday, the twenty-eighth, the Committee of the Whole considered and amended the document, then ordered it "fairly transcribed." On Saturday, the twenty-ninth, Richard Henry Lee wrote General Charles Lee: "I have been in this City a week where I have had the pleasure to see our new plan of Government go on well. This day will put a finishing hand to it. 'Tis very much of the democratic kind."[4] The Convention vote was unanimous.

Election of officers took place at once: Patrick Henry, by a vote of 60–45, defeated Thomas Nelson and assumed the honorific but largely powerless post of governor—the Convention had decided to omit the veto power.[†] John Page became president of the Council; Edmund Randolph, attorney general. When the first session of the Assembly convened in October, Edmund Pendleton was selected for the new government's office of real power, speaker of the House of Delegates. Virginia's delegation in Congress was reduced from seven to five, with Harrison and Braxton omitted.

But while the Constitution served the purposes of providing a quickly available structure of government, it was soon seen to be more of a restoration than a renovation. Mason's plan had proposed broadening the suffrage; Jefferson's would have made it close to universal for free male landholders through a grant of fifty acres to every "person of full age" who did not own that much. But the article as adopted stipulated that the right to vote "shall remain as exercised at present."

Jefferson would likewise have equalized the value of a vote by proportioning representation to population; the new constitution continued the traditional system of two representatives from each county, which weighted political power in favor of Tidewater with its large plantations and relatively small numbers of landowners, as against the far more numerous owners of small holdings in the Piedmont and the West.

Jefferson's plan provided that no person coming into the new state should be held in slavery. Had he been present at the vehement debate on the first sentence of the Bill of Rights, he might have withheld this for the time being; he was able to obtain passage of a nonimportation statute two years later.

Madison's article on religious freedom in the Bill of Rights required action to be taken on the position of the established church, and Jefferson would have taken it at once. The Convention, however, left this touchy subject untouched, and the Assembly dealt with it only piecemeal over a decade.

Beyond specific objections, Jefferson held that the making of the Constitution was beyond the powers of a convention that had not been chosen expressly for that purpose, and in any case the document should not have been put into effect without ratification by the people. He believed that a constitution should be framed and adopted in circumstances sufficiently exceptional and conspicuous to display its primacy over ordinary law; otherwise its provisions would have no permanent validity and be as subject to repeal as any act of the legislature.

Nevertheless, the Convention's resolutions of 15 May 1776 had coupled its instruction to its congressional delegates to move for independence in Philadelphia with a provision that its members should forthwith prepare a bill of rights and constitution in Williamsburg, and these documents could be justified under the congressional resolution of 10 May that urged "the respective assemblies and conventions of the United Colonies . . . to adopt such government as shall, in the opinion of the representatives of the people, best conduce to the happiness and safety of their constituents." The paragraph connecting Jefferson's preamble with the body of the Virginia constitution specifically stated: "By which several Acts of Misrule, the Government of this Country as formerly exercised under the Crown of Great Britain, is totally dissolved; We therefore, the Delegates and Representatives of the good People of Virginia, having maturely considered the Premises, and viewing with great concern the deplorable condition to which this once happy Country must be reduced, unless some regular adequate Mode of civil Polity is speedily adopted, and in Compliance with a Recommendation of the General Congress, do ordain and declare the future Form of Government of Virginia to be as followeth."[5]

Meanwhile, Mason, Richard Henry Lee, George Wythe, and Robert Carter Nicholas were appointed to propose a design for the new state's great seal. On 5 July, they submitted their report:

TO BE ENGRAVED ON THE GREAT SEAL

Virtus, the genius of the commonwealth, dressed like an *Amazon,* resting on a spear with one hand, and holding a sword in the other, and treading on TYRANNY, represented by a man prostrate, a crown fallen from his head, a broken chain in his left hand, and a scourge in his right.

In the exergon, the word VIRGINIA over the head of VIRTUS; and under-
neath the words *Sic Semper Tyrannis*.

On the reverse, a groupe.

LIBERTAS, with her wand and *pileus*.

On one side of her CERES, with the *cornucopia* in one hand, and an ear of
wheat in the other.

On the other side AETERNITAS, with the globe and phoenix.

In the exergon, these words:

DEUS NOBIS HAEC OTIA FECIT.[6]

  The last line met with objections. "But for god's sake what is the
Deus nobis haec *otia* fecit," Jefferson inquired of John Page; "If my
country really enjoys that *otium* [leisure], it is singular, as every other
colony seems to be hard struggling." Since a protracted search for an en-
graver, carried on by William Lee in London, delayed execution for two
years, Mason had ample time to change the offending phrase to the
single word: PERSEVERANDO.

  After this convention, Mason's stays at Gunston Hall were brief.
He continued to head the Fairfax County Committee of Safety, ex-

*George Wythe by John Trumbull, 1791; sketch made in Williamsburg preparatory to Trumbull's large canvas,* The Declaration of Independence *(courtesy, The Free Library of Philadelphia; photo, Charles P. Mills & Son)*

Geo Wythe Esq.
[Apr 25/91.] Williamsburg.

pediting the accumulation of military supplies after Alexandria's nervousness was increased by midsummer fire raids of Dunmore's fleet—in upper Stafford County, William Brent's house was among those destroyed. At the same time, from 1776 to 1781, in his longest period of sustained public service—and also perhaps the most diversified in the subjects with which he dealt—he represented Fairfax County in the House of Delegates at sessions that lasted from two to four months.

At its first session, in October 1776, the momentum of the Convention continued. Jefferson, having left the Congress in order to share in filling out the new structure of government, brought in a bill to set up the state's superior courts, and followed it by a measure authorizing establishment of a Committee of Law Revisors. By joint ballot, the two Houses selected a five-man committee under his chairmanship: the others were Speaker Pendleton, Wythe—who also resigned from Congress to work in Virginia—Mason, and Thomas Ludwell Lee. The first three were practicing attorneys; Lee and Mason were planters rather than lawyers, though Lee had read law at the Inner Temple and upon passage of Jefferson's bill was named a justice of the General Court, and Mason was considered a land law specialist because of his experience with the Ohio Company. Politically, Pendleton represented the conservatives; Wythe was in process of transition from right to left; Lee was a particular ally of Henry, who had not yet begun his transition from left to right.

When the committee met in Fredericksburg on 13 January 1777 to lay out its work, Pendleton's preference for procedure proved a surprise: instead of revising existing law piece by piece, he at first favored preparation of an entirely new code, and Lee supported him. But Mason's aide memoire begins:

The Common Law not to be medled with, except where Alterations are necessary.

The Statutes to be revised & digested, alterations proper for us to be made; the Diction, where obsolete or redundant, to be reformed: but otherwise to undergo as few Changes as possible.

The Acts of the English Commonwealth to be examined.

The Statutes to be divided into Periods: the Acts of Assembly, made on the same Subject, to be incorporated into them.

The Laws of the other Colonies to be examined, & any good ones to be adopted.[7]

The group agreed that bills be short: "not to insert any unnessessary Word, or omit a useful one," with laws made "on the Spur of the present Occasion" and innovative laws to be of limited duration. Mason noted members' specific accords on criminal law; inheritance; executions of court orders, in particular for debt and sureties; and land law. The death penalty was to be only for treason or murder, and suicide was "not to incur Forfeiture, but considered as a Disease"; corruption of blood was to be abolished. Procedure regarding pardons would be considered later.

While removal of legal carry-overs was urgent—in December, for instance, the act providing statutory salaries for Church of England clergy was suspended—there was opportunity to innovate at the same time.

Early in the session, Jefferson had brought in a bill abolishing entails; the committee now agreed on a new course of descents and distribution of estates, about which Jefferson later wrote:

I wished the commee to settle the leading principles of these, as a guide for me in framing them. . . . Mr. Pendleton wished to preserve the right of primogeniture, but seeing at once that that could not prevail, he proposed we should adopt the Hebrew principle, and give a double portion to the elder son. I observed, that if the elder son could eat twice as much, or do double work, it might be a natural evidence of his right to a double partition, but being on a par in his powers & wants, with his brothers and sisters, he should be on a par also in the partition of the patrimony, and such was the decision of the other members.[8]

Execution for debt was "not to be against the Body, unless Estate concealed; & agst. Estate made more easy." Quitrents to be abolished. Acquisitions of unappropriated lands to be entered with a surveyor and not more than four hundred acres in any county; no orders for land to issue from the governor and Council; lands irregularly acquired to be liable to caveat.

The work was divided into five parts, of which the fourth, consisting of "the residuary Part of the Virginia Laws, not taken up in either of the three first Parts; to which is added the criminal Law, and Land-

Law" was allotted to Mason, but with the proviso that "if he finds it too much, the other Gentlemen will take off his Hands any part he pleases."[9] With this general agreement and allocation, the group dispersed. Its *Report,* presented to the Assembly the following spring though not ordered printed until 1784, was chiefly the work of Jefferson, Wythe, and Pendleton: according to Jefferson, "Mr. Mason excused himself as, being no lawyer, he felt himself unqualified for the work, and he resigned soon after. Mr. Lee excused himself on the same ground, and died, indeed, in a short time."

That spring, a smallpox epidemic spread over northern Virginia. The Assembly elections, at which Philip Alexander was chosen as Mason's colleague, were so sparsely attended as to cause the results to be challenged. Economic activity in the area slowed to a near standstill: on 19 April, Mason wrote William Aylett: "the small Pox being at almost every one of our public warehouses renders a Tobacco purchase here, at this time, very difficult."

Mason's own innoculation was badly administered and only partially effective:* it prevented his attendance at the Assembly where, on 22 May, he was chosen in absentia a member of the Virginia delegation to Congress.† On 14 June, he declined the appointment in a letter to Wythe:

my arm which has been so much ulcerated where the inoculation was made, still continues so bad, that my being able to attend this session remains doubtful. I must therefore entreat the favor of you sir, to return my thanks to the Assembly for the honor they have been pleased to do me, in appointing me one of their delegates to Congress, and at the same time to inform them that I cannot by any means accept the appointment. My own domestic affairs are so circumstanced as not to admit of my continued absence from home, where a numerous family of children calls for my constant attention; nor do I think I have a right to vacate my seat in the house of delegates, without the consent of my constituents; and such of them as I have had the opportunity of consulting are adverse to it. Was this not the case, I must acknowledge I have other reasons for declining the appointment; which to avoid offence, I forbear giving.[10]

The final sentence of his letter conveyed veiled disapproval of the Assembly's action in omitting his friend, Richard Henry Lee, from the congressional delegation. Lee's enemies had been circulating the rumor that he was unpatriotically aiding the depreciation of Virginia's paper money by requiring his back country tenants to pay their rents in produce rather than in currency. (By the time the rumor reached Pendleton it had Lee demanding that "his tenants covenant to pay their rent in Specie.") At the same time, because of the long-standing Lee–Adams connection, Lee was accused of favoring New England's interests as opposed to Virginia's in the Congress.

The previous November, Lee had written Jefferson that innuendoes were circulating against him in the House; in February, he communicated his concern to Gunston Hall. On 4 March, Mason assured him that though he had heard the rumor he had dismissed it as "infamous Falsehood . . . I believe it has gained no Manner of Credit & don't think it's worth giving you a Moment's Uneasiness." But the gossip did not die. Lee sent long letters to Governor Henry and Council President Page, detailing the reasons why, in mid-1775, when emissions of paper money to pay for the war had barely begun, he had initiated agreements to accept produce as rent payments by tenants in Fauquier County who could not sell their crop because of the nonexportation association. (A year later, Loudoun County tenants petitioned the Assembly to grant them this particular form of relief.) Likewise defying "the poisonous tongue of Slander to produce a single instance on which I have preferred the interest of New England to that of Virga.," Lee returned to Williamsburg and demanded an investigation. After his appearance before a joint session, Col. John Banister, not one of Lee's partisans, wrote his brother-in-law Theodorick Bland: "Certainly no defence was ever made with more graceful eloquence, more manly firmness, equalness of temper, serenity, calmness and judgment, than this very accomplished speaker displayed on this occasion, and I am now of opinion he will be re-elected to his former station, instead of Mr. George Mason, who has resigned."[11]

Lee was not only exonerated but tendered a resolution thanking him for his services, written by Speaker George Wythe.* On 25 June, Lee was elected to Congress in the vacancy caused by Mason's withdrawal.

During the summer of 1777, on behalf of the Fairfax Committee of Safety, Mason made substantial tobacco purchases as new channels of trade and revenue opened and Virginia, no longer confined by the Navigation Acts, began direct exchange with European buyers, especially French and Dutch. The meeting point was the Caribbean Islands: ships from Bordeaux and Nantes in particular came to such Caribbean ports as St. Eustace and Martinique, there to exchange cargoes with Virginia captains bringing tobacco. In view of the British-and-loyalist blockade of Chesapeake Bay, such voyages were hazardous, but prices for successful deliveries were high; planters, having sold their tobacco outright at Virginia warehouses, were free of further risk; the state stood to realize substantial profits on cargoes that were not intercepted; and on their return voyages, captains could attempt to bring in vital supplies— arms, ammunition, salt.

In preparation for the autumn Assembly of 1777, Mason's Fairfax constituents set forth their priorities in an urgent communication to their delegates. They argued that the disruptive price level should be controlled by a general assessment to halt the depreciation of the currency: "we think the people are not only able to pay the tax, but that they will cheerfully submit to it." The Courts of Justice should be reopened: "the people would then pay their debts, or be legally compelled to it." Salt, being as unobtainable as it is essential, must be imported and provision made to supply persons who cannot afford it. (The British blockade had just intercepted six or seven merchantmen whose entire cargoes consisted of the scarce commodity.) A state insurance office to cover cargoes could increase imports and bring prices down. If these matters are seen to, "We might then expect to keep up an army. . . . In our present situation . . . this may be the last campaign."

Precise figures on inflation in the area appear in Lund Washington's record of price changes between 1776 and 1779: flour rose from 15/0 per hundredweight to £10.0.0; salt pork, from £5.0.0 to £80.0.0 per barrel; corn, from 2/0 to £4.0.0 per bushel. Craftsmen stopped working for wages in order to attempt self-sufficiency on their land: Lund wrote the general in the late winter of 1778 about one of the master carpenters employed on the enlargement of Mount Vernon: "I found he had very little thoughts of worckg. here much more—he said money woud not purchase the necessarys of Life and that he must endeavour to make them—findg. I coud do nothing better with him, I told him if he wou'd stick to his worck and endeavour to finish it—I wou'd make him a present at shearg. time of 40 Wt. of Wool and next Fall 30 Barrels of Corn—he has promised that he will be here very shortly and stick close to the worck, and that nothing but sickness shall take him from it."[12]

Desultory attendance at Assembly sessions—in Mason's case, usually due to ill health—began to give the body a bad repute. The fall meeting of 1777 was called for 20 October; a quorum was not present until the thirtieth. Mason, who had intended to leave on the twenty-sixth, was held up by bad weather and actually arrived on 14 November; his brother, Thomson, was brought in by the sergeant at arms ten days later; Jefferson first appeared on the last day of the month. The session dragged on and on until 24 January 1778; Pendleton called it "the most tedious I ever experienced." These delays, rather than inferior personnel, may have influenced the many letter writers who complained of being poorly represented, for practically all of the major figures of the past were delegates.*

Most of this session's agenda, and that of its immediate successors, consisted of war measures. The Declaration of Independence was a paper statement that five years of military effort were required to substantiate; all of the new state legislatures had continually to search for munitions, money, and men.

The disaster at Brandywine on 11 September 1777, with reports of drunkenness and bad conduct among Virginia's troops, followed by the loss of the battle of Germantown, where most of the 9th Virginia Regiment was taken prisoner, spread a gloom that, though temporarily brightened by news of the British surrender of Gen. John Burgoyne's army at Saratoga on 17 October, lasted through the winter.

In November, Washington's pleas to Patrick Henry and other governors, as he retreated to Valley Forge while the British extended to Philadelphia their previous occupation of New York, catalogued American inadequacies. On 23 December, he wrote the president of the Congress, "We have this day no less than 2,873 men in camp unfit for duty because they are barefooted and otherwise naked . . . unless some great change suddenly takes place . . . this Army must inevitably be reduced to one or other of these three things, Starve, dissolve, or disperse, in order to obtain subsistence in the best manner they can."[13*]

Thus confronted with grim actualities, the Virginia legislature roused itself, with Mason serving on drafting committees and as floor manager of a range of bills. One authorized the naming of commissioners "to have power and authority respectively to seize all linens, woollens, trimmings, tanned leather, hats, leather breeches, dressed deerskins, shoes, and stockings, proper for the use of the army, which may be found in the possession of any person or persons whatsoever."[14] A few weeks later Governor Henry was able to inform Washington that nine wagonloads of supplies and £15,000 worth of clothing were on their way. Another bill penalized preemptive buying of goods needed for the army by prospective profiteers; a third temporarily prohibited exports of beef, pork, and bacon in order to enable public contractors to obtain a supply; a fourth authorized seizures of salt.

Recruitment was even thornier. So much had been said, by Mason and others, to the effect that "a well regulated Militia . . . is the natural Strength and only safe & stable security of a free Government," that adoption of a draft law to supplement voluntary enlistments came hard. Yet current Virginia enlistments were scheduled to begin to expire in January and be complete by April, and the promised bounties in land and money seemed unlikely to retain these veterans in service. It was January 1778 before the legislature agreed on the recruitment measure that Mason had been carrying back and forth between the two Houses. In November, Pendleton calculated that it would produce 5,000 men; in March, Richard Henry Lee thought about 2,500. After riotous resistance in Loudoun County and grumbling and widespread evasion elsewhere, the actual yield in late May turned out to be 716 draftees or paid substitutes, of whom 83 melted into the landscape en route to camp.

The third major topic of Assembly debate, "Raising a Supply of Money for Publick Exigencies," proved the most intractable of all. The war had started with obligations from the French and Indian War still unredeemed; as new issues of treasury notes and interest-bearing certificates followed each other at an accelerating pace, the effective dates of the additional taxes voted to cover them were repeatedly deferred. In August 1777, Richard Henry Lee wrote Jefferson "the sum in circulation is immense and no corrective can be applied but Taxation"; two months later, Jacky Custis informed his stepfather that Mason was "preparing a remedy against the Depreciation of our Money which I think will do him great credit," and Washington replied: "I know of no person better qualified . . . than Colonel Mason, and shall be very happy to hear that he has taken it in hand. Long have I been persuaded of the indispensable necessity of a tax for the purpose of sinking the paper money, and why it has been delayed better politicians than I must account for."[15]

Mason's bill, brought in by a committee of which Thomas Nelson was chairman, constituted a complete overhaul of the tax system; all previous tax laws were repealed, and quitrents except those due Lord Fairfax were abolished. As passed in January after prolonged debate, it

*Paper Money*

remained in effect with only occasional revision through the war. An assessment of 0.5 percent of evaluated worth was to be placed on all property, not only on the previous tax base of land, slaves, and personal property, but on income as well. The proceeds were to be applied to Virginia's quota of the principal and interest due on treasury notes issued by the Continental Congress, to redemption of and interest on the treasury notes issued by the state, and to the state's annual operating expenses. To fill the gap until collections could begin, the treasurer was authorized to receive moneys loaned to the state by private citizens, issuing receipts in the form of certificates of the loan office that was concurrently established by another bill; if such loans proved inadequate, he could emit treasury notes up to $1,700,000, redeemable in December 1784.

But in Mason's view, the state's great unused resource, available for paying off its debt, providing bounties for its soldiers, and supporting the expenses of government, was its western lands. He and Jefferson obtained House approval of a resolution calling for establishment of a land office and the sale of public lands for these purposes. Their draft bill of January 1778 established a clear and uniform procedure for acquisitions: the office was to have a central registrar, appointed by the Assembly, from whom grants should issue; a surveyor in each county; and fair and true survey plats kept by the county court. At the same time, the bill offered some innovative incentives, to encourage the development of an agricultural society of family farms, settled by newly married couples, by soldiers, and by possessors of fifty-acre headrights.*

The Mason-Jefferson bill was unexpectedly stopped just short of adoption. It had been read twice and referred to the Committee of the Whole, but there it was suddenly killed by postponement beyond the end of the session. On the final day, to save what he could, Mason put through a resolution delaying sales of western lands for the present and limiting such sales to four hundred acres to a purchaser when resumed. With the interests of the Ohio Company in view, he also obtained a resolution authorizing the presentation to the legislature of claims to unpatented lands granted by order of a colonial governor and Council.

For more than a year, the land office bill and its companion measure on land titles languished; when they were revived in the spring of 1779, Mason was gloomy—and prophetic—to Richard Henry Lee about the changes that would precede their enactment. They had been "carried thro' a pretty numerous Committee, upon Principles of sound policy & Justice; the Fund, in Aid of our Taxes, arising from the Sale of the ba[c]k Lands, will be immense, if the Bill stands upon it's present Ground; but I understand both Bills are to be warmly opposed, & before they get thro' our Butcher's Shambles, the Committee of the Whole House, they will probably be mutilated & chop'd to Peices."[16]

Two weeks later, he was hoping that lost ground might be recovered on the floor of the Senate: amendments to the land title bill, "made Yesterday in the Committee by the Senate, at the Instance of their Speaker [Archibald Cary], are very absurd & unjust; they are to be reported to-morrow, & as the old Bruiser will then have his Mouth shut in the Chair, perhaps they may be set right."[17]

The land title bill, in which Mason had a personal interest both on behalf of the Ohio Company and as a speculator in headright certificates* came through with relatively little amendment, but on the land office bill, the conservatives, led by Pendleton and Harrison, won out over Mason and Jefferson. In addition to being mindful of their personal interests and those of the companies to which they belonged, these men believed that encouragement of settlement by individuals, such as Mason and Jefferson wanted, would reduce land values in the east by drawing off population there. For a related reason, Washington also disapproved: ready availability of such holdings would attract both soldiers currently in the army and prospective recruits. By stripping the measure of incentives to individual settlement, they converted it to the purposes of large-scale and absentee purchasers, some of whom subsequently acquired acreages measured in millions rather than hundreds of acres,† and the tax yield on which Mason had counted was likewise vitiated when huge holdings were paid for in depreciated currency.

Far more important to the future of Virginia's western lands, however, was the result of a confidential conversation that took place in December 1777 between Governor Henry and a young Virginian who had been familiar with the Kentucky region for some years, George Rogers Clark. Disinclined for security reasons to spread Clark's proposal widely, Henry communicated it only to the Council and to three men in the House, Mason, Jefferson, and the speaker. A guarded letter from the House members to Clark in early January promised legislative support for his military activities in the west that are described at length in the next chapter.

During the latter days of the 1777–78 session, less confidential conversations buzzed the corridors regarding a new involvement of Richard Henry Lee. The military defeats and retreats of the previous fall and the current sufferings of the Valley Forge winter were stirring mutterings about the commander-in-chief. In October, Congress had established a Board of War; at the end of November, General Horatio Gates, victor of Saratoga, was designated its president, and General Thomas Mifflin of Philadelphia a member. Both were unfriendly to Washington; still more inimical was Thomas Conway, an Irish soldier of fortune long in French service, who came to America in May 1777 and was at once named a brigadier by friends in Congress, to the displeasure of Washington and other American officers. In October, when it appeared likely that the same congressional friends were about to advance him to major general, Washington protested to Lee; how, he inquired, did Congress expect him to place the many foreigners they have promoted to the rank of field officers without destroying the morale of Americans of proved capacity already in the service? General Conway's merit as an officer "exists more in his own imagination, than in reality."[18]

Then, early in November, young James Wilkinson, in his cups, revealed the contents of a letter sent by Conway to Gates derogating the commander-in-chief; a listener transmitted the slur to Washington. The "Conway cabal" came into the open when the general dispatched to the author of the letter a pungently brief note: "Sir: A Letter which I receivd last Night, contain the following paragraph. In a Letter from Genl. Conway to Genl. Gates he says: 'Heaven has been determind to save your Country; or a weak General and bad Councellors would have ruind it.' I am Sir Yr. Hbl. Servt."[19]

Richard Henry Lee was known to be close to Generals Mifflin and Gates and others involved in this campaign of discreditation. Dr. James Craik, Washington's medical officer, informed his chief that "Base and villainous men, through chagrin, envy, or ambition, are endeavouring to lessn you in the minds of the people, and taking underhand methods to traduce your character . . . some of the eastern and southern members were at the bottom of it, particularly one, who had been said to be your enemy before, but denied it, Richard Henry Lee."[20]

By January, the general was sufficiently troubled to ask Lund Washington to make inquiries in Northern Virginia. On 18 February 1778, after consulting with Mason on his return from Williamsburg, Lund reported:

Colo. Mason* (who I shew'd your Letter of the 16th of janry.) tells me he was informd of the Cabal against you before he left Williamsburg, and some had hinted to him that R. H. Lee was one suspected of haveg. a Hand in it, and as they knew the intimacy subsistg. between them begd. that he woud talk to Lee and discover whether any thing of the Sort was in agitation or not—he did so—

*George Washington with the French Alliance in
hand, engraved by leMire from a painting by
L. lePaon belonging to the Marquis
de Lafayette
(courtesy, The Mount Vernon Ladies' Association)*

that Lee declares no such thing or even a hint has ever been mention'd in Congress, and that he shoud look upon it as one of the greatest misfortunes that coud befal this Continent shoud you by any means whatever give up the Command of the Army. . . .

Mason is of opinion it is a Tory Manuever, for he thinks no Friend to America can be an Enemy to you for by God which was his expression There is not nor ever was in the World A man who acted from a more Laudable and disinterested motive than you do. . . . Mason concluded by saying that he was convinced from the whole of his conversation with Lee, Harrison and other Members of Congress that a Faction in Congress agnst. you had never existed— our Conversation passd. in Alexandria before several gentlemen.[21]

With spring, the excitement died down. Mason's devotion to Washington continued, and this incident no more disturbed his friendship with Richard Henry Lee than his long-drawn-out dispute with William Lee, ending in a lawsuit, regarding some tobacco consigned to William at Richard Henry's request in 1775 and in Mason's view never adequately accounted for.

Spirits were shortly exalted by news of Franklin's successful negotiation of an alliance with France; Lafayette, from Paris, recommended celebration with "a grand, noisy feu de joy." The new mood appeared in Mason's letter after Lee was back in Congress:

American Prospects brighten every Day; nothing, I think, but the speedy Arrival of a strong British Squadron can save the Enemie's Fleet & Army at N. York; indeed as to their Fleet, I trust the Blow is already struck. We are apt to wish for Peace, I confess I am, altho' I am clearly of Opinion that War is the present Interest of these United States: The Union is yet incompleat, & will be so, until the Inhabitants of all the Territory from Cape Briton to the Missisippi are included in it; while G. Britain possesses Canada & West Florida, she will continually be setting the Indians upon us, & while she holds the Harbours of Augustine & Hallifax, especially the latter, we shall not be able to protect our Trade or Coasts from her Depredations; at least for many Years to come: the Possession of these two places wou'd save us more than half a Million a Year. . . . After "his most Christian Majesty, & Happiness & Prosperity to the French Nation," my next Toast shall be "long Life and Continuance in Office to the present British Ministry" in the first Bottle of good Claret I get; & I expect some by the first Ships from France.[22]

In the April 1778 elections, Mason acquired a new Assembly colleague, Jacky Custis.* Lund joyfully informed the general that "Custis was honorable elected a Delegate for this County last Monday. He got more than three times as many votes as Broadwater. Mason was first elected."[23]

But Mason missed the session altogether. Called for 4 May, it ended 1 June; Jacky Custis wrote his stepfather, "I have often wished my Colleague had been present. . . . He is most inexcusable in staying away. He got as far as Colo. Blackburn's and heard the House had broken up."[24] In John Augustine Washington's view, expressed to Richard Henry Lee, Mason's absence and the brevity of the session were related: "I have not heard particularly what our Assembly are about; but it is said it will be a short session, unless Col. Mason, who is not yet got down, should carve out more business for them than they have yet thought of."[25]

Early in October, Mason wrote a long letter to a correspondent abroad that summarizes his view of the course of public affairs up to this point in the Revolution. Its recipient is unknown—both address and close are lost; the text indicates that Mason had had no word of him for two years and that he was living "in a Country where you can spend your Time agreeably," from which he had written Mason the previous April.*

After transmitting family news, beginning with the death of his wife, Mason describes the events that canceled his intention to

spend the Remainder of my Days in privacy & Retirement with my children. . . . To shew you that I have not been an idle Spectator of this great Contest, and to amuse you with the Sentiments of an old Friend upon an important Subject I inclose you a Copy of the first Draught of the Declaration of Rights, just as it was drawn by me, & presented to the Virginia Convention, where it received few Alterations; some of them I think not for the better; this was the first thing of the kind upon the Continent, and has been closely imitated by all the other States. . . . We have laid our new Government upon a broad Foundation, & have endeavoured to provide the most effectual Securities for the essential Rights of human nature, both in Civil and Religious liberty; the People become every Day more & more attach'd to it; and I trust that neither the Power of Great Britain, nor the Power of Hell will be able to prevail against it.

There never was an idler or a falser Notion than that which the British Ministry have imposed upon the Nation "that this great Revolution has been the Work of a Faction, of a Junto of ambitious Men against the Sense of the People of America." On the Contrary, nothing has been done without the Approbation of the People, who have indeed out run their Leaders. . . . Equally false is the Assertion that Independence was originally designed here; things have gone such Lengths, that it is a Matter of Moonshine to us, whether Independence was at first intended, or not; and therefore we may now be believed. The truth is, we have been forced into it, as the only means of self-preservation. . . . To talk of replacing us in the Situation of 1763, as we first asked, is to the last Degree absurd, & impossible; they obstinately refused it, while it was in their power, and now, that it is out of their Power, they offer it. . . . Our Country has been made a scene of Desolation & Blood. Enormities & Cruelties have been committed here, which not only disgrace the British Name, but dishonour the human kind! . . . The Die is cast—the Rubicon is passed—and a Reconciliation with Great Britain, upon the Terms of returning to her Government is impossible.

No man was more warmly attach'd to the Hanover Family & the Whig Inter[e]st of England than I was, & few Men had stronger Prejudices in Favour of that Form of Government under which I was born & bred, or a greater Aversion to changing it. . . .

. . . but when Reconciliation became a lost Hope, when unconditional Submission, or effectual Resistance were the only Alternatives left us, when the last dutiful & humble petition from Congress received no other Answer than declaring us Rebels, and out of the King's protection, I from that Moment look'd forward to a Revolution & Independence, as the only means of Salvation; and will risque the last Penny of my Fortune, & the last Drop of my Blood upon the Issue. . . . I am not singular in my Opinions; these are the Sentiments of more than nine tenths of the best men in America.

God has been pleased to bless our Endeavours, in a Just Cause, with Remarkable Success. . . . American prospects brighten, and appearances are strongly in our Favour: the British Ministry must, & will acknowledge us independent States. . . .

*French ships off the New England coast, 17 August 1778, by Pierre Ozanne (courtesy, Library of Congress)*

I have thus given you a long and faithful, and I fear you will think a tedious account of the political state of affairs here; my opportunities of knowing them are equal to most men's, and the natural anxiety you must have to be well informed of the situation of your native country, at so important a crisis, will apologize for the trouble.[26]

While the "First Draught" of the Declaration of Rights enclosed with this letter is in Mason's hand, recent scholarship has observed that it is in fact a combination of committe print, notes, and memory, blending various stages of the development of the document (and including one word from the Declaration of Independence). Letter and enclosure eventually became part of the papers of Mason's son John.

An unfinished sentence dangles at the bottom of the last surviving sheet of this commentary on Virginia's first years of statehood: "We have had 200,000 acres of land laid off, marked and bounded in one survey for the Ohio. . . ." The break leaves undetermined whether any private inkling had reached Mason of the larger events in the West that had occurred under George Rogers Clark's leadership during the summer; Clark's official report of his first military successes did not reach Governor Henry in Williamsburg until the following month.

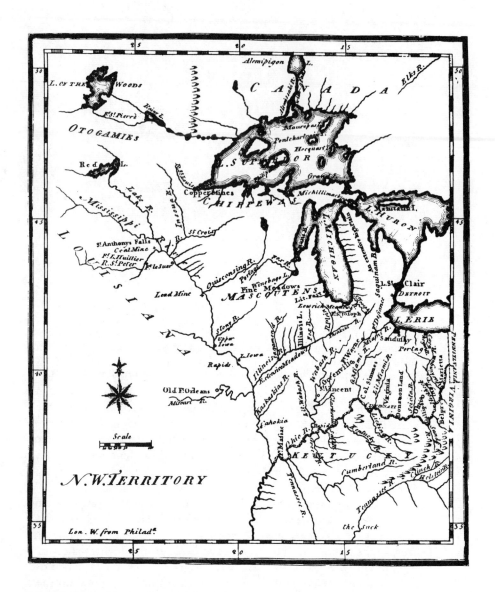

The Northwest Territory; map from Atlas
of the United States, 1795–1800 showing
Cahokia and St. Vincent
(courtesy, State Historical Society of Wisconsin)

# Chapter IX
# Half the Territory of the United States

*No eastern-living Virginian was as close as George Mason to the military action* by which the lands north of the Ohio were secured to the United States. The magnetism that the West exerted on him from his early youth was felt by many other planters, but to them the area was a distant extension of their Tidewater wealth, an expanse whose actual condition they only vaguely realized. Mason was second to none in speculation in choice tracts, but his perceptions bridged the usual gap between eastern men and the pioneers who lived beyond the Alleghenies, and there was an almost filial relationship between George Rogers Clark, the military leader who won the Northwest from the British, and his older friend and sponsor at Gunston Hall. Mason's attitude had none of the ambivalence exhibited by the European capitals toward the area, an ambivalence that had a counterpart at Williamsburg.

Viewed from London, Paris, or Madrid in the third quarter of the eighteenth century, the American colonies lay on the furthest fringes of transatlantic empire. Viewed from the Mississippi River, they were settlements on the eastern rim of a continent that was an empire in itself.

In the years just preceding the American Revolution, most of those in power in all three imperial capitals treated the interior of America as a faraway country of which they knew little, and their ignorance was indeed great. Yet there were always a few men of each nationality who, in following the inland rivers and traversing the mid-continent's forests and prairies, had recognized that the future lay under their feet.

After Louis XV, by the secret treaty of Ildefonso in 1762, consigned the Isle d'Orleans and the entire west bank of the Mississippi to his cousin, Charles III of Spain, Spanish ports appeared along the river as far up as St. Louis.

Informed by the explorations of priests and soldiers and denied Atlantic coastal access below the St. Lawrence by the English colonies, the French had early grasped the possibility of an inland empire stretching from Montreal to New Orleans. The age of canals was revolutionizing the internal commerce of Europe, and the St. Lawrence, the Great

Lakes, the Wabash, the Ohio, and the Mississippi offered a three-thousand-mile system requiring only a few portages for unrestricted transport of men and goods from one end to the other. But rivalry between commanders at the two terminals complicated its exploitation.

The British had always claimed title to land west of the Alleghenies: early colonial charters read "from sea to sea." And though the mountain barrier concentrated early settlement along the Atlantic coast, the richness of the westward-leading Mohawk Valley early attracted landowners of the upper Hudson, and Governor Spotswood led his Virginia Knights of the Golden Horseshoe to look beyond the Blue Ridge in 1716.

Yet while the governments of each of the imperial powers sent occasional encouragement to their military or civilian officials in middle America they never adequately supported them with money, goods for Indian trade, or troops other than in token numbers. The treaty concluding the Seven Years' War in 1763 expressed relative values on which all three contracting powers were agreed. The islands of the West Indies were sugar-rich and offered ports of call for triangular trade. The Spaniards were happy to exchange the Floridas for Cuba. By renouncing Canada and all territory east of the Mississippi except New Orleans, France regained such highly prized sites as Guadeloupe and Martinique. British merchants, convinced that the negotiators had let them down, urged on their government retrocession of Canada in exchange for some well-located islands.

After the peace, British officials replaced French at Quebec and Montreal; they had been in control at the Forks of the Ohio since General John Forbes recaptured the site in 1758 and changed the name from Fort Duquesne to Fort Pitt. In the west, British garrisons replaced French at Forts Le Boeuf, Detroit, etc. along the Great Lakes; at Vincennes on the Wabash; and at Kaskaskia and Cahokia east of the Mississippi in the Illinois country, though the population of these settlements, like that of the Spanish posts at Ste. Geneviève and St. Louis across the river, remained predominantly French. During the next decade, various English travelers, such as Thomas Hutchins, who covered the ground in the years 1764–75 and published mapped reports on the Illinois country in his *Topographical Description of Virginia, Pennsylvania, Maryland and North Carolina,* forcefully urged on a somewhat inattentive Whitehall the political advantages of control of the center of the continent and the long-term economic possibilities of the area.

Neither the Proclamation of 1763 forbidding British settlement west of the mountains nor the Quebec Act of 1774 extending the boundaries of that province over the entire transmontane area north of the Ohio and west to the Mississippi had been successful in holding back immigration. Families by the hundreds continued to push westward. Since pelts were of high quality where winters were severe, New Yorkers and Pennsylvanians engaged in the fur trade more persistently than their southern counterparts, but all alike were avid for rich acres. Proclamations might forbid and Indian tribes obstruct access to them, but once in possession, a family would fix a tenacious hold and fight to retain its own.*

In London, the keen eyes of Benjamin Franklin had discerned the imperial advantages of a consolidated North America early in the French and Indian War, as soon as British capture of Quebec insured French surrender of Canada. On 3 January 1760, he glowingly projected new possibilities to Lord Kames:

No one can rejoice more sincerely than I do on the Reduction of Canada; and this, not merely as I am a Colonist, but as I am a Briton. I have long been of Opinion, that the Foundations of the future Grandeur and Stability of the British Empire, lie in America; and tho' like other Foundations they are low and little seen, they are nevertheless, broad and Strong enough to support the greatest Political Structure Human Wisdom ever yet erected. I am therefore by no means for restoring Canada. If we keep it, all the Country from St. Laurence to Missisipi, will in another Century be fill'd with British People; Britain itself will become vastly more populous by immense Increase of its Commerce; the Atlantic Sea will be cover'd with your Trading Ships; and your naval Power thence continually increasing, will extend your Influence round the whole Globe, and awe the World! If the French remain in Canada, they will continually harass our Colonies by the Indians, impede if not prevent their Growth; your Progress to Greatness will at best be slow, and give room for many Accidents that may for ever prevent it, But I refrain, for I see you begin to think my Notions extravagant, and look upon them as the Ravings of a mad Prophet.[1]

The interest and implicit belief in the western country of two future presidents can be seen in a letter that James Monroe wrote to George Rogers Clark in 1782 and one that Washington wrote to Jefferson six years later. Monroe made Clark an offer of confidential correspondence, noting that as an official in Williamsburg he might be of use:

As I am altogether a stranger to you it may be necessary to inform you I am at present a member of ye Council & shall most probably continue in that office for three years. I have been educated to ye law & my interest & connections are at present in this part of ye country but have some thoughts of turning my attention toward yr quarter & perhaps sometime hence removing thither myself. I wish our correspondence to be private & as it shall be on my part conducted with intire confidence in you, so I wish you to do it in confidence that I shall be happy from ye opinion I have of yr merit to pay ye greatest attention to whatever you may propose which may tend to promote ye public interest & be honorable & advantageous to you.[2]

Washington assured Jefferson that ready access would soon be available:

Notwithstanding the real scarcity of money, and the difficulty of collecting it, the laborers employed by the Potomac Company have made very great progress in removing the obstructions at the Shenandoah, Seneca, and Great Falls; insomuch that, if this summer had not proved unusually rainy, and if we could have had a favorable autumn, the navigation might have been sufficiently opened (though not completed) for boats to have passed from Fort Cumberland to within nine miles of a shipping port, by the first of January next. There remains now no doubt of the practicability of the plan, or that, upon the ulterior operations being performed, this will become the great avenue into the western country.[3]

*Benjamin Franklin, mezzotint by*
*James McArdell after Benjamin Wilson,*
*1761*
*(courtesy, Benjamin Franklin Collection,*
*Yale University Library)*

Washington's enduring faith in this company is attested in his will: "I particularly recommend it to such of the Legatees . . . as can make it convenient, to take each a share of my stock in the Potomac Company in preference to the amount of what it might sell for, being thoroughly convinced myself that no uses to which money can be applied will be so productive as the Tolls arising from this navigation when in full operation (and this from the nature of things it must be 'ere long)."[4]

Mason and Franklin were leading opponents in the ensuing rivalry between Pennsylvania and Virginia, and between Pennsylvanians and Virginians, for the riches of the Ohio country. The jurisdictional disputes resulting from the vagueness of early charters had still not been cleared up: the line of demarcation between Maryland and Pennsylvania was fixed only when the English surveyors, Charles Mason and Jeremiah Dixon, ended the long-standing dispute between the Baltimores and the Penns during 1763–67; and since its westward extension, defining the Pennsylvania-Virginia boundary, was not agreed until 1784, the contested overlap at the strategic Forks of the Ohio continued to be a source of intercolonial and then interstate friction.

Virginians suffered a further affront when Whitehall, by the Quebec Act of 1774, extended the former boundary of New France south to the Ohio River, adopting the exact position that, when held by the French, had precipitated the French and Indian War; they were unlikely to forget that it was Virginia troops who had been sent to warn off the French and enforce colonial charters covering the region.

And in addition to the charter controversy, the rivalries of the quasi-public, quasi-private land companies below the governmental level, though not below the level of government interest, augmented the turmoil.

In 1773, in an attempt to recoup the damage done to the Ohio Company by the malfeasance of George Mercer, Mason undertook a new initiative based on the company's 1749 grant, and in so doing brought George Rogers Clark into the western service. He ordered a survey of a 200,000-acre tract south of the Ohio.

A commission for William Crawford as chief surveyor was obtained from the College of William and Mary before the end of the year, and, in 1774, Hancock Lee was appointed as Crawford's official assistant, with George Rogers Clark as one of his deputies.*

Hancock Lee, son of the Lees of Ditchley in Stafford County and a cousin of Richard Henry, had over the years experienced both the promise and the danger of the Kentucky country; he himself survived capture by Indians, but his cousin Hancock Taylor was mortally wounded by them in 1774 and his brother Willis shot in 1776.

George Rogers Clark passed his boyhood in Caroline County. His parents, from long-settled farm families in King and Queen County, had gone west to work two hundred acres adjacent to Peter Jefferson's Shadwell in Albemarle County, but on inheriting a larger farm, they moved back east when their second son was four.

He spent only a few years at school; at twelve, Donald Robertson, a Scot married to a relative of Mrs. Clark, declared him lacking in academic aptitude.* His father's ledgers credit him with raising his own crops at fifteen; at nineteen, when he was studying surveying with an uncle, he made his first trip west and placed a claim on the Fish Creek tributary of the Kanawha River. His enthralled descriptions, when he returned home for the winter, led his father to go out with him next spring, taking two slaves; in 1773, the young man adventured another 170 miles down the Ohio, put in a crop of seed corn, and visited the interior of Kentucky before coming home.† During Dunmore's War in 1774, he served as a captain of militia.

In the spring of 1775, on behalf of the Ohio Company, Lee and Clark laid off a tract of an estimated 200,000 acres (the area was actually some four times that size) which Mason described with enthusiasm: "They have got it all in one Tract, upon a large Creek, call'd Licking Creek; which falls into the Ohio River, on the South East Side, abt. 150 Miles below the Scioto River, & abt. 80 Miles above the Mouth of the Kentucky River; so that it is clear both of Henderson's & the Vandalia Company's Claim.‡ By all Accounts it is equal to any Land on this Continent, being exceedingly rich & level."[5] Mason's enthusiasm even withstood the surveyor's bill—£650 Virginia currency—for most of which he became liable when only three of the company's members paid the assessment of £50 sterling to which they had agreed.

But for a flaw in this survey, the Ohio Company would have realized its purpose, substantiated its claim, and brought wealth to its partners. The survey was defective because in 1772, the Virginia Assembly had organized the land west of the Kanawha River as Fincastle County. William Preston was its surveyor. The law required authorization by the official county surveyor for all surveys made in his county. Lee failed to obtain it, and Preston therefore declined to recognize his work.

From this body blow, the Ohio Company did not recover. In the autumn of 1778, Mason memorialized the Assembly to permit the company to pay ten shillings per hundred acres to be relieved of its corporate obligation to build and maintain a fort and prorate its assets among its members, but the members declined to take up the small number of shares owned in London, and the legislature failed to act. In 1779, the last year in which a company meeting is recorded, he petitioned the Assembly to validate the faulty survey, and, in 1781, Robert Carter backed him in another such effort, both unsuccessful.

Meanwhile, George Rogers Clark, hiring out to Hancock Lee for £80 per year plus the privilege of taking up land for himself as he worked, had stayed in the West and had begun to get into politics. In March 1775, a group of North Carolinians led by land speculator Judge Richard Henderson, with Daniel Boone among their number, purchased the land between the Kentucky and Cumberland rivers from the Cherokee Indians with the intent of erecting the proprietary colony of

Transylvania. Though Virginia claimed the area and North Carolina's Governor Martin castigated the project as an "infamous undertaking" by an "infamous company of Land Pyrates," the judge and his friends were able to elicit considerable support among settlers. Early in 1776, Clark went to Williamsburg to ascertain whether the Transylvania claim lay in Fincastle County. On returning, he found that a convention in Harrodsburg had repudiated Henderson, informally organized western Kentucky as a new county of Virginia, and elected him and John Gabriel Jones to represent them in Williamsburg.

In hopes of arriving while the 1776 Convention was still sitting, the two set out at once and alone; the trip proved a nightmare. They were reduced to walking speed when one horse foundered. Squelching through marsh in wet moccasins gave them the painful malady known as "scald feet." Indians appeared. Hobbling into Martin's Fort, they stood siege until the arrival of a party from Harrodsburg. On reaching Botetourt County, they learned the Convention had adjourned.

While Jones made a detour, Clark pushed on to Scotchtown in Hanover County to ask Virginia's newly elected governor for support in the hostilities he anticipated in the West. Patrick Henry sent him on to Williamsburg with a letter to the Council approving his request for five hundred pounds of powder; on 23 August, the Council agreed. Since the Virginia House of Delegates would reconvene in October, Clark and Jones decided to stay over and petition for legal recognition of their new county; in December, Fincastle was divided into three new counties, of which Kentucky was one.

The two men ran into trouble moving their five hundred pounds of powder downriver from Fort Pitt. They hid it on an island when Indians approached, but Jones was ambushed and killed when he went back with a party to recover it.

By the autumn of 1777, however, Clark had assembled a reassuring force of riflemen, pack horses, and mounted troops. This accomplished, he started east with an ambitious project; by skillful horse-trading along the way, he not only reached home on a good mount but with money in his saddlebags; investing it in shirts, a suit, and shoes, he made a fine entry into Williamsburg. His plan was to carry the war to the British by an attack that would secure the land north of the Ohio all the way from the Illinois country to Detroit. Governor Henry arranged for him to present his plan to the Council on 10 December; when asked to put it in writing, Clark declared it "would distress the garrisons at Detroit; it would fling the command of the two great rivers into our hands, which would enable us to get supplies of goods from the Spaniards and carry on trade with the Indians."[6]

The Council hesitated to take so major a decision without the Assembly's consent; at the same time it recognized the danger of word getting out if the plan were shared among so large a number. The final decision was to confide the entire scheme to the speaker and to two members of known western interests, Mason and Jefferson, while masking its purpose to the membership in general as a plan to defend Kentucky. So the House was asked to empower Henry to use troops against "western enemies"; he commissioned Clark a lieutenant colonel and supplied him with a treasury warrant for £1,200 Virginia currency and two sets of instructions: public orders to "proceed to Kentucky" and secret ones to capture Kaskaskia and other British outposts in the Illinois country. On 3 January 1778 the three House members who were fully informed addressed Clark a joint letter:

As some Indian Tribes, to the westward of the Mississippi, have lately, without any Provocation, massacred many of the Inhabitants upon the frontiers of this Commonwealth, in the most cruel & barbarous Manner, & it is intended to revenge the Injury & punish the Aggressors by carrying the War into their own Country

We congratulate you upon your Appointment to conduct so important an Enterprize in which we most heartily wish you Success; and we have no Doubt but some further Reward in Lands, in that Country, will be given to the Volunteers who shall engage in this Service, in addition to the usual Pay: if they are so fortunate [as] to succeed, we think it just & reasonable that each Volunteer entering as a common Soldier in this Expedition, shou'd be allowed three hundred Acres of Land, & the Officers in the usual Proportion, out of the Lands which may be conquered in the Country now in the Possession of the said Indians; so as not to interfere with the Claims of any friendly Indians, or of any People willing to become Subjects of this Commonwealth; and for this we think you may safely confide in the Justice & Generosity of the Virginia Assembly. We are Sir Yr. most Hble Servts.

G: Wythe
G Mason
Th: Jefferson[7]

Meanwhile, plans were also developing in the British headquarters of Lt. Col. Henry Hamilton, commandant at Detroit. In June 1777 he had received instructions from London to engage Indian allies for frontier war, since "to bring the war to a speedy issue and restore those deluded people to their former state of happiness and prosperity, are the favorite wishes of the Royal Breast."[8] To sweeten his approach with suitable presents, a consignment of sixteen gross of red-handled scalping knives was shipped to him from Quebec.

William Pitt might apostrophize Parliament: "Who is the man who dared to authorize and associate to our arms the tomahawk and scalping knife of the savage?" But in January 1778, Hamilton, whom the Americans nicknamed "The Hair Buyer," informed Sir Guy Carleton, from Detroit, "The Indians of this district have taken 34 prisoners, 17 of whom they delivered, and 81 scalps."[9]*

Clark moved first. In November 1778, Governor Henry received dispatches declaring his mission accomplished: the Illinois country was in American hands.

Jefferson sent congratulations: "Much solicitude will be felt for the result of your expedition to the Wabash; it will at least delay their expedition to our frontier Settlements; and if Successful, have an important bearing ultimately in Establishing our North Western boundary."[10] When informing the Virginia delegates in Congress of this

The Party of Savages went
with Orders not to spare Man
Woman or Child. To this cruel
Mandate even some of the Savages
made an Objection, respecting the
butchering the Women & Children
but they were told the Children
would make Soldiers, & the
Women would keep up the
Stock.

*Remembrancer Vol. 8. p. 77.*

Scalping Knives.
Crucifixes.
Tomahawks.

*"The Allies—*
*Par Nobile Fratrum!";*
*3 February 1780,*
*George III shares*
*a cannibal feast of*
*Americans with three*
*Indians while a bishop*
*arrives followed by a*
*sailor with scalping*
*knives*
(courtesy, The Trustees of
the British Museum)

development, Henry proposed continuing Clark's advance all the way to Detroit.

The past June, Congress had planned and appropriated for such an expedition with three thousand men and $10,000 in presents for the Delawares whose lands would be traversed; but towards the end of July, informed that supplies and horses could not be assembled in time, had canceled the plan. Washington, in spite of his long-standing awareness of the value of a successful campaign on the western front, was forced to disapprove not only this but other similar proposals at intervals during the balance of the war.

Thereafter, Clark experienced the same failure of support by authorities at a faraway capital that had frustrated and exasperated French, Spanish, and British commanders before him. A count of his own men showed them to be, on the average, over a thousand miles from home; at such a distance, government officials found frontier realities hard to visualize. The Assembly's lack of touch appeared that December when, after nearly two years with no pay, negligible supplies, and men arriving by tens in fulfilment of promises of hundreds, Clark received a ceremonial sword and the compliments of Virginia. He is said to have broken the sword across his knee and tossed the fragments into the Ohio River.* And just as he was about to set off on his 1778 campaign, Henry had commissioned him to buy—without scrimping on cost—a select group of stallions and mares from the Spanish settlements beyond the Mississippi and forward them, with suitable military protection, to the governor's farm in central Virginia.* Even Jefferson hoped he would have time to collect specimens from the Stone Age burial mounds near Lexington and the deposits of prehistoric mammal remains at Big Bone Lick.

But in George Mason, Clark recognized an eastern Virginian whose mind's eye could see the conditions under which he operated. It was to Mason, in November 1779, that he rendered the freshly written, first full account of his Illinois expedition, "too incredible for any Person to believe except those that are as well acquainted with me as you are or had experienced something similar to it."[11] Turning the pages of this seventy-five-page manuscript at Gunston Hall, Mason was a near-participant, episode by episode, in a campaign that became a legend of frontier war.

The *Memoirs* that Clark composed at Congressman John Brown's urging in the 1790s† expanded and extended the story, but the following excerpts from a letter,[12] written within a year of the events, conveyed to his older friend, while the sequence was still fresh, Clark's capacity for a grand design, his use of subterfuge, exhortation, and guile in supplement to or avoidance of actual military engagement, his skill in attaching the adherence of the French population in the captured towns, his parlays with the Indians, and the details of his incredible forced marches across frozen and flooded terrain in the dead of a midwestern winter.

I had since the beginning of the War taken pains to make myself acquainted with the true situation of the British posts on the Fronteers; and since find that I was not mistaken in my judgment—I was ordered to Attact the Illinois in Case of Success to car[r]y my Arms to any Quarter I pleased I was certain that with five hundred Men I could take the Illinois, and by my treating the Inhabitants as fellow Citizens, and shew them that I ment to protect rather than treat them as a Conquered People Engageing the Indians to our Interest &c. It might probably have so great an effect on their Country men at Detroyet, (they already disliked their Master,) that it would be an easy prey for me.

Clark's first objective was the town of Kaskaskia, which he took without a fight.

I got everything in Readiness on the 26th of June, set off from the Falls, double Man'd our Oars and proceeded day and Night until we run into the mouth of the Tenesse River the fourth day landed on an Island to prepare Ourselves for a March by Land, a few hours after we took a Boat of Hunters but eight days from Kaskaskias. . . . They were Englishmen, & appear'd to be in our Interest, their inteligence was not favorable, they asked leave to go on the Expedition, I granted it. . . . On the Evening of the 4th of July we got within three miles of the Town Kaskaskias, having a River of the same name to cross to the Town. After making ourselves ready for any thing that might happen, we marched after night to a Farm that was on the same side of the River about a mile above the Town, took the family Prisoners, & found plenty of Boats to Cross in; and in two hours Transported ourselves to the other Shore with the Greatest silence. I learned that they had some suspician of being attacked and had made some preparations, keeping out Spies, but they making no discoveries, had got off their Guards. I immediately divided my little Army into two Divisions ordered one to surround the Town, with the other I broke into the Fort, secured the Governour Mr. Rochblave in 15 minutes had every Street secured, sent Runners through the Town ordering the People on the pane of Death to keep close to their Houses, which they observ'd and before daylight had the whole disarmed. Nothing could excell the Confusion these People seemed to be in, being taught to expect nothing but Savage treatment from the Americans.

Summoning the ranking citizens, most of whom were French, Clark put the American cause to them in a favorable light, convincing them that he came as a liberator and assuring them of religious freedom.

I sent for all the Principal Men of the Town who came in as if to a Tribunal that was to determine their fate forever Cursing their fortune that they were not apprised of us time to have defended themselves. I told them that I was sorry to find that they had been taught to harbour so base an opinion of the Americans and their Cause: Explain'd the nature of the dispute to them in as clear a light as I was capable of, it was certain that they were a Conquered People and by the fate of War was at my mercy and that our Principal was to make those we Reduced free insted of enslaving them as they immagined. . . . No sooner had they heard this than Joy sparkled in their Eyes and [they] fell into Transports of Joy that really surprised me. As soon as they were a little moderated they told me that they had always been kept in the dark as to the dispute between America & Britain that they had never heard any thing before but what was prejuditial and tended to insence them against the Americans, that they were now convinced that it was a Cause they ought to Espouse. . . .

The Priest that had lately come from Canada had made himself a little acquainted with our dispute. . . . He asked if I would give him liberty to perform his duty in his Church. I told him that I had nothing to do with Churches more than to defend them from Insult. That by the laws of the State his Religion had as great Previledges as any other. This seem'd to compleat their happiness. . . .

Clark's next objective was the town of Cahokia.

In mean time I prepar'd a Detachment on Horse back, under Capt. Bowman to make a Descent on Cohos, about sixty miles up the Country; the Inhabitants told me that one of their Townsmen was enough to put me in possession of that place, by carrying the good news that the People would rejoice. However I did not altogether chuse to trust them, dispatched the Captain, Attended by a considerable number of the Inhabittants who got into the middle of the Town before they were discovered; the French Gentlemen Calling aloud to the People to submit to their happier fate, which they did with very little hesitation. A number of Indians being in town, on hearing of the Big knives [the Indian name for the Kentuckians], immediately made their Escape. . . . Our friends the Spanyards, [were] doing every thing in their power to convince me of their friendship. A Correspondance immediately commenced between the Governour and myself.

With Kaskaskia and Cahokia accepting him, Clark controlled the Illinois shores of the Mississippi. He then prepared to win over the one remaining settlement of any size, Vincennes, to the east on the Wabash.

Post St. Vincent, a Town about the Size of Williamsburg was the next Object in my view. As the whole [countryside] was appris'd of me, I was by no means able to march against it (the Governour a few months before going to Detroyet). . . . I pretended that I was about to send an Express to the falls of Ohio for a Body of Troops to Join me at a certain place in order to attact it. It soon had the desired effect. Advocates immediately appear'd among the people in their behalf. Mr. Jeboth, the Priest, to fully convince me of his Attachment offered to undertake to win that Town for me if I would permit him and let a few of them go; they made no doubt of gaining their friends at St. Vincents to my Interest; the Priest told me he would do himself, and gave me to understand, that although he had nothing to do with temporal business, that he would give them such hints in the Spiritual way that would be very conducive to the business.

Clark's strategy was to attach, or at least to neutralize, the Indians: "Domestick affairs being partly well settled the Indian Department came next the object of my attention. . . . It may appear otherwise to you, but [I] always thought we took the wrong method of treating with Indians, and strove as soon as possible to make myself acquainted with the French and Spanish mode which must be preferrable to ours, otherwise they could not possibly have such great influence among them."

At their Councils, Indian chiefs traditionally engaged in long parlays, usually delivered in person, but on occasion these were sent to the Council to be read aloud. Clark adopted this means of explaining the causes of the British–American war,

in the following manner. That a great many Years ago, our forefathers lived in England, but the King oppressed them in such a manner that they were obliged to Cross the great Waters to get out of his way; But he not being satisfied to loose so many Subjects sent Governours and Soldiers among them to make them obey his Laws, but told his Governours to treat them well and to take but little from them until they grew Populus, that then they would be able to pay a great deal. By the good treatment we got, we grew to be a great People and flourished fast. The King then wrote to his Governour & Officers that we had got Rich and numerous enough, that it was time to make us pay tribute, that he did not care how much they took, so as they left us enough to eat, and that he had sent them a great many Soldiers to make the Americans pay if they refused, that when they had made the Americans do as they pleased, they would then make the Indians pay likewise; But for fear the Indians should find it out by the Big Knives that the English intended to make them also pay, & Should get mad with the English for their treatment to their Neighbours the Big Knives, that they, his Governours should make us Quarrel &c. We bore their Taxes for many Years, at last they were so hard that if we killed a Deer they would take the Skin away and leave us only the Meat, and made us buy Blankets with Corn to fead their Soldiers with. By such usage we got Poor and was obliged to go naked; And at last we complained. The King got mad and made his Soldiers Kill some of our People and Burn some of our Villages. The Old Men then held a great Council and made the Tomahawk very sharp and put it into the hand of the young Men, told them to be strong & Strike the English as long as they could find one on this Island. They immediately struck and Killed a great many of the English. The French King hearing of it sent to the Americans and told them to be strong and fight the English like Men, that if they wanted help or Tomahawks he would furnish them &c. &c.

This Speech had a greater effect than I could have immagined, and did more service than a Regiment of Men cou'd have done.

Meanwhile, two of Clark's officers reached Vincennes, "entered the Fort and ordered them to surrender before they were appris'd About forty in number being made Prisoners. The Capt. made a Valuable

Treaty) Gave them their Liberty; this stroke compleated our Interest on the Wabache St. Vincents being a Post of great Importance, and not being able to spare many Men to Garrisson it I took uncommon pains intirely to Attach them to our Interest as well as the Inhabitants of the Illinois."

But Clark's tenure of Vincennes was brief. Governor Hamilton had left Detroit and was marching in his direction; the British regained the post on 17 December. Narrowly escaping capture, Clark pressed west to

the Town of Lapraryderush [La prairie des rochers] about twelve miles above Kaskaskias. The Gentlemen & Ladies immediately assembled at a Ball for our Entertainment; we spent the fore part of the night very agreeably; but about 12 Oclock there was a very sudden change by an Express Arriveing enforming us that Governour Hammilton was within three miles of Kaskaskias with eight hundred Men, and was determined to Attact the Fort that night. . . . I never saw greater confusion among a small Assembly than was at that time, every Person having their eyes on me as if my word was to determine their good or Evil fate. It required but a moments hesitation in me to form my Resolution. . . . I ordered our Horses Sadled in order if possible to get into the Fort before the Attact could be made. Those of the Company that had recovered their Surprise so far as to enable them to speak, begged of me not to attempt to Return, that the Town was certainly in possession of the Enemy and the Fort warmly Attacted. Some proposed Conveying me to the Spanish Shore; some one thing and some another. I thanked them for the Care they had of my Person, and told them it was the fate of War. . . . That I hoped they would not let the news Spoil our Divirsion sooner than was necessary, that we would divirt ourselves until our horses was ready, forced them to dance and endeavoured to appear as unconcerned as if no such thing was in Adjutation. This Conduct inspired the Young Men in such a manner that many of them was getting their Horses to Share fate with me. . . .

I sent off the Horsemen to St. Vincents to take a prisoner by which we might get intiligence, but found it impractable on account of the high waters; but in the hight of our anxiety on the evening of the 29th of Januy. 1779 Mr. Vague [Vigo] a Spanish Mercht. Arrived from St. Vincents, and was there the time of its being taken, and gave me every Intiligence that I could wish to have . . . (it was at this moment I would have bound myself seven years a Slave, to have had five hundred Troops).

Clark's next decision was so bold as to appear utterly foolhardy. He decided to march on Vincennes and take it back.

I considered the Inclemency of the season, the badness of the Roads &c. as an advantage to us, as they would be more off their Guard on all Quarters. I collected the Officers, told them the probability I thought there was of turning the scale in our favour. . . .

We were Conducted out of the Town by the Inhabitants: and Mr. Jeboth the Priest, who after a very suitable Discourse to the purpose, gave us all Absolution And we set out on a Forlorn hope indeed; for our whole Party with the Boats Crew consisted of only a little upwards of two hundred. . . . We had now a Rout before us of two hundred and Forty miles in length, through, I suppose one of the most beautiful Country in the world; but at this time in many parts flowing with water and exceading bad [for] marching. My greatest care was to divert the Men as much as possible in order to keep up their spirits. The first obstruction of any consequence I met with was on the 13th. Arriveing at the two little Wabachees although three miles asunder they now make but one, the flowed water between them being at Least three feet deep, and in many places four: Being near five miles to the opposite Hills, the shallowest place, except about one hundred Yards was three feet. This would have been enough to have stop'ed any set of men that was not in the same temper that we was. But in three days we contrived to cross, by building a large Canoe, ferried across the two Channels, the rest of the way we waded; Building scaffolds at each to lodge our Baggage on until the Horses Crossed to take them; it Rained nearly a third of our March; but we never halted for it. . . . From the spot we now lay on was about ten miles to Town, and every foot of the way put together that was not three feet and upwards under water would not have made the length of two miles and a half and not a mouthful of Provision. . . . If I was sensible that you wou'd let no Person see this relation I would give you a detail of our suffering for four days in crossing those waters, and the manner it was done; and I am sure that you wou'd Credit it. . . . But to our inexpressible Joy in the evening of the 23d. we got safe on Terra firma within half a League of the Fort, covered by a small Grove of Trees [and thus] had a full view of the wished for spot.

Sending a letter to the town by a prisoner he had taken, Clark waited "until near sunset, giving him time to get near the Town before we marched. As it was an open Plain from the Wood that covered us; I march'd time enough to be seen from the Town before dark but taking advantage of the Land, disposed the lines in such a manner that nothing but the Pavilions could be seen, having as many of them as would be sufficient for a thousand Men, which was observed by the Inhabitants, who . . . counted the different Colours and Judged our number accordingly."

Hamilton and his garrison inside the fort, having assumed initial firing to be by drunken Indians, were completely surprised.

About Eight o-clock in the morning I ordered the fireing to cease and sent a flag into the Garrisson with a hard Bill Recommended Mr. Hammilton to surrender his Garrisson & severe threats if he should destroy any Letters &c. He return'd an Answ. to this purpose; that the Garrisson was not disposed to be awed into any thing unbecomeing British Soldiers. The Attact was Renewed with greater Vigour than ever and continued for about two hours; I was determined to listen to no Terms whatever until I was in Possession of the Fort. . . . A flag appeared from the Fort with a Proposition from Mr. Hamilton for three days Cessation. A desire of a Conference with me immediately . . . after Some deliberation I sent Mr. Hamilton my Compliments, and beged leave to inform him that I should agree to no other terms than his surrendering himself and Garrisson Prisoners at discretion; but if he was desirous of a Conference with me I would meet him at the Church.

The conference was inconclusive, but in the evening Clark sent another demand for surrender, to which Hamilton acceded the next day. With the governor a prisoner and Detroit without a commandant, a chance to push the war to the borders of Canada lay open for the taking— had Clark had men and supplies: "Never was a Person more mortified than I was at this time to see so fair an oppertunity to push a Victory, Detroit lost for want of a few Men; knowing that they would immediately make greater Preparations expecting me. . . . I dispatched off Capt. Williams and Compy with Governour Hamilton, his principal Officers and a few Soldiers to the Falls of Ohio, to be sent to Williamsburg, and in a few days sent my letters to the Govourr."

Governor Henry transmitted the news to the speaker of the House:

I have enclosed a Letter for the perusal of the Assembly, from Colo. Clarke at the Illinois. This Letter among other things informs me of an Expedition which he had planned was determined to Execute, in order to recover Fort St. Vincent, which had been formerly taken by the British Troops, and garrisoned by those under the Colonel's Command. This Enterprise has succeeded to our utmost wishes, for the Garrison commanded by Henry Hamilton, Lieutenant Governor of Detroit, and consisting of British Regulars and a number of Volunteers were made Prisoners of War. Colo. Clarke has sent the Governor, with several officers and privates under a proper Guard, who have by this time arrived at New London, in the County of Bedford.[13]

In prefacing his first draft of history for Mason, Clark opened with a response to a now-lost letter or letters from Gunston Hall that must have contained some stern advice: "Continue to favour me with your valuable Lessons. Continue your Repremands as though I was your Son: when suspicious, think not that promotion or confer'd Honour will occation any unnecessary pride in me. You have infus'd too many of your Valuable precepts in me to be guilty of the like, or to shew any indifference to those that ought to be dear to me. It is with pleasure that I obey in transmitting to you a short sketch of my enterprise and proceeding in the Illinois as near as I can Recollect or gather from memorandums."[14]

Quite possibly, Mason worried earlier than most of Clark's friends about his increasingly excessive drinking.* Through the 1780s, whiskey became his refuge, first from frustration at his failure to receive permission for a campaign against Detroit, then from harassment in the courts by creditors to whom he had given drafts vouchered to the state of Virginia but never paid; and, as time went on, from bitterness at lack of recognition.

In the spring of 1779, the Assembly made good on the promise of a bounty to Clark and his soldiers in the Wythe-Mason-Jefferson letter. But thereafter, the state of Virginia failed to recompense the men who fought the western campaigns.† Clark had raised money where he could, signing drafts and putting up his own lands as security as long as they lasted; and so did others of his officers and associates. In

*One of the early vouchers tendered by George Rogers Clark to the Commonwealth of Virginia, 1779 (courtesy, Virginia State Library)*

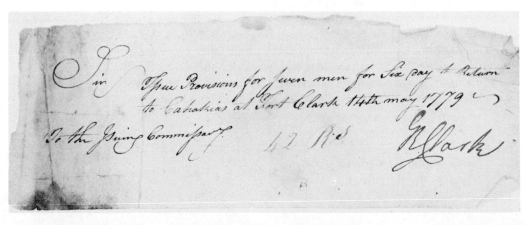

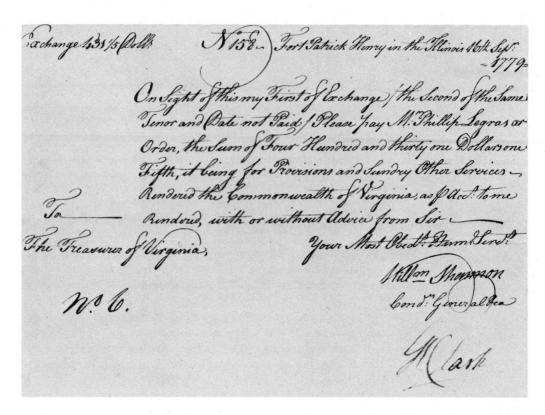

*A further voucher
tendered by George
Rogers Clark to the
Commonwealth of
Virginia, 1779
(courtesy, Virginia
State Library*

New Orleans, Oliver Pollock, who had furnished supplies on his own credit to the American and especially to the Virginian cause in the west, started the war an affluent merchant; he was bankrupt at its close.

When the British invaded eastern Virginia in 1780, Clark returned; Governor Jefferson made him a brigadier and he led troops against Benedict Arnold. But a projected march on Detroit from Fort Pitt, approved by Washington as part of a combined operation, petered out because of tardy American troop arrivals and Indian ambushes. The British remained in occupation of the Great Lakes forts and Detroit long after the signing of the peace treaty; the Indians correctly saw a threat to their reserved hunting grounds north of the Ohio as a swelling postwar tide of American settlers poured over the mountains into Kentucky. In the autumn of 1782, Clark led an unauthorized strike of Kentuckians across the river; he was thrown back and repulsed at the battle of Blue Licks where John Todd, Illinois County lieutenant, was killed and Daniel Boone wounded; recrossing the river, he laid waste the Indian town of Chillicothe. An anti-Clark faction formed; Benjamin Harrison, Virginia's new governor, welcomed its support at a time when he was replying to Clark's requests for payment with news that there were not four shillings in the state treasury. Jefferson, who himself had recently suffered some bitter moments, wryly wrote Clark that "you have enemies you must not doubt when you reflect that you have made yourself eminent. If you meant to escape malice you should have confined yourself within the sleepy line of regular duty."[15]

Mason, however, made a serious and partially successful effort to obtain recognition of Clark's services when Virginia's cession to Congress of the lands that Clark had conquered was under consideration during 1780 and 1781. Two of the seven conditions that he proposed to the Virginia congressional delegation through its member Joseph Jones were:

4thly. As Col. George Rogers Clarke planned and executed the secret expedition, by which the British posts were reduced, and was promised, if the enterprise succeeded, a liberal gratuity in lands in that country, for the officers and soldiers who first marched thither with him; that a quantity of land not exceeding one hundred and fifty thousand acres, be allowed and granted to the said officers and soldiers, to be laid off in one tract, the length of which not to exceed two-thirds of the breadth, in such place on the north-west side of the Ohio, as the majority of the officers shall choose, and to be afterwards divided among the said officers and soldiers, in due proportions according to the laws of Virginia.

5thly. That the said Col. George Rogers Clarke shall be permitted to hold, and shall have confirmed and granted to him, in fee simple for ever, without purchase money other than a nominal legal consideration, a certain tract of land, of seven miles and a half square, at the great falls of the Ohio, binding upon the river, upon the north-west side thereof, which hath been given him by the Wabache Indians for his services, and as testimony of their friendship to him, and of their attachment to the commonwealth of Virginia and the cause of America.[16]

Mason supported these conditions by reminding Jones that "the public faith stands pledged to Col. Clarke and his officers and men (in all about one hundred and eighty) . . . for a liberal reward in the lands they conquered"; by fixing garrisons behind the Indian towns they have deterred alliances with the British; they have protected the frontiers of the middle states; they have prevented the Spaniards from possessing themselves of the British posts and "meddling with the country on this side of the Mississippi, above the mouth of the Ohio," and fortified the American claim to the area in negotiating a treaty with Great Britain. Reemphasizing Clark's "enterprising genius, his great interest with the back inhabitants, his influence with the western Indians, and his knowledge of the country," Mason had "no doubt that Congress will cheerfully agree to the conditions in favor of Col. Clarke and his regiment."[17]

Jones was a member of the special congressional committee named to consider the matter; its September report accepted much of Mason's language. And while illness prevented Mason's attendance at the ensuing Assembly and the exercising of the leadership that he had hoped to exert there, the resolutions regarding cession of the Northwest Territory passed on 2 January 1781 contained the fourth, though not the fifth, of his points in Clark's favor, and this much remained in the definitive Act of Cession passed by the Virginia Assembly in 1783.

After the area above the Ohio had been organized by the Congress as the Northwest Territory in the winter of 1787–88, Mason, in

*Payment by the United States to Virginia for expenses incurred in the ceded Northwest Territory (courtesy, Virginia State Library)*

the legislature for the last time, tried once again. Virginia's claim on the central government for reimbursement of expenses "on account of the services of George Rogers Clark in the Illinois country" was before the Office of Illinois Accounts; in pursuance of a resolution of the House of Delegates, Mason persistently pressed the three commissioners for "any Estimate of the whole amount of the Sum to be reimbursed the Commonwealth by the United States."[18] The following May, $500,000 was agreed as the amount due Virginia. But Clark remained unreimbursed.*

A bright interval in 1783 collected all but one of the six Clark brothers—Lieutenant Richard was still in service in the West †—for a family gathering in Caroline County. Jonathan had been a lieutenant-colonel in the continental line; George Rogers was a brigadier general; the other three, Richard, Edmund, and John, were lieutenants. During the reunion, George Rogers and Edmund, the latter imprisoned at the taking of Charleston in 1780 but exchanged in 1782, stood sponsors at the christening of Jonathan's new child. John, though mortally infected with tuberculosis, was home from six years in captivity, most of it confined on a British prison ship after the battle of Germantown. Only thirteen-year-old William, whose exploits with Meriwether Lewis as a pioneer explorer in the Pacific Northwest still lay some years ahead, was not an officer.

But by this time, Clark's drinking had become serious in the eyes of not only his enemies but his close associates,‡ and he was east because he had been summoned by Governor Harrison to explain the Blue Licks defeat. Though there might be no money in the treasury, the governor wanted to know why the bankrupt Clark had not fortified the Mississippi.

In 1784, three months before the first Kentucky convention canvased the advantages of applying for separate statehood, Washington took a 680-mile trip to assess the western situation for himself; on his return, he appended these reflections to the journal of his ride:

No well informed Mind need be told, that the flanks and rear of the United territory are possessed by other powers, and formidable ones too—nor how necessary it is to apply the cement of interest to bind all parts of it together, by

*George Rogers Clark by Joseph H. Bush, 1818*
(courtesy, Locust Grove Division of Historic Homes, Inc., Louisville, Kentucky)

one indisoluble band—particularly the middle States with the Country immed-iately back of them—for what ties let me ask, should we have upon those people; and how entirely unconnected shod. we be with them if the Spaniards on their right or great Britain on their left, instead of throwing stumbling blocks in their way as they now do; should invite their trade and seek alliances with them? What, when they get strength, which will be sooner than is generally imagined (from the emigration of Foreigners who can have no predeliction for us, as well as from the removal of our own Citizens) may be the consequence of their having formed such connections and alliances; requires no uncommon foresight to predict.[19]

Clark's restiveness over the next years corroborated Washing-ton's concern. Mason's last known letter to him, an inquiry about Ken-tucky lands in the fall of 1786, ended, "it will always give me pleasure to hear of your health, & welfare; and to render you any acceptable service," but it came to a man burnt out and bitter at thirty-four. Clark fretted over the prolonged lack of government in the lands he had conquered—the vacuum was unfilled from 1783, when Virginia trans-ferred them to the United States, until passage of the Ordinance for the Northwest Territory in 1787. He hungered for recognition. He was without funds.

While the Virginia Assembly of 1792 was processing still another rejection of his claims, he wrote his brother Jonathan: "I have given the United States half the territory they possess, and for them to suffer me to remain in poverty, in consequence of it, will not redound much to their honor hereafter. If I meet with another rebuff I must rest contented with it, be industrious, and look out further for my future bread."[20] Clark did indeed "look out further," responding thereafter to offers of a commanding part in various of the separatist schemes for the mid-continent which were fostered by the foreign diplomats Gardoqui on behalf of Spain and Gênet on behalf of France.

But Kentucky's decision to apply for statehood and entry into the Union in 1792, the establishment of territorial government north of the Ohio under the Ordinance of 1787, and the lessening of Indian resistance after the British withdrew from the frontier forts in the north combined to secure for the United States the half of its territory that Clark had conquered.

# Chapter X
# Virginia at War

*While Clark was thrusting into the Illinois wilderness, the prevalence of profiteering and skulduggery in the settled area of Virginia weighed on the autumn Assembly session of 1778.* Mason was associated with a miscellany of legislation to curb current abuses. Grain was in short supply; in response to a plea from Congress "to prohibit the converting of . . . Bread, which was meant for the sustenance of Man into a Liquid poison for his Destruction," its use for distilling was temporarily forbidden. The existing act against profiteers—Washington called them "those murderers of our cause"—was strengthened. Depredations on American shipping by the loyalist Norfolk family of able seamen to whom Mason referred as "that infernal crew the Gutridge's," required further protection of Chesapeake Bay. As a reward for tipping officials off to the presence of a profitably operating counterfeiters' ring in Brunswick County,* emancipation was proposed for a slave named Kitt.

Mason came home to another winter of bad health, described to Jefferson in April: "I have been so roughly handled by the Gout this Winter (having had two Fits since I came from the Assembly, the last a most dangerous one in my Stomach) that I believe I shou'd have resolved to quit all public Business; had I not, just before, given my Word to some of my Constituents, that I wou'd serve them another Year."[1]

His son George, who was even more continually afflicted, decided to go to France in search of relief; Mason wrote Washington and Richard Henry Lee for letters of introduction.† Washington's long reply unburdened the thoughts of a beleaguered man:

. . . it would afford me very singular pleasure to be favoured at all times with your sentiments in a leizure hour, upon public matters of general concernment as well as those which more immediately respect your own State (if proper conveyance would render prudent a free communication). I am particularly desirous of it at this time, because I view things very differently, I fear, from what people in general do who seem to think the contest is at an end; and to make money, and get places, the only things now remaining to do. I have seen without dispondency (even for a moment) the hours which America have stiled her gloomy ones, but I have beheld no day since the commencement of hostilities that I have thought her liberties in such eminent danger as at present. . . . Our Enemy behold with exultation and joy how effectually we labour for their benefit; and from being in a state of absolute dispair, and on the point of evacuating America, are now on tiptoe. . . .

Were I to indluge my present feelings and give a loose to that freedom of expression which my unreserved friendship for you would prompt me to, I should say a great deal on this subject, but letters are liable to so many accidents. . . . I cannot refrain lamenting however in the most poignant terms, the fatal policy too prevalent in most of the States, of employing their ablest Men at home in posts of honor or profit, till the great national Interests are fixed upon a solid basis . . . where are our Men of abilities? Why do they not come forth to save their Country? Let this voice my dear Sir call upon you, Jefferson and others—do not from a mistaken opinion that we are about to set down under our own vine and our own fig tree let our hitherto noble struggle end in ignominy, believe me when I tell you there is danger of it. I have pretty good reasons for thinking, that Administration* a little while ago had resolved to give the matter up, and negotiate a peace with us upon almost any terms, but I shall be much mistaken if they do not now from the present state of our currency, dissentions, and other circumstances, push matters to the utmost extremity.[2]

Washington's plea to Mason, Jefferson, and others to take a larger part in continental public affairs was written when the Congress huddled uncomfortably in York, Pennsylvania, while the British occupied Philadelphia. On the earlier removal of that body to Baltimore in the winter of 1776–77, John Adams had mourned the absence of "Faces . . . that I saw in the first Congress . . . Mr. S. Adams, Mr. Sherman, Coll. Richard Henry Lee, Mr. Chase, and Mr. Paca, are all that remain. The rest are dead, resigned, deserted, or cutt up into Governors, etc. at home." By 1779, of Virginia's 1776 delegation other than Washington and Lee, Patrick Henry had been "cutt up" for three years as governor, and on 1 June Jefferson was "cutt up" to succeed him; Benjamin Harrison was speaker of the Virginia House; Pendleton was president of the Virginia Supreme Court of Appeals; Peyton Randolph and Richard Bland were dead.

Washington might urge men of abilities to "come forth to save their Country," but many held their country to be the sovereign state of Virginia. With varying degrees of intensity, the war induced a continental unity vis-à-vis the mother country, but interstate and regional diversity frequently fractured it, and there was no legal structure to give independent standing to the "country" that Washington had in mind.

Even the confederation of states whose formation Richard Henry Lee had moved in the 1776 Congress was still pending. John Dickinson's plan had been wrangled over for nearly sixteen months by the state delegations before agreement was reached in mid-November 1777. Within a year, eleven states had acceded to it; Delaware came in some months later. But for the proposed Articles of Confederation to go into effect, unanimity was required, and for almost two and a half more years, Maryland refrained from signing. In April 1779, in a caustic but accurate comment, Mason gauged this state's real purpose in holding up the articles to Richard Henry Lee: "I see the Maryland Declaration, upon the Subject of Confederation, & their modest Claim to part of the back Lands, after skulking in the Dark for several Months, has at last made it's Appearance."[3]

Maryland's delay in signing the articles had this aim in view: its congressional delegation stubbornly held to the position that the western lands must become the common property of all the states. Massachusetts, Connecticut, New York, Virginia, the Carolinas, and Georgia enjoyed substantial rights to such lands under their colonial charters; New Hampshire, Rhode Island, and the middle colonies—New Jersey, Pennsylvania, Delaware, Maryland—had none. At the same time, the land companies organized by citizens of the landless states such as the Whartons and Robert Morris in Pennsylvania and Thomas Johnson, William Paca, and George Morgan in Maryland, in partnership with such British subjects as former Governors Dunmore and Tryon and courtiers of comparable standing in London, had either made purchases from the Indians in the territories above and below the Ohio River or received encouragement from Whitehall to do so. Mason's prompt attendance at the spring session of the Virginia House of Delegates in 1779 was insured by the scheduling of a hearing on the claims of the Indiana Company. This company, which had members in Pennsylvania, Maryland, and Virginia, based its title on purchases from the Indians made in 1768 at the time of the Treaty of Fort Stanwix. Mason obtained a denial by the House of the validity of private purchases from any Indian nation.

Maryland's Governor Johnson took the line that since the area north of the Ohio that the Quebec Act of 1774 had transferred to the Province of Canada would be won back by the war effort of all the colonies, title to it should be vested in the confederation; Maryland would postpone signing the articles until the landholding states formally ceded their claims. As a result, the articles became binding only in 1781, when the war was almost over.

The confederation was in any case only a league—Article III declared it to be such and Article II specified retention by its members of their sovereignty, freedom, and independence, together with the tax power and the power to regulate commerce. The Congress was authorized to make war, to appoint representatives abroad, to conclude treaties and alliances, to manage Indian affairs, to borrow money on the credit of the United States, and to requisition men and money from the states. But it was without sanctions to secure compliance.

The confederation had no executive or judicial organs; it acted through committees of the Congress and by legislative decisions; voting was by states, with a two-thirds majority required on substantive matters. Not only members of state delegations but presidents of Congress came and went—Randolph of Virginia, Hancock of Massachusetts, Laurens of South Carolina. The one post filled with continuity was Washington's military command. Virginia's separate ratification of the French treaty of alliance in early June 1779 indicated the extent to which states considered themselves sovereigns; Mason informed Lee, who had resigned from Congress in disapproval and was living at home at Chantilly: "A Resolution has passed nem: con: for ratifieing the French Alliance, so far as is in the Power of this Commonwealth: after what has been written & published here, & considering that the Confederation is

*The newly erected Henrico County Courthouse, 1782, southwest corner of 22nd and Main, Richmond, wood engraving from a drawing by S. S. Kilburn in* Ballou's Dollar Monthly Magazine, *March 1862 (courtesy, The Valentine Museum, Richmond, Virginia)*

not yet acceded to by all the States, we thought this a necessary Measure."[4]

Early in this session, Mason became ill; Lee heard from him:

I am but just beginning to walk about, & attend the House, where I am indulged with being permitted to sit, when I have Occasion to speak, for I am not able to stand five Minutes at a time, & find myself fatigued, beyond Measure, by the Share which Necessity obliges me to bear in the public Business, since Mr. Jefferson (who is appointed Governor) has left the House. We go on, as usual, slowly, & are spending that time in Trifles & Whims, which ought to be applyed to the important Objects of restoring our Finances, & defending our Country: as a proof of this, a Bill has this Day passed the House for removing the Seat of Government, erecting magnificent Buildings &c. to be compleated in five Years.* I have Hopes it will be rejected, or at least the expensive part of it altered, or prolonged, in the Senate.[5]

Mason took a less gloomy view of the session's tax bill; he believed it improved the equity of levies. He likewise approved of a measure sequestering the estates of enemy aliens, and he thought the calibre of the delegates better. "The last Elections have mended our House, in Point of Abilities, but I fear not in sound Whigism & Republican Principles," yet "We are not likely to mend our Delegation in Congress; some of our best Men have refused to go, & others will not risque their Reputation with Men in whom they can't confide."[6] And on 19 June he added: "I inclose you a List of them; & I think you will hardly blame me for taking care, in time to keep out of such Company."†

An "indolent" subcommittee, whose members "have met, or rather failed to meet, at my Lodgings, every Morning & Evening for this Fortnight," is, he says, part of the cause of his remaining "in an indifferent State of Health, to which Vexation has not a little contributed." To prevent the House from melting away before its work was completed, he and John Page conspired in "a little Piece of Generalship . . . procuring an order that the Clerk shou'd grant no Certificate to any Member for his wages until the Assembly shou'd have adjourned;

unless upon Leave of Absence: some of the Fellows threat'ned and kick'd & strugled; but can't loosen the Knot."[7]

Mason blamed much of the quality of men elected to public office on voters' failure to exercise the franchise. His undated memorandum found in Jefferson's papers, *Remarks on the Proposed Bill for Regulating the Elections of Members of the General Assembly* suggests setting elections for all offices on the same day:

> The People, being wearied with too frequent Elections, seldom meet to chuse the Commissioners of the Tax, who are therefore generally appointed by the County Courts; this growing into Precedent, may encroach upon one of the fundamental, & most important Principles of the Constitution. . . . The Members of the late Assemblys have been the nominal, rather than the real Representatives of the People; many of them have been the Choice of a Handful, a Neighbourhood, or a Junto. An ignorant or obscure Man may have considerable Influence within a narrow Circle; but it will seldom extend thro' a County; unfortunately Elections are now so little attended to, that a factious bawling Fellow, who will make a Noise four or five miles round him, & prevail upon his party to attend, may carry an Election against a Man of ten times his Weight & Influence in the County, and Men of Modesty & Merit are discouraged from offering themselves . . . a Law therefore which wou'd bring the Body of the People to attend, & vote at their County Elections, wou'd be of the greatest importance to the State.[8]

Mason proposed levying fines on nonparticipants in an election, unless they had written excuses, with the tax assessors compiling lists of freeholders for the sheriff's use in collecting fines; any county where less than a majority (Mason first put less than two-thirds) of the eligible voters took part in the choice of Assembly delegates should be unrepresented for that year. Much of this thinking was used by Madison when he brought in a voting bill in 1785.

The spring Assembly of 1779 was given an advance look at agenda for the 1780s when Jefferson laid before the speaker the report of the Committee of Law Revisors. As intended, the document was no mere accommodation of the law to independent statehood; many of the 126 draft bills that accompanied it projected a new society built on the Declaration of Rights. Only a few of the measures passed at once; some of the most important were before the House for the better part of a decade. Jefferson's cherished proposal for a comprehensive system of general public education was not realized in his lifetime; he was an old man when the institution of higher learning in which his dream was to culminate took shape at Charlottesville, with him as architect, a quarter of a century after Mason's death.

Treatment of the church issue demonstrated the Assembly's gingerly approach to change. At the autumn session of 1779, repeal replaced annual suspension of the colonial law providing tithes for support of the Anglican clergy; Mason drafted the act. Even this small step was taken with a minimum of explanation. Mason had prefaced his bill with a statement of purpose[9] but his preamble was deleted in debate. A companion measure, also drafted by Mason, that vested the property of "the Church heretofore by Law established" in its members was killed in committee. Since the property of the established church had been purchased with taxes collected from the entire community, resistance to the measure may be explained by Jefferson's estimate a few years later that, while the majority of delegates were Anglicans, the majority of voters were dissenters. The larger question of disestablishment continued to be ignored for the better part of five years.

Mason's chief concern during the last wartime session that he attended—he was not well enough to go to Richmond for the autumn meeting of 1780 and then withdrew—was to attempt to halt the currency inflation that sucked public and private finance down into an everspreading morass. Tax receipts were meager; prices outran tax rates so fast that in December 1779 only some £110,000 remained in the treasury of a £1 million emission made in May, and requisitions by Congress lay unmet before the House.

The Ways and Means Committee's new tax bill stipulated payments in kind: "a tax of thirty pounds of tobacco, forty pounds of flour, fifteen pounds of hemp or two and a half bushels of Indian corn, at the option of the payer." Three-eighths of the commodities thus collected were to be reserved for the purchase of military supplies. A fund of £5 million current money was to be borrowed, with lenders receiving transferable certificates protected against further inflation by the proviso that 5 percent interest be paid "in such manner that the creditor may receive for his interest as much money as will purchase the same quantity of tobacco, that the interest of the money lent would have purchased at the time of the loan." In addition, a 2.5 percent duty was levied on sales of imported goods, a tax of 8/- per gallon on rum, and one of 6/- on spirits distilled from grain.

A week later, this proposal was supplemented, in a text annotated by Mason, by a £3 poll tax on free males over twenty-one and white servants, other than members of the armed forces; a £4 tax to be paid by owners on each of their slaves; a £30 to £40 tax on phaetons and coaches; and one of £10 on riding chairs. From the receipts anticipated from this measure, £1.5 million was earmarked to meet congressional requisitions, together with a like sum from the proceeds of sequestered estates, and £600,000 from the specific taxes levied at the preceding session.

Concurrently, the Commonwealth's treasurer was authorized to borrow the proposed fund of up to £5 million current money. The conversion rate of money and tobacco was set at 100 pounds of inspected tobacco to £30 current money; the inflationary gallop was recognized by a requirement that the grand juries of each year were to keep the ratio up to date.

These methods of raising—or attempting to raise—money were added to Mason's previous bill for securing new income through the sale of public lands. But the new taxes did not take immediate effect; the Committee of the Whole deferred collection for a year, and complaints by Alexandria merchants led Mason himself to propose a reduction of the vendor tax on imported goods from 2.5 percent to 2 percent as well as a deferral of its application date.

The following spring, Mason drafted a new appeal for money. As soon as word came that French troops and warships were on their way, Congress passed a $10 million assessment and apportioned to Virginia a quota of $1,953,200, to be paid within thirty days. Since no such sum could be raised that quickly through normal taxation, Mason's bill allowed persons who would advance money at once to discount the advance at 6 percent interest against their next tax bills; to persons advancing tobacco, replacement of similar quality, with 5 percent interest, was promised by 1 April 1781. Public tobacco to the value of £600,000 was ordered sold to swell this account.

By the end of the spring session of 1780, the South, for the first time, had become the war's active theater. In May 1779, British warships had appeared in Hampton Roads, landing troops to devastate both the Portsmouth shipyard and the docks at Suffolk, the state's military depot for dispatch of transatlantic cargoes and supplies to the southern armies via the Dismal Swamp and the North Carolina sounds. These forces shortly withdrew, but the offensive in South Carolina and Georgia which they went to join was appallingly successful. When Charleston fell on 12 May 1780, a large part of the American army in the South was taken prisoner.

As British troops invested the lower South, Virginia's defenselessness became alarmingly apparent; Mason drafted a long succession of bills designed to recruit, provision, and arm new forces—and to print more paper money.

In March 1780, Congress had resolved to retire $200 million continental currency at the rate of 40 to 1: the states were to issue new specie certificates, with Virginia's quota $1,666,666.66. Mason, together with Richard Henry Lee, now back in the Assembly, put the enabling legislation through with great difficulty. The miscellany of objects taxed showed that the bottom of the barrel had indeed been reached: 1/- on each glass window in every inhabited house; 20/- on every deed of conveyance to or mortgage on a town lot or tract of land of 400 acres or over and 10/- on lesser tracts; 8/- on every hogshead of tobacco exported; a penny a gallon on imported rum or spirits. Should the yield prove inadequate, the governor and council were authorized to sell the public buildings at Williamsburg, now no longer in use, and public lands nearby.

Three months later, the old Continental currency had shrunk in value from 40 to 1 to 77 to 1; nine months later, the ratio was 167 to 1, and the phrase "not worth a Continental" was bitterly current. By the time of Yorktown, a $1,000 Virginia treasury note was worth one Spanish dollar. When arbitrating a financial dispute in 1782, Mason referred to "Loan-Office certificates, as well as Paper Money, daily depreciating, and now of so little Estimation, that for my own part, I wou'd almost as soon receive Payment for a Sum of Money in a Bundle of last Year's News-Papers."[10]

In view of the growing chaos, a final piece of legislation from Mason's hand, prepared just before adjournment at the beginning of the summer of 1780, vested extraordinary powers in the governor and council: "Whereas in this time of publick danger, when a powerful and vindictive enemy are ravaging our southern sister states, and encouraged by success, are making a rapid progress towards our own borders, it has become highly expedient, as well to oppose the common enemy in general, as to provide for the safety and defence of this state in particular, to vest the executive with extraordinary powers for a limited time."[11]

The war news worsened. Many of Virginia's best continental troops were British prisoners. Shortly after the Charleston disaster, the brilliant British colonel, Banastre Tarleton, defeated a further contingent commanded by Col. Abraham Buford. On 16 August, Gen. Horatio Gates lost the battle of Camden; Gen. Johann Kalb, whom Washington had sent south with two thousand reinforcements from Maryland, was killed; the Virginia militia gave a miserable account of themselves; irreplaceable military stores and horses were captured. From the coast to the mountains, the Carolinas and Georgia were largely in British hands. The good news that arrived in October, when Col. Isaac Shelby, William Campbell, and John Sevier defeated a British-Tory force at King's Mountain, lightened the gloom, but this western victory only obliquely impeded Cornwallis's northern movement, and the same was true of the further American success at the Cowpens in January 1781, though it inflicted heavy losses.

Congress directed Washington to relieve General Gates of his command. When Maj. Gen. Nathanael Greene, his successor, came south in October 1780, he presented a letter from his commander-in-chief at Gunston Hall: "I can venture to introduce this Gentn. to you as a man of abilities bravery and coolness. He has a comprehensive knowledge of our affairs, and is a man of fortitude and resources. . . . With this character, I take the liberty of recommending him to your civilities and support for I have no doubt, from the embarrassed situation of Southern affairs —of his standing much in need of the latter from every Gentn. of Influence in the Assemblies of those states."[12]

Washington followed these amenities with strictures on the confederation's incurable inadequacies and insistence on the necessity of a stronger and more unified government:

As General Greene can give you the most perfect information, in detail of our present distresses, and further prospects, I shall content myself with giving the aggregate acct. of them. . . . We are without money, & have been so for a great length of time, without provision & forage except what is taken by Impress— without Cloathing—and shortly shall be (in a manner) without Men. In a word, we have lived upon expedients till we can live no longer. . . . If we mean to continue our struggles (& it is hoped we shall not relinquish our c[ause]) we must do it upon an entire new plan. We must have a permanent force. . . . We must at the same time contrive ways & means to aid our Taxes by Loans. . . . Our Civil government must likewise undergo a reform—ample powers must be lodged in Congress as the head of the Federal Union, adequate to all the purposes of War.[13]

As General Greene pressed on to see what could be saved in the

Carolinas, Virginia was again invested from the sea. In December, British ships landed a force at Norfolk commanded by traitor Benedict Arnold, now a British colonel; after occupying Portsmouth, he quickly pushed up the James on a warehouse-burning campaign. He was beaten off Williamsburg by a militia action, but welcomed at Westover by the widowed Philadelphia Tory, Maria Willing Byrd. Entering Richmond unopposed, he systematically destroyed warehouses and mills, the nearby foundry, and stores of arms and gunpowder. His troops fired a number of public buildings, looted private property. By 6 January 1781, the capital was a shambles. Returning to Portsmouth, Arnold wintered undisturbed, though Richard Henry Lee insisted that, with secrecy and dispatch, one ship-of-the-line and two frigates could be the means of delivering him into American hands.

On 27 March, British General William Phillips arrived in Norfolk with reinforcements. Combining these with Arnold's men, he moved inland to Williamsburg and on to Petersburg, where he set up headquarters after an unsuccessful holding attempt by Baron Steuben and raided north as far as Prince George. In the course of these operations, however, he took fever; he was ill in his headquarters when Lafayette, dispatched to Virginia by Washington, appeared above Petersburg and shelled the town. After his death a few days later, the command passed back to Arnold.

Meanwhile, Cornwallis was moving north. "Light-Horse Harry" Lee and his legion distinguished themselves in actions marking Greene's assumption of command; after Cornwallis withdrew to Wilmington to recover from his expensive victory at Guilford Courthouse on 15 March, the general and the colonel took the war back to South Carolina, where, on 8 September, they won the battle of Eutaw Springs. But Cornwallis did not rest long; on 25 April, he crossed the Virginia line, and by 19 May he was in Portsmouth in control of an intimidating array of troops, General Leslie having arrived from New York with further reinforcements.

On the allied side, Lafayette retreated north from Petersburg toward Fredericksburg, to protect the Falmouth arsenal and await the arrival of Gen. Anthony Wayne.

Mason's second and third sons, William and Thomson, took part in these events, the former in South Carolina and the latter on the James. In June, Mason described their military service to George in France. William had "commanded a Company of Voluntiers (75 fine young fellows from this Country). He had a rough Campaign of it,* and has acquired the Reputation of a vigilant & good officer; and I think is greatly improved by the Expedition. Your brother Thomson has lately returned from a Tour of Militia-Duty upon James River; He commanded a Platoon, in a pretty close Action at Williamsbourg, & behaved with proper Coolness & Intrepidity. He is now from Home, or wou'd have wrote to you."[14]

During the Carolina campaign, "Light-Horse Harry" Lee had

*Continental light dragoons, drawing by Jean-Baptiste-Antoine de Verger, 1781 (courtesy, The Anne S. K. Brown Military Collection, Brown University Library)*

thought highly enough of William to offer him a staff post, but Mason, while returning "my thanks for the very friendly part you have acted," refused permission because of a "domestic circumstance which will require his return as soon as his present term of service expires."[15] Mrs. Eilbeck's terminal illness ended in December; Mason wrote George six months later that she had "willed her Estate in the Manner she always intended . . . the Bulk of her Fortune to yr. Brother William."[16]

Meanwhile, in the midst of hostilities, the signing of the Articles of Confederation inched forward. Little by little, cession to the confederation of all state holdings of western lands was gaining adherents. In December 1779, the Virginia Assembly had sent a remonstrance chiding Congress for being willing to receive petitions from the Vandalia and

Indiana companies, observing that it had already offered to furnish lands in the area of these claims as bounties for the continental troops of the states that lacked western lands, and was "ready to listen to any just & reasonable propositions for removing the *Ostensible* causes of delay to the Complete Ratification of the Confederation."

In February 1780, New York passed a bill "to accelerate the federal alliance" by ceding some of its western holdings; in late June, Congress referred this act, the Virginia remonstrance, and Maryland's conditions to a committe of five, of which Joseph Jones was the Virginia member. In July, Mason's long letter to Jones informed him that the Virginia Assembly had ratified the boundary line between Pennsylvania and Virginia and suggested that Congress make a proposal regarding cession of Virginia's territory above the Ohio River. He pressed Jefferson, "The present is the season for accomplishing the great work of Confederation. If we suffer it to pass away I fear it will never return," and warned Madison: "I am certain there will be a strong opposition here to the cession of such an extensive territory. As I think I have some weight in our assembly, and more upon this than any other subject, I earnestly wish Congress may take up the consideration, and transmit reasonable proposals to our next session, that I may have an opportunity of giving them my aid; being anxious to do this last piece of service to the American union, before I quit the Assembly, which I am determined to do at the end of the next session."[17] In September, the committee urged "upon those states which can remove the embarrassment respecting the western country, a liberal surrender of a portion of their territorial claims," and Jones and Madison moved that such lands "shall be considered as a common fund."[18]

On 10 October, Congress resolved that the ceded territory "shall be disposed of for the common benefit of the United States and be settled and formed into distinct republican states, which shall become members of the federal union, and have the same rights of sovereignty, freedom and independence, as the other states."[19]

Though illness prevented Mason from being present to apply his weight that autumn, the Virginia Assembly voted for cession on 2 January 1781, and on 24 February, Maryland's delegates signed the Articles of Confederation, enabling Congress to set 1 March as the date of public announcement that the league was in force. When, in October 1783, Virginia's Assembly completed conveyance to Congress of its lands in what became the Northwest Territory, Mason's objectives for the area were achieved.

After five consecutive years of public service at the state level, with the end of 1780, Gunston Hall and Northern Virginia became the scene of Mason's life.

There were changes in his household. The children were growing up—in the autumn of 1781, he obtained a pass to the West Indies to permit the return home of his Scottish tutor, David Constable, who had lived at Gunston Hall since 1774. And in April 1780, he remarried.

That February, on his way back from the Assembly, he had been snowbound for some days at the Fredericksburg home of his cousin, James Mercer; writing him afterwards, Mason mentioned that as a Fairfax County justice, he had recently been kept busy signing marriage licenses: "This cold weather has set all the young Folks to providing Bedfellows. I have signed two or three Licenses every Day since I have been at Home. I wish I knew where to get a good one myself; for I find cold Sheets extreamly disagreeable."[20] By April, he had succeeded.

Sarah Brent, eldest daughter of the late George Brent of Woodstock, was a spinster of nearly Mason's age. On 8 April 1780, Mason and Sarah signed a covenant covering disposition of property during the marriage and to the surviving spouse; three days later, as Mason wrote in the family Bible, "George Mason of Gunston Hall in Fairfax County Virginia, aged abt. fifty four years, and his second Wife, Sarah Brent (D[aughter] of George Brent Esqr. of Woodstock in the County of Stafford) aged abou[t fifty] Years, were married on Tuesday the 11th Day of April in the Year 1780, [by] the Revd. Mr. James Scott, Rector of Dettingen Parish in the County of Prince William in Virginia."*

Shortly, Gunston Hall was replenished. In midsummer, the firm of John de Neufville & Son of Amsterdam invoiced sixteen chests, crates, barrels, and packs with contents to a value of £3,047.1.0 plus commissions and freight, addressed to Mason and shipped on board the *General Washington*. This order from Amsterdam illustrated the new turn American trade had taken. As soon as the colonies escaped from the British Navigation Acts, the tobacco previously delivered to Glasgow could be shipped directly to continental ports. The de Neufville firm was one of the largest purchasers in Holland. Similarly, the major quantities bought by the French Farmers General could be sent directly to Nantes and Bordeaux. These two French cities had long harbored commission houses from northern Europe, and American counterparts shortly appeared.†

In 1781, enemy raids disquieted the Northern Neck. In April, Mason urged the Virginia delegation in Congress to press for adoption of a duty on British imports from which to compensate owners for property damage and, before he sealed the letter, had reason to add the postscript: "Several of the Enemys Ships have been within two or three Miles of Alexandria; they have burn'd & plundered several Houses, & carryed off a great many Slaves; tho' I have hitherto been fortunate enough to lose no Part of my Property."[21]‡

Six weeks later the prospect of an attack on Gunston Hall alarmed him enough to send his family and household effects across the river to Mattawoman and inform George that

their Ships have been as high as Alexandria; but we are in daily expectation of sharing the same Fate with our Neighbours upon this, & the other Rivers; where many Familys have been suddenly reduced from Opulence to Indigence, particularly upon James River; the Enemy taking all the Slaves, Horses, Cattle, Furniture, & other Property, they can lay their Hands on; and what they can't carry away they wantonly destroy. We have removed our Furniture, backwards

"A Picturesque
View of the State
of the Nation
for February 1778";
while the British lion
sleeps, a Dutchman
flanked by French and
Spanish friends milks
a cow representing
British commerce while
the American Congress
saws off her horns
(courtesy,
Library of Congress)

& forwards, two or three times, upon different Alarms, by which it is very much damaged: great Part of it was pack'd up last Week, & sent to Maryland, where yr. Brother Thomson, & yr. Sisters now are.[22]

George showed at least one of his father's letters to the American ambassador in Paris; Franklin thought Mason's estimate of public affairs of 3 June 1781 of sufficient importance to pass on to the French foreign minister, the Comte de Vergennes; it is now bound in Correspondence Politique, Etats-Unis, vol. 17, ff. 52–53, Quai d'Orsay, Archives des Affaires Etrangères, Paris.

After recounting recent military events in Virginia and the Carolinas, Mason said:

We have had various Accounts of the sailing of a French Fleet, with a Body of Land Forces, for America. Should they really arrive it wou'd quickly change the Face of our Affairs, & infuse fresh Spirits, & Confidence; but it has been so long expected in vain, that little Credit is now given to Reports concerning it.

You know from your own Acquaintance in this Part of Virginia that the Bulk of the People here are staunch Whigs, strongly attached to the American Cause and well affected to the French Alliance; Yet they grow uneasy & restless, and begin to think that our Allies are spinning out the War in order to weaken America, as well as great Britain, and thereby leave us at the End of it, as dependent as possible upon themselves.

However unjust this Opinion may be, it is natural enough for Planters & Farmers, burdened with heavy Taxes, & frequently drag'd from their Familys upon military Duty, on the continual Alarms occasioned by the Superiority of the British Fleet. They see their Property daily exposed to Destruction, they see with what Facility the British Troops are removed from one Part of the Continent to another, and with what infinite Charge & Fatigue ours are, too late, obliged to follow; and they see too very plainly, that a strong French Fleet would have prevented all this.

If our Allies had a superior Fleet here, I Shou'd have no Doubt of a favourable Is[s]ue to the War, but without it, I fear we are deceiving both them & ourselves, in expecting we shall be able to keep our People much longer firm, in so unequal an Opposition to Great Britain.

France surely intends the Separation of these States, for ever, from Great Britain. It is highly her Interest to accomplish this, but by drawing out the Thread too fine & long, it may unexpectedly break in her Hands."[23]

Actually, the French fleet was well on its way: it had cleared the port of Brest on 22 March and was now in the West Indies. But Mason's letter substantiated the item that precedes it, a dispatch that the French minister, the Chevalier de la Luzerne, had sent to Paris in a numerical code. Luzerne affirms his own meticulous regard for security in keeping inviolate his secret knowledge that the fleet will soon arrive. Rochambeau, he says, has properly informed Washington—the Congress had voted the commander-in-chief liberty to receive, without passing on to its members, military intelligence whose diffusion might cause harm. But silence to other American friends entailed daily importunities: "For the last three or four months we have had to endure the disgruntlement and even the indirect reproaches of those who have pinned all their hopes on the arrival of the 2nd division; but that inconvenience is as nothing compared with the compromise of so important a secret."[24] Mason's letter gave Luzerne's superiors independent evidence of just how caustic some of the comment could be.

His alarm had increasing substance behind it. Since he was no longer a member of the Virginia Assembly, he missed the ignominious flight of the sparsely attended spring session of 1781, first from Richmond to Charlottesville, where Colonel Tarleton's troops nearly captured Governor Jefferson, Speaker Harrison, and Senate President Cary at Monticello, and then over the mountains to Staunton in the Shenandoah Valley. But the shakiness of the government was plain for all to see, and so was the precariousness of the military situation. By midsummer, the British dominated the entire state below Fredericksburg. Intending to move in for a coup de grace, Gen. Sir Henry Clinton directed Cornwallis to select a place to winter the British fleet. Cornwallis chose Yorktown and began to fortify Gloucester Point opposite.

But a countercoup was in the making. On news of the imminent arrival of de Grasse with his fleet and some three thousand fresh French troops, Washington, in concert with Rochambeau, determined to march with their combined forces to Virginia. On 26 August, de Grasse reached the Virginia Capes. On 5 September, the allied armies reached the head of Chesapeake Bay.

That same day, a British fleet, nineteen ships of the line under Admiral Graves, appeared outside Hampton Roads; de Grasse advanced to an engagement, which drove Graves to return to New York; the French admiral then moored inside the Capes below the Gloucester peninsula, and cut Cornwallis off from access to the sea.

*"View of the English
Fleet of 19 Sail
of the Line under
Rear Admiral Graves
Attacking the French
Fleet of 24 Sail
of the Line under
Count De Grafse
coming out of
the Chesapeak the
5th September 1781"*
(courtesy,
The National
Maritime Museum,
London)

The allied ground forces arrived, the siege of Yorktown began. On 19 October, the British army surrendered. Washington prepared a dispatch, "I have the Honor to inform Congress, that a Reduction of the British Army under the command of Lord Cornwallis, is most happily effected."

During the last six months of active warfare in Virginia, two successive chief executives incurred sufficient disapproval of their handling of the governorship for the Assembly to vote a formal investigation, the first for failure to act, the second for exceeding appointed powers.

At the end of his second gubernatorial term, at a time when the state was under maximum military pressure, Jefferson faded out of office. As early as October 1780, rumors of his desire to resign caused Pendleton to remark to Madison that it was "a little cowardly to quit our Posts in a bustling time,"[25] and Mason to urge his friend to reconsider: "I am much concerned to hear you intend, at the End of the present Campaign, to resign the Office of supreme Magistrate; I wish you cou'd be prevailed on to hold it at least, 'til after the next general Election; for I really dread the Choice which the present Assembly may make."[26] Jefferson did remain, but when his term ended on 1 June 1781, even though the government was in close-to-total disarray, he closed out his public business the next day.

After considering the merits of a dictatorship, the refugee Assembly at Staunton chose as governor the head of the Virginia militia, Thomas Nelson, Jr.; over the next months, he exercised on his own authority powers that were legally vested jointly in him and the Council. Indignant citizens reported and resisted arbitrary impressments of cattle, provisions, and equipment.*

Though ill, and at a distance,† Mason, who had drafted most of the acts of previous Assemblies granting extraordinary powers to the governor, became the catalyst of the next session's affirmation that constitutional limitations bound the chief executive and that the civilian was supreme over the military arm. He prepared the "Petition of the Freeholders and other Inhabitants of the Countys of Prince William (and Fairfax) in Behalf of Themselves, and their Fellow-Citizens" that brought matters to a head; it was referred to the Committee of the Whole House on the State of the Commonwealth on 10 December 1781.‡

Not since the catalog of British wrongs in the Declaration of Independence had so harsh a condemnation of official excesses been published: "Every Petty-Officer of Government, to indulge his own Caprice, or serve his private Interest, assumes a dispensing-Power over the Laws; a Crime for which, even in a monarchical Government, King Charles the first forfeited his Life, and James the second his Crown."[27]

Seized provisions, the allegations continued, had been sold to the French troops for specie and the specie misappropriated. Horses had been commandeered to mount troops from other states—Pennsylvania sent men down unmounted, "depending upon the extravagant and romantic Character of this Government." The clothing collected for Virginia's troops had been given to others or left undistributed. The embargo on exports had outlived its usefulness and should be repealed, so should laws making paper currency legal tender. Congress should be informed that this Commonwealth will not be burdened with more than its proper quota of charges and will insist on its proportionate benefits in loans of money and other advantages. Attendance at elections should be enforced by moderate penalties "as the most likely means of excluding Men of desperate Circumstances & Principles, and obtaining a wise and virtuous Legislature; which alone can recover the Confidence of the People, continue their Attachment to the Government, and give Stability, Reputation and Safety to the Commonwealth."[28]

Internal evidence shows this remonstrance to have been written after Yorktown, but it may have been circulating in Richmond in time to influence Governor Nelson's decision to resign—on grounds of ill health—on 29 November. (Pendleton considered his action due to vexation at seeing "his great Popularity so suddenly changed into general execration for having by his imprudent seizures, intercepted the Specie that was about to flow amongst the People."[29]) The Assembly's estimate of the seriousness of the situation was evidenced when it transferred the speaker of the House, Benjamin Harrison, to the governor's chair.

Yet because the success at Yorktown had terminated military dangers and because both of the castigated governors were now out of office, the House treated them gently. In mid-December, Jefferson, whom the necessity of facing charges had caused to miss serving as a congressional appointee for negotiation of the peace, was officially thanked for his "impartial, upright, and attentive administration whilst in office." Nelson requested and received a hearing "respecting such part of his conduct while Governor, as hath been arraigned in a memorial from the County of Prince William"; four days afterwards, Arthur Lee introduced a bill exonerating him, and the House passed an ex post facto law, "to indemnify Thomas Nelson, junior, esquire, late governor . . . and to legalize certain acts of his administration." The Assembly was pleased to treat wartime strains as bygones.

*ea service with Mason crest*
*ourtesy, Board of Regents of*
*unston Hall Plantation)*

# Chapter XI
# The Works of Peace

*News that preliminary peace terms had been signed in December 1781 enabled* the Virginia Assembly to turn to some of the positive legislation proposed by the law revisors. Mason's earliest public document, his *Scheme for Replevying Goods* in 1765, had been prefaced by an attack on the institution of slavery;* eight years later, when he prepared his *Extracts from the Virginia Charters*, he castigated it even more violently.† "Every Gentlemen here is born a Petty Tyrant. Practiced in Acts of Despotism & Cruelty, we become callous to the Dictates of Humanity, & all the finer feelings of the Soul. Taught to regard a part of our own Species in the most abject & contemptible Degree below us, we lose that Idea of the Dignity of Man, which the Hand of Nature implanted in us, for great & useful purposes."[1]

The law revisors had proposed that persons born of slave parents after the passage of the act should be free, provided with training for useful employment, and colonized outside the state at maturity. This proposal was not seriously considered, but, in 1781, the Assembly passed an act "directing the emancipation of certain slaves who have served as soldiers in this state" on the grounds that they, having "contributed towards the establishment of American liberty and independence, should enjoy the blessings of freedom as a reward for their toils and labours"; in 1782, an act legalized manumission by deed or will. Such a large slaveholder as Landon Carter drew up schedules for the gradual freeing of his considerable labor force during his lifetime; others, like Washington, specified manumission in their testaments.

Yet, except for small numbers of craftsmen and household servants, freed slaves normally possessed only rudimentary agricultural skills and had no access to land on which to use them. Resulting vagrancy and crime became an argument against manumission; a reaction against it set in. By 1784, petitions from various counties were urging repeal of the 1782 act, and, in 1806, further manumission was discouraged by a statute requiring freed slaves to leave the state within a year.

The will of George Mason's brother, Thomson, who died in 1785, was exceptional in considering economic needs while expressing the concern many gentlemen felt for their body servants, slaves who had often been their close companions over many years. Thomson specified that his Jack should be given a plot of land with suitable buildings and tools for small farming, directing "that my Executors and Heirs all join in protecting my said slave Jack, in all his just rights, and that he shall be subject to the Controul of no person whatsoever, and this provision I have made for him as a grateful acknowledgement of the Remarkable fidelity and Integrity with which he has conducted himself to me for twenty years and upwards."[2]

The situation was less complicated in areas on which the social and economic patterns of a slave society had not yet been fixed. Jefferson grasped an available opportunity in 1784 when he was chairman of the congressional committee to frame an ordinance for government of the western lands. The day Congress accepted the final terms under which Virginia ceded to the confederation its lands above the Ohio, he brought in a proposal covering not only the Northwest Territory but the entire area from the Great Lakes to the Gulf, east of the Mississippi and west of the mountains, even though Kentucky was an organized part of Virginia and the Carolinas and Georgia had not yet ceded their claims. In this region, he mapped boundaries for ten new states and applied to all the stipulation that "after the year 1800, of the Christian aera, there shall be neither slavery nor involuntary servitude in any of the said States, otherwise than in punishment of crimes, whereof the party shall have been convicted to have been personally guilty."[3]

If adopted, this proviso would have banned the institution in the areas where it was most profitable, such as the future states of Alabama and Mississippi, as well as further north, where the climate was more suitable to free labor. Congress rejected the measure by the narrowest of margins; the states' votes showed New England, New York, and Pennsylvania for; Maryland, Virginia, and South Carolina against; not voting were North Carolina, because evenly divided, and New Jersey, because only one delegate was present. Two delegates were absent because of illness: John Beatty of New Jersey, whose vote would have put that state in the affirmative, and James Monroe of Virginia, whose affirmative vote, with Jefferson's, would have cancelled the negatives of Samuel Hardy and Mason's cousin, John Fenton Mercer.

The ordinance for the Northwest Territory hung fire for three more years. In 1787, when a revised version, restricted to lands north of the Ohio, passed after Jefferson had gone to France, his antislavery clause, with omission of the phrase, "after the year 1800 of the Christian era," was incorporated; the institution was henceforth forbidden above the river.

In the mid-1780s, the religious freedom declared in the Virginia Bill of Rights became a reality in the state, with Jefferson the chief mover at the beginning of the campaign, Madison its sponsor at its end, and Mason assisting outside the legislative halls. The draft bill presented by the law revisors—and regarded by Jefferson as one of the three major achievements of his long life—read:

Well aware that . . . Almighty God hath created the mind free, and . . . that all attempts to influence it by temporal punishments, or burthens, or by civil in-

The public buildings
erected in 1780 on the
northwest corner of
Cary and 14th,
Richmond, as temporary
accommodation for the
state government, from
a drawing reproduced in
the Richmond Dispatch,
2 May 1885
(courtesy,
The Valentine Museum,
Richmond, Virginia)

capacitations, tend only to beget habits of hypocrisy and meanness . . . that to compel a man to furnish contributions of money for the propagation of opinion which he disbelieves *and abhors*, is sinful and tyrannical . . . that our civil rights have no dependence on our religious opinions . . . and finally, that truth is great and will prevail if left to herself. . . .

We the General Assembly of Virginia do enact that . . . all men shall be free to profess, and by argument to maintain, their opinions in matters of religion, and that the same shall in no wise diminish, enlarge, or affect their civil capacities.[4]

When first introduced in 1779, this bill failed to pass. An alliance between consistent conservatives, like Edmund Pendleton, and former radicals in process of turning conservative, like Richard Henry Lee and Patrick Henry, with Henry as its skillful and persuasive leader, began to form around a proposal for state support of religion in general under a general assessment act. Financial aid obtained by tithes assessed on the entire population, like those formerly levied to fund the established Church of England, was to be prorated among all denominations.

Because the established church, with its compulsory attendance and tax support, had been the Virginia institution most visibly connected with the British social structure, during and after the war it had suffered a catastrophic decline. Clergy, left to rely on the voluntary support of dwindling congregations, turned to other professions; services became irregular. The Reverend Mr. Massey resigned as Pohick's clerk of the vestry in 1777; the minutes of sporadic vestry meetings over the next seven years concerned only the vestry's actions as overseers of the poor. The February 1784 meeting that accepted Washington's resignation was the last attended by Mason.*

Other religious denominations, however, were flourishing, and in the October Assembly of 1784, by a vote of 47–32, the House, responding to petitions from various counties, proposed "a moderate assessment for the support of the Christian religion" and chose Patrick Henry chairman of the committee to draft a bill. The measure passed its second reading and was scheduled for final consideration with every prospect of success: Henry's oratory could bend the House to his will, and he supported this bill with a devotion that might have surprised his reverend namesake and other clergy associated in the Parson's Cause.

Playing for time by pleading that so vital a measure should not be pushed through at a single Assembly session, Madison forestalled a third reading: by a vote of 45–38, the bill was put over to the following autumn. The eleven-month delay also presented opportunity for Madison to get Henry out of the House by elevating him to the governor's chair and for the bill to be argued and explained in the counties.

Mason, George Nicholas, and others of its opponents urged Madison to draw up a *Memorial and Remonstrance* for wide circulation and signature. The statement, published without naming the author, reaffirmed the position of Madison's article on religious freedom in the Bill of Rights: "We maintain therefore that in matters of Religion, no man's right is abridged by the institution of Civil Society, and that Religion is wholly exempt from its cognizance."[5]

Mason had the document printed in Alexandria, with space for signatures at the end, and circulated it actively in the Northern Neck; many longhand copies were also distributed, especially in the Shenandoah Valley.

In seeking signatures, both Mason and Madison had some disappointments. On 2 October 1785, Mason sent a copy to his neighbor at Mount Vernon, inviting his signature and that of Dr. Stuart. The very next day, Washington dispatched a rather equivocal reply:

Altho' no man's sentiments are more opposed to *any kind* of restraint upon religious principles than mine are; yet I must confess, that I am not amongst the number of those who are so much alarmed at the thoughts of making People pay towards the support of that which they profess. . . . As the matter now stands, I wish an assessment had never been agitated, and as it has gone so far, that the Bill could die an easy death; because I think it will be productive of more quiet to the State, than by enacting it into a Law; which in my opinion, would be impolitic, admitting there is a decided majority for it, to the disquiet of respectable minority.[6]

He also did not sign the Fairfax County petition against the bill presented next month at the new session of the Assembly.†

On the other hand, when Mason sent a copy of the *Remonstrance* to Robert Carter at Nomini, he approached a man already active against the general assessment bill: "The Violence offered therein to the Declaration of Rights and the presumptious Aid intended to Christ's Visible Church, below, were very alarming—and in the month of last June I joined Some persons in the four lower Counties in this Neck in Offering to the People, there, a Petition addressed to the General Assembly, noting therein Some Reasons against the Bill and praying that it might be rejected."[7]

Mason left to Madison the attempt to secure Richard Henry Lee's signature and its foreseeable rebuff: "he must be a very inattentive observer in our Country, who does not see that avarice is accomplishing the destruction of religion, for want of a legal obligation to contribute something to its support."[8]

Over the state as a whole, sentiment shifted during the summer. The Methodists, who earlier had declared themselves "not Dissenters, but a Religious Society in Communion with the Church of England" and therefore in favor of state support, reversed their official view. Presbyterians in various counties, notably Hanover, rescinded previous declarations. Washington had his wish: by the time the Assembly met, the majority against assessment was so apparent that the general assessment bill was never called up for a vote.

The way was thus clear at last for passage of Jefferson's 1779 Statute for Religious Freedom, and Madison was quick to seize the opportunity. On 17 November, Patrick Henry was elected to the governorship. Jefferson's bill cleared the House in December; after minor adjustments, the Senate assented. On 19 January 1786, Speaker Benjamin Harrison presented the engrossed copy to the governor for signature, and Henry had no choice but to affix his name.

While such specific pieces of reform legislation were being enacted in the mid-1780s, attention turned to the desirability of a general revision of the constitution of 1776. No one regarded the document as sacrosanct; within weeks of its adoption Wythe had assured Jefferson that changes were required and he was the man to make them, and Pendleton had set forth the preference of a conservative for a structure in which the traditional ruling class should have a firmer hold on power.

Jefferson not only had a number of specific objections to the document, but he had always regretted that the 1776 Convention had not been chosen by the people for the express purpose of drafting a fundamental framework to stand above ordinary law. Accordingly, in the spring of 1783, he wrote Madison that "A Convention for the amendment of our Constitution having been much the topic of conversation for some time, I have turned my thoughts to the amendments necessary,"[9] and prepared a complete draft.

Mason's attitude toward revision was obviously a factor; in letters that crossed, Jefferson, still in Congress at Annapolis, inquired on 11 December 1783 if Madison had visited Gunston on his way home: "You have seen G. M. I hope, and had much conversation with him. What are his sentiments as to the amendment of our constitution?

What amendments would he approve? Is he determined to sleep on, or will he rouse and be active? I wish to hear from you on this subject."[10]

Meanwhile, from Orange, Madison, with the italicized words in code, had reported to his friend: "I took *Col. Mason* in my way *and had an evening's conversation with him. . . . On the article of a convention* for *revising our form of government he was sound and ripe and I think would not decline* a participation *in the work*."[11]

In fact, however, Mason had previously decided that the state had higher priorities for immediate action than constitutional revision. On 6 May 1783 he had written Patrick Henry, who, after skipping a session, was about to return to the legislature:* "We are told that the present Assembly intend to dissolve themselves, in order to make way for a General Convention, to new-model the Constitution of Government. Will such a Measure be proper, without a Requisition from a Majority of the People? . . . at any Rate, will it not be better to defer it a Year or two, until the present Ferment (occasioned by the late sudden Change) has subsided, and Men's Minds have had time to cool?"[12]

Foremost among Mason's immediate concerns were the continuing problems of Virginia's public finances, augmented now by that of paying the prerevolutionary debts owed by Virginians to British merchants. The preliminary articles of peace had stipulated that no obstacles be put in the way of collection, and final agreement could be wrecked by nonobservance of this article; yet sentiment among debtors was strong for default.

Virginia had started the war with a low level of public debt; by 1774, a determined policy of redemption of the £540,000 of paper money issued during the Seven Years War and two subsequent issues totaling £40,000 had reduced the state's outstanding obligations to £54,391. But an unfavorable balance of trade, occasioned by private purchases of British goods, had by 1783 reached a point where bullion was moving out of Virginia, and Treasurer Nicholas could not continue redemption of outstanding paper. That spring Virginia currency was quoted in London at a 30 percent discount against the pound sterling.

The volume of private debt that had occasioned the adverse balance was estimated by Jefferson at roughly £2 million when the Revolution started; the estimate of the British merchants to their government in 1791 totaled over £300,000 more. Virginia's debt exceeded the combined debts of the four other southern states.

Repayment was complicated by the act passed in 1777 that had permitted debts due British subjects to be paid into the state loan office, with the state auditor issuing a certificate of payment and the state assuming responsibility for subsequent transfer to the creditor. In the interval between 1777 and 1780, when Virginia's currency had depreciated to a point where the law was suspended, 552 payments were made. Their face value was £275,000, but because of depreciation their actual sterling value was nearer £15,000.

The de facto cancellation represented by these payments, however, was a relatively small fraction of what was owed. A policy of total repudiation was forming in the minds of the debtors whose entire debt was still outstanding; sensing the availability of a political constituency on the issue, Patrick Henry became their leader.

Though, during the spring of 1783, Mason had been "for a long time disabled, by a very sore Finger, from holding a Pen," by the first week in May, his hurt had healed; in a burst of activity, he communicated his concern over finance to such correspondents as William Cabell in Amherst, Henry Tazewell in Williamsburg, and Arthur Campbell in Kentucky, all of whom, as well as his brother, Thomson, were members of the Assembly; his influence was apparent in Fairfax County's instructions to its delegates, Alexander Henderson and Charles Broadwater, and in two subsequent petitions to the legislature signed by substantial numbers of Fairfax freeholders, one on the debts and the other on control of credit.

The petition on the debts proposed that the public assume the entire amount due, with refunds to persons who had paid into the loan office made at the specie rather than the nominal value of their payments, even though "some of them have not paid the Value of six Pence in the Pound." The basic question of repayment of private obligations could then be considered as a whole.

Mason flayed the sentiment for default:

In Conversation upon this Subject, we sometimes hear a very absurd Question—"If we are now to pay the Debts due to the British Merchants, what have we been fighting for all this while?"—Surely not to avoid our Debts; but to rescue our Country from the Oppression & Tyranny of the British Government, and secure the Rights and Liberty of ourselves & our Posterity. . . . The Ministry in Great Britain, as well as the Torys here, have indeed constantly accused us of engaging in the War to avoid the Payment of our Debts; but every honest Man has denyed so injurious a Charge, with Indignation."[13]

Washington, Madison, and Mason stood together as two opposing factions developed in Virginia composed of those who did and those who did not favor payment of private obligations to British creditors. But Mason diverged from the other two when a division occurred between those who did and those who did not favor providing the central government with a direct source of funds with which to pay the public debt of the United States. Alexander Hamilton had advocated a grant of independent tax powers since 1779, when he outlined a plan to enlarge the Articles of Confederation, conveying to the Congress powers to lay and collect taxes, establish banks, regulate commerce, and exercise powers of enforcement on the states.

Between 1781 and 1783, Congress had requisitioned the states for $10 million to pay interest on the French and Dutch loans; by June 1784, it had received only $1.5 million. Congressional finance committees wrestled with proposals for alternatives to requisition. In February 1781, the states were unsuccessfully requested "to vest a power in Congress to levy a five per cent ad valorem duty on imports, to be collected by its own revenue agents." The proposal was revived in 1783 when demobilization of the army approached: long unpaid men were unlikely to disband without demur. Hamilton, who strongly favored the impost, thought grumbling by the troops might be a good thing: "If no excesses take place I shall not be sorry that ill-humours have appeared." He queried Washington: "There are dangerous prejudices in the particular states opposed to those measures which alone can give stability and prosperity to the Union. There is a fatal opposition to Continental views. Necessity alone can work a reform. But how to apply it and how keep it within salutary bounds?"[14]

Year by year, to Mason and others, Washington had more and more firmly urged the grant of new powers: when news came of the definitive conclusion of peace, he assured Hamilton: "No man in the United States is, or can be more deeply impressed with the necessity of a reform in our present Confederation than myself. No man perhaps has felt the bad effects of it more sensibly."[15] During ceremonies at Annapolis on 22 December 1783, his last act as general of the army reiterated this concern: at the dinner preceding the ball in his honor, after the thirteen scheduled toasts had been drunk, he volunteered one more: "Competent powers to Congress for general purposes!"

But Congress received no new powers. Mason's opposition to the impost illustrated what Madison, who was strongly in favor of it, had in 1783 termed his "heterodoxy" in being "too little impressed with either the necessity or the proper means of preserving the Confederacy." Mason's "fatal opposition to Continental views" was boldly written into Fairfax County's instructions to its Assembly delegates:

We desire and instruct you strenuously to oppose all encroachments of the American Congress upon the sovereignty and jurisdiction of the separate States; and every assumption of power, not expressly vested in them, by the Articles of Confederation. If experience shall prove that further powers are necessary and safe, they can be granted only by additional articles to the Confederation. . . .

And in particular we desire and instruct you to oppose any attempts which may be made by Congress to obtain a perpetual revenue, or the appointment of revenue officers. . . .

We like not the language of the late address from Congress to the different States, and of the report of their committee upon the subject of revenue. . . . The very style is alarming. The proposed duties may be proper, but the separate States only can safely have *the power of levying taxes*. Congress should not have even the appearance of such a power. . . . When the same man, or set of men, holds both the sword and the purse, there is an end of liberty.[16]

The problems of the "half-starved, limping government, always moving on crutches and tottering every step," of which Washington predicted the worst consequences in 1784, began to affect the conduct of foreign affairs. Returning to America as chargé d'affaires in 1785 after a year's leave in France, Chevalier Louis-Guillaume Otto, in a "Mémoire" to the Comte de Vergennes, answered the question: *Will the Congress be in a position to pay portions of the principal and interest due to His Majesty?* with a bleak estimate:

It is easy to see that, in the actual state of American finances, it would be impossible to get, beyond the annual expenses of the government, the interest and portions of the principal due us. . . . Congress's means are extremely limited and the criminal obstinacy of the state of Rhodeisland in refusing a 5 per cent tax [the impost] deprives it of the only resource which was left to fulfill its obligations. Taxes furnish barely a sixth of the estimated returns, and among the debts of the United States there is one even more sacred than ours, that of the army . . . it is impossible that they will not first try to satisfy these brave men who in the most critical periods displayed a courage, a patriotism, and a perseverance of which there is no other example in history.[17]

By 1785, John Adams was in London and Thomas Jefferson in France as ministers appointed by the United States, but when the former broached the possibility of a commercial treaty, the British foreign minister pointedly inquired whether he meant one treaty or thirteen. In midsummer of 1786, Charles Pinckney of South Carolina brought in a series of proposed amendments to the confederation, whose opening article would have vested in Congress exclusive power of regulating commerce and laying and collecting duties on imports and exports (though with the resulting funds accruing to the individual states); but it died without consideration.

Yet in the second half of the 1780s, these pressing public problems did not prevent individual enjoyment of postwar domestic tranquility. From New England to Virginia, men whose names had become nationally known during the Revolution embellished their physical surroundings and settled—they were growing older—into an establishment* of which order was a pleasant and increasingly prized feature. John Brown's new brick mansion in Providence, Rhode Island, had an address that symbolized the trend: it stood (and stands) on the corner of Power and Benefit streets. At Thomaston, Maine, in the early 1790s, Ebenezer Alden built Montpelier for General John Knox, founding father of the Cincinnati, the postwar association of former Continental and French officers, and Washington's secretary of war. In Quincy, Massachusetts, in 1787, John and Abigail Adams moved from their barn-red house with white trim, on the same grounds as the house where he was born, to the commodious structure more than a mile away which became the seat of the Adams dynasty. In New York, Gouverneur Morris bought Morrisania from his half-brother. In Philadelphia, by the early 1780s, Robert Morris had acquired the house sequestered from Richard Penn, Pennsylvania's last proprietor; George Grieve, translator of *Travels in North America in the Years 1780, 1781, and 1782* by the Marquis de Chastellux, noted him as "the first who has introduced the luxury of hot-houses, and ice-houses on the continent. He has likewise purchased the elegant country house formerly occupied by the traitor, Arnold, nor is his luxury to be outdone by any commercial voluptuary of London."[18] Yet Morris commissioned Pierre l'Enfant to build him a still more stately marble mansion

*Mount Vernon*
*by an unknown artist,*
*c. 1792; the earliest-*
*known artist's rendering*
*(courtesy, The*
*Mount Vernon Ladies'*
*Association)*

after he relinquished this house for the use of Washington as president in 1790.

At Mount Vernon, Washington, in bucolic relaxation, completed the interior of his "new room," framed by Lund* during his absence: the entablature over the doors displayed the tools of agriculture, crossed rakes and scythes, while his English friend, Samuel Vaughan, who sketched the layout of house and garden in 1787, sent him a marble mantel carved with pastoral scenes from his own estate in Wansted. The Washingtons were indeed in need of banqueting space—the flow of visitors that began with the freshet of north-bound French officers in the early summer of 1782[†] did not cease during his lifetime.

Jefferson undertook a Palladian reconstruction of Monticello as soon as he returned from France in 1789; among the many friends and neighbors to whom he dispensed architectural advice was Madison, who added wings to Montpelier in anticipation of his marriage to Dolley Payne Todd in 1794. Somewhat later, James Monroe's Oak Hill signaled that family's rise from his grandfather's overseership at John Mercer's Marlborough. With the exception of Jefferson, whose fascination with architecture never interfered with his agrarian philosophy, these men of property formed a national constituency for a politics of stability.

While there were no external additions to Gunston Hall during the years when other men's mansions were expanding, Mason was

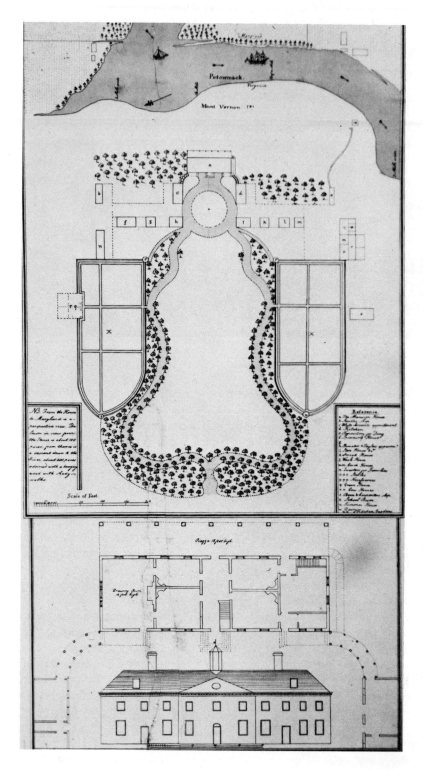

*Mount Vernon,
nineteenth-century
lithograph by
R. von Glumer after
Samuel Vaughan,
1787*
*(courtesy, The
Mount Vernon Ladies'
Association)*

comfortably busy adding to his domestic possessions and settling his sons on new estates.

At this time, he ordered from London silver displaying the family's English connections. When his son John was abroad at the end of the decade, silversmith Joshua Johnson gave him a copy of the order: "The Mason arms of the Stratford-upon-Avon in Warwickshire, and the Thompson arms of Yorkshire quartered together, with the following motto, *Pro Republica Semper*, to be engraved on such pieces of silver as will properly admit of it, and the crest of the said arms upon the other pieces. The above Mason arms are, viz: a point with three battlements charged with as many fleurs-de-lis, on the middle battlement a dove with wings displayed proper, and may be easily found in the Herald's office, where they are more particularly described." The crest of these arms is to be seen on the tea and coffee services now at Gunston Hall; the arms are described in Burke's *General Armory*.

All of Mason's children lived nearby. Of the four girls, Nancy became the wife of Rinaldo Johnson of Aquasco, Maryland. Mary Thomson's husband was John Cooke of West Farm in Stafford, and Betsey's, William Thornton of The Cottage in King George County. Sally, married to Daniel McCarty of Cedar Grove, lived closest to Gunston Hall. Grandchildren were born—and died. In February 1785, when Sally lost a little daughter, Mason advised:

> I most sincerely condole with you for the loss of your dear little girl, but it is our duty to submit with all the resignation human nature is capable of to the dispensation of Divine Providence which bestows upon us our blessings, and consequently has a right to take them away. . . . Your dear baby has died innocent and blameless, and has been called away by an all wise and merciful Creator, most probably from a life of misery and misfortune, and most certainly to one of happiness and bliss. . . . I would by all means advise you to lose a little blood without delay, and to take two or three times a day twenty or thirty drops of spirits of lavender of which I send you some by the bearer. I am, my dear child, Your affectionate father.[19]

The eldest and youngest sons married sisters. In March 1784, Mason sent Arthur Lee a letter to "be delivered you by my Son George; who comes to Annapolis, I believe, to furnish himself with some matrimonial aparatus." George, Jr.,'s wife was Elizabeth Mary Ann Barnes of Barnesfield in King George County; almost a decade later, her younger sister Sarah married George's younger brother Thomas. William likewise found a wife in King George, Ann Stuart of another Cedar Grove. Thomson's Sarah Chichester, of Newington, was a Fairfax County girl. John went furthest afield for a bride: his Anna Maria Murray came from Annapolis.

Two of Mason's sons became proprietors of existing properties: William's Mattawoman in Maryland had belonged to his maternal grandparents, and Thomas, when grown, took over the Mason estate at Woodbridge with its ferry over the Occoquan opposite Colchester. But young George's home, Lexington, below Gunston on the Dogue's

Neck peninsula, was new, and so was Thomson's Hollin Hall, adjacent to the Mount Vernon acres between Dogue's Run and Little Hunting Creek; it repeated the name of the seventeenth-century home of the Thomsons near Ripon in Yorkshire; John Mason's house with its fine garden on Analostan Island opposite Georgetown was built shortly after his father's death.

In addition to holdings in the vicinity, Mason expected to leave his family very considerable tracts in the west. His last letter to George before the latter's return from abroad in 1783 brought good news: "I have got all my back-Lands judiciously located, in one Body, upon Panther Creek, a Branch of Green River. . . . I expect the surveys will be compleated this Winter; I have been once or twice disappointed in making my Surveys, by the Incursions of the Indians; which has run me to great Expence. These Lands will cost me, by the time the Title is compleated, not less than £1,000 Specie; but if I can secure & settle them, they will, in twenty years, be worth forty or fifty thousand Pounds to my Family."[20]*

Yet even in a society where individuals enjoyed a large measure of economic self-sufficiency, personal tranquility could not be sustained in the midst of growing public disintegration. In flushed exercise of their sovereign powers, the states were inhibiting trade by commercial restrictions that blocked the passage of farm produce from New Jersey into New York, brought Pennsylvanians into armed conflict with Connecticut settlers in the Wyoming Valley, exacerbated boundary disputes, and infused new vitality into ancient conflicting claims regarding waterways. Pennsylvania proposed to join the Delaware and Chesapeake Bays by a canal across the northern tip of Delaware. Navigation in general and the Potomac Company's projected canal connecting the Potomac and the Ohio were in lively dispute between Virginia and Maryland.

Mason began to consider a return to public life; his letters to a number of Assembly members in May 1783 included a paragraph such as this:

"It gave me much Satisfaction to see your Name again in the List of the Members of the Assembly. I retired from public Business from a thorough Conviction that it was not in my Power to do any Good, & very much disgusted with Measures, which appeared to me inconsistent with common Policy and Justice. I see from the Acts which have been passed since, the same System has still been pursued; Yet this has not extinguished my Love for my Country; and if I recover tollerable Health, and shou'd find just Cause to think I can do any important public Service, I will return again to the Assembly. I have great Hopes from a State of Peace & Tranquility."[21]

Yet, as the spring election of 1784 approached, he sent an irate note to his friend Martin Cockburn: "I have been lately inform'd that some People intend to open a Pole for me at the Election to-morrow for this County. I hope this will not be offered; for as I have repeatedly declared that I can not serve the County, at this time, as one of it's Representatives, I shou'd look upon such Attempt, in no other Light than as an oppressive & unjust Invasion of my personal Liberty; and was I to be elected under such Circumstances, I shoud most certainly refuse to act."[22]

Passage by the 1784 session of a Port Act limiting the landings of ships not owned by Virginians roused Mason to write a pamphlet condemning the measure, but it was 1786 before he accepted election to the Assembly, and then, as Washington's diary shows, rather to his neighbor's surprise. "The suffrages of the people fell upon col. Mason and Doctr. Stuart—on the first contrary to, and after he had declared he could not serve—and on the other whilst he was absent at Richmond—Captn. West who had offered his services & was present, was rejected—the votes were—for Colo. Mason, 109—For Doctr. Stuart, 105—and for Captn. West 84."[23]

Mason wryly notified John Harvie, "My County has once more sent me into the Assembly, very contrary to my Inclination, & to every Remonstrance I cou'd make against it. If the present House of Delegates is composed of such Materials as the two or three last, I despair of being able to do any essential public Service. The only agreeable Reflection that presents itself to me, on the Occasion is, that I shall meet with some of my old Assembly Friends."[24]

A difficult agenda awaited him, and on some issues his friends were not sure where he stood. Virginians in Congress were very worried about Jay's negotiations with Gardoqui as they affected navigation of the Mississippi. A commercial connection with Spain was generally desired throughout the confederation, but a sectional split occurred when Spain attempted to exact as part of its price for a treaty an agreement under which Americans would forego use of the Mississippi as a channel of overseas commerce. The eastern states, having no stake in the matter, were entirely willing to accept this restriction; to the southern states, especially to the Kentuckians of Virginia, use of the river constituted a vital interest. Henry Lee summarized the split to Washington:

It is suggested that the project of the treaty will become the subject of deliberation in the Assembly of Virginia. . . . The eastern states consider a commercial connexion with Spain, as the only remedy for the distresses which oppress their citizens, most of which they say flow from the decay of their commerce. In this opinion they have been joined by two of the middle states. On the other hand, Virginia has with equal zeal opposed the connection, because the project involves expressly the disuse of the navigation of the Mississippi for a given time, and eventually they think will sacrifice our right to it. . . . Should this matter come before our Assembly, much will depend on Mr. Mason's sentiment.[25]

On the monetary problem, Mason's friends had no doubts of his help. The previous August, Madison had briefed Jefferson on the pressures for new issues of paper in various states, including Virginia: "My hopes rest chiefly on the exertions of Col. Mason, and the failure of experiments elsewhere,"[26] and in April he again deplored the "strong itch beginning to return for paper money. Mr. Henry is said to have the measure in contemplation, and to be laying his train for it already. He will however be powerfully opposed by Col. Mason, if he should be elected and be able to serve, by Monroe and Marshal, and Ludwell Lee (son of R. H. L.) who are already elected."[27] To these two friends, Mason's election brought rejoicing; Madison wrote: "A great many changes have taken place in the late elections. The principal acquisitions are Col. George Mason who I am told was pressed into the service at the instigation of Genl. Washington,* Genl. Nelson, Mann Page. . . . Among the many good things which may be expected from Col. Mason, we may reckon perhaps an effort to review our Constitution. The loss of the port bill will certainly be one condition on which we are to receive his valuable assistance."

On one subject, however, Madison still felt the doubt he had expressed to Jefferson three years previously: "I am not without fears . . . concerning his federal ideas. The last time I saw him he seemed to have come about a good deal towards the policy of giving Congress the management of Trade. But he has been led so far out of the right way that a thorough return can scarcely be hoped for. On all other great points, the Revised Code, the Assize bill, taxation, paper money, &c. his abilities will be inestimable."[28]

Yet when the time came, "the longest and most severe Fit of the Gout, I ever experienced" kept Mason from attending the session. On 4 December, Madison forecast to Jefferson the likelihood that he would miss the entire session: "Repeal of the port bill has not yet been attempted. Col. Mason has been waited for as the hero of the Attack. As it is become uncertain whether he will be down at all, the question will probably be brought forward in a few days. The repeal were he present would be morally certain. Under the disadvantage of his absence, it is more than probable. The question of British debts has also awaited his patronage. I am unable to say what the present temper is on that subject, nothing having passed that could make trial of it."[29]

Yet for the time being, Madison's forebodings seemed exaggerated; in the autumn of 1785, Mason had not only been appointed by the Assembly but had been in sufficiently good health to serve as a Virginia commissioner at the first of the consultations on interstate trade disputes, which expanded into the Constitutional Convention at Philadelphia. And in May of 1787, accepting appointment to Virginia's delegation, he set out on the longest journey he ever took from Gunston Hall.

# Chapter XII
# Building the Federal Structure

*Mason and Madison were the only two men to be appointed commissioners to all three of the successive meetings from which the federal constitution emerged: the negotiations between Maryland and Virginia on trade and navigation of the Potomac leading to the Mount Vernon Convention of 1785; the enlarged interstate discussion of trade questions at Annapolis in 1786; and the constitution-making convention at Philadelphia in 1787. Yet neither man attended the complete series; through an administrative oversight, Madison was not notified of his appointment to the first, and illness forced Mason to be excused from service at the second.\* Both were present at the third.*

The terms of Maryland's first charter had included jurisdiction over the Potomac to the high-tide mark on the Virginia shore, and on the attainment of separate statehood Virginia had left this stipulation unchallenged, though Virginian sailing ships traded from port to port along the waters dividing the two states, and fishermen, oystermen, and clam-diggers from the Old Dominion practiced their craft, disputatiously, in likely depths and profitable shallows. The location and operation of lighthouses, the designation of ports of entry and customs inspections, the rules of navigation, and, during the Revolution, the maintenance of shore batteries and other means of defense caused more or less continual friction. In 1778, commissioners to mitigate these discords had been appointed by the Virginia Assembly, but the British blockade shortly reduced activity in bay and river.

By June 1784, the revival of trade had renewed the need for consultation. The Virginia Assembly named Mason, Edmund Randolph, Alexander Henderson, and James Madison to meet with Maryland representatives and "frame such liberal and equitable regulations . . . as may be mutually advantageous." But Governor Henry's office neglected to notify the delegation either of its appointment or of the time and place of meeting proposed by Maryland's governor; as a result, the arrival of Daniel of St. Thomas Jenifer, Thomas Stone, and Samuel Chase in Alexandria in March 1785 required hasty action; Washington and Mason had quickly to fill the breach. Mason wrote Madison afterwards: "I shou'd not have known that I was one of the Persons appointed, had I not, by mere Accident two or three Days before the Meeting, been informed of it, by two of the Maryland Commissioners writing to me, that they shou'd endeavour to take my House in their Way, and go with me to Alexandria."[1]

Alexander Henderson was in Alexandria; he, Mason, and the Marylanders waited several days for the two missing Virginians. When a letter from Randolph to Mason on another matter indicated he knew nothing of the conference, Mason and Henderson proceeded on behalf of Virginia: papers in Washington's possession on parallel negotiations with Pennsylvania indicated that any two commissioners could legally act.

On Washington's invitation, the conference adjourned to Mount Vernon; on 24 March, he "sent my carriage to Alexandria for Col. Mason according to appointment, who came in about dusk"; the others arrived about one o'clock the next day. Over the ensuing weekend, terms were worked out, and Mason returned to Gunston in Washington's carriage, sending back with the coachman "some young shoots of the Persian Jessamine and Guelder rose."*

Mason and Henderson transmitted the results of the conversations to the speaker of the House. They had negotiated a twelve-point accord covering navigation, port duties, fishing rights, safety measures, and jurisdiction over trials of piracies, violations of commercial regulations, or other crimes occurring on the water. They had prepared an address to the president of the Pennsylvania Council, describing plans of Maryland and Virginia to extend navigation of the Potomac westward and to open a road from the head of navigation to the waters running into the Ohio and requesting Pennsylvania's concurrence in the use of those parts of the Ohio and its branches lying within Pennsylvania, goods using this route to enjoy free transit other than maintenance tolls. After returning to Maryland, the delegates of that state gave notice of the Mount Vernon Compact to Delaware and invited its official participation in a similar measure for upper Chesapeake Bay.

The commissioners likewise urged application to Congress for permission to enter into an interstate compact for naval protection, for agreement on the value of foreign gold and silver coins passing as specie in the two states, for legal procedures affecting commercial instruments, and for a schedule of duties on imports and exports, all these matters to be reviewed annually at a regular meeting of representatives of the two states.

But it then developed that the Virginia Assembly had stipulated the participation of three Virginia commissioners, not two, in the making of the compact and that instead of covering the Potomac, the Pokomoke, and the relevant parts of Chesapeake Bay, the agreement was to have been confined to the Potomac. Mason complained to Madison that he supposed "This blundering Business . . . will give me the Trouble & Expence of a Journey to Richmond, next Session, to appologize for, & explain our Conduct."[2] But he was felled by gout, Maryland ratified the compact without dissent, and Madison managed Virginia's ratification so deftly that the House approved it as it stood by the end of December.

Greatly encouraged, Madison promptly proposed another and more inclusive conference: on the final day of its session in January 1786, the House authorized a call for a gathering at which, in the words of Governor Henry's invitation, commissioners should "take into consideration the Trade of the UNITED STATES to examine the relative Situations and Trade of the said States to consider how far an uniform System in their commercial Regulations may be necessary to their common Interest and their permanent Harmony."[3] Annapolis was selected as the site, and the date set for 11 September.

Attendance was disappointing. Only a dozen men, representing the five states of Virginia, Pennsylvania, Delaware, New Jersey, and New York, actually arrived. The three Virginians present were Randolph, Madison, and St. George Tucker. Alexander Hamilton was there from New York, prepared to lead the pressure for stronger central institutions on which he and Washington had been determined from the war years.

Because of "so partial and defective a representation," after waiting four days for further arrivals the delegates concluded that they should refrain from action. But with John Dickinson in the chair, they expressed "their earnest and unanimous wish, that speedy measures may be taken, to effect a general meeting, of the States, in a future Convention. . . . In this persuasion, your Commissioners submit an opinion, that the Idea of extending the powers of their Deputies, to other objects, than those of Commerce . . . will deserve to be incorporated into that of a future Convention."[4] Accepting a report pre-

*"Britain's State Pilot," 1779, showing figures representing France, Spain, and the Netherlands, with Lord North in the boat*
*(courtesy, The Trustees of the British Museum)*

pared by Hamilton, it was voted to seek a meeting at Philadelphia on the second Monday in May 1787 "to devise such further provisions as shall appear to them necessary to render the constitution of the Foederal Government adequate for the exigencies of the Union; and to report such an Act for that purpose to the United States in Congress assembled, as when agreed to, by them, and afterwards confirmed by the Legislatures of every State, will effectually provide for the same."[5]

Preparations for this convention figured largely in the dispatches sent to their governments by the diplomats that the European powers, after recognizing American independence, had sent to New York to keep an eye on events—and on each other.* In point of service, the senior diplomat was the Chevalier Louis-Guillaume Otto, who had been secretary to the French Minister from 1779 to 1784. Pieter Johan van Berckel represented the Dutch Estates General. Spain's Don Diego Gardoqui was less concerned about general developments than about his prolonged negotiations with the confederation's secretary of state, John Jay, on a treaty of navigation and commerce. Great Britain, though accepting John Adams as minister to the Court of St. James in 1785, reciprocated only by consular appointments until 1792, naming John (after 1789, Sir John) Temple, who had three generations of New England connections behind him, as consul general.

For several years before 1787, these observers had reported in chorus the disintegration of the new nation, especially its financial difficulties. By 1787, Otto regarded the Congress as "actually only a phantom of sovereignty, destitute of powers, of energy, and of respect";[6] Temple, alarmed by the violence of Shays's rebellion, when farmers in the western part of Massachusetts presented their grievances at pitchfork point, closed the courts, and seized the Springfield arsenal, declared, "It is plain my Lord Things cannot long remain as they are; there is an universal Relaxation of Law & Justice, and a total want of Energy thro'out the States." Temple was not sanguine that the disintegration could be reversed at Philadelphia: "So many different sentiments and clashing interests will probably meet in contact upon the occasion, that great doubts are justly entertained whether any measure will be unanimously adopted by the convention; or, if that should happen, whether all the States will ratify and abide by what the delegates determine upon."[7] Otto shared his alarm, "A radical vice afflicts the structure of these states, one which will always oppose a perfect union: in reality, these states have no pressing desire to be under a single head. Their political aims, limited to their commercial interests, incite in them a reciprocal aversion and jealousy, passions which during the war were absorbed by enthusiasm for liberty and independence, but which now begin to revive in full force."[8] Yet he was impressed by the caliber of the men coming to Philadelphia: "even in Europe a more impressive assembly in respect to talents, familiarity with affairs, disinterestedness and patriotism will never have been seen. General Washington, Dr. Franklin and a large number of other personages as distinguished if less well known in Europe, have been summoned."[9]

Virginia and six other states had already named delegates by 21 February 1787 when Congress formally authorized a convention "for the sole and express purpose of revising the Articles of Confederation"; thereafter five of the remaining six did so. Only Rhode Island, torn by factional enmities, did not participate.*

The Virginia delegation, chosen by the Assembly on 4 December 1786, originally consisted of Washington, Madison, Wythe, Henry, the newly elected governor Edmund Randolph, John Blair, and Mason. When Patrick Henry, indifferent to the need of a stronger central government, declined membership, Randolph offered the post to Thomas Nelson and, when he refused, to Richard Henry Lee, who pled both ill health and a conviction that no member of Congress should sit in the Convention.[†] Randolph then named Dr. James McClurg, a man without previous political experience—he had been Virginia's wartime head of hospitals.

Until mid-March, Washington's acceptance was in doubt. The date and place of the meeting presented him with a problem. On resigning his commission, he had declared his firm intention to retire. He had notified the Society of the Cincinnati that he would not accept reelection and would not attend their triennial convention scheduled for Philadelphia at the same time as the political gathering. More important than this, Shays's rebellion had just been put down by armed force at the battle of Petersham, and Washington believed "there are combustibles in every State which a spark might set fire to." If the Philadelphia meeting turned out to be as sparsely attended as the Annapolis session, of which he had harbored great hopes, or if its labors failed to arrest the current disintegration, he would have staked his prestige and lost. Not until 9 April did he unenthusiastically confirm to Randolph his intention to attend, hoping, he said, "for the best."

In this mood, he started north on 9 May in advance of the rest of the Virginia delegation, riding through a rain-soaked countryside in order to put in an appearance at the Cincinnati meeting before the Convention opened. Four days later he made a triumphal entry into Philadelphia, escorted from Chester by senior officers of his old command, joined by cavalry detachments outside the city, and heralded on arrival by artillery salvos, bell-ringing, and citizen crowds. His courtesy call on Franklin, now president of Pennsylvania's unicameral Assembly, united two men who had not seen each other since 1776.

Washington had expected to lodge at Mrs. House's, a genteel establishment long favored by Virginia members of Congress, but the Robert Morrises so strongly pressed an invitation to stay at their imposing home that the general made it his headquarters.

To avoid any slipup, Governor Randolph had written Mason three times telling him of his appointment and urging him to attend; an invitation to Randolph to stop at Gunston on his way north accom-

*View of the City of Philadelphia, drawn by Joseph Holland, etched by Gilbert Fox, 1797 (courtesy, The Historical Society of Pennsylvania)*

panied Mason's unqualified acceptance. However, at the Convention's scheduled opening on 14 May, only representatives of the host state and two Virginians, Washington and Madison, appeared. Swollen streams and mired roads were partly responsible: before nightfall, Randolph, Wythe, Blair, and McClurg rode or drove into town, and the arrival of Mason, accompanied by his son, John,* completed the Virginia roster on Thursday, the seventeenth. Yet it was not until Friday, the twenty-fifth, that enough representatives were present for the Convention to organize; by that time, at least one member had appeared from all states except New Hampshire, Connecticut, and Maryland.†

During the interval, Mason informed his son George, the Virginia delegation took advantage of the opportunity, to "meet & confer together two or three Hours, every Day; in order to form a Correspondence of Sentiments"; it was from the ideas advanced in these six- or seven-man discussions that the Virginia Plan, introduced on 29 May by Governor Randolph, took shape, and Mason's description suggests an accord in which he fully joined. Likewise, "for Form's Sake, and to see what new Deputies are arrived, & to grow into some Acquaintance with each other, [we] regularly meet, every Day, at 3 O'Clock P:M: at the State-house."[10]

They were comfortably settled at the Indian Queen on 4th Street, "where we are very well accommodated, & have a good Room to ourselves, & are charged only 25s. Pensylva. Curry. ♃ Day, including our Servants & Horses, exclusive of Club in Liquor, & extra Charges; so that I hope I shall be able to defray my Expences with my public Allowance; & more than that I do not wish."[11]

The delegation also called upon the president of Pennsylvania; Mason assured George, who had taken a letter of introduction on his trip to France, that Dr. Franklin "enquired very particularly & kindly after you."[12]

And they engaged in some sightseeing: on their first Sunday in town, Mason and the others, except Washington who went the following week, attended the Roman Catholic Church, "more out of Compliment than Religion, & more out of Curiosity than compliment." Mason reacted as a low-church eighteenth-century Anglican:

There was a numerous Congregation; but an indifferent Preacher, I believe a Foreigner. . . . Altho' I have been in a Roman Catholic Chappel before, I was struck with the Solemnity of the Aparatus, & cou'd not help remarking how much every thing was calculated to warm the Imagination, & captivate the Senses. No wonder that this shou'd be the popular Religion of Europe. The Church Musick was exceeding fine; but while I was pleased with the Air of Solemnity so generally diffused thro' the Church, I was somewhat disgusted with the frequent Tinckling of a little Bell; which put me in Mind of the drawing up the Curtain for a Puppet-Shew. I wonder they have not substituted some more solemn & deep-toned Instrument.[13]

The Indian Queen was so solidly booked that, when Mrs. Randolph joined her husband and they took larger lodgings nearby, a scramble ensued for the vacated place. George Read of Delaware, regretting that his own room was too small to take a second bed, hurried John Dickinson to reserve Randolph's previous quarters.*

The only negative note in Mason's letters during this period concerned the strenuous wining and dining of delegates undertaken by the fashionable world of Philadelphia. Washington might enjoy taking tea with the Samuel Powels or the Benjamin Chews, attending a concert after dinner at the Morrises or visiting General Thomas Mifflin's country estate, but a single week of social protocol was more than enough for Mason: "It is impossible to judge how long we shall be detained here, but from present appearances I fear until July, if not later. I begin to grow heartily tired of the etiquette and nonsense so fashionable in this city. It would take me some months to make myself master of them, and that it should require months to learn what is not worth remembering as many minutes, is to me so discouraging a circumstance as determines me to give myself no manner of trouble about them."[14]

Wherever he was, Mason's thoughts were never far from his home, and about half of a letter to George at this time concerns George's current building operations and those planned for Thomson: "You are mistaken in thinking Paper will be as cheap as plaistering; because nothing will be saved by the Paper, but the third coat of Plaister; however as you prefer it, I will endeavour to procure it."[15]

But though he might rail at Philadelphia's frivolities and miss life at Gunston Hall, when the Convention opened on 25 May and Robert Morris's sole recorded utterance during its sessions, proposing the election of a president, brought Washington unanimously to the chair,* Mason was in a very positive mood.

His first letter to George, on 20 May, and an almost identical one to Arthur Lee the next day, advanced cautious optimism:

I have reason to hope there will be greater Unanimity, & less Opposition, except from the little States, than was at first apprehended. The most prevalent Idea, in the principal States seems to be a total Alteration of the present foederal System and substituting a great National Council, or Parliament, consisting of two Branches of the Legislature, founded upon the Principles of equal proportionate Representation, with full legislative Powers upon all the Objects of the Union; and an Executive: and to make the several State Legislatures subordinate to the National, by giving the latter the Power of a Negative upon all such Laws, as they shall judge contrary to the Interest of the foederal Union. It is easy to foresee that there will be much Difficulty in organizing a Government upon this great Scale, & at the same time reserving to the State Legislatures a sufficient Portion of Power for promoting & securing the Prosperity & Happiness of their respective Citizens. Yet, with a proper Degree of Coolness, Liberality, & Candour (very rare Commodities by the Bye) I doubt not but it may be effected.[16]

This confidence continued: on 1 June he impressed upon his son the long-term significance of what he and his colleagues were about to do and his appreciation of their capacities:

When I first came here, judging from casual Conversations with Gentlmen from the different States, I was very apprehensive that, soured & disgusted with the unexpected Evils we had experienced from the democratic Principles of our Governments, we shou'd be apt to run into the opposite Extreme . . . tho' I have the Pleasure to find, in the Convention, many Men of firm Republican Principles. America has certainly, upon this Occasion, drawn forth her first Characters; there are upon this Convention many Gentlemen of the most respectable Abilities; and, so far as I can yet discover, of the purest Intentions. The Eyes of the United States are turn'd upon this Assembly, & their Expectations raised to a very anxious Degree. May God grant we may be able to gratify them, by establishing a wise & just Government. . . . The Revolt from Great Britain, & the Formations of our new Governments at that time, were nothing compared with the great Business now before us. There was then a certain Degree of Enthusiasm, which inspired & supported the Mind; but to view, thro the calm sedate Medium of Reason, the Influence which the Establishments now proposed may have upon the Happiness or Misery of Millions yet unborn, is an Object of such Magnitude, as absorbs, & in a Manner suspends the Operations of the human Understanding.[17]

Mason's affirmative attitude doubtless profitted from the exceptional period of good health that he enjoyed that summer. He was present at the opening of the Convention and at its close, and the records of its debates show him to have been in consistent attendance during the more than three and a half months of its sitting. The impression of vigor that he conveyed to fellow-delegates was set

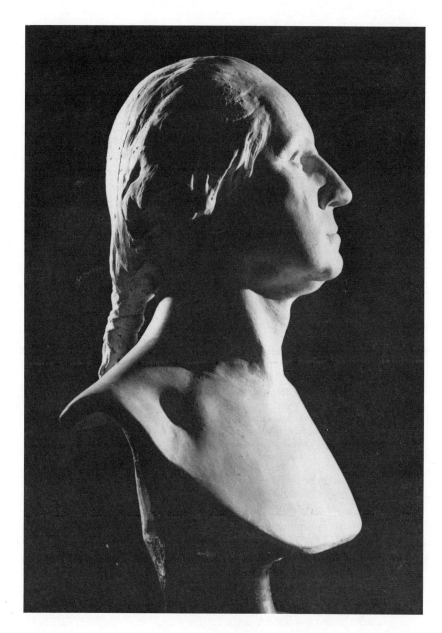

*Original clay bust of George Washington,
modeled from life at Mount Vernon by
Jean Antoine Houdon, 1785*
(courtesy, The Mount Vernon Ladies'
Association; photo, Marler)

down by William Pierce of Georgia: "Mr. Mason is a Gentleman of remarkable strong powers, and possesses a clear and copious understanding. He is able and convincing in debate, steady and firm in his principles, and undoubtedly one of the best politicians in America. Mr. Mason is about 60 years old, with a fine strong constitution."[18]

Among other impressions, an engaging picture of the delegates, including Mason, in the early days of the Convention, came from a lobbyist. Manasseh Cutler of Massachusetts represented the Ohio Company of Associates, formed the previous year in Boston by veterans who hoped their holdings of continental certificates could be applied at par to the purchase of a large tract in the new Northwest Territory. He had hovered around Congress in New York until it completed the Northwest Ordinance and had been a signatory to a government contract that then took up 1.5 million acres along the north bank of the Ohio at 66⅔ cents per acre. Afterwards he moved on to Philadelphia and put up at the Indian Queen:

This tavern is situated in Third Street, between Market Street and Chestnut Street, and is not far from the center of the city. It is kept in an elegant style, and consists of a large pile of buildings, with many spacious halls, and numerous small apartments, appropriated for lodging rooms....

Being told, while I was at tea, that a number of the Members of the Continental Convention . . . lodged in this house, and that two of them were from Massachusetts, immediately after tea, I sent into their Hall (for they live by themselves) to Mr. Strong and requested to speak with him. . . . Mr. Strong very politely introduced me to Mr. Gorham, of Charlestown, Mass; Mr. Madison and Mr. Mason and his son, of Virginia; Governor Martin, Hon. Hugh Williamson, of North Carolina; the Hon. John Rutledge and Mr. Pinckney, of South Carolina; Mr. Hamilton, of New York, who were lodgers in the house, and to several other gentlemen who were spending the evening with them.[19]

During this visit, Cutler twice ran up against the Convention's decision to meet in closed session. To George, Mason had anticipated adoption of such a rule: "It is expected our doors will be shut, and communications upon the business of the Convention be forbidden during its sitting. This I think myself a proper precaution to prevent mistakes and misrepresentation until the business shall have been completed, when the whole may have a very different complexion from that in which the several crude and indigested parts might in their first shape appear if submitted to the public eye."[20]

Cutler's first encounter with security occurred during a call on Dr. Franklin:

We found him in his Garden, sitting upon a grass plat under a very large Mulberry, with several other gentlemen and two or three ladies. . . . The Doctor showed me a curiosity he had just received, and with which he was much pleased. It was a snake with two heads, preserved in a large vial. . . . The Doctor mentioned the situation of this snake, if it was traveling among bushes, and one head should choose to go on one side of the stem of a bush and the other head should prefer the other side, and that neither of the heads would consent to come back or give way to the other. He was then going to mention a humorous matter that had that day taken place in Convention, in consequence of his comparing the snake to America, for he seemed to forget that everything in Convention was to be kept a profound secret; but the secrecy of Convention matters was suggested to him, which stopped him, and deprived me of the story he was going to tell.

He then found security measures in full force at the state house:

This is a noble building; the architecture is in a richer and grander style than any public building I have before seen. The first story is not an open walk, as is usual in buildings of this kind. In the middle, however, is a very broad cross-aisle, and the floor above supported by two rows of pillars. From this aisle is a broad opening to a large hall, toward the west end, which opening is supported by arches and pillars. In this Hall the Courts are held, and, as you pass the aisle, you have a full view of the Court. The Supreme Court was now sitting. This bench consists of only three judges. Their robes are scarlet; the lawyers, black. The Chief Judge, Mr. McKean, was sitting with his hat on, which is the custom, but struck me as being very odd, and seemed to derogate from the dignity of a judge. The hall east of the aisle is employed for public business. The chamber over it is now occupied by the Continental Convention, which is now sitting, but sentries are planted without and within—to prevent any person from approaching near—who appear to be very alert in the performance of their duty."[21]

*"View of the State-House at Philadelphia," 1793, showing tower as it was during 1781-1829; the Congress Hall at the right, where the new government met during the 1790s, was begun in 1787 and completed in early 1790*
*(courtesy, The Historical Society of Pennsylvania)*

When the Convention began serious business on 28 May and a committee headed by Wythe brought in proposed rules for the conduct of debate, Mason again exhibited the political sensitivity which had impressed William Pierce: in addition to approving the holding of debates in closed session, he, with William King of Massachusetts, successfully deleted a rule that would have permitted members to call for recorded votes as questions were discussed: "Such a record of the opinions of members would be an obstacle to a change of them on conviction; and in case of its being hereafter promulged must furnish handles to the adversaries of the Result of the Meeting."[22]

Likewise, the Virginia delegation helped postpone the emergence of one critical and inescapable conflict. Mason had observed to George on arrival that the instructions of some delegates, mostly from the small states, confined them to modification of the Articles of Confederation only and specified insistence that Convention decisions follow the voting rules that obtained under the articles, with votes taken by states on the principle of one sovereign, one vote. Pennsylvania's Philadelphia representatives were inclined to precipitate an early confrontation on this issue, but the rules as adopted merely declared that, for the Convention to act, not less than seven states must be represented.

Substantive matters first came before the body on 29 May, when Governor Randolph, as leader of the Virginia delegation, presented the plan on which he and his colleagues had been working since their arrival. As no other delegation had a comprehensive proposal ready, the Virginia Plan became the Convention's agenda. The experience of six of the seven men who had produced it comprised the main events of the recent American past. Mason was the major author of the first written constitution of modern times and of the bill of rights that preceded it. Madison, young as he was in 1776, was even then author of the innovative article on religious liberty; in 1784, he had thoughtfully drafted proposed revisions for the Virginia constitution; and now, at thirty-six, he was entering his full maturity, ready to become the major shaper of the new national document. Washington, as the man of all in America who had experienced most acutely the ineffectiveness of the confederation, was present to apply steady and documented pressure for adequate powers to the central government. Of the three lawyers, Wythe had behind him not only his long career as law professor at William and Mary but his congressional service at the time of the Declaration of Independence, his membership on Virginia's Committee of Law Revisors, and his speakership of the Virginia House of Delegates. Blair had been on the committee to prepare Virginia's bill of rights and constitution and was currently a judge of the state's Court of Appeals. Randolph had been his state's first attorney general, had led its delegation to the Annapolis Convention the previous year, and was now governor. Only McClurg, the physician, was without political credentials.

The plan that had taken form in the exchanges of this intimate group, as Mason had forecast to George when they began to work on it, went far beyond revision of the Articles of Confederation.* While there is no record of the talks at the Indian Queen, Mason's early participation in the Convention debates is a record of support of the document brought forward by Randolph. As of this date, he gave no evidence of the "heterodoxy" in being "too little impressed with either the necessity or the proper means of preserving the confederacy" which Madison reported to Jefferson after his visit to Gunston Hall four years earlier. On the contrary, he joined the discussion of clause after clause as a vigorous proponent of the establishment of a national government to replace the current league of sovereign states. In its initial provision, the Virginia Plan departed from the Articles of Confederation: it contemplated voting in a bicameral national legislature by state representatives whose numbers were proportioned either to existing state quotas of financial contribution to the confederation or to the number of free inhabitants of the states. The derivation of governmental power from the people was to be plainly evidenced by popular election, in the states, of the members of the lower house. These members were to be of a specified minimum age, to be salaried, and to be ineligible to other state or United States offices during their terms of service and for a specified period thereafter. In order to insure rotation in office, they were to be incapable of reelection for a specified time after serving their terms; and while in office they were to be subject to recall.

Where the lower house was designed to reflect popular sentiment, the upper house was to encourage stability. It was to be elected by the lower house from candidates of a specified minimum age nominated by the respective state legislatures. As in the lower house, members were to be salaried. Their terms were to be long enough to insure independence; they were to have the same ineligibilities as the lower house.

Both branches could initiate legislation; together, they were not only to enjoy the legislative powers vested in Congress under the Articles of Confederation but also "to legislate in all cases to which the separate States are incompetent, or in which the harmony of the United States may be interrupted by the exercise of individual Legislation."[23]

The executive, elected by the national legislature, should administer the powers of the central government for a specified term only; after this term, the executive should be ineligible for reelection. The powers conferred should be those vested in Congress under the confederation, together with a general authority over national law. Together with appropriate members of the national judiciary, the executive should serve as a revisory council to examine all acts of the national legislature before they took effect and to review any disallowances of acts of state legislatures; its decisions, however, should be subject to reversal by a vote of a specified portion of the national legislature.

A national judiciary should be established as the third major division of government, with inferior courts of first instance and supreme appellate tribunals. Judges of these courts were to be chosen by the national legislature and to hold office during good behavior. Their jurisdiction should extend to cases of piracies, felonies, etc., committed on the high seas; cases between foreigners and citizens of the United States; cases respecting collection of the revenue; impeachments of national officers; and a broad category described as "questions which may involve the national peace and harmony."[24]

In addition to the establishment of the three branches of government along these general lines, the Virginia Plan proposed provision for admission of new states into the union and guarantees to each state of a republican form of government. The Congress as existing under the Articles of Confederation should remain in being until the new articles of union were adopted. Amendments to the Articles of Confederation offered for acceptance by the present Convention and approved by Congress should be submitted to the states; their legislatures should convene popularly elected special assemblies for the purpose of ratification.

This plan, together with one by Charles Pinckney of South Carolina, based on the amendments to the Articles of Confederation he had proposed in Congress the previous year, was ordered submitted to the Convention, sitting under the chairmanship of Nathaniel Gorham of Massachusetts as a Committee of the Whole to consider the state of the American Union. In numbers almost daily augmented by new arrivals, the delegates then began to wrestle with the Virginians' proposals.

Since the Convention discussed in camera, contemporary evidence of what was said must be sought in the tersely stated official *Journal* published some years later and in members' private notes. Of these, Madison's are both the fullest and the most complete—he was present daily throughout the deliberations.* Much briefer and more fragmentary records, covering shorter periods of attendance, were kept by delegates Robert Yates of New York, who left the meeting in early July; Rufus King of Massachusetts; James McHenry of Maryland; William Pierce of Georgia; William Paterson of New Jersey; and Alexander Hamilton of New York; a few memoranda and drafts of speeches were found among Mason's papers. Together, they display in considerable detail the disorderly, detailed, day-to-day argument from which major determinations eventually emerged.

At one time or another, fifty-five of the seventy-three appointed delegates attended the sessions.† Technically, the Philadelphia Convention was a meeting of sovereign states; their accredited representatives approached each other as members of an alliance hitherto united in a loose confederacy. Yet Elbridge Gerry of Massachusetts correctly declared the states to be "neither the same Nation nor different Nations. We ought not therefore to pursue the one or the other of these ideas too closely."[25]

The most solid basis for unity was the common colonial experience. Delegates may have had only casual dealings with leaders in colonies other than their immediate neighbors, but all had had dealings with Whitehall. Likewise, almost without exception, they shared a record of first-hand, practical service in local government, and while differences in manners and mores separated the expertise of a selectman of a New England town from that of a gentleman justice of a southern county court, both were familiar with a broadly similar range of political issues. The great majority had served in the legislature of their colony or state, and over half were either attorneys or judges.

Three-quarters of the membership had taken part in the pre-revolutionary Continental Congress or the Congress of the Confederation; eight were signers of the Declaration of Independence; six, of the draft Articles of Confederation; seven, of the Annapolis Convention.

John Dickinson could advisedly counsel, "experience must be our only guide. Reason may mislead us."

The military past of about half of those in attendance added another dimension of unity: four delegates had been on Washington's immediate staff; more than a dozen others had been officers in the continental line, and a like number, officers of state militia. Ten were members of the Cincinnati. No one was more aware than they of the absence of a firm political center, of the confederation's weak civilian conduct of the war, its inability to supply men, material, and money, even money to pay the fighting men.

Most of the officers, moreover, in campaigning up and down the coast, had had opportunity to make themselves familiar with the daily life, customs, and circumstances of the several states. A certain number of civilians, too, and Madison in particular, had acquired friendships and experience outside their native jurisdictions through travel or education away from home; John Witherspoon could look down the delegate list and note the names of nine Princeton men.

In the limited geographic range of his familiarity, Mason was one of a minority: over the years, he had been unable to accept membership in his state's delegation to Congress, and this journey to Philadelphia was his first venture beyond the Virginia-Maryland area in which he was at home.

As the meeting got under way, while there was ready agreement that the confederation had proved itself inadequate, a common view had to be sought as to whether the confederation's successor should be a federal or a unitary structure. According to Yates, Randolph "candidly confessed" his plan "not intended for a federal government—he meant a strong *consolidated* union, in which the idea of states should be nearly annihilated";[26] and Delegate Gouverneur Morris of Pennsylvania, according to Madison, "explained the distinction between a *federal* and *national, supreme,* Govt.; the former being a mere compact resting on the good faith of the parties; the latter being a compleat and *compulsive* operation."[27] On the other hand, Delegate Roger Sherman, just in from Connecticut, seemed to Madison not to be "disposed to Make too great inroads on the existing system; intimating as one reason, that it would be wrong to lose every amendment, by inserting such as would not be agreed by the States."[28]

The New Yorkers had been authorized to attend the meeting in the exact words used by the Congress in calling it, "for the sole and express purpose of revising the Articles of Confederation"; two of the three men appointed, John Lansing, Jr., and Robert Yates, retired from the Convention in early July, subsequently advising their governor that "we have been reduced to the disagreeable alternative, of either exceeding the powers delegated to us, and giving our assent to measures which we conceive destructive to the political happiness of the citizens of the United States, or opposing our opinions to that of a body of respectable men, to whom these citizens had given the most unequivocal proofs of confidence."[29]

Virginia's credentials were far more flexible; "Mr. Mason observed that the present confederation was not only deficient in not providing for coercion & punishment agst. delinquent States; but argued very cogently that punishment could not in the nature of things be executed on the States collectively, and therefore that such a Govt. was necessary as could directly operate on individuals, and would punish those only whose guilt required it."[30]

Delegates differed vigorously on how direct the popular participation in government should be. Mason's 1 June letter to George was accurate: popular tumults, especially Shays's rebellion, had caused a reaction against democracy, particularly in New England, where earlier it had been most broadly practiced. As soon as the Convention turned to the proposition that the lower house of the national legislature be elected by the people of the states, Connecticut's Sherman declared his preference for choice by the state legislatures: "the people . . . should have as little to do as may be about the Government. They want information and are constantly liable to be misled."[31] Gerry of Massachusetts agreed: "The evils we experience flow from the excess of democracy. The people do not want virtue; but are the dupes of pretended patriots. . . . He had . . . been too republican heretofore: he was still however republican, but had been taught by experience the danger of the levilling spirit."[32]

Mason and Madison countered this view:* the former declared the lower house "was to be the grand depository of the democratic principle of the Govt.,"[33] and the latter, while approving "refining the popular appointments by successive filtrations" in the upper house, the executive, and the judiciary, held that "the great fabric to be raised would be more stable and durable if it should rest on the solid foundation of the people themselves, than if it should stand merely on the pillars of the Legislatures."[34]

The limits of democracy were considered in another context during decisions on the tenure of members of the upper house and the executive. If the persons in such places were to hold office during good behavior, a close-knit ruling group would almost inevitably establish itself; indeed if the executive powers were exercised by one man, his tenure would amount to a life monarchy. Such a prospect was congenial to those who, like Alexander Hamilton, cherished a great admiration for the British Constitution; the plan of government that he presented in a major speech during the third week of discussion envisaged "The supreme Executive authority of the United States to be vested in a Governour to be elected to serve during good behaviour."[35] Nor was Hamilton's royalism solitary: Gouverneur Morris approved life tenure for the executive, and Mason's twenty-eight-year-old cousin, John Francis Mercer, who after a wealthy marriage moved across the Potomac in 1785 and between 6 and 17 August attended the Convention as a Maryland delegate, was believed to be an out-and-out Royalist. Outside the Convention, Arthur Lee evidenced Royalist inclinations when he wrote young Thomas Shippen in England: "It is now manifest that we have not the public virtue and private temperance which are necessary to the establishment at least of free Republics; but that we have courage, enterprize and high mindedness enough to make a great and even illustrious people, under one Sovereignty consisting of an imperial head, a Senate for life, and an elective house of Comms."[36]

Whitehall was aware of this sentiment. Thomas Townshend, Viscount Sydney, alerted Lord Dorchester, former commander-in-chief in America and current governor of Quebec:

The report of an intention on the part of America to apply for a sovereign of the house of Hanover has been circulated here; and should an application of that nature be made, it will require a very nice consideration in what manner so important a subject should be treated . . . it will upon all accounts be advisable that any influence which your lordship may possess should be exerted to discourage the strengthening their alliance with the house of Bourbon, which must naturally follow were a sovereign to be chosen from any branch of that family.[37]

Opinion favored a fairly strong executive. At the opening of the Revolution, in reaction against the British king and the royal governors who acted in his name, most state constitutions had provided governorships in which the incumbent was little more than a figurehead, denied even a veto. In the same spirit, the Articles of Confederation had stipulated that no individual should be president for more than one year in every three. But the weakness and instability of such leadership was patent, and, unless the executive had a measure of independence, the doctrine of the balance of powers, affirmed by many state constitutions, became a demonstrable fiction.

The frequency with which Convention delegates changed their minds on the powers of the executive indicates the genuineness with which a meeting of minds was sought. The records of debate show members concurring, deferring, comparing, reconsidering, reconciling. Interspersed with other topics, the presidency was considered on twenty-one separate days. Thirty votes were taken on the method of choosing the chief executive; the electoral college system, first proposed on 19 July, was not adopted until 4 September.

Two other major problems, by contrast, were approached from adversary positions, with disagreement so profound and so unyielding as to threaten dissolution of the Convention. The first of these to surface concerned proper representation in the national legislature of states ranging in power and population from Virginia, Pennsylvania, and Massachusetts to Delaware and Rhode Island. As Mason had told George, Delaware's delegates came with a fixed position on this question—one state, one vote. Their strict instructions indicated the strength of the small states' fears lest they be overwhelmed. In introducing the New Jersey Plan as the small states' alternative to the Virginia Plan on 9 June, the governor, William Paterson, declared that "the proposition for a proportional representation" in the legislature struck at the existence of the lesser states and that "the small States would never agree to it."[38] The large state delegations were just as unwilling to see ignored an actual inequality whose extremes bracketed a population ratio of 10 to 1.

Yet the proportional representation favored by the large states contained its own difficulties: proportional to what? Population, wealth, and the existing schedule of quotas for contributions to the confederacy had all been suggested as a basis for calculations. Inseparable from such figures was the thorny question of slavery. A slave was a man; a slave was a property. How should he be counted? The great concentration of slaves was in the South. States without slaves would not accept the preponderance given to states with them by an enumeration that counted the men of both races. Yet to consider the white population alone would underrecord the effective weight of a state like South Carolina, where the 1790 census showed a white population of 140,178 and a black population of 108,895. Reconciliation of large and small state interests appeared intractable, almost insoluble.

Dr. Franklin's rare interventions in debate were frequently ceremonial. On 28 June, he rose to propose that in view of current discords, sessions be opened with prayer: "If a sparrow cannot fall to the ground without his notice, is it probable that an empire can rise without his aid?"[39] Hamilton and others objected that recourse to this practice at so late a date might alert outsiders to dissension within; Randolph disposed of the matter by suggesting the appropriateness of a Fourth of July sermon. Whether out of ignorance or because of a delicate suggestion, the *Pennsylvania Packet* of 19 July carried a widely copied item: "So great is the unanimity, we hear, that prevails in the Convention, upon all great federal subjects, that it has been proposed to call the room in which they assemble—Unanimity Hall."

The first outlines of a solution appeared when, by a vote of 6–4, with one state divided, the Convention proposed that "The right of suffrage in the first branch of the Legislature of the United States ought not to be according to the rule established in the articles of confederation, but according to some equitable ratio of representation,"[40] and Oliver Ellsworth of Connecticut moved that "in the second branch . . . each state shall have an equal vote."

Opening the debate, his colleague, William Samuel Johnson, said:

The fact is that the States do exist as political Societies, and a Govt. is to be formed for them in their political capacity, as well as for the individuals composing them. Does it not seem to follow, that if the States as such are to exist they must be armed with some power of self-defence. This is the idea of (Col. Mason) who appears to have looked to the bottom of this matter. . . . On the whole he thought as in some respects the States are to be considered in their political capacity, and in others as districts of individual citizens, the two ideas embraced on different sides, instead of being opposed to each other, ought to be combined; that in *one* branch the *people*, ought to be represented; in the *other, the States.*[41]

On 2 July, when with one state divided, a tie vote on Ellsworth's motion denied it passage, a Grand Committee, of one member from each state, was chosen by ballot to seek a way out of the impasse during the brief Independence Day recess. Mason was the Virginia member.

The major political compromise that enabled the Convention to move forward emerged from the inventiveness of this group, in which Roger Sherman substituted for Ellsworth, who had been taken ill. The Connecticut delegation proffered twin proposals on condition that both be adopted:

I. That in the 1st branch of the Legislature each of the States now in the Union shall be allowed 1 member for every 40,000 inhabitants of the description reported in the 7th Resolution of the Come. of the whole House: that each State not containing that number shall be allowed 1 member: that all bills for raising or appropriating money, and for fixing the Salaries of the Officers of the Governt. of the U. States shall originate in the 1st branch of the Legislature, and shall not be altered or amended by the 2d branch: and that no money shall be drawn from the public Treasury, but in pursuance of appropriations to be originated in the 1st branch.

II. that in the 2d branch each State shall have an equal vote.[42]

The proposals were promptly attacked. Madison "conceived that the Convention was reduced to the alternative of either departing from justice in order to conciliate the smaller States, and the minority of the people of the U. S. or of displeasing these by justly gratifying the larger States and the majority of the people."[43]

Gouverneur Morris, who had grown up in New York but was now a citizen of Pennsylvania, declared that "the whole aspect of it to be wrong. He came here as a Representative of America; he flattered himself he came here in some degree as a Representative of the whole human race; for the whole human race will be affected by the proceedings of this Convention. . . . State attachments, and State importance have been the bane of this Country. . . . Who can say whether he himself, much less whether his children, will the next year be an inhabitant of this or that State."[44]

On the side of the small states, Gunning Bedford, Jr., of New Jersey defended the proposition regarding the upper house: "the lesser States have thought it necessary to have a security somewhere. . . . In order to obtain this, the smaller have conceded as to the first branch, and as to money bills. If they be not gratified by correspondent concessions as to the 2d. branch is it to be supposed they will ever accede to the plan."[45]

Elbridge Gerry interceded for a greater spirit of accommodation: "If no compromise should take place what will be the consequence. . . . If we do not come to some agreement among ourselves some foreign sword will probably do the work for us."[46] To which, on behalf of the committee, Mason added:

The Report was meant not as specific propositions to be adopted, but merely as a general ground of accomodation. . . . However liable the Report might be to objections, he thought it preferable to an appeal to the world by the different sides, as had been talked of by some Gentlemen. It could not be more inconvenient to any gentleman to remain absent from his private affairs, than it was for him: but he would bury his bones in this city rather than expose his Country to the Consequences of a dissolution of the Convention without any thing being done.[47]

From this beginning, the legislative bodies that later in the Convention were named the House of Representatives and the Senate took form.

The extent to which, as of mid-July, Mason was in the forefront of the proponents of the Convention's plan was witnessed by a North Carolina delegate, William Blount, himself disgruntled with the course of the debate. His colleagues, he complained, "were in Sentiment with Virginia who seemed to take the lead. Madison at their Head tho Randolph and Mason also great."[48]

While far less divisive than the achievement of balance between the small states and the large, the relation between existing states and new ones to the west was also a subject of spirited canvass.

Vermont and Kentucky were visibly preparing to request statehood: they would eventually be followed by others, numerous and populous enough to outweigh the original thirteen. News of covert negotiations between western settlers and the Spanish had for several years alerted easterners to a possible breakaway of this territory. Its continued adherence to the United States was clearly to be desired, but some in the Convention were fully prepared to establish a new colonialism beyond the Appalachians. Gouverneur Morris wanted a Congress "so fixed as to secure to the Atlantic States a prevalence in the National Councils." Mason, who crossed swords with Morris more and more often, declared himself decidedly of opinion that if such states "made a part of the Union, they ought to be subject to no unfavorable discriminations"; Morris held to his view that "the Busy haunts of men not the remote wilderness, was the proper School of political Talents. If the Western people get the power into their hands they will ruin the Atlantic interests."[49]

The second problem to be debated from fixed positions with intransigent heat had its root in sectional economic interests. New England lived off its trade, the South off its staples. Northern prosperity came from the sea, from the carrying trade, from fishing on the Grand Banks, from foreign manufactures imported in New England bottoms. Southern prosperity came from the land, chiefly from exports of commodities raised on plantations cultivated by slave labor. From the beginning, this difference had underlain much discussion, though the clash it occasioned occurred fairly late in the debates. Madison, in early speeches on the conflict between small states and large, had observed that congressional voting records showed how infrequently the pros and cons on an issue represented voting according to state size; far more often, they reflected economic interests, and these divided rather than united the three most powerful states. Massachusetts depended on its fish; Pennsylvania on its flour; Virginia on its tobacco. "The great danger to our general government," he said, "*is the great southern and northern interests of the continent, being opposed to each other.*"[50]

The issue might have come up much earlier than it did if Mason had actually delivered a speech that in drafted form was found in his papers. On 4 June, temporary absence from the hall caused him to miss

*James Madison by Gilbert Stuart
(courtesy, Bowdoin College Museum of Art,
Brunswick, Maine)*

an important vote when the Convention decided that the executive power should be exercised by one man rather than by three. Madison recorded seven states for the motion, three against; Virginia's aye was by a close vote, with Madison, McClurg, and Washington in favor, Randolph and Blair against, and the other two paired: "Col. Mason being no, but not in house, Mr. Wythe ay but gone home."[51] In support of a three-man executive that would have institutionalized sectionalism, Mason had intended to urge:

> Have not the different parts of this extensive government, the several States of which it is composed a right to expect an equal participation in the Executive, as the best means of securing an equal attention to their interests? Should an insurrection, a rebellion or invasion happen in New Hampshire when the single supreme magistrate is a citizen of Georgia, would not the people of New Hampshire naturally ascribe any delay in defending them to such a circumstance and *vice versa*? If the Executive is vested in three persons, one chosen from the Northern, one from the Middle, and one from the Southern States, will it not contribute to quiet the minds of the people and convince them that there will be proper attention paid to their respective concerns? Will not three men so chosen bring with them, into office, a more perfect and extensive knowledge of the real interests of this great Union?[52]

But the sectional fissure did not open until the Convention—in a debate that caused a profound change in Mason's attitude toward the entire document—reached the question of what commercial powers should be exercised by the central government. Should it be allowed to pass acts regulating commerce by a simple majority? The staple states were alarmed lest excessive export duties be voted by representatives of states whose economies did not depend on exports. Should it be empowered to prohibit, or at least to tax, the importation of slaves? The arithmetic of legislative representation showed this to be possible.

New England was adamant that special voting rules such as requirement of a two-thirds or even a three-fourths majority should not limit enactment of duties and other trade regulations. South Carolina and Georgia were just as determined that the basis of their economies must not be subject to destruction by an unconcerned majority.

On 21 August a full-scale debate canvassed drafts of two related sections: "No tax or duty shall be laid by the Legislature on articles exported from any State; nor on the migration or importation of such persons as the several states shall think proper to admit; nor shall such migration or importation be prohibited. . . . No navigation act shall be passed without the assent of two-thirds of the members present in each House."[53]

Connecticut delegates feared that the power to tax exports was likely "to engender incurable jealousies"; Williamson of North Carolina pointed to Virginia's taxation of his state's tobacco when exported through Virginia ports as an instance of the evil of such a power. Mason stated "a principle often advanced & in which he concurred, that 'a majority when interested will oppress the minority' ";[54] the eight northern states with interests different from the five southern states would have 36 votes to 29 in the lower house. Other southerners affirmed that acceptance of a majority rule would "destroy the last hope of an adoption of the plan" in their area. Gouverneur Morris tried to dismiss the issue—"These local considerations ought not to impede the general interest."

Telling counterargument stressed the relation between the central government's possession of power over foreign trade and its effectiveness in the conduct of foreign policy. Wilson of Pennsylvania said that "a power over exports might be more effectual than that over imports in obtaining beneficial treaties of commerce,"[55] and Madison supported it on this and two other grounds: tariffs would be necessary not only for "procuring equitable regulations from other nations"[56] but also as a means of securing revenue for the central government and protecting the development of domestic manufactures.

As voting approached and resistance to the conferring of such power visibly stiffened, Clymer of Pennsylvania hazarded a proposal to confine commercial regulations to measures for securing revenue. It failed. Madison then attempted to save at least something by supporting the wording of the second proposal under consideration: restriction of the passage of trade measures by requirement of a two-thirds majority in each house was, he said, "a lesser evil than total prohibition."[57] Even this lost by a division of five states to six;* Virginia was in the negative, with Madison and Washington outvoted by Mason, Randolph, and Blair.

When discussion shifted to the clause forbidding regulation of the migration and importation of persons—the reference was to slaves—tempers rose, and a sharp division appeared between the states of the Upper South, Maryland and Virginia, where the slave population more than reproduced itself, and those of the Deep South, South Carolina and Georgia, whose supply depended on imports. Luther Martin of Maryland declared that "it was inconsistent with the principles of the revolution and dishonorable to the American character to have such a feature in the Constitution;"[58] he favored a power to prohibit or tax the importation of slaves because he thought the clause as it now stood would favor the traffic. He attempted to bulwark his argument by a general appeal: the increase of slavery, under the prospective rules for apportionment of representatives in the lower house, would increase the number of members from the southern states, yet slavery "weakened one part of the Union which the other parts were bound to protect."[59]

Rutledge of South Carolina replied in anger that "Religion & humanity had nothing to do with this question—Interest alone is the governing principle with Nations—The true question at present is whether the Southn. States shall or shall not be parties to the Union,"[60] and his colleague Pinckney declared: "South Carolina can never receive the plan if it prohibits the slave trade. In every proposed extension of the powers of Congress, that State has expressly & watchfully excepted that of meddling with the importation of negroes."[61]

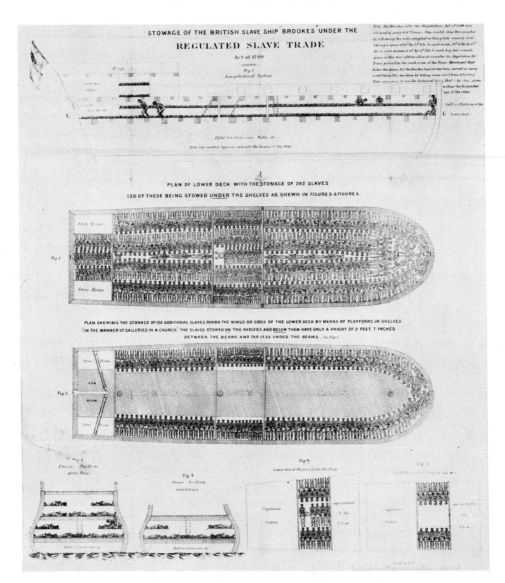

*"Stowage of the British Slave Ship 'Brookes' under the Regulated Slave Trade Act of 1788"*
(courtesy, Library of Congress)

Ellsworth and Sherman of Connecticut attempted peacemaking: the former suggested that the states were the best judges of their particular interests; since the slavery question had been avoided under the confederation, he saw no greater necessity for bringing it into the new plan. Sherman observed that "the abolition of slavery seemed to be going on in the U.S. & that the good sense of the several States would probably by degrees compleat it";[62] he proposed leaving the clause as it stood in the interest of having as few objections as possible to the proposed scheme of government.

But Mason, bent on using the new document to limit the institution that he had abhorred from his earliest years in public service, lashed out in pungent opposition:

This infernal trafic originated in the avarice of British Merchants. The British Govt. constantly checked the attempts of Virginia to put a stop to it. The present question concerns not the importing states alone but the whole Union. The evil of having slaves was experienced during the late war. Had slaves been treated as they might have been by the Enemy, they would have proved dangerous instruments in their hands. . . . Maryland & Virginia he said had already prohibited the importation of slaves expressly. N. Carolina had done the same in substance. All this would be in vain if S. Carolina & Georgia be at liberty to import. The Western people are already calling out for slaves for their new lands; and will fill that Country with Slaves if they can be got thro' S. Carolina & Georgia. Slavery discourages arts & manufactures. The poor despise labor when performed by slaves. They prevent the immigration of Whites, who really enrich & strengthen a Country. They produce the most pernicious effect on manners. Every master of slaves is born a petty tyrant. They bring the judgment of heaven on a Country. As nations can not be rewarded or punished in the next world they must be in this. By an inevitable chain of causes & effects providence punishes national sins, by national calamities. He lamented that some of our Eastern brethren had from a lust of gain embarked in this nefarious traffic. As to the States being in possession of the Right to import, this was the case with many other rights, now to be properly given up. He held it essential in every point of view, that the Genl. Govt. should have power to prevent the increase of slavery.[63]

The debate ended in recommittal. A Grand Committee was named, this time with Madison as the Virginia member. Gouverneur Morris remarked: "These things may form a bargain among the Northern & Southern States."[64]

The bargain was duly made. Its terms enabled the Convention to move forward, but they deferred to the long future the decision that the delegates were currently unable to take. The Grand Committee offered as substitute wording on the importation of slaves: "The migration or importation of such persons as the several States now existing shall think proper to admit, shall not be prohibited by the Legislature prior to the year 1800—but a Tax or Duty may be imposed on such migration or importation at a rate not exceeding the average of the Duties laid on Imports."[65]

At the same time, it proposed that the section requiring a two-thirds majority for passage of navigation acts be struck. Defending the committee's action, Madison argued that abuse of power by the majority was improbable, while the benefit of an unrestricted authority in international negotiations was certainly great. Mason countered: "If the Govt. is to be lasting, it must be founded in the confidence & affections of the people, and must be so constructed as to obtain these. The *Majority* will be governed by their interests. The Southern States are the minority in both Houses."[66] Randolph, in the first open indication of a breach, declared that "there were features so odious in the Constitution as it now stands, that he doubted whether he should be able to agree to it."[67] Yet when the states voted, the House unanimously supported excision of the section.

The two adversary issues of the Convention were thus differently resolved. Political balance of the small states and the large was achieved by a brilliant innovation of which Mason heartily approved. Economic balance between the sections was obtained by a deal in which continuance of the slave trade was countenanced, and a simple majority became sufficient for enactment of export and import duties. Mason lost on both counts, and the double defeat was reflected in his attitude thereafter.

By midsummer, empathies and antipathies among the delegates began to be discernible. Few members were in either complete accord or complete disagreement on the issues, but congenialities had been discovered and differences in general attitude were underscored as the days went on.

Among colleagues outside the Virginia delegation, Elbridge Gerry of Massachusetts emerged as a man with whom, as the weeks went on, Mason progressively saw eye to eye on many points and Gouverneur Morris as a man with whom he was in frequent disagreement.

Gerry's early political career closely resembled Mason's own. Son of a Marblehead merchant family, he had served in the Massachusetts General Court, on the Committee of Correspondence, and then in the Provincial Congress of Massachusetts, always a close associate of Sam and John Adams. As a member of the Confederation Congress, he was an early advocate of independence. He and Mason shared a puritan streak; in their respective states both had urged passage of sumptuary laws. In this Convention, Pierce described him as "a Man of property . . . very much a gentleman in his principles and manners . . . connected and sometimes clear in his arguments." He was chairman of the Grand Committee that achieved the political compromise. As the debates proceeded, he and Mason developed together the doubts that led both to withhold their names from the final document.

Gouverneur Morris was the son of the second lord of New York's manor of Morrisania and his French second wife—her surname was Gouverneur. A conservative aristocrat with a leaning toward monarchy, he felt a devotion to the interests of the rich and well born and an aversion to democracy. Witty, gracious, and detached, he was both a man of the world and a man-about-town—his limp was attributed to a carriage accident during a precipitate departure from the home of an unexpectedly returning husband. Though his family was sharply divided by the Revolution—he and two half-brothers affiliated with the American cause while his mother became a Loyalist and another half-brother a British major general—he served in New York's Provincial Congress and constitution-making Provisional Assembly, where he successfully supported religious toleration but failed to obtain abolition of slavery. Defeated for office in 1779, he moved to Philadelphia and in the early 1780s assisted the unrelated Robert Morris when the latter was the confederation's superintendent of finance; from then on, the two were associates in many business ventures. His elegance included a felicity of language that made him the leading draftsman of the Committee of Style when the Constitution was given its final polish. Morris expressed

*Elbridge Gerry, etched by Albert Rosenthal after a 1797 miniature (courtesy, Russell W. Knight)*

his views in debate more often than any other Convention member. He and Mason clashed throughout the session.

As delegates sweltered in the sticky heat of a Philadelphia summer, assembling to the sound of Washington's gavel at ten in the morning and keeping at their work until three or four in the afternoon, they could often have endorsed John Quincy Adams's next-generation comment that the Constitution was "extorted from the grinding necessities of a reluctant nation." Progress was glacial; agreement ground forward at uneven rates, throwing aside periodic dumps of pulverized material. As early as the second week of June, Washington sighed when he wrote home for a fresh supply of clothing, "I see no end to my staying here."[68]

Yet by 27 July, when the Convention named Rutledge, Randolph, Gorham, Ellsworth, and Wilson as a Committee of Detail to bring order to the miscellany of scattered motions it had passed, material for a constitution was in hand. The Convention recessed for ten days while the committee drafted.

For those not so engaged, the break afforded a welcome respite. Washington's diary shows him driving out in Gouverneur Morris's phaeton to spend a night at a farm on part of the old Valley Forge encampment; riding over formerly bitter ground, he saw where the ploughshare had replaced the sword as he made inquiries about a standing crop of buckwheat. When he revisited Trenton, he inspected the new ironworks there.

Randolph was at work with the committee; McClurg had left for home. How Mason, his son, and the other Virginians spent their time is not known; his friend Elbridge Gerry, with his wife and new baby, went to New York: "we improved the Oppertunity to take an airing. I have left them there, by the advice of all her Friends, as the Heat of Philadelphia in the Month of August might prove injurious to our Infant."[69]

When members reassembled, they received a printed draft and began a clause-by-clause review. Supplementing this text, on 18 August a considerable list of additional powers to be exercised by the national legislature was submitted to the Committee of Detail, and thereafter several committees with one member from each state were chosen to prepare revised versions of a number of sections. Mason represented Virginia in groups considering means to secure the payment of the public debt and provide protection to creditors of the government; advising on the organization of the militia and the relative responsibilities of the central and the state governments in respect to troops; and allaying fears of the Maryland delegates regarding the uniform application, from state to state, of duties, imposts, and excises.

By 8 September, the document had been sufficiently refined to be transmitted to a Committee of Style consisting of Johnson, Hamilton, Gouverneur Morris, Madison, and King. Toward the end of his life, Madison affirmed: "The *finish* given to the style and arrangement of the Constitution fairly belongs to the pen of Mr. Morris."[70] Morris himself had written Timothy Pickering: "That instrument was written by the fingers, which write this letter."[71]

On 12 September, the committee laid before the Convention a printed version; review of this document then completed the debates.

# Chapter XIII
# Mason's Change of Attitude

*Individual members' contributions to the Convention proceedings fell into three* periods: the early substantive considerations of desirable structure for a central government and powers to be exercised under it; clause-by-clause examination of the version presented by the Committee of Detail; and efforts to obtain last-minute revisions when the Constitution came from the Committee of Style, preparatory to the signing that took place on 17 September. Mason's was a prominent voice in all three.

In the early weeks of discussion, as a member of the group that prepared the Virginia Plan, Mason advanced and defended proposals and opinions with regard to the structure of all three branches of government. From the beginning, he emphasized the importance of executive independence. Had he thought direct election of the executive by the people practicable, he would have been for it, but by mid-July, he said: "The extent of the Country renders it impossible that the people can have the requisite capacity to judge of the respective pretensions of the Candidates,"[1] and still later, he remarked: "A popular election in any form, as Mr. Gerry has observed, would throw the appointment into the hands of the Cincinnati, a Society for the members of which he had a great respect; but which he never wished to have a preponderating influence in the Govt."[2*]

While he preferred a three-man executive, he accepted the Convention's early decision for one man; he urged a single seven-year term as a means of giving him independence of the legislature. In late July, when tenure was again considered, he supported an unsuccessful proposal by Pinckney that would have limited eligibility to six years in any twelve.

On 4 June, he vigorously resisted a proposal that the executive serve during good behavior: "We are not indeed constituting a British Government, but a more dangerous monarchy, an elective one. . . . Do gentlemen mean to pave the way to hereditary Monarchy? Do they flatter themselves that the people will ever consent to such an innovation? If they do I venture to tell them, they are mistaken."[3] When the subject came up again in mid-July, he again urged its rejection: "He considered an Executive during good behavior as a softer name only for an Executive for life. And that the next would be an easy step to hereditary Monarchy."[4]

He preferred election of the executive by the national legislature to choice by a special group of electors. Extolling the merits of rotation in office in terms almost identical with those of his Fairfax County papers, he regarded "the very palladium of Civil Liberty, that the great officers of State, and particularly the Executive should at fixed periods return to that mass from which they were at first taken, in order that they may feel & respect those rights & interests, which are again to be personally valuable to them."[5] When he moved once again for a single seven-year term, the motion carried 7 to 3, but was reversed later in favor of a four-year term, with reeligibility and choice by a body of electors.

Mason provided the wording that, in Article II, sec. 4, still covers cases of malfeasance in office. At one of the Convention's first meetings he had urged that "Some mode of displacing an unfit magistrate is rendered indispensable by the fallibility of those who choose, as well as by the corruptibility of the man chosen";[6] on 20 July, he returned to the subject: "No point is of more importance than that the right of impeachment should be continued. Shall any man be above Justice? Above all shall that man be above it, who can commit the most extensive injustice? When great crimes were committed he was for punishing the principal as well as the Coadjutors."[7] On 8 September, he proposed that impeachment should not be confined to cases of treason and bribery but include "maladministration" as well. When members considered the word too general, he substituted the phrase familiar from English law, "high crimes & misdemesnors agst. the State."[8] The phrase "agst. the State" was first changed to "against the United States" and then dropped altogether in the final polishing by the Committee of Style. Thus amended, Mason's wording governed the impeachment processes of 1868 and 1974.

Consideration of treason raised the touchy subject of sovereignty in a federal structure. Mason observed that "The United States will have a qualified sovereignty only. The individual States will retain a part of the Sovereignty. An Act may be treason agst. a particular State which is not so agst. the U. States. He cited the Rebellion of Bacon in Virginia as an illustration of the doctrine."[9] In order to sharpen the definition of treason, he moved the insertion of the words "giving them aid and comfort" after "enemies of the United States." All but three states approved, and the insertion remained, appearing as Article III, sec. 3.

Mason's final observation on the powers of the executive concerned the veto power. "To guard against too great an impediment to the repeal of laws," he proposed that the legislature should be able to override a presidential veto by a two-thirds rather than a three-fourths majority. His motion carried, but without Virginia's vote: his and Randolph's approval was outweighed by the disapproval of Madison, Washington, and Blair.

Mason was a consistent advocate of a revisory council, in which the president and members of the judiciary would review laws before they went into effect. He approved it as a means of keeping the purse and the sword from lying in the same hands, of giving more weight to the executive, and of making further use of the judges: "Their aid will be the more valuable as they are in the habit and practice of considering laws in their true principles, and in all their consequences."[10]

He was very dubious of the value of a vice-president. As late as 7 September, he proposed substituting for the office a six-man privy council, chosen by the Senate: it would afford regional representation, with two members drawn from each of the country's three main sections. Without an advisory body, "we were about to try an experiment on which the most despotic Government had never ventured. The Grand Signor himself had his Divan."[11] Though Franklin supported him—"He thought a Council would not only be a check on a bad President, but be a relief to a good one"—only three delegations voted for the proposal.

Mason thought the size of the House of Representatives, as originally proposed, too small: its quorum would be thirty-eight and a majority of a quorum twenty. Virginia's ten representatives would contrast with Rhode Island's and Delaware's one each. "This was certainly too small a number to make laws for America. They would neither bring with them all the necessary information relative to various local interests, nor possess the necessary confidence of the people."[12] He and Gerry supported a motion by Madison to double the number; it failed at the time, but their point carried on 17 September with the last change in the Constitution's text.

The Virginia Plan had specified that representatives should be salaried; Mason emphasized the importance of their stipends coming from the national government not the states, lest inequality embarrass or parsimony cause only inferior persons to be willing to serve. He was firmly committed to popular elections of representatives: "Whatever inconveniency may attend the democratic principle, it must actuate one part of the Govt. It is the only security for the rights of the people."[13] He was also for biennial elections.

In the debate as to how representation should be proportioned, Mason insisted that "numbers of inhabitants; though not always a precise standard of wealth, was sufficiently so for every substantial purpose."[14] He opposed counting slaves equally with whites: "It was certain that the slaves were valuable, as they raised the value of land, increased the exports & imports, and of course the revenue, would supply the means of feeding & supporting an army, and might in cases of emergency become themselves soldiers. As in these important respects they were useful to the community at large, they ought not to be excluded from the estimate of Representation. He could not however regard them as equal to freemen and could not vote for them as such."[15]

When Rutledge urged that both property and population be weighed, Mason objected to it as "something too indefinite & impracticable."[16] He thought a provision to allow representation in accordance with taxes paid by the states would be just in principle, but in application it might push the national legislature toward requisitions. It was in the context of these considerations that Ellsworth first proposed all of the free male population and three-fifths of the slaves as a basis for representation; passed over at the time, it was later adopted.[17]

With regard to qualifications for service in the House of Representatives, Mason urged that members be required to own land and to be free of debt to the United States, citing English property qualifications. He approved a minimum age limit of twenty-five years: "every man carried with him in his own experience a scale for measuring the deficiency of young politicians; since he would if interrogated be obliged to declare that his political opinions at the age of 21. were too crude & erroneous to merit an influence on public measures. It had been said that Congs. had proved a good school for our young men. It might be so for any thing he knew but if it were, he chose that they should bear the expence of their own education."[18] He proposed that representatives be citizens of seven-years standing rather than three; that they conform to fixed requirements of state residency; that they not be permitted to hold state and federal office concurrently or leave their congressional seats in order to take federal office: "Instead of excluding merit, the ineligibility will keep out corruption, by excluding office-hunters."[19]

Representatives should be elected by direct ballot—Mason reiterated this position when Pinckney moved that the manner of choice be left to the state legislatures. He was for an extension of the franchise; a freehold qualification was a carry-over from English practice and not the only suitable criterion. "The true idea in his opinion was that every man having evidence of attachment to & permanent common interest with the Society ought to share in all its rights & privileges. Was this qualification restrained to freeholders? . . . Ought the merchant, the monied man, the parent of a number of children whose fortunes are to be pursued in his own Country, to be viewed as suspicious characters, and unworthy to be trusted with the common rights of their fellow Citizens[?]"[20]

In the selection of senators, he was for election by the state legislatures and against choice by the lower house or by groups of states; he thought three senators to a state too many; he approved a property qualification, a minimum age of thirty, six-year terms with one-third going out biennially, and a citizenship requirement of fourteen years.

In the division of powers between the houses, the lower house must originate money bills; the Senate must not have the power to tax or to appropriate. One of Mason's longest speeches was in support of a motion by Randolph to restrict the tax power to "the purpose of revenue only" and prohibit amendment of finance measures by the Senate. Congress rather than the president should have power to declare war and should regulate the national militia (he disapproved of a standing army). The laws of the United States should be paramount to state laws.

On several occasions, Mason advocated with minimum success a congressional power to enact sumptuary laws whose effect would curb imports of luxury goods and so help correct the nation's unfavorable trade balance and debt structure: "It was objected . . . that they were contrary to nature. This was a vulgar error. The love of distinction it is true is natural; but the object of sumptuary laws is not to extinguish this principle but to give it a proper direction."[21]

In respect to the judiciary, Mason strongly approved appointment of judges by Congress rather than by the executive. A document on the structure and powers of the courts, written in another hand (perhaps Blair's) with corrections by Mason, shows his interest in provisions regarding the role of the courts in litigation arising from land claims. Mason emphatically desired ratification of the Constitution by specially elected state conventions rather than by the state legislatures, with adoption by nine states required to put the document into effect.

In mid-July, he made a motion on the location of the national capital, to "prevent the seat of the Natl. Govt. being in the same City or town with the Seat of Govt. of any State longer than until the necessary public buildings could be erected."[22] However, he withdrew it when Gouverneur Morris expressed fear that it would antagonize citizens of Philadelphia and New York against the entire plan.

Through most of August, Mason maintained his position of positive participation. Only after the deal on commercial regulations and the slave trade did his speeches, along with those of various other delegates, begin to show a growing restiveness. On the thirty first, Luther Martin of Maryland and Gerry of Massachusetts delivered broad attacks on the document as a whole. When the Convention took up the article that would submit the plan to Congress, Mason, who on 5 July had declared that he would rather "bury his bones in this city" than have the Convention disperse with nothing done, seconded Gerry's motion to postpone consideration: "he would sooner chop off his right hand than put it to the Constitution as it now stands. He wished to see some points not yet decided brought to a decision, before being compelled to give a final opinion on this article. Should these points be improperly settled, his wish would then be to bring the whole subject before another general Convention."[23] Support for a second convention appeared from diverse quarters: Gouverneur Morris had long favored one because he believed it would bring in a more highly centralized and vigorous government plan; Randolph urged it as a means of allowing state conventions to propose amendments to the present plan.

By this date, Mason and others with objections began to hold informal conversations; Mason handed a list of proposed revisions to the Maryland delegation, soliciting their support on the grounds that "if the alterations could be obtained, the system would be unexceptionable." Luther Martin subsequently described meetings held in Philadelphia while delegates were still sitting:

Some time in the month of August, a number of members who considered the system, as then under consideration, and likely to be adopted, extremely exceptionable, and of a tendency to destroy the rights and liberties of the United States, thought it advisable to meet together in the evenings. . . . Mr. Gerry was the first who proposed this measure to me . . . and wished we might assemble at my lodgings; but not having a room convenient we fixed upon another place. There Mr. Gerry and Mr. Mason did hold meetings; but with them also met the delegates from New Jersey and Connecticut, a part of the delegation from Delaware, an honorable member from South Carolina, one other from Georgia and myself.[24]

Mason was further alienated on 12 September when the Convention as a whole and his own delegation in particular dealt him a major humiliation. It came after he expressed an emphatic wish for the plan to be "prefaced with a Bill of Rights, & would second a Motion if made for the purpose. It would give great quiet to the people; and with the aid of the State declarations, a bill might be prepared in a few hours."[25] Gerry concurred in the idea, moving, with Mason as a seconder, for a committee to prepare a bill of rights.

Sherman, while affirming the importance of securing the rights of the people, observed that "The State Declarations of Rights are not repealed by this Constitution; and being in force are sufficient"; Mason countered that "The Laws of the United States are to be paramount to State Bills of Rights."

When Gerry's motion was voted on, out of deference to him the contrary-minded Massachusetts delegation abstained. The Virginia delegation did not abstain on Mason's account. Of the ten states voting, all repudiated the author of the first American bill of rights with a unanimous no.

Mason was now an opponent of adoption of the Constitution in its current form. On the day of his snub on a bill of rights, the Committee of Style brought in its report. The notes on Gerry's copy of this print show that his friend had by this time worked out a coherent list of objections to it. Kate Mason Rowland, Mason's nineteenth-century biographer, published his reasons for withholding his signature as she found them, in his hand, on the back of his own copy; its whereabouts is not now known. But with one paragraph transposed, the wording of her transcript appears, headed merely "Objections," in Elbridge Gerry's handwriting on the blank pages of his copy.

Two or three of the latter sections contained exaggerated warnings of gloom and doom, such as the declarations that since states will in fact resort to ex post facto laws if exigencies require them, the Constitution's prohibition of them will encourage other breaches; that the Congress may extend its powers indefinitely under its own construction of the general clause; or that this government, starting as a moderate aristocracy, will end either as a monarchy or as a corrupt and tyrannical rule of the few. But the main body of the document presents a formidable list of arguable points:

There is no declaration of rights, and the laws of the general government being paramount, the declarations in the separate states are no security.

The inadequate size of the House of Representatives affords the shadow rather than the substance of representation.

Though the senators are not representatives of the people or amenable to them, they can originate and alter money bills, including the salaries of the officers whom they appoint in conjunction with the president; make treaties; try impeachments. These powers, together with the duration of their terms and their status as a continuing body, will destroy all balance in government.

The judiciary as proposed will absorb and destroy the state judiciaries and impede the attainment of justice by the poor.

The president has no constitutional council. From this defect spring the improper powers of the Senate and the unnecessary office of the vice-president, who as president of the Senate dangerously blends executive and legislative powers.

The unrestrained power of the president in granting pardons for treason may be exercised to screen from punishment those whom he has secretly instigated to commit crimes, and thereby prevent a discovery of his own guilt.

The declaration that all treaties are supreme law of the land gives the executive and the Senate an exclusive power of legislation.

The capacity of a bare majority to make commercial and navigation laws may bring ruin to the five southern states which a requirement of a two-thirds vote could have prevented; the state legislatures are restrained from taxing their own exports and the general legislature from prohibiting importation of slaves for twenty-odd years.

There is no section preserving liberty of the press or trial by jury in civil cases, nor is there one concerning the danger of standing armies in time of peace.

The range of these objections clearly forecast that when the time came to sign the Constitution, Mason would withhold his name.

On the morning of 13 September, the Convention's obvious business was to take up the report of the Committee of Style. Mason impeded its start.

Madison's impatience colored his reporting when Mason opened the day with an attempt to revive his proposal for sumptuary laws: "After descanting on the extravagance of our manners . . . he moved that a Committee be appointed to report articles of Association for encouraging . . . oeconomy frugality and also american manufactures."[27] The conciliatory chairman of the Committee of Style courteously seconded the motion; with Mason as its chairman, a committee of five was appointed and the proposal died.

Mason then asked for action on his previous day's motion that congressional control over commerce not preclude the states from laying duties to cover export inspection costs. It passed, with Madison acidly observing, "There was no debate." Only when these obstructions were out of the way could the convention take up the Committee of Style's report.

During the three-day, clause-by-clause consideration that followed, Mason and Gerry acted in frequent concert. Yet the Virginia delegation did not show a consistent division, with proponents Madison, Washington, and Blair voting one way and dissentients Randolph and Mason, the other: on the fourteenth, Madison records three consecutive —and losing—votes in which Virginia voted aye without a recorded division among delegation members. The first, supported only by Virginia and Georgia, was on a motion concerning congressional power to charter companies; the second, on a motion by Madison and Pinckney, "to establish an University, in which no preferences or distinctions should be allowed on account of religion," on which ten states voted 4 to 6 against, with Connecticut divided; and the last, on a proposal moved by Mason, seconded by Randolph, and supported by Madison on which Virginia and Georgia again found themselves alone that would have warned against standing armies in time of peace. But when Mason sought to distinguish between criminal and civil cases in prohibiting ex post facto laws, all states voted no.

On the fifteenth Randolph initiated a confused debate by moving to except cases of treason from the president's power to grant reprieves and pardons: "The President may himself be guilty. The Traytors may be his own instruments."[28] Mason seconded. Morris, Wilson, and King were against confiding the power to the legislature; if the executive "be himself a party to the guilt he can be impeached and prosecuted." Madison proposed associating the Senate with the president as a council of advice. Randolph and Mason were against bringing in the Senate. In the end, the motion lost.

Near the close of the day, as a vote neared on the Constitution as a whole, Randolph proposed referring the plan to state conventions for suggested amendments, with final revision to be made at a second constitutional convention. "Should this proposition be disregarded, it would he said be impossible for him to put his name to the instrument. Whether he should oppose it afterwards he would not then decide but he would not deprive himself of the freedom to do so in his own State, if that course should be prescribed by his final judgment."[29]

Seconding the motion, Mason indicated his own inability to sign: he "followed Mr. Randolph in animadversions on the dangerous power and structure of the Government. . . . This Constitution had been formed without the knowledge or idea of the people. A second Convention will know more of the sense of the people, and be able to provide a system more consonant to it. It was improper to say to the people, take this or nothing. As the Constitution now stands, he could neither give it his support or vote in Virginia; and he could not sign here what he could not support there. With the expedient of another Convention as proposed, he could sign."[30] After Pinckney responded with counterarguments, Gerry declared that he too would withhold his name. A motion for a second convention was advanced by Randolph, only to be defeated by a unanimous no, and on a motion to agree to the Constitution as it stood, a majority of each state delegation voted aye.

On Monday 17 September, after the engrossed Constitution

*Edmund Randolph by an unknown artist after an original now lost*
*(courtesy, The Virginia Historical Society)*

was read, Franklin requested Wilson to read on his behalf a speech inviting all delegates to sign: "I doubt . . . whether any other Convention we can obtain may be able to make a better Constitution . . . and I think it will astonish our enemies, who are waiting with confidence to hear that our councils are confounded. . . . I cannot help expressing a wish that every member of the Convention who may still have objections to it, would with me, on this occasion doubt a little of his own infallibility— and to make manifest our unanimity, put his name to this instrument."[31]

Franklin also offered a suggestion thought up by Gouvernour Morris as a device for presenting a united front: that the Constitution be declared "Done in Convention, by the unanimous consent of *the States* present."[32]

Morris overtly urged this proposal when Randolph confessed his continued inability to sign; Hugh Williamson of North Carolina, with the misgivings of his colleague William Blount in mind, suggested that individuals be asked to sign only the letter transmitting the document to Congress. But individual signature was preferred.

One last alteration of the text was then proposed by Gorham and seconded by King and Carroll: it increased the size of the House of Representatives by raising its numbers from a ratio of 1–40,000 to 1–30,000; as Washington rose to put the question he broke the silence he had maintained as chairman throughout proceedings to express his satisfaction with the change.

On the final day, Hamilton put in a dramatic appearance: he had previously asked Rufus King to "let me know when your *conclusion* is at hand: for I would choose to be present at that time." He pressed for unanimity: "A few characters of consequence, by opposing or even refusing to sign the Constitution, might do infinite mischief. . . . No man's ideas were more remote from the plan than his own . . . but is it possible to deliberate between anarchy and Convulsion on one side and the chance of good to be expected from the plan on the other."[33]

Randolph recognized that "in refusing to sign the Constitution, he took a step which might be the most awful of his life, but it was dictated by his conscience, and it was not possible for him to hesitate, much less, to change."[34] Gerry resented the Franklin-Morris proposal as "levelled at himself and the other gentlemen who meant not to sign."[35] Mason made no statement.

After all others present had affixed their names and Franklin had uttered a closing homily, the Convention adjourned sine die. Washington's diary sums up that 17 September:

Met in Convention when the Constitution received the unanimous assent of 11 States and Colo. Hamilton's from New York (the only delegate from thence in Convention) and was subscribed to by every member present except Govr. Randolph and Colo. Mason from Virginia, and Mr. Gerry from Massachusetts. The business being thus closed, the Members adjourned to the City Tavern, dined together and took a cordial leave of each other; after which I returned to my lodgings, did some business with, and received the papers from the Secretary of the Convention, and retired to meditate on the momentous w[or]k which had been executed, after not less than five, for a large part of the time six, and sometimes 7 hours sitting every day, [except] sundays & the ten days adjournment to give a comee. opportunity and time to arrange the business, for more than four months.[36]

Next morning the secretary to the Convention set out for New York by the 10 A.M. stage, conveying the Convention's plan to Congress. In the offices of the *Pennsylvania Packet,* typesetters, in a stint that broke speed records, were picking type fast enough to present the complete document in the issue of 19 September. Those delegates who did not immediately leave for home were busily weighing down midweek mail pouches with letters to their friends. The struggle for and against ratification had already begun.

Factional divisions in the state legislatures were certain to bias consideration of the new plan irrespective of its merits; disapproving members were already known to be organizing opposition. Yates and

*"Convention at Philadelphia, 1787,"* woodcut

Lansing, allies of Governor Clinton, had retired to New York in disgruntlement early in the Philadelphia deliberations. Luther Martin had gone back to Maryland in late August with fire in his eye. Gerry's attitude would be potent in Massachusetts, Mason's in Virginia, as would Governor Randolph's on whichever side he threw his weight in his final decision.

On 18 September, Mason forwarded his "Objections" to Richard Henry Lee in Congress; before leaving Philadelphia, he consulted with Pennsylvania opponents of the document,* though a few weeks later he was irate when a version of his "Objections" appeared in Philadelphia printed "very incorrectly, without my Approbation, or Privity."

Likewise on the eighteenth, Randolph sent a copy of the Constitution to Acting Governor Beverley Randolph in Richmond with the information: "Altho' the names of Colo. Mason and myself are not subscribed, it is not, therefore, to be concluded that we are opposed to its adoption. Our reasons for not subscribing will be better explained at large, and on a personal interview, than by letter."[37]

On the twentieth, Gerry sent the text of the Constitution to John Adams in London: "There were only three dissentients Governor Randolph and Colonel Mason from Virginia and your friend who now addresses you from Massachusetts . . . time must determine the fate of this production which with a check on standing armies in a time of peace and on an arbitrary administration of the powers vested in the legislature would have met with my approval."[38]

On 26 September, the Connecticut proponents of the Constitution, Ellsworth and Sherman, supplied Governor Huntington with copies of the document and argument on its behalf.

In New York, on delivery of the plan, such powerful members of Congress as Richard Henry Lee and William Grayson of the Virginia delegation, together with Nathan Dane of Massachusetts, mounted an attempt to transmit it to the states with a minimum of enthusiasm. But since nearly a third of the thirty-three members who took part in the congressional debate on the document had been members of the Convention, formal action had to await their return.

Edward Carrington urgently summoned Madison to resume his congressional seat and strengthen the positive side of the argument:

I take this precaution to apprise you that the same schism which unfortunately happened in our State in Philadelphia, threatens us here also—one of our Colleagues Mr. R. H. Lee is forming propositions for essential alterations in the Constitution, which will, in effect, be to oppose it.—Another, Mr. Grayson, dislikes it, and is, at best for giving it only a silent passage to the States. Mr. H. Lee joins me in opinion that it ought to be warmly recommended to ensure its adoption.[39]

When Madison arrived, he found that Lee and Dane had declared the Convention to have acted ultra vires; the proposed Constitution could by no means be regarded as a revision of the Articles of Confederation, and a revision was what Congress had ordered it to prepare. And as a second line of opposition, Lee was proposing attachment of amendments before transmission, including a bill of rights "& several other things corresponding with the ideas of Colonel Mason."[40*] But while Lee circulated his amendments outside the Congress and Grayson sent similar views to William Short, Jefferson's aide, in Paris, Lee's covering letter to Mason admitted that in Congress their efforts failed: "I availed myself of the Right to amend, & moved the Amendments copy of which I send herewith & called the ayes and nays to fix them on the journal. This greatly alarmed the Majority & vexed them extremely. . . . They found it most eligible at last to transmit it [the plan] merely, without approving or disapproving; provided nothing but the transmission should appear on the Journal . . . they took the opportunity of inserting the word *Unanimously,* which applied only to simple transmission, hoping to have it mistaken for an Unanimous approbation."[41]

In this manner, the draft Constitution became subject to the judgment of the states.

# Chapter XIV
# For and Against

*Mason returned to Gunston Hall lacerated in body as well as in spirit. Between* Philadelphia and Baltimore a road accident injured both him and his guest and passenger, the Maryland delegate James McHenry.

Mrs. McHenry had impatiently expected her husband on 18 September; a mild reproach greeted him in a note as he passed through Baltimore: "From the middle of the afternoon, with a listening ear I was attentive to every sound, expecting that I should presently catch that of your voice, or feet approaching, but no sound so pleasing was to be heard." Yet she admitted having received word that he might be arriving later: "I have indeed got a letter which prevents my being apprehensive that any accident has happened to you."[1]

On a pot-holed stretch of road, the vehicle had suddenly tipped over, throwing both men out on the ground. Daniel Carroll, who was not far behind them, caught up and zestfully reported the occurrence to Madison: "I overtook him [Mason] & the Majr. on the road: By the time they had reached within 9 Miles of Baltimore, they had exhausted all the stories of their youth &ca. and had entered into a discusn. of the rights to the Western World. You know they are champions on opposite sides of this question.* The Major having pushed the Col hard on the Charters of Virginia the latter had just wax'd warm, when his Charateer put an end to the dispute, by jumbling their Honors together by an oversett. I came up soon after. they were both hurt—the Col. most so. he lost blood at Baltimore, & is well."[2]

Washington too had a lucky escape on his way home. With Blair as his carriage companion, he hastened off on the eighteenth, impatient to reach Mount Vernon. Near Head of Elk, he decided to use a rickety bridge when they reached an impassable ford. To lighten the load, he and Blair got out and crossed on foot. But when the vehicle started over, the flooring of the bridge collapsed under one of the horses, and the animal's frightened lunges threatened to drag the other horse and chariot after him. Help arrived in time to save the equipage, but the *Delaware Gazette* worried publicly about "a life so dear to the country."

Carroll dismissed Mason's fall a bit lightly: several weeks later, after Washington had condoled with him on 7 October, Mason said he was still feeling its effects: "I got very much hurt in my Neck & Head, by the unlucky Accident on the road; it is now wearing off, tho' at times still uneasy to me."[3][†]

Citizens of Fairfax County learned about Mason's attitude toward the Constitution while the Convention was still sitting. Joseph Jones passed the gossip on to Madison: "Some stories I have heard since my return and on my visit to Alexandria, make me apprehensive there is not that unanimity in your councils I hoped for . . . it is *whispered* here, there is great disagreement among the gentlemen of our delegation, that the general and yourself on a very important question were together, Mr. M——n alone and singular in his opinion and the other two gentlemen holding different sentiments."[4]

County sentiment strongly favored the document, and Dr. David Stuart, the county's other Assembly delegate, warmly shared Washington's approval. Immediately after Mason's return, Fairfax freeholders, the chief Alexandria merchants prominent among them, signed instructions to their delegates to propose "an immediate Convocation" to secure "the speedy Adoption of the System of Government recommended by the late General Convention." Mason quickly assured Washington that he would cooperate: "I take the Liberty to enclose you my Objections to the new Constitution of Government; which a little Moderation & Temper, in the latter End of the Convention, might have removed. I am however most decidedly of Opinion that it ought to be submitted to a Convention chosen by the People, for that special Purpose; and shou'd any attempt be made to prevent the calling such a convention here, such a Measure shall have every Opposition in my Power to give it."[5]

A letter from a gentleman in Petersburg, reprinted in the *Pennsylvania Packet* of 10 November, described the Assembly proceedings. Francis Corbin, who approved the Constitution, opened the session and moved the calling of a ratifying convention. Patrick Henry insisted that the call should envisage amendment of the document: "There were errors and defects in the Constitution, and he therefore proposed the addition of some words to Mr. Corbin's resolutions by which the power of proposing amendments might be given." Countering him, John Marshall urged the Assembly not to interject its opinions: "He thought, with Mr. Nicholas, that the people should have no reason to suppose that their Legislature disapproved the new federal government" and therefore proposed "That a Convention should be called and that the new Constitution should be laid before them for their free and ample discussion."

This the Assembly did, but with very deliberate speed, delaying Virginia's choice of delegates until the regular elections of the forthcoming spring and setting 1 June 1788 as the Convention date. Mason sent Washington a copy of the resolutions, observing that "the Assembly have given time for full Examination & Discussion . . . and have avoided giving any Opinion of their own upon the Subject."[6*]

Most conventions were held earlier. Delaware's was the first, ratifying unanimously on 7 December 1787. Pennsylvania's adopted by a vote of 46 to 23 on 12 December. New Jersey's on 18 December and

Georgia's on 2 January 1788 were both unanimous; on 9 January, Connecticut's vote was 128 to 40.

The Massachusetts convention, in the first really close contest, ratified by 187 to 168 on 6 February. New Hampshire's first session on 13 February found many delegates bound by Anti-Federalist instructions and adjourned to 3 June to give time for some of these to be changed. Maryland voted 63 to 11 on 28 April; South Carolina, 149 to 73 on 23 May.

In the three remaining states, Virginia's convention call was for 1 June, New York's for 17 June, North Carolina's for 21 July. (While Rhode Island had sent no delegates to Philadelphia, the document was forwarded to its government for signature; but the state remained outside the system until 1790.)

Though the Constitution was to come into force on adherence by nine states, geographical realities precluded effective government if participating states were separated from each other by nonparticipants—if New England were cut off at the New York border, or the Deep South isolated at the North Carolina or the Virginia line. Moreover, Virginia and New York were among the larger states; if their wealth and population were subtracted from the whole, the United States would be seriously diminished. The size and location of these as-yet-undecided states, and the stature of the personalities opposing each other in their conventions, charged the approaching sessions with tension.

The earlier debates and the public prints had thoroughly canvassed the pros and cons of each disputed section of the document; most of the best minds that had been at Philadelphia furnished public commentary. James Wilson made a masterly presentation of the new plan at a public meeting in Philadelphia on 6 October 1787. Charles Pinckney's pamphlet, "Observations on the Plan of Government Submitted to the Federal Convention," produced in the first half of October, was shortly reprinted in the South Carolina *State Gazette*. In November, Roger Sherman began "Letters of a Countryman," and Oliver Ellsworth started a series of articles, signed "A Landholder," in the Connecticut *Courant*. In Virginia, week after week from early winter to June 1788, the Richmond *Independent Chronicle* and other papers carried profederalist material and reprinted supportive articles originating elsewhere. Dickinson's "Letters of Fabius" began early in 1788 and continued through the spring.

Greatest in weight among all the expositions and recommendations offered the American public during the time of the state conventions was *The Federalist,* essays signed "Publius" which were first printed in New York journals from October 1787 to August 1788, the joint work of three men from the two larger states that were late to ratify, Alexander Hamilton and John Jay* of New York and James Madison of Virginia. Reprints by Virginia's local presses were soon advertised in Richmond's *Independent Chronicle*.

For the opposition, Mason's "Objections" influenced the argument from one end of the country to the other. "Centinel's" letters in the Pennsylvania *Independent Gazette* induced angry refutation; Luther Martin's long attack before the Maryland Assembly on 29 November was reprinted in Dunlap's *Maryland Gazette and Baltimore Advertiser* and republished as an Anti-Federalist pamphlet; he named "The favorers of monarchy, and those who voted the total abolition of State governments" as the cause, in great measure of "the objections of those honorable members, Mr. Mason and Mr. Gerry."

In every thing that tended to give the *large States* power over the *smaller*, the *first* of these gentlemen could not forget he belonged to the *Ancient Dominion*, nor could the latter forget, that he represented Old Massachusetts. That part of the system, which tended to give those States power over the others, met with their *perfect approbation;* but, when they viewed it charged with *such powers,* as would *destroy all State governments,* their own as well as the rest,—when they saw a president so constituted as to differ from a monarch scarcely but in name, and having it in his power to become such in reality when he pleased; they being *republicans* and *federalists,* as far as an attachment to their own States would permit them, they warmly and zealously opposed those parts of the system.[7]

Much of the published attack on opponents of the Constitution was highly personal, and most of it centered on Mason. On 17 October, the Pennsylvania *Journal* published a story repeated by the Massachusetts *Gazette* on 26 October to the effect that Alexandria's mayor and council had warned Mason on his return from Philadelphia to leave town at once or his safety would be endangered by the populace; the allegation circulated for a month before the *Gazette* published a retraction on 20 November.

The *New Haven Gazette* of 6 December contrasted Mason and Washington: "Where was Mr. George Mason from 1775 to 1783—what was the part he then took? Of his colleague, who did *sign* the Constitution the *admiring world* well knows." Richard Henry Lee and Randolph, along with Mason, were targets of "Old State Soldier," "Cassius" (James Sullivan of Massachusetts), "Valerius," "Civis Rusticus," and "A Plain Dealer." In October, the Connecticut *Courant* reprinted a Philadelphia dispatch "that the Federalists should be distinguished hereafter by the name of Washingtonians, and the Antifederalists by the name of Shayites, in every part of the United States"; "A Plain Dealer" ridiculed Randolph's change of attitude after Massachusetts ratified in February as a blind willingness to ride with any majority.

In some cities, Anti-Federalists sought advantage by publishing Mason's "Objections" in truncated form. When northern papers cut all reference to his disapproval of the power of Congress to regulate commerce by a simple majority, Madison remarked to Washington, "Tricks of this sort are not uncommon with the Enemies of the new Constitution. Col. Mason's objections were as I am told published in Boston mutilated of that which pointed at the regulation of Commerce."[8] This omission attracted attention when Oliver Ellsworth's widely reprinted "Landholder Letter No. VI" insisted that the determining factor in Mason's opposition was the defeat of the requirement of a two-thirds majority in the commerce clause: "Just at the close of the Convention, whose proceedings in general were zealously supported by Mr. Mason, he moved for a clause that no navigation act should ever be passed but with the consent of two-thirds of both branches; urging that a navigation act might otherwise be passed excluding foreign bottoms from carrying American produce to market, and throw a monopoly of the carrying business into the hands of the eastern states. . . . The loss of this question determined Mr. Mason against the signing the doings of the convention."[9]

On 12 March, Old State Soldier's "Communication No. 3" in the Richmond *Independent Chronicle* deplored the "barefaced impudence" of Lee and Mason: "As for Mr. Mason, poor old man, he appears to have worn his judgment entirely threadbare and ragged in the service of his country."

Private letters were even more cutting: in March, Nicholas Gilman of Virginia alarmed John Sullivan of New Hampshire: "Had it been pleasing to the preserver of Man, in the Super abundance of his tender mercies, to have removed P——y with M——n [Patrick Henry and Mason] to the regions of darkness, I am induced to think the new System of government would have been adopted—but the delay in our backsliding State has rendered it much more doubtful in my mind than it had been at any period since the Completion of the plan."[10]

(The lasting personal strains that developed are instanced by Lund Washington's letter of 6 March 1789, telling the general of a rumor in Stafford that "we shoud have a very pretty President at the head of our new Government, one Who had pd. his Debts within the time of the War with paper Money, altho it had been lent to him in specie. Now Sir if this report be true you may readily tell where it originated and proves beyond a Dobt that Colo. Mason is no Friend of yours . . . they believed the report was first propagated by Colo. Coock who is Colo. Masons son in Law."[11])

The sharpness of personal invective and hot response led Franklin to communicate one of his homilies to the *Federal Gazette:*

I beg I may not be understood to infer, that our general Convention was divinely inspired when it form'd the new federal Constitution, merely because that Constitution has been unreasonably and vehemently opposed; yet I must own I have so much Faith in the general Government of the World by Providence, that I can hardly conceive a Transaction of such momentous Importance to the Welfare of Millions now existing, and to exist in the Posterity of a great Nation, should be suffered to pass without being in some degree influenc'd, guided and governed by that omnipotent, omnipresent & beneficent Ruler, in whom all inferior Spirits live & move and have their Being.[12]

And while few other estimates of the document were this extravagant, many convention members held views approximating the closing paragraphs of the notes James McHenry took at Philadelphia:

Being opposed to many parts of the system I make a remark why I signed it and mean to support it.

1sly I distrust my own judgement, especially as it is opposite to the opinion of a majority of gentlemen whose abilities and patriotism are of the first cast; and as I have had already frequent occasions to be convinced that I have not always judged right.

2dly Alterations may be obtained, it being provided that the concurrence of ⅔ of the Congress may at any time introduce them.

3dly Comparing the inconveniences and the evils which we labor under and may experience from the present confederation, and the little good we can expect from it—with the possible evils and probable benefits and advantages promised us by the new system, I am clear that I ought to give it all the support in my power.[13]

Sober consideration was given Mason's "Objections" by such thoughtful members as Wilson and Madison; Washington forwarded an Alexandria reprint of Wilson's Philadelphia speech to David Stuart, then attending the Assembly in Richmond, with the recommendation: "As the enclosed advertiser contains a speech of Mr. Wilson's (as able, candid and honest a member as in Convention) which will place most of —M.— objections in their true point of light, I send it to you—the republication will (if you can get it done) be Serviceable at this Juncture."[14]

Madison profoundly believed that the agenda before the country was to adopt this constitution, rather than to consider how to form a better one. While the document was the work of many men, his relation to it put him in much the position occupied by Mason and Jefferson during discussion of their respective documents in 1776: he inevitably felt that alterations would not be for the better. And beyond his personal involvement, he was accurately and acutely aware that time was working on the side of disintegration, both in terms of support for the proposed frame of government and in terms of the cost to the country of continuing ungoverned.

He therefore reminded Washington that most of Mason's objections had not, so far as he recalled, been actively pressed during the debate; that his desire for a larger House of Representatives had been met on the last day of the Convention; that his group of objections to the Senate article and his related objection to the office of the vice-president had been "very faintly urged" at the time. Madison also recalled Mason as having acquiesced in the allowance of an interval permitting the importation of slaves and in the prohibition of the laying of export duties by the states.

While admitting that he himself had been in favor of an advisory council to the president, Madison suggested that the form proposed by Mason, with the Senate's power of appointment to executive offices transferred to it, would have occasioned outcry among Mason's own associates. In regard to Mason's objections to the judicial article, Madison insisted that relatively few cases would be matters of federal cognizance. He said he failed to understand Mason's statement that the Constitution does not secure the common law. As a former member of the Virginia Committee of Law Revisors, Mason should well know that both common law and statute law change with the times—abolition of primogeniture and of the ecclesiastical establishment were cases in point.

Since the Convention had provided for future alterations of the Constitution through the amending process once the government was organized, Madison insisted that this, rather than exposure of the entire document to a second convention, was the desirable method of change.

In the eight states where ratification was not unanimous, the issue of prior versus subsequent amendment became the crux of the debate, with eventual favor given to the latter course. Since excisions or alterations of clauses already in the document presented greater difficulties than additions to it, two of the latter, as time went on, began to acquire an especially broad basis of support. There was practical unanimity for the explicit statement that powers not specifically granted to the central government were reserved to the states; and in state after state a desire was voiced for a federal equivalent of the guarantees assured individuals by the states' bills of rights. At Philadelphia, Mason's attempt to secure this addition had been unanimously voted down, but it accumulated unifying approval as the ratification process progressed.

In Pennsylvania, the first state to ratify by a divided vote and to offer amendments, "The Address and Reasons of Dissent" prepared by the minority of the Convention for their constituents headed its list of objections with "The omission of a Bill of Rights ascertaining and fundamentally establishing those unalienable and personal rights of men, without the full, free and secure enjoyment of which there can be no liberty, and over which it is not necessary for a good government to have the control."[15] Subsequent debaters took the argument from there.

The choices as initially presented were either ratification of the document as it stood, or insistence on amendment prior to ratification. The Massachusetts convention, the second to ratify by a divided vote, invented another choice that became the turning point in acceptance of the document. Jefferson called it "the much better plan of Massachusets and which had never occurred to me": to vote for ratification while strongly recommending to the new government's immediate attention an appended list of desired amendments. The development of this alternative was achieved by the parliamentary skill of the Massachusetts Federalists.

Two major divisions, both of them duplicated in other major states, were apparent among the members who assembled in Boston on 9 January 1788. One was a division between generations. The men who had been leaders during the 1765–76 decade, who had raised liberty trees, cried, "Give me liberty or give me death," heaved crates of tea into Boston Harbor—the Christopher Gadsdens, the Patrick Henrys, the Isaac Searses, the Sam Adamses—held with Thomas Paine that "government like clothes is the badge of lost innocence." They wanted a minimum, not more. Sam Adams, on entering the Massachusetts convention, exclaimed, "I stumble at the threshold. I meet with a national government, instead of a Federal Union of Sovereign States." Even the men with greater executive experience or more social prestige than these—the James Warrens, the Elbridge Gerrys, the John Hancocks, the George Clintons, the Benjamin Harrisons, the Richard Henry Lees— but men whose entry into public life, like theirs, dated from the early revolutionary years, were chary of the extension of public power. While

*Samuel Adams by John Singleton Copley,*
*c. 1770–1772*
*(courtesy, Museum of Fine Arts, Boston)*

there were older men who from colonial days had been well-disposed to forces and institutions making for order and stability—Pendleton in civilian affairs in Virginia, Washington in the army—the ranking Federalists were young. In the year of the Stamp Act, Madison was fourteen; "Light-Horse Harry" Lee, nine; Jay, twenty; Hamilton, about eight. Their elders had come on stage in a period when liberty was the heart's desire; they themselves had made their entrances when war-and-postwar disintegration was the conspicuous danger, and order the greatest good.

The second division was between the eastern and the western parts of the states. Amos Singletary of Worcester County represented the small farmers of Massachusetts—and the area of Shays's Rebellion—when he said: "These lawyers, and men of learning, and monied men that talk so finely . . . expect to be the managers of this constitution, and get all the power and all the money into their own hands, and then they will swallow up all us little folks, like the great *Leviathan,* Mr. President, yes, just as the whale swallowed up *Jonah.* This is what I am afraid of."[16]

The wealth and prestige of Boston were indeed in evidence. Yet the choice of a presiding officer represented a balance: the state's president, John Hancock, enjoyed an uncontested status as the city's ranking merchant, but an equally uncontested record as a risk-taking protagonist of liberty in the early revolutionary years. The Federalists showed themselves prepared to lean over backward to assure all views being heard. Five days after the meeting assembled, a motion invited Gerry, who was not a delegate, "to take a seat in the Convention, to answer any questions of fact from time to time, that the Convention may ask, respecting the passing of the Constitution."

During the three weeks of debate that followed, the Anti-Federalists were thought to gain the edge. The Federalists' counter-strategy first appeared at the close of the morning session of 30 January. Immediately after a motion was made to ratify, Hancock declared the noon recess. When members reassembled, he inquired whether "the introduction of some amendments would not be attended with the happiest consequences."[17] The effect on the opposition was immediate: Sam Adams was on his feet to declare: "I feel myself happy in contemplating the idea,"[18] and when a set of amendments, drafted by Theophilus Parsons but introduced as from Hancock, was brought forward, he moved a committee for their consideration. On 4 February, with the endorsement of fifteen of its twenty-four members, nine proposed changes were presented to the body as a whole; two days later, when Sam Adams brought in more, he refrained from an adversary stance in presenting them. Hancock then revealed a new formula: he proposed ratification now, but with the nine committee amendments appended for urgent consideration by the new government. The convention accepted the formula by a vote of 187 to 168.*

An hour after the vote, General Henry Jackson jubilated to General Henry Knox, who as secretary-general of the Society of the Cincinnati was serving as a communications center for news of the constitution's prospects:

HUZZA—HUZZA—

as you must be anxious & to keep you from suspence a moment I have the *extream pleasure* to inform you, that the grand question was put this Afternoon at 5 OClock by yeas & nays, and was *in favor* of the Constitution by a Majority of 19. . . . I attended in the Gallery from 9 OC in the morning until within a half an hour since, & eat my dinner there on *Gingerbread & Cheese* which I sent forth a boy to buy in a Neighbouring Shop. . . .

The moment the *Ratification* was declared outdoors, the whole of the Bells in Town were set a Ringing.[19]

Up and down the seaboard, the new formula, coupled with adherence by another of the three most important states, had an electric effect. Observant diplomats agreed with the analysis of their Dutch colleague, P. J. van Berckel:

It is all too likely that the same would have been absolutely rejected in Massachusetts had not Governor Hancock as President of the Convention proposed some changes whereby the rights of the people are more precisely stipulated and insured. . . . The Federalists consider these changes as merely pro forma and stand them in the wind.

The Anti-federalists look at them as a forerunner of all such changes and amendments . . . and have no doubt that the states of New York, Maryland and Virginia will not only recommend these to their representatives in the new government, but will give them express instructions on other things which they deem necessary to the preservation of liberty and independence. Thus it seems that the people of the State of Massachusetts have shown the way along which both parties will finally unite.[20]

Madison heartened Washington with "the favorable result of the Convention at Boston. The amendments are a blemish, but are in the least offensive form." He sent the news to Jefferson with the comment: "The decision of Massts. will give the turn in favor of the Constitution unless an idea should prevail or the fact should appear, that the voice of the State is opposed to the result of its Convention."[21] Following a swing through Virginia, Col. Edward Carrington held ratification in Massachusetts to have been "perhaps the most important event that ever took place in America . . . had she rejected I am certain there would not have been the most remote chance of its adoption in Virginia."[22]

On 28 April, Washington explained the significance of the new formula to Lafayette:

The opinion of Mr. Jefferson and yourself is certainly a wise one, that the Constitution ought by all means to be accepted by nine States before any attempt should be made to procure amendments . . . with prudence in temper and a spirit of moderation, every essential alteration may in the process of time, be expected. You will doubtless have seen, that it was owing to this conciliatory and patriotic principle, that the convention of Massachusetts adopted the constitution in toto, but recommended a number of specific alterations, and quieting explanations as an early, serious, and unremitting subject of attention.[23]

As the stage was set for the forthcoming drama in Virginia, two

*John Hancock by John Singleton Copley,*
*1765*
*(courtesy, Museum of Fine Arts, Boston)*

major personalities—Washington and Jefferson—stood, and remained, in the wings.

The delicacy of Washington's position derived from the open secret that if a new government were established, the presidency would be his. When the New York *Daily Advertiser* proposed the idea nine days after the Philadelphia Convention closed and the two Philadelphia papers promptly followed, they were merely putting into print what was in all men's minds, overtly expressed again in the Richmond *Independent Chronicle*'s Extraordinary Issue of 23 April. Pierce Butler of Georgia wrote a relative that he did not think the executive powers would have been made so great "had not many of the members cast their eyes towards General Washington as President; and shaped their Ideas of the Powers to be given to a President, by their opinions of his Virtue."[24]

The master of Mount Vernon had to walk a narrow line between apparent indifference and alleged office-seeking: he wrote Lafayette, "In answer to the observations you make on the probability of my election to the Presidency, (knowing me as you do) I need only to say, that it has no enticing charms, and no fascinating allurements for me. However, it might not be decent for me to say I would refuse to accept, or even to speak much about an appointment, which may never take place."[25]

His participation was therefore restricted to a voluminous private* correspondence, carried on with the help of his former aide, David Humphreys, who lived at Mount Vernon through the winter and spring. On 1 January 1788, he assessed to Jefferson the opposition anticipated in Virginia: "many influential characters here have taken a decided part against it, among whom are Mr. Henry, Colo. Mason, Govr. Randolph and Colo. R. H. Lee; but from every information which I have been able to obtain, I think there will be a majority in its favor notwithstanding their dissention."[26] His reply of 8 January 1788 to Governor Randolph, who had sent him a copy of his "Letter . . . on the Federal Constitution," was given much credit for the governor's change of position: "There are some things in the new form, I will readily acknowledge, wch. never did, and I am persuaded never will, obtain my *cordial* approbation, but I then did conceive, and do now most firmly believe, that, in the aggregate, it is the best Constitution that can be obtained at this Epocha, and that this, or a dissolution of the Union awaits our choice, and are the only alternatives before us."[27]

During the Richmond Convention, Washington's silent, approving absence was no less potent than his silent, approving presence had been at Philadelphia. "Be assured his influence carried this government,"[28] Monroe, who voted against it, wrote Jefferson when it was all over; from the same position, William Grayson declared, "I think that were it not for one great character in America, so many would not be for this government."[29]

In Paris, Jefferson awaited publication of the Constitution with avid impatience. Many Virginia friends—Washington, Madison, Carrington, Monroe—had described the start of the Philadelphia proceedings to him, but once debate was under way, he had heard no more. On 30 August 1787, he complained to John Adams: "I have news from America as late as July 19, nothing had then transpired from the Federal convention. I am sorry they began their deliberations by so abominable a precedent as that of tying up the tongues of their members. . . . I have no doubt that all their other measures will be good & wise. it is really an assembly of demigods."[30]

Jefferson stood between the generations. In 1765, he had been twenty-two. His first political experience, in Virginia's "Movement Party," had aligned him with Henry, Mason, Richard Henry Lee; and his Declaration of Independence was the apex of the architecture of liberty constructed during the revolutionary years. And now in Paris, accredited to a monarchy that was no less absolute for having been the friend of the fledgling United States, he again saw daily evidence of the evils of too concentrated power. The mood of 1787–88 in France was like that of the early 1770s in America, a time of revolution almost but not quite begun. The French period corresponding to that in which the Philadelphia document was framed, with the forces of order moving in to arrest national disintegration, lay five years in the future at Thermidor.

The ambassador's old colleagues kept his eagerness for news in mind: a letter of 6 September from Madison began: "As the Convention will shortly rise I should feel little scruple in disclosing what will be public here, before it could reach you, were it practicable for me to guard by Cypher against an intermediate discovery."[31] But he went on to indicate the broad outlines of the draft that had just come from the Committee of Style, and on 24 October, from New York, he forwarded a copy of the actual document,* naming the Virginians who refused to sign and the prospects of ratification there:

It will not escape you that three names only from Virginia are subscribed to the Act. Mr. Wythe did not return after the death of his lady. Docr. M'Clurg left the Convention some time before the adjournment. The Governour and Col. Mason refused to be parties to it. Mr. Gerry was the only other member who refused. . . . Col. Mason left Philada. in an exceeding ill humour indeed. A number of little circumstances arising in part from the impatience which prevailed towards the close of the business, conspired to whet his acrimony. He returned to Virginia with a fixed disposition to prevent the adoption of the plan if possible. . . . His conduct has given great umbrage to the County of Fairfax, and particularly to the Town of Alexandria. He . . . will probably be either not deputed to the Convention, or be tied up by express instructions.

My information from Virginia is as yet extremely imperfect. I have a letter from Genl. Washington which speaks favorably of the impression within a circle of some extent; and another from Chancellor Pendleton which expresses his full acceptance of the plan, and the popularity of it in his district, I am told also that Innes and Marshall are patrons of it. In the opposite scale are Mr. James Mercer, Mr. R. H. Lee, Docr. Lee and their connections of course, Mr. M. Page according to Report, and most of the Judges & Bar of the general Court. The part which Mr. Henry will take is unknown here. Much will depend on it. I had taken it for granted from a variety of circumstances that he wd. be in the opposition, and still think that will be the case. There are reports however which favor a contrary supposition.[32]

The further correspondence between Madison and Jefferson displays both the growth in Jefferson's appreciation of the urgency of acceptance of the Constitution and the extent to which his unswerving insistence on a bill of rights pressed Madison toward a new attitude. On first reading, Jefferson was inclined to approve Randolph's proposal for a second convention following consideration of the document in the states. On 20 December 1787, after listing the many features of the plan that he liked, he continued:

I will now add what I do not like. First the omission of a bill of rights providing clearly and without the aid of sophisms for freedom of religion, freedom of the press, protection against standing armies, restriction against monopolies, the eternal and unremitting force of the habeas corpus laws, and trials by jury in all matters of fact triable by the laws of the land and not by the laws of Nations . . . a bill of rights is what the people are entitled to against every government on earth, general or particular, and what no just government should refuse, or rest on inference.[33]

By the first week of February 1788, in letters to William Stephens Smith, Madison, and Alexander Donald, Jefferson had changed his position enough to suggest a form of immediate but conditional ratification that was widely quoted in the Virginia Convention: "Were I in America, I would advocate it warmly till nine should have adopted, and then as warmly take the other side to convince the remaining four that they ought not to come into it till the declaration of rights is annexed to it."[34]

The contests for Convention seats at the March elections were hard fought. Richard Henry Lee, whom Mason had urged to offer, excused himself on grounds of health and remained an active letter-writer at Chantilly. The strong Federalist sentiment in the Northern Neck would have given him a very tough contest. Since it was clear that Mason would experience similar difficulties as a candidate in Fairfax, his plans were the subject of lively conjecture. On 8 October 1787, Lambert Cadwalader of New Jersey, who greatly approved of the Constitution and was correspondingly sanguine of its adoption, forecast that Mason would either not be chosen or would be instructed to agree to adoption. On 12 January 1788, Colonel Carrington reported to General Knox that "Colo. Mason is decidedly discarded by a Majority of his late constituents in Fairfax County—so conscious is he that they will not elect him for the Convention that, he has declared himself a Candidate for a Neighbouring County [Stafford] where he is invited by some characters of influence who are with him in opinion; but it is supposed he will not succeed in the election."[35]

Yet a month later David Stuart, in an estimate of the county situation for Washington, wondered if Mason might try from Fairfax after all: "I have just returned from a tour round most of the county. . . . I have found that Pope and Chichester [Mason's son-in-law] in particular have been very active in alarming the people. The latter Gentleman and myself were near meeting at several houses—He had his pockets full of Mason's objections; which he leaves wherever he calls. . . . I almost thi[nk] that Mason, doubtful of his election in Stafford will offer for

*Major General Henry Knox by*
*Charles Peale Polk*
*(courtesy, National Portrait Gallery,*
*Smithsonian Institution, Washington, D.C.)*

this County . . . he might have been satisfied with the publication of his objections, without taking the pains to [lodge] them at every house."[36]

In the end, Mason won narrowly in Stafford, where two Federalist candidates split the proratification vote. Roger West replaced him as Fairfax representative in the Assembly.

As soon as the election results were in hand, speculation burgeoned on the probable vote in the Convention. Mason's estimate agreed with the general view that the men who would assemble in Richmond would be very equally divided between ayes and nays. Madison felt a dozen votes would be decisive. Washington wrote Jay that the Federalists hoped for a majority of twenty but that they were apprehensive of "the arts that may yet be practised, to excite alarm with the members from the western district."[37]

Blair Smith, president of Hampden-Sydney College, shared Washington's concern about the west and advised Madison that Patrick Henry, easily elected despite opposition in Prince Edward County, was stirring up discontent in Kentucky, whose fourteen delegates might well be decisive in the final vote. Kentucky's Anti-Federalist sentiment was fired by resentment against John Jay's recent negotiations with Spain. Other geographic divisions among delegates had less specific cause and were of longer standing: the Federalists lived chiefly in Tidewater, the Northern Neck, and the Shenandoah Valley; the Anti-Federalists in the Southside, the Piedmont, and the area beyond the Alleghenies. The latter were predominantly small farmers, advocates of paper money, debtors—Patrick Henry's natural constituency; the former were merchants, plantation owners, lawyers, and in the Valley, Presbyterians eager for stability.

Mason's temper as he set forth for Richmond is reflected in his letter of 26 May to Jefferson, in which he enclosed a printed copy of his "Objections":*

I make no Doubt that you have long ago received Copys of the new Constitution of Government. . . . Upon the most mature Consideration I was capable of, and from Motives of sincere Patriotism, I was under the Necessity of refusing my Signature, as one of the Virginia Delegates; and drew up some general Objections; which I intended to offer, by Way of Protest; but was discouraged from doing so, by the precipitate, & intemperate, not to say indecent Manner, in which the Business was conducted, during the last Week of the Convention, after the Patrons of this new plan found they had a decided Majority in their Favour, which was obtained by a Compromise between the Eastern, and the two Southern States, to permit the latter to continue the Importation of Slaves for twenty odd Years; a more favourite Object with them than the Liberty and Happiness of the People. . . . From the best Information I have had, the Members of the Virginia Convention are so equally divided upon the Subject, that no Man can, at present, form any certain Judgement of the Issue. There seems to be a great Majority for Amendments; but many are for ratifying first, and amending afterwards. This Idea appears to me so utterly absurd, that I can not think any Man of sense candid, in Proposing it.[38]†

# Chapter XV
# Ratification with a Bill of Rights

*When the Virginia Convention gathered in Richmond, leaders of both persua-*
sions lodged side by side at the Swan, a one-story wooden building
whose long porch fronted Broad Street between 8th and 9th—Mason
and Henry were there, and so were Madison and Pendleton.* All had
ridden or driven into town through fetlock-deep dust—Virginia was
wilting in a hot tobacco-killing drought.

The opening session was held in the Public Buildings, the three-
story wooden structure on the corner of Cary and 14th streets built in
1780 to house the government when the capital moved from Williamsburg. But the crowds were such that Mason proposed a shift to the
more spacious new Academy† in the center of the square bounded by
Broad, Marshall, 11th, and 12th streets.

Pendleton, now Virginia's chief justice, was chosen chairman.
Sixty-seven and frail, dependent on his crutch in moving about, he was
permitted to remain seated when addressing the house. Wythe, now
judge of the Court of Chancery, presided over the greater part of the
debates as chairman of the Committee of the Whole—these two old
antagonists now found themselves in accord for ratification. The twenty-
four-member, geographically representative Committee of Privileges
and Elections closely balanced the two parties: Anti-Federalist Benjamin Harrison was chairman and Mason the second man named, but
friends of the Constitution were thought to have a two-man advantage.

The appointment of a shorthand reporter raised objections.
Mason opposed it as contrary to parliamentary usage—and also because
he believed that David Robertson of Petersburg, the man selected, was
a Federalist. Many members were critical of the published result: Robertson was not centrally seated and found the words of speakers
with weak voices, like Madison, hard to catch; from time to time he
simply noted that he could not hear.‡

The contrast between this Convention and that at Philadelphia
could hardly have been greater. Spasmodic attendance by most of the
fifty-five men who appeared at Philadelphia at one time or another
reduced that assembly to a group of comfortable size for discussion.
The twenty-eight counties organized in Virginia since independence

*Edmund Pendleton*
*by Thomas Sully*
*after a miniature*
*by William Mercer*
*(courtesy, The Virginia*
*Historical Society)*

raised the delegate roll at Richmond to 170 as compared with the 129 Constitutionmakers who assembled at Williamsburg in 1776, and their attendance was faithful. In Philadelphia, secrecy had been the rule, and members only were present. In Richmond, press and public packed themselves around the official participants.

The Richmond session, moreover, instead of being a search for viable new ideas and common ground, was essentially an adversary proceeding. Members of both sides had previously affirmed themselves willing to accommodate, but the subject before this house was to give a clear-cut yes or no answer on whether to ratify, at once, the Constitution in the form submitted. Each side claimed to represent a majority of popular sentiment, though for the most part more modestly than Patrick Henry, who declared himself "satisfied four-fifths of our inhabitants are opposed to the new scheme of government. Indeed, in the part of this country lying south of James River, I am confident nine-tenths are opposed to it."[1]

The forthcoming debates were therefore seen as a contest in which reason or exhortation,* or a combination of the two, would lead a few delegates to change their views if personally free or go against their instructions if elected under instruction. The Convention had a courtroom atmosphere, with the case for and against ratification being argued before an attentive jury; the impression was enhanced by the jury-like attitude of the great majority of the delegates. Robertson may have occasionally omitted minor entries in the debates, but on non-procedural matters he records the speeches of fewer than twenty men; at least 150 of the 170 delegates were auditors up to the moment of the vote.

Counsel for each side were evenly matched. In addition to Pendleton and Wythe, Madison, "Light-Horse Harry" Lee, George Nicholas, John Marshall, James Innes, Francis Corbin, and Charles Clay were known to be for ratification. Henry, Mason, Benjamin Harrison, William Grayson, John Tyler, James Monroe, and John Dawson were known to oppose it, at least until modifications were made.

The great uncertainty was the governor: Edmund Randolph had not signed in Philadelphia, and in the autumn his "Letter . . . on the Federal Constitution" was critical of the document; but he had never closed the door to its support, and growing rumor now named him in its favor. In January, he had urged Madison to attend: "You must come in. Some people in Orange are opposed to your politicks. Your election to the convention is, I believe sure; but I beg you not to hazard it by being absent at the time."[2]

Counsel for ratification enjoyed a great advantage—each speech buttressed their argument with cumulative effect. The argument of the principal opposition counsel, on the contrary, was bifurcated at its core: Mason and Henry proceeded from different premises. To Henry, the Constitution was a catastrophe; to Mason, a first draft in need of revision.

From the time the Philadelphia Convention was first proposed, Henry had been against a strengthened central government, root and branch; when challenged as to why he did not accept the Assembly's offer of membership in the Virginia delegation and work for a document that he could support, he is said to have dismissed the query with "I smelt a rat."

Mason's opposition had indeed hardened in the heat of the attacks on him in recent months. On 22 April, Madison told Jefferson: "Col. M——n is growing every day more bitter, and outrageous in his efforts to carry his point; and will probably in the end be thrown by the violence of his passions into the politics of Mr. H——y."[3] Some two weeks earlier Nicholas had said, "I have reason to believe his sentiments are much changed which I attribute to two causes: first the irritation he feels from the hard things that have been said of him, and secondly to a vain opinion he entertains (which has industriously been supported by some particular characters) that he has influence enough to dictate a constitution to Virginia, and through her to the rest of the Union."[4]

Yet while the two chief opponents were in constant consultation, and memoirs of participants recalled their daily morning walks together from the Swan to the Academy, arm in arm, both prior to the Convention and again and again at the close of his speeches there, Mason stated that if his specific objections were met, the document would have his support.

Henry was the opponent whom the Federalists really feared. In March, Colonel Carrington had deplored to General Knox: "the danger is, that a great proportion of the Assembly will be so overborn by the declamatory powers of Mr. Henry as to be deceived into his measures although their ultimate views may be intirely different. it is held out by Mr. Henry and his demagogues that Virga. is so important that she can bring nine or even 12 States to her measures."[5]

Carrington's estimate was just: when Henry addressed the Convention, the scene became a theater rather than a court. At fifty-three he was a bit stooped; he wore wire-rimmed spectacles; he had a nervous mannerism of twirling his skimpy brown wig. But the magnetic eye, the cadence of a voice that played on his audience like a musical instrument, and the compelling elocutionary style absorbed in youth from evangelist George Whitefield were now no less potent than when fourteen years earlier Mason called him "the most powerful speaker I ever heard." Madison dreaded the impact of such eloquence; again and again, the entire assemblage trembled to Henry's words.

The Federalists were delighted when, at the opening session, the dignified figure of Mason, his white hair set off by a black suit, advanced to offer a motion that set the agenda in exactly the mold that Madison preferred. As an advocate of reasoned consideration, Mason proposed that the Convention, acting as a Committee of the Whole, take up the Constitution clause by clause. "Light-Horse Harry" Lee was impatient of the suggestion: every one, he said, was familiar with the document, and the Convention must finish its work before the Virginia Assembly session set for 23 June. But members approved Mason's motion, and on that basis debate was ordered begun.

Madison correctly believed that a clause-by-clause procedure would not suit Henry's style, but Henry's intent never to allow himself to be confined by it was evident as soon as the group gathered the next morning. He rose to challenge the making of the document as ultra vires—the Philadelphia delegates had not amended the Articles of Confederation, and that was what the Congress had instructed them to do.

I consider myself as the servant of the people of this Commonwealth, as a centinel over their rights, liberty, and happiness. I represent their feelings when I say, that they are exceedingly uneasy. . . . If our situation be thus uneasy, whence has arisen this fearful jeopardy? It arises from this fatal system—it arises from a proposal to change our government:—A proposal that goes to the utter annihilation of the most solemn engagements of the States. . . . That this is a consolidated Government is demonstrably clear, and the danger of such a Government, is, to my mind, very striking. I have the highest veneration for those Gentlemen,—but, Sir, give me leave to demand, what right had they to say, *"We, the people?"* My political curiosity, exclusive of my anxious solicitude for

*Attempts at the features of Patrick Henry.—*

*Sketches of Patrick Henry, traced by Thomas Crawford from the sketchbook of Benjamin Henry Latrobe (courtesy, The Papers of Benjamin Henry Latrobe, Maryland Historical Society)*

the public welfare, leads me to ask, who authorized them to speak the language of, *We, the people,* instead of, *We, the States?* States are the characteristics, and the soul of a confederation. If the states be not the agents of this compact, it must be one great consolidated, National Government, of the people of all the States.[6]

Although throughout the sessions, neither Wythe nor Pendleton made a great effort to hold a tight parliamentary rein, in this case, Pendleton downed Henry with a ruling that since the Congress of the Confederation had submitted this Constitution to this convention with a request for a vote, debate should go forward.

For a brief interval, members then followed agreed procedure; the clerk read the preamble and first two sections of Article I and George Nicholas—squat, fat, and bald, sometimes caricatured as a plum pudding with legs, but a speaker whom Henry respected—addressed himself for two hours to the provisions for the House of Representatives.

As soon as he ended, the portly, personable governor rose. Dismissing Henry's objection to "We, the people" as "one of the most trivial that will be made to the Convention"—a government that was to be for the people could well start with that phrase—he made the awaited announcement that placed him on the Federalist side. Mindful that eight states had now acceded to the Constitution, and though there were amendments he thought desirable, he was prepared to support the document as it stood: "As with me the only question has ever been, between previous, and subsequent amendments, so will I express my apprehensions, that the postponement of this Convention, to so late a day, has extinguished the probability of the former without inevitable ruin to the Union, and the Union is the anchor of our political salvation."[7]

In the hush of realization of the weight of this announcement, Mason took the floor for substantive debate. To convert "what was formerly a confederation, to a consolidated government" he declared, is "to annihilate totally the state governments"; while no man was a greater friend to a firm union, he nevertheless doubted that a general national government could effectively control "so extensive a country, abounding in such a variety of climates, etc." The tax power should be given to Congress only for use if and when the states fail to comply with requisitions. He forecast his opposition to the judiciary article. But in closing, he wished for "such amendments and such only, as are necessary to secure the dearest rights of the people."[8]

Madison then stood up, a small figure in blue and buff with ruffled lace, hat in hand and notes in hat. Reserving his further remarks for the next morning, he urged on the Convention the importance of following its agreed procedure.

That night members set down their first estimates of the situation. Madison cheered Washington, who sent word on to John Jay: the first days of the Convention had been "as auspicious as could possibly have been expected." From the opposition, William Grayson conceded to Nathan Dane, "We are alarmed. We do not despond."

On 5 June, however, Madison lay ill at the Swan and could not speak as scheduled. Pendleton took his place to refute both of the previous Anti-Federalist speakers: the Constitution would be the shield and protector of liberty and would "not intermeddle with the local particular affairs of the states." "Light-Horse Harry" charged into the lists, accusing Henry of appealing to members' fears: "I trust he is come to judge, and not to alarm." An aroused Henry rose for a speech lasting more than three hours, a rising crescendo of rhetorical questions in defense of the liberties assured by the Bill of Rights:

The rights of conscience, of trial by jury, liberty of the press, all your immunities and franchises, all pretentions to human rights and privileges, are rendered insecure, if not lost, by this change so loudly talked of by some, and inconsiderately by others. Is this tame relinquishment of rights worthy of freemen? Is it worthy of that manly fortitude that ought to characterize republicans: It is said eight States have adopted this plan. I declare that if twelve States and an half had adopted it, I would with manly firmness, and in spite of an erring world, reject it. You are not to inquire how your trade may be increased, nor how you are to become a great and powerful people, but how your liberties can be secured; for liberty ought to be the direct end of your government. . . . Liberty the greatest of all earthly blessings—give us that precious jewel, and you may take everything else: But I am fearful I have lived long enough to become an old-fashioned fellow.[9]

Next morning, the Federalists seized the initiative, putting up a succession of three of their weightiest speakers—Randolph, Madison, and Nicholas—to counter this major attack. They cataloged the weaknesses that had made changes in the confederation necessary; Nicholas remarked that "as there can be no liberty without government, it must be as dangerous to make power too little as too great." The now-recovered Madison presented a closely reasoned review and counseled against the confusion that would attend amendment before ratification.

Pressure on the Anti-Federalists continued on the seventh, when Francis Corbin raised the touchy question of how, without a strong government possessed of independent tax powers, payments could be made on the confederation's international debts: "How long, Sirs, shall we be able by fair promises to satisfy these creditors? How long can we amuse by idle words those who are amply possessed of the means of doing themselves justice?" Randolph again summarized the defects of the confederation, and Madison reviewed the weaknesses of all confederations from the time of the Greeks.

Responding, Henry declared that the Virginia bill of rights contained maxims of liberty which must be preserved. He raised the specter of the federal excise man and the probable lavishness of a central government.

On Saturday, Randolph observed that Mason was absent from the House—it was the following Wednesday before he spoke again. Madison's report to Washington revealed what was going on: "Oswald of Philada., has been here with letters of the antifederal leaders from N. York and probably Philada. He staid a very short time here during which he was occasionally closeted with H——y and M—a—on &c."[10]

The New York Convention was scheduled to open on 17 June; in preparation, that state's Federal Republican Committee, of which Gen. John Lamb was chairman, had asked the Richmond Committee of Opposition to let him have copies of amendments that they were prepared to back. Mason was at work on a draft. He, Grayson, and Henry all wrote Lamb on the ninth; Colonel Oswald carried the agreed amendments back by hand a few days later. Mason said: "Although there is a general Concurrence in the Convention of this State that Amendments are necessary, yet, the Members are so equally divided with respect to the Time and Manner of obtaining them, that it cannot now be ascertained whether the Majority will be on our Side or not; if it should be so, I have no doubt but that an Official Communication will immediately take place between the Convention of this State and yours."[11]

During these conferences, Henry, unlike Mason, continued to attend the sessions, where the extent to which Randolph was becoming a stalwart Federalist irked him. His observation that it now "appeared the system once execrated by the honorable member must be adopted, let its defects be ever so glaring" brought Randolph angrily to his feet. Such a remark, he thundered, was "incompatible with the least shadow of friendship"; if their friendship must fall, "let it fall like Lucifer, never to rise again." He threw on the table a letter to his constituents, to be available, he said, "for the inspection of the curious and the malicious." Henry promptly named Col. William Cabell of Amherst as his second, and for some hours members held their breaths lest there be a duel.

On the tenth, Monroe made his initial entry into the discussion, dwelling on the powers proper for a central government; he thought the doctrine that all powers not ceded were retained by the states an illusion unless specifically declared, and John Marshall rose to defend the thesis that a union of purse and sword was inevitable under any government.

When Mason next spoke, on the tax power, he obliquely called attention to a powerful Federalist presence making itself felt outside the Convention doors. Both of the Morrises, the Great Financier and his associate had come to town and were known to be attentively following the debates.

In the course of examining what type of tax structure could be anticipated if an independent tax power were given to the central government, Mason quoted from a 1782 report in which Robert Morris suggested to the Congress that, in addition to a land tax and a poll tax, a tax on spirits "will be a means of compelling vice to support the cause of virtue, and, like the poll tax, will draw from the idle and dissolute that contribution to the public service which they will not otherwise make."[12] Though Robertson reported, "Mr. Mason declared that he did not mean to make the smallest reflection on Mr. Morris,* but introduced his letter to shew what taxes would probably be laid," "Light-Horse Harry" rebuked the maker of this sally: "Does he imagine that he that can raise the loudest laugh is the soundest reasoner?"

Much of the week of 9–13 June was spent on a question as touchy for the Federalists as that of the confederation's debts was for their opponents: the navigation of the Mississippi as affected by the treaty power. The 7 to 5 vote by which Congress had authorized Jay to yield navigation rights for twenty-five years had been a straight vote of the northern and central states against those of the South. On the ninth, Henry warned: "If a bare majority of Congress can make laws the situation of our western states is dreadful." Three days later, he linked the Mississippi question to the main issue: "We are told that, in order to secure the navigation of that river, it was necessary to give it up for twenty-five years to the Spaniards, and that thereafter we should enjoy it forever, without interruption from them. The argument resembles that which recommends adopting first and then amending."[13]

Grayson and Tyler, both of whom had been in Congress at the time of the decision, supported him. Corbin began a riposte, but as he spoke, the long drought broke; a shattering storm drowned his words and forced the Convention to adjourn.

With this debate, the Anti-Federalists reached the peak of their strength. Ten of the fourteen Kentucky delegates voted against the Constitution. In his weekend situation estimate, Madison thought "the business is in the most ticklish state that can be imagined"; he expected a very small majority indeed and perhaps not on the Federalist side. Similarly, Theodorick Bland informed Arthur Lee that each side was claiming a majority of from three to eight but that he suspected there was "a decided majority for interior amendments, that is who do

*Robert Morris by an unknown artist,*
*c. 1782*
*(courtesy, Independence National*
*Historical Park, Philadelphia)*

not think it prudent to mount a high-blooded, fiery steed, without a bridle."[14]

On the morning of the fourteenth, word passed from mouth to mouth that Pendleton was ill; Anti-Federalist John Tyler was voted temporarily into the chair. The week's debate ranged over various topics: the federal power over the militia and the dangers of a standing army, the election and the impeachment of the president, the treaty power, the judiciary article. Mason was a frequent participant in all of these considerations; in addition, he took occasion to express once more his abhorrence of slavery, to insist that the office of the vice-president was unnecessary and dangerous, and to raise a specter of crime in the federally controlled ten-mile square:

This ten miles square . . . may set at defiance the laws of the surrounding states, and may, like the custom of the superstitious days of our ancestors, become the sanctuary of the blackest crimes. Here the federal courts are to sit. We have heard a good deal said of justice. . . . What sort of a jury shall we have within the ten miles square? The immediate creatures of the government. What chance will poor men get, where congress have power of legislating in all cases whatever, and where judges and juries may be under their influence, and bound to support their operations?[15]

On the sixteenth, with Pendleton back in the Convention, Mason reverted to the doctrine of reserved powers: "That congress should have power to provide for the general welfare of the union, I grant. But I wish a clause in the constitution with respect to all powers which are not granted, that they are retained by the states. Otherwise the power of providing for the general welfare may be perverted to its destruction."[16]

When the first clause of the ninth section, comprising the terms of the deal at Philadelphia between the North and the South, came up on the seventeenth, Mason delivered one of his final speeches on slavery:

This is a fatal section, which has created more dangers than any other. The first clause, allows the importation of slaves for twenty years. Under the royal government, this evil was looked upon as a great oppression, and many attempts were made to prevent it; but the interest of the African merchants prevented its prohibition. No sooner did the revolution take place, than it was thought of. It was one of the great causes of our separation from Great-Britain. Its exclusion has been a principal object of this state, and of most of the states in the union. The augmentation of slaves weakens the states; and such a trade is diabolical in itself, and disgraceful to mankind. Yet by this constitution it is continued for twenty years. As much as I value an union of all the states, I would not admit the southern states into the union, unless they agreed to the discontinuance of this disgraceful trade, because it would bring weakness and not strength to the union.[17]

Madison's reply reminded Mason that the Deep South would not have come in without the clause and that a twenty-year limit was an improvement on the absence of any restriction of slavery under the Articles of Confederation.

When the judiciary article was canvassed on the nineteenth, Mason declared that with the scope allowed in this proviso there would be no limit to federal power. It would destroy the states, rendering them mean and contemptible. It would apply " 'To controversies between a state, and the citizens of another state'. . . . Is this state to be brought to the bar of justice like a delinquent individual? Is the sovereignty of the state to be arraigned like a culprit, or private offender. . . . What is to be done if a judgment be obtained against a state. . . . It would be ludicrous to say, that you could put the state's body in jail. . . . A power which cannot be executed, ought not to be granted."[18]

Rising to refute Mason next day, Marshall declared: "With respect to disputes between a state and the citizens of another state, its jurisdiction has been decried with unusual vehemence. I hope no gentleman will think that a state will be called at the bar of the federal court. . . . It is not rational to suppose that the sovereign power shall be dragged before a court. The intent is to enable States to recover claims of individuals residing in other States. I contend this construction is warranted by the words. I see a difficulty in making a state a defendant, which does not prevent its being a plaintiff."[19]

(Marshall was wrong. It took the eleventh amendment to the Constitution to meet Mason's point, for the U.S. Supreme Court, in its first major case, *Chisholm* v. *Georgia,* ruled that a state could be sued. Proposed in March 1794 and ratified four years later, this amendment reads: "The judicial power of the United States shall not be construed to extend to any suit in law or equity, commenced or prosecuted against one of the United States by citizens of another state, or by citizens or subjects of any foreign state.")

Situation estimates at the end of this, the final week of debate, were far from dogmatic. On the nineteenth, Federalist Archibald Stuart of Augusta calculated to John Breckinridge of Albemarle that only six delegates were still uncommitted, "any three of whom will give us a Majority, the fate of Virga. is thus suspended upon a Single Hare."[20]

But once the judiciary article was out of the way, Madison felt better. Even on the twentieth, his arithmetic had comforted Hamilton: "At present, it is calculated that we still retain a majority of three or four if we can weather the storm against the part under consideration, I shall hold the danger to be pretty well over."[21] His letter of the twenty-third to Washington announced Anti-Federalist "despair: Col. Mason in particular talked in a style which no other sentiment could have produced. He held out the idea of civil convulsions as the effects of obtruding the Government on the people. He was answered by several and concluded with declaring his determination for himself to acquiesce in the event whatever it might be."[22]

As the clause-by-clause debate reached its latter stages, the desirability of following the lead of Massachusetts in presenting an agreed list of subsequent amendments had begun to gain ground among advocates of both persuasions, with a bill of rights at the top of the list. Henry's almost daily warnings of the peril of omitting such guarantees were beginning to have a cumulative effect. Proponents of the Constitution still argued that the document already contained adequate protection—Nicholas brought Mason indignantly to his feet when he declared, "But, sir, this bill of rights was no security. It is but a paper check." Madison, if more on tactical than on substantive grounds, was slowly turning toward inclusion of such a bill.

A second increasingly accepted idea was to extend the concept of individual rights to states' rights, by giving assurance that the states retained all powers not expressly granted to the central government.

The approach of the Assembly session applied pressure to terminate. On 24 June, Wythe, relinquishing the chair of the Committee on the Whole, proposed ratification.

Henry responded by introducing fifteen prior amendments, essentially the ones concerted by the Opposition Committee in the 9–14 June period. Randolph disproved their necessity, item by item: "I ask you, if it be not better to adopt, and run the chance of amending it hereafter, than run the risk of endangering the Union? The Confederation is gone; It has no authority. If, in this situation, we reject the Constitution, the Union will be dissolved."[23] Mason, Monroe's brother-in-law John Dawson, and Grayson countered him: Dawson averred that the cup of slavery which would be pressed to the lips of the people by the adoption of the Constitution, was "not sweetened, whether administered by the hand of a Turk, a Briton, or an American";[24] less dramatically, Grayson stressed the dangers of a continent divided between accepting and nonaccepting states.

Henry's last speech before the curtain went down was enhanced by special stage effects of sound and light:

When I see beyond the horrison that binds human eyes, and look at the final consummation of all human things, and see those intelligent beings which inhabit the aetherial mansions, reviewing the political decisions and revolutions which in the progress of time will happen in America, and the consequent happiness or misery of mankind—I am led to believe that much of the account on one side or the other, will depend on what we now decide. Our own happiness alone is not affected by the event—All nations are interested in the determination. We have it in our power to secure the happiness of one half of the human race. Its adoption may involve the misery of the other hemispheres.[25]

Robertson's text breaks off: "Here a violent storm arose, which put the house in such disorder, that Mr. *Henry* was obliged to conclude." Nicholas proposed the question for decision the next day.

In the early speeches on the twenty-fifth, Nicholas and Harrison, Madison and Monroe alternated in advocacy of subsequent or prior amendments. James Innes then declaimed in favor of immediate ratification so stirringly that Henry generously complimented an "eloquence splendid, magnificent and sufficient to shake the human mind."

Two of the final speakers were heard with special attention by vote-estimators: Adam Stephen of the mountain county of Berkeley and Zachariah Johnston of Augusta in the critical Shenandoah Valley. They declared themselves in favor. Quickly sensing the political significance of what they said, Henry announced, "I wish not to go on to violence, but will wait with hopes that the spirit which predominated in the revolution is not yet gone. . . . I shall therefore patiently wait in expectation of seeing that Government changed so as to be compatible with the safety, liberty and happiness, of the people."[26]

Randolph ended the debate.

As members prepared to cast their ballots, twin resolutions were brought forward. The first moved ratification with the proviso that such amendments as the Convention agreed upon would be recommended for consideration by the first Congress to assemble under the new plan. The second, a substitute for the preceding, moved that before ratification a bill of rights and other amendments should be submitted to the other states for their consideration and action.

Five votes proved enough to determine the issue. The substitute motion fell short: ayes 80, nays 88. The original motion was then carried: ayes 89, nays 79. By a majority of ten, Virginia had ratified the Constitution. A motion by George Mason, seconded by Patrick Henry, moved that the ayes and nays be made a matter of record.

A five-man committee of Federalists was appointed to prepare a form of ratification. A twenty-man group, drawn from both sides and including Henry and Mason, was named to report a list of amendments; two days later it presented a twenty-article bill of rights, repeating much of the bill that Mason had drafted twelve years previously, and twenty other amendments, largely the list that Henry had offered for adoption. All were accepted.

The news reached Alexandria on the evening of 27 June; the next day, at Wise's Tavern, in Washington's presence, thirteen toasts terminated a festive dinner, punctuated by cannon shot.

Until the wee hours of the following morning, Alexandrians assumed that Virginia's constituted the ninth and decisive accession. But a dispatch rider who then reached town brought word that New Hampshire had had the honor, by a majority of 11, on the twenty-first. Virginia was the tenth state.

In New York, the parade down Broadway that celebrated the Constitution's entry into force served also as an instrument of psychological warfare; that state's Convention was still sitting at Poughkeepsie, and Yates and Lansing were in active opposition there. The forward-looking Hamilton was making the most of the celebration in New York City. The New York ratification, on 30 July, was by a three-vote margin, 30 to 27.* The fifteen-year-old Princeton student, John Randolph (later known as Randolph of Roanoke), sent his father an eyewitness description of the festivities:

a very grand Procession . . . proceeded . . . down Broadway thro' Wall Street . . . to the Foederal Green . . . where there were tables set for more than five Thousand poeple to Dine—two Oxen were roasted whole and several cows and Sheep . . . there were ten tables, set out to represent the ten States which had acceded to the Constitution, all which were concentered together at one end like the sticks of a Fan; where they joined were seated all the Congress with the president in the middle. The Procession was very beautiful and well conducted.

Every trade and profession had a Colour emblematical of it. The cheif of the Bakers were drawn on a stage on which they were seen mixing their bread; the apprentices all in white followed with ready baked Cakes. The Coopers followed making barrels and the apprentices follow with a keg under the arm of each. next came the Brewers bringing hogshead of beer along with a little Bacchus a stride a Cask holding a large Goblet in his hand . . . to the honor of New York be it spoken that among 8000 people who were said to have dined together on the green there was not a single Drunken Man or fight to be seen.[27]

In Virginia, by contrast, the celebration was low-keyed; the Richmond Convention had a disagreeable aftermath. On 27 June, Madison notified Washington:

The Convention came to a final adjournment today. The inclosed is a copy of their Act of ratification with the yeas & nays. A variety of amendments have been since recommended; several of them highly objectionable, but which could not be parried. The Minority are to sign an address this evening which is announced to be of a peace-making complexion. Having not seen it I can give no opinion of my own. I wish it may not have a further object.[28]

According to "A Spectator of the Meeting," in the *Independent Chronicle* of 9 July, it did in fact have a further object: Anti-Federalists who attended expecting an address "to reconcile the minds of their constituents" were offered a document "tending to irritate rather than to quiet the public mind." Some of those present walked out. Benjamin Harrison, backed by Tyler and Lawson, moved that no action be taken; "Mr. Mason discovering their sentiments to prevail generally, prudently and with temper withdrew his address."

The meeting had more background than appeared in this report. The Assembly, as soon as it had a quorum on the twenty-fifth, took formal cognizance of a letter communicated to it by the governor the day before. Dated 8 May, it had been written to Randolph by Governor George Clinton of New York proposing cooperative action between their two states to secure prior amendments. The Anti-Federalists, who enjoyed an ample majority in the Assembly under Patrick Henry's leadership, considered themselves to have been tricked. When they sent a committee to hear the governor's reasons for withholding it until the Virginia Convention was over, Randolph's explanation was unconvincing: on receipt of the letter, he had submitted it to the Council for a ruling as to whether it was a public or a private communication; when the Council decided that it was public, he had felt bound to keep it until the Assembly met.*

In the autumn, the Assembly's choice of Virginia's first pair of U.S. senators showed it to be unreconciled. The vote that sent two ranking Anti-Federalists to New York was: Richard Henry Lee, 98; William Grayson, 86; James Madison, 77.[†]

During the months before the inauguration of the new government, correspondence between Madison in New York and Jefferson in Paris further examined the limitations and the strengths of a bill of rights.

On 17 October, Madison sent Jefferson a pamphlet that collected

New York parade in
honor of the adoption
of the federal
Constitution
(courtesy,
Emmet Collection,
Manuscripts and
Archives Division,
The New York Public
Library, Astor,
Lenox and Tilden
Foundations)

all the alterations of the Constitution that had been proposed saying:
"not a few, particularly in Virginia have contended for the proposed
alterations from the most honorable & patriotic motives. . . . My own
opinion has always been in favor of a bill of rights; provided it be so
framed as not to imply powers not meant to be included in the enumeration. At the same time I have never thought the omission a material
defect, nor been anxious to supply it even by subsequent amendment,
for any other reason than that it is anxiously desired by others." Illus-
trating from his campaign on behalf of Jefferson's beloved Statute for
Religious Freedom three years before, he forced Jefferson's attention to
the vulnerability of a bill of rights to the tyranny of a majority:

> Repeated violations of these parchment barriers have been committed by
> overbearing majorities in every State. In Virginia I have seen the bill of rights
> violated in every instance where it has been opposed to a popular current. Not-
> withstanding the explicit provision contained in that instrument for the rights
> of Conscience, it is well known that a religious establishment wd. have taken
> place in that State, if the Legislative majority had found as they expected. . . .
> Wherever the real power in a Government lies, there is the danger of oppression.
> In our Governments the real power lies in the majority of the Community, and
> the invasion of private rights is *chiefly* to be apprehended, not from acts of
> Government contrary to the sense of its constituents, but from acts in which
> the Government is the mere instrument of the major number of the Constitu-
> ents. This is a truth of great importance, but not yet sufficiently attended to.[29]

Replying on 15 March 1789, Jefferson in turn directed Madison's
attention to the value of a bill of rights as a point of reference that would
assure the judiciary a firm independent status and give reality to the
separation of powers:

In the arguments in favor of a declaration of rights, you omit one which has great weight with me, the legal check which it puts into the hands of the judiciary. This is a body, which if rendered independent, and kept strictly to their own department merits great confidence for their learning and integrity. In fact what degree of confidence would be too much for a body composed of such men as Wythe, Blair, and Pendleton? On characters like these the "civium ardor prava jubentium" would make no impression. I am happy to find that on the whole you are a friend to this amendment. The Declaration of rights is like all other human blessings alloyed with some inconveniences, and not accomplishing fully it's object. But the good in this instance vastly overweighs the evil.[30]

Within weeks after the federal House of Representatives organized, on 4 May 1789, Madison announced that he would very shortly "bring on the subject of amendments to the constitution,"* and on 8 June, he presented a list comprising most of the items common to the proposals submitted by the several states; after these had lain before the House for six weeks, a select committee of a member from each of the eleven states that had so far ratified was appointed to consider not only Madison's condensation but the complete lists forwarded by the states.†

The most important change proposed by this committee was to present Madison's suggestions, which he had envisaged as insertions in the body of the Constitution, in the form of a list of separate amendments to the document. On 24 August, seventeen proposals were sent to the Senate for concurrence.

By 9 September, the Senate had reduced the number of articles to twelve and considerably improved their style. On 23 September, the conference report of the two bodies was presented to the House by Madison and to the Senate by Ellsworth. Two days later, President Washington received the document for transmission to the states.

The first two of the twelve articles submitted for state ratification concerned internal matters: one set the future relation between the number of members of the House of Representatives and the population; the other required that an election intervene between a vote changing the salaries of senators and representatives and the entry into force of the change. Neither was adopted. But all of Articles III through XII were approved. The first eight of these constituted a bill of rights closely parallel to Mason's Virginia declaration of 1776; Article XI affirmed that enumeration of certain rights in the Constitution did not affect the retention of others by the people, and Article XII specifically stated that all powers not delegated to the United States by the Constitution or prohibited by it to the states were retained by the states or by the people. In a little over two years, state ratifications imbedded these in the federal document. Virginia's adherence on 15 December 1791 was the final necessary vote.‡

In considerable part through the intransigence of the man who wrote the first state declaration, a bill of rights had been incorporated in the new nation's fundamental law. Mason's leading objection to the document drafted at Philadelphia had been eliminated with the active concurrence of the colleague who was its chief architect.

# Chapter XVI
# The French Counterpart

*Simultaneously, in the summer of 1789, Mason's Virginia Bill of Rights of 1776* became a progenitor of two such declarations proclaimed in the name of an entire nation—the first amendments to the Constitution of the United States, and the French *Déclaration des droits de l'homme*.

On 8 June, in New York, the American House of Representatives heard Madison present his recommended amendments to the document under which the new national government had become a reality three months before. On 11 July, three thousand miles away in Paris, the French Constituent Assembly heard the Marquis de Lafayette present his *Déclaration européene des droits de l'homme et du citoyen,** whose nine articles were combined with similar proposals from other sources in the *Déclaration des droits de l'homme* adopted by the Assembly on 27 August and promulgated by Louis XVI on 3 November.

It was fitting that Lafayette should be the link between the two. During 1784–85, while he was in the United States on his first postwar visit, his letters to his wife, Adrienne de Noailles, frequently transmitted instructions regarding the newly purchased residence on the left bank of the Seine into which they were about to move. Among these, he asked her to order twin picture frames, to serve a symbolic purpose in his study. One was to contain the engrossed copy of the Declaration of Independence that he had just ordered through Franklin's grandson; he wanted "to have it engraved in golden letters at the most conspicuous part of my cabinet, and when I wish to put myself in spirits, I will look at it and most voluptously read it over."[1] The other frame was to remain empty, awaiting, Lafayette said, the day when France should proclaim a similar document.

The theory of the French Revolution had been complete for some years before its outbreak. In spite of the surveillance of the Bourbon court and in spite of periodic necessity to seek a printer in Holland or take temporary refuge in England, the intellectuals of the time were amazingly unrestrained in both their letters and their conversation. To many who engaged in such discussions, and to some in powerful places who protected them, the transfer of revolutionary ideas into revolutionary action seemed remote: Lafayette's uncle, the comte de Ségur, later explained, "We thought it was only a warfare of pen and word, which to us appeared quite devoid of danger to the superior existence that we enjoyed."

The entourage of the king was even more oblivious of their coming downfall. The courtiers playing at shepherds and shepherdesses in Marie Antoinette's *petit hameau* would have been horrified by the commercial and fiscal program that the physiocrat economist, Pierre Samuel du Pont, suggested to Voltaire in 1769 to relieve the sufferings of French agriculture:

Paris is full of people who don't want to hear any mention of freedom of commerce. They say it will lead to freedom of thought. They are wrong; on the contrary, it will be one of the fruits of freedom to think and to write. They also say that restrictions [of trade] are not harmful to everyone; and that without the exclusive privileges which they establish, five or six million peasants would perhaps enjoy a far better soup, and a million proprietors fewer debts and difficulties, but that it would necessitate dismantling two hundred coaches that now circulate in Paris. It would be a good thing to do away with another three hundred if one were engaged in enriching the king by a form of taxation that would not ruin the People. Counting four horses, a master, and three servants per equipage, and adding them all together, you see, Monsieur, four thousand powerful animals, ready to be my enemies. It doesn't take nearly that many to persecute and destroy a poor man. I've always warned my wife that in marrying a reasonably honest citizen, brave enough to write about the public good, she should never be too sure of sleeping with him.[2]

Du Pont's semiserious style typified the cover under which early proposals for reform were advanced, but by 1788, the time for starker statements had arrived. The American ambassador was then in his element. In 1776, Jefferson had missed the Virginia Convention because of his service in the Continental Congress; in 1787, he had missed the Philadelphia Convention because of his French ambassadorship. But now, while theoretically an observer of revolutionary constitution-making in Paris, as giver of advice to long-time friends and as host for crucial consultations, he became in effect a participant.

In the winter of 1788–89, his zest for a French bill of rights, based on the Virginia pattern, leaps from the pages of letter after letter. On 20 December 1788, he announced to James Currie: "All the world is occupied at present in framing, every one his own plan of a bill of rights,"[3] and on 12 January 1789, he repeated to Madison, "Every body here is trying their hand at forming declarations of rights. As something of that kind is going on with you also, I send you two specimens from hence."[4]

One of the specimens was Lafayette's. For the next six months the ambassador and the marquis worked together; Lafayette's note to Jefferson of 9 July shows that the ambassador was suggesting changes down to the moment before Lafayette introduced his bill: "To Morrow I present my bill of rights about the middle of the sitting. Be pleased to Consider it Again, and Make Your observations."[5]

Their collaboration, however, was far from being the only channel of communication of American ideas to French revolutionary thought. During the 1780s, the American colony in Paris was numerous and well-informed; the successive ambassadors—Franklin until 1785 and Jefferson thereafter—were merely the ranking members of a group

*Déclaration des droits de l'homme et du citoyen, 1789*
*(courtesy, Service Photographique, Bibliothèque nationale, Paris)*

that included, for longer or shorter periods, John Adams, Henry Laurens, Silas Deane, the Lees, Mazzei, Gouverneur Morris, Tom Paine, and the very considerable number of children of the American Revolution who visited France in the 1780s—John Adams's son, John Quincy; Franklin's grand-nephew, Jonathan Williams, Jr.; Mason's sons, George and John; Dr. Shippen's son, Thomas Lee; young Edward Rutledge, and many more.

American experience was likewise available through the printed word. The American bills of rights had been at hand for a decade in the *Recueil des lois constitutives des colonies anglaises confédérées sous la dénomination de 'Etats-Unis de l'Amérique septentrionale,' auquel on a joint les acts d'Indépendance, de confédération et d'autres acts du Congrès général, dédié à M. le D. Franklin,* published in Paris in 1778. Paine's *Common Sense* had been promptly translated, as was *The Federalist* after the Philadelphia Convention.

Jefferson's *Notes on Virginia,* begun at Monticello in response to questions by the French diplomat, Barbé-Marbois, had been printed in English in Paris in 1785; a French translation by the Abbé Morellet came out in 1787, to the dissatisfaction of the author, who sent the abbé a list of seventy errors, "the correction of which is indispensable." Nevertheless, the translation was widely read.

Numerous French commentaries and travelogues included Brissot de Warville's *De la France et des Etats-Unis* in 1787 and his three-volume *Nouveau Voyage dans Les Etats-Unis* five years later. Between 1760 and 1790, twenty-six European commentaries on America circulated in three languages, and fifteen in four: French, English, German, and Dutch.*

In addition, word-of-mouth, eye-witness accounts of American bills of rights, constitutions, and initial government operations could be had from French officers who had served in America during the Revolution; many had maintained ties by joining the French Society of the Cincinnati at the close of the war. In extraordinary numbers, these young aristocrats were elected to the States General of 1789 as representatives of the noblesse.

A dilemma confronted them. Jefferson was Lafayette's mentor in the *crise de conscience* the young nobleman experienced in May 1789, one shared by a very considerable number of his fellow-officers. As a representative of the noblesse, he was bound by a firm mandate to insist that voting be by social orders rather than by individuals: the votes of the two privileged groups in the realm, the nobility and the clergy, would thus counterbalance the vote of the bourgeois Third Estate. When the Third Estate refused to accept the arrangement, successfully insisting on a merger of the orders, with decisions made on the basis of one man, one vote, Jefferson wrote Washington:

I am in great pain for the M. de la Fayette. His principles you know are clearly with the people. But having been elected for the noblesse of Auvergne, they have laid him under express instructions to vote for the decision by orders and

*Lafayette as commander of the French National Guard,*
*color etching by Hoffman, 1790*
*(courtesy, Virginia State Library)*

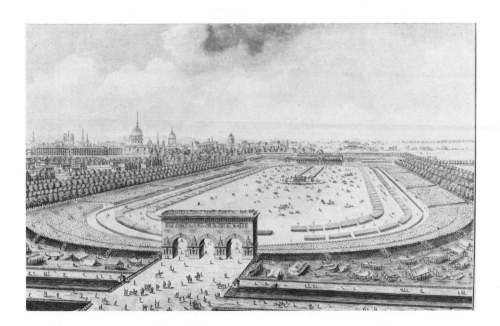

*"Vue du Champ de Mars, le 14 Juillet, 1790"*

*(courtesy, Service Photographique, Bibliothèque nationale, Paris)*

not persons. This would ruin him with the tiers etat, and it is not possible he should continue long to give satisfaction to the noblesse. I have not hesitated to press on him to burn his instructions and follow his conscience as the only sure clue which will eternally guide a man clear of all doubts and inconsistencies.[6]

The French officers' dilemma could be attributed to the difference between the social and political structure which they had observed in America and the French structure in which they were now called upon to act. In America, they had witnessed the establishment of a series of popular republics; a union of these republics had been the object of the recent national convention in Philadelphia. Here in Paris, they represented a privileged feudal order in a nation ruled by an absolute king. It was clear to Jefferson that in such circumstances a change to a constitutional monarchy, not a republic, was the most that could be safely attempted. He correctly believed that a country not yet emerged from feudalism was unready for more and that, if more were tried, social disruption would follow. However philosophically reasonable these young nobles thought citizenship in a republic to be, it was more than the fabric of Bourbon society could permit them. Their position was tenable only as long as they were working on the constitution whose acceptance the Assembly secured from the king on 14 September 1791.

But Louis had already lost the confidence of the nation by his attempt to leave the country the previous June in a flight halted only by chance recognition at Varennes. A specially summoned national convention abolished royalty on 21 September 1792; thereafter all chances for an orderly political transition vanished; and on 21 January 1793, hope of a constitutional monarchy went to the guillotine with the king.

A title was then a man's undoing; in a citizens' republic, a nobleman was out of place. As the anarchic violence of the Terror racked republican France; almost to a man, by year's end, 1793, the aristocrat-officers—Lafayette included—were in hiding, in exile, in prison, listed for beheading or already dead.

Their position, their dilemma, and their fate were shared by others who had not been in America but who admired the American experience in the light of world history. Notable among these was Marie Jean Antoine-Nicholas de Caritat, Marquis de Condorcet. A distinguished mathematician and philosopher, he was of exceptional influence in the formation of the French declaration of rights; he readied a draft as soon as the fusion of the States General created the National Assembly. When the Legislative Assembly succeeded it in 1791, he was elected a member and shortly chosen president. Yet in July 1793, he was forced into hiding; in March 1794, he was arrested; next morning he was found dead in his cell.

Condorcet's writings attributed an importance to the American Revolution endorsed by most of his colleagues. Yet the American bills of rights and the French declaration, even though they contained many of the same ideas and even phrases, had somewhat different premises. The French declaration emphasized universals rather than specifics, abstract rights to which man was entitled by his humanity. In his "Eloge de Franklin," Condorcet said that in most American states "a declaration of the rights of man sets the limits that nature and justice impose on the powers of society—a sublime idea, of which the ancient compacts between peoples and kings were only a first beginning, of which France should give the prior example to the Old World."[7]

The cousins and parents of the French declaration were the philosophers Voltaire and Rousseau, the encyclopedists, the physiocrats; its nurseries were the Thirty Club, the Masonic Lodge of the Nine Sisters, the salons where radical ideas could be discussed in freedom among friends, including a number of senior Americans. In additon to Condorcet, the circle included Turgot, the duc de la Rochefoucauld, the Rolands, Brissot de Warville.

In their thinking, the American Revolution was not just a historical event on the European periphery; it was an ideological force in the mainstream of human progress. Tom Paine, who avoided jail in England by fleeing to France in 1787, caught the different set of mind in his *Rights of Man,* published with Condorcet's encouragement and with its second part dedicated to Lafayette:

No beginning could be made in Asia, Africa, or Europe, to reform the political condition of man. Freedom had been hunted around the Globe. . . . But such is the irresistible nature of truth, that all it asks . . . is the liberty of appearing. . . . The independence of America, considered merely as a separation from England, would have been a matter but of little importance, had it not been accompanied by a revolution in the principles and practise of governments. She made a stand, not for herself only, but for the world. . . . America was the only spot in the political world where the principles of universal reformation could begin.[8]

Condorcet himself, in his posthumously published *Sketch for an Historical Picture of the Progress of the Human Mind,* attested the European impact of this revolution in very similar terms. The American cause, he said, had been "pleaded before the tribunal of opinion in the presence of all Europe. The rights of man were firmly sustained and developed, without restrictions or reservations, in writings that circulated from the shores of the Neva to those of the Guadalquivir. This document penetrated the most enslaved countries, the most remote villages, whose inhabitants were astonished to learn that they had rights. They learned to value those rights, now that they knew that other men had dared to assert and defend them."[9]

And in his *Ideas on Despotism,* he credited to George Mason the first statement of the rights of man in systematic form: "The first Declaration of Rights that is entitled to be called such is that of Virginia . . . its author is entitled to the eternal gratitude of mankind."[10]

In Jefferson's letter to Madison at the beginning of 1789, he said of Lafayette's declaration of rights, "You will see that it contains the essential principles of ours accomodated as much as could be to the actual state of affairs here."[11] Comparison of the eighteen articles of Mason's bill and the seventeen of the *Déclaration des droits de l'homme* as finally adopted corroborates him. (Given in full in Appendix 5, p. 341.) Some of the articles of the *Déclaration*, beginning with the first three, come close to being transcripts: men are born free; government exists to maintain their inalienable rights; sovereignty resides in the nation. The seventh, ninth, tenth, and eleventh—on due process, freedom of thought (even religious), of speech, of writing and publishing ideas and opinions—are likewise close parallels; both documents affirm the importance of the separation of powers. On the other hand, the rights of revolution, as expressed by Mason in the second part of his third article and phrased by Jefferson in the Declaration of Independence, "whenever any Form of Government becomes destructive of these Ends, it is the Right of the People to alter or to abolish it," could hardly be affirmed in the face of a monarch.

Many of the clauses of the two documents differed in whether they were addressed to a grievance that currently existed or to one that might occur: Mason's statement that "no man, or set of men, are entitled to . . . privileges from the community, but in consideration of publick services" was a safeguard against the future appearance in America of privileges that existed in England; the French insistence on *la carrière ouverte aux talents* was an attack on the current social structure of France.

The philosophical difference between the French and the American approach is clearest in the definitions of law and the specification of legal procedures in the two documents; where the Virginians extolled trial by jury and rejected excessive bail and fines, cruel and unusual punishments, general warrants, etc., the French were concerned to recognize law as the expression of the general will and liberty as the power to do whatever is not injurious to others. Both castigated ex post facto laws.

While the Virginians held standing armies in peace-time to be "dangerous to liberty," the French accepted the necessity of a "public force" in order to guarantee the rights of man and were chiefly concerned that the tax required for its support and for the expenses of administration should be "assesed equally on all citizens in proportion to their means," that public agents should be accountable, and that citizens or their representatives should have the right to ascertain the necessity of levies and to consent to the modes of their application.

The two declarations differed in their attitude toward property. Mason specified means of access to it rather than ownership of it as a natural right. When commenting on Lafayette's second draft, Jefferson bracketed the words *le droit de propriété* for suggested removal. Mason's bill and the French declaration as adopted are alike in declaring that no man's property should be taken for public use without due process of law, but the French prohibition is preceded by the phrase "Since property is a sacred and inviolable right."

At Gunston Hall, George Mason could follow French events through the public prints, but during the constructive years—the first phase—of the French Revolution, he also had a private window on its course through the eyes of his fourth son, John, who was a member of a mercantile partnership in Bordeaux from 1788 through 1791 and a faithful correspondent—a considerable collection of his letters survives. Since he was in Paris during sessions of the States General, he could respond to his father's request to "give me the best Description you can of their appearance; their proceedings, & what is likely to be the result."

*"Wha Wants Me?"; (Tom Paine),*
*26 December 1792*
*(courtesy, The Trustees of the British Museum)*

*The French Counterpart* [309]

During 1786–87, John had acquired business experience in Alexandria with the merchant William Hartshorne and, in the autumn of 1787, had made a trip on behalf of the firm to Boston, bearing a letter from his father to Elbridge Gerry and renewing acquaintance from Philadelphia days. In 1788, he entered into partnership with James and Joseph Fenwick of Maryland and sailed for France the end of June while his father was still at the Virginia ratifying convention. Each of the three young men put up £1000 capital; James minded the American end of the business while the others were abroad. The nicely balanced firm represented the two chief sources of tobacco, with Fenwick a Catholic Marylander and Mason a Protestant Virginian; both affiliations were helpful in Bordeaux. Counseled by the older generation in each family to "give no Credit, nor ever advance more than the Value of Effects in their Hands for any Man," their prospects were good.

Before departing, John had visited all of the ranking American cities except Charleston, but in Bordeaux he found a metropolis on a different scale. The late-eighteenth-century splendor of the second city of France was at once solid evidence and symbol of the new power in the realm, the commercial and financial element, the emergent bourgeoisie.

In the reigns of Louis XV and Louis XVI, entire sections had been renewed in the current architectural mode. The medieval defense walls were taken down; the former sites of their massive gates, except for the Porte de la Grosse Cloche, were embellished with classic triumphal arches. To remodel the waterfront Jacques Gabriel was brought from Paris in 1720 to design the Place Royale at the apex of the bow-shaped curve of the Garonne River; in 1755, Gabriel's son, designer of the Place de la Concorde in Paris, completed twin structures to house the tax bureau and the bourse around an oval whose centerpiece was Lemoyne's equestrian statue of Louis XV. In the interior of the city, long tree-lined avenues were flanked by new houses of contemporary architecture, their balconies adorned with superb iron work, their doors with massive knockers of intricate design.

After interruption of building during the Seven Years' War, funds elicited from the commercial community commissioned architect Victor Louis to design the thirteen-hundred-seat Grand Théâtre, above whose classic peristyle statues of Venus, Juno, Minerva, and the Nine Muses looked down on the Place de la Comédie. John Adams, on his first trip to the city in 1778, attended a performance of *Les Deux Avares* at the Comédie and "went to the Opera, where the Scenery, the Dancing the Music, afforded me a very chearfull, sprightly amusement, having never seen any thing of the kind before."[12]

Ecclesiastical construction paralleled secular renewal: J. Etienne and R. F. Bonfin, rivals of Victor Louis, erected a new archbishopric. Other magnificent private mansions were commissioned by members of the nobility or ranking bankers, merchants, and shippers. All this was in process or just recently completed when John Mason arrived.

But from the practical standpoint of the foreign commercial community, the greatest change during the city's reconstruction was the demolition of the Chateau Trompette. Louis XIV had been shrewdly suspicious of cities; toward the end of the seventeenth century, he commissioned military architect Vauban to extend a tremendous fort around the fifteenth-century palace of Charles VII, and thereafter royally appointed governors and commandants of troops kept an eye on the rising Bordeaux bourgeoisie from this stronghold.

As soon as its walls were leveled, the area north of it, the Quartier des Chartrons, where previously were only open fields and a Chartreux monastery, developed into a section of business offices and residences of merchants from Europe and America. Three-story houses with iron-grilled balconies made the tree-lined Allée des Chartrons one of the loveliest streets of Bordeaux; it was here, at no. 15 (no. 35 today), that the young partners, Fenwick and Mason, set up housekeeping, to the great satisfaction of George Mason, who on 14 May 1789 wrote John: "I hope to hear soon that you & Mr. Fenwick have got to House-keeping; for as your Business is now grown considerable, & there are, of course, many Captains of Ships & others to whom it will be necessary for you to shew Civilities, I can't think House-keeping will be any great Addition to your Expences; and I am sure it will give some Respectability to your House; besides that it must be much more agreeable than living in a boarding-House."[13]

The partnership throve. Young Mason's years in Bordeaux coincided with the peak of the port's eighteenth-century prosperity. In 1788, 253 vessels, totaling 75,000 tons, sailed outbound for French colonies, chiefly in the West Indies, and 242, totaling 72,000 tons, arrived. The Almanach of Commerce for 1791, cataloging alphabetically the ships of the port engaged in colonial commerce, lists 39 under the letter "A" alone. Their names reflect the sunny economic skies the merchants were enjoying—14 are "aimable," from *L'Aimable Aimée* of 150 tons to *L'Aimable Marianne* of 600. The major European nations were at peace; seaborne commerce moved freely.

Fenwick was pleased with his new associate:

Mr. Mason is just such a disposition—principals—understanding &c &c as I could have wish'd him to have—you therefore may conclude we shall suit extreemly well together. He is *industrious* attentive *frugal* & *reasonable*,—he has courage to form resolutions & spirit to adhere to them—he does not count a

*Bordeaux prior to the demolition of the Chateau Trompette*
(courtesy,
The Mariners Museum,
Newport News, Virginia)

sou on his expected fortune from his father nor assumes nothing from his name or connexions.

I govern & rule in every instance & at same time adopt his plans follow his advice & go according to his direction & wishes.[14]

Yet along with his attention to the affairs of his firm, Mason saw a good bit of France, the Low Countries, and England. An autobiographic note among his papers tells, "While I was abroad I travelled between February and June 1789 thro the north of France (remaining some months in Paris), Brabant, Holland and part of England remaining in London about a month, and between —— 1790 and —— 1791 while south of France visiting Montauban, Toulouse, Carcassonne, Montpelier, Marseilles, Hyères, Avignon, Nîmes, Aix."[15]

George Mason interested himself in every detail of his son's business. He disapproved of the acceptance of an offer from a London merchant to extend a £1,000 line of credit to the firm—was this done by Mr. Fenwick without John's participation? "The Custom of drawing, & re-drawing being the most dangerous, in my Opinion, of all mercantile Expedients." He continued to urge strict adherence to the principle of giving no credits: "By giving extensive Credits you may, indeed, acquire a large Fortune, upon Paper; but you will never have one any where else."[16]

To astonish or amuse his son's colleagues, Mason sent John, at intervals, various forms of wildlife: mockingbirds, cardinals, deer, and, particularly, opossums with which to puzzle French naturalists:

We have now got a female Opossom, who is too far advanced in her Pregnancy, to bear a Sea-voyage; the Young ones being almost ready to drop off the Teats, as they are vulgarly (but I believe erroniously) called. We intend to keep her, until she has raised her Brood; I expect they will be perfectly tame, & when they are sufficiently grown up, we will send you some of them; which will give a fair Chance of their breeding in France. . . . I will hereafter send you my Conjectures upon this extraordinary Mode of Generation so different from that of other Animals, that the fact is neither understood, or believed in Europe.[17]

To enhance the firm's prestige, Mason set about obtaining the American consulship in Bordeaux for Joseph Fenwick:

your Brother George & I are both of Opinion, that it will be proper to make the Application for him, in Preference to you, for several Reasons . . . and above all, because we wou'd avoid giving the smallest cause for any Jealousy, or misunderstanding between you. You may therefore assure Mr. Fenwick that what Interest I may have, with our new Rulers shall be most cordially exerted in his Favour . . . tho' I have no Reason to expect my Interest will have much Weight in the new Government, having, as you know, warmly opposed it, in it's present Shape, both in the federal Convention, & our own. In my opinion, a Letter of Recommendation from our Minister, Mr. Jefferson, wou'd have a good Effect.[18]

He wrote Washington on Fenwick's behalf in June 1789; on hearing from Jefferson that the appointment was made, he notified John that it "was principally oweing to my Interest with our Friend Mr. Jefferson (now American Secretary of State) from whom I had a Letter upon the Subject, immediately upon the matter being fixed. I hope it will be of considerable Service to your House; and I have no

*Bordeaux harbor
by Pierre Lacour,
1804, showing
the Maison Fenwick
at the corner of the
Place du Port
(courtesy, Musée
des Arts Decoratifs,
Bordeaux)*

Doubt of Mr. Fenwick's Attention, & propriety of Conduct in the Office."[19]

During the course of these negotiations, Fenwick made a trip to the United States, touring the coast from Maryland to New Hampshire in the interest of business contacts. On his return to France, he embarked on a building venture of a scope worthy of Bordeaux. Engaging the Paris architect, J.-B. Dufart, who had designed the Autel de la Patrie in the Champ de Mars for the mass celebrations of the early Revolution, he commissioned the Maison Fenwick, to occupy the corner where the Allée des Chartrons reached the harbor at the Place du Port. Intended as both a residence and the U. S. consulate, this spacious four-story structure was planned to house shops on the ground floor and offices and living quarters above.

The building, only slightly remodeled, is intact today: pillars flank the arcaded central doorway, with prows of ships sculptured in stone on either side. The reception rooms, reached by an elaborate staircase, open through French doors onto iron-grilled balconies across both east and south facades. Rising from the roof, twin turrets, balanced above the east and the west halves of the building, are topped by windowed cupolas—very like those of the New England sea-captains' homes that Fenwick had just seen—from which the entire sweep of city and harbor can be surveyed. Joseph Fenwick passed the rest of his life in Bordeaux, and while both politically and economically there were some anxious moments in the 1790s,* the property remained in his hands and those of his son until 1858.†

Even more central to the life of France than Bordeaux's primacy in overseas commerce during John's period of residence was the direc-

*Entrance to the Maison Fenwick*
*(by author)*

tion given by its principal men to the first phase of the Revolution, the period when the bourgeoisie came into its own. When the old royal provinces were subdivided, the area around Bordeaux became the Département de la Gironde, and the dominant national figures in Paris were known as the Girondins. So John had immediate opportunity to observe and even to join in the revolutionary action at its source.

The future split between the moderate revolutionary thinkers, the Girondins, who were comparable to George Mason's associates in America, and the radicals of the 1793 Terror, the Montagnards, who were comparable to the Shaysites of Massachusetts but unlike them succeeded in seizing power, was early visible in two of Bordeaux's political clubs. That known as Amis de la Liberté et l'Egalité attracted the radicals; the membership of the Amis de la Constitution was a roster of ranking Girondins.

In September 1789, Mason, who frequently forwarded John's political reports to New York, sent Samuel Griffin John's mid-June account of the struggle of the orders in the States General:

> The third Estate (as hitherto called) have in their last Address to the King, taken a new Style, and called themselves "VOS COMMUNES" in which they tell him, in very spirited Terms, that they must insist upon the other two orders . . . determining upon what Principles they will go on with the public Business; otherwise they will proceed without them, and convince his Majesty that they speak the Language of the Nation. These People seem to have catched the Flame of American Freedom; and in protecting the Rights & Liberty of others; have learned to assert their own.[20]

In mid-July, John was himself in correspondence with Jefferson; the ambassador was then seeking transportation home to take up his post as secretary of state. Three days before the storming of the Bastille

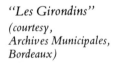

*"Les Girondins"*
(courtesy,
Archives Municipales,
Bordeaux)

on 14 July, John offered him passage in the *Washington,* "destined for Potomac but can touch at Norfolk"; two days after the event, Jefferson replied that he could not leave at once because more pressing matters prevented his obtaining the permission to depart that was required by diplomatic protocol:

Great events have taken place within these few days. Yesterday the king went without any cortege but his two brothers to the States General and spoke to them in very honest and conciliatory terms; such as in my opinion amount to a surrender at discretion. The temper of this city is too much heated at present to view them in that light, and therefore they keep on the watch and go on in organizing their armed Bourgeoisie. But I have not a single doubt of the sincerity of the King, and that there will not be another disagreeable act from him. He has promised to send away the troops.[21]

(But next day, Jefferson was writing Tom Paine: "A more dangerous scenes of war I never saw in America than what Paris has presented for 5. days past."[22])

At the time, Bordeaux remained calm, but on 11 May 1790, John reported that the city was suddenly "more agitated than I have seen it since the first flame of patriotism in July." The issue was religious liberty. On 19 April, the Assembly had passed a decree, declaring "the Legislature ought not, nor could not meddle with the Consciences of men and their religious creed"; during the debate a member had declared that all religions should be obliged to read annually, and post in their churches, the immortal declaration of the Virginia Assembly on freedom of worship, and Condorcet had extolled its terms. Thereafter, John continued, the aristocratic and Catholic party "drew up a form of violent protest against this blasphemous & heretic act as they were pleased to call it . . . & sent it abroad to stir up the People." Five members from Bordeaux—three from the noblesse and two from the clergy— signed this protest; when the news reached the National Coffee House it roused a cry "*a la lanterne & a feu,*" and those present resolved "that five effigies made of Straw & sewed in Canvas . . . should be hung in due form to five lanterns in the Street chapeau Rouge between the Exchange and the Comedy house . . . this was executed about 7 o'clock in the Evening amidst many thousand applauding and shouting Spectators. They hung an hour and were then taken down & burnt with their Protestation on a Pile prepared in the middle of the Street for the Purpose."[23]

Other cities were comparably inflamed. John added news from day to day. At Montaubon, upriver between Bordeaux and Toulouse, where the aristocratic party had defeated the popular side in a municipal election, fighting broke out on 10 May, the day appointed for inventory of the goods of the church preparatory to the civil constitution of the clergy. In Bordeaux, "Gentlemen Merchants & Principals of houses of Commerce are prayed to allow each one of their young Men of the Counting house to make the present Campaign & to continue their wages & reserve their Places during their absence"; some fifteen thousand volunteers marched toward Montaubon but returned without an

*"Premier Registre des Verbaux de la Société des Amis de la Constitution depuis le 16 avril 1790 jusqu'au 10 juillet 1791; Sceance Ordinnaire Du Samedy 31 Juillet 1790"* shows the admission of *"Mr. Masson"* (John Mason) into the club (courtesy, Archives départementales de la Gironde, Bordeaux)

engagement. John blurted out his feelings: "Let us then expect that the Murders I am going to tell you of at Montaubon will call forth the Vengeance of the Good People to make such examples of that damnable Party—those execrable monks and cursed nobles—as may deter from attempting anything further."[24]

By the end of April, the young man had sworn overt adherence to the Revolution, and Mason approved:

I think, from your last Accounts, the Revolution in France has advanced too far to be now overset, & hope that their Constitution of Government, so constant to the Rights of human Nature, will be firmly & permanently established.* I think you judged properly in taking the oath under the new Constitution. I see no objection that a Friend of Liberty, & sacred Rights of Mankind, cou'd have to taking, cordially & sincerely, the Oath to such a Government; perhaps it is a Duty in every Man who receives protection from it; nor does it appear to me to interfere with the Dutys you owe your own Country. The Refusal of the British Merchants in Bourdeaux is a Specimen of British Pride & Mulishness, for which that Nation is so remarkable.[25]

John soon went further: on Saturday, 31 July 1790, the minute book of the Amis de la Constitution listed the admission of fifteen new members. Fourteen were French, but the name heading the list was "Mr. Masson."[26] On 10 January 1791, George Mason closed a long account to the secretary of state with a touch of pride: "My son John was admitted, about the latter End of last Summer, a Member of the great Constitutional Committee for the City of Bordeaux; an Appointment with which I am very well pleased; not only as it shews that he is well known & esteemed in the City, but as it will make him acquainted with some of the first Characters in that Part of the Kingdom, and will be the Means of much Information and Improvement."[27]

By the time of Terror, John had left France. In 1791, he was already planning to return home and open a commission house of his own on the Potomac. On 16 April, in the last letter addressed to Bordeaux, his father informed him that an Act of Congress had located the permanent seat of the national government on the Potomac River and that the Ten Mile Square included both Alexandria—and Mason's 2,000-acre tract above it—on the Virginia side and Georgetown on the Maryland side. John landed at Norfolk in midsummer 1791 and shortly established his business office in Georgetown. By the end of the decade he and Anna Maria Murray, his Annapolis bride, were placing the furniture and engravings he had brought from France in their new brick house on Analostan Island, designing one of the formal gardens fashionable towards the century's end, assembling trees for the orchard, and importing some of the first Merino sheep to be introduced in America.

# Chapter XVII
# Legacies

*During John's years abroad, Mason rusticated at Gunston Hall in the retirement* of which he had long talked. His days were largely taken up with family affairs. In 1791 he declined John Francis Mercer's request for him to purchase Marlborough on the ground that he was overextended: "Payment of my Daughter's Fortunes, the building for, & setling two of my Sons, and raising Capitals in Trade for two others, has required, & will require, all the Money I am able to command."[1]

By this time, George and William were planters in their own rights; his father attributed George's improved health to the beneficent effects of the warm sulphur springs in Augusta County, where both of these sons had resorted during August in 1790 and 1791.

Within the year, Thomson's new house was ready for its interior finish. Mason asked John to get a man "to take the Dimensions of the four Chimneys, for which he wants free Stone Chimney-Peices, and also of the Fire-Place in his best Room, & give Directions for a Marble Chimney-Peice, to be sent for to England; unless one of those you have to dispose of will suit it." Thomson had become collector of customs in Alexandria in 1789.

Of the two younger sons, John's future as a merchant seemed assured, though when he first came back, his extensive imports on the *Washington* ran into sufficient difficulties under the federal tonnage act. Mason, while acidly remarking that the information against them had been laid by "a poor Devil of a Scotchman, as ravenous as a famished Cat," advised him to go to Philadelphia to wait upon the secretary of the treasury with an explanation. Between him and his father, the bonds of affection were very close, and Mason's many letters to him in Georgetown show that as the father became more and more confined to Gunston Hall, he depended on his son to carry out many commissions. Thomas, who would shortly come of age, was something of a problem. He had been placed with William Hodgson, a Londoner who emigrated to Alexandria in 1790 and opened a mercantile house after serving two years in Newgate prison during the war for his pro-American political views, but to his father's annoyance, Thomas proved to be neither the business man nor the correspondent that John was. Mason complained to John of unanswered letters and then of receiving one "expressing his great Desire of being established in some Business upon his own Account; at the same time expressing much Disgust at the Business & Profession of a Merchant; which after the time he has spent in the Pursuit, and which too was his own choice; shewed a Fickleness of Disposition, & want of Steadiness, that may prove highly injurious to him." Mason had intended to send him to Bordeaux for some foreign experience, but "To tell you the Truth, I am almost out of Conceit of sending another Son to Europe; for Fear of giving him a Distaste to his own Country. This is generally the Case with such Americans as have spent much time in Europe; it is, in some measure, the case with yourself; I can see it with great Concern (and it is the only thing I have to regret in you) for in my Opinion, there can hardly be a greater Misfortune, than a Man's having a Distaste to that Country, in which all his connections are, and in which he is to spend his life."[2] So Thomas worked for William Hartshorne in Alexandria for a time just as John had done; eventually, he settled on the family plantation at Woodbridge.

Mason continued to supervise his plantation. He was among the wealthiest men in Virginia: the tax lists for 1787–88 show him with real estate holdings in Fairfax County alone of 7,649 acres and taxable personal property in 118 slaves, 63 horses, 116 cattle, and a four-wheeled carriage.[3]

But he gradually withdrew from outside activities in the locality. In 1789, he resigned as justice of the Fairfax County Court,* though because he had fallen out with the Alexandria merchants, holding them to exert too much influence in county affairs, he engaged in the attempt—successful a decade later—to get the courthouse moved out of Alexandria to a more central location.

He still took the enjoyment of any Virginia gentleman in entertaining guests. With his sons and daughters all nearby, frequent family parties brought the young people and their children home. He extended hospitality to travelers: when William Loughton Smith visited his way down the coast from New York to Charleston in 1791, he wrote in his diary: "Sunday I remained at Mount Vernon and left on Monday, and proceeded to the Seat of Colonel Mason, about thirteen miles on the Potomac; the ride a pleasant one, a hilly country, well-wooded and romantic. Colonel George Mason is a gentleman of considerable eminence in the political line in this state. I arrived at his house about dinner time, and staied with him until the next morning. The house is rather an ancient brick building, with a neat garden, at the end of which is a high natural terrace which commands the Potomac; the ground about is rough and unimproved."[4] And he sent invitations to friends in the Congress and the new administration to stop at Gunston on their way to and from Philadelphia, for he followed closely current developments in national affairs.

Before Washington left Mount Vernon to assume the presidency, the two old neighbors engaged in a conversation recorded only by a terse line in Washington's diary for 2 November 1788: "Mr. George Mason came here to dinner and returned in the evening."†[5] That is their last known visit. Since his decision not to support the Constitution, Mason had necessarily been aware of the strain between Washington and himself; to John in Bordeaux, in 1789, he both regretted the result and defended the cause:

You know the friendship which has long existed (indeed from our early youth) between General Washington and myself. I believe there are few men in whom he placed greater confidence; but it is possible my opposition to the new government . . . may have altered the case. In this important trust, I am truly conscious of having acted from the purest motives of honesty, and love to my country . . . and I would not forfeit the approbation of my own mind for the approbation of any man or all the men upon earth. My conduct as a public man, through the whole of the late glorious Revolution, has been such as, I trust, will administer comfort to me in those moments when I shall most want it, and smooth the bed of death.[6]

He had gone out of his way to restore relations; in June 1789, he had closed a letter to the president in New York, "And sho'd anything occur, in which I can render you any Service here, I beg you will command me, without Reserve, as I can truly say there is not a Man in the World, who more sincerely wishes you every Felicity."[7]

While resumption of the old intimacy between two people who felt as strongly as each of these did on a matter that both regarded as of central importance was probably not possible, the loyalty to Washington of the men who represented him locally in his absence, such as Lund Washington and Tobias Lear, did nothing to close the breach. Lear's exchange of letters with Mason in July 1789 about a former coachman who had applied to Washington for employment could hardly have been stiffer.

Mason had likewise been anxious that disagreements with Madison in the conventions should not leave a permanent scar. In January 1791, he sent messages by Jefferson: "He is one of the few Men, whom from a pretty thorough Acquaintance, I really esteem; tho' I have been apprehensive some late Difference (and it has only been a late one) on political Questions had caused a Coolness between us. I am sure it has not on my Part; for if I know my own Heart, I have more Liberality than to think the worse of a Friend for a Disagreement on any theoretical Opinions."[8]

Jefferson's prompt reply repudiated the idea of a breach: "I had no occasion to sound Mr. Madison on your fears expressed in your letter. I knew before, as possessing his sentiments fully on that subject, that his value for you was undiminished. I have always heard him say that tho' you and he appeared to differ in your systems, yet you were in truth nearer together than most persons who were classed under the same appellation. You may quiet yourself in the assurance of possessing his complete esteem."[9]

Madison's introduction of proposed amendments to the Constitution at the opening of the first session of Congress had brought great reassurance to Gunston Hall: on 8 September 1789, Mason told Congressman Samuel Griffin: "I have received much Satisfaction from the

Amendments to the federal Constitution, which have lately passed the House of Representatives; I hope they will also pass the Senate. With two or three further Amendments . . . I cou'd chearfully put my Hand & Heart to the new Government." [10]*

In March 1790, after Senator William Grayson died at Dumfries on his way to New York, Governor Beverley Randolph sent Mason an urgent commission to fill out Grayson's unexpired term: "The very important subjects now before congress so interesting to America in general and more especially to your native State call for the counsels of the wisest of her citizens." [11]

Mason declined; "my present State of Health (if I had no other Objection) rendering me unable to discharge the Duties of the Office. . . . In such a Situation, even if I was now in New York it wou'd not be in my Power to render our Country any essential Service, and I can't reconcile myself to the Idea of receiving the Publick's Money for Nothing." [12] The senatorial appointment went to James Monroe.

Mason's health was indeed bad,† and it worsened. The exceptionally severe winter of 1791–92 made his long attack of gout especially painful; when summer came, the whole family, including the slaves, was laid up with chills and fever. After the fever passed, Mason caught a chest cold. On 10 September, he informed John of the sorry state of the entire establishment:

I am very unwell myself, with an exceeding troublesome Cough; which a Night or two ago was so bad, as to entirely prevent my sleeping. . . . Mrs. Mason is much as when you left us; still unable to walk a Step. . . . Your Sister Betsy & your Brother William, have been both very ill . . . they are now better; having missed their Fevers, for the last two or three Days. Our Servants are almost all laid up with bad Fevers; there are not enough of them well, to take Care of the Sick. I hardly remember so sickly a Season. [13]

At the end of the month, however, Mason could sit up enough to receive a visitor whose coming he had long anticipated. Since Jefferson's return from France, the two had looked forward to a talk. Their first attempt had ended in disappointment: on 16 March 1790, Mason gently chided Jefferson for having gone by without pausing on his way to be sworn in as Washington's secretary of state: "Until I heard of your passing thro' Colchester, a few Days ago, I had flattered myself with having the Pleasure of seeing you at Gunston . . . and of personally congratulating you, upon your Return to your native Country." [14]

Jefferson quickly explained his absence: "the roads being so bad that I was obliged to leave my own carriage to get along as it could, and to take my passage in the stage, I could not deviate from the stage road. I should have been happy in a conversation with you on the subject of our new government, of which, tho' I approve of the mass, I would wish to see some amendments, further than those which have been proposed, and fixing it more surely on a republican basis." [15]

The following January, Mason renewed his invitation: "There is a particular Circumstance, tho' its Consequences have been little attended to, or thought of, which is continually sapping and contaminating

*James Monroe by John Vanderlyn,*
*c. 1816*
*(courtesy, National Portrait Gallery,*
*Smithsonian Institution, Washington, D.C.)*

THE CONTRAST
1792

BRITISH LIBERTY.

FRENCH LIBERTY

RELIGION.        MORALITY.
LOYALTY OBEDIENCE TO THE LAWS
INDEPENDANCE PERSONAL SECURITY
JUSTICE INHERITANCE PROTECTION
PROPERTY INDUSTRY NATIONAL PROSPERITY
HAPPINESS

ATHEISM        PERIURY
REBELLION TREASON ANARCHY MURDER
EQUALITY MADNESS CRUELTY INJUSTICE
TREACHERY INGRATITUDE IDLENESS
FAMINE NATIONAL & PRIVATE RUIN.
MISERY

WHICH IS BEST

*"The Contrast,
1792": British and
French liberty as seen
through British eyes
(courtesy, The Trustees of
the British Museum)*

the Republicanism of the United States, and if not timely altered, will corrupt the rising Generation."[16]

Jefferson, intrigued, guessed at the nature of the "circumstance": "What is it? What is said in our country of the fiscal arrangements now going on? . . . Whether these measures be right or wrong abstractedly, more attention should be paid to the general opinion. However, all will pass, the excise will pass, the bank will pass. The only corrective of what is amiss in our present government will be the augmentation of the numbers in the lower house, so as to get a more agricultural representation, which may put that interest above that of the stock-jobbers."[17]

Actually, Jefferson's guess concerned a subject that, far from being "little attended to," was on all men's tongues. Hamilton had become secretary of the treasury in circumstances peculiarly favorable to his view that the government should be as much like the British system as possible: he looked on Washington as head of state and himself as the equivalent of prime minister. The early Cabinet offered him little competition. Jefferson did not reach New York to take office as secretary of state for months after the new government was organized. At the War Office, Knox was an old soldier, and Attorney General Randolph a pliable individual. Washington was fifty-seven; Hamilton, in the ambitious vigor of his early thirties, engagingly and forcefully pressed policy on his chief.

By the end of 1791, he had prepared a fully developed fiscal and economic program and laid it before Congress in four major reports: he proposed funding of the United States debt at full value; assumption by the national government of the revolutionary debts of the states; creation of a bank similar to the Bank of England to facilitate industry and commerce; and enactment of a protective tariff to fence off the domestic market for finished goods. All would foreseeably solidify the approval of the urban well-to-do.

Mason's views on these proposals were pungently expressed to Senator Monroe: "Our new Government is a Government of Stock-jobbing and Favourtism. It required no extraordinary Degree of Penetration, to forsee that it wou'd be so, from it's Formation. If any Man, of common Sense, doubts the first . . . let him attentively read the Secretary of the Treasury's Reports upon the Debt of the United States, and upon the Bank; and consider the Tendency, Spirit, and necessary Operation of the whole funding System."[18]

Both national and state securities had been largely bought up by men of capital at vastly depreciated prices, and while assumption might be good news in some states, it was not so in Virginia. Madison confirmed to Pendleton that the commonwealth, although it had already made progress in retiring its own obligations from its own resources, would become liable for a prorated share of the outstanding debt of states that had accomplished far less. Jefferson, convinced that congressional sentiment in favor of assumption was accumulating, suggested to Mason: "Perhaps its opponents would be wiser to be less confident in their success, & to compromise by agreeing to assume state debts still due to individuals, on condition of assuming to the states at the same time what they have paid individuals."[19]

In this controversy, the first outlines of political parties began to emerge; lasting difference of purpose began to separate those bent on solidifying support of the federal government among the well-to-do in the commercial centers by economic and fiscal policies to their benefit and those of a more agrarian and democratic cast of mind.

Washington, the man in the middle of rising partisan spirit, was well aware of the resistance to Hamilton's proposals in Virginia; on 20 July 1792, from Mount Vernon, he sent Hamilton a list of objections that he had encountered—it was copied almost verbatim from one Jefferson had sent him two months earlier. He headed his covering letter "(Private and Confidential)" noting that he sent it "in strict confidence, and with frankness and freedom":

On my way home, and since my arrival here, I have endeavoured to learn from sensible and moderate men, known friends to the Government, the sentiments which are entertained of public measures. These all agree that the Country is prosperous and happy; but they seem to be alarmed at that system of policy, and those interpretations of the Constitution which have taken place in Congress. Others, less friendly perhaps to the Government and more disposed to arraign the conduct of its Officers (among whom may be classed my neighbour, and quandom friend Colo. M.) go further, and enumerate a variety of matters, wch. as well as I can recollect, may be adduced under the following heads.[20]

*Alexander Hamilton by John Trumbull,*
*1792*
(courtesy, National Gallery of Art, Washington,
D.C., gift of the Avalon Foundation)

*Thomas Jefferson*
*by Charles Willson Peale, c. 1791*
*(courtesy, Independence National Historical*
*Park, Philadelphia)*

Hamilton's energetic reply of August 18 enclosed a rebuttal that runs to thirty printed pages. He hotly denied that assumption "has furnished effectual means of corrupting such a portion of the legislature, as turns the balance between honest Voters whichever way it is desired,"[21] declaring:

As far as I know, there is not a member of the Legislature who can properly be called a Stock-jobber or a paper Dealer. . . .

It is strange perversion of ideas, and as novel as it is extraordinary, that men should be deemed corrupt & criminal for becoming proprietors in the funds of their Country. Yet I believe the number of members of Congress is very small who have ever been considerably proprietors in the funds.

As to improper speculations on measures depending before Congress, I believe there never was any *body* of men freer from them.[22]*

He rejected with similar force the charge that advocates of strong central government were moving toward monarchy.† "There is not a man at present in either branch of the Legislature who, that I recollect, had held language in the Convention favourable to Monarchy."[23]‡

On the regional aspects of assumption, he

regretted that party discriminations are so far Geographical as they have been; and that ideas of a severance of the Union are creeping in both North and South. . . . It happened that Mr. Maddison and some other distinguished characters of the South started in opposition to the Assumption. The high opinion entertained of them made it be taken for granted in that quarter, that the opposition would be successful. . . . Hence it happened that the inhabitants of the Southern States sustained a considerable loss by the opposition to the assumption from Southern Gentlemen, and their too great confidence in the efficacy of that opposition.[24]

Whatever Mason had intended earlier, these aspects of federal policy were the main feature of the tour d'horizon that he and Jefferson conducted when, on Sunday, 30 September 1792, the northbound secretary of state turned off the highway into Gunston Hall. They first rambled over events at the Philadelphia Convention, about which, according to Jefferson's abbreviated notes of the conversation, Mason's memory was sometimes faulty. But when they came to the debt question, his proposals were sharp and clear:

He said he considd Hamilton as having done us more injury than Gr. Britain & all her fleets & armies. That his (Mason's) plan of settling our debt would have been something in this way. He would have laid as much tax as could be paid without oppressing the people. Particularly he would have laid an impost of about the amount of the first laid by Congress, but somewhat different in several of it's articles. He would have suspended all application of it one year during which an office should have been open to register unalienated certificates.§ At the end of the year he would have appropriated this revenue. 1st. To pay the civil list. 2. The interest of these certif. 3. Instalments of the principal. 4. A surplus to buy up the alienated certificates still avoiding to make any other provision for these last. By the time the unalienated certificates should have been all paid, he supposed half the alienated ones would have been bought up at market. He would then have proceeded to redeem the residue of them.[25]

Mason's appearance wrenched Jefferson's heart. From Georgetown, he wrote Madison: "I called at Gunstonhall, the proprietor just recovering from a dreadful attack of the cholic. He was perfectly communicative, but I could not, in discretion, let him talk as much as he was disposed."[26]

When Jefferson turned his horse's head to the main road—his next stop was Mount Vernon—the two friends parted for the last time. Mason had engaged in his final canvass of public affairs. On the following Sunday afternoon, 7 October, he died.

Jefferson learned of the event only after reaching Philadelphia; Senator Monroe, who was northbound when it happened and who also had intended to pay Mason a visit, wrote him on 16 October: "You have before this I presume heard of the death of Colo. Geo. Mason wh. was abt. the 8th. of this month of the gout in the stomach. His patriotic virtues thru the revolution will ever be remembered by the citizens of this country, and his death at the present moment will be sensibly felt by the republican interest."[27]

James Mercer informed the president; on 1 November, Washington briefly condoled: "I will also unite my regret to yours for the death of our old friend, and acquaintance Colo. Mason."[28]

Mason died as a private person, not a public figure. He was buried in the family graveyard south of the house. Most newspaper files of the period are broken; an obituary appears in Maryland's *Journal and Baltimore Advertiser* of 2 November, and Alexandria's *Columbia Mirror and Alexandria Advocate* of 28 November quotes from his will. London's *Gentleman's Magazine* announced his death in its January 1793 issue.

Mason left two sorts of legacy, as a Virginia gentleman and as a political thinker. His will, probated in Fairfax Court House on 16 October,[29] was the unchanged document that he had written nearly twenty years earlier, following the death of his first wife. Because of his marriage contract of 8 April 1780 with Sarah Brent, entitling her to a life interest in four hundred acres of his Dogue's Neck land, "in lieu and in full Satisfaction of her Dower & legal Share" of his estate if she survived him, no later revision had been necessary.

Major provisions had been carried out during his lifetime; the specified payments of fortunes for his daughters when they married and the distribution of lands to his sons had largely taken place. George, Jr.,'s Lexington plantation was on the Dogue's Neck tract that now became his together with title to Gunston Hall; the principal residence thus descended to the first born, even though Mason specifically stated that all of his bequests were in fee simple, with none of the property entailed. William received Maryland properties adjacent to the Eilbeck estate that he had inherited from his maternal grandparents; Thomson, the lands near his new house adjacent to the Mount Vernon holdings along Little Hunting Creek; John, Analostan Island and the acreage opposite it along the Potomac's Virginia shore; Thomas, the Woodbridge estate below the Occoquan River in Prince William County and further tracts in Charles County, Maryland.

In designating his personal property, Mason gave named groups of slaves and their offspring to each of his children; he divided among the boys the furniture and books at Gunston Hall, specifying for George his gold watch and certain pieces of silver, including the silver bowl given by Mason's mother which had been used for the baptisms of all the children.

He ordered mourning rings for various friends and relatives and a suit of mourning for his cousins Miss Bronaugh and the Cockburns. He named as executors his son, George, and Martin Cockburn, requesting the Reverend Mr. Massey to advise them and asking that they "will excuse the trouble I now give them, when they reflect upon the Necessaty that dying men are under of thus imploying the care and kindness of the living"; to requite them for their trouble, they were to have £10 a year from his estate, "to be laid out by them in private charitys, upon such as they shall Judge worthey objects." He asked that marble tombstones be erected to his mother and father and his wife, Ann, in case he had not already done so.

Mason's will, however, fell short of his intentions in respect to western lands. He left George his stock in the Ohio Company; a small sum from its accounts remained in his hands when he died, and as late as May 1792, he had corresponded with his cousin, John Francis Mercer, his attorney for several suits in Maryland, regarding a company tract known as Pleasant Valley. This tract, long in litigation, was thought to represent the terminal transaction in the company's affairs when his heirs, finally successful, disposed of it some forty years later.

A far larger area, claimed by Mason in his personal capacity, was likewise in litigation for a decade after his death, the tract on the Panther Creek tributary of the Green River in western Kentucky which he had been so careful to have properly surveyed and had estimated to George twelve years earlier as possibly being worth some £40,000 to £50,000 by the end of the century. In the spring of 1780, Hancock Lee surveyed contiguous tracts on this creek for Mason, William Moore, and James Madison, Sr. Beginning with 8,400 acres in Mason's name, he used his description of this section as a base for the rest: 8,300 acres more for Mason, and 10,000 each for the other two purchasers. That October, an error was discovered: the key tract lay four miles above the junction of Panther Creek and the Green River and not, as described, four miles above the forks of Panther Creek. Mason corrected the error, filing a special entry at the Jefferson County Courthouse; the surveys were recorded; the state of Virginia was paid for the land.

Next April, however, one George Wilson filed papers on 40,926 acres adjacent to Mason's 8,400 acres and, in March 1785, entered a caveat against Mason's 8,300 acres and all of Moore's and Madison's tracts as conflicting with his own. A trip west by Mason's son, William, in 1784 had failed to clear the matter up; John Coffer, who accompanied him, testified in 1795 that on their return, Mason termed Wilson's action "a bare-faced piece of knavery and infamous combination between Wilson and some of the Surveyors."

When the case came to trial, the evidence suggested such chican-

*Gunston Hall graveyard*
*(by author)*

ery. Wilson had two partners, Christopher Greenup and John Handley; the latter was deputy county surveyor and, as such, thoroughly familiar with the land records. A courthouse employee testified that these men had studied the Mason survey "in the late hours of the night and that he held a candle to give them light."

Kentucky obtained statehood in 1792; in 1800, the case was renewed, with a cross-caveat filed in the name of Mason's minor grandson, George's son Richard, before the United States District Court for the Kentucky District. In May 1801, with Judge Harry Innes presiding, this court ruled decisively in Mason's favor.* Innes observed that Wilson had had "notice before he made his entry that Mason had appropriated the land"; he cited Lord Hardwicke's finding that "the taking of a legal estate after notice of a prior right makes a person mala fide purchaser, and is a species of fraud." Wilson appealed the decision to the United States Supreme Court.

In 1801, President Adams named John Marshall chief justice; *Wilson* v. *Mason* was on the docket of Marshall's first winter term and is reported in 1 Cranch 45–103. Wilson's lawyer was the flamboyant Joseph H. Daveiss, the first western attorney to plead in Washington; without education until his teens, he had read law in Kentucky with George Nicholas. Using his very considerable fluency in quotation, he based his argument on Lord Kames's discussion of error in his *Principles of Equity*.† His Lordship distinguished between taking advantage of another man's error in order to avoid damage to one's self, *in damno evitando,* and doing so in order to secure gain, *in lucro capitando*. With respect to the former, he said, "No man is conscious of wrong, where he takes advantage of an error committed by another to save himself from loss: if there must be a loss, common sense dictates, that it ought to rest upon the person who has erred, however innocently rather than upon him who has not erred." This Daveiss quoted, but Marshall, when preparing the opinion of the court, apparently did not notice that Daveiss failed to complete the quotation. Kames continued his paragraph with a sentence directly refuting what Wilson had pled: "But *in lucro capitando,* the moral sense teaches a different lesson; which is that no man ought to take advantage of another's error to make a gain by it."[30] The verdict awarded the tract to Wilson. Shortly, the fact materialized that Daveiss was not an attorney for a claimant to this land; he was its owner. Soon the land was all in the family: through marriage within months to Marshall's sister, Ann, Daveiss became the chief justice's brother-in-law.

The tangible goods distributed under Mason's will transmitted his possessions as the Virginia planter and benevolent parent recalled by his son, John, among his childhood memories. But John also recalled his father as the source of new political ideas, and toward the end of the first quarter of the nineteenth century, the younger generation attempted to enhance this legacy by gathering a fuller record from Mason's political friends and associates who were still alive.

George Mason, Jr., had survived his father only briefly, dying in

1796, but his son George actively pursued a correspondence with men who had known his grandfather. In the forgiving mellowness of old age, Madison in 1827 wrote of their relationship:

My first acquaintance with him was in the convention of Va. of 1776. . . . Being young and inexperienced I had of course but little agency in those proceedings. I retained however a perfect impression that he was a leading champion for the Instruction [for independence]; that he was the author of the Declaration as originally drawn, and with very slight variations adopted; and that he was the Master Builder of the Constitution, & its main expositor & supporter throughout the discussion. . . .

The public situation in which I had the best opportunity of being acquainted with the genius, the opinions & the public labours of your grandfather was that of our co-service in the Convention of 1787 . . . none who differed from him on some points will deny that he sustained throughout the proceedings of the body the high character of a powerful Reasoner, a profound Statesman and a devoted Republican.

My private intercourse with him was chiefly on occasional visits to Gunston when journeying to & fro from the North, in which his conversations were always a feast to me.[31]

In 1821, in retirement at Monticello, Jefferson paid a comparable tribute to Mason in his *Autobiography*:

I had many occasional and strenuous coadjutors in debate, and one most steadfast, able and zealous; who was himself a host. This was George Mason, a man of the first order of wisdom among those who acted on the theatre of the revolution, of expansive mind, profound judgment, cogent in argument, learned in the lore of our former constitution, and earnest for the republican change on democratic principles. His elocution was neither flowing nor smooth; but his language was strong, his manner most impressive, and strengthened by a dash of biting cynicism, when provocation made it seasonable.[32]

Like that of his worldly goods, much of Mason's intangible legacy as a political thinker was passed on in his lifetime—in his state, in the nation, and to the world at large.

The adoption of written constitutions in the American states during the third quarter of the eighteenth century introduced the modern governmental era. The political theory and practice that appeared in the British-American colonies as separation from the mother country neared was an affirmation with worldwide application, first in the European revolutions and reforms that began in France in 1789 and continued down the nineteenth century, and then in colonial revolts on other continents.

The succession of New World constitutions of which Virginia's, with Mason as its chief architect, was the first, declared the source of political authority to be the people, and spelled out, for an increasingly literate electorate to read, the functions of the state, its powers, and the limitations on those powers. And in addition to making clear what a government was entitled to do, most of them were prefaced by a list of individual rights of the citizens under their jurisdiction, rights that government should in no case infringe, rights whose maintenance was government's primary reason for being. Mason wrote the first of these lists. He was fond of saying that good government required "frequent recurrence to fundamental principles"; his declaration of rights posted the principles where all might see.

They were seen, in his time, in the transfer of revolutionary ideas from the New World to the Old. For the ensuing two hundred years, they have likewise been seen down the decades in this country. It is true, as Madison observed to Jefferson and as George Nicholas declared to a wrathful Mason in the Virginia Convention of 1788, that a willful majority, given power, can make a scrap of paper of a bill of rights, and the twentieth century has seen this done. But it is also true that the existence of such a bill has permitted emergent perceptions of justice to cite its articles as standards in the measurement of what is as against what should be, and the twentieth century has seen this done, too.

It has seen ample corroboration of Jefferson's observation to Madison in 1789 that the existence of a national bill of rights would assure reality to the balance of governmental powers by giving the judiciary a function coordinate in importance with those of the other two branches. The twentieth-century judicial tempering of absolute power in economic affairs to the advantage of the common man is one case in point. Judicial recognition of the civil rights of the country's minority populations is another.

That is not to say that Mason's views were necessarily consonant with as wide a use of the institutions of central government as the middle years of the twentieth century have witnessed. The spectacle of the descendants of the Hamiltonians wishing to return the powers of the federal government to the states, while the descendants of the Jeffersonians enthusiastically extend them at the national capital, is a contemporary paradox, and Mason was so much a Jeffersonian of his own time as to worry Madison by his "heterodoxy . . . in being too little impressed with either the necessity or the proper means" of preserving a central focus of the national life.

Partly because he was a very local man and partly because of the generation gap between him and all of his chief colleagues, except Washington, that set his formative years deeper than theirs in the colonial experience, to Mason, more than to the others, Virginia was in the beginning and remained, "my Country." The doctrine of interposition and nullification which Jefferson developed in the Kentucky Resolutions of 1798 drew on his resources and so did the theory of states' rights as enlarged during the next 160 years.

The enlargement was again a paradox. A number of Mason's colleagues believed that his opposition to the Constitution was caused as much by the mid-Convention bargain on commercial legislation and the slave trade as by the absence of a national bill of rights, and his last conversation with Jefferson showed it to have been at least a major factor. After telling Jefferson that the Constitution, as agreed to until a fortnight before the Convention rose, was such as he could have set his hand and heart to, the objection on which he dwelt was this economic deal, whose terms made him a double loser. Sanction of slavery stayed in, and requirement of a two-thirds majority on tariffs was traded off to obtain it. And politicians of subsequent decades transposed his arguments for a state's right to protect its commerce into support for the South's attempt first to protect its "peculiar institution," and then to mount a massive resistance to interracial change.

The political images of Mason transmitted in the memoirs of his son, John, enhance the respect due him and many of the revolutionary generation for the disinterestedness of their devotion to public affairs. More than others of his contemporaries, Mason was untouched by political ambition. After Ann Eilbeck's death, a prompt remarriage in the prevailing mode would have freed him from the care of his young family to accept appointment as a Virginia delegate to the Continental and the Confederation Congress and to serve more consecutively in office in Williamsburg and Richmond. He preferred Gunston Hall.

Likewise, the economic interpreter of history finds such biographies as Mason's difficult to fit into his thesis. The plantation life at Gunston Hall and elsewhere in Virginia was a more than adequate source of economic well-being and the scene of deeply rooted human contentment. Its disruption offered no material gain; it was costly not only to the owners' fortunes—Mason estimated to George in 1783 that his losses from the war amounted to at least £10,000 sterling—but to their private pursuit of happiness.

Yet because they regarded their liberties as infringed, these gentlemen became revolutionaries. Among Mason's intangible legacies, the most moving is the passage in his will that transmits the compass of his life's direction, public and private, in a final message to his sons:

> I recommend it to my sons, from my own Experience in Life, to prefer the happiness of independance & a private Station to the troubles and Vexations of Public Business; but if either their own inclination or the Necessity of the times shou'd engage them in Public Affairs, I charge them, on a Fathers Blessing, never to let the motives of private Interest or ambition to induce them to betray, nor the terrors of Poverty and disgrace, or the fear of danger or of death deter them from Asserting the liberty of their Country, and endeavouring to transmit to their posterity those Sacred rights to which themselves were born.[33]

Five years later, describing intervening events to friends overseas, Mason said of the transition from a colony to statehood in Virginia, "Taking a retrospective view of what is passed, we seem to have been treading upon enchanted Ground." At a similar interval after the Philadelphia Convention, his final conversation with Jefferson expressed a less favorable attitude toward the formation of the Federal Constitution. Yet at a distance of two hundred years, his "retrospective view" is applicable to the entire period of the emergence of the United States, and his determined insistence that a bill of rights was necessary for the nation as well as for the states is in generous measure responsible.

# Appendix 1
## First Draft of the Virginia Declaration of Rights

*(Written by George Mason as a member of the committee to prepare a bill of rights and constitution for Virginia, to which he was appointed on 18 May 1776, and sent by Thomas Ludwell Lee, probably with the post of 25 May from Williamsburg, to his brother, Richard Henry Lee, in Congress in Philadelphia. The first ten articles are in Mason's hand, the remainder of the document in Lee's.)*

A Declaration of Rights, made by the Representatives of the good People of Virginia, assembled in full Convention; and recommended to Posterity as the Basis and Foundation of Government.

That all Men are born equally free and independent, and have certain inherent natural Rights, of which they can not by any Compact, deprive or divest their Posterity; among which are the Enjoyment of Life and Liberty, with the Means of acquiring and possessing Property, and pursueing and obtaining Happiness and Safety.

That Power is, by God and Nature, vested in, and consequently derived from the People; that Magistrates are their Trustees and Servants, and at all times amenable to them.

That Government is, or ought to be, instituted for the common Benefit and Security of the People, Nation, or Community. Of all the various Modes and Forms of Government, that is best, which is capable of producing the greatest Degree of Happiness and Safety, and is most effectually secured against the Danger of mal-administration. And that whenever any Government shall be found inadequate, or contrary to these Purposes, a Majority of the Community had an indubitable, inalianable and indefeasible Right to reform, alter or abolish it, in such Manner as shall be judged most conducive to the Public Weal.

That no Man, or Set of Men are entitled to exclusive or separate Emoluments or Privileges from the Community, but in Consideration of public Services; which not being descendible, or hereditary, the Idea of a Man born a Magistrate, a Legislator, or a Judge is unnatural and absurd.

That the legislative and executive Powers of the State shoud be seperate and distinct from the judicative; and that the Members of the two first may be restraind from Oppression, by feeling and participating the Burthens they may lay upon the People; they should, at fixed Periods be reduced to a private Station, and returned, by frequent, certain and regular Elections, into that Body from which they were taken.

That no part of a Man's Property can be taken from him, or applied to public uses, without the Consent of himself, or his legal Representatives; nor are the People bound by any Laws, but such as they have in like Manner assented to for their common Good.

That in all capital or criminal Prosecutions, a Man hath a right to demand the Cause and Nature of his Accusation, to be confronted with the Accusers or Witnesses, to call for Evidence in his favour, and to a speedy Tryal by a Jury of his Vicinage; without whose unanimous Consent, he can not be found guilty, nor can he be compelled to give Evidence against himself. And that no Man, except in times of actual Invasion or Insurrection, can be imprisoned upon Suspicion of Crimes against the State, unsupported by Legal Evidence.

That no free Government, or the Blessings of Liberty can be preserved to any People, but by a firm adherence to Justice, Moderation, Temperance, Frugality, and Virtue and by frequent Recurrence to fundamental Principles.

That as Religion, or the Duty which we owe to our divine and omnipotent Creator, and the Manner of discharging it, can be governed only by Reason and Conviction, not by Force or Violence; and therefore that all Men shou'd enjoy the fullest Toleration in the Exercise of Religion, according to the Dictates of Conscience, unpunished and unrestrained by the Magistrate, unless under Colour of Religion, any Man disturb the Peace, the Happiness, or Safety of Society, or of Individuals. And that it is the mutual Duty of all, to practice Christian Forbearance, Love and Charity towards Each other.

That in all controversies respecting Property, and in Suits between Man and Man, the ancient Tryal by Jury is preferable to any other, and ought to be held sacred.

That the freedom of the press, being the great bulwark of Liberty, can never be restrained but in a despotic government.

That laws having a retrospect to crimes, & punishing offences committed before the existence of such laws, are generally dangerous, and ought to be avoided.

N. B. It is proposed to make some alteration in this last article when reported to the house. Perhaps somewhat like the following

That all laws having a retrospect to crimes, & punishing offences committed before the existence of such laws are dangerous, and ought to be avoided, except in cases of great, & evident necessity, when safety of the state absolutely requires them. This is thought to state with more precision the doctrine

respecting ex post facto laws & to signify to posterity that it is considered not so much as a law of right, as the great law of necessity, which by the well known maxim is— allowed to supersede all human institutions.

Another is agreed to in committee condemning the use of general warrants; & one other to prevent the suspension of laws, or the execution of them.

The above clauses, with some small alterations, & the addition of one, or two more, have already been agreed to in the Committee appointed to prepare a declaration of rights; when this business is finished in the house, the committee will proceed to the ordinance of government.

T. L. Lee

(Mason Papers, Library of Congress, Washington, D.C., and George Mason, *The Papers of George Mason, 1725–1792,* ed. Robert A. Rutland, 3 vols. [Chapel Hill: University of North Carolina Press, 1971], 1:276–78.)

# Appendix 2
## Printed Committee Draft of the Virginia Declaration of Rights

*(Submitted 27 May 1776; published in Dixon & Hunter's Virginia Gazette on 1 June, and in the Pennsylvania Evening Post of 6 June, from which it was widely recopied up and down the coast.)*

A DECLARATION *of* RIGHTS *made by the representatives of the good people of* Virginia, *assembled in full and free Convention; which rights do pertain to us, and our posterity, as the basis and foundation of government.*

1. THAT all men are born equally free and independent, and have certain inherent natural rights, of which they cannot, by any compact, deprive or divest their posterity; among which are, the enjoyment of life and liberty, with the means of acquiring and possessing property, and pursuing and obtaining happiness and safety.

2. That all power is vested in, and consequently derived from, the people; that magistrates are their trustees and servants, and at all times amenable to them.

3. That government is, or ought to be, instituted for the common benefit, protection, and

security, of the people, nation or community, of all the various modes and forms of government that is best, which is capable of producing the greatest degree of happiness and safety, and is most effectually secured against the danger of mal-administration; and that whenever any government shall be found inadequate or contrary to these purposes, a majority of the community hath an indubitable, unalienable, indefeasible right, to reform, alter, or abolish it, in such manner as shall be judged most conducive to the publick Weal.

4. That no man, or set of men, are entitled to exclusive or separate emoluments or privileges from the community, but in consideration of publick services, which, not being descendible, or hereditary, the idea of a man born a magistrate, a legislator, or a judge, is unnatural and absurd.

5. That the legislative and executive powers of the state should be separate and distinct from the judicative; and that the members of the two first may be restrained from oppression, by feeling and participating the burthens of the people, they should,

at fixed periods, be reduced to a private station, return into that body from which they were (originally) taken, (and the vacancies be supplied) by frequent, certain, and regular elections.

6. That elections of members to serve as representatives of the people, in assembly, ought to be free; and that all men, having sufficient evidence of permanent common interest with, and attachment to, the community, have the right of suffrage.

7. That no part of a man's property can be taken from him, or applied to publick uses, without his own consent, or that of his legal representatives; nor are the people bound by any laws but such as they have, in like manner, assented to, for their common good.

8. That all power of suspending laws, or the execution of laws, by any authority without consent of the representatives of the people, is injurious to their rights, and ought not to be exercised.

9. That laws having retrospect to crimes, and punishing offences, committed before the existence of such laws, are generally oppressive, and ought to be avoided.

10. That in all capital or criminal prosecutions a man hath a right to demand the cause and nature of his accusation, to be confronted with the accusers or witnesses, to call for evidence in his favour, and to a speedy trial by an impartial jury of his vicinage, without whose unanimous consent he cannot be found guilty, nor can he be compelled to give evidence against himself that no man be deprived of his liberty except by the law of the land, or the judgment of his peers.

11. That excessive bail ought not to be required, nor excessive fines impossed, nor cruel and unusual punishments inflicted.

12. That warrants unsupported by evidence, whereby any officer or messenger may be commanded or required to search suspected places, or to seize any person or persons, his or their property, not particularly described, are grievous and oppressive, and ought not to be granted.

13. That in controversies respecting property, and in suits between man and man, the ancient trial by jury is preferable to any other, and ought to be held sacred.

14. That the freedom of the press is one of the great bulwarks of liberty, and can never be restrained but by despotick governments.

15. That a well regulated militia, composed of the body of the people, trained to arms, is the proper, natural, and safe defence of a free state; that standing armies, in time of peace, should be avoided, as dangerous to liberty; and that, in all cases, the military should be under strict subordination to, and governed by, the civil power.

16. That the people have a right to uniform government; and therefore, that no government separate from, or independent of, the government of Virginia, ought, of right, to be erected or established within the limits thereof.

17. That no free government, or the blessing of liberty, can be preserved to any people but by a firm adherence to justice, moderation, temperance, frugality, and virtue, and by frequent recurrence to fundamental principles.

18. That religion, or the duty which we owe to our CREATOR, and the manner of discharging it, can be directed only by reason and conviction, not by force or violence; and therefore, that all men should enjoy the fullest toleration in the exercise of religion, according to the dictates of conscience, unpunished and unrestrained by the magistrate, unless, under colour of religion, any man disturb the peace, the happiness, or safety of society. And that it is the mutual duty of all to practice Christian forbearance, love, and charity, towards each other.

# Appendix 3
## Final Version of the Virginia Declaration of Rights

*(Adopted 12 June 1776; printed in Purdie's Virginia Gazette on 14 June and Dixon & Hunter's Virginia Gazette on 15 June.)*

A DECLARATION OF RIGHTS made by the Representatives of the good people of VIRGINIA, assembled in full and free Convention; which rights do pertain to them and their posterity, as the basis and foundation of Government.

1. That all men are by nature equally free and independent, and have certain inherent rights, of which, when they enter into a state of society, they cannot, by any compact, deprive or divest their posterity; namely, the enjoyment of life and liberty, with the means of acquiring and possessing property, and pursuing and obtaining happiness and safety.

2. That all power is vested in, and consequently derived from, the People; that magistrates are their trustees and servants, and at all times amenable to them.

3. That Government is, or ought to be, instituted for the common benefit, protection, and security of the people, nation, or community;—of all the various modes and forms of Government that is best which is capable of producing the greatest degree of happiness and safety, and is most effectually secured against the danger of mal-administration;—and that, whenever any Government shall be found inadequate or contrary to these purposes, a majority of the community hath an indubitable, unalienable, and indefeasible right, to reform, alter, or abolish it, in such manner as shall be judged most conducive to the publick weal.

4. That no man, or set of men, are entitled to exclusive or separate emoluments and privileges from the community, but in consideration of publick services; which, not being descendible, neither ought the offices of Magistrate, Legislator, or Judge to be hereditary.

5. That the Legislative and Executive powers of the State should be separate and distinct from the Judicative; and, that the members of the two first may be restrained from oppression, by feeling and participating the burdens of the people, they should, at fixed periods, be reduced to a private station, return into that body from which they were originally taken, and the vacancies be supplied by frequent, certain, and regular elections, in which all, or any part of the former members, to be again eligible, or ineligible, as the law shall direct.

6. That elections of members to serve as Representatives of the people, in Assembly, ought to be free; and that all men, having sufficient evidence of permanent common interest with, and attachment to, the community, have the right of suffrage, and cannot be taxed or deprived of their property for publick uses without their own consent or that of their Representative so elected, nor bound by any law to which they have not, in like manner, assented, for the public good.

7. That all power of suspending laws, or the execution of laws, by any authority, without consent of the Representatives of the people, is injurious to their rights, and ought not to be exercised.

8. That in all capital or criminal prosecutions a man hath a right to demand the cause and nature of his accusation, to be confronted with the accusers and witnesses, to call for evidence in his favour, and to a speedy trial by an impartial jury of his vicinage, without whose unanimous consent he cannot be found guilty, nor can he be compelled to give evidence against himself; that no man be deprived of his liberty except by the law of the land, or the judgment of his peers.

9. That excessive bail ought not to be required, nor excessive fines imposed, nor cruel and unusual punishments inflicted.

10. That general warrants, whereby any officer or messenger may be commanded to search suspected places without evidence of a fact committed, or to seize any person or persons not named, or whose offence is not particularly described and supported by evidence, are grievous and oppressive, and ought not to be granted.

11. That in controversies respecting property, and in suits between man and man, the ancient trial by Jury is preferable to any other, and ought to be held sacred.

12. That the freedom of the Press is one of the greatest bulwarks of liberty, and can never be restrained but by despotick Governments.

13. That a well-regulated Militia, composed of the body of the people, trained to arms, is the proper, natural, and safe defence of a free State; that Standing Armies, in time of peace, should be avoided as dangerous to liberty; and that, in all cases, the military should be under strict subordination to, and governed by, the civil power.

14. That the people have a right to uniform Government; and, therefore, that no Government separate from, or independent of, the Government of *Virginia*, ought to be erected or established within the limits thereof.

15. That no free Government, or the blessing of liberty, can be preserved to any people but by a firm adherence to justice, moderation, temperance, frugality, and virtue, and by frequent recurrence to fundamental principles.

16. That Religion, or the duty which we owe to our *Creator*, and the manner of discharging it, can be directed only by reason and conviction, not by force or violence; and, therefore, all men are equally entitled to the free exercise of religion, according to the dictates of conscience; and that it is the mutual duty of all to practise Christian forbearance, love, and charity, towards each other.

# Appendix 4
## The Bill of Rights Contained in the Declaration of Independence

*(Adopted by the Congress of the Confederation on 4 July 1776, the declaration prefaced its bill of particulars enumerating the colonies' grievances with a brief statement of the purpose for which "Governments are instituted among Men.")*

WHEN in the Course of human Events, it becomes necessary for one People to dissolve the Political Bands which have connected them with another, and to assume among the Powers of the Earth, the separate and equal Station to which the Laws of Nature and of Nature's God entitle them, a decent Respect to the Opinions of Mankind requires that they should declare the causes which impel them to the Separation.

We hold these Truths to be self-evident, that all Men are created equal, that they are endowed by their Creator with certain unalienable Rights, that among these are Life, Liberty and the Pursuit of Happiness.—That to secure these Rights, Governments are instituted among Men, deriving their just Powers from the Consent of the Governed, that whenever any Form of Government becomes destructive of these Ends, it is the Right of the People to alter or to abolish it, and to institute new Government, laying its Foundation on such Principles, and organizing its Powers in such Form, as to them shall seem most likely to effect their Safety and Happiness.

# Appendix 5
## Declaration of the Rights of Man and Citizen

*(Adopted by the National Constituent Assembly of France on 26 August 1789, accepted by the king on 3 October, promulgated on 3 November. For the French text, see "La Déclaration des droits de l'homme et du citoyen," in Jacques Godechot, La Pensée revolutionnaire en France et en Europe, 1780–1799 [Paris: Colin, 1964], pp. 115–18.)*

The representatives of the French people, organized in National Assembly, considering that ignorance, forgetfulness, or contempt of the rights of man are the sole causes of public misfortunes and of the corruption of governments, have resolved to set forth in a solemn declaration the natural, inalienable, and sacred rights of man, in order that such declaration, continually before all members of the social body, may be a perpetual reminder of their rights and duties; in order that the acts of the legislative power and those of the executive power may constantly be compared with the aim of every political institution and may accordingly be more respected; in order that the demands of the citizens, founded henceforth upon simple and incontestable principles, may always be directed towards the maintenance of the Constitution and the welfare of all.

Accordingly, the National Assembly recognizes and proclaims, in the presence and under the auspices of the Supreme Being, the following rights of man and citizen.

1. Men are born and remain free and equal in rights; social distinctions may be based only upon general usefulness.

2. The aim of every political association is the preservation of the natural and inalienable rights of man; these rights are liberty, property, security, and resistance to oppression.

3. The source of all sovereignty resides essentially in the nation; no group, no individual may exercise authority not emanating expressly therefrom.

4. Liberty consists of the power to do whatever is not injurious to others; thus the enjoyment of the natural rights of every man has for its limits only those that assure other members of society the enjoyment of those same rights; such limits may be determined only by law.

5. The law has the right to forbid only actions which are injurious to society. Whatever is not forbidden by law may not be prevented, and no one may be constrained to do what it does not prescribe.

6. Law is the expression of the general will; all citizens have the right to concur personally, or through their representatives, in its formation; it must be the same for all, whether it protects or punishes. All citizens, being equal before it, are equally admissible to all public offices, positions, and employments, according to their capacity, and without other distinction than that of virtues and talents.

7. No man may be accused, arrested, or detained except in the cases determined by law, and according to the forms prescribed thereby. Whoever solicit, expedite, or execute arbitrary orders, or have them executed, must be punished; but every citizen summoned or apprehended in pursuance of the law must obey immediately; he renders himself culpable by resistance.

8. The law is to establish only penalties that are absolutely and obviously necessary; and no one may be punished except by virtue of a law established and promulgated prior to the offence and legally applied.

9. Since every man is presumed innocent until declared guilty, if arrest be deemed indispensable, all unnecessary severity for securing the person of the accused must be severely repressed by law.

10. No one is to be disquieted because of his opinion, even religious, provided their manifestation does not disturb the public order established by law.

11. Free communication of ideas and opinions is one of the most precious of the rights of man. Consequently, every citizen may speak, write, and print freely, subject to responsibility for the abuse of such liberty in the cases determined by law.

12. The guarantee of the rights of man and citizen necessitates a public force; such a force, therefore, is instituted for the advantage of all and not for the particular benefit of those to whom it is entrusted.

13. For the maintenance of the public force and for the expenses of administration a common tax is indispensable; it must be assessed equally on all citizens in proportion to their means.

14. Citizens have the right to ascertain, by themselves or through their representatives, the necessity of the public tax, to consent to it freely, to supervise its use, and to determine its quota, assessment, payment, and duration.

15. Society has the right to require of every public agent an accounting of his administration.

16. Every society in which the guarantee of rights is not assured or the separation of powers is not determined has no constitution at all.

17. Since property is a sacred and inviolable right, no one may be deprived thereof unless a legally established public necessity obviously requires it, and upon condition of a just and previous indemnity.

# Appendix 6
## The First Ten Amendments to the Constitution of the United States

*(Twelve amendments were submitted to the states by joint resolution of Congress adopted 25 September 1789; by the end of 1791, ten of them (numbers 3 through 12) were ratified by the requisite three-fourths of the states and became part of the Constitution.)*

ARTICLE I. Congress shall make no law respecting an establishment of religion, or prohibiting the free exercise thereof; or abridging the freedom of speech, or of the press; or the right of the people peaceably to assemble, and to petition the Government for a redress of grievances.

ARTICLE II. A well-regulated militia, being necessary to the security of a free State, the right of the people to keep and bear arms, shall not be infringed.

ARTICLE III. No soldier shall, in time of peace be quartered in any house, without the consent of the owner, nor in time of war, but in a manner to be prescribed by law.

ARTICLE IV. The right of the people to be secure in their persons, houses, papers, and effects, against unreasonable searches and seizures, shall not be violated, and no warrants shall issue, but upon probable cause, supported by oath or affirmation, and particularly describing the place to be searched, and the persons or things to be seized.

ARTICLE V. No person shall be held to answer for a capital, or otherwise infamous crime, unless on a presentment or indictment of a Grand Jury, except in cases arising in the land or naval forces, or in the militia, when in actual service in time of war or public danger; nor shall any person be subject for the same offense to be twice put in jeopardy of life or limb; nor shall be compelled in any criminal case to be a witness against himself, nor be deprived of life, liberty, or property, without due process of law; nor shall private property be taken for public use without just compensation.

ARTICLE VI. In all criminal prosecutions, the accused shall enjoy the right to a speedy and public trial, by an impartial jury of the State and district wherein the crime shall have been committed, which district shall have been previously ascertained by law, and to be informed of the nature and cause of the accusation; to be confronted with the witnesses against him; to have compulsory process for obtaining witnesses in his favor, and to have the assistance of counsel for his defense.

ARTICLE VII. In suits at common law, where the value in controversy shall exceed twenty dollars, the right of trial by jury shall be preserved, and no fact tried by a jury shall be otherwise re-examined in any court of the United States, than according to the rules of the common law.

ARTICLE VIII. Excessive bail shall not be required, nor excessive fines imposed, nor cruel and unusual punishments inflicted.

ARTICLE IX. The enumeration in the Constitution, of certain rights, shall not be construed to deny or disparage others retained by the people.

ARTICLE X. The powers not delegated to the United States by the Constitution, nor prohibited by it to the States, are reserved to the States respectively, or to the people.

# Notes

vii  *St. George Tucker to William Wirt, 4 April 1813, MS 1274, Maryland Historical Society, Baltimore, Md.

3  *Gunston's prefix indicates the possessive of a personal name. From 1368 to the end of the century, the abbot of Croxden, one of the two great Cistercian houses in this part of Staffordshire, was named William Gunston; among his numerous foundations was a leper hospital near Gunston, whose site is still known as Leper House Farm.

†When Lichfield Cathedral was rebuilt at the Restoration, a militant symbol of Royalist faith was the eleven-foot stone statue of Charles II, crowned and holding scepter and orb, placed to dominate the cathedral close at the apex of the nave gable of the cathedral's west front; it held this position from 1669 to 1860, when the architect of another renovation substituted a figure of Christ in Majesty.

4  *For the patents, see Westmoreland County, Va., Deeds and Wills Book I, pp. 50, 84, and 196–97. Nell Marion Nugent, comp., *Cavaliers and Pioneers: Abstracts of Virginia Land Patents and Grants, 1623–1800* (Richmond: Dietz Press, 1934), pp. 297–98 and 332, describes the locations of the Fowke and Mason lands. The suit between Tho. Doggus and John Gresham, 25 November 1652, in which one George Mason was a juryman, is recorded in Westmoreland County, Va., Order Book, 1652–1665, p. 7a. The first paragraph of Thomas Fowke's will, in Deeds and Wills Book I, p. 196, reads: "In the name of God amen I Thomas Fowke of the County of Westmoreld. in Virginia Gentleman being of perfect mind and memory praised be god for the same doe make this my last will and Testament in manner and form following First I bequeath my soul into the hands of Almighty God my creator hoping by the death and passion of Jesus Christ his only son my alone saviour to receive forgiveness of all my sins and after this life ended to enjoy everlasting happiness in the Kingdom of heaven my body I give to the earth if I die upon land otherwise where it shall please god to Call for me being now bound to sea for my worldly estate which god in his mercy hath blessed me withall, I give and bequeath as following."

7  *In the early eighteenth century, Virginia's governorship was frequently a sinecure held by an English nobleman who never set foot in the colony; the duties of the office were performed by a lieutenant, but locally these men bore the title of governor.

9  *For details, see George MacLaren Brydon, *Virginia's Mother Church and the Political Conditions under Which It Grew*, 2 vols. (Richmond: Virginia Historical Society, 1947–52), 1:372–73.

†Giles Brent had been Maryland's treasurer; Margaret and Mary were the first women to become landholders there in their own right, calling their acres Sisters Freehold. Margaret, who became a lawyer, created a furore in 1648 by demanding a seat in the Assembly as attorney for Lord Baltimore and executrix of the late governor, his cousin Leonard Calvert. Her application was denied. In 1650 the Brent family withdrew across the river to Virginia, pointedly giving the name of Peace to their new plantation in Stafford.

16  *Robert Beverley listed imports in discussing drinkables: "Their Small-drink is either Wine and Water, Beer, Milk and Water, or Water alone. Their richer sort generally brew their Small-Beer with Malt, which they have from *England,* though they have as good Barley of their own, as any in the World; but for want of the convenience of Malt-Houses, the Inhabitants take no care to sow it. The poorer sort brew their Beer with Mollasses and Bran; with *Indian* Corn Malted by drying in a Stove; with Persimmons dried in Cakes, and baked; with Potatoes; with the green stalks of *Indian* Corn cut small, and bruised; with Pompions; and with the *Batates Canadensis,* or *Jerusalem Artichoke,* which some People plant purposely for that use, but this is the least esteem'd, of all the sorts before mention'd.

"Their Strong Drink is *Madera* Wine, which is a Noble strong Wine; and Punch, made either with Rum from the *Caribee* Islands, or Brandy distilled from their Apples, and Peaches; besides *French-Brandy,* Wine, and strong Beer, which they have constantly from England." (Robert Beverley, *The History and Present State of Virginia,* ed. with intro. Louis B. Wright [Chapel Hill: University of North Carolina Press, 1947], p. 293.)

17  *The Clyde's great shipbuilding days began only with the age of steam: though the first locally built sailing ship to go to America went in 1718, as Glasgow merchants accumulated fleets, they generally bought elsewhere.

26  *Now in the Virginia State Library.

†Now in the Bucks County Historical Society Library, Doylestown, Pennsylvania, and cited at length in C. Malcolm Watkins, *The Cultural History of Marlborough, Virginia* (Washington, D.C.: Smithsonian Institution Press, 1968).

31     *See Louis B. Wright, *The First Gentlemen of Virginia* (San Marino, Calif.: Huntington Library, 1940).

32     *Sir Thomas Littleton was justice of the Court of Common Pleas in Henry VII's time.

34     *The tolls were four pence for a man and the same for a horse.

35     *Postal rates reflected the difficulties of overland delivery: a letter from London to New York cost 1/-, but from New York to Williamsburg, 1/3.
    †Original in the Public Library, Alexandria, Virginia.

37     *The site of Pittsburgh.

38     *The site of Cumberland.
    †Gist's notes whetted his readers' land hunger. On Sunday, 17 February 1751, he "Crossed the little Miamee River, and altering our Course South West twenty five Miles to the big Miamee River opposite Twigtwee Town. All the way from the Shannoah Town to this place (except the first twenty miles which is broken) is fine rich level Land, well timbered with large walnut ash sugar trees cherry trees &c; it is well watered with a great number of little streams or rivulets and full of beautiful natural meadows, covered with wild rye blue grass and clover and abounds with Turkeys, deer, elks, and most sorts of game particularly Buffaloes, thirty or forty of which are frequently seen feeding in one meadow. In short it wants nothing but cultivation to make it a most delightfull countrey." (Lois Mulkearn, ed., *George Mercer Papers Relating to the Ohio Company of Virginia* [Pittsburgh: University of Pittsburgh Press, 1944], pp. 257–58.)

41     *Now at Gunston Hall.
    †Ninety years later, their son, John, wrote that the originals "now in my possession in the month of May, 1840, are so defaced and mutilated by time and damp rooms, as that the features can no longer be traced with accuracy—but from which were taken, in the year 1811, under my supervision—when they (originals) were yet perfect, or nearly so, three several setts of copies, by Monsieur D. W. Boudet . . . which were justly deemed . . . close and accurate copies, as well in the lineaments and features of the faces . . . and in the drapery—in which last were exactly, in contour and in fashion preserved the depicted dresses shown on the originals." Boudet was a French refugee who had been a pupil of David. All three sets of copies have survived; Ann's auburn hair, combed high away from forehead and ears, but with long curls brought forward over her shoulders, contrasts with her blue dress and its filmy lace at sleeves and neck. Two ornate buttons accentuate the opening of her bodice; she holds a rose between thumb and forefinger of her left hand.

47     *Hugh Jones, in *The Present State of Virginia*, ed. Richard L. Morton (Chapel Hill: University of North Carolina Press, 1956), p. 87, listed three kinds of white servants, those working for agreed wages, those working under indenture, and "those convicts or felons that are transported, whose room they [Virginians] had much rather have than their company; for abundance of them do great mischiefs, commit robbery and murder, and spoil servants, that were before very good: But they frequently

there meet with the end they deserved at home, though indeed some of them prove indifferent good."

    Reporting the Lee fire to the Lords of Trade on 26 March 1729, Governor Gooch used the occasion to complain: "the secret Robberies and other villainous Attempts of a more pernicious Crew of transported Felons, are yet more intollerable; witness the Dwelling House and Out Houses of Mr. Thomas Lee which in the night time were set on fire by these villains and in an instant burnt to the ground, a young White Woman burnt in her bed, the Gentleman, his wife and three children very providentially getting out at a window, with nothing on but their Shifts and Shirts on their backs, which was all they saved, not two minuits before the House fell in: and this was done by those Rogues because as a Justice of the Peace, upon complaint made to him, he had granted a warrant for apprehending some of them. They are not yet discovered. In consideration of this gentleman's misfortune, which he is not well able to bear, and as it rises from the discharge of his duty as Magistrate, I have been prevailed upon to intercede with your Lordships, that his case may be recommended to his Majesty, for his royal Bounty of two or three hundred Pounds towards lessening his loss, which was the more considerable by a very good collection of books." (PRO, CO, 5:1317. Transcripts of Crown-copyright records in the Public Record Office, London, appear by permission of the Controller of Her Majesty's Stationery Office, London.)

51     *On 18 April 1775, Robert Adam wrote his brother, John, forecasting competition from "his taste for Bas relieves, Ornaments, & decorations of Buildings. He both knows well & draws exquisitely." (John Harris, *Sir William Chambers, Knight of the Polar Star* [London: Zwemmer, 1970], p. 7.)

55     *Hunting was also done on foot. Robert Beverley's early eighteenth-century description of a coon hunt lost no validity in later years: "It is perform'd a Foot, with small Dogs in the Night, by the Light of the Moon or Stars. Thus in Summertime they find an abundance of Raccoons, Opossums, and Foxes in the Corn-Fields, and about their Plantations: but at other times, they must go into the Woods for them. The Method is to go out with three or four Dogs, and as soon as they come to the place, they bid the Dogs seek out, and all the Company follow immediately. Where-ever a Dog barks, you may depend on finding the Game; and this Alarm, draws both Men and Dogs that way. If this Sport be in the Woods, the Game by that time you come near it, is perhaps mounted to the top of an high Tree, and then they detach a nimble Fellow up after it, who must have a scuffle with the Beast, before he can throw it down to the Dogs; and then the Sport increases, to see the Vermine encounter those little Currs. In this sort of Hunting, they also carry their great Dogs out with them, because Wolves, Bears, Panthers, Wild-Cats, and all other Beasts of Prey, are abroad in the Night." (Robert Beverley, *The History and Present State of Virginia*, ed. with intro. Louis B.

Wright [Chapel Hill: University of North Carolina Press, 1947], pp, 309–10.)

† Washington was steward of the Alexandria Jockey Club.

62 *On 1 June 1787, when Mason was attending the Constitutional Convention in Philadelphia, a postscript to a letter to his son George gave a few further details of his workroom: "I wou'd thank you to desire Thomson to send me, if he can find it, the Plan I drew, two or three Years ago, for equalizing the Virginia Land Tax; which I have promised a Copy of to the North Carolina Delegates. I believe he will find it among the loose Papers on the right hand Division of the second Drawer in my Desk & Book Case, in the little Parlour. & I shou'd be glad to have the Strictures I wrote some time ago, upon the Port Bill but where it is I don't remember; it lay among the loose Papers in one of the dining Room Windows; which, a little before I left Home, I tied up in a Bundle and I believe put into one of the Pigeon-holes in the Book Case in the Dining-Room; but am not certain. Pray desire him, in looking over the Papers, not to dissort them; but make them up again together, in the same separate Bundles; & where any of the Bundles are endorsed, to make them up again with the Endorsations on the Out Side." (George Mason, *The Papers of George Mason, 1725–1792*, ed. Robert A. Rutland, 3 vols. [Chapel Hill: University of North Carolina Press, 1971], 3:893.)

66 *Thomas Adams, a Virginia merchant in Fleet Street known to be soft-hearted toward needy fellow colonists, was a frequent recipient of his desperate appeals: "My dear Adams, you must by some means or other procure me £50 by Tuesday morning, or I must go to the Dogs. The note I mentioned to you formerly falls due on that day. . . . I shall ask no more from you till Anderson arrives who I hope will bring me half a hundred puncheons of Shannandoah [tobacco], which will honestly pay all my Debts. . . . If you can by any means negotiate the note I send I shall be strong enough by the time it falls due, tho' at present I give you my oath I have not a Brace of pounds in the world, nor do I know where to get Them unless you or Brown will help me." (*Virginia Magazine of History and Biography* 17, no. 3, [July 1909]: 326–27.) In 1767, Mercer eloped, penniless, with a presumptive heiress; she came to Virginia with him early in 1768 only to die in Richmond shortly after arrival. He returned to England, once more to dangle for office under the Crown.

67 *In December, Mason wondered whether their correspondence was being intercepted by "some S——l who knows our Hand-writing."

76 *Of this hostelry, John Davis wrote: "It was easier landing at *Alexandria* in *America*, than *Alexandria* in *Egypt;* and I found elegant accomodations at *Gadesby's* hotel. It is observable that *Gadesby* keeps the best house of entertainment in the United States. . . .

"The splendour of *Gadesby's* hotel not suiting my finances, I removed to a public-house kept by a *Dutchman,* whose *Frow* was a curious

creature. I insert a specimen of her talk: This hot weather makes a body feel odd. How long would a body be going from *Washington* to *Baltimore*? How the mosquitoes bite a body, &c. But I left the body of my landlady to approach that of her daughter whose body resembled one of those protuberant figures which Rubens loved to depict." (John Davis, *Travels of Four Years and a Half in the United States of America, 1798, 1799, 1800, 1801 and 1802,* ed. A. J. Morrison [New York: Henry Holt & Co., 1909], pp. 244–45.)

79 *In the case brought by Messrs. Sydenham & Hodgson *v.* George Mason, Gent. on 21 July 1763, the jury decided that "the Plaintiff take nothing by his Bill but for his false clamour be in mercy and that the said Defendant go thereof without day and recover against the Plaintiff his costs by him in this behalf sustained." (Fairfax County, Va., Minute Book, 1756–63, part 2, f. 904.) In the case of Mason *v.* Sewell, 17 October 1770, the estate of Sewell, who had been in debtor's prison for twenty days, was sold. It consisted of "1 flock bed, 2 blankets, 1 rug, 1 hog, 1 gun, 2 plates, 1 basen, 1 iron pott, some earthenware, 1 chest, some pewter spoons, 5/- owing from William Ferguson, 1 water pail, 1 frying pan, 1 pr. flesh forks, 2 or 3 old knives and forks, 2 rugs, 1 pr. horse fleems." (Fairfax County, Va., Order Book, 1770–72, f. 121.) The yield was 21/3.

† In May 1770, Jane Morrison, servant of Benjamin Sebastian, was presented for a baseborn mulatto child; in November, the judges ruled: "The churchwardens of Fairfax Parish recover against the said Jane for the use of the said Parish £15 and if not paid at the expiration of her servitude to be sold by the churchwardens of the said parish for the time being for five years for the use of the said parish." (Ibid., f. 17.)

‡ In the case of Our Sovereign Lord the King *v.* Franklin Perry on an indictment, the jury found Perry guilty of a felony: "Therefore it is considered and ordered that the Sheriff give the said Franklin Perry ten lashes on the bare back at the public whipping post and that he be committed until he gives security for payment and costs." (Ibid., f. 219.)

§ On 7 April 1759, with eight justices present, Toney, a Negro man slave, was accused of "feloniously breaking the house and stealing sundry goods the property of Michael Rhine of the value of 21/11 and committing a rape on the body of Jane the wife of John Evans being arraigned in open court for the said Facts pleaded not guilty and thereupon the witnesses against him being sworn and examined and consideration of the same being had, the court are of the opinion that the said Toney is guilty of the said Facts therefore it is considered that the said Toney go from hence to the prison and from thence to the place of execution there to be hanged by the neck til he be dead, on the 18th day of this instant and that his body afterwards be hung in chains." (Fairfax County, Va., Minute Book, 1756–63, part 1, f. 332.) A few years later, some of Mason's slaves were executed; in dunning his former neighbor, John Posey, Washington mentioned: "Colo. Mason hath several times spoke to me on Acct. of your Bond (to wh. I am a Security) since he wrote to you himself; and I shoud presume, must now have greater Calls for the Money than he himself apprehended, in as much as he has been disappointed of receiving £350 of the Publick for his executed Negroes." (George Washington, *The Writings of George Washington, 1745–1799*, ed. John C. Fitzpatrick, 39 vols. [Washington, D.C.: U.S. Government Printing Office, 1931–44], 2:507.

84 *Such cushions were placed on the lectern of the pulpit.

87 *After the start of the Revolution, when Mazzei returned to Europe to seek aid for the United States, John Adams testified to his effectiveness in a letter to Jefferson: "I know nothing of this Gentleman, but what I have learned of him here. His great affection for you Mr. Wythe, Mr. Mason, and other choice Spirits in Virginia, recommended him to me. I know not in what light he Stands in your Part: but here, as far as I have had opportunity to see and hear, he has been usefull to Us. He kept good Company and a good deal of it. He talks a great deal, and was a zealous defender of our Affairs. His Variety of Languages, and his Knowledge of American affairs, gave him advantages which he did not neglect." ( John Adams to Thomas Jefferson from Paris, 29 June 1780; not given in John Adams *The Works of John Adams,* ed. Charles Francis Adams, 10 vols. [Boston: Little, Brown & Co., 1856] but reproduced in Thomas Jefferson, *The Papers of Thomas Jefferson,* ed. Julian P. Boyd, 19 vols. to date [Princeton: Princeton University Press, 1950–], 3:468–70.)
† Even in the midst of the Revolution, exchanges of garden rareties went on; when Mason dispatched his son William in search of arms for his company, he used the opportunity to send Jefferson "a few of the Portugal, & best kind of rare-ripe Peach Stones. Almost all my Portugal peaches were stolen this Year, before they were ripe; but I saved the few Stones I send you myself, & know they are the true Sort. I have observed this kind of Peach requires more Care than most others, & if the Trees are not tended, & the Ground cultivated, the Fruit is apt to be coarse & harsh; with due Culture the Peaches are the finest I ever tasted. . . . The sooner the Peach Stones are planted, the better; if it is deferred 'til late in the Winter, very few will come up next Spring; they shou'd be secured from the Moles by Slabs, or some such thing, let into the Ground." (George Mason, *The Papers of George Mason, 1725–1792,* ed. Robert A. Rutland, 3 vols. [Chapel Hill: University of North Carolina Press, 1971], 2:676.)

89 *In fact, though some people never forgave Lee for bringing up the matter, all was not well. The paper currency issued to finance Virginia's military operations during the French and Indian War was scheduled to be retired and destroyed as notes of various maturities came due for redemption. But because many substantial planters were very short of cash,

Robinson had not been burning the notes; he had permitted his friends to borrow upon them, depositing security in the treasury. Only £369,000 of a total issue, 1754–62, of £539,000 had been called in and burned. Cary's commission of inquiry had not gone behind Robinson's word—the facts came out only after the treasurer's death the following year, when Robert Carter Nicholas, who accepted the post after persuading the Assembly to separate it from that of speaker, came upon the securities deposited by Robinson's friends. On 9 April 1767, the chairman of a new commission of inquiry, Richard Bland, announced Robinson's defalcation, after his administrators had made a payment to the treasury, as totaling £102,019.5.7. The loan office proposal, if enacted, would have enabled Robinson to extricate himself.

Nine years later, in the Continental Congress, John Adams learned of the lasting effect of Lee's action: "Mr. Wythe told me, that Thomas Lee, the elder Brother [actually the father] of Richard Henry was the delight of the Eyes of Virginia and by far the most popular Man they had. But that Richard Lee was not. I asked the reason, for Mr. Lee appeared a Scholar, a Gentleman, a Man of uncommon Eloquence, and an agreeable Man. Mr. Wythe said all this was true but Mr. Lee had when he was very young and when he first came into the House of Burgesses moved and urged on an Inquiry into the State of the Treasury which was found deficient in a large Sum, which had been lent by the Treasurer to many of the more influential Families of the Country, who found themselves exposed, and had never forgiven Mr. Lee." ( John Adams, *Diary and Autobiography of John Adams,* ed. Lyman Butterfield, 4 vols. [Cambridge, Mass.: Belknap Press of Harvard University Press, 1961], 3:367–68.)
† A captain had made a fast voyage: the House of Commons had not passed the measure until 27 February, and royal assent had not been given until 22 March.

96 *He also begged "your Care of the inclosed Letters." These may have been private messages for Washington to deliver to friends in Williamsburg. On the other hand, they may have been the two communications signed "Atticus" that shortly appeared in the Maryland and the Virginia *Gazette;* in his 5 April letter, Mason had mentioned work already begun on a draft and invited Washington's ideas. Whoever did the actual writing, these letters must have originated in the Ross-Mason-Washington group, plus whomever else they had added to their number— perhaps Richard Henry Lee, who like Washington and unlike Mason was a burgess at this time. The second "Atticus" article was an expansion of the reasoning in Mason's letter to Washington of 5 April, even to the repetition of certain phrases.

101 *In retrospect, Jefferson's *Autobiography* chronicled its origin: "Not thinking our old & leading members up to the point of forwardness & zeal which the times required, Mr. Henry, R. H. Lee, Francis L. Lee, Mr. Carr & myself agreed to meet in the evening in a private room of the Raleigh to consult on the

state of things. . . . We were all sensible that the most urgent of all measures was that of coming to an understanding with all the other colonies, to consider the British claims as a common cause to all, & to produce an unity of action: and for this purpose that a commee of correspondce in each colony would be the best instrument for intercommunication: and that their first measure would probably be to propose a meeting of deputies from every colony at some central place, who should be charged with the direction of the measures which should be taken by all." (Thomas Jefferson, *The Writings of Thomas Jefferson,* ed. Paul Leicester Ford, 10 vols. [New York and London: G. P. Putnam's Sons, 1892–99], 1:9–10.)

106  *Cf. Mason's letter to a correspondent in England in December 1770: "The Americans have the warmest Affection for the present Royal Family; the strongest Attachment to the British Government & Constitution; they have experienced it's Blessings & prefer it to any that does or ever did exist; while they are protected in the Injoyment of [its] Advantages they will never wish to change, there are not five Men of Sense in America who wou'd accept of Independence if it was offered." (George Mason, *The Papers of George Mason, 1725–1792,* ed. Robert A. Rutland, 3 vols. [Chapel Hill: University of North Carolina Press, 1971], 1:129.)

108  *The position against nonexportation, with which Washington was in personal accord, was spelled out in the Convention's instructions to Virginia's delegates to the Congress: "The earnest desire we have to make as quick and full payment as possible of our debts to Great Britain, and to avoid the heavy injury that would arise to this country from the earlier adoption of the non-exportation plan, after the people have already applied so much of their labor to the perfection of the present crop, by which means they have been prevented from pursuing other methods of clothing and supporting their families, have rendered it necessary to restrain you in this article of non-exportation; but it is our desire that you cordially cooperate with our sister Colonies in General Congress, in such other just and proper methods as they or the majority shall deem necessary for the accomplishment of these valuable ends." (*American Archives,* comp. Peter Force, 9 vols. [Washington, D.C.: published under an Act of Congress, 1837–53], 4th ser. 1:689–90.)

109  *John Adams's diary for 3 September 1774, tells of meeting Lee at the Philadelphia home of his sister, Mrs. Thomas Shippen: "Breakfasted at Dr. Shippens: Dr. Witherspoon was there. Col. R. H. Lee lodges there; he is a masterly man. This Mr. Lee is a brother of the sheriff of London, and of Dr. Arthur Lee, and of Mrs. Shippen; they are all sensible and deep thinkers. . . . Spent the evening at Mr. Mifflin's with Lee and Harrison from Virginia, the two Rutledges, Dr. Witherspoon, Dr. Shippen, Dr. Steptoe, and another gentleman; an elegant supper, and we drank sentiments till eleven o'clock. Lee and Harrison were very high. Lee had dined with Mr. Dickinson and drank Burgundy the whole after-

noon." (John Adams, *Diary and Autobiography of John Adams,* ed. Lyman Butterfield, 4 vols. [Cambridge, Mass.: Belknap Press of Harvard University Press, 1961], 2:120–21.)

110  *The choice of blue and buff was new. The uniform worn by Washington in the French and Indian War and as a member of the Continental Congress in 1774–75 was that shown in his 1772 portrait by Charles Willson Peale.

112  *George Mason, Jr., recently come of age, joined the Fairfax Independent Company and was chosen an ensign in 1774; when the independent companies were grouped into minute regiments the next year, he became a captain of foot. In 1776, the Committee of Safety issued him a warrant to obtain two guns for "a detachment of his minute Company marched to Hampton." But his persistent illnesses, of the same kind and even more frequent than his father's, soon took him out of military service.

119  *Lee won by one vote over Carter Braxton, 37 to 36.

121  *In London, like other Loyalists prominent in their colonies when the Revolution broke and aghast at the increasing unlikelihood of a restoration, Galloway and the Tories with whom he associated came to regard the British military effort as desultory enough to suggest that Sir William Howe was serving the domestic political interests of the Whigs. This view, accepted by that high Tory, the Reverend Charles Wesley, diverted Wesley from hymn-writing to the composition of a long satirical poem, *The American War,* contrasting Howe's leadership with that of Washington. Written apparently in 1782 and printed for the first time in 1975, it reads in part:

How can th' indignant muse forbear
The different leaders to compare?
One in the soft'ning Town she sees,
Dissolv'd in luxury and ease,
With fulness of superfluous bread,
With choicest delicacies fed,
Suffering his friends to fall oppressed
And die, for furnishing the feast:
The other, self-supported Chief,
Without supply, without relief,
Demands an Enemy's applause
So worthy of a nobler cause,
The lord of an unconquered mind
Can in himself resources find,
(What present times will scarce conceive
Or late posterity believe),
Can raise an army with his foot,
Or build a camp out of a hut,
Repelling at each gaping flaw
The wintry blast with mud and straw.
  Behold him with his burrough'd host,
Four thousand feeble men at most,
Whose numbers every hour decrease
Reduc'd by famine and disease,
Who starv'd and sick and dying lie
Exposed to the inclement sky.
The sharpest frost for months sustain
The billowing snow, and pouring rain,

And nothing could their courage quell
Who pain and death disdain'd to feel.
(Charles Wesley, *The American War* [London: The
Keepsake Press, 1975], ll. 509–37.)

122 *With Mason, John Dalton headed Alexandria's
service of military supply; whenever the British
raided up the Potomac, Alexander Henderson
prudently went into hiding lest he be shot.
†So did men who had acquired a reputation for
sharp dealing—in 1771 William Lee had charged
Scottish merchants in general with being "something
like the stinking and troublesome weed we called
in Virginia wild onion."
‡For descriptions of this and other new buildings,
see John Gibson, *The History of Glasgow* (Glasgow:
Chapman and Duncan, 1777), pp. 144–51.

123 *The firm at its height had five stores in Virginia
and seven in Maryland; as early as the Seven Years'
War it owned twenty-five vessels, and its then
trading turnover of half a million pounds yearly
had doubled by the time of the Revolution.

124 *Fleming's letters and ledger books are in the archives of the Cumberland County Record Office
at Carlisle. They cover the years 1772–75 and
1783–88.

125 *For instance, the *Mally* of Whitehaven, Captain
Mitchison, master, sailed 6 April 1775, arrived at
Norfolk, loaded, and was in Whitehaven again on
5 July; sailed again on 12 July and was home once
more on 21 November.
†See T. M. Devine, "Glasgow Merchants and the
Collapse of the Tobacco Trade 1775–1783," *Scottish Historical Review* 52, no. 153 (April 1973):1.
‡Yet in terms of economic leverage on Glasgow's
economy, Mason's nonexportation objective was
very partially attained. When the last ship made
harbor in 1775, most of the major firms possessed
ample stockpiles of tobacco. Individual hardships
occurred, especially among the smaller businesses,
and the massive failures of the Buchanan firm in
Glasgow and the firm of How & Younger in Whitehaven, though only partially related to the tobacco
business, were catastrophic to many investors.
But the capital gains realized over the next few
years from their supplies on hand enabled the
tobacco lords and the city's economy generally
to fund entries into new lines after the war.

When the price of tobacco had risen from
three to six pence a pound, it seemed to the Cunninghame partners that the time had come to take
their profit and sell—to all, that is, except William
Cunninghame. At that price, he bought the others
out. When he sold, the price had passed three
shillings sixpence; its peak was eight shillings.

128 *At Frederick, he was outraged to be "dragged,
bound with cords, before the Committee, which
consisted of a taylor, a leather breeches-maker, a
shoemaker, a gingerbread-baker, a butcher, and two
publicans.

"The greatest part of them being Germans, I
really underwent a most curious examination, nearly
to the following effect. 'Got tamm you' (says one)
'howsh darsht you make an exshkape from dist

honorablsh Committish?' 'For flucht der dyvel (says
another) Howsh can you shstand sho shtyff for King
Shorsh akainsht dish koontery?' 'Sacramenter (roars
out another) Dish Committish will make Shorsh
knoa howsh to behave himself.' 'By Goat (bawls the
butcher) Ich would kill all de Enklish tives, as soon as
Ich vould kill van ox, or van cow.'

"After they had all exhausted themfelves by
haranguing in this manner, they insisted that I should
answer them.

"I replied, 'that I could have very little to say
to them, having no intention of employing either of
them; as when I wanted cloaths I should apply to
another taylor; and to other persons also for leather
breeches as well as for shoes or boots; that I never eat
gingerbread; and had an aversion to butchers and
publicans, whenever they stepped aside from the line
of their proper occupations; and, that as I conceived
they had as little business with me as I with them,
requested they would detain me no longer.' "
(J. F. D. Smyth, *A Tour in the United States of America,*
2 vols. [London: Robinson, Robson, and Sewell,
1784; New York: The Arno Press, Inc. 1968],
2:274–75.)

130 *Colonial Virginia's great seal consisted of the royal
coat of arms above the legend: "En dat Virginia
Quartam."

131 *Rush's Commonplace Book for 8 June 1809,
on Paine's death repeats that *Common Sense* was
written "at my request. I gave it its name. He
possessed a wonderful talent of writing to the tempers and feelings of the people." (Commonplace
Book, p. 222, MSS, American Philosophical Society
Library, Philadelphia, Pa.)

137 *Yet the James City electors had instructed their
delegates, Nicholas and William Norvell to move
"towards dissolving the connexion between
American and Great-Britain, totally, finally, and
irrevocably," and the instruction had been carried
both in Purdie's *Virginia Gazette* of 26 April and the
*Pennsylvania Evening Post* of 11 May.

142 *Edmund Randolph, writing at the end of the century, corroborated this statement: "A very large
committee was nominated to prepare the proper
instruments and many projects of a bill of rights
and constitution discovered the ardor for political
notice rather than a ripeness in political wisdom.
That proposed by George Mason swallowed up all
the rest by fixing the grounds and plan, which after
great discussion and correction, were finally ratified."
(Edmund Randolph, *History of Virginia,* ed. with
intro. Arthur H. Shaffer [Charlottesville: University
Press of Virginia, 1970], p. 252.)
†Edward Rutledge's angry South Carolinian reaction
to Lee's motion, expressed to John Jay on 8 June,
illustrated the value of delay: "The Congress
sat till 7 o'clock this evening in consequence of a
motion of R. H. Lee's rendering ourselves free and
independant States. The sensible part of the House
opposed the Motion—they had no objection to
forming a Scheme of a Treaty which they would
send to France by proper Persons and uniting this
Continent by a Confederacy; they saw no Wisdom

in a *Declaration* of Independence, nor any other Purpose to be enforced by it, but placing ourselves in the Power of those with whom we mean to treat, giving our Enemy Notice of our Intentions before we had taken any steps to execute them and thereby enabling them to counteract us in our Intentions and rendering ourselves ridiculous in the Eyes of foreign powers by attempting to bring them into an Union with us before we had united with each other. For daily experience evinces that the Inhabitants of every Colony consider themselves at Liberty to do as they please upon almost every occasion. And a Man must have the Impudence of a New Englander to propose in our present disjointed state any Treaty (honorable to us) to a Nation now at peace. No reason could be assigned for pressing into this Measure, but the reason of every Madman, a shew of our spirit." (Edmund Cody Burnett, ed. *Letters of Members of the Continental Congress,* 8 vols. [Washington, D.C.: Carnegie Institution of Washington, 1921–36], 1:477–78.)

150 *The distinction was pungently stated a few years later by Thomas Paine in his *Rights of Man:* "Toleration is not the *opposite* of intoleration, but is the *counterfeit* of it. Both are despotisms. The one assumes to itself the right of withholding liberty of conscience, and the other of granting it." (Thomas Paine, *The Works of Thomas Paine,* 2 vols. [Philadelphia: Carey, 1797], 2:77–78.)

151 *Mrs. Hutchinson's affirmation, in her exchange with Deputy Governor Thomas Dudley and another magistrate, when the executives of Massachusetts Bay, the chief ministers, and the elders sat as a synod to examine her beliefs, exemplified the basic tenet of Madison's declaration:

> Mrs. Hutchinson. "Now if you do condemn me for speaking what in my conscience I know to be the truth I must commit myself unto the Lord."
> Mr. Nowell (a magistrate and a founder of Boston's First Church). "How do you know that that was the Spirit?"
> Mrs. Hutchinson. "How did Abraham know that it was God that bid him offer his son, being a breach of the sixth commandment?"
> The Deputy Governor. "By an immediate voice."
> Mrs. Hutchinson. "So to me by an immediate revelation."
> The Deputy Governor. "How! an immediate revelation?"
> Mrs. Hutchinson. "By the voice of his own spirit in my soul."

(Thomas Hutchinson, *The History of Massachusetts Bay,* ed. Lawrence Shaw Mayo, 2 vols. [Cambridge, Mass: Harvard University Press, 1936], 2:383–84.)

157 *Joseph Reed of Philadelphia had written General Washington in March, "It is said that the Virginians are so alarmed at the idea of independence that they have sent Mr. Braxton on purpose to turn the vote of that Colony, if any question on that subject should come before Congress." (William B. Reed,

*Life and Correspondence of Joseph Reed,* 2 vols. [Philadelphia: Lindsay and Blakiston, 1847], 1:173.) Braxton had been chosen to fill the vacancy in Virginia's congressional delegation caused by the death of Peyton Randolph in the autumn of 1775; he sat from 23 February 1776 until the new election. Married to a daughter of the last royal receiver general for Virginia, kinsman of the conservative and in some cases Tory-minded Carters, and go-between in the confrontation of Patrick Henry and Governor Dunmore in the powder incident, Braxton nevertheless signed the Declaration of Independence. Because of his pamphlet, however, he was not re-appointed to the Congress in 1776.

160 *Writing as an old man in 1825, Jefferson took less credit than was his due; he said Pendleton informed him that, after days of debate in which the plan was "disputed inch by inch," members "could not, from mere lassitude, have been induced to open the instrument again; but that, being pleased with the Preamble of mine, they adopted it in the House, by way of Amendment to the Report of the Committee; and thus my Preamble became tacked to the work of George Mason." (Thomas Jefferson, *The Papers of Thomas Jefferson,* ed. Julian P. Boyd, 19 vols. to date [Princeton: Princeton University Press, 1950–], 1:384.) But it was Jefferson who gave the Senate its name; new material integrated into the body of the text included his section on the western lands, specifying Virginia's boundaries as fixed by the 1609 charter.
†Emergency war powers, however, were conferred on the governor and Council at the end of the year, in a bill drafted by Mason.

165 *Nevertheless, Mason firmly believed in such preventative measures: in the winter Assembly session he brought in a bill regulating innoculations and penalizing infected persons who spread the disease.
†Mason was actually elected twice at this session: after Thomas Nelson resigned, the Assembly first chose him to complete the unexpired term; on 22 May, it selected Harrison, Mason, Jones, Harvie, and Francis Lightfoot Lee as the new delegates.

166 *A new election to the speakership had been required when Edmund Pendleton was temporarily removed from public life by a fall from his horse that irreparably injured one hip—after a slow and partial recovery, this handsome but heavy-set man moved with a crutch for the rest of his days. The ensuing three-man race pitted Wythe, nominated by Jefferson, against Robert Carter Nicholas and Benjamin Harrison. Two ballots were required before a narrow decision installed Wythe. The winner was careful to extend an olive branch to his predecessor: on 15 May, Pendleton wrote William Woodford that Wythe "declared From the chair that he considered his appointment as *Vicarious* only, and that he was to restore it to me as soon as I was able to Attend." (Edmund Pendleton, *Letters and Papers of Edmund Pendleton, 1734–1803,* coll. and ed. David John Mays, 2 vols. [Charlottesville: University Press of Virginia, 1967], 1:209.)

167 *Madison was in Williamsburg as a frustrated mem-

ber of the Council (a body which he described as "the grave of useful talents"); he had been defeated for the House because he disapproved of treating voters on election day and lost to a less dry candidate.

168 *A French dispatch to the Quai d'Orsay in 1778 estimated: "America has lost in the war between 40 and 90 thousand men of its most useful class; only the smaller part fell to the steel of the enemy; disease, hunger, lack of clothing and of care took off the rest." (Correspondence Politique, Etats-Unis, 1778, vol. 17, f. 415, Archives des Affaires Etrangères, Paris.)

169 *Such rights accrued to newly arrived immigrants; they could also be purchased from persons not intending to use them. Most of Mason's extensive acquisitions represented purchase of such rights.

170 *Land Office Warrant No. 1, of 10 June 1779, witnessed Mason's alacrity with regard to his personal claims beyond the mountains: it is for 8,100 acres due him on importation certificates.
† During the last two decades of the century, 101 grantees held 10,000–20,000 acres; 64 held 25,000–50,000; 41 held 50,000–100,000; and 44 over 100,000. Henry Banks, of the firm of Hunter, Banks & Co., opposite the Virginia State Capitol, held 528,770 acres in five of the counties now in West Virginia, plus an additional 100,000 in Montgomery and Wythe, 200,000 in Russell jointly with Richard Smith, and 362,954 on the Ohio in Jefferson County jointly with Philip Barbour. Robert Morris of Philadelphia held 1.3 million acres on the Big Sandy, Tug, and Guyandott rivers; 200,000 on the Greenbriar, Gouley, and Birch; and 30,038 on branches of the Monongahela and Big Sandy jointly with Wilson Cary Nicholas, whose personal holdings in Montgomery, Russell, and Wythe counties totaled 1.1 million acres, plus 50,000 in Greenbrier. (George E. Lewis, *The Indiana Company, 1763–1798: A Study in 18th Century Frontier Land Speculation and Business Venture* [Glendale, Calif.: Arthur H. Clark Co., 1941], pp. 136ff.)

171 *Mason had paid a visit to Lee's home at the turn of the year: Richard Henry wrote his brother Francis from Chantilly on 3 January: "My health is much better, but I have not got my cloaths made—We are miserably off here for Taylors, and my winter apparatus very bad. My friend Colo. Geo. Mason has been a week here and keeps me from going into some necessary preparatives for my return to Philadelphia." (Lee Papers, microfilm, University of Virginia.)

173 *Married to Eleanor Calvert of Maryland in 1776, he had just completed his house, Abingdon, north of Alexandria; to this holding he shortly added the property that became Arlington.

174 *Mason's nineteenth-century biographer, Kate Mason Rowland, assumed the unknown addressee to have been George Mercer in England; Robert A. Rutland, the editor of *The Papers of George Mason,* suggested a young member of the Brent family then in England for his education. A third possibility might be an older recipient living on the Continent, in Holland or France.

181 *Clark's letter announcing his appointment to his brother Jonathan is in Jonathan Clark Papers, Virginia and Kentucky, etc., 1728–79, Draper MSS 1L16, State Historical Society of Wisconsin, Madison, Wis. How early, and in what circumstances, the Mason and the Clark families first knew each other is uncertain. The account book of Edmund Clark, who kept stores at Newmarket and Hanover, shows Mason as a customer in his latter years, but early documentation is lacking.

182 *Robertson's account books for those years show James Madison, John Tyler, and Clark's older brother, Jonathan, to have been more persistent students; his meticulous entries are followed, on occasion, by the notation: "Deo Gratia & Gloria, All paid." (*Virginia Magazine of History and Biography* 33, no. 2 [April 1925]: 194ff.; *VMHB* 2, no. 3 [July 1925]: 288ff.; *VMHB* 34, no. 2 [April 1926]: 141ff.; and *VMHB* 34, no. 3 [July 1926]: 232.)
† A considerable collection of George Rogers Clark's letters to his brother Jonathan describing these trips is in the Jonathan Clark Papers, Virginia and Kentucky, etc., 1728–79, Draper MSS 1L, State Historical Society of Wisconsin, Madison, Wis.
‡ Judge Henderson of North Carolina was attempting to found a new colony in the west, while the same purpose animated a group of Pennsylvanians and Londoners in the present area of West Virginia.

184 *A few months earlier, the Continental Congress had authorized Washington to seek Indian allies but reversed itself when Col. George Morgan, commissioner of Indian Affairs for the Middle Department, urged the greater advantages of securing Indian neutrality through a treaty under which the Indians would permit unopposed passage by American troops. Congressional negotiations to this end failed when a western settler murdered Chief Cornstalk of the Shawnee and redoubled the Indian anger incited by the murder of Mingo Chief Logan's family a year and a half before.

185 *On 20 February 1812, through the efforts of Charles Fenton Mercer, the Virginia Assembly voted Clark a second sword, whose blade was inscribed: "A tribute to courage and patriotism, presented by the State of Virginia to her beloved son, General George Rogers Clark, who by the conquest of the Illinois and Vincennes, extended her empire, and aided in defence of her liberties." (Mercer's letter of 1 September 1848, Draper MSS, 12J36, State Historical Society of Wisconsin, Madison, Wis.)

186 *"I would not have you value the cost of the Horses or the expense of sending them in. . . . Get good men to bring them to New Castle Town in Hanover & give them handsome wages to secure their taking pains to bring them safe & have particular care of the Horses. . . . I want true Spanish Blood & the Mares to be large as you can get, & not old. Don't lose a moment in agreeing for the Mares, for vast Numbers of People are about to go out after them from here, & will soon pick them all up & raise the price very high." (*Official Letters of the Governors of Virginia,* ed. H. R. McElwaine, 3 vols. [Richmond: n.p.], 1:323–24.)

†Brown wrote Clark on 5 July 1789, urging him to write his story and saying Madison would help. Clark replied that "In the Winter of 1779, on the request of Col. G. Mason of Fairfax, I wrote him a pamphlet that contained great part of our proceedings up to that time. I have wrote to him for it, in hopes that he might find it among his old papers, but have got no answer from him." (George Rogers Clark, *George Rogers Clark Papers, 1771–1781,* ed. James A. James [Springfield, Ill: Illinois State Historical Library, 1912], pp. 622–23.) Brown then assured him, "By next post, I shall write Colo. Mason for the pamphlet you mention and should it come to hand I shall be careful to forward it to you by the first opportunity." (Clark Manuscripts, Draper MSS 2 J 17, State Historical Society of Wisconsin, Madison, Wis.) Mason, however, did not relinquish the MSS; it descended in the family for some time and is now in The Filson Club archives in Louisville. For a discussion of Clark's manuscript, see George Mason, *The Papers of George Mason, 1725–1792,* ed. Robert A. Rutland, 3 vols. (Chapel Hill: University of North Carolina Press, 1971), 2:588–90.

191 *The availability of whiskey, whether for trade with the Indians, for distribution to the troops, or for personal use, is witnessed by a receipt in the archives of The Filson Club, signed by George Rogers Clark and attested by John Clark: "Received of Majr. G. Walls fifty nine Gallons of whisky Consind. to me by Majr. J. P. Duvall which I promise to pay the Value at the time of Receiving of it Fort Nelson Feby 1st 1783."
†Virginia's auditor insisted that Clark had failed to present vouchers for a considerable part of his expenditures. But in 1913, they were found in the attic of the Capitol.

194 *In 1812, six years before Clark died, Virginia awarded him an annuity of $400; and twenty years after his death contributed $30,000 to his estate.
†He never came home. In March 1784, he set out alone from Louisville for Vincennes. His horse and saddlebags were found on the bank of the White River.
‡Typical accusations and justifications of his conduct are in two letters written in October 1782: Col. Arthur Campbell to Col. William Davies, "Genl. Clarke is in that country [Kentucky] but he has lost the confidence of the people, and it is said become a Sot; perhaps something worse"; and Col. Joseph Crockett to Governor Harrison, "as for Genl: Clark's conduct, last campaign whilst I had the *honor* to serve under his com'd (as touching his military character) I cannot think he is *deserving censure.* his greatest misfortune & loss of usefull operation of the campaign, was the want of men." *(Calendar of Virginia State Papers and Other Manuscripts Preserved in the Capitol at Richmond, 1652–1869,* 11 vols., ed. vol. 3 William P. Palmer and Sherwin McRae [Richmond: R. F. Walker, Superintendent of Public Printing, 1875–93], 3:337, 358–59.)

197 *In November, Richard Henry Lee exploded to Patrick Henry: "Already the continental emissions exceed in a sevenfold proportion the sum necessary for medium; the State emissions added, greatly increase the evil. It would be well if this were all, but the forgeries of our currency are still more mischievous. They depricate not only by increasing the quantity, but by creating universal diffidence concerning the whole paper fabric. In my opinion these Miscreants who forge our money are as much more criminal than most other offenders as parricide exceeds murder." (Richard Henry Lee to Patrick Henry, 15 November 1778, (Myers MS 2137), Manuscripts & Archives Division, The New York Public Library, Astor, Lenox and Tilden Foundations, New York, N.Y.
†George departed with warm letters of recommendation to Lafayette and Franklin from Washington and to John Adams and Arthur Lee from Richard Henry.

198 *After Burgoyne's defeat at Saratoga, the British had considered a settlement. Measures introduced by Lord North in Parliament in November, though diminished by the king's refusal to entertain any possibility of independence, might have been thoughtfully reviewed in America in the midst of the Valley Forge winter had they been promptly passed. Postponement during the long parliamentary Christmas recess, however, brought them to an affirmative vote only on 11 February 1778, and that was eleven days after Franklin's long-sought treaty of commerce and alliance with France had been signed in Paris.

200 *In 1780, a move to Richmond occurred in spite of Mason's opposition; it was desired by members from the Piedmont and mountain counties on the grounds of convenience as well as by those fearful of British attack from the water.
†Both Jones and Henry declined; the delegation as finally set up consisted of Mason's cousin, James Mercer, who likewise withdrew by the end of the year, Edmund Randolph, William Fitzhugh, Meriwether Smith, and Cyrus Griffin.

Foreign observers of the congressional scene agreed with Mason's strictures; in December 1785, a French dispatch commented on the rule restricting the service of members to no more than three years: "Young men of great talent but little experience commence to gain places in Congress which becomes a school of politics for them but do not add much consistency to the delegates presence. As a result, Monseigneur, a great insouciance prevails— delegates absent themselves for the most trivial reasons." (Correspondence Politique, Etats-Unis, 1785, vol. 30, f. 475, Archives des Affaires Etrangères, Paris.)

Gijsbert Karel van Hogendorp, cousin of the Dutch envoy, reported: "What is even more afflicting is that the members being to a less extent men who possess the confidence of the nation than men who are willing to accept the commission, it has come about that Congress is composed of young men, rich and frivolous, of old countrymen, uninformed in the affairs of the world, of officers who, having no longer a military occupation, offer themselves to the council of the nation (perhaps through vanity), of advocates who arrive only at a time when the state which appoints them has need of their services in a particular dispute—and very little of men who, endowed with virtuous principles and necesary knowledge, have sufficient patriotism to sacrifice their private views in the public interest." (Translated in Edmund Cody Burnett, ed., *Letters of Members of the Continental Congress,* 8 vols. [Washington, D.C.: Carnegie Institute of Washington, 1921–36], 7:495n.)

205   *The "Return of the 2d S. C. Regiment of Foot" for 8 April and for 2 May 1780 (Draper MSS IVV33 and 43, State Historical Society of Wisconsin, Madison, Wis.) show a Capt. Mason as "sick" and as "in Genl. Hospital" on those dates; the captain is not otherwise identified.

208   *The Anglican ceremony ignored Sarah's Catholicism.
†When George Mason, Jr., was abroad during 1779–81, his father chided him for having "made so slow progress in the French language; it is owing to your conversing too much among your own Countrymen, & to your not accustoming yourself to write french" and remarked that "I can not but think you judged extreamly ill, in spending so much time in Nantes; where you cou'd expect no great Improvement, either in Health, Knowledge, or Manners." (George Mason, *The Papers of George Mason, 1725–1792,* ed. Robert A. Rutland, 3 vols. [Chapel Hill: University of North Carolina Press, 1971], 2:691.) A number of young Americans were conspicuous profligates there; Thomas Morris, young half-brother of the Great Financier, was made American consul in 1777 and, according to one correspondent, "turned out the greatest drunkard the world ever produced." (Benjamin Franklin, *Writings of Benjamin Franklin,* 10 vols., ed., with life and intro. Albert Henry Smyth [New York: Macmillan, 1907; New York: Haskell House, 1970], 7:13 n.) He wrote finis to his alcoholism during a debauch in 1778 and left the American accounts in sorry disarray.
‡Henry Lee, Prince William County lieutenant, wrote Governor Jefferson on 9 April that the Goodriches had sent a privateer's tender up the river with twenty-one men, who plundered, took off Negroes on both sides, and intended to burn Mount Vernon and Gunston. A lucky shift of the wind had prevented their landing and made possible the capture of a number of them, including the captain, now lodged in Alexandria jail. *(Calendar of Virginia State Papers,* 11 vols., eds. vol. 2 William P. Palmer and Sherwin McRae [Richmond: R. F. Walker, Superintendent of Public Printing, 1875–93], 2:22.)

212   *As early as the previous May, Mason had alerted Jefferson to unrest resulting from "vague, and (as I apprehend) illegal Instructions," applied "very differently in the different Countys, according to each Mans Interpretation of Instructions which no Man understands; this, if not timely prevented by clear and precise orders from the Executive, will in many Instances, occasion Law Suits, & in some, most probably Violence." (George Mason, *The Papers of George Mason, 1725–1792,* ed. Robert A. Rutland, 3 vols.

[Chapel Hill: University of North Carolina Press, 1971], 2:685.) Under Nelson, the situation worsened.
†John Harvie had hoped for Mason's return to the Assembly: "Doctor Arthur Lee is Chosen a Member, and I have heard that Mr. Mason will again Consent to Serve. The Assistance of men of Real Abilities I should hope will be a Stimulous to others of like Character to lend their aid to the tottering Condition of the Commonwealth." (Thomas Jefferson, *The Papers of Thomas Jefferson,* ed. Julian P. Boyd, 19 vols. to date [Princeton: Princeton University Press, 1950–], 6:133.
‡A milder but comparable petition from Frederick County was introduced on 22 November.

214   *Earlier than Mason, Richard Henry Lee had made an even stronger statement: "The importation of slaves into this colony has been, and will be attended with effects, dangerous, both to our political and moral interests. When it is observed that some of our neighboring colonies, though much later than ourselves in point of settlement, are now far beyond us in improvements, to what, sir, can we attribute this strange, this unhappy truth: The reason seems to be this: that with their whites they import arts and agriculture, whilst we, with our blacks, exclude both." (Cazenove G. Lee, Jr., *Lee Chronicle,* comp. and ed. Dorothy Mills Parker [New York: New York University Press, 1957], p. 124.)
†A copy of the Bill to Prevent the Importation of Slaves, &c., introduced 16 June 1777 by Isaac Zane of Frederick County, has marginal notes in Mason's handwriting; it is in the archives of the Virginia State Library.

217   *Washington's diary for 2 October 1785, after he had become a parishioner of Christ Church, Alexandria, indicates the infrequency with which Pohick was used: "Went with Fanny Bassett, Burwell Bassett, Doctr. Stuart, G. A. Washington, Mr. Shaw and Nelly Custis to Pohick Church; to hear a Mr. Thompson preach, who returned home with us to Dinner, where I found Revd. Mr. Jones, formerly a Chaplin in one of the Pennsylvania Regiments.

"After we were in Bed (about eleven Oclock in the Evening, Mr. Houdon, sent from Paris by Doctr. Franklin and Mr. Jefferson to take my Bust, in behalf of the State of Virginia, with three young men assistants, introduced by a Mr. Perin a French Gentleman of Alexandria arrived here by water from the latter place."

Fannie Bassett, Martha Washington's niece, was at Mount Vernon preparatory to her marriage to George Augustine Washington two weeks later: Washington's diary shows the groom and her brother going "to the Clerk's office & thence to Colo. Mason's for a license" on 14 October, and next day, "after the candles were lighted George Augustine Washington and Frances Bassett were married." Dr. David Stuart had become an in-law by marrying Eleanor Calvert Custis, widow of Martha's son, Jacky, after Jacky died of fever contracted at the siege of Yorktown. (George Washington, *The Diaries of George Washington, 1748–1799,* ed. John C. Fitzpatrick, 4 vols. [Boston and New York:

Houghton Mifflin Co., 1925], 2:433.)

† Mason accepted Washington's refusal with good grace: a month later a letter to him begins: "The Bearer waits on you with Side of Venison (the first we have killed this Season) which I beg your Acceptance of." (George Mason, *The Papers of George Mason, 1725–1792*, ed. Robert A. Rutland, 3 vols. [Chapel Hill: University of North Carolina Press, 1971], 2:833.)

219 *Henry's resumption of House leadership caused agitation for a constitutional convention to die down. With the underlined words in code, Jefferson suggested to Madison from Paris on 8 December 1784: *"While Mr. Henry lives* another bad constitution would be formed and saddled forever on us. What we have to do I think is *devoutly* to *pray* for his *death."* (Thomas Jefferson, *The Papers of Thomas Jefferson,* ed. Julian P. Boyd, 19 vols. to date [Princeton: Princeton University Press, 1950–], 7:558.)

222 *Barbé-Marbois, reporting to the French government on the Fourth of July ceremony of 1785, observed that "the magistrates begin to distinguish themselves from the people at large by wearing clothes of special cut and color. Some congress delegates dress in black, and these distinctions, even though modest, call forth sarcasm on the part of those who would like to level everything." (Correspondence Politique, Etats-Unis, 1785, vol. 30, f. 115, Archives des Affaires Etrangères, Paris.)

223 *Lund himself, married in 1782 and now settled at modest but comfortable Hayfield a few miles southwest of Mount Vernon, was fulfilling the hope he had confided to Washington in 1776: "I never expect to be Rich, my only Wish, or ambition has been to save so much out of my wages during the time I have served you and others, as woud be sufficient to purchase a small Farm in some part of the Countrey where the produce of it wou'd enable me to live and give a Neighbour Beef, & Toddy." (Lund Washington to George Washington, 15 February 1776, Collections, The Mount Vernon Ladies' Association.)
† Part of the set of china from his own factory that the Comte de Custine presented to Mrs. Washington, hostess in her husband's absence, can be seen at Mount Vernon today.

226 *Mason's memorandum of 10 September 1782 regarding the surveys directed: "As it is of the utmost Importance to have the Lands so described & bounded, as to be easily found hereafter I wish to have the Beginning of each Tract very particularly described, any remarkable Object noted, & the beginning Tree or Trees of each Tract mark'd G. MASON . . . it will also be necessary, in running the Lines, to mention the Distance at which the Course crosses any large Run or remarkable Water-Course; such Precautions as these will . . . prevent Disputes." (George Mason, *The Papers of George Mason, 1725–1792,* ed. Robert A. Rutland, 3 vols. [Chapel Hill: University of North Carolina Press, 1971], 2:744.)

Mason's preoccupation with these lands was the subject of unkindly comment in a letter from Lund Washington to George Washington that same spring regarding the election of Fairfax County representatives in the House of Delegates. Sometime earlier, Charles Broadwater's lack of suitability had been mutually agreed upon at Mount Vernon and Gunston Hall, but the loyal Lund imputed to Mason a part in Broadwater's elimination of Dr. David Stuart: "On Monday last was our election for Assembly men when Broadwater was elected in preference to Doctor Stuart who is allowed by all who know him to be a man of the first education and abilities among us. He is a modest man and did not go much among the people, only made his intention known to the heads of the people. It was very tight polling between Broadwater and Stuart the former carried it by only 3 votes. There were some who woud have blushed to vote against Stewart and therefore did not vote at all. . . . Mason was not present but he had said he shoud vote for Broadwater although he was a very ignorant man and the other a very clever man. It is believed that Henderson [the other delegate] did not chose to have any one there who coud oppose him in any thing and as to Mason whose whole mind is taken up with saving and accumulating wealth he has long found out that Stuart is no friend to monopolizing lands." (Lund Washington to George Washington, 23 April 1783, Collections, The Mount Vernon Ladies' Association.)

228 *A few weeks earlier, Jefferson had heard from James Currie that "Madison is reelected for his County after considerable opposition; at the Instance of Genl. Washington, I have been told, old George Mason comes in and several new Members from whom considerable things are expected in our critical situation." (Thomas Jefferson, *The Papers of Thomas Jefferson,* ed. Julian P. Boyd, 19 vols. to date [Princeton: Princeton University Press, 1950–], 10:109.)

229 *The Annapolis meeting took place in September; in late November, Mason wrote an Alexandria merchant that he had been "constantly confined for more than a month, & the greatest part of the Time with the Gout in both feet; & am still very lame in one of my Feet. If it pleases God to restore me tollerable Health, I will still attend the Assembly; there being several things in Agitation there, which I think will be very injurious to the public." (George Mason, *The Papers of George Mason, 1725–1792,* ed. Robert A. Rutland, 3 vols. [Chapel Hill: University of North Carolina Press, 1971], 2:858.)

230 *Viburnum Opulus sterile,* a variety of the European cranberry bush. Planted two days later in the shrubberies, they flowered in May.

232 *John Temple, Britain's consul general, commented to the Marquis of Carmarthen: "A French Minister is, I am informed, expected in the next Packet from France, and he will not, I dare say, come with Empty Pockets, no bad policy to these indigent States; but, it is with pleasure I can perceive, that all uncorrupted sensible Americans behold with dislike, & even detestation, the part that faithless Court have, for a long time, acted in the Netherlands, &, after all their incendiary projects, have left those ignorant Wrong-headed Dutchmen to shift for themselves." (PRO,

FO, 4/6, no. 27. Transcripts of Crown-copyright records in the Public Record Office, London, appear by permission of the Controller of Her Majesty's Stationery Office, London.)

233 *Just before the Convention met, a committee of Rhode Island merchants, led by the Brown brothers of Providence, expressed their regret at the failure of their legislature to name representatives and promised to exert themselves on behalf of approval by their state of whatever measures might be adopted.

†Lee's actual reasons went deeper. He believed that such powers as the right to make treaties and the right to issue paper money should be vested in Congress but was firmly in favor of the states retaining their powers over commerce. He admitted that the efforts of Congress to raise money by apportioning quotas to the states had worked badly yet opposed an award to the central government of power to raise funds directly: "the difficulty certainly is, how to give this power in such a manner as that it may only be used for good, and not abused to bad, purposes." (R. H. Lee to Mason, 15 May 1787, Lee Papers, microfilm, University of Virginia.)

234 *Mason apparently had a plan for John, who the previous year had begun to gain business experience with the Alexandria merchant, William Hartshorne; he wrote George, "I have not yet been able to do anything respecting your brother John, and fear I shall meet with much difficulty on that subject," but nothing materialized in Philadelphia. John went to France next year as junior partner in a firm at Bordeaux. (George Mason, *The Papers of George Mason, 1725–1792*, ed. Robert A. Rutland, 3 vols. [Chapel Hill: University of North Carolina Press, 1971], 3:884.)

†Connecticut's appointees arrived early the next week, but in Maryland, Daniel Carroll wrote a friend, "Yesterday the General Assembly appointed me one of the Deputies for this State to attend the Foederal Convention in Phila. As this appointment was neither wished for, or expected by me, & I have been detained from home all last Winter, & 6 weeks this Spring, it will be some time before I can enter on the execution of this Trust. I dare not think of residing in Philada. during the summer months." New Hampshire's delegates had not really been expected, since the state's empty treasury was unable to supply them with funds, but importunate summons from other small states finally brought them in at the end of June. (Max Farrand, ed., *The Records of the Federal Convention of 1787*, rev. ed., 4 vols. [New Haven and London: Yale University Press, 1966], 4:62–63.)

235 *Application was also made on behalf of Elbridge Gerry, but he rented a house when he became a family man.

236 *Franklin had planned to make this motion, since otherwise, as chief executive of the host state and the senior Convention delegate by many years, he might have been presumed a candidate, but bad weather and weakness kept him home.

240 *Less than two weeks after the Virginia Plan was introduced, the resourceful Chevalier Otto sent the Quai d'Orsay a complete and detailed description of it, observing that "what is afoot is an entire recasting of the constitution. . . . Only rarely is one a spectator at a political event of the importance of this one, and it is difficult to confine to a few pages the agenda which should determine the future happiness, power, and energy of a nascent empire." (Correspondence Politique, Etats-Unis, 1787, vol. 32, f. 275, Archives des Affaires Etrangères, Paris.)

242 *Quotations in the following text are from these notes unless otherwise identified. For a quarter of a century after the Convention their existence was unknown; writing to John Adams regarding records of debates in the Congress and during the Convention on 11 August 1815, Jefferson inquired: "Do you know that there exists in manuscript the ablest work of this kind ever yet executed, of the debates of the constitutional convention of Philadelphia in 1788? The whole of everything said and done there was taken down by Mr. Madison, with a labor and exactness beyond comprehension." On 24 August, Adams replied, "Mr. Madison's Notes of the Convention of 1787 or 1788 are consistent with his indefatigable Character. I shall never see them, but I hope Posterity will." The official *Journal* of the Convention was printed in 1819; in 1821, Madison began preparation of his notes for posthumous publication. After his death in 1836 the Library of Congress bought the manuscript; its first, and partial publication took place in 1840. (*The Adams-Jefferson Letters*, ed. Lester J. Cappon, 2 vols. [Chapel Hill: University of North Carolina Press, 1959], 2:453, 455.)

†While many attended only sporadically, the single formal resignation was that of Wythe; at the end of the first week of debates, he was called home by the fatal illness of his wife and he resigned on 16 June. On 30 June, Mason suggested to Acting Governor Beverley Randolph the appointment of Francis Corbin, who was currently in Philadelphia, but no action was taken to fill the vacant place.

244 *Pierce's notes show Mason "of the opinion that the appointment of the Legislature coming from the people would make the representation actual, but if it came from the State Legislatures it will be only virtual." (Max Farrand, ed., *The Records of the Federal Convention of 1787*, rev. ed., 4 vols. [New Haven and London: Yale University Press, 1966], 1:57.)

251 *During the latter part of the Convention, New Hampshire was present and voting, but New York was not (two of its three delegates had withdrawn, and Hamilton's attendance was sporadic); the normal vote was thus reduced to eleven states.

257 *Before the emergence of national political parties in the next decade, the Society of the Cincinnati was the only private group, except for the Masonic order, with a nation-wide membership.

267 *The advantages of quick adoption stimulated Pennsylvania's proratification party to call a convention at once; on 28 September a motion in the Assembly proposed election of members within ten days. When

opposition members attempted to deny the House a quorum by staying away, a mob dragged them in and held them down in their seats while votes were taken. The Convention date was set for 20 November. Washington wrote Madison that Mason "has I am informed rendered himself obnoxious in Philadelphia by the pains he took to disseminate his objections among some of the leaders of the seceding members of the Legislature of that State." (George Washington, *The Writings of George Washington, 1745–1799*, ed. John C. Fitzpatrick, 39 vols. [Washington, D.C.: U.S. Government Printing Office, 1931–44], 29:285.)

268 *Washington observed that the "political tenets of Colo. M. and Col. R. H. L. are always in unison." (Ibid., 29:285.)

269 *Any discussion of the lands beyond the Alleghenies between a Marylander and a Virginian was sure to be touchy.
†Later in October, at the Assembly session, Archibald Stuart thought he still appeared shaken. During the debate on the Port Bill: "Masons Arguments in the Reply were vague & inconclusive in short, altho he is sometimes much admired for great strength of Mind Orginality of Expression & for the Comprehensive view which he takes of his subjects yet upon that Occasion he fell far short of the general Expectation, & I fear the Effects of Age have sometimes been discoverable in him." (Archibald Stuart to James Madison, 2 November 1787, Madison Papers, Library of Congress, Washington, D.C.)

270 *The two men, as they had done over the years, signed themselves "Your affecte. & obt. Servt." The time had not come when Washington wrote: "With some, to have differed in sentiment is to have passed the Rubicon of their friendship." (George Washington, *The Writings of George Washington, 1745–1799*, ed. John C. Fitzpatrick, 39 vols. [Washington, D.C.: U.S. Government Printing Office, 1931–44], 29:431.) While Virginia papers quoted Mason as declaring during the session, "I would have lost this hand before it should have marked my name to the new government" (Petersburg, Virginia, *Gazette* of 1 November and *Virginia Journal* of 8 November), Governor Randolph wrote Madison that "Mr. Mason has declared in Assembly that although he is for amendments, he will not quit the Union even if they should not be made."

271 *Jay had been disappointed of election to the New York delegation to Philadelphia; he gave vigorous support to the Constitution, first in five essays collected in his *Address to the People of New York on the Constitution*, then as one of the authors of *The Federalist*, and finally as a leader of the state ratifying convention.

277 *Announcement of the result brought conciliatory statements from a number of strong Anti-Federalists, typified by Mr. Widgery of New Gloucester: he "should return to his constituents, and inform them that he had opposed the adoption of the Constitution; but that he had been overruled, and that it had been carried by a majority of wise and understanding men; that he should endeavor to sow the seeds of union

and peace among the people he represented." (*Debates, Resolutions and Other Proceedings of the Convention of the Commonwealth of Massachusetts . . .* [Boston: Oliver & Monroe and Joshua Cushing, 1809], p. 217.)

280 *His wrath was formidable when his letters were not treated as private. The zealous Federalist, Charles Carter of Shirley, copied and showed in confidence to a friend excerpts from Washington's letter to him of 14 December 1787. When Washington discovered it had reached the press, a swift rebuke assured Carter, "Could I have supposed that the contents of a private letter (marked with evident haste) would have composed a newspaper paragraph, I certainly should have taken some pains to dress the sentiments . . . in less exceptionable language." (George Washington, *The Writings of George Washington, 1745–1799*, ed. John C. Fitzpatrick, 39 vols. [Washington, D.C.: U.S. Government Printing Office, 1931–44], 29:380.)

281 *Washington and John Adams's son-in-law had done so some weeks earlier.

284 *To replace the incorrect Philadelphia version, Mason had had copies printed himself. *The Virginia Journal and Alexandria Advertiser* reproduced them in November 1787, the Richmond *Virginia Independent Chronicle* in early December. The *Chronicle*'s printer, Augustine Davis, also bound the pamphlet with others as *VARIOUS EXTRACTS on the Federal Government, Proposed by a Convention held at Philadelphia*.
†Though the fact was not yet known, Jefferson had by this time departed from his initial views on adoption. In letters to Edward Carrington on 27 May and William Carmichael on 3 June (Thomas Jefferson, *The Papers of Thomas Jefferson*, ed. Julian P. Boyd, 19 vols. to date [Princeton: Princeton University Press, 1950– ], 13:208, 232) he endorsed the Massachusetts formula. Madison's letter to Randolph of 2 July first revealed his change of view: "I find that he is becoming more and more a friend to the new Constitution, his objections being gradually dispelled by his own further reflections on the subject. He particularly renounced his opinion concerning the expediency of a ratification by 9 & a refusal by 4 States, considering the mode pursued by Massts. as the only rational one, but disapproving some of the alterations recommended by that State. He will see still more room for disapprobation in the reconsideration of other States. The defects of the Constitution which he continues to criticize are the omission of a bill of rights, and of the principle of rotation at least of the Ex. Departmt." (James Madison, *The Writings of James Madison*, ed. Gaillard Hunt, 9 vols. [New York and London: G. P. Putnam's Sons, 1900–1910], 5:235.)

285 *In the autumn of 1787, Richard Henry Lee had counseled Mason: "If you are in correspondence with our Chancellor Pendelton it will be of much use to furnish him with the objections, and if he approved our plan, his opinion will have great weight with our Convention." (Lee Papers, Virginia Historical Society.) But Pendleton approved the Constitution.

†When in America during 1777–78, the Chevalier Alexandre Maria Quesnay de Beaurepaire, grandson of the physiocrat-economist who invented the phrase *laissez faire,* had responded to the suggestion of John Page of Rosewell that an American institution comparable to the Royal Academies of London, Paris, and Brussels be seated in Richmond, with branches in Baltimore, Philadelphia, and New York. The cornerstone was laid with Masonic ceremony in 1786, but the French Revolution ended the venture.

‡Madison later described the precautions he took on behalf of his private reporting at Philadelphia: "I chose a seat in front of the presiding member with the other members, on my right & left hand. In this favorable position for hearing all that passed, I noted in terms legible & in abbreviations & marks intelligible to myself what was read from the Chair or spoken by the members; and losing not a moment unnecessarily between the adjournment & reassembling of the Convention I was enabled to write out my daily notes during the session or within a few finishing days after its close." (Max Farrand, ed., *The Records of the Federal Convention of 1787,* rev. ed., 4 vols. [New Haven and London: Yale University Press, 1966], 3:550.)

287 *Much later, John Marshall was reported as reminiscing: "If I were called upon to say who of all the men I have known had the greatest power to convince, I should perhaps say Mr. Madison, while Mr. Henry had without a doubt the greatest power to persuade." (William Wirt Henry, *Patrick Henry: Life, Correspondence, and Speeches,* 3 vols. [New York: Charles Scribner's Sons, 1891], 2:376.)

292 *Morris was unperturbed; on the twelfth, he wrote Gen. Horatio Gates: "The Convention here are hard at work day by day the debates are supported with ability & pursued with ardour on both sides & the knowing ones pronounce that the Event is doubtfull, each Side pretend to count a Majority in their own Favour & following the example I am inclined to think that the Constitution will be adopted by Virginia." (12 June 1788, Emmet Collection MS 9471, Manuscripts and Archives Division, The New York Public Library, Astor, Lenox and Tilden Foundations, New York, N.Y.) Next day, however, Gouverneur Morris was less sanguine to Hamilton: the debates "were not going so well in this State as the Friends of America could wish"; but he counseled optimism: "My Religion steps in where my Understanding falters and I feel Faith as I lose Confidence." (Alexander Hamilton, *The Papers of Alexander Hamilton,* ed. Harold C. Syrett, 19 vols. to date [New York and London: Columbia University Press, 1961–], 5:7.)

297 *The close vote in several important states worried the diplomats: British Consul George Miller, in Charleston, felt that "the small Majority by which it was carried in the two latter States [Virginia and New York], as well as in some of the others, gives room to apprehend it may not be submitted to with that chearfulness which might be wished." (PRO, FO, 4/6, no. 231, 15 August 1788. Transcripts of

Crown-copyright records in the Public Record Office, London, appear by permission of the Controller of Her Majesty's Stationery Office, London.)

298 *In a private letter a few months later, Mason compared Randolph to the arch-traitor of the Revolution. The recent gubernatorial election, he said, had put a new man "in the Room of young A——ld." (George Mason, *The Papers of George Mason, 1725–1792,* ed. Robert A. Rutland, 3 vols. [Chapel Hill: University of North Carolina Press, 1971], 3:1136.)

†Henry even banished Madison from this Assembly by getting him sent to New York as a delegate to the dying session of the confederation. And when the lines for the state's new federal congressional districts were drawn, the area around Orange was not laid out for Madison's electoral comfort, though his constituents sent him to the House of Representatives by a margin of some three hundred votes over James Monroe.

300 *By a margin of one day in the case of Virginia, and two days in the case of New York, he got his announcement into the record ahead of requests from those states for the calling of a second convention.

†Agreeing with Samuel Osgood of New York, who said he considered the first Congress as a second convention, Congressman Elbridge Gerry attempted unsuccessfully to have the House as a whole consider all suggestions; there were some three hundred, covering about a hundred subjects.

‡Virginia was the eleventh and last necessary state, because between 1789 and 1791 the adherence of North Carolina and Rhode Island to the Union and the admission of Vermont as the first new state had raised the number of members to fourteen.

301 *On 12 July, Jefferson wrote Richard Price that the recently convened States General of France "are in quiet possession of the powers of the nation, and have begun the great work of building up a constitution. . . . The Declaration of the rights of man, which constitutes the 1st. chapter of this work, was brought in the day before yesterday." (Thomas Jefferson, *The Papers of Thomas Jefferson,* ed. Julian P. Boyd, 19 vols. to date [Princeton: Princeton University Press, 1950–], 15:271.)

304 *See Jacques Godechot, *Les Revolutions (1770–1799)* Paris: Presses Universitaires de France, Nouvelle Clio No. 36, 1963), p. 103.

313 *Shipping figures for the mid-90s show the deadly impact of war on Bordeaux's commerce. Whenever Britain and France were at odds, the long estuaries leading to Nantes and Bordeaux became pockets whose open ends could be closed by a few well-gunned British warships. By 1792, the city's tonnage was reduced to 169 ships of 51,000 tons outbound, and 201 ships of 66,000 tons inbound; during the later 1790s, Fenwick's correspondence with the city council shows him hard put to find money to complete his new house and pay the taxes on it. In 1801, a German observer recorded the desolation caused by the Napoleonic wars: "Bordeaux' ancient splendor is no more. . . . Many Merchants throng the bourse, but most of them go there only out of

habit—business dealings are rare. The domestic wine trade is the only one that has not disappeared."
† The eighteenth-century terra-cotta bust "America" from the Maison Fenwick, now in the Bordeaux Musée d'Art Ancien, was donated by the subsequent owners, the family of Pelleport-Burète.

317   *Mason's previous letter to John had worried: "I heartily wish the french Nation Success . . . but I dread the Consequences of their Affairs remaining so long in an unsetled State. Their Finances, their Commerce, & some of their most important Interests, must suffer exceedingly by it; besides the Risque of the most respectable Part of the People (which is always found in the Middle Walks of Life) being disgusted, and worn down, with so long a Scene of Doubt & Uncertainty, not to say Anarchy." (George Mason, *The Papers of George Mason, 1725–1792,* ed. Robert A. Rutland, 3 vols. [Chapel Hill: University of North Carolina Press, 1971], 3:1199.)

320   *See Fairfax County, Va., Court Orders, 1788–92, part 1, p. 175, for his letter of resignation, desiring that his retirement be made a matter of record, "that I not be subjected to censure for refusing to execute the Dutys of an office, which I no longer hold."
† That was one of the days when the Mount Vernon establishment served two dinners. Washington's entry, without specifying how long Mason remained, continues: "After dinner, word was brot. from Alexandria that the Minister of France was arrived there and intended down here to dinner. Accordingly, a little before Sun setting he (the Count de Moustiers, his Sister, the Marchioness de Brehan, the Marquis her son and Mr. du Ponts came in)." Actually, the Marchioness was both Moustier's sister-in-law and his mistress; their relationship was a factor in his subsequent removal.

322   *Yet on the same day that Mason wrote Griffin, Washington wrote Dr. Craik: "I always expected, that the Gentleman, whose name you have mentioned would mark his opposition to the new government with consistency. Pride on the one hand, and want of manly candor on the other, will not I am certain let him acknowledge an error in his opinions respecting it though conviction should flash on his mind as strongly as a ray of light. If certain characters which you have also mentioned [Cockburn and Richard Chichester] should tread *blindfold* in his steps it would be matter of no wonder to me. They are in the habit of thinking that everything he says and does is right, and (if capable) they will

not judge for themselves." (George Washington, *The Writings of George Washington, 1745–1799,* ed. John C. Fitzpatrick, 39 vols. [Washington, D.C.: U.S. Government Printing Office, 1931–44], 30:396–97.)
† In the postscript of a letter to Jefferson at this time, he explained a two-week delay in its dispatch: "This Letter was intended to have been forwarded the day on which it is dated; but I was suddenly seized with a repeated Attack of the Gout (after having been confined for near two months before) which rendered me unable to sit up, or attend to any thing, for several Days." (George Mason, *The Papers of George Mason, 1725–1792,* ed. Robert A. Rutland, 3 vols. [Chapel Hill: University of North Carolina Press, 1971], 3:1191.)

328   *Of fourteen senators who favored assumption, at least ten held securities, and of thirty-two House members, at least twenty-one did so.
† The appointment of Gouverneur Morris, whose affection for monarchy was well known, to succeed Jefferson as U.S. minister to revolutionary France had outraged many. Mason's comment was: "to send, upon such an Occasion, a Man, who is known to execrate such a Government is rather a Novelty in the diplomatic Code. . . . I can reconcile it with Propriety, only by applying Mr. Pope's Maxim— Whatever is, is right." (George Mason, *The Papers of George Mason, 1725-1792,* ed. Robert A. Rutland, 3 vols. [Chapel Hill: University of North Carolina Press, 1971], 3:1257.)
‡ But Cabinet member Hamilton had done so. See Max Farrand, ed., *The Records of the Federal Convention of 1787,* rev. ed., 4 vols. (New Haven and London: Yale University Press, 1966), 1:288–90, 424.
§ Certificates were known as "alienated" and "unalienated," depending on whether they had been bought up by speculators or remained in the hands of their original holders. Mason's distinction would have provided sure compensation for the latter while leaving returns on the former largely to the play of market forces.

322   *A transcript is in the archives of The Filson Club in Louisville.
† In the first edition, 1760, there is an "Index of Principles to be explained or mentioned in this Work"; it includes the following maxim: "One is permitted to take advantage of another's error in *damno evitando,* not in *lucro capitando.*" See pp. 26, 27, 32.

# References

## CHAPTER I

1. Hugh Jones, *The Present State of Virginia,* ed. Richard L. Morton (Chapel Hill: University of North Carolina Press, 1956), pp. 64–65.

2. Devereux Jarratt, *The Life of the Reverend Devereux Jarratt* (Baltimore: Warner & Hanna, 1806), pp. 13–14.

3. Jones, *Present State of Virginia,* pp. 96–97.

4. Fairfax Harrison, *Landmarks of Old Prince William,* intro. John Melville Jennings (Berryville, Va.: Chesapeake Book Club, 1964), p. 131.

5. William Fitzhugh, *William Fitzhugh and His Chesapeake World, 1676–1701,* ed. Richard Beale Davis (Chapel Hill: University of North Carolina Press, 1963), pp. 286, 288.

6. Ibid., p. 291.

7. Samuel Rowlands, *The Knave of Clubbs* (London, 1611), p. 34.

8. Sarah August Dickson, *Panacea or Precious Bane: Tobacco in Sixteenth Century Literature,* Publication No. 5, Arents Tobacco Collection (New York: New York Public Library, 1954), p. 156.

9. Isaac Hawkins Brown, *Of Smoking: Four Poems in Praise of Tobacco, An Imitation of the Style of Four Modern Poets, viz. Alexander Pope, Esq., Ambrose Philips, Esq., Dr. Young, Mr. Thoms* (London: Curll, 1736), pp. 7–8.

10. George Mason, *The Papers of George Mason, 1725–1792,* ed. Robert A. Rutland, 3 vols. (Chapel Hill: University of North Carolina Press, 1971), 1:61–62.

11. Robert Beverley, *History and Present State of Virginia,* ed. Louis B. Wright (Chapel Hill: University of North Carolina Press, 1947), p. 272.

12. *Virginia Magazine of History and Biography* 36, no. 3 (July 1928): 220–21. See discussion of this letter in Pierre Marambaud, *William Byrd of Westover, 1674–1744* (Charlottesville: University Press of Virginia, 1971), p. 283.

13. Kate Mason Rowland, *The Life of George Mason, 1725–1792,* 2 vols. (New York and London: G. P. Putnam's Sons, 1892), 1:35.

14. Ibid.

15. Fitzhugh, *Chesapeake World,* p. 256.

16. Ibid., p. 244.

17. Frances Norton Mason, ed., *John Norton & Sons, Merchants of Virginia, Being the Papers from Their Counting House for the Years 1750–1795* (Richmond: Dietz Press, 1937), pp. 94, 123–24.

18. John Gibson, *The History of Glasgow* (Glasgow: Chapman & Duncan, 1777), p. 212.

## CHAPTER II

1. *Virginia Magazine of History and Biography* 32, no. 1 (January 1924): 27.

2. Lois Mulkearn, ed., *George Mercer Papers Relating to the Ohio Company of Virginia* (Pittsburgh: University of Pittsburgh Press, 1944), p. 204.

3. Ibid.

4. *Executive Journals of the Council of Colonial Virginia,* 6 vols., various eds. (Richmond: Virginia State Library, 1925–66); vol. 4 (25 October 1721 to 28 October 1739), ed. H. R. McElwaine, 1930, p. 328.

5. Ibid., vol. 5 (1 November 1739 to 7 May 1754), ed. Wilmer L. Hall, 1945, p. 434.

6. George Mason, *The George Mason Papers, 1725–1792,* ed. Robert A. Rutland, 3 vols. (Chapel Hill: University of North Carolina Press, 1971), 1:159.

7. Mulkearn, *George Mercer Papers,* pp. 200–201.

8. Richard L. Perry, ed., *Sources of Our Liberties: Documentary Origins of Individual Liberties in the United States Constitution and the Bill of Rights* (Chicago: American Bar Foundation, 1959), p. 66n.

9. John Davis, *Travels of Four Years and a Half in the United States of America, 1798, 1799, 1800, 1801 and 1802,* ed. A. J. Morrison (New York: Henry Holt & Co., 1909), pp. 267–68.

10. Philip Vickers Fithian, *Journal & Letters of Philip Vickers Fithian, 1773–1774,* ed. with intro. Hunter Dickinson Farish (Williamsburg: Colonial Williamsburg, Inc., 1943), pp. 220–21.

11. Mason, *Papers,* 1:11.

12. Cited by Richard K. MacMaster, "Instructions to a Tobacco Planter, 1725," *Maryland Historical Magazine* 63, no. 1 (Spring 1968): 177–78.

13. Mason, *Papers,* 1:20.

14. William Fitzhugh, *William Fitzhugh and His Chesapeake World, 1676–1701,* ed. Richard Beale Davis (Chapel Hill: University of North Carolina Press, 1963), p. 366.

15. Facsimile of *Encyclopaedia Britannica,* 1771 edition, 3 vols. (Chicago: Encyclopedia Britannica, Inc., 1968), 3:126–27.

16. Mason, *Papers,* 1:271.


CHAPTER III

1. George Mason, *The Papers of George Mason, 1725–1792,* ed. Robert A. Rutland, 3 vols. (Chapel Hill: University of North Carolina Press, 1971), 1:45–46.

2. John Mason, John Mason Papers, microfilm, Manuscripts Division, Library of Congress, Washinton, D.C.

3. Stafford County, Va., Deed Book S, 1780–1786, ff. 318–19.

4. Fairfax Harrison, "The Equine FFVs," *Virginia Magazine of Biography and History* 35, no. 4 (October 1927): 351. For description of Old Janus see *American Turf Register and Sporting Magazine,* 15 vols. (Baltimore: 1829–38; New York: 1839–44), 3:272; "An Advocate of the Turf," *Annals of the Turf* (The Petersburg Intelligencer, 1833); Patrick Nisbett Edgar, *The American Race-Turf Register* (New York: Press of Henry Mason, 1833).

5. George Washington, *The Diaries of George Washington, 1748–1799,* ed. John C. Fitzpatrick, 4 vols. (Boston and New York: Houghton Mifflin Co., 1925), 2:455.

6. Mason, *Papers,* 1:42–43.

7. John Mason Papers.

8. Mason, *Papers,* 1:130–31.

9. John Mason Papers.

10. Ibid.

11. Ibid.


CHAPTER IV

1. George Washington, *The Writings of George Washington, 1745–1799,* ed. John C. Fitzpatrick, 39 vols. (Washington, D.C.: U.S. Government Printing Office, 1931–44), 1:193.

2. Ibid., p. 463.

3. George Mason, *George Mason Papers, 1725–1792,* ed. Robert A. Rutland, 3 vols. (Chapel Hill: University of North Carolina Press, 1971), 1:224.

4. Jane Carson, ed., *We Were There: Descriptions of Williamsburg, 1699–1859* (Charlottesville: University Press of Virginia, 1965), pp. 15–16.

5. Paul Leicester Ford, ed., *The True George Washington* (Freeport, N.Y.: Books for Libraries Press, 1971), p. 299.

6. Washington, *Writings,* 2:185.

7. Mason, *Papers,* 1:41.

8. Ibid., p. 220.

9. Washington, *Writings,* 2:475.

10. George Washington, *The Diaries of George Washington, 1748–1799,* ed. John C. Fitzpatrick, 4 vols. (Boston and New York: Houghton Mifflin Co., 1925), 1:349–50.

11. Mason, *Papers,* 1:185.

12. Alexandria, Va., Town Trustees' Minute Book, passim.

13. Fairfax County, Va., Court Orders, 1768–70, p. 132.

14. Ibid., p. 133.

15. Ibid., p. 135.

16. Ibid.

17. George Washington, Washington Papers, microfilm ser. 4, reel 32, Manuscript Division, Library of Congress, Washington, D.C.

18. Truro Parish, Va., Truro Parish Vestry Book, 3 and 4 February 1766, ff. 109–15 passim; 3 March 1769, ff. 137–41 passim; 5 June 1772, f. 153; 14 June 1773; 24 and 25 February 1774, ff. 162, 164, Manuscript Division, Library of Congress, Washington, D.C.

19. George Whitefield, *A Continuation of the Rev. Mr. Whitefield's Journal from His Embarking after the Embargo to His Arrival at Savannah in Georgia* (London: W. Strahan for James Hunter, 1740), p. 63.

20. Landon Carter, *The Diary of Col. Landon Carter of Sabine Hall, 1752–1778,* ed. with intro. Jack P. Greene, 2 vols. (Charlottesville: University Press of Virginia, 1965), 2:671.

21. Thomas Jefferson, *Thomas Jefferson's Garden Book, 1766–1824,* annot. Edwin Morris Betts (Philadelphia: American Philosophical Society, 1944), p. 55.

22. Jonathan Clark Papers, Virginia and Kentucky, etc., 1728–79, Draper MSS IL313, State Historical Society of Wisconsin, Madison, Wis.

23. Carter, *Diary,* 2:831.

24. Washington, *Writings,* 3:127.

25. Mason, *Papers,* 1:234.

26. Ibid., p. 227.


CHAPTER V

1. *Journals of the House of Burgesses of Virginia, 1761–1765,* ed. John Pendleton Kennedy (Richmond: Virginia State Library, 1907), p. lxvii.

2. "Journal of a French Traveller in the Colonies, 1765," *American Historical Review* 26 (1920–21): 745.

3. Thomas Jefferson, *The Writings of Thomas Jefferson*, ed. Paul Leicester Ford, 10 vols. (New York and London: G. P. Putnam's Sons, 1892–99), 1:404.

4. George Mason, *The Papers of George Mason, 1725–1792*, ed. Robert A. Rutland, 3 vols. (Chapel Hill: University of North Carolina Press, 1971), 1:60–61.

5. *Journals of the House of Burgesses of Virginia, 1761–1765*, p. lxix.

6. *Virginia Magazine of History and Biography* 30, no. 1 (January 1922): 82.

7. *Journals of the House of Burgesses of Virginia, 1761–1765*, pp. lxx, lxxii.

8. Mason, *Papers*, 1:66.

9. Ibid., p. 69.

10. George Washington, *The Writings of George Washington, 1745–1799*, ed. John C. Fitzpatrick, 39 vols. (Washington, D.C.: U.S. Government Printing Office, 1931–44), 2:500–501.

11. Mason, *Papers*, 1:99.

12. Ibid., p. 102.

13. Ibid., p. 110.

14. *Journals of the House of Burgesses of Virginia, 1766–1769*, ed. John Pendleton Kennedy (Richmond: Virginia State Library, 1906), p. 227.

15. Mason, *Papers*, 1:116–17.

16. John Mason Papers, microfilm, Manuscript Division, Library of Congress, Washington, D.C.


*CHAPTER VI*

1. George Mason, *The Papers of George Mason, 1725–1792*, ed. Robert A. Rutland, 3 vols. (Chapel Hill: University of North Carolina Press, 1971), 1:190.

2. *Journals of the House of Burgesses of Virginia, 1773–1776*, ed. John Pendleton Kennedy (Richmond: Virginia State Library, 1905), p. 124.

3. Mason, *Papers*, 1:191.

4. Ibid., p. 192.

5. George Washington, *The Diaries of George Washington, 1748–1799*, ed. John C. Fitzpatrick, 4 vols. (Boston and New York: Houghton Mifflin Co., 1925), 2:156.

6. J. F. D. Smyth, *A Tour in the United States of America*, 2 vols. (London: Robinson, Robson, and Sewell, 1784; reprint New York: The Arno Press Inc., 1968), 1:65–68 passim.

7. Robert Munford, *The Candidates: Or, The Humours of a Virginia Election*, ed. with intro. Jay B. Hubbell and Douglass Adair (Williamsburg: Institute of Early American History and Culture, 1948), p. 43.

8. George Washington, *The Writings of George Washington, 1745–1799*, ed. John C. Fitzpatrick, 39 vols. (Washington, D.C.: U.S. Government Printing Office, 1931–44), 3:227n.

9. Ibid., pp. 227–28.

10. Washington, *Diaries*, 2:160.

11. Nicholas Cresswell, *The Journal of Nicholas Cresswell, 1774–1777* (New York: Dial Press, 1924), pp. 27–28.

12. Washington, *Diaries*, 2:157.

13. Mason, *Papers*, 1:201–7 passim.

14. Washington, *Writings*, 2:501.

15. Mason, *Papers*, 1:209.

16. MSS list, published with permission of Francis L. Berkeley, Jr., Charlottesville, Va.

17. *Virginia Magazine of History and Biography* 15, no. 4 (April 1908): 355–57.

18. Mason, *Papers*, 1:235.

19. Burton J. Hendrick, *The Lees of Virginia* (Boston: Little, Brown & Co., 1935), p. 170.

20. Mason, *Papers*, 1:210–11.

21. Ibid., p. 212.

22. Ibid., p. 229.

23. Ibid., pp. 229–31 passim.

24. Ibid., p. 239.

25. Ibid., p. 241.

26. Ibid., p. 250.

27. Edmund Pendleton, *Letters and Papers of Edmund Pendleton, 1734–1803*, coll. and ed. David John Mays, 2 vols. (Charlottesville: University Press of Virginia, 1967), 1:110.

28. Mason, *Papers*, 1:255.

29. Ibid.

30. Ibid., p. 250.

31. Washington, *Writings*, 20:318.

32. Ibid., 27:58n.

33. Charles Fenton James, *Documentary History of the Struggle for Religious Liberty in Virginia* (Lynchburg, Va., 1900; New York: Da Capo Press, 1971), p. 76.

34. James Parker to Charles Steuart, 7 June 1774, Charles Steuart Papers, National Library of Scotland, Edinburgh.

35. Henry Fleming to Messrs. Fisher & Bragg, 17 November 1774, Henry Fleming, Correspondence and Ledger Books, 1772–75 and 1783–88, Cumberland County Record Office, Carlisle, England.

36. Mason, *Papers*, 1:253.

37. Cresswell, *Journal*, p. 1.

38. Ibid., pp. 44–45.

39. Ibid., p. 201.

40. Smyth, *Tour*, 2:205–6.

41. Ibid., p. 229.

42. Ibid., pp. 248–49.

43. Mason, *Papers*, 1:258–59.

44. Ibid., p. 261.

45. John Locke, *Two Treatises of Government* (Dublin, 1794), p. 254.

46. Benjamin Rush, *The Autobiography of Benjamin Rush,* ed. with intro. George W. Corner (Westport, Conn.: Greenwood Press, 1948), p. 114.

47. Washington, *Writings,* 4:297.


CHAPTER VII

1. John Adams to Mercy Warren, 8 January 1776, *The Warren-Adams Letters,* Massachusetts Historical Society *Publications* 72, 2 vols. (Boston, 1917) 1:201–3.

2. Landon Carter, *The Diary of Col. Landon Carter of Sabine Hall, 1752–1778,* ed. with intro. Jack P. Greene, 2 vols. (Charlottesville: University Press of Virginia, 1965), 2:980.

3. Edmund Randolph, *History of Virginia,* ed. Arthur H. Shaffer (Charlottesville: University Press of Virginia, 1970), pp. 233–34.

4. George Mason, *The Papers of George Mason, 1725–1792,* ed. Robert A. Rutland, 3 vols. (Chapel Hill: University of North Carolina Press, 1971), 1:256.

5. Lund Washington to George Washington, 29 October 1775, Collections, The Mount Vernon Ladies' Association.

6. Ibid.

7. Ibid., 17 January 1776.

8. Mason, *Papers,* 1:267.

9. Thomas Jefferson, *The Writings of Thomas Jefferson,* ed. Paul Leicester Ford, 10 vols. (New York and London: G. P. Putnam's Sons, 1892–99), 1:80.

10. Mason, *Papers,* 1:260.

11. Lund Washington to George Washington, 31 January 1776, Collections, The Mount Vernon Ladies' Association.

12. Mason, *Papers,* 1:267.

13. Carter, *Diary,* 2:1007.

14. Edmund Cody Burnett, ed., *Letters of Members of the Continental Congress,* 8 vols. (Washington, D.C.: Carnegie Institution of Washington, 1921–36), 1:416–17.

15. *Virginia Magazine of History and Biography* 34, no. 2 (April 1926): 185.

16. *William and Mary Quarterly,* 1st ser. 19, no. 4 (April 1911): 254.

17. Robert Brent to Richard Henry Lee, 28 April 1776, Lee Papers, University of Virginia, Charlottesville, Va.

18. Edmund Pendleton, *Letters and Papers of Edmund Pendleton, 1734–1803,* coll. and ed. David John Mays, 2 vols. (Charlottesville: University Press of Virginia, 1967), 1:179.

19. Mason, *Papers,* 1:271–72.

20. Pendleton, *Letters and Papers,* 1:179.

21. Jefferson, *Writings,* 10:306–7.

22. Thomas Jefferson, *The Papers of Thomas Jefferson,* ed. Julian P. Boyd, 19 vols. to date (Princeton: Princeton University Press, 1950–), 1:292.

23. *Adams Family Correspondence,* ed. Lyman Butterfield, 2 vols. (Cambridge, Mass.: Belknap Press of Harvard University Press, 1963), 2:30–31.

24. Bernard Mayo, *Jefferson Himself* (Charlottesville: University Press of Virginia, 1942), p. 71.

25. Mason, *Papers,* 1:277, 278.

26. Thomas Ludwell Lee to Richard Henry Lee, 1 June 1776, Lee Papers, University of Virginia, Charlottesville, Va.

27. James Madison, *The James Madison Papers,* ed. vols. 1–6 William T. Hutchinson and William M. E. Rachal; ed. vol. 7 to date, Robert A. Rutland and William M. E. Rachal (Chicago and London: University of Chicago Press, 1962–), 1:106.

28. Madison, *Papers,* 1:174.

29. Ibid., pp. 174–75.

30. See Margaret A. Judson, *The Political Thought of Sir Henry Vane the Younger* (Philadelphia: University of Pennsylvania Press, 1969).

31. Sir William Scott, who as Lord Stowell was judge of the Court of Admiralty, 1798–1828, cited in Sir William Holdsworth, *A History of English Law,* 16 vols. (Boston: Little, Brown & Co., 1938), 12:583n.

32. Benjamin Franklin, *The Papers of Benjamin Franklin,* ed. Leonard W. Labaree, 17 vols. to date (New Haven and London: Yale University Press, 1959–), 1:103–4.

33. Henry Home, Lord Kames, *Essays on the Principles of Morality and Natural Religion* (Edinburgh: Kincaid and Donaldson, 1751), p. 108.

34. Henry Home, Lord Kames, *Historical Law Tracts,* 2nd ed. (London: A. Millar, 1761; Edinburgh: Kincaid and Bell, 1761), Tract III, *History of Property,* p. 143.

35. For texts of the various state declarations, see Bernard Schwartz, *The Bill of Rights: A Documentary History,* 2 vols. (New York, Toronto, London, Sydney: Chelsea House in assoc. with McGraw-Hill Book Co., 1971), 1:231–379.


CHAPTER VIII

1. Richard Henry Lee to Edmund Pendleton, 12 May 1776, Lee Papers, University of Virginia, Charlottesville, Va.

2. Edmund Pendleton, *Letters and Papers of Edmund Pendleton, 1734–1803,* coll. and ed. David John Mays, 2 vols. (Charlottesville: University Press of Virginia, 1967), 1:177.

3. Thomas Jefferson, *The Papers of Thomas Jefferson,* ed. Julian P. Boyd, 19 vols. to date (Princeton: Princeton University Press, 1950–), 1:476–77.

4. Richard Henry Lee to Gen. Charles Lee, 29 June 1776, The New-York Historical Society, New York, N.Y.

5. Jefferson, *Papers,* 1:379.

6. Commonwealth of Virginia, *Proceedings of Convention,* 5 July 1776.

7. George Mason, *The Papers of George Mason, 1725–1792,* ed. Robert A. Rutland, 3 vols. (Chapel Hill: University of North Carolina Press, 1971), 1:327.

8. Thomas Jefferson, *The Writings of Thomas Jefferson,* ed. Paul Leicester Ford, 10 vols. (New York and London: G. P. Putnam's Sons, 1892–99), 1:68–69.

9. Mason, *Papers,* 1:331.

10. Ibid., p. 345.

11. Charles Campbell, ed., *The Bland Papers* (Petersburg, Va.: E. and J. Ruffin, 1840–43), p. 58.

12. Lund Washington to George Washington, 18 March 1778, Collections, The Mount Vernon Ladies' Association.

13. George Washington, *The Writings of George Washington, 1745–1799,* ed. John C. Fitzpatrick, 39 vols. (Washington, D.C.: U.S. Government Printing Office, 1931–44), 10:192–93.

14. Mason, *Papers,* 1:355.

15. Washington, *Writings,* 10:60.

16. Mason, *Papers,* 2:507.

17. Ibid., p. 522.

18. Washington, *Writings,* 9:388.

19. Ibid., 10:29.

20. Edmund Cody Burnett, *The Continental Congress* (New York: The Macmillan Co., 1941; New York: W. W. Norton & Co., 1964), p. 285.

21. Lund Washington to George Washington, 18 February 1778, Collections, The Mount Vernon Ladies' Association.

22. Mason, *Papers,* 1:429–30.

23. Lund Washington to George Washington, 22 April 1778, Collections, The Mount Vernon Ladies' Association.

24. John Parke Custis to George Washington, 17 June 1778, Custis Papers, Virginia Historical Society, Richmond, Va.

25. John Augustine Washington to Richard Henry Lee, 26 May 1778, Lee Papers, University of Virginia, Charlottesville, Va.

26. Mason, *Papers,* 1:434–37 passim.

CHAPTER IX
1. Benjamin Franklin, *The Papers of Benjamin Franklin,* ed. Leonard W. Labaree, 17 vols. to date (New Haven and London: Yale University Press, 1959–), 9:6–7.

2. James Monroe to George Rogers Clark, 26 June 1782, Draper MSS 52J23, State Historical Society of Wisconsin, Madison, Wis.

3. George Washington, *The Writings of George Washington, 1745–1799,* ed. John C. Fitzpatrick, 39 vols. (Washington, D.C.: U.S. Government Printing Office, 1931–44), 11:317.

4. Fairfax County, Va., Will Book Liber H, no. 1, p. 2.

5. George Mason, *The Papers of George Mason, 1725–1792,* ed. Robert A. Rutland, 3 vols. (Chapel Hill: University of North Carolina Press, 1971), 1:263.

6. Frederick Palmer, *Clark of the Ohio: A Life of George Rogers Clark* (New York: Dodd, Mead & Co., 1929), p. 154.

7. Mason, *Papers,* 1:409–10.

8. Palmer, *Clark of the Ohio,* p. 124.

9. Ibid., p. 172.

10. Thomas Jefferson, *The Papers of Thomas Jefferson,* ed. Julian P. Boyd, 19 vols. to date (Princeton: Princeton University Press, 1950–), 2:246.

11. Mason, *Papers,* 2:576.

12. Ibid., pp. 556–81 passim.

13. *Calendar of Virginia State Papers and Other Manuscripts Preserved in the Capitol at Richmond 1652–1869,* 11 vols., ed. vol. 1 William P. Palmer (Richmond: R. F. Walker, Superintendent of Public Printing, 1875–93), 1:319–20.

14. Mason, *Papers,* 2:555

15. Jefferson, *Papers,* 6:204–5.

16. Mason, *Papers,* 2:657.

17. Ibid., pp. 659–60.

18. "In the House of Delegates the 7th of January 1788," Records of the U.S. Department of State, Miscellaneous Papers, documents relating to the claim of Virginia on account of the services of George Rogers Clark in the Illinois Country, National Archives, Washington, D.C.

19. George Washington, *The Diaries of George Washington, 1748–1799,* ed. John C. Fitzpatrick, 4 vols. (Boston and New York: Houghton Mifflin Co., 1925), 2:326.

20. George Rogers Clark to Gen. Jonathan Clark, 11 May 1792, copy in State Historical Society of Wisconsin, published in Walter Hayden English, *Conquest of the Country Northwest of the River Ohio, 1778–1783, and Life of Gen. George Rogers Clark,* 2 vols. in 1 (Indianapolis and Kansas City: Bobbs-Merrill Co., 1896; reprint, New York: The Arno Press, Inc., 1971), p. 790.

CHAPTER X

1. George Mason, *The Papers of George Mason, 1725–1792,* ed. Robert A. Rutland, 3 vols. (Chapel Hill: University of North Carolina Press, 1971), 2:495.

2. George Washington, *The Writings of George Washington, 1745–1799,* ed. John C. Fitzpatrick, 39 vols. (Washington, D.C.: U.S. Government Printing Office, 1931–44), 14:299–301.

3. Mason, *Papers,* 2:498.

4. Ibid., p. 507.

5. Ibid.

6. Ibid., p. 508.

7. Ibid., p. 523.

8. Ibid., p. 630.

9. Ibid., p. 553.

10. Ibid., p. 713.

11. Ibid., pp. 639–40.

12. Washington, *Writings,* 20:241.

13. Ibid., p. 242.

14. Mason, *Papers,* 2:692–93.

15. Ibid., p. 680.

16. Ibid., p. 689.

17. Ibid., pp. 661–62.

18. Edmund Cody Burnett, ed. *Letters of Members of the Continental Congress,* 8 vols. (Washington, D.C.: Carnegie Institution of Washington, 1921–36), 5:xxxix and xl.

19. Ibid., p. xli.

20. Mason, *Papers,* 2:618.

21. Ibid., p. 683.

22. Ibid., p. 690.

23. Ibid., pp. 693–94.

24. Correspondence Politique, Etats-Unis, 1781, vol. 17, ff. 49 and 50, Archives des Affaires Etrangères, Paris.

25. Edmund Pendleton, *Letters and Papers of Edmund Pendleton, 1734–1803,* coll. and ed. David John Mays, 2 vols. (Charlottesville: University of Virginia, 1967), 1:321.

26. Mason, *Papers,* 2:676.

27. Ibid., p. 707.

28. Ibid., p. 711.

29. Pendleton, *Letters and Papers,* 2:381.


CHAPTER XI

1. George Mason, *The Papers of George Mason, 1725–1792,* ed. Robert A. Rutland, 3 vols. (Chapel Hill: University of North Carolina Press, 1971), 1:173.

2. Stafford County, Va., Deed Book S, 1780–86, f. 319.

3. Thomas Jefferson, *The Papers of Thomas Jefferson,* ed. Julian P. Boyd, 19 vols. to date (Princeton: Princeton University Press, 1950–), 6:608.

4. Ibid., 2:545–46.

5. James Madison, *The James Madison Papers,* eds. vols. 1–6 William T. Hutchinson and William M. E. Rachal; vol. 7 to date, Robert A. Rutland and William M. E. Rachal (Chicago and London: University of Chicago Press, 1962–), 7:118.

6. George Washington, *The Writings of George Washington, 1745–1799,* ed. John C. Fitzpatrick, 39 vols. (Washington, D.C.: U.S. Government Printing Office, 1931–44), 2:832.

7. Mason, *Papers,* 2:833.

8. Richard Henry Lee, *The Letters of Richard Henry Lee,* ed. James Curtis Ballagh, 2 vols. (New York: The Macmillan Co., 1911–14), 2:304.

9. Jefferson, *Papers,* 6:277.

10. Ibid., p. 381.

11. James Madison to Thos. Jefferson, 10 December 1783, Madison Papers, Manuscript Division, Library of Congress, Washington, D.C.

12. Mason, *Papers,* 2:770.

13. Ibid., pp. 776–77.

14. Edmund Cody Burnett, *The Continental Congress* (New York: The Macmillan Co., 1941; New York: W. W. Norton & Co., 1964), p. 561.

15. Washington, *Writings,* 26:277.

16. Mason, *Papers,* 2:781.

17. Louis-Guillaume Otto, "Mémoire," trans. Paul E. Sifton, *William and Mary Quarterly,* 3rd ser. 22, no. 4 (October 1965): 629–30.

18. Marquis de Chastellux, *Travels in America in the Years 1780, 1781, and 1782,* 2 vols., rev. trans., intro., and notes, Howard C. Rice, Jr. (Chapel Hill: University of North Carolina Press, 1963), p. 301.

19. Mason, *Papers,* 2:810.

20. Ibid., p. 762.

21. Ibid., pp. 775–76.

22. Ibid., p. 799.

23. George Washington, *The Diaries of George Washington, 1748–1799,* ed. John C. Fitzpatrick, 4 vols. (Boston and New York: Houghton Mifflin Co.,1925), 2:419.

24. Mason, *Papers,* 2:855.

25. Edmund Cody Burnett, *Letters of Members of the Continental Congress,* 8 vols. (Washington, D.C.: Carnegie Institution of Washington, 1921–36), 8:481–83 passim.

26. James Madison, *The Writings of James Madison,* ed. Gaillard Hunt, 9 vols. (New York and London: G. P. Putnam's Sons, 1900–1910), 2:261.

27. Jefferson, *Papers,* 11:310 (the last paragraph of this letter, here quoted, is omitted in Madison, *Writings.*)

28. Madison, *Writings,* 2:237–38.

29. Ibid., pp. 293–95.

CHAPTER XII
1. George Mason, *The Papers of George Mason,
1725–1792,* ed. Robert A. Rutland, 3 vols.
(Chapel Hill: University of North Carolina Press,
1971), 2:826.
2. Ibid., p. 827.
3. Ibid., p. 844.
4. U.S. Sesquicentennial Commission, *History
and Formation of the Union under the Constitution*
(Washington, D.C.: U.S. Government Printing
Office, 1941), pp. 41–42.
5. Ibid., p. 43.
6. Max Farrand, ed., *The Records of the Federal
Convention of 1787,* rev. ed., 4 vols. (New Haven and
London: Yale University Press, 1966), 3:15.
7. PRO, FO, 4/5, pt. 1, p. 163. Transcripts of
Crown-copyright records in the Public Record
Office, London, appear by permission of the
Controller of Her Majesty's Stationery Office,
London.
8. Farrand, *Records,* 3:16.
9. Ibid., p. 15.
10. Mason, *Papers,* 3:880.
11. Ibid., p. 881.
12. Ibid.
13. Ibid.
14. Ibid., p. 884.
15. Ibid., p. 891.
16. Ibid., p. 880.
17. Ibid., pp. 892–93.
18. Farrand, *Records,* 3:94.
19. Ibid., p. 58.
20. Mason, *Papers,* 3:884.
21. Farrand, *Records,* 3:58–59.
22. Ibid., 1:10.
23. Ibid., p. 21.
24. Ibid., p. 22.
25. Ibid., p. 532.
26. Ibid., p. 24.
27. Ibid., p. 34
28. Ibid., p. 35.
29. Ibid., 3:244–45.
30. Ibid., 1:34.
31. Ibid., p. 48.
32. Ibid.
33. Ibid.
34. Ibid., p. 50.
35. Ibid., p. 292.
36. Arthur Lee to Thomas Shippen, Jr., 7 May
1787, Burton J. Hendrick, *The Lees of Virginia* (Boston: Little, Brown & Co., 1935), p. 369.
37. Farrand, *Records,* 3:80–81.
38. Ibid., 1:177–78.
39. Ibid., p. 451.
40. Ibid., p. 460.

41. Ibid., pp. 461–62.
42. Ibid., p. 526.
43. Ibid., pp. 527–28.
44. Ibid., pp. 529–31 passim.
45. Ibid., p. 531.
46. Ibid., p. 532.
47. Ibid., pp. 532–33.
48. Edmund Cody Burnett, ed., *Letters of
Members of the Continental Congress,* 8 vols. (Washington, D.C.: Carnegie Institution of Washington,
1921–36), 8:624.
49. Farrand, *Records,* 1:533–34, 583.
50. Ibid., p. 476.
51. Ibid., p. 97.
52. Ibid., p. 113.
53. Ibid., 2:183.
54. Ibid., p. 362.
55. Ibid.
56. Ibid., p. 361.
57. Ibid., p. 363.
58. Ibid., p. 364.
59. Ibid.
60. Ibid.
61. Ibid.
62. Ibid., pp. 369–70.
63. Ibid., p. 370.
64. Ibid., p. 374.
65. Ibid., p. 396.
66. Ibid., p. 451.
67. Ibid., p. 452.
68. George Washington, *The Writings of George
Washington, 1745–1799,* ed. John C. Fitzpatrick,
39 vols. (Washington, D.C.: U.S. Government
Printing Office, 1931–44), 29:228.
69. Elbridge Gerry to Samuel R. Gerry, 12
August 1787, Gerry Papers, f. 54, Massachusetts
Historical Society, Boston, Mass.
70. Farrand, *Records,* 3:499.
71. Ibid., p. 420.


CHAPTER XIII
1. George Mason, *The Papers of George Mason,
1725–1792,* ed. Robert A. Rutland, 3 vols.
(Chapel Hill: University of North Carolina Press,
1971), 3:925.
2. Ibid., p. 931.
3. Ibid., p. 899.
4. Ibid., p. 926.
5. Ibid., pp. 931–32.
6. Ibid., p. 895.
7. Ibid., p. 927.
8. Ibid., p. 980.
9. Ibid., p. 963.
10. Ibid., p. 928.

11. Ibid., p. 979.

12. Ibid., p. 922.

13. Ibid., p. 910.

14. Ibid., p. 923.

15. Ibid.

16. Ibid., p. 924.

17. Max Farrand, ed., *The Records of the Federal Convention of 1787*, rev. ed., 4 vols. (New Haven and London: Yale University Press, 1966), 1:594.

18. Mason, *Papers*, 3:912.

19. Ibid., p. 975.

20. Ibid., pp. 949–50.

21. Ibid., p. 962.

22. Ibid., p. 933.

23. Ibid., pp. 973–74.

24. *Maryland Journal and Baltimore Advertiser*, 18 March 1788.

25. Mason, *Papers*, 3:981.

26. Farrand, *Records*, 2:588.

27. Ibid., p. 606.

28. Ibid., p. 626.

29. Ibid., p. 631.

30. Ibid., p. 632.

31. Ibid., pp. 642–43.

32. Ibid., p. 643.

33. Ibid., pp. 645–46.

34. Ibid., p. 646.

35. Ibid., p. 647.

36. George Washington, *The Diaries of George Washington, 1748–1799*, ed. John C. Fitzpatrick, 4 vols. (Boston and New York: Houghton Mifflin Co., 1925), 3:236–37.

37. Farrand, *Records*, 3:83.

38. Elbridge Gerry, Gerry Papers, Manuscript Division, Library of Congress, Washington, D.C.

39. Farrand, *Records*, 3:99.

40. James Madison, *The Writings of James Madison*, ed. Gaillard Hunt, 9 vols. (New York and London: G. P. Putnam's Sons, 1900–1910), 5:4–5.

41. Richard Henry Lee to George Mason, 1 October 1787, Lee Papers, Virginia Historical Society, Richmond, Va.


*CHAPTER XIV*

1. Margaret C. McHenry to James McHenry, 18 September 1787, MS 647, McHenry Papers, Maryland Historical Society, Baltimore, Md.

2. Daniel Carroll to James Madison, 28 October 1787, Madison Papers, Manuscript Division, Library of Congress, Washington, D.C.

3. George Mason, *The Papers of George Mason, 1725–1792*, ed. Robert A. Rutland, 3 vols. (Chapel Hill: University of North Carolina Press, 1971), 3:1001.

4. Max Farrand, ed., *The Records of the Federal Convention of 1787*, rev. ed., 4 vols. (New Haven and London: Yale University Press, 1966), 3:80.

5. Mason, *Papers*, 3:1001–2.

6. Ibid., p. 1011.

7. Farrand, *Records*, 3:180–81.

8. Ibid., p. 168.

9. Ibid., pp. 164–65.

10. Edmund Cody Burnett, ed., *Letters of Members of the Continental Congress*, 8 vols. (Washington, D.C.: Carnegie Institution of Washington, 1921–36), 8:709.

11. Lund Washington to George Washington, 6 March 1789, Collections, The Mount Vernon Ladies' Association.

12. Farrand, *Records*, 3:296–97.

13. Ibid., 2:649–50.

14. Ibid., 3:128.

15. Bernard Schwartz, ed., *The Bill of Rights: A Documentary History*, 2 vols. (New York, Toronto, London, Sydney: Chelsea House in association with McGraw-Hill Book Co., 1971), 2:668.

16. *Debates, Resolutions and other Proceedings of the Convention of the Commonwealth of Massachusetts. . .* (Boston: Oliver & Monroe and Joshua Cushing, 1809), p. 137.

17. Ibid., p. 161.

18. Ibid., p. 162.

19. Gen. Henry Jackson to Gen. Henry Knox, 6 February 1788, Knox Papers, Massachusetts Historical Society, Boston, Mass.

20. *Algemeen Ryksarchief Staten-Generaal*, Liassen No. 7130, f. 289, The Hague.

21. James Madison, *The Writings of James Madison*, ed. Gaillard Hunt, 9 vols. (New York and London: G. P. Putnam's Sons, 1900–1910), 5:100, 102–3.

22. Col. Edward Carrington to Gen. Henry Knox, 13 March 1788, Knox Papers, Massachusetts Historical Society, Boston, Mass.

23. George Washington, *The Writings of George Washington, 1745–1799*, ed. John C. Fitzpatrick, 39 vols. (Washington, D.C.: The U.S. Government Printing Office, 1931–44), 29:478.

24. Farrand, *Records*, 3:302.

25. Washington, *Writings*, 29:479.

26. Ibid., p. 350.

27. Ibid., pp. 357–58.

28. James Monroe, *The Writings of James Monroe*, ed. Stanislaus Murray Hamilton, 7 vols. (New York, 1898; New York: AMS Press, 1969), 1:186.

29. Jonathan Elliot, ed., *The Debates in the Several State Conventions on the Adoption of the Federal Constitution*, Vol. III, *The Debates in the Convention of the Commonwealth of Virginia* (Philadelphia: J. B. Lippincott Co., 1881), p. 616.

30. Farrand, *Records*, 3:76.

31. Ibid., p. 77.

32. Madison, *Writings,* 5:33–37 passim.

33. Thomas Jefferson, *The Papers of Thomas Jefferson,* ed. Julian P. Boyd, 19 vols. to date (Princeton: Princeton University Press, 1950–), 12:480.

34. Ibid., p. 558.

35. Col. Edward Carrington to Gen. Henry Knox, 12 January 1788, Knox Papers, Massachusetts Historical Society, Boston, Mass.

36. George Washington, Washington Papers, Microfilm Reel 97 (ser. 4), Manuscript Division, Library of Congress, Washington, D.C.

37. Washington, *Writings,* 29:514.

38. Mason, *Papers,* 3:1044–46.

CHAPTER XV

1. William Wirt Henry, *Patrick Henry: Life, Correspondence and Speeches,* 3 vols. (New York: Charles Scribner's Sons, 1891), 2:342.

2. Edmund Randolph to James Madison, 3 January 1788, Emmet Collection MS 9537, Manuscripts and Archives Division, The New York Public Library, Astor, Lenox and Tilden Foundations, New York, N.Y.

3. James Madison, *The Writings of James Madison,* ed. Gaillard Hunt, 9 vols. (New York and London: G. P. Putnam's Sons, 1900–1910), 5:121.

4. Max Farrand, ed., *The Records of the Federal Convention of 1787,* rev. ed., 4 vols. (New York and London: Yale University, 1966), 3:296.

5. Col. Edward Carrington to Gen. Henry Knox, 13 March 1788, Knox Papers, Massachusetts Historical Society, Boston, Mass.

6. David Robertson, comp., *Debates and Other Proceedings of the Convention of Virginia . . . June, 1788,* 3 vols. (Petersburg: Hunter and Prentis, vol. 1, 1788; Prentis, vols. 2–3, 1789), 1:35–36.

7. Ibid., p. 39.

8. George Mason, *The Papers of George Mason, 1725–1792,* ed. Robert A. Rutland, 3 vols. (Chapel Hill: University of North Carolina Press, 1971), 3:1050, 1054.

9. Robertson, *Debates,* 1:56–57.

10. Madison, *Writings,* 5:179n.

11. Mason, *Papers,* 3:1058.

12. Francis Wharton, ed., *The Revolutionary Diplomatic Correspondence of the United States,* 6 vols. (Washington, D.C.: U.S. Government Printing Office, 1889), 5:630.

13. Henry, *Patrick Henry,* 2:360.

14. Theodorick Bland to Arthur Lee, 13 June 1788, Richard H. Lee, *Life of Arthur Lee,* 2 vols. (Boston: Wells and Lilly, 1829), 2:337–38.

15. Mason, *Papers,* 3:1082.

16. Ibid., pp. 1083–84.

17. Ibid., p. 1086.

18. Ibid., p. 1106.

19. Robertson, *Debates,* 3:127–28.

20. Archibald Stuart to John Breckinridge, 19 June 1788, Breckinridge Papers, Manuscript Division, Library of Congress, Washington, D.C.

21. Madison, *Writings,* 5:216.

22. Ibid., p. 226.

23. Robertson, *Debates,* 3:170–71.

24. Ibid., pp. 178–79.

25. Ibid., p. 189.

26. Ibid., p. 212.

27. Randolph of Roanoke to his stepfather, St. George Tucker, 30 July 1788, Emmet Collection MS 9582, Manuscripts & Archives Division, The New York Public Library, Astor, Lenox and Tilden Foundations, New York, N.Y.

28. Madison, *Writings,* 5:234.

29. Ibid., pp. 271–72.

30. Thomas Jefferson, *The Papers of Thomas Jefferson,* ed. Julian P. Boyd, 19 vols. to date (Princeton: Princeton University Press, 1950–), 14:659.

CHAPTER XVI

1. Marie Joseph Paul Yves Roch Gilbert du Motier, Marquis de Lafayette, to William Temple Franklin, 19 November 1783, Franklin Papers, vol. CV, no. 152, American Philosophical Society, Philadelphia, Pa.

2. Pierre Samuel du Pont to Voltaire, 1 September 1769, MSS Cde 236, f. 4, Bibliothèque Nationale, Paris.

3. Thomas Jefferson, *The Papers of Thomas Jefferson,* ed. Julian P. Boyd, 19 vols. to date (Princeton: Princeton University Press, 1950–), 14:366.

4. Ibid., p. 437.

5. Ibid., 15:255.

6. Ibid., pp. 118–19.

7. Marie Jean Antoine-Nicholas de Caritat, Marquis de Condorcet, "Eloge de Franklin," *Oeuvres,* ed. A. Condorcet O'Connor and F. Arago, 12 vols. (Paris: Didot Franks, 1847–49), 3:399–400.

8. Thomas Paine, *The Works of Thomas Paine,* 2 vols. (Philadelphia: Carey, 1797), 2:149.

9. Condorcet, "Esquisse d'un tableau," *Oeuvres,* 6:199.

10. "Idées sur le despotisme," ibid., 9:168.

11. Jefferson, *Papers,* 14:437.

12. John Adams, *Diary and Autobiography of John Adams,* ed. Lyman Butterfield, 4 vols. (Cambridge, Mass.: Belknap Press of Harvard University Press, 1961), 2:293–94.

13. George Mason, *The Papers of George Mason, 1725–1792,* ed. Robert A. Rutland, 3 vols. (Chapel Hill: University of North Carolina Press, 1971), 3:1151.

14. Joseph Fenwick to Capt. Ignatius Fenwick, 11 October 1788, Fenwick Papers, MS 1011, Maryland Historical Society, Baltimore, Md.

15. John Mason, John Mason Papers, microfilm, Manuscript Division, Library of Congress, Washington, D.C.

16. Mason, *Papers,* 3:1138.

17. Ibid., p. 1153.

18. Ibid., pp. 1136–37.

19. Ibid., p. 1204.

20. Ibid., pp. 1171–72.

21. Jefferson, *Papers,* 15:278.

22. Ibid., p. 279.

23. Mason, *Papers,* 3:1194–95.

24. Ibid., pp. 1196, 1198.

25. Ibid., pp. 1203–4.

26. Premier registre des Verbaux de la Société des amis de la Constitution depuis le 16 avril 1790 jusqu'au 10 juillet 1791, 31 juillet 1790, Archives départementales, Bordeaux, France.

27. Mason, *Papers,* 3:1217.

CHAPTER XVII

1. George Mason, *The Papers of George Mason, 1725–1792,* ed. Robert A. Rutland, 3 vols. (Chapel Hill: University of North Carolina Press, 1971), 3:1236.

2. Ibid., p. 1269.

3. Jackson T. Main, "The One Hundred," *William and Mary Quarterly,* 3rd ser. 11, no. 3 (July 1954): 354–84.

4. William Loughton Smith, "Journal of William Loughton Smith from Philadelphia to Charleston, April-May, 1791," Massachusetts Historical Society, *Proceedings* 51 (October 1917): 64.

5. George Washington, *The Diaries of George Washington, 1748–1799,* ed. John C. Fitzpatrick, 4 vols. (Boston and New York: Houghton Mifflin Co., 1925), 3:440–41.

6. Mason, *Papers,* 3:1142.

7. Ibid., pp. 1160–61.

8. Ibid., p. 1218.

9. Thomas Jefferson, *The Writings of Thomas Jefferson,* ed. Paul Leicester Ford, 10 vols. (New York and London: G. P. Putnam's Sons, 1892–99), 6:186–87.

10. Mason, *Papers,* 3:1172.

11. Ibid., p. 1191.

12. Ibid., p. 1192.

13. Ibid., p. 1273.

14. Ibid., pp. 1188–89.

15. Jefferson, *Papers,* 16:493.

16. Mason, *Papers,* 3:1218.

17. Jefferson, *Writings,* 6:186.

18. Mason, *Papers,* 3:1256–57.

19. Jefferson, *Papers,* 16:493.

20. George Washington, *The Writings of George Washington, 1745–1799,* ed. John C. Fitzpatrick, 39 vols. (Washington, D.C.: U.S. Government Printing Office, 1931–44), 32:95.

21. Ibid., p. 97.

22. Alexander Hamilton, *The Papers of Alexander Hamilton,* ed. Harold C. Syrett, 19 vols. to date (New York and London: Columbia University Press, 1961–), 12:249–50.

23. Ibid., p. 254.

24. Ibid., pp. 254, 257.

25. Jefferson, *Writings,* 1:202.

26. Ibid., 6:114.

27. James Monroe, *The Writings of James Monroe,* ed. Stanislaus Murray Hamilton, 7 vols. (New York, 1898; New York: AMS Press, 1969), 1:245–46.

28. Washington, *Writings,* 32:200.

29. Fairfax County, Va., Will Book F, No. 1.

30. Henry Home, Lord Kames, *Principles of Equity,* 2nd ed. (London: A. Millar, 1776; Edinburgh: Kincaid & Bell, 1776), p. 36.

31. James Madison, *The Writings of James Madison,* ed. Gaillard Hunt, 9 vols. (New York and London: G. P. Putnam's Sons, 1900–10), 9:293–95.

32. Jefferson, *Writings,* 1:65.

33. Mason, *Papers,* 1:159.

# Index

## A

Abridgments of laws in force in Va., 27; Mercer's *Abridgment,* 27–28
Adam, Robert, 73
Adams, Abigail, 146, 222
Adams, John, 130, 165, 222, 254, 267, 281, 332; as Mass. delegate to First Continental Congress, 109; on preference for republic, 133; on Declaration of Independence, 142, 146; principal author of Massachusetts Declaration of Rights, 154–55; *Thoughts on Government,* 156–57, 159; on composition of Congress, 198; ambassador to London, 222, 232; in Paris, 304; in Bordeaux, 310
Adams, John Quincy, 255; in Paris, 304
Adams, Samuel, 95, 110, 254, 275, 277; Mass. delegate to First Continental Congress, 109; and the Lees, 110; in Mass. ratifying convention, 275
Aderton, Joseph, 40
Albemarle County, Va., 38, 108, 181, 295
Alden, Ebenezer, 222
Alexander, Gerald, 34
Alexander, Philip: trustee of Alexandria, 34; elected to Va. Assembly, 165
Alexandria, Va., 35, 63, 64, 69, 73, 74, 80, 84, 85, 86, 114, 122, 128, 163, 202, 208, 217, 229, 230, 270, 272, 274, 281, 297, 310, 318, 319, 320, 329; establishment of, 18, 33–34; Mason a trustee of, 63, 75; growth of, 75–77; formation of municipal government of, 76; county court moved to, 76–77
Alleghany Mountains, 153, 177, 178, 284
Amendments: prior vs. subsequent as issue of ratification, 275, 295. *See also* Constitution (U.S.)
*American Congress* (ship), 136
Amherst, Lord Jeffrey, 66
Amis de la Constitution, 315; John Mason a member of, 318
Amis de la Liberté et l'Egalité, 315
Analostan Island, 34, 226, 318; John Mason inherits, 329
Anglican clergy, in Va., 7–9; payment of, in tobacco, 72; affluence among, 73, 122; loyalists among, 122; tithes for, repealed, 201; disposal of property of, 201–2. *See also* Parson's Cause; Church of England
Annapolis, Md., 45, 95, 156, 221, 225, 229, 318
Annapolis Convention, 231, 242; failure of, 231, 233; and call for Federal Convention, 231–2
Anti-Federalists, 278; in N.H., 271; publications by, 272; in Mass., 277; in Ky., 284; in Va., 284, 285, 290, 291, 292, 299; in Piedmont, 284; in Southside, Va., 284
Appalachian Mountains, 65, 248
Aquia Church, 54, 60
Aquia Creek, 47, 80
Araby. *See* Mattawoman

Architecture: in England in early eighteenth century, 44–45; brick used in colonial Va., 47; wood used in, 47; Chinese influence, 50–51
"Arms of Fairfax" tavern (Colchester), 35
Arnold, Benedict, 192, 222; as British colonel, 205; at Westover, 205; destroys Richmond, 205
Arrell, David, 76, 103
Atkinson, Roger, 108
Augusta County, 38, 39, 295, 296, 319
Aylett, William, 165

## B

Bacon's Rebellion, 4, 258
Balance of powers: debated in Federal Convention, 245. *See also* Constitution (U.S.); Separation of powers
Ballendine, John: *Proposals,* 87
Baltimore, the lords, 9, 39, 181
Baltimore, Md., 269; Confederation Congress meeting in, 198
Banister, Col. John, 166
Banks: establishment of, Hamilton's plan for, 220, 325
Baptists: in Va., 85, 86
Barbadoes, 34, 72. *See also* Analostan Island
Barbé-Marbois, François, marquis de, 304
Barnes, Elizabeth Mary Ann: marriage to George Mason's son George, 225
Barnes, Sarah: marriage to Thomas Mason, 225
Bartlett, Josiah, 146
Bastille: storming of, 315–16
Bratty, John, 215
Beaumarchais, Pierre Augustin Caron de, 109
Bedford, duke of, 37
Bedford, Gunning, Jr., 247
Belhaven: supplanted by Alexandria, 34.
Belvoir, 34, 47, 60, 121
Berckel, Pieter Johan van, 232; on Mass. ratification formula, 278
Berkeley, Edmund, 108
Berkeley, Sir William, 47
Berkeley County, 296
Beverley, Robert: *History and Present State of Virginia,* 13; on slavery, 13; *Abridgment of the Public Laws of Virginia,* 27
Big Knives, 187; Indian name for Kentuckians, 188
Bill of Rights (American States): in Va., 147–53; in other colonies, 153–55; translated into French, 304
Bill of Rights (England) of 1689, 24, 32; influence on Virginia Declaration of Rights, 148
Bill of Rights (U.S.): relation to Va. Declaration of Rights, 300; amended to Constitution, 300
Bladensburg, Md., 95
Blainville, Pierre Joseph Céloron de, 63
Blair, Rev. James, 8, 10

Blair, John, Sr.: acting governor of Va., 99; death of, 120
Blair, John, Jr., 95, 149, 261, 264, 269, 300; delegate to Federal Convention, 233, 234; and Va. constitution, 240; judge of Va. Court of Appeals, 240; against one-man executive, 250; against proposed trade measures, 251; against Mason's proposal for overriding presidential veto, 258
Bland, Richard, 114; elected to First Continental Congress, 108; declined election to Second Continental Congress, 118; elected to Va. Committee of Safety, 120; death of, 198
Bland, Theodorick, 166, 292; on outcome of Va. ratifying convention, 292, 291
Blount, William, 248, 265
Blue Licks, battle of, 192, 194
Blue Ridge Mountains, 23, 153, 178
Board of Custom Commissioners of the Revenue (Boston), 95
Board of Trade and Plantations (London), 23, 94; and Ohio Co., 37, 66
Board of War: established by Confederation Congress, 172
Boggess, Robert, 55, 56, 82; vestryman of Pohick Church, 55; race course managed by, 55
Boone, Daniel, 182; wounded at Blue Licks, 192
Bordeaux, 166, 208, 315, 316, 318, 320, 321; description of, in late eighteenth century, 310–11; primacy of, in overseas commerce, 311, 313
Boscobel, 3, 4
Boston, 95, 102, 107, 109, 121, 238, 275, 277, 310; fatalities in, 98; closing of port of, 101, 106–7; relief to, 103, 106; destruction of tea in, 107; held by General Gage, 109, 116; evacuated by Gage, 121; American recovery of, 136
*Boston Gazette*, 90
Boston Port Act, 101, 106
Botetourt, Norborne Berkeley, baron de, 66, 95, 98; named governor of Va., 95; dissolves House of Burgesses, 95; death of, 99
Bouquet, Col. Henry, 65
Bourbon court, 301, 306
Bowdoin, James, 133
Braddock, Gen. Edward, 64, 88
Bradford, William, 150
Brandywine, battle of, 167
Braxton, Carter, 116, 124, 160; election to Va. Committee of Safety, 120; on continental unity and foreign support, 138; on Va. congressional delegation, 157; *Address to the Convention,* aristocratic government proposal of, 157
Breckinridge, John, 295
Brent, George, 9, 10, 208; and Catholics in Stafford, 9
Brent, Giles, 9, 18
Brent, Robert, 137
Brent, Sarah: marriage to George Mason, 208. *See also* Mason, Sarah Brent
Brent, William: elected to Va. Convention of 1776, 137; house of, destroyed by Dunmore's fleet, 163
Brent family, 9, 11, 26, 60
Brewood, 3
Broadwater, Charles, 104, 105, 108, 220
Bronaugh, Jeremiah, 33
Bronaugh, Simpha Rosa, 64

Bronaugh, William, 64
Brown, Congressman John, 186
Brown, John, 222
Brown, Isaac Hawkins: *Of Smoking,* 12
Bruton Parish, 80
Bruton Parish Church, 140
Buchanan, Andrew, 124
Buchanan family, 16, 17
Buckland, James, 44
Buckland, John, 44
Buckland, William, 44, 49, 51; architectural influences on, 44–45; indentured to George Mason, 45; portrait of, 45; architectural books owned by, 45, 47, influence of Chinese design on, 50–51
Buford, Col. Abraham, 204
Bull, William, 120
Burgoyne, Gen. John: surrender at Saratoga, 167
Burnaby, Andrew, 69 *Travels Through the Middle Settlements,* 35; description of Williamsburg by, 71
Butler, Pierce, 280
Byrd, Maria Willing, 205
Byrd, William II, 13, 25
Byrd, William III, 120

C
Cabell, William, 220; elected to Va. Committee of Safety, 120; named as Henry's second in threatened duel with Randolph, 291
Cadwalader, Lambert, 282
Cahokia, 178; taken by Gorge Rogers Clark, 187
Calvert, George, Lord Baltimore, 9
Campbell, Arthur, 220
Camden, battle of, 204
Cameron, Lt. Allen, 128
Cameron parish, 33
Camm, Rev. John, 72
Campbell, William, 204
Canada, 199; British replace French in, 178; French surrender of, 179
Canals, 177–78, 181–226
"Candidus": response to *Common Sense,* 133
Cape Company, The, 99
Cape Hatteras, 122
Caribbean Islands, 166
Carleton, Sir Guy, 184
Carlyle, John, 69, 73, 75; trustee of Alexandria, 34; in French and Indian War, 64; as Presbyterian, 86
Carlyle, Sarah Fairfax, 34
Carlyle House Conference, 88
Caroline County, 86, 181, 194
Carr, Dabney, 110
Carrington, Edward, 268, 280, 282; on Mass. ratification formula, 278; on Henry's oratorical powers, 288
Carrington, Paul, 124, 136; elected to Va. Committee of Safety, 120
Carroll, Daniel, 266, 269
Carter, Charles, 137
Carter, Landon, 37, 47, 214; diary of, 72, 86, 136; response to *Commn Sense,* 133–34
Carter, Robert, 36, 66, 74, 182; letter book of, 37; response to Madison's *Memorial and Remonstrance,* 217–18; opposition to general assessment bill, 217–18
Carter, Robert Wormeley, 37

Cary, Archibald, 89, 108, 138, 170, 210; chairman, committee on, Va. constitution and bill of rights, 139
Cary, Sally: marries George William Fairfax, 60
Cary Committee, 140, 142, 147, 156, 158
"Cassius," 272
*Catherine* (ship), 35
Catholics: in Md., 9; in Va., 9, 77; barred from public office, 77
Cedar Grove, 60, 225
"Centinel's" letters, 271
Chalmers, James: *Plain Truth,* 133
Chambers, William: *Designs for Chinese Buildings,* 51
Chantilly, 282
Chapman, Nathaniel, 37
Charles I (Eng.), 9, 11, 12, 32, 151
Charles II (Eng.), 3–4, 11
Charles III (Spain), 177
Charles VII (France), 311
Charles County, Md., 11, 39, 40, 41, 56, 129, 329
Charleston, S.C., 84, 121, 133, 310, 320; occupation of, 122, 194; fall of, 203, 204
Charlotte County: instructions to delegates, 136–37
Charlottesville, Va., 201, 210
Chase, Samuel, 229
Chastellux, François Jean, marquis de: *Travels in North America,* 222
Cherokee Indians, 68, 182
Chesapeake Bay, 4, 5, 122, 127, 128, 210, 226, 230; British blockade of, 166; protection of, 197
Chesapeake Capes, 17
Chew, Benjamin, 235
Chew, Joseph, 119
Chichester, Sarah: marries Thomson Mason, 225
Chickamuxen Creek, 11, 25
Chillicothe: Clarke destroys, 192
Chippendale, Thomas, 50
*Chisholm* v. *Georgia,* 295
Chopawamsic, 25, 30, 74
Christ Church, Alexandria, 80
Church of England: established church in Va., 7, 8, 122; attendance at required by law, 8, 79; churches in Fairfax County, 84; statutory salaries to clergy suspended, 164; during and after Revolution, 216–18. *See also* Anglican clergy
Civil War (England), 3
"Civis Rusticus," 272
Clark, Edmund, 194
Clark, George Rogers, 175, 177–96 passim; Va. support for military activities of, 170, 172; and Mason, 177; account of Illinois expedition of, 186–91
Clark, John, Sr., 86
Clark, John, Jr., 194
Clark, Jonathan, 86, 194, 196
Clark, Richard, 194
Clark, William, 194
Clay, Charles, 287
Clergy, Anglican. *See* Anglican clergy
Clermont, 73
Clinton, George, 267, 275, 298
Clinton, Gen. Sir Henry, 210
Clyde, River (Scotland), 16, 17, 124
Cockburn, Martin, 59, 82, 84, 101, 112, 118, 226; and Mason, 59–60; and Mason's children, 100; as executor

of Mason's will, 330
Coffer, John, 330
Coke, Sir Edward, 31–32; *Reports,* 31; *Abridgment of Littleton,* 32
Colchester, Va., 35, 36, 47, 68, 122, 225, 322; establishment of, 18; incorporation of, 34–35
Colden, Cadwalader, 120
Colle, 87
College of New Jersey, 85, 150. *See also* Princeton University
*Columbia Mirror and Gentleman's Magazine,* 329
Committee of Law Revisors (Va.), 163–65, 214, 240, 274; *Report* of, 165, 214, 215
Committees of Correspondence, 102, 110; created in Va., 110
*Common Sense* (Paine), 131; publication of, 131; effect of publication of, 133–34; translated into French, 304
Condorcet, Antoine Nicholas, marquis de, 307, 308, 316; and French declaration of rights, 307; death of, 307; influence of American Revolution on, 307; "Eloge de Franklin," 307; *Sketch for an Historical Picture of the Progress of the Human Mind,* 308; on European impact of the American Revolution, 308; *Ideas on Despotism,* 308; on George Mason, 308
Confederation, 138, 206, 221, 227, 242, 296; definition of, 199; and western lands, 198–99, 206; weaknesses of, 199, 204, 221–22, 240, 243, 244, 274, 290–91; Washington on, 204; in force, 207; debts of, 291, 292
Confederation, Articles of, 206, 220, 240, 241, 242, 243, 246, 288, 294; unanimity required for ratification of, 198, Maryland's delay in signing, 198–99; become binding in 1781, 199, 207; powers to states and Congress under, 199; revision of, authorized by Congress, 233, 238; voting rules under, 238–39; Va. plan on ratification of amendments to, 241–42; on tenure of president, 245; and slavery, 294
Confederation Congress, 127, 128, 184, 185, 204, 230, 242, 254, 335; in York, Pa., 198; in Baltimore, 198; requisitions states, 202, 203, 220; resolution of, on ceded territory, 207; proposal by Jefferson on slavery in new states, 215; prohibits slavery in Northwest Territory, 215, in Annapolis, 218; powers of under Articles of Confederation, 199, 221, 222, 228; and tax powers, 220–21; authorizes Federal Convention, 233; and Mississippi navigation rights, 292
Connecticut, 133, 154, 226, 234, 243, 246, 252, 262, 264; colonial charter of, 199; proposals in Federal Convention, 247, 250; proponents of Constitution in, 267–68; ratifies Constitution, 271
Connolly, John, 128–29; Connolly affair, 129
Constable, David, 207
Constituent Assembly (France), 301, 306
Constitution (U.S.), 24, 155, 229, 266, 268, 301; objections to final draft of, 261–63; adopted by majority of state delegations to Federal Convention, 264; struggle for ratification of, 266–68, 271–97 passim; opposition to, 266–67, 268, 270, 271, 272, 274; departure of, from Articles of Confederation, 268, 288; ratification of, by state conventions, 270–71; publications for and against, 271, 272; provision for amending, 274–75; and reservation of powers to states, 275; Mass. formula for ratification of, 275, 277; challenged as ultra vires, 288; judiciary article of,

294–95; eleventh amendment to, 295; first ten amendments to, ratified by states, 300. *See also* Anti-Federalists, Federal Convention, Federalists

Continental Congress, First, 110, 114, 121, 242, 302, 335; Va. resolution to call, 102, 108; call for in Fairfax Resolves, 107; permits exports in exchange for ammunition, 118; adjournment of, 143

Continental Congress, Second, 136, 143; calls for General Fast, 140; receives Va. resolution for independence, 142; Jefferson becomes draftsman of declaration, 142–43; votes on Lee's motion, 146; debates wording, 146–47; completes document, 147

Conway, Thomas, 172

Cooke, John, 225

Copein, William, 80, 82

Corbin, Francis, 270, 287, 291, 292

Corbin, Richard, 93, 120

Cornwallis, Charles Cornwallis, marquess of, 204, 205; defeated at Yorktown, 210

*Courant* (Conn.), 271

Cowpens, battle of, 204

Craik, Dr. James, 172

Crawford, William, 181

Cresap, Thomas, 37, 38

Cresswell, Nicholas, 105, 126–27

Croghan, George, 39, 128

Cromwell, Oliver, 3, 101, 151

Cumberland, Prince Henry-Frederick, duke of, 95

Cumberland County: instructions to delegates, 136

Cunninghame, William, 123

Currency: depreciation of, 166, 168, 170, 203, 219; retired by Congress, 203. *See also* Inflation

Currie, James, 302

Custis, John Parke (Jacky), 168, 173

Custis, Martha Dandridge: marries George Washington, 60. *See also* Washington, Martha Dandridge Custis

Custis, Patsy, 61

Cutler, Manasseh, 238, 239

D

Dade, Francis, 78–79

Dalton, John, 34, 75, 135; on Fairfax Committee of Surveillance, 99; and Potomac Navy, 135

Dane, Nathan, 268, 290

Darrell, Sampson, 78

Daveiss, Joseph H., 332

Davies, Samuel, 85, 150

Davis, John, 35

Dawson, John, 287, 296

Deane, Silas, 304

de Berdt, Dennys, 110

Debt assumption: Hamilton's plans for, 325, 328; objections to, in Va., 325

*Déclaration des droits l'homme*, 301; influence of American documents on, 155; and *Déclaration européene*, 301; adopted by Frence Assembly, 301; emphasis of on universals, 307; and Va. Declaration of Rights, 308–9

*Déclaration européene*, 301, 302

Declaration of independence (Va.), 138–39; divided reactions to, 136; timing of, 138

Declaration of Independence, 146–47, 152, 167, 175, 212, 240, 242, 281, 301, 308; committee chosen to draft, 142; influence of Va. Declaration of Rights on, 146; S.C. and Pa. against on first vote, 146; unanimous endorsement of, 146; debate on Jefferson's draft of, 146–47

Declaration of Rights and Grievances (Stamp Act Crisis), 91

Declaratory Act, 93–94, 98; Mason's response to, 94

Deep South, 251, 271, 294

Delaware, 121, 153, 198, 199, 226, 231, 235, 245, 259, 262; divided on first vote for independence, 146; delegation to Federal Convention, 245; first to ratify Constitution, 270

Delaware Declaration of Rights, 151

*Delaware Gazette,* 269

Delaware Indians, 65, 185

Dering, William, 30

Detroit, 128, 178, 183, 184, 185, 187, 190; failure of plan to take, 192; British occupation of, 192

Dickinson, John, 110, 235, 243; "Letters from a Farmer in Pennsylvania," 95; plan of for confederation, 198; chairs Annapolis Convention, 231; "Letters of Fabius," 271

Digges, Dudley, 110, 120, 138

Dinwiddie, Robert, 38, 64, 65, 66, 72, 74, 93; and Ohio Company, 38–39, 66

Disestablishment, 202; Madison on, 150–51, 152; opposition to, 150; accomplished, 215–18

Dixon, Jeremiah, 181

Dixon and Hunter's *Virginia Gazette*, 148–49; Braxton's government plan published in, 157

Dobbs, Arthur, 37

Doeg Indians, 4

Dogue's Neck, 22, 35, 39, 41, 43, 47, 56, 59, 225–26, 329; Mason settles in, 33, 41

Donald, Alexander, 282

Dorchester, Guy Carleton, baron, 245

Dufart, J.-B., 313

Dulany, Daniel, 112, 121; *Considerations,* 121

Dumfries, 35, 60, 69, 73, 122, 322; establishment of, 18, 33; Mason as a trustee of, 33, 39; county seat of Prince William, 36; description of life in, 36–37; manufacturing in, 37; decline of, 73; nonimportation and nonexportation resolves adopted at, 102

Dunlap's *Maryland Gazette and Baltimore Advertiser*, 271

*Dunmore* (ship), 35

Dunmore, John Murray, earl of, 120, 128, 135, 199; made governor of Va., 99, 102; dissolves House of Burgesses, 102, 103, 124; invests Norfolk, 109, 131; removes guns and ammunition from Williamsburg, 116; summons House of Burgesses, 116; retreats to *Fowey,* 116; driven off, 127; and Connolly affair, 128–29; declares martial law, 134; raids of, 134, 163; and Governor Eden of Md., 156

"Dunmore's Indian War," 116, 182

Du Pont, Pierre Samuel, 302

E

Eastern Shore, (Va.), 5

East India Company, 107

Eden, Governor (Md.), 156

Edgar, Joanna, 40

Edgar, John, 40

Edgar, Sarah. *See* Eilbeck, Sarah Edgar
Egremont, Sir Charles Wyndham, earl of, 13
Eilbeck, Ann. *See* Mason, Ann Eilbeck
Eilbeck, Sarah Edgar, 41; death of, 74, 206
Eilbeck, William, 40–41; death of, 74
Electoral college, 245
Ellicott family, 35
Ellsworth, Oliver, 246, 247, 268; proposes avoidance of slavery question, 252; on Committee of Detail, 256; proposal on proportionment of representation, 259–60; letters signed "A Landholder," 271; "Landholder Letter No. VI," 272–73; presents U.S. constitutional amendments to Senate, 300
Ellzey, William, 68
Enlightenment, Age of, 33, 130
Entail, 11, 153, 164
Eutaw Springs, battle of, 205
Executive branch. *See* Presidency (U.S.)
Exports, 16; cessation of tobacco, 107, 122–25; debate on taxation of, in Federal Convention, 250
Ex post facto laws: Va. Declaration of Rights on, 148; Mason on, 148, 262, 264

*F*
Fairfax, Bryan, 104, 106
Fairfax, George William, 60, 68, 69, 82, 84, 91; as trustee of Alexandria, 34; and Ohio Company, 37; marries Sally Cary, 60; as patriot, 121
Fairfax, Thomas, Lord, 11, 33, 39; as trustee of Alexandria, 34; death of, 121
Fairfax, William, 34, 47, 64; as trustee of Alexandria, 34; and Ohio Company, 37, 38; as head of Governor's Council, 38; son Henry, 64
Fairfax County Committee of Safety, 105, 112, 116, 129, 134, 135, 162, 166; Mason chairs, 110; Washington chairs, 112; taxes tithables for ammunition, 112; resolution of on militia, 112, 114; and military protection of coasts, 135; warns of need to stockpile salt, 135
Fairfax Committee of Surveillance, 99
Fairfax County, 33, 35, 55, 56, 63, 68, 69, 76, 79, 89, 91, 104, 135, 147, 166, 208, 217, 220, 221, 225, 258, 270, 281, 282, 284, 320, 329; formation of, 33; building of churches in, 80–82, 84; aid to Boston, 103; and petitions on debts and on credit control, 220; resentment of toward Mason, 270; calls for ratifying convention, 270; favors Constitution, 270
Fairfax County Committe of Correspondence, 126
Fairfax Independent Company of Volunteers: articles of associaton of, 110, 112; issue of election of officers in, 114–15
Fairfax parish, 79, 84, 86
Fairfax Resolves, 102, 103, 105, 130, 159; Mason and, 102, 105–7; on regulation of trade, 106; on taxes for defense of British Empire, 106; on taxation and representation, 106; on retention of colonial status, 106; on nonimportation, 107, 108; on continental union, 107; on slave trade, 107; on nonexportation, 107, 108; on court judgments for debt, 107
Falls Church, 80, 82
Farmers General (French), 17, 208
Fauquier, Francis, 65, 66, 72, 82, 89, 91, 92, 93; dissolves House of Burgesses, 91; death of, 95

Fauquier County, 109, 166; formation of, 5
Federal Convention, 229, 232–56 passim, 287, 302, 304, 306, 328; authorized by Congress, 233; Va. delegation to, 233; closed sessions of, 238–39, 242; voting rules governing, 239–40; Virginia Plan introduced in, 240–42; *Journal* of, 242; bases for unity in, 242–43; goes beyond revision of Articles of Confederation, 243; debate in, on popular participation in government, 244, 245; debate in, on tenure in upper house and executive, 244–45, 257–58; royalist sentiment in, 244–45; debate in, on powers of executive, 245; debate in, on electoral college, 245; debate in, on representation in legislature, 245–48; New Jersey Plan introduced in, 245; large vs. small states in, 245–46, 253–54; issue of slavery in, 246, 251–53, 254, 259; debate in, on relation of existing to new states, 248; new colonialism in, 248; sectionalism in, 248, 250–51; decides on one-man executive, 250, 257; debate in, on regulation of commerce, 250–51; South vs. North in, 250–51, 254; debate in, on relation of foreign policy and trade, 251; Committee of Detail, 256, 257, 258; Committee of Style, 256, 257, 262, 263; treason considered in, 258, 264; impeachment considered in, 258; power to override presidential veto considered in, 258; revisory council considered in, 258–59; vice-presidency considered in, 259; size of House of Representatives considered in, 259, 266, 274; salaries of representatives considered in, 259; elections of representatives considered in, 259, 260; proportionment of representation considered in, 259–60; qualifications for service in House of Representatives considered in, 260; extension of franchise considered in, 260; election of senators considered in, 260; qualifications for senators considered in, 260; on separation of powers, 260; tax power considered in, 260; on Congress's power to declare war, 260; and supremacy of U.S. over state law, 260; appointment of judges considered in, 261; and structure and powers of courts, 261; emergence of opposition in, 261–63; refusal to consider addition of a bill of rights, 262; sumptuary laws disapproved, 263; considers Committee of Style report, 263–64; on congressional power to charter companies, 264; on establishment of a university, 264; on standing armies, 264; on ex post facto laws, 264; on second convention, 264; Constitution signed in, 266; declared to have acted ultra vires, 268, 288–89; provides for amending Constitution, 274–75; contrast to Va. ratifying convention, 285–86
*Federal Gazette,* 273
*Federalist, The,* 271; translated into French, 304
Federalists, 278, 288, 292; publications by, 271, 272; in Mass., 275, 277; youth of, 277; in Northern Neck of Va., 282, 284; in Stafford County, 284; in Va., 284, 285, 288, 289, 290–91, 292, 295–96, 297; in Tidewater, Va., 284; in Shenandoah Valley, 284; and Patrick Henry, 288; and treaty power and navigation of Mississippi, 292
Fenwick, James, 310
Fenwick, Joseph, 310, 311, 312; in Bordeaux, 310, 312–13; on John Mason, 311–12; American consul in Bordeaux, 312–13
Fincastle County, 182, 183

Fithian, Philip: description of Dumfries life by, 36–37

Fitzhugh, Mary Mason, 64

Fitzhugh, William, 9, 10, 11, 18, 20, 21, 43; feoffee of Marlborough, 18

Fitzhugh, William III, 64

Five Knights' Case, 32

Fleming, Henry, 124

Fleming, Thomas, 76

Fleming, William, 136, 158

Forbes, Gen. John, 65, 178

Fort Cumberland, 64, 66, 87

Fort Duquesne, 64; recapture of by British, 65; renamed Fort Pitt, 65, 178. *See also* Fort Pitt

Fort Le Boeuf, 64, 72, 178

Fort Loudoun, 64

Fort Necessity, 64

Fort Pitt, 65, 128, 178, 183, 192

Fort Stanwix, treaty of, 199

*Fowey* (ship), 116

Fowke, Gerard, 3, 4, 56

Fowke, Susanna, 4

Fowke, Thomas, 4

Fowke family, 3, 4, 9

France, 3, 16, 313, 322; treaty of alliance with colonies, 173, 199, 281; Va. ratifies treaty of alliance with, 199; early proposals of reform in, 302; feudalism in, 306; royalty abolished in, 306; establishment of republic in, 307; Reign of Terror in, 307, 315, 318; National Assembly created in, 307; Legislative Assembly created in, 307

Franklin, Benjamin, 67, 110, 146–47, 209, 232, 233, 235, 238–39, 246, 266, 301, 302; as Pa. delegate to First Continental Congress, 109; and Thomas Paine, 130; and Declaration of Independence, 142; consoles Jefferson, 146–47; on Lord Kames, 152–53; negotiates alliance with France, 173; on consolidation of North America, 179; opposes Mason in Ohio country, 181; supports Mason's idea for privy council, 259; on Constitution, 265, 273

Franklin, William, 120

Frederick, Md., 128

Frederick County (Va.), 23, 39, 68, 69, 91

Fredericksburg, 116, 164 205 208 210

French, Daniel, 82, 99; death of, 82, 84

French and Indian War, 103, 168, 179, 181, 219, 310; disputes leading to, 63; called Seven Years' War in Europe, 64; taxation of colonies to support, 64; treaty ending, 66, 178

French fleet, 209–10

French Revolution, 301; American contributions to the *Déclaration des droits de l'homme,* 302–4, 308; contrast in philosophies, 308–9; dilemma of titled officers with American experience, 304–7; John Mason's reports on, 309, 315–18

French settlements in America, 177–78

French troops, 203; arrival of in America, 210

Fry, Col. Joshua, 64; and Loyal and Greenbriar Land companies, 38

G

Gadsby's tavern (Alexandria), 76

Gadsden, Christopher, 133, 275

Gage, Gen. Thomas, 109, 116; holds Boston, 109;

evacuates Boston, 121

Galloway, Joseph, 121

Gallow's Hill, 76

Gardoqui, Don Diego, 196, 227, 232; negotiations with John Jay, 227, 232

*Gaspee* incident, 101

Gates, Gen. Horatio, 172, 204

*General Armory* (Burke): on Mason arms, 225

*General Washington* (ship), 208

*Gentleman's Magazine,* 31; announcement of Mason's death in, 329

*Gentlemen's and Builders Repository on Architecture Displayed, Designs Regulated and Drawn by E. Hoppus, The,* 45, 47

Georgetown, Md., 73, 226, 318, 319, 328; establishment of, 18, 34

Georgia, 13, 154, 238, 242, 262, 264, 280; attempt to prohibit slavery in, 13; colonial charter of, 199; British offensive in, 203, 204; on voting rules for trade regulation, 250; slavery in, 251; ratifies constitution, 271

Germain, Lord George, 156

Germantown, battle of, 167, 194

Gerry, Elbridge, 242, 247, 256, 257, 261, 262, 267, 272, 275, 281, 310; on election of lower house, 244; and Mason, 254, 261, 263, 264; early political career of, 254; withholds signature from Constitution, 254, 264, 266; on size of House of Representatives, 259; opposed to constitution, 261, 267; moves to postpone consideration of constitution, 261; and Bill of Rights, 262; and Mass. ratifying convention, 277

Gibbs, James: *Book of Architecture,* 44

Gibson, Walter, 16

Gilman, Nicholas, 273

Gironde, Département de la, 315

Girondins (France), 315

Gist, Christopher: and Ohio Company, 38, 64; explores Ohio River, 38; and French and Indian War, 64

Glasgow, 16–17, 34, 35, 125; shipbuilding in, 16; and tobacco trade, 16–17, 18, 23; tobacco aristocracy of, 16–17; Mercer's *Abridgment* published in, 28; reaction of to American Revolution, 122–24

Glasgow Merchants House, 18

Glassford, John, 16, 35, 123

Glorious Revolution of 1688, 9, 24, 32, 130

Gooch, William, 37

Goodrich family: loyalists, 122, 197

Gorham, Nathaniel, 238, 242, 266; as chairman of Committee of the Whole in Federal Convention, 242

Governor's Council (Va.), 10, 28, 66, 68, 92; royal selection for, 7; and John Mercer, 28; veto of loan bill by, 89

Graham, John, 33

Grain: production of in Virginia, 73–74; shortages of, 197; distilling of forbidden, 197

Grand Ohio Company, 67

Grasse, Admiral François Joseph Paul, comte de, 210

Graves, Rear Admiral Thomas, 210

Grayson, William, 268, 290, 291, 292, 296; Anti-Federalist, 280; against ratification of the Constitution, 287; as U.S. senator from Va., 298; death of, 322

Great Lakes, 177–78, 215; British occupation of forts on, 192

Great Meadows, battle of, 64
Green, Rev. Charles, 33, 59, 73, 76, 81
Greenbriar Land Company, 32, 38
Greene, Maj. Gen. Nathanael, 204–5
Greenock (Scotland), 17
Greenway Court, 34
Grenville, George, 88
Grieve, George, 222
Griffin, Samuel, 315, 321
Guilford Courthouse, battle of, 205
Gunston, (Staffordshire, Eng.), 3, 56
Gunston Hall, 3, 23, 24, 43, 45–62 passim, 64, 74, 79, 99,
   100, 109, 162, 165, 177, 186, 191, 204, 207, 208, 218,
   223, 225, 228, 230, 233, 236, 240, 269, 309, 319, 320,
   321, 322, 328, 329, 330, 335; exterior of, 47–48;
   interior of, 49–53; grounds of, 54, 58–59; as working
   plantation, 55–56; origin of name of, 56; replenishing
   of, 208; prospect of attack on, 208–9
Gunston Hall (Charles County, Md.), 56

H
Hagerstown, Md., 128
Hamilton, Alexander, 220, 232, 238, 242, 246, 277, 295;
   on independent tax powers, 220; on regulation of
   banks, 220; on regulation of commerce, 220; favors
   import duty, 221; at Annapolis Convention, 231;
   royalism of, 244, 324; on Committe of Style, 256; plea
   of for unanimity in signing Constitution, 266; The
   Federalist, 271; and ratification celebration in New
   York City, 297; as secretary of the treasury, 324;
   economic proposals of, 324–25; defends debt
   assumption plan, 328
Hamilton, Lt. Col. Henry, 184; plans to engage Indians
   as British allies, 184; regains Vincennes, 189;
   surrenders to George Rogers Clark, 190, 191
Hammond, Matthias, 45
Hampden-Sydney College, 284
Hampshire County, 23, 69
Hampton Roads, 5, 122, 210; British warships in, 203
Hanbury, John, 37
Hancock, John, 275, 278; as president of Congress, 133,
   199; signs Declaration of Independence, 147; as
   president of Mass., 277
Hanover County, 73, 85, 98, 90, 182, 218; Virginia
   Committee of Safety meets in, 134
Hanover County Committee, 116
Hanoverians, 11
Hanover Presbytery, 85
Hardwicke, Philip Yorke, earl of, 332
Hardy, Samuel, 215
Harrison, Benjamin, 95, 160, 170, 194, 210, 218, 275,
   299; elected to First Continental Congress, 108;
   elected to Second Continental Congress, 118;
   governor of Va., 192, 212; speaker of Va. House, 198;
   in Va. ratifying convention, 285; Anti-Federalist, 285;
   against ratification of the Constitution, 287; on prior
   amendment of the Constitution, 296
Harrodsburg, 183
Hartshorne, William, 310, 320
Harvie, John, 38, 227
Headright certificates, 9, 169, 170
Henderson, Alexander, 35, 56, 84, 123, 220; as Fairfax

County justice, 56; and nonimportation, 99; as
   delegate to Md. trade negotiation, 229, 230
Henderson, Judge Richard: land speculation of, 182–83
Henry, Patrick, 85, 95, 101, 116, 124, 137, 153, 157, 163,
   166, 167, 170, 175, 183, 184, 273, 275, 280, 281, 284,
   285, 286, 289, 296, 297, 298; and Parson's Cause, 73,
   89, 217; eloquence of, 73, 89, 101, 114, 143, 217, 288,
   290, 296; elected to House of Burgesses from Louisa
   County, 89; speech against Stamp Act, 89–90;
   dismissal of from House of Burgesses, 90; elected to
   First Continental Congress, 108; and Va. Committee
   of Correspondence, 110; at Va. Convention of 1775,
   114; as governor of Va., 127, 160, 183, 198, 217, 218;
   in Va. Convention of 1776, 138; on continental unity,
   143; on disestablishment, 150; on Braxton's
   governmental plan, 157; and George Rogers Clark,
   183, 184–85, 185–86, 191; turns conservative, 216; and
   state support of religion, 216; and general assessment
   act, 216; and Statute for Religious Freedom, 218; and
   debts to British subjects, 220; on issuing new paper
   money, 228; calls for interstate trade conference, 231;
   declines election to Federal Convention, 233, 287; and
   amendment of Constitution, 270; against ratification
   of Constitution, 287; against strong central
   government, 287; challenges Constitution as ultra
   vires, 288–89; on liberties assured by bill of rights,
   290, 291, 295; threat of duel with Edmund Randolph,
   291; on Mississippi navigation rights, 292; introduces
   Constitutional amendments, 296; concedes to
   Federalists in Va. ratifying convention, 296–97
Hesselius, John, 41
Hewitt, Richard, 30
Hillsborough, Wills Hill, viscount, 98
Hodgson, William, 319
Hollin Hall, 7, 226
Holt's Creek, 56
House of Burgesses (Va.), 5, 7, 8, 10, 13, 23, 25, 63, 69,
   72, 77, 87, 88, 95, 96, 102, 108, 116; attempts to
   regulate tobacco, 17; and establishment of towns, 18,
   33–34; Mason a member of, 63, 68; elections to, 68,
   69, 89; and proposal to seek loan from England, 88;
   Committee on Privileges and Elections, 98, 90;
   resolutions of against Stamp Act, 89–90; dissolved by
   Fauquier, 91; denounces transporting of Mass.
   citizens for trial, 95; dissolved by Botetourt, 95;
   petitions king, 98; sets fast day, 101; dissolved by
   Dunmore, 102, 103, 124; final meetings of, 116
House of Commons, 10, 31, 95; and Five Knights' Case,
   31–32
House of Lords, 10, 124–25
House of Representatives (U.S.), 248, 300, 301; Va. plan
   on election of, 241; Mason on, 244; debate on
   representation in Federal Convention, 245–48; Conn.
   proposal on, 247; origination of appropriations in,
   247, 260; size of, 259, 266, 274; salaries of, 259;
   qualifications for service in, 260; election of by direct
   ballot, 260; organization of, 300; consideration of
   amendments by, 300; sends proposed amendments to
   Senate, 300
How, Peter, 40
Howe, General Sir William, 121, 136
Howe, Admiral Richard, earl, 127

Humphreys, David, 280
Hunting Creek, 34
Huntington, Gov. Samuel (Conn.), 268
Hutchins, Thomas, 178; *Topographical Description,* 178
Hutchinson, Anne, 151
Hutchinson, Thomas, 120

I

Ildefonso, treaty of, 177
Impeachment: considered in Federal Convention, 258
Imports, 16; availability of in colonial Va., 35; debate on taxation of, in Federal Convention, 250; Mason advocates sumptuary laws to curb, 260–61
Independence Day, 247
*Independent Chronicle* (Richmond), 273, 280, 298; profederalist material in, 271; *The Federalist* advertised in, 271
*Independent Gazette* (Pa.), 272
Indiana Company, 199, 207
Indian Queen tavern (Alexandria), 76
Indian Queen tavern (Philadelphia), 235, 238, 240
Indians, 4, 39, 64, 66, 183, 186; along Potomac, 4; trade with, 178; in Northwest Territory, 179, 184; British plan to engage as allies, 184; George Rogers Clark neutralizes, 188; destroy town of Chillicothe, 192; purchases of land from, 199. *See also* Cherokee Indians, Delaware Indians, Doeg Indians, Iroquois Indians, Potomac Indians, Susquehannock Indians, Wabache Indians
Inflation, 167, 168, 202, 203
Innes, Harry, 332
Innes, James, 287, 296
Iroquois Indians, 37

J

Jackson, Gen. Henry, 277, 278
James I, 12, 90
James II, 9
James River, 5, 23, 116, 205
Jamestown, 6, 7, 47
Jarratt, Rev. Devereux, 6
Jay, John, 277, 284, 290; Mississippi negotiations with Spain, 227, 284, 292; *The Federalist,* 271
Jenifer, Daniel of St. Thomas, 229
Jefferson, Peter, 181; and Loyal and Greenbriar land companies, 38
Jefferson, Thomas, 87, 90, 101, 108, 114, 116, 127, 135, 137, 142, 147, 149, 152, 153, 165, 167, 168, 179, 197, 198, 200, 202, 210, 219, 227, 240, 274, 278, 281, 284, 298, 302, 308, 309, 312, 315, 321, 329, 334; *Garden Book,* 59, 86; "Summary View of the Rights of British America," 108, 130; as draftsman of Declaration of Independence, 142–43, 281; and Va. Committee of Correspondence, 110; elected to Second Continental Congress, 118; on importance of Va. affairs, 143, 146, 163; influence of Va. Declaration of Rights on, 146; and debate on draft of Declaration of Independence, 146–47; and Va. constitution, 146, 157–58, 160, 161; and preamble to Va. constitution, 158, 160; on suffrage, 160; on representation, 160; on slavery, 161, 215; and nonimportation statute, 161; on Va. seal, 161; and bill on superior courts, 163; and Committee of Law Revisors, 163, 164, 165, 201; and

bill abolishing entails, 164; and land office bill, 169–70; and George Rogers Clark, 172, 183–84, 192–93; and western lands, 183; as Va. governor, 192, 198; proposes general public education, 201; Va. Assembly investigation of, 211, 213; as ambassador to France, 215, 222, 268, 280–81; and religious freedom, 215–16, 218; correspondence of, with Madison, 218–19, 282, 299–300, 302, 308, 328; Statute for Religious Freedom, 218, 299; and reconstruction of Monticello, 223; on Mass. ratification formula, 275; Va. and ratification struggle, 280–82; on proposal for second convention, 282; favors conditional ratification, 282; and bill of rights, 282, 298–99, 299–300; on judiciary, 299–300; on separation of powers, 299; participates in French revolutionary constitution-making, 302; on French bill of rights, 302; and Lafayette, 302, 304, 306; *Notes on Virginia,* 304; on constitutional monarchy in France, 306; on Lafayette's *Déclaration,* 308; as American secretary of state, 312, 315, 322, 324; on French Revolution, 316; on U.S. fiscal policy, 324; on representation in lower house, 324; on Hamilton's debt assumption plan, 325; last visit of, with Mason, 328–29; tribute to Mason, 333; *Autobiography,* 333
Johnson, Joshua, 225
Johnson, Rinaldo: marries Nancy Mason, 225
Johnson, Samuel, 109
Johnson, Thomas, 87, 199
Johnson, William Samuel, 246, 256
Johnston, George, 98, 91
Johnston, Zachariah, 296
Jones, Gabriel, 69
Jones, Rev. Hugh, 8; *Present State of Virginia,* 3
Jones, Inigo, 44
Jones, John Gabriel, 183
Jones, Joseph, 193, 207, 270
*Journal and Baltimore Advertiser:* Mason's obituary in, 329
Judiciary (U.S.): Va. plan on, 241; Mason on, 261, 263, 294–95; constitutional article on, 294–95; Jefferson on, 299–300

K

Kalb, Gen. Johann, 204
Kames, Henry Home, Lord, 152–53, 179, 332; *Principles of Equity,* 152–53, 332; *Historical Law Tracts,* 153
Kanawha River, 23, 63, 182
Kaskaskia, 178; Clark's secret plans to take, 184; captured by Clark, 186–87
Kent, William: *Designs of Inigo Jones, The,* 44–45
Kentuckians: called Big Knives by Indians, 188; and commercial treaty with Spain, 227
Kentucky, 153, 170, 181, 182, 184, 192, 196, 215, 220, 248, 330, 332; organized as Va. county, 183; applies for statehood, 194, 196; Anti-Federalists in, 284, 292; delegates vote against ratification of Constitution, 292; statehood of, 332
Kentucky Resolutions of 1789, 334
Kentucky River, 23, 182
King, Rufus, 264, 266; notes of, on Federal Convention, 242; on Committee of Style, 256
King, William, 239, 256, 264, 266
King's Mountain, battle of, 204
Kirk, James, 126

Knights of the Golden Horseshoe, 23, 178
Knox, Gen. Henry, 278, 282, 288, 324

L

Lafayette, Marie Joseph Paul, marquis de, 173, 301, 307, 309; shells Petersburg, 205; to Fredericksburg, 205; presents *Déclaration européene*, 301, 302; and Jefferson, 302, 304; crisis of conscience, 304
Lamb, Gen. John, 291
Land office bill (Va.), 169–70
Land title bill (Va.), 170
Langdon, John, 146
Langley, Batty: *City and Country Builder's and Workman's Treasury of Design*, 47; *Gothic Architecture*, 48; *Design*, 82
Lansing, John, Jr., 243; opposed to Constitution, 267, 297
Laurens, Henry: as president of Congress, 199; in Paris, 304
Lear, Tobias, 321
Lee, Arthur, 69, 225, 236, 292; "Monitor's Letters," 95; in London, 109; writings of, 109–10; as deputy to Franklin, 110; as London agent for Va. and Mass., 110; royalist inclinations of, 244–45
Lee, Gen. Charles, 160; as commander of Southern Division, 138
Lee, Francis Lightfoot, 101, 108, 127, 136; in House of Burgesses, 69; as delegate to Second Continental Congress, 119
Lee, Hancock, 181, 182, 330
Lee, Henry, 69, 137, 227
Lee, "Light-Horse Harry," 205, 277, 288, 290, 292; for ratification of the Constitution, 287
Lee, Ludwell, 228
Lee, Philip Ludwell, 69, 120
Lee, "Squire Richard," 69
Lee, Richard Henry, 43, 68, 88, 95, 98, 101, 102, 114, 124, 137, 147, 149, 153, 156, 160, 168, 170, 173, 181, 197, 198, 199, 205, 218, 267, 268, 272, 273, 275, 280, 281; and Mason's *Extracts from the Virginia Charters*, 68; and Ohio Company, 68; in House of Burgesses, 69; and inquiry into John Robinson's accounts, 88 89; elected to First continental Congress, 108, 109; and Samuel Adams, 110; elected to Second Continental Congress, 118; on continental unity and foreign aid, 138; moves to declare independence, 142, 146; "Government Scheme," 157, 159; denounces Braxton's plan of government, 157; and Va. seal, 161; investigation of, 165–66; elected to Congress, 166; and discreditation campaign against Washington, 172–73; in Va. Assembly, 203; turns conservative, 216; declines as delegate to Federal Convention, 233; active opponent of Constitution, 268, 282; elected U.S. senator from Va., 298
Lee, Thomas, 47, 69; and Ohio Company, 23, 37; as president of Va. Council, 37; as acting governor of Va., 37, 39; and treaty with Iroquois Indians, 37; death of, 38; as presiding judge of Westmoreland County, 47
Lee, Thomas Ludwell, 142, 147, 149; in House of Burgesses, 69; elected to Va. Committee of Safety, 120; and Va. Declaration of Rights, 147, 148, 149; and Committee of Law Revisors, 163, 164, 165; named

justice of General Court, 163; death of, 165
Lee, William, 69, 86, 110, 162, 173; in London, 109; marriage of, 109; as sheriff of London, 109; as British alderman from Aldgate,109
Lee, Willis, 181
*Leeds*, H.M.S., 91
Leesburg, 76, 127
Legislative branch. *See* House of Representatives (U.S.)
Leslie, Gov. Alexander, 205
Lewis, Meriwether, 194
Little Hunting Creek, 47, 226, 329
Livingston, Robert R., 142
Locke, John, 151, 152, 159; and Glorious Revolution in England, 130; social compact of, 130; *Essay on Toleration*, 150
London, 8, 16, 17, 23, 44, 95, 109, 124, 177, 184, 199, 329; Thomson Mason in, 44
London, Bishop of, 8, 84
London Company, 31
*London Public Ledger*, 94
Long ordinary (Dumfries), 36
Loudoun County, 26, 69, 127, 166; formation of, 5, 76; land purchases in by Ann Thomson Mason, 22–23; resistance to recruitment in, 168
Louis XIV, 9, 311
Louis XV, 310
Louis XVI, 301, 302, 306, 310
Louisa County, 89, 90
Loyalists, 120–29; in Va.; 120, 121, 126–29, 197; among clergy, 122
Loyal Land Company, 23, 38
Loyalty oath: drafted by Mason and Josiah Parker, 118; required in 1777, 118
Ludwell, Hannah Phillipa: marries William Lee, 109
Luzerne, Chevalier de la, 210

M

McCarty, Daniel, 60, 82, 84; marries Sarah Mason, 60, 225
McClurg, Dr. James, 240, 256, 281; as delegate to Federal Convention, 233, 234; for one-man executive, 250
McHenry, James, 269; notes on Federal Convention of, 242; and support of constitution, 273–74
Madison, James, Sr., 330
Madison, James, 153, 155, 207, 211, 218, 219, 220, 223, 229, 238, 240, 243, 248, 263, 264, 268, 269, 270, 271, 274, 277, 280, 284, 285, 287, 288, 290, 291, 294, 295, 300, 302, 328, 33; in Va. Convention of 1776, 138; on Cary Committee, 140; article on religious freedom, 149, 150–51, 152; at Princeton, 150; and Va. Declaration of Rights, 150–51, 161; and voting bill of 1785, 201; and Statute for Religious Freedom, 215; general assessment bill, 216–17; *Memorial and Remonstrance*, 217-18; on Mason's views on revising Va. constitution, 218–19, 221; on payment of British creditors, 220; marries Dolley Payne Todd, 223; on issuing new paper money, 227–28; appointed to Md. trade negotiation, 229; and Mount Vernon Compact, 230; at Annapolis Convention, 231; at Federal Convention, 233 234; and Virginia Plan, 240; and Va. constitution, 240; notes of, on Federal Convention, 242; on House of Representatives, 244, 247, 259; on

economic sectionalism, 248; on one-man executive, 250; on foreign trade and foreign policy, 251; on tariffs, 251; on trade measures, 251; on abuse of power by majority, 253; on international negotiations, 253; on Committee of Style, 256; and proposal on overriding presidential veto, 258; *The Federalist*, 271; onnecessity of ratifying Constitution, 274; on Mason's objections to Constitution, 274–75; on amendment process, 274–75; on Mass. ratification formula, 278; correspondence of, with Jefferson, 278, 281–82, 287, 298–99; predictions of, on Va. ratification vote, 284, 292, 295; reports Va. ratifying convention to George Washington, 291, 295, 298; on bill of rights, 296, 298–99; on power of majority, 299; proposes U.S. constitutional amendments to House of Representatives, 300, 301, 321; Mason's esteem for, 321; on Hamilton's debt assumption plan, 325; recollects Mason, 333

Magna Charta, 32

Manley, John, 84

Manumission, 214

Marketing: methods of in colonial Va., 16, 17–18, 19–20

Marlborough, 26, 28, 30, 31, 33, 41, 45, 47, 74, 223, 319

Marlborough, duke of, 18

Marshall, Ann: marries Joseph H. Daveiss, 332

Marshall, John, 228, 270, 281; on union of purse and sword, 292; on state suits in Supreme Court, 295; as U.S. chief justice, 332

Martin, Luther, 238; on slave trade, 251; opposed to Constitution, 261, 267; Anti-Federalist publications of, 272

Martin, Rev. Thomas, 149–50

Martin, Thomas Bryan, 69

Martinique, 166, 178

Maryland, 9, 23, 39, 64, 112, 121, 128, 130, 153, 156, 199, 204, 215, 226, 232, 242, 261, 278, 310, 313; delays signing Articles of Confederation, 198–99, 207; slavery in, 251; first charter of, 229; trade dispute with Va., 228, 229; ratifies Constitution, 271

*Maryland Gazette*, 41, 76, 90–91

Mason, Ann Eilbeck (1734–73), 52–53, 330; marriage of, 39–40, 41; portrait of, 41; as seen by son John, 52–53; death of, 99–100, 174, 329, 335

Mason, Ann Eilbeck (1755–1814), 59, 100; marries Rinaldo Johnson, 225

Mason, Ann Thomson, 7, 34; purchases land, 22–23; widowed, 25; manages estate, 25–26; records of, 25–26, 30; death of, 74

Mason, Catherine. *See* Mercer, Catherine Mason

Mason, Charles: surveyor of Mason-Dixon line, 181

Mason, Elizabeth (b. 1768), 59, 322; marries William Thornton, 225

Mason, Elizabeth Waugh, 10, 26

Mason, French, 55

Mason, George (c. 1629–86), 4, 9; emigrates to Va., 3, 4; and Potomac Indians, 4; county lieutenant of Stafford County, 6; in House of Burgesses, 7

Mason, George (c. 1660–1716): county lieutenant of Stafford County, 6; as ardent Whig, 9; and John Waugh, 9–10; marries Elizabeth Waugh, 10, 26; feoffee of town of Marlborough, 18

Mason, George (1690–1735), 40; militia lieutenant of Stafford County, 6; in House of Burgesses, 7; 10;

honorary burgess of Glasgow, 18–19; acquires land, 22; moves to Maryland, 11, 22; and Knights of the Golden Horseshoe, 23; death of, 25

Mason, George (1725–92), 3, 6, 23, 25, 26, 60, 62, 85, 94, 101, 108, 124, 153, 154, 155, 166, 174, 182, 197, 198, 211, 214, 216, 218, 219, 221, 223, 226, 229, 233, 238, 243, 244, 248, 262, 264, 266, 268, 269, 270, 273, 274, 280, 281, 282, 298, 312, 315, 319, 322, 324, 333; on slavery, 13, 107, 214, 252–53, 259, 263, 294; birth of, 22, 25; and Ohio Company, 23, 37–38, 39, 63, 66, 67–68, 75, 163, 170, 181, 182; and Va. Declaration of Rights, 24, 142, 146, 147, 148, 149, 152, 262, 333–34; education of, 30–31, 32, 33; town trustee of Dumfries, 33, 39, 102; trustee of Alexandria, 34, 63, 77; and George Washington, 36, 41, 43, 55, 63, 68, 74–75, 77, 79, 82, 86, 87, 91, 96, 102, 104, 105, 107, 108, 112, 114, 119, 134–35, 135–36, 173, 207, 270, 320–21; and western lands, 38, 63, 168–69, 177, 183, 199, 207, 330, 332; as planter, 39, 55–56, 59–60, 73, 86, 87; as Truro vestryman, 39, 63, 79, 82; marries Ann Eilbeck, 39–40, 41; portrait of, 41; and Richard Henry Lee, 43, 69, 98–99, 109, 140, 142, 165–66, 170, 173, 198, 199–200; poor health of, 43, 134, 167, 193, 197, 200, 228, 322; and Martin Cockburn, 59–60, 101–2, 118–119, 226–27; relationship of, with family, 62, 100, 101–2, 118, 165, 225; as Fairfax justice, 63, 77, 208; and Stamp Act, 63, 88, 91; in House of Burgesses, 63, 68, 72; and French and Indian War, 64, 65; designation as colonel, 64–65; and building of Pohick Church, 82, 84; and Declaratory Act, 94; and nonimportation resolution, 95; advocates nonexportation, 96, 125; on Fairfax Committee of Surveillance, 99; loses wife, 99–100; will of, 100, 329–30, 332, 335; on Patrick Henry, 101, 288; and Fairfax Resolves, 102, 105, 107, 130; on Fairfax Committee of Safety, 105, 112, 126, 134–35, 162–63, 166; and Fairfax Independent Company of Volunteers, 110; on election of military officers, 114–15; and loyalty oath, 118, 126; on Va. Committee of Safety, 118, 119, 120; and Connolly affair, 128–29; and military defense of Va., 134, 135, 136; in Va. Convention of 1776, 137; on Cary Committee, 140, 142; on foreign alliances, 140; on general warrants, 148; on uniform system of government in Va., 148; on ex post facto laws, 148, 264; on religious toleration, 149, 150, 215; on right of access to property, 152, 309; writes as "Aristides," 156; and Va. constitution, 158–59, 160, 218, 219, 333; on separation of powers, 158, 159, 260, 263; on right of suffrage, 159, 160; influences on political thought of, 159; and Va. seal, 161, 162; in Va. House of Delegates, 163, 200; on Committee of Law Revisors, 163, 164, 165; declines appointment to Congress, 165; and Va. Assembly, 166–70 passim, 173, 199–201, 227; on militia, 168, 203, 263; and tax measures, 168–69, 202, 203, 208, 221, 263; and land office bill, 169–70; and land title bill, 170; and George Rogers Clark, 172, 177, 181, 183–84, 186, 191, 193–94; and Ohio country, 181; on Maryland's refusal to sign Articles of Confederation, 198; on Va. treaty of alliance with France, 199–200; on regulation of elections, 201, 212; and Madison, 201, 207, 229, 321; death of, 201, 329; and repeal of tithes to Anglican church, 201; and

Anglican church property bill, 201; and inflation, 202, 203; and paper money, 203, 228; letters to son George, 205, 208–10, 226 234, 235–36, 238, 239, 244, 245; on Confederation, 207, 221, 244; remarries, 207–8; "Petition of Freeholders," 212; on the executive, 212, 250, 257-58; on civilian supremacy over military, 212; on embargo on exports, 212; *Scheme for Replevying Goods*, 214; *Extracts from the Virginia Charters*, 214; and general assessment bill, 217; and Va. public finances, 219, 220; opposed to congressional impost, 221; on state sovereignty, 221, 290, 295; domestic life of, 223, 225; arms of, 225; and Port Act of 1784, 227; and Federal Convention, 228, 233, 236, 238, 239; and Md. trade negotiation, 228, 229–30; and Mount Vernon Compact, 230; on Philadelphia social life, 235, 236; and Va. Plan, 240, 257; on House of Representatives, 244, 246, 247, 259, 260, 262; on admission of new states, 248; on oppression of minority by majority, 250, 253; against proposed trade measures, 251; and Elbridge Gerry, 254, 261, 310; and Gouvernour Morris, 248, 254, 25; favors sumptuary laws, 254, 260–61, 263; withholds signature from Constitution, 254, 262, 263, 264, 281; on impeachment, 258; on treason, 258, 263, 264; on power to override presidential veto, 258; on vice-presidency, 259, 263, 274, 294; proposes privy council, 259, 263; on extension of franchise, 260; on Senate, 260, 263, 274; on Congress's tax power, 260, 290, 292; on Congress's power to declare war, 260; on judiciary, 261, 263, 274, 290, 294-95; on ratification of Constitution, 261; on location of national capital, 261; favors second Federal Convention, 261, 264; proposes bill of rights, 262; on supremacy of U.S. over state laws, 262; opposition to Constitution, 262-63, 267, 270, 272, 274, 282, 284, 287, 312; on treaties, 263; on commercial and navigation laws, 263, 272; on freedom of press, 263; on trial by jury, 263; and Va. ratifying convention, 284–97 passim; on Mass. ratifying formula, 284; and proposed amendments to Constitution, 291, 321–22; on crime in new U.S. capital, 294; on doctrine of reserved powers, 294; on rights of revolution, 308; letters to son John, 311, 312, 317–18, 319, 321, 322; obtains consulship for Joseph Fenwick, 312–13; retirement or, 319, 320; wealth of, 320; on debt assumption, 328; *Wilson* v. *Mason,* 332; Madison's and Jefferson's recollections of, 333; advice to sons in will, 335

Mason, George (1753–96), 30, 59, 75, 99, 112, 208, 209, 210, 225, 226, 234, 235, 236, 238, 239, 240, 244, 245, 312, 329, 332, 333; poor health of, 197; in France, 197, 205; marries Elizabeth May Ann Barnes, 225; and Lexington, 225–26; in Paris, 304; as planter, 319; as executor of father's will, 330; death of, 332-33

Mason, George (1786–1834), 333

Mason, James (infant), 99

Mason, John, 54, 59, 225; memoirs of, 51–52, 53–54, 55–56, 58–60, 61–62, 63, 100, 332, 335; education of, 54; on his mother's death, 100; papers of, 175; marries Anna Maria Murray, 225, 318; and Analostan Island, 226, 329; at Federal Convention with father, 234, 238, 256; in Paris, 304, 309; in Bordeaux, 309, 310, 311–12, 313, 315–18; letters from France, 309, 315–17; travels in Europe, 312; swears adherence to French

Revolution, 317; joins Amis de la Constitution, 318; as merchant in Georgetown, 319

Mason, Mary, 25, 26, 74. *See also* Selden, Mary Mason

Mason, Mary, 59; marries John Cooke, 225

Mason Richard (infant), 99

Mason, Richard (grandson), 332

Mason, Sarah, 59; marries Daniel McCarty, 60

Mason, Sarah Brent, 329; marriage to George Mason of Gunston Hall, 208; illness of, 322

Mason, Simpha Rosa Enfield, 33, 64

Mason, Thomas, 36, 54, 59, 87, 99, 319–20; education of, 54; marries Sarah Barnes, 225; and Woodbridge, 225, 329

Mason, Thomson (1733–85), 25, 26, 45, 94, 95, 108, 126–27, 167, 220; to London, 31, 44; will of, 54, 214–15; in House of Burgesses, 68; proposes declaration of rights, 94; letters to *Virginia Gazette*, 108, 130

Mason, Thomson (1759–1820), 235, 329; birth of, 59; in Revolution, 205; marries Sarah Chichester, 225; and Hollin Hall, 226; as customs collector in Alexandria, 319

Mason, Westwood, 54

Mason, William, 59, 322, 329; in S.C. in Revolution, 205, 206; marries Ann Stuart, 225; and Mattawoman, 225; as planter, 319; trip west, 330

Mason, William Temple, 54

Mason-Dixon line, 181

Mason family, 9, 11

Masonic Lodge of the Nine Sisters, 307

Massachusetts, 64, 88, 102, 109, 130, 151, 154, 232, 238, 239, 242, 245, 267, 268, 272, 277, 315; and Stamp Act crisis, 95; loyalists in, 120; Declaration of Rights, 154–55; colonial charter of, 199; fish as staple of, 248; Committee of Correspondence, 254; General Court, 254; Provincial Congress, 254; ratifies Constitution, 271, 275, 277–78, 295; Federalists in, 275, 277; Anti-Federalists in, 275, 277

*Massachusetts Gazette*, 272

Massey, Lee, 73, 81–82, 99, 216–17, 330

Mattawoman, 41, 59, 225

Mattawoman Creek, 40, 41

Maury, James, 73

Mayflower Compact, 130

Mayo, John 136

Mazzei, Philip, 87; in Paris, 304

*Memorial and Remonstrance* (Madison), 217–18

Mercer, Ann Roy, 30

Mercer, Catherine Mason, 26

Mercer, George, 30, 75; in French and Indian War, 64, 91; as Ohio Company's London agent, 66–68, 69, 91, 181; *The Case of the Ohio Company*, 66; in House of Burgesses, 69; as Va. stamp distributor, 91–93

Mercer, Capt. James, 64

Mercer, James, 75, 87, 108, 116, 208, 281, 329; in French and Indian war, 64; on Va. Committee of Safety, 120

Mercer, John, 26–30, 34, 36, 47, 72, 80, 100, 223; as coguardian of Mason children, 26; emigrates to Va., 26; marries Catherine Mason, 26; *Abridgment*, 27–28, 32; as gentleman justice, 28; builds mansion at Marlborough, 28; as Va. gentleman, 28, 30; library of, 30, 31–32, 33, 45, 159; and Ohio Company, 38; sons of, 64; death of, 75

Mercer, John Fendall, 64
Mercer, John Fenton, 215
Mercer, John Francis, 244, 319, 330; royalism of, 244; in Federal Convention, 244
Methodists, in Va., 218
Mifflin, Gen. Thomas, 172, 235
Mills, James, 30
Mississippi River, 23, 177, 178, 184, 187, 193, 194, 215; demand for unrestricted navigation on, 24; Spanish ports on, 177; Jay's negotiations over navigation of, 227, 292
Mohawk Valley, 178
Moncure, John, 41, 60, 73, 80
Monroe, James, 215, 223, 228, 280, 296; grandfather an overseer, 22, 223; interest of, in western lands, 179; in Va. ratifying convention, against ratification of Constitution, 280, 287; on proper powers of central government, 292; on prior amendment, 296; appointment to U.S. Senate, 322; on Mason's death, 329
Montagnards (France), 315
Monticello, 87; reconstruction of, 223
Montpelier, 150, 222, 223
Montreal, 63, 178
Montrose, 41
Moore, Jeremiah, 85–86
Moore, William, 330
Morgan, George, 199
Morrellet, Abbe: translates Jefferson's Notes on Virginia, 304
Morris, Gouverneur, 222, 243, 251, 253, 254–55, 256, 264, 265 266; royalism of, 244; Federalism of, 247; favors dominance of Atlantic states, 248; and Mason, 248, 254, 255; a conservative aristocrat, 254; supports religious toleration, 254; moves from New York to Philadelphia, 247, 254; favors second Federal Convention, 261; in Va., 292; in Paris, 304
Morris, Robert, 199, 222–233, 235, 236, 254; in Va., 292; and tax on spirits, 292
Morrisania, 222, 254
Mount Airy, 37
Mount Pleasant, 47
Mount Vernon, 47, 74, 75, 79, 100, 108, 112, 114, 136, 167, 217, 223, 226, 269, 280, 320, 325, 329; inherited by George Washington, 41; managed by Lund Washington, 134
Mount Vernon Convention of 1785, 229, 230
Munford, Col. Robert; The Candidates, 103, 104
Murray, Anna Maria: marries John Mason, 225, 318
My Lord's Island. See Analostan Island

N
Nantes, 166, 208
Navigation Acts, 88, 125, 166, 208
Nelson, Thomas, 108, 124, 160; as secretary of colony of Va., 38; and Ohio Company, 38; and Greenbriar Land Company, 38
Nelson, Thomas, Jr., 137, 138, 168, 228; on mood for independence in Va., 137; as governor of Va., 212; Assembly investigation of, 211, 212, 213; declines to participate in Federal Convention, 233
Nelson, William, 98, 99
New England, 85, 101, 151, 215, 222, 242, 244, 248, 271; on voting rules for regulation of trade, 250
New France, 63, 181
New Hampshire, 154, 199, 232, 273, 313; framing of constitution in, 155; ratifies Constitution, 297
New Haven Gazette, 272
New Jersey, 121, 130, 154, 199, 215, 226, 231, 242, 247, 262, 282; loyalists in, 120; ratifies Constitution, 270
New Jersey Plan: alternative to Va. Plan, 245
New Orleans, 177, 178
Newport Mercury, 90
New York, 64, 121, 130, 154, 207, 210, 215, 226, 231, 242, 261, 267, 268, 278, 291, 297, 315, 320, 321, 324; loyalists in, 120; occupation of, 122, 167; abstains on first vote for independence, 146; Provincial Congress of, 146, 238, 254; colonial charter of, 199; cedes western lands, 207; delegation to Federal Convention, 243; Provisional Assembly of, 254; ratifying convention, 271, 291; Federal Republican Committee, 291; celebration of Constitution's entry into force, 297–98; ratifies Constitution, 297
New York Committee of Safety, 133
New York Daily Advertiser, 280
Nicholas, George, 290, 291, 292, 296, 332, 334; for ratification of the Constitution, 287, 296; on House of Representatives, 289; on subsequent amendment, 296
Nicholas, Robert Carter, 95, 102, 108, 114, 121, 137, 219, 270; in Va. Convention of 1776, 138; opposed to declaring independence, 138; opposed to Article 1 of Va. Declaration of Rights, 149; opposed to disestablishment, 150; and Va. seal, 161; opposed to general assessment bill, 217
Nomini Hall, 36, 217
Nonexportation, 107, 166, 212; advocated by Mason, 96, 118, 122; resolves, 102; in Va. Convention of 1775, 118; effect of, on tobacco trade, 125
Nonimportation, 107, 122; agreements on, 95–96; association, 95, 98, 99; formation of county committees to enforce, 99; Fairfax Resolves call for, 105, 108; statute supported by Jefferson, 161
Norfolk, 6, 47, 122, 124, 128, 316, 318; held by Dunmore, 109; loyalists in, 122, 197; British troops land at, 205
North: economic sectionalism of, 248; trade in, 248; debate over supremacy of, 250–51, 253; vs. South, 250–51
North, Frederick, earl of Guilford, 98; "Olive Branch" resolutions of, 116
North Carolina, 130, 154, 203, 215, 248; organization of land companies in, 23; colonial charter of, 199; in British hands, 204; ratifying convention, 271
North Carolinians: ventures in western lands, 68, 182-83
Northern Neck (Va.), 3, 4, 6, 34, 38, 73, 91, 102, 121, 217; migration to, 3, 6; plantations in, 11; feudal law in, 11; residents of, and Ohio Company, 23, 37; British raids in, 208; Federalist sentiment in, 282
Northumberland County, 4–5
Northwest Ordinance, 196, 215, 238
Northwest Territory, 177–96 passim, 207, 238; won by George Rogers Clark, 177; British and European ignorance about, 177; British claims to, 178; immigration into, 178; jurisdictional disputes over, 181; ceded to Congress, 193; government established in, 196, 215

O

Oak Hill, 223
Occoquan, 35, 73, 329; mills at, 36
Occoquan Plantation, 34
Occoquan River, 22, 25, 32, 34, 35, 56, 73, 225, 329
Ocracoke Inlet, 122
Office of Illinois Accounts, 194
Oglethorpe, James Edward, 13
Ohio, Forks of the, 37, 38, 39, 63, 64, 178; Pa.-Va. dispute over, 39, 181
Ohio Company, 23, 37–39, 63–68, 73, 75, 181, 182, 330; approved by Board of Trade, 37; Northern Neck participants in, 37; Moon as treasurer, 37; reorganization of, 38, 72; and dispute over Ohio River land, 63–65; British imperial policy and, 65; merger with Grand Ohio Company, 67; Lee and Clark survey for, 181, 182; dissolution of, 182, 330
Ohio River, 23, 38, 39, 63, 177, 178, 181, 182, 185, 187, 192, 193, 199, 207, 215, 226, 230, 238; disputes over claims to, 39; French claims to land on, 63, 64; British claims to land on, 64; Va. claims to land on, 68
"Old State Soldier," 272; "Communication No. 3," 273
Osborne, Richard, 34
Oswald, Col. Eleazer, 291
Otto, Chevalier Louis-Guillaume, 221–22, 232–33
Overseers, 21–22
Overwharton parish, 9, 41, 73, 80

P

Paca William, 199
Pagan, John, 34
Page, John, Jr., 138, 162, 166, 200; indebtedness of, 21; on Va. Committee of Safety, 120; in Va. Convention of 1776, 137; as president of Va. Council, 160
Page, Mann, 21, 47, 228, 281
Paine, Thomas, 130–31, 134, 275, 316; Common Sense, 130; editor of Pennsylvania Magazine, 131; in Paris, 304; Rights of Man, 307
Palladio, Andrea, 44, 47, 58
Panther Creek, 330
Paper money, 88; depreciation of, in Va., 165, 168–69, 203, 219, 228
Paris, 177, 210, 301, 309, 310, 313, 315, 316; American colony in, 302, 304
Parker, Hugh, 37–38
Parker, James, 124
Parker, Josiah, 118, 126
Parks, William, 27, 30
Parsons, Theophilus, 277
Parson's Cause, 72–73, 217; Patrick Henry and, 73
Paterson, William: notes of, on Federal Convention, 242; introduces N.J. Plan, 245
Payne, Daniel, 37
Payne, Edward, 80, 82
Payne, William, 68
Peale, Charles Willson, 41, 45
Pendleton, Edmund, 116, 119, 124, 139, 142, 157, 165, 167, 168, 170, 211, 212, 216, 277, 281, 285, 290, 294, 300, 325; and Loyal and Greenbriar land companies, 38; in First Continental Congress, 108; on Va. Committee of Safety, 120; as president of Va. Convention of 1776, 138; and Va. Declaration of Rights, 149; opposed to disestablishment, 150; on

Braxton's plan of government, 157; as speaker of Va. House of Delegates, 160; on Committee of Law Revisors, 163, 164, 165; as president of Va. Supreme Court of Appeals, 198, 285; and state support of religion, 216; and general assessment act, 216; conservative preference of, 218; and Va. ratifying convention, 285; for ratification of Constitution, 284, 287; defends legality of making of Constitution, 289
Penn, John 120
Penn, Richard, 222
Penn family, 39, 181
Pennsylvania, 39, 64, 65, 121, 130, 154, 199, 212, 215, 226, 230, 231, 240, 245, 251; organization of land companies in, 23; charter of, 39; claims to western lands, 66; loyalists in, 120; bill of rights, 154; rivalry with Va. for Ohio country, 181; flour as staple of, 248; opponents of Constitution in, 267; ratifies Constitution, 270
Pennsylvania Evening Post, 137, 139, 142
Pennsylvania, Gazette, 92
Pennsylvania Journal, 272
Pennsylvania Magazine, 131
Pennsylvania Packet, 246, 266, 270
Perry, Franklin, 78
Petersburg, 108, 285; British headquarters in, 205
Petersham, battle of, 233
Petition of Right of 1629, 24, 32
Philadelphia, 62, 74, 85, 110, 112, 116, 121, 127, 128, 130, 131, 133, 137, 139, 157, 172, 199, 222, 238, 240, 243, 261, 267, 269, 271, 280, 285, 286, 288, 291, 294, 302, 304, 306, 310, 319, 320, 328, 329; land speculators, 66–67; Merchants' Association, 95–96; First Continental Congress meets in, 108, 109; British occupation of, 121, 122, 167, 198; Federal Convention to meet at, 232; social life of, 235, 236
Phillips, Gen William, 205
Phipps, Rev. John, 30
Pickering, Timothy, 256
Piedmont, 161; production of wheat in, 73; Anti-Federalists in, 284
Pierce, William, 239; on Mason, 238; notes of, on Federal Convention, 242; on Elbridge Gerry, 254
Pinckney Charles, 222, 238, 264; proposes plan for amendment of Articles of Confederation, 242; on slave trade, 251; proposal of, on executive eligibility, 257; against second Federal Convention, 264; "Observations on the Plan of Government," 271
Pitt, William, 184
"Plain Dealer, A," 272
Plain Truth, 133
Pleasants, Samuel, 108
Pohick Bay, 60
Pohick Church, 82, 84, 99, 105, 216, 217
Pohick Creek, 49, 56, 82
Pokomoke River, 230
Political parties, 334; emergence of outlines of, 325
Pollock, Oliver, 192
Port Act of 1784, 227, 228
Portsmouth, Va., 203; British occupation of, 205
Port Tobacco, Md., 18
Posey, John, 75, 82
Posey, Milly, 61
Potomac Church, 54

Potomac Company, 226
Potomac Creek, 18, 22, 74
Potomac Indians, 4
Potomac River, 4, 5, 6, 9, 11, 18, 22, 23, 25, 26, 34, 38,
    40, 41, 43, 47, 49, 56, 73, 87, 122, 124, 128, 226, 229,
    230, 244, 316, 318, 320, 329; settlement along, 4;
    defense of, 135; jurisdictional dispute over, 229; and
    the Mount Vernon convention, 229–30
Poughkeepsie, N.Y., 297
Powel, Samuel, 235
Presbyterians: in Va., 85, 86, 122, 218, 284
Presidency (U.S.): debate on tenure of, 244–45; debate
    on powers of, 245; Va. Plan on, 241; Mason on,
    257–58; and impeachment, 258; power to override
    veto by, 258
Press, freedom of, 148–49
Preston, William, 182
Primogeniture, 11, 26, 153, 274
Prince Edward County, 284
Prince George County, , 5, 103, 205
Prince George's County, Md., 40
Princeton University, 85, 150, 243, 297
Prince William County, 27, 35, 69, 102, 137, 208, 213,
    329; formation of, 5, 33
Proclamation of 1763, 66, 91, 178
Profiteering, 197; bill prohibiting in Va., 168, 197
"Publius," 271
Purdie, Alexander, 116
Purdie & Dixon's *Gazette*, 87
Purdie's *Virginia Gazette*, 140, 149, 157, 159

Q

Quantico Creek, 25, 34
Quebec, 64, 178, 179, 184, 245
Quebec Act of 1774, 178, 199; extends New France
    borders, 181
Quitrents, 38, 164; in Northern Neck, 11; and Lord
    Fairfax, 121

R

*Rainbow*, H.M.S., 92
Rainbow Inn (Alexandria), 76
Raleigh Tavern (Williamsburg), 25, 102, 124; mantel
    motto, 25
Ramsay, William, 116, 118; trustee of Alexandria, 34;
    lord mayor of Alexandria, 76
Randolph, Beverley, 322; acting governor of Va., 267
Randolph, Edmund, 138, 230, 231, 233, 234, 235, 240,
    246, 248, 264, 267, 272, 280, 281, 290, 291, 297;
    patriot, 120; attorney general of Va., 160, 240;
    delegate to Md. trade negotiation, 229; delegate to
    Federal Convention, 233, 234; delegate to Annapolis
    Convention, 240; presents Va. Plan to Federal
    Convention, 240; governor of Va., 240; on federal
    government, 243; against one-man executive, 250;
    against proposed trade measures, 251; on Committee
    of Detail, 256; views on ratification uncertain, 253,
    287; for Mason's proposal on overriding presidential
    veto, 258; motion to restrict tax powers to revenue
    only, 260; favors second federal convention, 261, 264,
    282; on pardons for treason, 264; proposes referring
    Constitution to states for suggested amendments,
    264; inability to sign Constitution, 265, 266, 281, 287;

opposed to Constitution, 267; "Letter . . . on the
    Federal Constitution," 280, 287; declares in favor of
    ratification, 289–90, 291; on defects of confederation,
    291; Henry threatens duel with, 291; disapproves
    Henry's amendments, 296; as U.S. attorney general,
    324
Randolph, John: loyalist, 120; returns to England, 120
Randolph, John ("Randolph of Roanoke"): description
    of New York ratification celebration, 297–98
Randolph, Peyton, 72, 90, 99, 102, 116; attorney general
    of Va., 72; elected to First Continental Congress, 108;
    elected to Second Continental Congress, 118; patriot,
    120; death of, 138, 198
Rappahannock River, 4, 5, 6, 35
Raspberry Plain, 26, 126–27
Read, George, 235
Read, Isaac, 136
Rebels: King declares colonists, 130, 156
*Recruiting Officer, The*, 36
Reed, Joseph, 131
Religion: in colonial Va., 7–10, 84–86; proposal for state
    support of, in Va., 216
Religious freedom, 149–52; Madison and, 149, 150, 215;
    in Va., 215; Mason and, 215; Committee of Law
    Revisors recommendation on, 215–16; statute for,
    218, 299, as issue in France, 316
Religious toleration: in Virginia Declaration of Rights,
    148; Madison on, 150–51; Sir Henry Vane on, 151–52
Restoration (England), 3, 4, 32
Revenue Act of 1764, 88; impact on New England, 88
Revenue Act of 1767, 94–96
Revisory Council: Mason on, 258–59
Revolution (U.S.), 6, 60, 61, 62, 177, 219, 222, 245;
    background of leaders of, 25; crises leading to, 63;
    negotiation of peace, 213, 214; preliminary articles of
    peace, 219; conclusion of, 221; French officers in, 304;
    global influence of, 307–8; European ramifications of,
    333
Rhode Island, 101, 154, 199, 245, 259; refusal to levy tax,
    222; refusal to participate in Federal Convention, 233;
    outside federal system, 271
Richards, Mourning, 80
Richmond, 62, 267, 274, 335; Va. Convention of 1775
    scheduled for, 110; capital of Va. moved to, 200, 285;
    Arnold's troops damage, 205; Va. ratifying
    convention held in, 284, 285, 286
Ripon (England), 7, 226
Ripon Lodge, 60
Ritchie family, 16, 17
Robertson, David, 285, 287, 296
Robertson, Donald, 182
Robinson, John, 35, 38; speaker of House of Burgesses,
    72; treasurer of colonial Va., 72; inquiry into accounts
    of, 88–89
Rochambeau, 210
Rochefoucauld, Jean Baptiste Donatien de Vimeur,
    comte, 307
Rock Creek, 22, 34
Rodney, Caesar, 146
Roland, Jean Marie, 307
Romney, Va., 23
Rosewell, 21, 47, 137
Ross, David, 95

Ross, Hector, 36
Rousseau, Jean Jacques, 130, 307
Rowland, Kate Mason: biographer of George Mason, 19, 262
Rowland, Samuel, 12
Roy, Ann. *See* Mercer, Ann Roy
Royal George tavern (Alexandria), 76
Royalists: in England during British civil war, 3; in Federal Convention, 244–45; Hamilton on, 328
Rush, Benjamin, and Thomas Paine, 131
Rutledge, Edward, 146
Rutledge, Edward, Jr., in Paris, 304
Rutledge, John, 238; on slave trade, 251; on Committee of Detail, 256; and proportionment of representation, 259

S
Sabine Hall, 47
Ste. Geneviève, 178
St. Eustace, 166
St. Lawrence River, 177
St. Louis, 177, 178
St. Paul's Cathedral, 44
Salmon, William: *Palladio Londonensis, The*, 47, 50
Salt: shortage of, 135, 166; exemption from nonimportation, 135; British interception of, 166; seizures of, authorized by Va. legislature, 168
Sandys, George: translations of Ovid by, 31
Saratoga, battle of, 167
Savannah, Ga., 84
Scarlet, Martin, 10
Scioto River, 38, 182
Scotchtown, 183
Scotland: included in United Kingdom, 16
Scott, Rev. Andrew, 73
Scott, Rev. James, 72, 73, 100, 208; and Ohio Co., 73
Scottish merchants, 16, 18, 122–25; in Va., 18, 125–26
Sears, Isaac, 133, 275
Sears, William Bernard, 82, 84
Sectionalism: in Federal Convention, economic, 248; and commercial powers of central government, 250–51; North–South, 248, 250–53; within states, 277
Ségur, Henri François, comte de, 301
Selden, Mary Mason, 74
Selden, Col. Samuel, 74
Semple, James, 36
Senate (U.S.), 248; Va. plan on election of, 241; debate on election of, in Federal Convention, 244, 246; Conn. proposal on, 247; Mason on election of, 260; Mason on qualifications for, 260; consideration of amendments by, 300
Separation of powers: in Virginia Declaration of Rights, 148; Adams on, 156; Jefferson on, 299
Seven Years' War. *See* French and Indian War
Sevier, John, 204
Shadwell, 181
Shakespeare, 31
Sharpe, Governor (Md.), 92
Shaysites, 272, 315
Shays's Rebellion, 232, 233, 244
Shelburne, Lord, 109
Shelby, Col. Isaac, 204
Shenandoah Valley, 210, 217, 296; Federalists in, 284

Sherman, Roger, 243, 262, 268; on committee to draft Declaration of Independence, 142; on election of lower house, 244; on committee on legislative representation, 247; in slave trade debate in Federal Convention, 252; "Letters of a Countryman," 271
Shippen, Thomas, 245
Shippen, Thomas Lee: in Paris, 304
Shirley, William, 64; and capture of Louisburg, 64; and French and Indian War, 64; governor of Mass., 88
Short, William: aide to Jefferson, 268
Singletary, Amos, 277
Slavery, 149, 214–15: in Va., 12–13; opposition to, in Va., 12–13, 253, 294; laws against traffic in, in colonial Virginia, 13; in Va. Convention of 1776, 149; proposal to outlaw, in new states, 215; prohibited in Northwest Territory, 215; as issue in Federal Convention, 246; in Upper South, 251; in Deep South, 251; process of abolition of, 252; Mason on, 259, 294
Slaves, 7, 12, 13, 16, 21, 22, 26, 134; in Tidewater, 12; and overseers, 22; at Gunston Hall, 60; freed, 214; and Federal Convention, 251–53; Mason on importation of, 294
Smith, Blair, 284
Smith, Edward, 40
Smith, Meriwether, 158
Smith, William, Jr.: chief justice of N.Y., 120–21
Smith, William Loughton, 320
Smith, William Stephens, 282
Smyth, J. F. D., 105; *Tour in the United States of America*, 103; on Va. social structure, 103–4; loyalist, 128; plot with John Connolly, 128–29
Society of the Cincinnati, 222, 233, 243, 257, 278; in France, 304
South: as theater of Revolution, 203; British troops in, 203; economic sectionalism of, in Federal Convention, 248; agriculture in, 248; vs. North, 250–51; and Miss. navigation rights, 292
South Carolina, 154, 215, 222, 262; loyalists in, 120; against independence on first vote in Second Continental Congress, 146; adoption of state constitution in, 154; freedom of religion in, 154; colonial charter of, 199, British offensive in, 203, 204; on voting rules for trade regulation, 250; slavery in, 251; ratification of Constitution, 271
South Carolina *State Gazette*, 271
Southside, Va.: Anti-Federalists in, 284
Spanish settlements: in America, 177, 178
Specie: scarcity of, in colonial Va., 12, 74
*Spectator*, 31
Speirs, Alexander, 16, 17
Spotswood, Gov. Alexander, 7; expedition westward, 32, 178
Springfield, 59, 60
Stafford County, 9, 11, 18, 28, 33, 35, 41, 54, 69, 73, 137, 163, 181, 225, 273, 282, 284; formation of, 5; Whig–Tory tensions in, 9; Anglican–Catholic tensions in, 9–10; George Mason's purchases of land in, 22; John Mercer gentleman justice in, 28; Thomson Mason elected to House of Burgesses in, 68; Mason elected to Va. Convention of 1788 in, 284
Stamp Act Congress (New York), 91; Declaration of Rights and Grievances of, 91
Stamp Act of 1765, 63, 66, 88, 89, 92, 93, 121, 277;

continental resistence to, 63, 88; Mason's response to, 88; Patrick Henry's repudiation of, 89–90; House of Burgesses resolutions in response to, 89–90; George Mercer as Va. stamp distributor, 91–93; repeal of, 93, 94, 95

States General (France), 304, 307, 309, 315

State sovereignty: under Articles of Confederation, 199; exercise of, inhibits trade, 226; and boundary disputes, 226; and claims on waterways, 226; Mason on, 258

States' rights, 296, 334

Staunton, 210

Stephen, Adam, 296

Steuben, Frederick William Augustus, baron von, 205

Stewart, Charles, 124

Stratford, 37, 47, 153

Stone, Thomas, 229

Stuart, Ann: marriage to William Mason, 225

Stuart, Archibald, 295

Stuart, Dr. David, 270, 274, 282, 284

Stuart, James: *Antiquities of Athens*, 45

Stuarts (England), 3, 9, 11, 24

Stumpy Point (Md.), 11, 25

Suffolk, 203

Sugar Act. *See* Revenue Act of 1764

Sullivan, James: as "Cassius," 272

Sullivan, John, 273

Sumptuary laws: Mason for, 254, 260–61, 263; Gerry for, 254

Supreme Court (U.S.), 295, 332

Susquehannock Indians, 4

Swan inn (Richmond), 285, 288, 290

Swedish East India Co., 51

*T*

Tabb, John: elected to Va. Committee of Safety, 120

Tariffs: proposed in Federal Convention, 251

Tarleton, Col. Banastre, 204, 210

Taxation: and representation, 24; of colonies to support French and Indian War, 64, 88; British policy of, 66; parliamentary, of colonies, 88, 90, 91, 93–94, 102, 106; by Va., of N.C. tobacco, 250

Taxes: parish, 7; public (Va.), 7; personal property (Va.), 7, 169, 202; poll (in Va.), 7, 202, 292; for land patents, 74; in kind, to provide military supplies, 202; on sale of imported goods, 202; on rum and spirits, 202, 203; on slaves, 202; on spirits, 292; on windows, 203; on deeds, 203; on exported tobacco, 203; power to levy and collect, 220–21, 222; land, 292

Taylor, John: and Ohio Co., 37

Taylor, Hancock, 181; death of, 181

Tazewell, Henry, 220

Tea: tax on, 94; tax retained, 98, 107

Temple, John, 232; on difficulties of unification of states, 232

Test Act, 77

Thermidor, 281

Thomson, Stevens, 7

Thomson, Sir William, 7

Thornton, William, 225

Thoroughgood, Adam, 47

Tidewater (Va.), 11, 23, 87, 90, 109; growth of tobacco in, 12; plantations in, 12; slaves in, 12; use of brick in

building, 47; political power of, 160–61; wealth of, 177; Federalists in, 284

Tobacco: in colonial Va., 11–12, 16, 72, 73; as legal tender, 12, 72, 74, 203; Va. trade of, with Glasgow, 16–17; government inspection of, 17; warehouses for, 17–18, 19; marketing of, 17–18, 19–20; and fertility of land, 21; planting of, 21; payment of clergy salaries in, 72; effect of grain production on, 74; nonexportation of, 107, 122, 125; effect of embargo on, 125; direct trade with Europe, 166, 208

Todd, John: killed in battle of Blue Licks, 192

Tories: in Stafford County, 9; in Va., 137, 205. *See also* Loyalists

Towns: emergence of, in colonial Va., 18, 19; establishment of, by Assembly, 33–34

Townshend, Charles, 94; ideas of, on colonial government, 94; death of, 94

Townshend, Thomas, Viscount Sydney, 245

Townshend Acts: repeal of, 98

Trade, colonial: with Scotland, 16, 18; U.S., directly with Europe, 208

Transylvania: plans for creation of, 182–83

Treason: considered in Federal Convention, 258; Mason's definition of, 258

Treasury certificates, 202

Treaty power, and navigation of Mississippi River, 292

Trent, William, 64; and Ohio Co., 64

Triplett, Thomas, 108

Truro parish, 8, 73, 79–80; George Mason IV on vestry of, 33, 63; vestry of, 39, 68, 81–82, 84; tithes in, 80; church building of, 80–84

Tryon, Governor, 199

Tucker, St. George, vii, 231; at Annapolis Convention, 231

Two Penny Act, 72; disallowed by king, 72, 73

Tyler, John, 292, 299; against ratification, 287; Anti-Federalist, 294

*U*

United States, first use of term, 147

*V*

"Valerius," 272

Valley Forge, 135, 172, 256; Washington retreats to, 167

Vandalia, 67

Vandalia Company, 182, 206

Vane, Sir Henry the Younger, 151–52

Vaughan, Samuel, 223

Vergennes, Charles Gravier, comte de, 221

Vermont, 154, 248; declaration of rights, 154

Vice-president: Mason on, 259, 294; considered in Federal Convention, 259

Vincennes, 178; taken by George Rogers Clark, 187–89; British troops regain, 189; retaken by Clark, 189–90, 191

Virginia, 219, 222, 226, 245, 259, 264, 267, 268, 278; English society reproduced in, 4, 6, 10–11; geography of, 5; application of law in, 7; Catholicism in, 9; colonial economy of, 11–12; marketing of tobacco in, 17–18, 19–20; charters of, 39, 199, 269; leadership of, in declaring independence, 136; governmental structure of, 158–59; seal of, 161–62; war in, 203–13 passim; and tobacco trade with Europe, 166; and rivalry with Pa. over Ohio country, 181; British invasion of, 192; cedes western lands, 193, 207; ratifies treaty of alliance with France, 199; and commercial treaty with Spain, 227; and trade dispute with Md., 228, 229; delegation to Federal Convention, 244, 262, 263–64; tobacco as staple in, 248; slavery in, 251; ratification struggle in, 278–97 passim; opposition to ratification of Constitution in, 280; "Movement Party," 281; Federalists in, 282, 284, 285, 288, 289, 290–91, 292, 295–96, 297; Anti-Federalists in, 284, 285, 290, 291, 292, 299; ratifies Constitution, 297; ratification celebration in, 299; ratifies amendments to Constitution, 300

Virginia, University of, 201

Virginia Assembly, 165, 166, 168, 182, 206, 207, 217, 218, 220; first session of, 160; and religious freedom, 161; appoints Committee of Law Revisions, 163; and war measures, 167, 168–69, 203–4; bill prohibiting profiteering, 168; bill authorizing seizures of salt, 168; establishes loan office, 169; and George Rogers Clark, 185, 191; Act of Cessation of Northwest Territory, 193, 207, 215; forbids distilling of grain, 197; report of Committee of Law Revisors presented to, 201; and Church of England, 201–2; taxes imposed by, 202; ratifies Pa.-Va. boundary, 207; flight of, to Charlottesville, 210; flight of, to Staunton, 210, 212; investigates Jefferson, 211, 213; investigates Thomas Nelson, Jr., 211, 212, 213; frees slaves, 214; legalizes manumission, 214; Port Act of 1784, 227; names delegates to Md. trade negotiations, 229; calls for Annapolis Convention, 231; selects delegates to Federal Convention, 233; delays ratifying convention, 270

Virginia Committe of Safety, 120, 126, 138; creation of, 119, 120; meets in Hanover, 134; *Journal* of, 135; *The Account Book* of, 135

Virginia Constitution, 156, 161, 240; called for by Va. convention of 1776, 138, 139; Richard Henry Lee's plan for, 157; Carter Braxton's plan for, 157; Mason major author of, 158; Jefferson's proposals for, 157–58, 160; preamble by Jefferson, 158, 160, 161; adopted by convention, 160; election of officers under, 160

Virginia Convention of 1774, 102, 108, 110; proposal of Continental Congress at, 108; nonimportation agreement proposed at, 108; authorizes county militias, 110

Virginia Convention of 1775, 110, 114, 118–20, 135; Committe to Prepare a Plan for a Militia, 114; and defense of colony, 114, 119; and nonexportation ordinance, 118–20; on taxes, 119; creates Va. Committee of Safety, 119; factionalism in, 119; as Va. chief executive, 120; defers consideration of loyalty oath, 126

Virginia Convention of 1776, 136, 150, 158, 161, 163, 302; election of delegates to, 136, 137–38; conservative control of, 138; Committe on Privileges and Elections, 138; Committee on Propositions and Grievances, 138; votes unanimously to declare independence, 138; and Va. Declaration of Rights, 148–49; denies safe passage to Gov. Eden, 156; frames state constitution, 156; adopts constitution, 160

Virginia Declaration of Rights, 32, 147–51, 156, 158, 161, 175, 201, 215, 217, 291, 308; called for in Va. Convention of 1776, 138, 139; Mason drafts, 142, 147, 240; published in *Pennsylvania Evening Post*, 142; on equality, 147; on separation of powers, 148; on freedom of elections, 148; on militia, 148, 309; and unusual punishments, 148, 308; and excessive bail, 148, 308; unanimous passage of, 149; Madison's contribution to, 149; on due process, 148; on property, 148, 152, 309; on freedom of the press, 148; on general warrants, 148, 308; on ex post facto laws, 148, 308; influence of, on other states, 153–55; and U.S. Bill of Rights, 300, 301; progenitor of French, *Déclaration*, 301; and *Déclaration des droits de l'homme*, 308–9

*Virginia Gazette*, 30, 92, 94, 95, 101, 102, 108, 116, 155. See also Dixon & Hunter's *Virginia Gazette*, Purdie's *Virginia Gazette*

Virginia Plan, 234, 240–42, 257; formation of, 234; as Federal Convention agenda, 240; on bicameral legislature, 240–41; on executive, 241; on national judiciary, 241; on admission of new states, 241; guarantees to states, 241; on amending Articles of Confederation, 241–42; on representatives' salaries, 259

Virginia ratifying convention, 270, 271, 285–97 passim, 310; meets in Richmond, 280, 285; contest for seats in, 282, 284; Committee on Privileges and Elections, 285; Committee of the Whole, 285, 288; contrast to Federal Convention, 285–86; as adversary proceeding, 286–87; influence of, on N.Y. convention, 291; Mass. formula and, 295; bill of rights and constitutional amendments approved by, 297; minority report of, 298

Virginia Statute for Religious Freedom, 218, 299; influence of, on French revolutionaries, 316; Condorcet on, 316

Voltaire, François Marie Arouet de, 130, 302, 307

*W*

Wabache Indians, 193
Wabash River, 178, 184
Wagener, Peter, 35, 82, 99
Wagener, Thomas, 65
Wahanganoche, 4
Wait, William, 82
Walker, Dr. Thomas, 38
Walpole, Thomas, 67
Warren, James, 275
Warren, Dr. Josiah, 109
Warren, Mercy Otis, 133
Warrenton, Va., 109
Warville, Brissot de, 307; *Nouveau Voyage dans les Etats-Unis*, 304; *De la France et des Etats-Unis*, 304
*Washington* (ship), 316, 319
Washington, Ann Fairfax, 34
Washington, Augustine: and Ohio Company, 37
Washington, George, 43, 68, 84, 101, 114, 119, 121, 129, 167, 192, 196, 197, 198, 204, 207, 210, 217, 218, 220, 221, 222, 223, 228, 230, 231, 232, 235, 243, 255, 264, 269, 272, 274, 277, 278, 281, 284, 291, 297, 298, 312, 322, 324, 334; diary of, 36, 55, 59, 100, 102, 103, 105, 227, 256, 266, 320; and Mason, 36, 41, 63, 68, 74–75, 77, 79, 82, 86, 86, 91, 95, 102, 104, 105, 107, 108, 112,

197–98, 204, 320–21, 325, 329; and Ohio Company, 39, 64; inherits Mount Vernon, 41; marries Martha Dandridge Custis, 60; as military commander, 64–65, 116, 135, 167–68, 185, 199; in House of Burgesses, 69, 72, 91; as planter, 73–74, 86, 87; as Alexandria trustee, 76; as Fairfax County justice, 77, 78; on Truro vestry, 79; on nonimportation, 96; on Fairfax committee of surveillance, 99, on Fairfax Committee of Safety, 105; elected to First Continental Congress, 108; and Fairfax Independent Company of Volunteers, 110; and Fairfax County Committee, 112, 116; on *Common Sense*, 131; at Valley Forge, 135, 167; on American military inadequacies, 167–68; against land office bill, 170; campaign of discreditation against, 172–73; and western lands, 179; and Potomac Company, 179, 181; will of, 181, 214; on unification, 194, 196; on confederation, 204, 221; on British surrender at Yorktown, 211; and Federal Convention, 233, 234, 236; and Virginia Plan, 240; for one-man executive, 250; for trade measures, 251; against proposal for overriding presidential veto, 258; on House of Representatives, 266; approves Constitution, 270; on Mass. ratifying formula, 278; and Va. ratifying struggle, 280, 284; on opposition to ratification of Constitution in Va., 280; as first president, 300; and Hamilton's debt assumption plan, 325

Washington, John Augustine, 138, 173
Washington, Lawrence, 37, 41, 72, 124; and Ohio Company, 23, 37; as trustee of Alexandria, 34; death of, 38, 41
Washington, Lund, 84, 173, 223; manages Mount Vernon, 134; letters to George Washington, 134, 135, 167, 273; records inflation in Va., 167; on discreditation campaign against George Washington, 172–73; loyalty to George Washington, 321
Washington, Martha Dandridge Custis, 60, 100
Waugh, David, 26
Waugh, Elizabeth. *See* Mason, Elizabeth Waugh
Waugh, John, 9–10, 26
Wayne, Gen. Anthony, 205
Wesley brothers, 84
West, Hugh, 33, 34
West, John, 68, 99, 104
West, Roger, 284
Western lands, 22–24, 170; cession of, to Confederation, 198–99, 206, 207. *See also* Ohio Company
West Indies, 178, 207, 210, 311
Westmoreland County, 4, 5, 47, 69, 91, 102; nonimportation and nonexportation proposals in, 102
Westover, 13, 25, 205
West Virginia, 67
Wharton family, 67, 199
Whigs, 9, 109, 120; in Va., 9, 10
Whitefield, George, 84, 288
Whitehall, 13, 44, 66, 89, 93, 178, 181, 199, 242, 245;

disallows Va. prohibition of slavery, 13
Whitehaven, 16, 17, 20, 127
White Plains, N.Y., 146
Wilkes, John, 109
Wilkinson, James, 172
*William* (ship), 128
William and Mary, 9
William and Mary, College of, 3, 8, 30, 90, 99, 181, 240
Williams, Jonathan, Jr., 304
Williamsburg, 6, 7, 23, 25, 27, 28, 38, 47, 62, 66, 69, 79, 80, 87, 88, 89, 91, 95, 96, 101, 102, 103, 105, 108, 109, 116, 124, 128, 135, 136, 140, 146, 147, 157, 166, 175, 179, 183, 190, 203, 220, 285, 286, 335; first printing press at, 27; description of, by Andrew Burnaby, 71; British troops beaten off, 205
Williamson, Hugh, 238, 250, 265
Wills Creek, 38, 66
Wilson, George, 330, 332
Wilson, James, 130, 264, 271, 274; on relation of foreign trade and policy, 251; on Committee of Detail, 256; Philadelphia speech of, 271, 274
*Wilson v. Mason*, 332
Winchester, 23, 34, 64, 69, 74, 121
Wise's tavern (Alexandria), 297
Witherspoon, John, 150, 243
Wood, James, 69
Woodbridge, 225, 320, 329
Woodford, William, 30
Woodstock, 60, 208
Worcester, battle of, 3
Worshipful Company of Joiners, 44, 45
Wren, Christopher, 44
Wren, James, 82
Writs of assistance, 88
Wyoming Valley, 226
Wythe, George, 156, 160, 163, 165, 166, 218, 281, 289, 300; elected to Second Continental Congress, 118; and Va. seal, 161; on Committee of Law Revisors, 163, 165, 240; speaker of Va. House of Delegates, 166, 240; and George Rogers Clark, 184; a delegate to Federal Convention, 233, 234, 239, 240; and Va. Plan, 240; against one-man executive, 250; judge of the Court of Chancery, 285; chairman of the Committee of the Whole in Va. ratifying convention, 285; for ratification, 287; proposes ratification, 296

Y
Yates, Robert, 243; notes of, on Federal Convention, 242, 243; opposes Constitution, 266–67, 297
York, Pa.: Congress meets in, 198
York County, 110
York River, 5, 91
Yorkshire (Eng.), 7, 121, 226
Yorktown, 99, 137, 203, 212, 213; British surrender at, 210

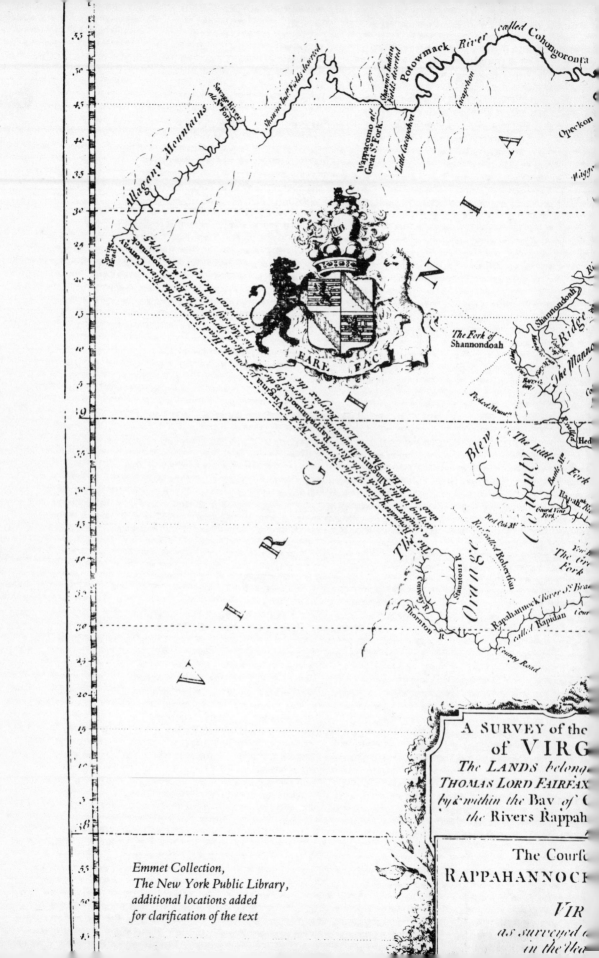

Potowmack River called Cohongoronta

Wappacomo or Great S. Fork

Little Cacapehon

Cacapehon

Manna Indian Fields deserted

Shanan Ind. Fields deserted

Savage River als N. Fork

Allagany Mountains

Spring Head

EARL FAC

N I A

V I R G

V I R

VIRGINIA

Opeckon

Wagg

Shannondoah

Ridge

The Manna

The Fork of Shannondoah

Blew

The Little

Fork

Batt. Br.

Rappah. Riv.

Gourd Vine Fork

The Gr. Fork

Blew Ridge

Picked Mounn.

Robertson

Red Oak Mn.

Riv. called Robertson

Orange County

Conway R.

Staunton R.

Thornton R.

Rappahannock River S. Bra.

called Rapidan

County Road

Hed

Yow

Cour.

A SURVEY of the
of VIRG

The LANDS belong.
THOMAS LORD FAIRFAX
by & within the Bay of C
the Rivers Rappah

The Cours
RAPPAHANNOC

VIR
as surveyed
in the Yea